'Constitutional Royalism' is one of the most familiar yet least often examined of all the political labels found in the historiography of the English Revolution. This book fills a gap by investigating the leading Constitutional Royalists who rallied to King Charles I in 1642 while consistently urging him to reach an 'accommodation' with Parliament.

These Royalists' early careers reveal that a commitment to the rule of law and a relative lack of 'godly' zeal were the characteristic predictors of Constitutional Royalism in the Civil War. Such attitudes explain why many of them criticised the policies of the King's personal rule, but also why they joined the King in 1642 and tried to achieve a negotiated settlement thereafter. The central chapters examine their role in the peace talks of the 1640s and assess why those talks broke down. The final part of the book traces the Constitutional Royalists through the Interregnum – during which they consciously withdrew from public life – to the Restoration, when many of them returned to prominence and saw their ideas vindicated. A concluding chapter reviews the long-term legacy of Constitutional Royalism and its specific contribution to the politics of the English Revolution. Throughout, the story of the Constitutional Royalists is set within the wider context of seventeenth-century English political history and thought.

Cambridge Studies in Early Modern British History

CONSTITUTIONAL ROYALISM AND THE SEARCH FOR SETTLEMENT, *c.* 1640–1649

Cambridge Studies in Early Modern British History

Series editors

ANTHONY FLETCHER
Professor of Modern History, University of Durham

JOHN GUY
Professor of Modern History, University of St Andrews

and JOHN MORRILL
Reader in Early Modern History, University of Cambridge, and Fellow and Tutor of Selwyn College

This is a series of monographs and studies covering many aspects of the history of the British Isles between the late fifteenth century and the early eighteenth century. It includes the work of established scholars and pioneering work by a new generation of scholars. It includes both reviews and revisions of major topics and books, which open up new historical terrain or which reveal startling new perspectives on familiar subjects. All the volumes set detailed research into our broader perspectives and the books are intended for the use of students as well as of their teachers.

For a list of titles in the series, see end of book.

CONSTITUTIONAL ROYALISM AND THE SEARCH FOR SETTLEMENT, c. 1640–1649

DAVID L. SMITH

Selwyn College, Cambridge

CAMBRIDGE
UNIVERSITY PRESS

PUBLISHED BY THE PRESS SYNDICATE OF THE UNIVERSITY OF CAMBRIDGE
The Pitt Building, Trumpington Street, Cambridge, United Kingdom

CAMBRIDGE UNIVERSITY PRESS
The Edinburgh Building, Cambridge CB2 2RU, UK
40 West 20th Street, New York NY 10011–4211, USA
477 Williamstown Road, Port Melbourne, VIC 3207, Australia
Ruiz de Alarcón 13, 28014 Madrid, Spain
Dock House, The Waterfront, Cape Town 8001, South Africa

http://www.cambridge.org

First published 1994
First paperback edition 2002

A catalogue record for this book is available from the British Library

Library of Congress Cataloguing in Publication data
Smith, David L.
Constitutional royalism and the search for settlement, *c*. 1640–1649 / David L. Smith
p.   cm. – (Cambridge studies in early modern British history)
Includes bibliographical references and index.
ISBN 0 521 41056 8
1. Great Britain – Politics and government – 1642–1649.
2. Great Britain – Politics and government – 1625–1649.
3. Monarchy – Great Britain – History – 17th century.
4. Great Britain – Constitutional history.
I. Title. II. Series.
DA415.S62 1994
941.06′2–dc20   93-34969   CIP

ISBN 0 521 41056 8 hardback
ISBN 0 521 89339 9 paperback

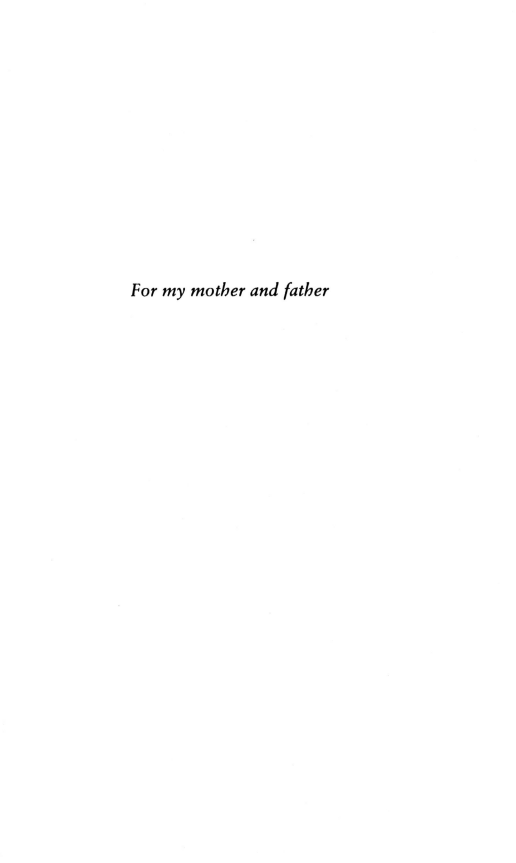

For my mother and father

CONTENTS

ACKNOWLEDGEMENTS

Since I embarked upon research in October 1986 I have accumulated debts to many institutions and individuals. I received generous financial support from the British Academy, which awarded me a Senior State Studentship, and especially from my *alma mater*, Selwyn College, Cambridge. I am deeply grateful to the Master and Fellows for electing me to a Research Scholarship, to the Centenary Research Fellowship and latterly to an Official Fellowship. Above all, I wish to thank them for enabling me to work in such an agreeable and stimulating environment. It is a rare institution which can grant someone equally happy and rewarding experiences as undergraduate, postgraduate and Fellow.

By far my greatest academic creditor is John Morrill. The manifold debts which I have incurred during the preparation of this book are but the latest in a long line extending over more than a decade. It was he who first introduced me to Stuart Britain as an undergraduate, and later supervised my doctoral dissertation, completed in 1990. Since then, he has continued to provide a characteristic blend of advice, encouragement and constructive criticism. Without his unfailing generosity, inspiration and friendship this book could not possibly have been written.

I also wish to thank Anthony Fletcher for providing many valuable and detailed comments on the first draft of this book. Nicholas Cranfield, Ian Gentles, Mark Goldie, John MacCafferty, Patrick Owen, John Scally and Daniel Woolf all read various sections in draft and made numerous helpful suggestions and criticisms. Between them, they have saved me from more errors and infelicities than I like to contemplate. It goes without saying that the failings of the finished work are entirely my own responsibility.

In developing this project beyond my original dissertation, I profited greatly from the advice of my two examiners, Gerald Aylmer and Derek Hirst. In addition, I am indebted to the following for giving me references and/or helpful guidance on specific points: John Adamson, Sabrina Alcorn-Baron, Ian Atherton, David Bevington, Martin Butler, Richard Cust, Colin Davis, Sir Geoffrey Elton, Ken Fincham, Simon Groenveld, John Guy, Caroline Hibbard, Patrick Higgins, Maija Jansson, Mark

Kishlansky, Peter Lake, Sheila Lambert, Keith Lindley, Patrick Little, Anthony Milton, Craig Rose, Conrad Russell, Peter Salt, Kevin Sharpe, Quentin Skinner, Richard Strier, Christopher Thompson, the late John M. Wallace, Ian Ward and Jenny Wormald. I also owe thanks to the staff of Cambridge University Press, and especially William Davies, for their assistance and support.

The formulation of my more general ideas on the politics of early Stuart England has benefited enormously from many conversations with other members of the Early Modern British History seminar and the Tudor seminar at Cambridge, and of the Tudor and Stuart seminar at the Institute of Historical Research. I have also gained immensely from supervising Cambridge undergraduates over the past six years, and from teaching two courses at the University of Chicago during the Spring Quarter of 1991. These enjoyable experiences have left me in no doubt that teaching and research belong together.

I wish to record my gratitude to James Jones and Alan Davidson for allowing me to read material prior to publication; to Sir Lyonel Tollemache, for granting me access to the Tollemache MS at Buckminster Park; to Viscount De L'Isle, for permitting me to consult his family muniments at the Centre for Kentish Studies; to the Leeds Castle Foundation, and especially David Cleggett, for sending me xeroxes of the Fairfax MS at Leeds Castle; to Christopher Thompson for giving me a copy of his invaluable transcript of Walter Yonge's diary; and to the Beinecke Library at Yale for providing a xerox of the commonplace book of Sir John Strangways.

The staffs of many other libraries and archives have assisted me courteously, knowledgeably, and with seemingly infinite patience. I owe a particular debt to Donald Gibson at the Centre for Kentish Studies; to Harry Cobb at the House of Lords Record Office; to Mary Robertson at the Henry E. Huntington Library, San Marino, where I spent a pleasantly productive month during the summer of 1991; and above all to the staff who run the Manuscripts Room and the Rare Books Room in the Cambridge University Library.

I have left my overriding debt until last. Without my parents' constant encouragement, support and willing sacrifices over the years this book would never have come to exist. I dedicate it to them, with love and gratitude.

ABBREVIATIONS

APC	*The Acts of the Privy Council of England, 1542–1631,* ed. J. R. Dasent, E. G. Atkinson, J. V. Lyle, R. F. Monger and P. A. Penfold (46 vols., 1890–1964)
BL	British Library
BL, TT	British Library, Thomason Tracts
Bodl. Lib.	Bodleian Library, Oxford
CJ	*Journals of the House of Commons* (1803–)
CKS	Centre for Kentish Studies
Clarendon, *History*	Edward, Earl of Clarendon, *The History of the Rebellion and Civil Wars in England,* ed. W. Dunn Macray (6 vols., Oxford, 1888)
Clarendon, *Life*	Edward, Earl of Clarendon, *The Life of Edward, Earl of Clarendon . . . Written by himself* (3 vols., Oxford, 1827)
Clarendon SP	*State Papers collected by Edward, Earl of Clarendon* (3 vols., Oxford, 1757)
Cope	Esther S. Cope, ed., *Proceedings of the Short Parliament of 1640* (Camden Society, 4th series, 19, 1977)
CSPV	*Calendar of State Papers Venetian,* ed. Rawdon Brown, Horatio F. Brown and Allen B. Hinds (40 vols., 1864–1940)
CUL	Cambridge University Library
D'Ewes (C)	*The Journal of Sir Simonds D'Ewes from the first recess of the Long Parliament to the withdrawal of King Charles from London,* ed. Willson H. Coates (New Haven, 1942; repr. Hamden, 1970)
D'Ewes (N)	*The Journal of Sir Simonds D'Ewes from the beginning of the Long Parliament to the opening of the trial of the Earl of Strafford,* ed. Wallace Notestein (New Haven, 1923)
DNB	*Dictionary of National Biography,* ed. L. Stephen and Sidney Lee (63 vols., 1885–1900)

EHR	*English Historical Review*
Gardiner, *Civil War*	S. R. Gardiner, *History of the Great Civil War, 1642–1649* (4 vols., 1893)
Gardiner, *Documents*	S. R. Gardiner, ed., *Constitutional Documents of the Puritan Revolution, 1625–1660* (3rd edition, Oxford, 1906)
Gardiner, *History*	S. R. Gardiner, *History of England from the Accession of James I to the outbreak of the Civil War, 1603–1642* (10 vols., 1883–4)
HJ	*Historical Journal*
HMC	Historical Manuscripts Commission
JBS	*Journal of British Studies*
LJ	*Journals of the House of Lords* (1846)
Maltby	*The Short Parliament (1640) Diary of Sir Thomas Aston*, ed. Judith D. Maltby (Camden Society, 4th series, 35, 1988)
MP	Main Papers of the House of Lords (at the House of Lords Record Office)
P & P	*Past and Present*
PJ	Willson H. Coates, Anne Steele Young and Vernon F. Snow, ed., *The Private Journals of the Long Parliament* (3 vols., New Haven and London, 1982–92)
	vol. I, 3 January to 5 March 1642 (1982)
	vol. II, 7 March to 1 June 1642 (1987)
	vol. III, 2 June to 17 September 1642 (1992)
PRO	Public Record Office
RO	Record Office
Rushworth	John Rushworth, *Historical Collections of private passages of State* (8 vols., 1680–1701)
Russell, *Causes*	Conrad Russell, *The Causes of the English Civil War* (Oxford, 1990)
Russell, *FBM*	Conrad Russell, *The Fall of the British Monarchies, 1637–1642* (Oxford, 1991)
Russell, *Parliaments*	Conrad Russell, *Parliaments and English Politics, 1621–1629* (Oxford, 1979)
SP	State Papers (at the Public Record Office)
STC	A. W. Pollard and G. R. Redgrave, ed., *A Short-Title Catalogue of Books Printed in England, Scotland and Ireland and of English Books Printed Abroad, 1475–1640* (2nd edition, ed. W. A. Jackson, F. S. Ferguson and K. F. Pantzer, 2 vols., 1976–86)

STC (News)	C. Nelson and M. Seccombe, ed., *British Newspapers and Periodicals, 1641–1700: A Short-Title Catalogue of Serials Printed in England, Scotland, Ireland and British America* (New York, 1987)
TRHS	*Transactions of the Royal Historical Society*
Two Diaries	Maija Jansson, ed., *Two Diaries of the Long Parliament* (Gloucester and New York, 1984)
Wing	Donald Wing, ed., *A Short-Title Catalogue of Books Printed in England, Scotland, Ireland, Wales and British America and of English Books Printed Abroad, 1641–1700* (2nd edition, 3 vols., New York, 1972–88)

A NOTE ON QUOTATIONS, SOURCES, DATES AND TERMINOLOGY

Throughout this book, quotations from primary sources are as in the original, except that I have extended the standard abbreviated forms and adapted some extreme punctuation to modern usage.

All dates are in Old Style, except that the year is regarded as beginning on 1 January rather than 25 March.

In the footnotes and bibliography, the place of publication of books cited is London unless otherwise stated.

My use of the term 'England', 'English' etc. calls for brief explanation. In the course of this study, I explore the attitudes of Constitutional Royalists towards the Crown's relations with distinctively English institutions such as the Church of England, the common law of England, and the English Parliament. I certainly do not wish to fall foul of the charge of Anglocentricity. But I have had to use 'England', 'English' etc. wherever institutions, relationships or structures specific to England are discussed. In such contexts, the words 'Britain' and 'British' do not accurately convey the perspective of Constitutional Royalists, and would therefore impede rather than assist a reconstruction of their ideas.

Part I

THE ORIGINS OF CONSTITUTIONAL ROYALISM

————————— ⫷ 1 ⫸ —————————

Introduction: themes, debates, sources

I

'Constitutional Royalism' is one of the most familiar yet least often examined of all the political labels found in the historiography and literary criticism of the English Revolution. The term is most commonly used to describe a group of moderate Royalists who became prominent among
Charles I's advisers in 1641–2. The leading exponents are usually identified
as Edward Hyde, Viscount Falkland and Sir John Culpepper; and their
ideas are thought to revolve around a concept of limited monarchy which
ruled under the law, and a wish to preserve the existing structures of the
Church of England. These were the people who guided Charles I's more
conciliatory actions in 1641–2, and whose political attitudes found their
classic expression in the King's *Answer to the XIX Propositions*. Neither
historical nor literary scholars appear to doubt the *existence* of Constitutional Royalism as a phenomenon during the twelve months before the
outbreak of the English Civil War.[1]

But all this in turn prompts two further questions. First, how numerous
and how co-ordinated were the Constitutional Royalists in 1641–2? We as
yet know very little about whether there were other figures of similar
outlook beyond the three leading characters, or about the extent to which
they operated as a coherent political grouping. Did they rally behind a firm
set of policies and propositions, or do their contrasting emphases make it
inappropriate to lump them together into a single group? Second, whatever
became of these people after 1642? How far were their attitudes applicable
to the politics of the Civil War period, and what was their role in successive peace negotiations? Was there such a thing as Constitutional Royalism
during the remainder of the 1640s, or was it purely a transient product of

[1] See especially B. H. G. Wormald, *Clarendon: Politics, History and Religion, 1640–1660*
(Cambridge, 1951; repr. 1989), pp. 3, 81, 122, 150, 154; Corinne Comstock Weston, 'The
theory of mixed monarchy under Charles I and After', *EHR*, 75 (1960), 426–43, at 430;
John Morrill's own introduction, in *Reactions to the English Civil War, 1642–1649*, ed.
John Morrill (1982), p. 7; John M. Wallace, '*Coopers Hill*: the manifesto of parliamentary
royalism, 1641', *ELH, A Journal of English Literary History*, 41 (1974), 494–540, at 534.

3

1641–2? None of these questions has so far been addressed by historians, and the aim of this monograph is to offer some answers to them.

We immediately face a serious problem of taxonomy. How do we decide who should be classified as a Constitutional Royalist? The obvious danger is that of deciding in advance who should be in our sample, analysing their beliefs, and then using the results to define Constitutional Royalism. Such an argument would be tautological. There is also the hazard of imposing an artificial construct upon the historical reality. Since the term was not used by contemporaries, there is the problem of projecting an anachronistic category back on to the evidence. Finally, we must tread a delicate path between teasing out the ideas and attitudes which people held in common, and transforming them into a monolithic group. It is important to remain sensitive to their similarities without losing sight of their differences.

With all this in mind, I have used two rules of thumb for including an individual in this study. Both of these are as close to objective tests as I can devise. They seem to me to minimise the role of the observer – which inevitably distorts the view of the past under observation – and to work with the grain of the surviving evidence. The first criterion is prominence in royal counsels during the twelve months before the *Answer to the XIX Propositions*, and especially between January and August 1642. The most important of these figures were the Marquess of Hertford, the Earl of Southampton, Lord Seymour of Trowbridge, Viscount Falkland, Sir John Culpepper, Sir John Strangways and Edward Hyde. This list includes the three figures usually identified as the leading theorists of Constitutional Royalism on the eve of the Civil War, together with several other political heavyweights who have received rather less attention. All of these figures were close to Charles I during the period which culminated in the *Answer*, and many of them held senior offices.

My second criterion has been a frequent and prominent involvement on the King's behalf in successive peace negotiations throughout the period 1642–8. This is a rather more problematic litmus test. If we included every Royalist who ever acted as a peace commissioner, or who played an occasional role as a go-between, or who claimed to desire peace, we would end up with an immensely long list. Furthermore, the list would include people like Sir John Berkeley and John Ashburnham, who facilitated negotiations in 1647 but who had earlier been willing to contemplate violence against Parliament in a way which clearly sets them apart from men like Hyde, Falkland and Culpepper. People such as Berkeley and Ashburnham cannot straightforwardly be classified as Constitutional Royalists. Instead, we can identify one large cluster of individuals who regularly participated in negotiations, or urged the King to offer conciliatory terms, and several others who had splintered off from the coalition of 1641–2. The larger group comprises six moderate Royalist nobles who often acted as a team: the Duke of Richmond, the Marquess of Hertford, the Earls of Southampton, Lindsey and Dorset, and Lord Seymour. By 1646 another, smaller group had emerged which included Culpepper. But by this time he was working closely with two figures who had earlier been implicated in the first Army Plot, and whose subsequent commitment to royal concessions appears to have been for mainly tactical reasons: Henry Jermyn and John Ashburnham. We will need to assess how far this represented a change of attitude on Culpepper's part. During 1646–8 these two circles seem to have operated largely independently of each other, the former remaining in England, the latter with the exiled court in France. Hyde, it seems, became an isolated figure during the later 1640s, and lived quietly on Jersey, preoccupied with writing his *History*. Between them, these two criteria give us a sample of ten figures who may tentatively be classed as Constitutional Royalists: Hyde, Falkland, Culpepper, Seymour, Strangways, Hertford, Richmond, Southampton, Dorset and Lindsey. I make no claim that this list includes *all* those who could possibly be classified as Constitutional Royalists, or even that it represents a distinct and self-contained group. But I do think it comprises the leading exponents of an identifiable set of attitudes and priorities.

We will see throughout this book that the activities and alignments of these people fluctuated enormously during the decade of the Civil Wars. Nothing could indicate more clearly that we are examining political processes before 'the age of parties'. For much of the time, they were, so to speak, *aligned* but not *co-ordinated*. They shared extensive areas of common ground, while retaining considerable differences of emphasis. The constellations of people who worked closely together mutated constantly over time. Yet these ten figures retained a similar outlook throughout this period, a fact which is underlined by the appointment of all those who survived to senior public office in 1660.[2] To take either a narrower or a broader sample of individuals would tend to obscure this very important element of continuity within royal counsels.

II

The classification of individuals is not the only problem we face. The name 'Constitutional Royalism' itself requires some further exploration and justification. At first sight, it looks like a contradiction in terms. Is it possible to be loyal to both a monarch and a constitution? Do not the ideas of monarchy – which emphasise the rule of an individual – and of

---

[2] See below, pp. 295–7.

constitutionalism – with their emphasis on political and legal norms which transcend the individual – naturally pull in opposite directions? Logically, this may well be true; but two points should immediately be made to set this paradox in its proper historical perspective.

First, the notion of 'constitutional monarchy' has been a recurrent theme in England's political development. (For my use of the term 'England' see my note on p. xvi.) Even today, this remains England's official form of government. The monarchy, though bound by constitutional conventions, retains surprising importance, and it has been convincingly argued that its contemporary political strength 'does not lie in the power it has, but in the power that it denies to others'.[3] Historically, the really remarkable feature of the English monarchy has been its ability to adapt to changing political contexts, and to play convincing roles within wholly contrasted constitutional frameworks. Since the high Middle Ages, it has displayed a versatility of monarchical form in a way which is almost unique. This exceptionally long and distinctive pattern of development demonstrates the viability of ideas of 'constitutional monarchy' and gives them a compelling claim to be studied. The resilience of such ideas is shown particularly vividly by their survival during the years of the English Revolution, and their resurgence after the Restoration.

This leads us neatly into the second point. The belief that royal and constitutional patterns of government are logically opposed is very much a modern one. It is one aspect of the ideas of the Enlightenment, and was reinforced in the later eighteenth century by the American and French Revolutions. However, I shall argue in this book that this belief was virtually unknown in early seventeenth-century England. Indeed, it was axiomatic for most people in the decades before the Civil Wars that the monarch and the constitution were integrally and symbiotically bound together. The famous commonplace of the 'body politic', with the monarch as head and the nation as body and members, illustrates this perfectly. Today, we instinctively analyse politics in terms of checks and balances, in terms of one authority *limiting* another. It takes a real effort of imagination to empathise with people who assumed that politics was an harmonious process in which different sources of authority complemented and reinforced each other. This outlook was among the principal hallmarks of the Constitutional Royalists of the 1640s, and meant that they never found their beliefs self-contradictory.

Although many of its underlying assumptions had long-established antecedents, the emergence of Constitutional Royalism took place within a very specific political and ideological context. It was designed to answer a

[3] This aphorism is Antony Jay's, quoted in Anthony Sampson, *The Changing Anatomy of Britain* (2nd edition, 1983), pp. 6–7.

particular problem posed by a particular king: Charles I. Chapter 2 will analyse the early Stuart constitution and the contrasting ways in which James I and Charles I managed it. It will argue that Charles I's personality and political style were peculiarly likely to expose the latent tensions within the constitution and to upset the delicate balance of the Church. His passion for order and definition proved disastrous in a system which depended on the maintenance of grey areas, and caused serious divisions within the political nation by the end of the 1630s. In particular, they raised the question of whether the constitution needed to be defined in order to protect it from a monarch like Charles I, or whether such definition would alter its fundamental nature.

Constitutional Royalism emerged during 1641–2 as one of several possible answers to that question. Its basic premises were that royal powers and constitutional government were inherently compatible; that Charles I could be trusted to rule legally and to abide by the safeguards against non-parliamentary government erected in 1640–1; that limitations on his power to choose advisers and military commanders were antithetical to monarchy; and that the existing structures of the Church of England were an intrinsic part of the constitution which should be preserved from 'root-and-branch' reform. Chapter 3 examines the early careers of our sample of ten Constitutional Royalists. It traces their activities during the 1620s and 1630s, and explores whether we can pinpoint any activities and beliefs which serve as predictors of their Constitutional Royalism. Chapter 4 then charts how they emerged as Royalists during the early 1640s. This chapter stresses the importance of attitudes towards the rule of law and the future of the Church in persuading these people to rally behind the King. It concludes with a discussion of why moderate Royalists and moderate Parliamentarians were unable to coalesce and form a united middle ground during the summer of 1642.

After the outbreak of the Civil War, the Constitutional Royalists are best defined as those among the King's followers who consistently sought to further peace negotiations with Parliament. This was not necessarily incompatible with senior military command; nor did it ever entail a preference for unconditional surrender; it primarily involved a readiness to keep talking. The core of this book consists of a detailed analysis of the role of Constitutional Royalists in these successive negotiations. Chapter 5 provides a chronological outline of the talks, and looks at both the formal treaties at Oxford (1643), Uxbridge (1645), Newcastle (1646), over the *Heads of the Proposals* (1647), and at Newport (1648), and also at the various informal contacts between the King's followers and Parliament during the years of Civil War. Chapter 6 then identifies seven crucial issues which impeded the progress of these negotiations: the nature of religion

and church government; the command of the militia; the powers and privileges of Parliament; the relationship between royal authority and the
common law; the choice of royal advisers and the composition of the Privy
Council; the fate of Royalist 'delinquents'; and the question of the King's
'honour and conscience'. It will look at each sticking-point in turn, discussing whether there was a Constitutional Royalist position on it, and trying
to explain why agreement with Parliamentary negotiators proved so
elusive. Part Two of the book concludes with an examination of eight
writers whose publications during the 1640s offered a theoretical justification for the political activities of the Constitutional Royalists. Their
ideas will be contrasted with those of other writers who defended the
concept of absolute monarchy.

Part Three seeks to locate Constitutional Royalism within a longer time-
frame. It begins by telling the story of what happened to the various
Constitutional Royalists during the Interregnum (chapter 8). I shall suggest
that the dominant note – expressed in poetry as well as in political practice
– was one of quiescence and withdrawal rather than any attempt to subvert
the republican régimes. In the following chapter I draw the camera lens out
to an even wider angle, and examine the legacy of Constitutional Royalism
after 1660. This is inevitably a broader, more speculative section, and
argues that Constitutional Royalism was a crucial influence upon the
Restoration settlement. It shaped the government's policies during the
1660s, and made an important contribution to the outcome of both the
Exclusion Crisis and the Glorious Revolution. In a looser sense, the values
and attitudes characteristic of Constitutional Royalism may be traced well
into the eighteenth century, and they thus assisted the gradual evolution of
England's modern constitutional monarchy. The final chapter draws
together the threads of the argument and summarises the significance of
Constitutional Royalism for our view of the English Civil Wars, and of
English political history in general.

III

Let us now turn to examine the current state of research on the Royalist
party during the 1640s. Conrad Russell has recently drawn attention to the
relative paucity of work on the King's followers in the English Civil Wars:
'It is the English Royalists, not the English Parliamentarians, who are the
real peculiarity we should be attempting to explain ... The intellectual and
social antecedents of Royalism have not yet been studied with the care
which has for many generations been lavished on the Parliamentarians,
and the result is that we do not know nearly as well what continuities

informed Royalism as we do what continuities informed its opponents.'[4] This book cannot claim to fill that lacuna, but instead seeks to reconstruct the development of one particular strand of Royalism. That strand is not entirely virgin territory, and along the way we will engage with a number of historiographical controversies.

In general, work on Constitutional Royalism over the last forty years can be divided into two categories. First, we have a series of books and articles which locate it within the context of theories of mixed government. Perhaps the most influential of these is Margaret Judson's *The Crisis of the Constitution*.[5] This presents a fine analysis of several key Royalist writers of the Civil War years, whose work I address in chapter 7.[6] The book is excellent in charting how hitherto blurred issues became clear during the 1640s. However, it does tend to see the reigns of James I and Charles I as a monolith, and therefore to play down the significance of 1625 as a turning-point.[7] As will become clear from chapter 2, I believe it would be hard to exaggerate the significance of the contrasts between James I and Charles I. The distinctiveness of the Caroline period emerges with rather more definition in the work of Corinne Comstock Weston.[8] This is particularly helpful because it places Constitutional Royalism within an immensely long historical context, and traces its influence right up to the Great Reform Act of 1832. 'Mixed monarchy' ideas are seen to have had a long and important legacy in English politics. Weston's writings also contain a very detailed analysis of that key document in the evolution of Constitutional Royalism, the King's *Answer to the XIX Propositions*.[9] The *Answer* is now one of the best understood expressions of the Constitutional Royalist outlook, for it also forms the subject of the greater part of Michael Mendle's *Dangerous Positions*.[10] This provides the most authoritative account to date of the composition of the *Answer*, and also explains

---

[4] Russell, *FBM*, pp. 526, 532.
[5] Margaret Atwood Judson, *The Crisis of the Constitution: An Essay in Constitutional and Political Thought in England, 1603–1645* (New Brunswick, NJ, 1949).
[6] *Ibid.*, pp. 385–436.
[7] E.g. this synoptic statement: ' . . . the reader of this book will recall the fact that during the period from 1603 to 1640 royalist policy and thought had been aggressive': *ibid.*, p. 385.
[8] See especially Weston, 'Theory of mixed monarchy'; *English Constitutional Theory and the House of Lords, 1556–1832* (1965), especially pp. 23–43; 'England: ancient constitution and common law', in *The Cambridge History of Political Thought, 1450–1700*, ed. J. H. Burns and Mark Goldie (Cambridge, 1991), pp. 374–411; Weston and Janelle Renfrow Greenberg, *Subjects and Sovereigns* (Cambridge, 1981).
[9] The text of the King's *Answer to the XIX Propositions* may be found in Rushworth, IV, 725–35.
[10] Michael Mendle, *Dangerous Positions: Mixed Government, the Estates of the Realm, and the Making of the Answer to the XIX Propositions* (Alabama, 1985), especially pp. 5–20, 171–83.

its relationship to contemporary estates theory. On the evolution of Royalist thought after 1642, however, older work has retained its value remarkably well. In particular, John Sanderson's recent study of 'the philosophical basis of the English Civil War'[11] complements – but does not supersede
– the survey of early seventeenth-century political thought by J. W. Allen,
although sadly the latter only goes up to 1644.[12] Richard Tuck's new
account marks an important departure from previous approaches because
it locates Royalist writings within the context of European political theory
and moral philosophy.[13] We also have two excellent studies of the thought
of John Bramhall;[14] and a valuable analysis of the intellectual traditions
which lie behind Royalist thought.[15] All in all, then, there is a sizeable
corpus of work upon which to build when reconstructing the emergence of
Constitutional Royalism as a political ideology.

   We know far less about how that ideology was translated into practice.
There is no detailed account of the peace negotiations of the 1640s from a
Royalist perspective. Instead, all we have is a tightly focused debate about
the composition of the Royalist party at Oxford. Ian Roy began this in the
early 1960s with his doctoral thesis on 'the Royalist army in the first Civil
War', and an important article derived from it.[16] Roy suggested that three
main factional groupings had emerged by early 1644: 'Swordsmen', 'Courtiers' and 'Civilians'.[17] He saw Queen Henrietta Maria, Lord George
Digby and John Ashburnham as among the consistent opponents of compromise, but argued that the initiative gradually passed to the 'Swordsmen', led by Prince Rupert.[18] In 1981, Ronald Hutton modified this picture
by identifying the three principal Royalist factions as 'moderates' (led by
the Earls of Hertford, Southampton and Lindsey); 'ultra-Royalists'
(especially Digby, Ashburnham, Henry Jermyn and Henry Percy); and a
group of military hard-liners which coalesced around Prince Rupert.[19]
Hutton suggested that the repeated failure of peace negotiations undermined the position of the moderates, and gave the initiative to an 'ultra-

[11] John Sanderson, *'But the People's Creatures': The philosophical basis of the English Civil War* (Manchester, 1989), pp. 38–85.
[12] J. W. Allen, *English Political Thought, 1603–1660*, vol. I: *1603–1644* (1938), 488–521.
[13] Richard Tuck, *Philosophy and Government, 1572–1651* (Cambridge, 1993), pp. 260–78.
[14] J. W. Daly, 'John Bramhall and the theoretical problems of Royalist moderation', *JBS*, 11 (1971), 26–44; John Sanderson, 'Serpent-Salve, 1643: the Royalism of John Bramhall', *Journal of Ecclesiastical History*, 25 (1974), 1–14.
[15] J. W. Daly, 'The origins and shaping of English Royalist thought', *Historical Papers/ Communications Historiques* (1974), pp. 15–35.
[16] I. Roy, 'The Royalist army in the First Civil War' (DPhil thesis, University of Oxford, 1963), especially pp. 78–96; 'The Royalist Council of War, 1642–6', *Bulletin of the Institute of Historical Research*, 35 (1962), 150–68.
[17] Roy, 'Royalist army', pp. 78–85.   [18] *Ibid.*, pp. 86–96.
[19] Ronald Hutton, 'The structure of the Royalist Party, 1642–6', *HJ*, 24 (1981), especially 554–7, 562–3.

Royalist axis' consisting of the second and third groups. A few years later, James Daly challenged these arguments, and suggested that factional alignments among leading Royalists were never as clear cut as Roy and Hutton assumed.[20] Daly pointed out that moderates such as Hertford and Lindsey also held military commissions, while a 'hard-liner' like Digby did not automatically oppose all negotiations. Many of these points are very persuasive. However, it will be the argument of this book that the flexibility of individuals, and the fluidity of their factional loyalties, did not preclude the existence of distinct and separable attitudes towards the conduct of the Civil War. There was a consistent Constitutional Royalist *outlook*, even if the factional alignments of its exponents shifted during the course of the 1640s.

I have deliberately left the most important post-war work on Constitutional Royalism until last. Brian Wormald's *Clarendon* stands alone not just because of its extraordinarily subtle and perceptive reconstruction of Hyde's political and religious beliefs, but also because it remains the only attempt to bridge the gulf between Constitutional Royalism in theory and in practice. This was a study of Hyde both as a politician and as an historian. Many of Wormald's arguments have since become axiomatic to our view of the 1640s. He revealed the epistemological problems posed by Clarendon's *History of the Rebellion*, and the extent to which this work involved retrospective self-justification.[21] Above all, he demonstrated that many Royalists also remained in a broad sense 'Parliamentarians', while a decision to remain at Westminster did not necessarily imply a hatred of monarchy. The categories 'Royalist' and 'Parliamentarian' were thus shown to be much less watertight than the 'Whig' historians supposed. Unfortunately, Wormald's lead was never followed up. We have no collective study of Constitutional Royalism during the Civil War, let alone biographies of its leading exponents. Moderate Royalists have consistently received less attention than the 'Cavaliers' and 'Swordsmen'. Apart from Wormald's study, there are only two post-war biographies of Clarendon.[22] Interest in Falkland focuses on his leadership of the Great Tew circle, and we have had no biography of him since 1940.[23] This compares with four biographies of Prince Rupert and one of Hopton.[24] In recent years, several

[20] J. W. Daly, 'The implications of Royalist politics, 1642–6', *HJ*, 27 (1984), 745–55.
[21] On the reliability of the *History*, see also Ronald Hutton, 'Clarendon's *History of the Rebellion*', *EHR*, 97 (1982), 70–88.
[22] R. W. Harris, *Clarendon and the English Revolution* (1983); Richard Ollard, *Clarendon and his Friends* (1987). Ollard is strongest for the period after 1649.
[23] Kurt Weber, *Lucius Cary, Second Viscount Falkland* (New York, 1940). On the Great Tew circle, see especially Hugh Trevor-Roper, *Catholics, Anglicans and Puritans* (1987), pp. 166–230.
[24] B. E. Fergusson, *Rupert of the Rhine* (1952); G. M. Thomson, *Warrior Prince: Prince Rupert of the Rhine* (1976); P. Morrah, *Prince Rupert of the Rhine* (1976); M. Ashley,

books on the recruitment, membership and organisation of Royalist armies
have also been published.[25] By contrast, there are no biographies of figures
such as Richmond, Hertford, Southampton, Lindsey, Seymour, Strangways and Culpepper.[26] We also lack an account of their collective involvement in peace negotiations. In general Charles's followers have been less
fully studied than those who remained with Parliament.[27] Wormald's
splendid book stands curiously alone on the historiographical landscape,
and it deserves to have stimulated rather more studies in the same area. I
hope that this monograph may go some way towards redressing the
imbalance.

IV

Lastly, a word about the primary sources on which this study is based.
Broadly, these may be divided into five categories. First, there are the reminiscences, correspondence and personal papers of our leading protagonists.
By far the most famous memoirs are of course Clarendon's *History of the
Rebellion* and his autobiographical *Life*.[28] Despite all the problems of – to
put it kindly – a less than perfect memory, these remain a marvellous evocation of Hyde's values and frame of mind, as well as an unrivalled source
of information about the shifting relationships between the King's followers. He gives beautiful pen-portraits of all the main Royalists.[29] These
works are complemented by the voluminous collection of Hyde's papers,
covering the years from 1608 to 1689, now in the Bodleian Library.[30] A
selection from these was published in the eighteenth century, but often

---

Rupert of the Rhine (1976); and F. T. R. Edgar, *Sir Ralph Hopton: The King's Man in the
West, 1642–52* (Oxford, 1968).

[25] Most notably P. R. Newman, *Royalist Officers in England and Wales, 1642–1660: A
Biographical Dictionary* (1981); Ronald Hutton, *The Royalist War Effort, 1642–1646*
(Harlow, 1982); and J. Malcolm, *Caesar's Due: Loyalty and King Charles, 1642–6* (1983).

[26] For Dorset's career during the 1640s, see David L. Smith, '"The more posed and wise
advice": the fourth Earl of Dorset and the English Civil Wars', *HJ*, 34 (1991), 797–829;
and 'The political career of Edward Sackville, fourth Earl of Dorset (1590–1652)' (PhD
thesis, University of Cambridge, 1990).

[27] This disparity is evident in Gardiner, *Civil War*, and has not been corrected since. We
have major studies of political developments at Westminster during the 1640s – such as
David Underdown, *Pride's Purge: Politics in the Puritan Revolution* (Oxford, 1971); and
Blair Worden, *The Rump Parliament, 1648–53* (Cambridge, 1974) – and of the Parliamentarian armies, especially M. A. Kishlansky, *The Rise of the New Model Army* (Cambridge, 1979). It would also be fair to say that the majority of the county studies published
during the 1960s and 1970s have examined Parliamentarian rather than Royalist areas.

[28] Clarendon, *History; Life*.

[29] Cf. M. W. Brownley, *Clarendon and the Rhetoric of Historical Form* (Philadelphia,
1985), pp. 145–85.

[30] Bodl. Lib., MSS Clarendon 1–93 form the so-called Clarendon State Papers.

there is no substitute for going back to the originals.[31] Hyde became an historian, and realised the importance of preserving for posterity the materials generated by his career. But he was not entirely alone in this respect. Dorset's papers contain extensive correspondence relating to Royalist politics during the 1630s and 1640s.[32] The smaller collections of Strangways (his letters at the Dorset Record Office, and a vitally important commonplace book in the Beinecke Library at Yale),[33] and the scattered papers of the Seymours are particularly illuminating.[34]

Second, there are a number of diaries, memoirs and collections of papers by other important figures which throw floods of light on Constitutional Royalism. Of those in print, the diary of Sir William Dugdale and Sir Edward Walker's *Historical Discourses* are especially informative about politics at Oxford during the first Civil War.[35] Walker was secretary of the King's Council of War, and many of his working papers survive, although this archive is exceptionally scattered.[36] The very important papers of Sir Edward Nicholas, Secretary of State from November 1641, are now contained in three separate deposits, in the British Library, at Guildford and at Christ Church, Oxford.[37] Finally, the Coke correspondence – which has recently become available in the British Library[38] – tells us a great deal about the coalescence of Constitutional Royalists around the King during the months preceding the outbreak of civil war.

The third category looks paradoxical: it consists of the sources relating to Parliament during the 1640s. But in fact these are indispensable for an accurate picture of Royalist politics and policies. The official *Journals* of the two Houses – and especially those of the House of Lords – print most of the formal papers exchanged during successive peace treaties. The majority of these can also be found in Rushworth's *Historical Collections*,

---

[31] *Clarendon SP.*
[32] These are mainly to be found in the Sackville, Bourchier and Cranfield sections of CKS, U 269 (Sackville MS).
[33] Dorset RO, D 124 (Fox-Strangways [Earls of Ilchester] MS); Beinecke Library, Yale University, Osborn MS b. 304 (commonplace book of Sir John Strangways).
[34] For the present study, the most important collections of Seymour material are: Longleat House, Warminster, Wiltshire, Seymour MS; Devon RO, Seymour of Berry Pomeroy MS, 1392 M/L16; and Wiltshire RO, Ailesbury MS, WRO 1300.
[35] *The Life, Diary and Correspondence of Sir William Dugdale*, ed. W. Hamper (1827); Edward Walker, *Historical Discourses* (1705).
[36] The main collections are BL, Add. MS 37998; Harl. MSS 6802–6804, 6851, 6852; Stowe MS 580; Bodl. Lib., MSS Ashmole 1110–1112, 1132; House of Lords RO, Historical Collection MS 65.
[37] BL, Egerton MSS 2533–2562 (many of which were published by the Camden Society in four volumes between 1886 and 1920); Surrey RO, Guildford Muniment Room, Bray Deposits 52/2/19, 85/5/2; Christ Church Muniment Room, Oxford, Evelyn Collection, Nicholas Box.
[38] BL, Add. MSS 64870–64924 (Coke MS, series I); Add. MSS 69868–69935 (Coke MS, series II); Add. MS 69936–69998 (Coke MS, series III).

although his thematic organisation of material into what John Morrill has called 'subject clusters' destroys any sense of chronological progression.[39] The *Journals* also tell us much about informal talks between the two sides: who acted as mediators, what terms were offered, and why they came to be rejected. These *Journals* must be supplemented by the many volumes of working papers generated by the Houses of Parliament during the 1640s, now among the so-called Main Papers in the House of Lords Record Office,[40] and also by the many private diaries kept by MPs.[41] The latter are critically important in uncovering how Constitutional Royalists converged in 1641–2, and why they ultimately felt impelled to leave Westminster. There are many discrepancies between them, and it is therefore difficult to know how closely they reproduce a speaker's original words. My policy throughout has been wherever possible to select passages recorded by more than one diarist – taking this to be a reasonably good indication that something analogous was once uttered – and then to cite the most lucid available version. Another helpful but still underused source are the papers of Speaker Lenthall, now among the Nalson and Tanner collections in the Bodleian Library.[42] These often cast important sidelights on political dynamics at Westminster, and also contain intriguing material about Royalist activities during the Interregnum. There is further important information to be gleaned from the various classes of State Papers in the Public Record Office, especially the State Papers Domestic and the papers of the Committee for Compounding with Royalist delinquents.[43]

Fourth, I have examined the main Royalist pamphlets and tracts of the Civil War period, and tried to assess how far their ideas influenced – and were informed by – political practice. While writers such as Maxwell, Hudson, Filmer and Hobbes may be classified as 'absolutist' Royalists with reasonable confidence, the positions of several others appear to resemble that of our Constitutional Royalists. The most prolific of these were John Bramhall, Sir Charles Dallison, Dudley Digges the younger, Henry Ferne, James Howell, David Jenkins, Jasper Mayne and Sir John Spelman; I analyse some of their principal works written during the 1640s in chapter 7.

Lastly, I make some use throughout this study of the various newsbooks published during the Civil Wars in both London and Oxford. These are a

---

[39] John Rushworth, *Historical Collections of private passages of State* (8 vols., 1680–1701); John Morrill, *The Nature of the English Revolution* (Harlow, 1993), p. 285, n. 1.
[40] MP.
[41] The main printed diaries of the Long Parliament are: D'Ewes (N); D'Ewes (C); *PJ*, I–III; and *Two Diaries*. The main MS diaries are found listed in the Bibliography, under British Library and Bodleian Library.
[42] Bodl. Lib., MSS Dep. c. 152–76 (Nalson MS); MSS Tanner 51–66 (letters and papers).
[43] PRO, SP 16 and 23 respectively.

very problematic source. Their purpose was often to persuade as much as to inform, and many of their statements can be shown from other documents to be distorted or false. None the less, they do tell us something about how the two sides wished to be seen – this is after all the main purpose of propaganda – and they sometimes contain information which cannot be gleaned anywhere else. Of the Royalist newsbooks, the most valuable is *Mercurius Aulicus*, written by Sir John Berkenhead. Its combination of reportage, gossip and speculation makes it a useful source. However, it seems essential when consulting both this and the London newsbooks not to place weight on their statements unless they are corroborated by other contemporary evidence.

All these classes of primary material really come into their own after 1640, and some only begin during the years of civil war. But if we are to interpret them correctly, we must first examine the state of England in the early seventeenth century. For only then can we understand the broad context within which Constitutional Royalism emerged.

—————————————————— 《 2 》——————————————————

Context: the early Stuarts and the early Stuart constitution

It is a truism that we can only fully understand the events which gripped England during the 1640s by first understanding the nature of English politics and government in the opening decades of the seventeenth century. But an investigation of Constitutional Royalism underlines this rather obvious point with unusual force. For it represented – in both theory and practice – a very specific response to a particular set of political circumstances. It could only have emerged within those circumstances; and it cannot be explained in isolation from them. The purpose of this chapter is to sketch the broad outline of those circumstances, and thus explore the problem which Constitutional Royalism attempted to resolve. We will look in turn at the nature of the English constitution in the early seventeenth century; at the contrasting ways in which the first two Stuarts managed that constitution; and at the political and religious tensions which had emerged by the later 1630s.

The English monarchy as it had evolved by 1603 was in many ways unusual by European standards. A combination of relatively confined geographical frontiers and the ambition of successive medieval monarchs had enabled the institutions of government and the law to achieve an exceptional degree of centralisation by the end of the Middle Ages. The existence (from the twelfth century) of a law that was genuinely 'common' to almost all of England, and (from the thirteenth) of a Parliament which plausibly claimed to be 'the body of the whole realm' gave England a head start in the process of national consolidation which characterised early modern Europe.[1] The Reformation further accentuated this divergence between English and continental patterns. Uniquely, it was imposed by the authority of the King-in-Parliament, not by that of the Crown alone. There is no exact continental parallel to this, or to the final eradication of

[1] There is a vast body of literature on this theme. For some contrasting accounts, see J. P. Cooper, *Land, Men and Beliefs*, ed. G. E. Aylmer and J. S. Morrill (1983), p. 109; Brian Manning, 'The nobles, the people, and the constitution', *P&P*, 9 (1956), 42–64; H. G. Koenigsberger, *Politicians and Virtuosi* (1986), pp. 1–25; Robert Bartlett, 'Lordship and law in medieval England', *JBS*, 30 (1991), 449–54; and Geoffrey Elton, *The English* (Oxford, 1992), pp. 55–60, 99–110.

palatinate jurisdictions (especially those of Chester and Durham) which accompanied it during the crowded decade of the 1530s.[2] When the preamble to the Act of Appeals (1533) stated that 'this realm of England is an empire' it asserted a freedom of action for the monarch and Parliament in both domestic and international affairs which was unique in Europe.[3]

This supremacy of King-in-Parliament in turn reflects what was perhaps the most distinctive feature of the constitution which the Stuarts inherited in 1603. It was exceptional in laying claim to be both a 'personal' monarchy and a 'mixed' monarchy. In constitutional terms, this gave the monarchy a Janus-like quality which could prove a source of both strength and (as we shall see) weakness. In one sense English monarchy was still what it had been throughout the Middle Ages and what most of its con-tinental neighbours unambiguously remained: a personal monarchy in which the monarch ruled as well as reigned. Much recent research has demonstrated the vital importance of the personalities of successive monarchs in influencing the nature of political processes and decisions. As Kevin Sharpe has written, 'in the seventeenth century the succession of a new monarch was still the fundamental change in the political climate'.[4] Moreover, the monarch remained the ultimate source of patronage and of public authority. All public offices, at both national and local levels, were held on royal commissions and exercised in the monarch's name. The Court did not just provide a splendid setting for the monarch; it emerges from recent research as a vital nerve-centre of political discussion, intrigue and decision making.[5] Those who enjoyed personal access to the monarch commonly wielded disproportionate influence over the formation and implementation of policy, while the heir to the throne often became the rallying point for those who felt excluded under the current sovereign.

Powerful ideologies existed to legitimate and reinforce such a situation. It may be inappropriate to apply Walter Ullmann's phrase 'a descending conception' of power to early modern England;[6] but a resilient belief in

[2] Compare the continental patterns discussed in Euan Cameron, *The European Reformation* (Oxford, 1991), especially pp. 267–91.
[3] The Act of Appeals (24 Hen. VIII, c. 12) is printed in full in G. R. Elton, ed., *The Tudor Constitution* (2nd edition, Cambridge, 1982), pp. 353–8; the quotation is at p. 353. Cf. Walter Ullmann, '"This Realm of England is an Empire"', *Journal of Ecclesiastical History*, 30 (1979), 175–203.
[4] Kevin Sharpe, 'The image of virtue: the court and household of Charles I, 1625–1642', in *The English Court from the Wars of the Roses to the Civil War*, ed. David Starkey (Harlow, 1987), p. 226. Cf. Kevin Sharpe, *The Personal Rule of Charles I* (New Haven and London, 1992), p. 179.
[5] See especially *The English Court*, Starkey, *passim*; but see also the ensuing debate: G. R. Elton, 'Tudor government', *HJ*, 31 (1988), 425–34; David Starkey, 'A reply: Tudor government: the facts', *HJ*, 31 (1988), 921–31.
[6] For this term, see Walter Ullmann, *Principles of Government and Politics in the Middle Ages* (2nd edition, 1966), p. 20.

'the divinity that doth hedge a king' is very easy to document. Johann Sommerville has shown that theories of kingship by divine right – which held that monarchs derived their powers from God, that they were answerable to Him alone, and that they could not therefore be lawfully resisted – 'existed in the minds of many Englishmen, not just in the ravings of a few eccentric clerics'.[7] This was a political culture which accepted the necessity for royal discretionary powers outside the definition of the common law (labelled generically the royal 'prerogative'); which perceived the crown as the natural apex of the political hierarchy; and which perpetuated beliefs in the healing powers of monarchs which had been attributed to the English and French monarchies since the end of the Dark Ages. The very fact that scrofula came to be known as the 'King's Evil' catches something of the quasi-divine character of monarchy in early modern England.[8]

Yet this tradition did not exist in isolation. During the sixteenth century, theorists who defended the notion of limited monarchy emerged in a number of continental states. One of the most influential works in France, for example, was Claude de Seyssel's *The Monarchy of France* (1515), which analysed French kingship in terms of a series of 'bridles' upon the monarch's authority.[9] In England, this tradition of limited monarchy dated back at least to the thirteenth-century legist Henry de Bracton, who formulated the principle *debet rex esse sub lege*.[10] The view of monarchy under the law was powerfully endorsed in the late fifteenth century by the work of Chief Justice Sir John Fortescue, which described the English monarchy as *dominium politicum et regale* (constitutional monarchy) in contradistinction to *dominium regale* (absolute monarchy).[11] This principle was enshrined by the reforms of the 1530s which established the legislative supremacy of statutes passed by a 'mixed sovereign' consisting of the King-in-

---

[7] J. P. Sommerville, *Politics and Ideology in England, 1603–1640* (Harlow, 1986), p. 46.
[8] On this subject the classic work remains Marc Bloch, *Les rois thaumaturges* (Strasburg, 1924); but see also Judith Richards, '"His Nowe Majestie" and the English monarchy: the kingship of Charles I before 1640', *P&P*, 113 (1986), 77–81. For Charles I's proclamations regulating the ceremony of 'touching' for the 'King's Evil', see J. F. Larkin, ed., *Stuart Royal Proclamations*, vol. II: *Royal Proclamations of King Charles I, 1625–46* (Oxford, 1983), 44–5, 238–9, 256–8, 349–50, 416–17, 433–4, 446–7, 466–7, 504–5, 552–3, 574–5, 621–2, 629–30, 693–4.
[9] Quentin Skinner, *The Foundations of Modern Political Thought* (2 vols., Cambridge, 1978), II, 260–7.
[10] Elton, *Tudor Constitution*, p. 13. This tradition in English political and constitutional thought might be traced back even earlier: see J. C. Holt, *Magna Carta and Medieval Government* (1985), pp. 1–22.
[11] Elton, *Tudor Constitution*, p. 13. Cf. Koenigsberger, *Politicians and Virtuosi*, pp. 1–25; Gerald Harriss, 'Political society and the growth of government in late medieval England', *P&P*, 138 (1993), 28–57; and Michael Mendle, 'Parliamentary sovereignty: a very English absolutism', in *Political Discourse in Early Modern Britain*, ed. Nicholas Phillipson and Quentin Skinner (Cambridge, 1993), pp. 101–11.

Parliament.[12] By 1559, Bishop John Aylmer of London could describe the English constitution in terms which anticipate some of the views expressed by Constitutional Royalists during the 1640s: 'the regiment of Englande is not a mere monarchie, as some for lacke of consideracion thinke, nor a meere oligarchie, nor democratie, but a rule mixte of all these, wherein ech one of these have or should have like authoritie'.[13] England, it seemed, had managed to attain the benefits of strong monarchical rule while avoiding its attendant dangers. When Richard Hooker commended 'their wisdom by whom the foundations of this Commonwealth have been laid; wherein, though no manner person or cause be unsubject to the King's power, yet so is the power of the King over all and in all limited that unto all his proceedings the law itself is a rule', he embraced a secularised view of the English as an 'elect nation' which amounted to saying that England had managed to have its constitutional cake and eat it.[14]

Unfortunately, at the heart of this attractive paradigm of royal government by both divine right and popular consent lay a logical contradiction. If the powers of either the sovereign or subjects (or at any rate of their representatives in Parliament) were extended to their full potential, they would inevitably become incompatible. Tudor and early Stuart political theory sought to avert this possibility by insisting repeatedly on a natural harmony between monarch and subject. One of the greatest achievements of 'revisionism' has been to demonstrate how deeply this harmony was perceived as normative in early modern English politics. The idea of conflict between monarch and people appeared unnatural and abhorrent; instead contemporaries concentrated on celebrating the intuitive rapport between them. As Henry VIII told both Houses of Parliament in 1542: 'we at no time stand so highly in our estate royal as in the time of Parliament, wherein we as head and you as members are conjoined and knit together into one body politic'.[15] The supremacy of statute and the much weaker powers accorded to proclamations meant that the Tudors and early Stuarts wielded far greater power when acting with Parliament than when acting alone. Yet there were absolutely no cast-iron guarantees of this 'special relationship'. What if the monarch and Parliament should fall out? What if the royal prerogative and the common law should come into conflict?

---

[12] The phrase 'mixed sovereign' was coined by Sir Geoffrey Elton: e.g. G. R. Elton, *Studies in Tudor and Stuart Politics and Government* (4 vols., Cambridge, 1974–92), II, 213; *England under the Tudors* (3rd edition, 1991), p. 482.

[13] John Aylmer, *An Harborowe for Faithfull and Trewe Subiectes* (Strasburg, 1559), sigs. H2[v]–H3[r] (*STC*, 1005).

[14] Richard Hooker, *Of the Laws of Ecclesiastical Polity*, ed. Arthur Stephen McGrade (Cambridge, 1989), p. 147 (Book VIII, c. 2 [13]).

[15] These words come from Henry VIII's speech regarding Ferrers' Case, quoted in Elton, *Tudor Constitution*, p. 277.

Contemporary constitutional thought offered no answer. All it asserted was that the monarch *should* act *pro bono publico* not *pro bono suo*, and that the royal prerogative and the common law were therefore innately symbiotic.[16] It was possible to believe that both existed by divine right.[17] As Chief Justice Hobart declared in 1623: 'The prerogative laws are ... the law of the realm for the king, as the common law is the law of the realm of the subject'.[18] This meant that the locus of ultimate sovereignty was never identified, and there was no machinery for arbitration if these two sources of authority collided.

It needs stressing that this system of government, often called the 'ancient constitution', was not inherently unstable.[19] It had many attractions as a form of mixed government in which no single source of authority was able to act without restraint, and in which different 'divine rights' could co-exist in harmonious order.[20] But, as John Reeve has argued, 'the working of the English constitution depended upon avoiding the activation of the various potential conflicts contained within it'.[21] To put it another way, this was a system which relied for its smooth running on the maintenance of grey areas. It required politicians to become so taken with the benefits of balance and harmony that they lost sight of the logical flaws and contradictions within the constitution.

Recent research on the reigns of Elizabeth I and James I strongly suggests that this was far from an impossible ideal. Both these monarchs displayed considerable skill in their handling of the political nation. Time and again, they projected a sense that they wanted what their leading subjects wanted. Their management of Parliament illustrates this very clearly. Without losing sight of the evident disagreements which emerged during Elizabethan Parliaments – especially over religion, over law reform and over the 'common weal' – it remains true that relations between the monarch and the political élite were never in danger of breaking down

---

[16] Cf. John Morrill, *The Nature of the English Revolution* (Harlow, 1993), pp. 4–5, 50, 409–11, 416.

[17] Conrad Russell, 'Divine rights in the early seventeenth century', in *Public Duty and Private Conscience in Seventeenth-Century England: Essays Presented to G. E. Aylmer*, ed. John Morrill, Paul Slack and Daniel Woolf (Oxford, 1993), pp. 111–12.

[18] Quoted in Derek Hirst, *Authority and Conflict: England, 1603–1658* (1986), p. 27.

[19] For contrasting discussions of the origins and assumptions of the 'ancient constitution', see Sommerville, *Politics and Ideology*, pp. 86–111; J. P. Kenyon, ed., *The Stuart Constitution* (2nd edition, Cambridge, 1986), pp. 7–110; J. G. A. Pocock, *The Ancient Constitution and the Feudal Law* (2nd edition, Cambridge, 1987), especially pp. 30–69, 255–305; William Klein, 'The ancient constitution revisited', in *Political Discourse in Early Modern Britain*, Phillipson and Skinner, pp. 23–44; and above all Glenn Burgess, *The Politics of the Ancient Constitution: An Introduction to English Political Thought, 1603–1642* (1992), *passim*.

[20] Russell, 'Divine rights', pp. 104–7.

[21] L. J. Reeve, *Charles I and the Road to Personal Rule* (Cambridge, 1989), p. 178.

completely.[22] As Sir Geoffrey Elton has written, Elizabeth's 'golden speech' of 30 November 1601, in which she declared 'that never thought was cherished in my heart that tended not to my people's good', 'symbolises the essential unity of Crown and Commons, of queen and people, upon which the Tudor constitution rested'.[23] The crucial skill was not to *avoid* disagreements over specific policies but rather to make them pall beside the underlying unanimity between a monarch and a people devoted to the good of each other.

James I possessed these abilities to a far greater degree than was once thought. This was a monarch well able to live with grey areas; a man whose personality and private life equipped him to cope with ambivalence. There was something deeply appropriate about a king who coveted the title of *rex pacificus* ruling this constitution with all its fudges and blurred distinctions. It is certainly true that his initial dealings with the English Parliament betrayed a lack of tact; that his personal appearance and behaviour belied his high-flown rhetoric of kingship; that he could rage and fume against the House of Commons, as in 1614, when he told the Spanish ambassador Gondomar that he was 'surprised that [his] ancestors should ever have allowed such an institution to come into existence', or in 1621 when he tore the House's Protestation out of the Commons' Journal.[24] Yet through it all, he remained willing to summon Parliaments regularly and to listen to their advice. He admitted to Gondomar in the same breath that he was 'obliged to put up with what' he could not 'get rid of'.[25] Very few members of very few Jacobean Parliaments actually feared for the future of the institution. Near the start of his reign, James told the Houses that if the Gunpowder Plot had succeeded, 'mine end should have been with the most honourable and best company, and in that most honourable and fittest place for a king to be in'.[26] Near his actual end, after the troubled session of 1621, he could still remark that 'the House of Commons at this time have showed greater love, and used me with more respect in all their proceedings than ever any House of Commons have heretofore done to me'.[27] There is no reason to doubt Conrad Russell's fundamental observation that 'in general, the story of 1621 and 1624

[22] For this picture of Elizabethan Parliaments, see especially G. R. Elton, *The Parliament of England, 1559–1581* (Cambridge, 1986); Michael A. R. Graves, *Elizabethan Parliaments, 1559–1601* (Harlow, 1987); D. M. Dean and N. L. Jones, ed., *The Parliaments of Elizabethan England* (Oxford and Cambridge, MA, 1990); and the essays in N. Jones and D. Dean, ed., *Parliamentary History*, 8 (1989), part ii (special issue, 'Interest groups and legislation in Elizabethan Parliaments: Essays presented to Sir Geoffrey Elton').
[23] Elton, *Tudor Constitution*, p. 312. An extract from Elizabeth's 'golden speech' is printed at pp. 325–6.
[24] For James's remark to Gondomar, see Gardiner, *History*, II, 251; for his tearing of the Protestation out of the Commons' Journal in 1621, see Russell, *Parliaments*, pp. 141–4.
[25] Gardiner, *History*, II, 251.   [26] *LJ*, II, 359.   [27] *LJ*, III, 69.

suggests that not very much was wrong with relations between Crown and Parliament'.[28] It is striking how closely these words resemble Sir Geoffrey Elton's summing up of Elizabeth I's relations with her Parliaments.

The continuities between Elizabeth I and James I extended far beyond this knack for working effectively with Parliaments. Their subjects' perception that both monarchs ruled *pro bono publico* was greatly strengthened by their approach to two key areas: the common law, and the Church of England. Here, as with Parliament, 1603 proved much less of a turning-point than historians once believed.[29]

There are no known instances of Elizabeth I's trying to influence, let alone pervert, the due processes of the common law. Contemporaries felt entirely confident that the prerogative and the common law complemented and reinforced each other. A good example is found in the writing of Sir Thomas Smith, who asserted in the 1560s that 'diverse ... rights and pre-eminences the prince hath which be called prerogatives royal ... which be declared particularly in the books of the common laws of England'.[30] Discretionary powers were not abused: 'as Smith explained, *legibus solutus* meant to the Tudors a right to dispense with the law if equity required it, a necessary point of flexibility'.[31]

It seems that James I acted in the same spirit. At no time did he 'assert that he could override the common law at will'.[32] The opening phrases of his speech to Parliament on 21 March 1610 might at first sight suggest a belief in divine right monarchy: 'the state of monarchy is the supremest thing upon earth; for kings are not only God's lieutenants upon earth, and sit upon God's throne, but even by God himself they are called gods'.[33] However, it is vital to notice the distinction which James then made 'between the state of kings in their first original, and ... the state of settled kings and monarchies that do at this time govern in civil kingdoms'. The latter was characterised by monarchical rule under a system of laws – laws

which are properly made by the king only, but at the rogation of the people, the king's grant being obtained thereunto. And so the king came to be *lex loquens*, after a sort, binding himself by a double oath to the observation of the fundamental laws of the kingdom: tacitly, as by being a king, and so bound to protect as well the people as the laws of his kingdom; and expressly, by his oath at his coronation. So ... every just king in a settled kingdom is bound to observe that paction made to his people by his laws, in framing his government agreeable thereto ... [34]

---

[28] Russell, *Parliaments*, p. 419.
[29] For a survey and powerful critique of the view that 1603 marked a watershed, see e.g. Elton, *Studies*, II, 164–82.
[30] Quoted in Elton, *Tudor Constitution*, p. 20.   [31] *Ibid.*, p. 18.
[32] Burgess, *Politics of the Ancient Constitution*, p. 155.
[33] Quoted in Kenyon, *Stuart Constitution*, p. 11.   [34] *Ibid.*, p. 12.

This passage takes us to the heart of James's vision of the ancient constitution, and reveals much about why he proved able to manage it so successfully. Its picture of a sovereign law-giver who yet ruled according to the fundamental laws of the kingdom shows considerable sensitivity to the ambivalences of the English polity.[35] As Glenn Burgess has written, James's speech was 'an appeal to consensus – that is to an agreed theoretical framework'.[36] Logically, the system was riddled with contradictions. Yet, when managed in this benign spirit, it proved workable. There were strict limits to James's interference in common law actions. The closest call was probably Bate's Case (1606), but even here, James left the Judges of the Court of Exchequer to reach their own verdict without royal intimidation.[37] Indeed, the King upheld the divine right of judges,[38] and was 'careful to argue that impositions by prerogative were not a threat to common law because they were applied only in areas beyond the territorial jurisdiction of the English common law'.[39] Throughout his reign, James's conscience and sense of duty made him adhere strictly to the terms of his coronation oath;[40] and his own words carry great conviction: 'never king was in all his time more careful to have his laws duly observed, and himself to govern thereafter, than I'.[41]

Another area in which there were marked continuities between Elizabeth and James lay in their management of the Church of England. This was, of course, intimately related to the first two areas: Protestantism was the 'true religion by law established'; it was protected and enforced by the Acts of Supremacy and Uniformity passed by Elizabeth's first Parliament. This made it impossible to separate issues affecting the Church from those bearing on the law and the constitution, a consequence of the particular nature of the English Reformation which added a further dimension to the close relationship between politics and religion in early modern Europe.[42] Furthermore, the wide spectrum of religious opinion among English Protestants (not to mention the survival of a resilient Catholic minority) meant that the Church of England required as delicate a balancing act on the monarch's part as did the management of secular government and the law. To favour one strand of religious opinion over another would be disastrous. Elizabeth I and James I both proved singularly adept at this

[35] Cf. Paul Christianson, 'Royal and parliamentary voices on the ancient constitution, *c.* 1604–1621', in *The Mental World of the Jacobean Court*, ed. Linda Levy Peck (Cambridge, 1991), especially pp. 76–8.
[36] Burgess, *Politics of the Ancient Constitution*, p. 148.
[37] For a detailed account of Bate's Case, see Gardiner, *History*, II, 6–10.
[38] Russell, 'Divine rights', pp. 107–8.
[39] Burgess, *Politics of the Ancient Constitution*, p. 141.
[40] Kevin Sharpe, 'Private conscience and public duty in the writings of James VI and I', in *Public Duty and Private Conscience*, Morrill *et al.*, pp. 85–7.
[41] Kenyon, *Stuart Constitution*, p. 12.   [42] For this, cf. Russell, *Causes*, pp. 62–3.

balancing act. Elizabeth was determined to preserve 'the quietness of the Church reformed' against pressure from both 'right' and 'left':[43] she suspended Archbishop Grindal for not suppressing Puritan 'prophesyings'; and in 1595 refused Whitgift permission to promulgate the Lambeth Articles in order to avoid further divisive debates over predestination.[44] She was, initially, one of the very few staunch defenders of this 'Church but halfly reformed', yet her careful protection allowed the Church to strike deep roots by 1603. Similarly, James I emerges from the recent work of Kenneth Fincham and Peter Lake as an enlightened Governor of the Church who sought to woo moderate Catholics and moderate Puritans and to welcome a plurality of religious opinion within the broad framework of a national Church. He 'was a monarch dedicated to the principle of religious unity'[45] who maintained stability in a Church which was never doctrinally monolithic.[46] Perhaps James's most skilful ploy – in which he surpassed even Gloriana – was to ensure that nearly all varieties of opinion could secure promotion within the ecclesiastical hierarchy. The Church of Elizabeth and James was one from which very few ever felt excluded or wished to separate.[47]

All these similarities of policy and method between the last Tudor and the first Stuart surely suggest that the change of dynasty in 1603 was much less of a watershed than has sometimes been argued. We may well obtain a truer picture by concentrating on the elements of continuity which unite the period 1558–1625; those which encouraged many during the 1640s to speak of James and Elizabeth in the same breath. Perhaps we can even highlight the considerable amount of common ground between their two reigns by using the term 'Jacobethan' to describe this period.

---

[43] For the quotation, see Elton, *Tudor Constitution*, p. 454; for Elizabeth's management of the Church, see especially Patrick Collinson, *The Religion of Protestants* (Oxford, 1982), pp. 1–38; Christopher Haigh, *Elizabeth I* (Harlow, 1988), pp. 27–46.

[44] Grindal's suspension is described in Patrick Collinson, *Archbishop Grindal, 1519–1583* (1979), pp. 233–65. Contrasting accounts of the controversy over the Lambeth Articles may be found in H. C. Porter, *Reformation and Reaction in Tudor Cambridge* (Cambridge, 1958), pp. 364–75; Peter Lake, *Moderate Puritans and the Elizabethan Church* (Cambridge, 1982), pp. 218–42; and Peter White, *Predestination, Policy and Polemic: Conflict and Consensus in the English Church from the Reformation to the English Civil War* (Cambridge, 1992), pp. 101–10.

[45] Kenneth Fincham and Peter Lake, 'The ecclesiastical policy of King James I', *JBS*, 24 (1985), 169–207, at 187. See also 'The ecclesiastical policies of James I and Charles I', in *The Early Stuart Church, 1603–1642*, ed. Kenneth Fincham (1993), especially pp. 23–36.

[46] This theme, and especially the lack of consensus over the doctrine of predestination, is explored in White, *Predestination, Policy and Polemic*, especially pp. 60–214; and 'The via media in the early Stuart Church', in *Early Stuart Church*, Fincham, pp. 211–30.

[47] This view of the Jacobean Church is based especially on Fincham and Lake, 'Ecclesiastical policy of James I'; 'Ecclesiastical policies of James I and Charles I'; Kenneth Fincham, *Prelate as Pastor: The Episcopate of James I* (Oxford, 1990); Peter Lake, 'Calvi-

The parallels between Elizabeth and James are thrown into high relief when we turn to the reign of Charles I. As we saw above, the arrival of a new monarch was always a pivotal moment for this political system. In a personal monarchy the personality of the monarch remained of fundamental importance. In a mixed monarchy, however, it was essential that the monarch's personality should 'mix' well with the personalities of the leading subjects. The constitution possessed no machinery to secure this 'mixing' if it did not occur naturally. Unfortunately, in almost every aspect of policy Charles I proved less suited to co-operate with his leading subjects in governing the English Church and State than his two immediate predecessors. I will argue shortly that 1625 marked a turning-point in the monarch's handling of Parliament, the common law and the Church. But first, I want to examine three personality traits which rendered Charles poorly equipped to rule the 'ancient constitution': a passion for order and definition, an inability to trust others, and a lack of political instinct. There is perhaps a danger that the following account will seem unduly one-sided. But it is deliberately partial because I want to focus on those personal attributes of Charles I which revealed the fault-lines in the early Stuart constitution; or – to change the metaphor – which led him to work against the grain of the political system rather than with it.

All three of these characteristics stemmed in large part from a fundamental insecurity and lack of confidence. Conrad Russell has argued plausibly that 'a constant nagging doubt about his status and capacity ... underlay many of Charles's less fortunate political characteristics'.[48] It would be difficult to imagine a more damaging weakness in this particular political context, for it required plenty of self-confidence to govern the English constitution, with its delicate balances, its compromises, its grey areas. Only a genuinely confident ruler could cope with the poorly defined ground rules of such a system. Charles – for reasons which are now almost impossible to recover – lacked such confidence. Instead, he 'always sought to define the point at issue'.[49] Had this predilection been confined to drawing up vast tomes of Household ordinances – prescribing in minute detail the meals granted to Court officials, the keys allocated to various servants or the regulations necessary to reduce embezzlement – it might have proved harmless enough.[50] But when translated into the sphere of public policy it became extremely dangerous in a constitution which depended so heavily on blurred distinctions. Those grey areas made it

nism and the English Church, 1570–1635', *P&P*, 114 (1987), 32–76; Collinson, *Religion of Protestants*, pp. 1–38.
[48] Russell, *Causes*, pp. 204–5.
[49] Reeve, *Road to Personal Rule*, p. 178. Cf. Sharpe, *Personal Rule*, pp. 182–3, 191–6, 198.
[50] For a discussion of these ordinances, see Sharpe, 'Image of virtue', pp. 229–48; and *Personal Rule*, pp. 209–40.

virtually impossible to produce a definition of political, legal or ecclesiastical authority which could command universal agreement. Instead, by defining his own position, Charles forced others to define theirs, and this process caused growing rifts between the King and many of his leading subjects.

This was all the more disastrous because Charles found it extremely difficult to trust others. The work of Richard Cust in particular has revealed Charles's deep anxieties about his subjects' loyalty, and demonstrated that these dated back to the opening years of his reign.[51] Charles seemed unable to attribute to his critics anything but the most subversive intentions. He assumed that those who disagreed with him were 'wicked spirits' or 'malignants'.[52] Furthermore, criticism seems consistently to have taken him by surprise. This in turn reflected Charles's marked lack of political instinct. As John Reeve has written, Charles 'had no conception of the art of the possible and was unreceptive and ill at ease in the world of affairs ... in a fundamental sense, [he] did not understand the use of power'.[53] Another aspect of Charles's poor political skills was the fact that, in the words of Conrad Russell, 'he tended to have a somewhat two-dimensional view of other people, and therefore to lack skill in predicting their reactions'.[54] This helps to explain why he so frequently granted concessions too late for them to do any good.[55] Taken together, all these traits meant that Charles was neither a natural negotiator nor a natural politician. They proved deeply destabilising when applied to Parliament, to the legal system and to the Church.

Thanks to the research of Conrad Russell, Richard Cust and John Reeve, we are now very well informed about the Parliaments of 1625–9. It seems clear that political and religious tension escalated to new levels during the second half of the 1620s. How far can this be attributed to the change of monarch in 1625? At first sight, Charles I's declared vision of Parliaments was nothing if not orthodox. As he put it in 1640:

These meetings and assemblies were in their first originall and in the practise of all succeeding ages ordained and held as pledges and testimonies of affection between the King and his people, the King for his part graciously hearing and reddressing such grievances as his people in humble and dutifull manner shall represent unto him, and the subjects on their part ... supplying His Majesty upon all extraordinary occasions.[56]

[51] Richard Cust, *The Forced Loan and English Politics, 1626–1628* (Oxford, 1987), pp. 325–8; cf. Russell, *Causes*, pp. 202–3.
[52] Cust, *Forced Loan*, p. 22; Russell, *Causes*, p. 203.
[53] Reeve, *Road to Personal Rule*, p. 176.
[54] Russell, *Causes*, p. 206.   [55] Cf. *ibid.*, pp. 208–9.
[56] *His Majesties Declaration to all his loving subjects on the causes which moved him to dissolve the last Parliament* (1640), p. 49 (CUL, Syn. 7. 64. 73/43).

But this passage does not, I suggest, offer the insight into Charles's mind, or the blueprint for his actions, that the speech of 21 March 1610 does for his father. A more promising candidate for such a text is probably the draft declaration for the Parliament of 1628, recently edited by Richard Cust.[57] This was drawn up by Attorney-General Sir Robert Heath but never actually issued. However, there seems no reason to doubt that it accurately reflected the King's own wishes. In a most revealing passage, it summed up the Parliament which had passed the Petition of Right as follows:

By the event we find that some of the members of that house [of commons], blinded with a popular applause, have, under the specious shew of redeeminge the libertye of the subject, indevoured to destroye our just powre of soveraignty, trusted unto us by God almighty, and which we, by the assistaunce of his divine grace, neather doe, nor ever did, intend to use but for the good and protection of our people, wherby they have soe diverted that which was the mayne ende of ther assembling, our timely supplyes for the common safetye of us all, that the parliament, having nowe satt full sixe weeks … they have not given soe much as one reeding to the bill by which those nominall subsidyes should be graunted and really confirmed unto us.[58]

This passage is covered with Charles's fingerprints: the insistence that he only intended the good of his subjects; the belief that all criticism sprang from a subversive minority who sought to 'destroye' his 'soveraignty'; and the sense that the main purpose of Parliaments was to grant supply. It reflects a view of Parliament less as the monarch's 'great council' than as a revenue-voting body, and thus marks a vital step away from the 'Jacobethan' ideal. Such a view certainly contrasts with that of John Pym, for whom 'bills [were] the end of a Parliament'.[59] But it makes it very easy to see why Charles – faced with Parliaments reluctant to vote supply – decided first to raise money by alternative methods (the Forced Loan), and then, at the end of the 1620s, to abandon Parliaments altogether. He was not prepared to keep going with Parliaments if they failed to grant supply. When he embarked on the Personal Rule, it was because he had actually come to prefer non-parliamentary forms of government.[60]

It is sometimes suggested that here the contrast with James I was more apparent than real.[61] After all, with the exception of the Addled Parliament (1614), Parliament did not meet between 1610 and 1621; and no statutes

[57] Richard Cust, 'Charles I and a draft Declaration for the 1628 Parliament', *Historical Research*, 63 (1990), 143–61. The original of this draft is PRO, SP 16/138/45i. See also Richard Cust, 'Charles I, the Privy Council and the Parliament of 1628', *TRHS*, 6th series, 2 (1992), 38–40, 49–50.
[58] Cust, 'Charles I and a draft Declaration', 160.
[59] Quoted in Conrad Russell, *Unrevolutionary England, 1603–1642* (1990), p. 217. Sir Geoffrey Elton regards this as 'an admirable and memorable definition' of a Parliament: Elton, *Parliament*, p. 25.
[60] The growth of this preference is charted in detail in Reeve, *Road to Personal Rule*, *passim*; and in Sharpe, *Personal Rule*, pp. 8–62.
[61] See, for example, Sharpe, *Personal Rule*, p. 603.

were passed during these eleven years. But it cannot be emphasised too much that the circumstances of these two eleven-year periods were completely different. The Jacobean case coincided with a period of international peace predicated on the Dutch–Spanish truce of 1609. In peacetime, Parliaments became less necessary. But as soon as conflict resumed in the late 1610s, James quickly summoned a Parliament. It was otherwise under Charles I. He took the decision to dissolve Parliament in March 1629 and *then* withdrew from the Thirty Years' War under the terms of the Treaties of Susa (April 1629) and Madrid (November 1630).[62] This chronology reveals the crucial difference: under James I prolonged peace rendered Parliaments dispensable; under Charles I, a conscious decision to rule without Parliaments preceded and necessitated a pacific foreign policy. Contemporary members of Parliament did not fail to draw their own conclusions. As Sir Benjamin Rudyerd correctly perceived in 1628: 'This is the crisis of Parliaments: we shall know by this if Parliaments live or die.'[63]

One of the functions of the Houses of Parliament was to sit as a court of law, and it is therefore unsurprising to find that these contrasts hold good when we compare James's and Charles's handling of the legal system. Whereas James never departed from his pledge of 1610 to observe 'the fundamental laws of the kingdom', Charles showed no such scruples. Over the last decade, several studies have revealed his readiness time and again to subvert the workings of the common law in order to secure his preferred judgements.[64] This work has culminated in Glenn Burgess's recent study, which concludes that 'unlike his father, Charles made only the most unconvincing claims to be ruling by the law' and 'muddled the language of absolute prerogative with that of the common law'.[65] The alternative interpretation, which argues that there was 'a staunchly legalistic strain to Charles's theory and practice of kingship', does not tell the whole story.[66] Against it, two episodes will serve to illustrate Charles's 'impatience . . . of following legal forms and procedures' and his willingness instead to erect a 'legal tyranny'.[67]

[62] These treaties are discussed in Reeve, *Road to Personal Rule*, pp. 51–2, 242–62; and in Sharpe, *Personal Rule*, pp. 65–70.
[63] J.A. Manning, ed., *Memoirs of Sir Benjamin Rudyerd* (1841), p. 114. For further discussion of Rudyerd see below, pp. 35–6, 99–100, 104. I am hoping to carry out further research on this topic in the future.
[64] Reeve, *Road to Personal Rule*; 'The arguments in King's Bench in 1629 concerning the imprisonment of John Selden and other Members of the House of Commons', *JBS*, 25 (1986), 264–87; John Guy, 'The origins of the Petition of Right reconsidered', *HJ*, 25 (1982), 289–312; Cust, *Forced Loan*.
[65] Burgess, *Politics of the Ancient Constitution*, p. 213.
[66] Sharpe, *Personal Rule*, pp. 194–6, 659–65, 931–2; quotation at p. 195.
[67] Burgess, *Politics of the Ancient Constitution*, p. 200. For a discussion of how the term 'legal tyranny' – taken from Charles I's final letter to the Prince of Wales in January 1649 – accurately describes the King's own actions during the later 1620s, see Morrill, *Nature of the English Revolution*, pp. 287–91.

First, when the Five Knights were tried in the Court of King's Bench in 1627 for refusing to pay the Forced Loan, Charles was determined that the judges should not discuss his right to imprison for non-payment, but instead should endorse his right to imprison without cause shown in national emergencies. The King was furious when the judges simply entered a 'rule of court' which could not serve as a precedent, and ordered Attorney-General Heath to change the ruling into a binding judgement. The House of Lords was horrified to learn from Buckingham that Heath 'had a check from the King' to commit this wholly illegal act.[68]

Second, in 1629 the Commons investigated why the printed form of the Petition of Right differed from that passed by both Houses, and now included the King's first – and unacceptable – answer within the body of the text. Moreover, the King's printer had originally given the Petition of Right a statute number, but this had been obliterated by a pumice-stone to make its statutory force less certain. Both changes were blatantly illegal; and again it emerged that both had been personally authorised by the King.[69]

There is no evidence that such actions had any parallel under James I. Unlike his father, Charles I was willing to use emergency powers to override the common law. And by claiming that right for himself, he forced others to define their own positions with a novel precision.[70] The happy commonplaces about a natural symbiosis between royal prerogative and common law began to give way, during the later 1620s, to sentiments such as those voiced by Henry Sherman in 1628: 'I never knew the prerogative but as a part of the common law.'[71] Pym, in very similar language, refused to recognise any royal power 'distinct . . . from the power of the law'.[72] Sir Thomas Wentworth, perceiving the threat which this posed to orthodox beliefs about the relationship between prerogative and law declared: 'I hope it shall never be stirred here whether the King be above the law or the law above the King.'[73] When that question became even thinkable, one of the cardinal assumptions underpinning the 'ancient constitution' had begun to unravel. And it was Charles's actions which were responsible for its being thinkable by 1628.[74]

If this was Charles's attitude towards the law, we would hardly expect

[68] Guy, 'Origins of Petition of Right'; and Burgess, *Politics of the Ancient Constitution*, pp. 191–4. For this quotation, see F. H. Relf, ed., *Notes of the Debates in the House of Lords, 1621–9* (Camden Society, 3rd series, 42, 1929), 93.
[69] Morrill, *Nature of the English Revolution*, p. 289.
[70] Cf. Burgess, *Politics of the Ancient Constitution*, pp. 213–14.
[71] Mary Frear Keeler, M. J. Cole and W. B. Bidwell, ed., *Proceedings in Parliament, 1628* (6 vols., New Haven, 1977–83), III, 99.
[72] *Ibid.*, 494.   [73] *Ibid.*, 98–9.
[74] Cf. Burgess, *Politics of the Ancient Constitution*, p. 200.

him to treat the 'Church by law established' with any greater respect. While it would be inappropriate here to offer a detailed account of the religious policies of the later 1620s and 1630s, it is nevertheless vital to explore how Charles and Laud sought to alter the Church of England, how they deviated from 'Jacobethan' practices, and therefore why 1625 marked a critical turning-point in the ecclesiastical as well as the parliamentary and legal history of England.[75] This is all the more necessary because such an interpretation is by no means universally accepted.[76]

The fact that William Laud became Archbishop of Canterbury at all surely reflected the change of monarch. It would almost certainly never have happened under James I, who only appointed Laud Bishop of St David's in 1621 very reluctantly and warned Buckingham darkly 'take him to you, but on my soul you will repent it'.[77] Laud was but one of a string of high church clerics promoted to senior positions in the mid- and late 1620s. By 1628, the archbishopric of York, the bishoprics of London, Durham, Chichester, Bath and Wells, Carlisle, Ely, Exeter, Coventry and Lichfield, Norwich, Oxford, Rochester and Winchester, and many senior deaneries and livings were occupied by divines of a Laudian persuasion.[78] Dr George Morley who, when asked 'what the Arminians held', quipped that 'they held all the best bishoprics and deaneries in England', was making a significant point.[79] Certainly there are signs that this trend began in James's later years.[80] It is also true that three of the leading members of the Durham House group – Laud, Matthew Wren and John Cosin – were first accepted at Court between 1621 and 1624. But, as Hugh Trevor-Roper has pointed out, they were accepted 'not by King James, but by the Prince of Wales and the Duke of Buckingham'.[81] Like the promotions of other

[75] For interpretations which see 1625 as a watershed, see especially Nicholas Tyacke, 'Puritanism, Arminianism and counter-revolution', in *The Origins of the English Civil War*, ed. Conrad Russell (1973), pp. 119–43; *Anti-Calvinists: The Rise of English Arminianism, c. 1590–1640* (Oxford, 1987); Lake, 'Calvinism and the English Church'; Russell, *Causes*, pp. 58–130; Julian Davies, *The Caroline Captivity of the Church* (Oxford, 1992); and *Early Stuart Church*, Fincham, especially chapters 1–4 and 7.

[76] Arguments which stress the continuities across 1625 were adumbrated in Kevin Sharpe, 'Archbishop Laud', *History Today*, 33 (1983), 26–30; and Peter White, 'The rise of Arminianism reconsidered', *P&P*, 101 (1983), 34–54. They have now been developed at length in White, *Predestination, Policy and Polemic*; 'Via media'; and Sharpe, *Personal Rule*, especially pp. 275–402.

[77] John Hacket, *Scrinia Reserata: A Memorial Offer'd to the Great Deservings of John Williams, D.D.* (1693), Part I, 64 (Wing, H 171).

[78] This statement is based on an examination of the lists of English archbishops and bishops in E. B. Fryde, D. E. Greenway, S. Porter and I. Roy, ed., *Handbook of British Chronology* (3rd edition, 1986), pp. 213–84. Cf. Kenneth Fincham, 'Episcopal government, 1603–40', in *Early Stuart Church*, Fincham, pp. 71–91.

[79] Clarendon, *Life*, I, 56.

[80] See the discussion in Sheila Lambert, 'Richard Montagu, Arminianism and censorship', *P&P*, 124 (1989), especially 36–43.

[81] Hugh Trevor-Roper, *Catholics, Anglicans and Puritans* (1987), pp. 60–1.

'Arminian' divines before March 1625, their emergence reflects not so much a change of heart on James's part as the increasing influence of Prince Charles and Buckingham as the King's health and political will deteriorated. Furthermore, there was a crucial difference between James's willingness throughout his reign to promote *some* high church clerics to bishoprics (which was essential to preserve a balance within the ecclesiastical hierarchy) and Charles's desire to promote *only* such clerics (which irrevocably upset that balance).

There is abundant evidence that contemporaries perceived a major change in official religious policy during the years after 1625. Under James, very few doubted that their ruler was a Calvinist. In 1629, Pym even tried to include James in a list of 'Fathers of the Church'.[82] As John Morrill has written, 'most "hotter sort of protestants" were integrated into the Jacobean church and state. Puritan magistrates and churchwardens abound ... There was no incompatibility between serving God and the Crown.'[83] By contrast, the policies of Charles and Laud conflicted dramatically with the expectations and assumptions of many people. There may not have been a systematic attack on the doctrine of predestination.[84] But the magnitude and visibility of the changes in churches up and down England have recently been convincingly analysed by Andrew Foster and Peter Lake.[85] The Laudians extended existing arguments for conformity to enforce their own view of the rites and ceremonies of the Church.[86] The insistence that the altar be moved to the east wall of the church and railed in; the concern for 'order' and 'decency'; the obsessive pursuit of 'the beauty of holiness'; the emphasis on the sacraments as a more efficacious channel of God's grace than the sermon; the suppression of many Puritan lectureships – all these marked the use of royal discretionary powers to narrow the boundaries of legitimate belief and turned religious innovation into a standing issue. There is no parallel under James or Elizabeth to the resolution passed by the Commons on 2 March 1629: 'Whosoever shall bring in innovation of religion, or by favour or countenance seek to extend or introduce popery or Arminianism, or other opinion disagreeing from the true and orthodox Church, shall be reputed a capital enemy to this kingdom and commonwealth.'[87] The urgency of this resolution is reflected in its position at the head of the Commons' Protestation. To argue that

---

[82] Russell, *Parliaments*, p. 420.   [83] Morrill, *Nature of the English Revolution*, p. 52.
[84] White, *Predestination, Policy and Polemic*, pp. 238–312.
[85] Andrew Foster, 'Church policies of the 1630s', in *Conflict in Early Stuart England*, ed. Richard Cust and Ann Hughes (Harlow, 1989), pp. 193–223; Peter Lake, 'The Laudian style: order, uniformity and the pursuit of the beauty of holiness in the 1630s', in *Early Stuart Church*, Fincham, pp. 161–85.
[86] Peter Lake, 'The Laudians and the argument from authority', in *Court, Country and Culture*, ed. B. Y. Kunze and D. D. Brautigam (Rochester, NY, 1992), pp. 149–75.
[87] Rushworth, I, 670.

Laud perceived himself less as an innovator than as a 'traditionalist' enforcing neglected aspects of the Elizabethan Church settlement is probably true, but cannot explain why so many contemporaries sensed a definite change of direction from the late 1620s. It was not how Laud saw himself, but how others saw him, which proved so destabilising.[88] It would be difficult to adduce a 'Jacobethan' parallel to the words of Harbottle Grimston in April 1640: 'The Commonwealth hath bin miserably torne and macerated, and all proprieties and liberties shaken: the Church distracted, the Gospell and Professors of it persecuted.'[89]

Such intemperate language was a distinctively Caroline phenomenon; and it did not come out of a blue sky in 1640. A number of recent studies – including Ann Hughes on Thomas Dugard, Peter Salt on Sir Edward Dering, and John Fielding on Thomas Woodford[90] – have reconstructed 'godly' responses to Charles I's religious policies. They show that (just as in the parliamentary and legal spheres) the King's passion for definition in religious matters – his search for unity through uniformity[91] – forced others to define their own positions. Furthermore, it is vital to recognise Charles's personal commitment to these policies. Not only did he annotate Laud's annual metropolitical reports in meticulous detail, often urging him to report back on the most specific matters;[92] he also intervened at crucial moments to assert his personal authority on particular points of doctrine or practice. Two examples illustrate this dramatically. First, in 1633 Charles stopped the Court of Arches from hearing complaints from the parishioners of St Gregory's church, London, against the repositioning of their communion table against the east wall of the chancel. Instead, he transferred the case to the Privy Council where he could himself act as judge and publicly affirm his policy on the position of the altar.[93] Second, in 1640 he put pressure on Convocation to include the famous 'etcetera

---

[88] Cf. Sharpe, *Personal Rule*, especially pp. 284–92.

[89] Harbottle Grimston, *Master Grimston his worthy and learned Speech ... concerning troubles abroad and grievances at home* (1641), sig. A3 (Wing, G 2051).

[90] Ann Hughes, 'Thomas Dugard and his circle in the 1630s – a "parliamentary-puritan" connexion?', *HJ*, 29 (1986), 771–93; S. P. Salt, 'The origins of Sir Edward Dering's attack on the Ecclesiastical Hierarchy, c. 1625–1640', *HJ*, 30 (1987), 21–52; John Fielding, 'Opposition to the Personal Rule of Charles I: the diary of Robert Woodford, 1637–1641', *HJ*, 31 (1988), 769–88.

[91] Cf. Davies, *Caroline Captivity of the Church*, especially pp. 5–45; and Lake, 'Laudian style'.

[92] The originals of these reports are preserved in Lambeth Palace Library, MS 943 (Laud papers). For printed versions of the reports for 1636–9, see *The Works of William Laud*, ed. W. Scott (7 vols., Oxford, 1847–60), V, 336–70. The King's annotations are discussed in Sharpe, *Personal Rule*, p. 201; Fincham and Lake, 'Ecclesiastical policies of James I and Charles I', pp. 44–7; and Davies, *Caroline Captivity of the Church*, pp. 31–2.

[93] For a detailed account of the St Gregory's case, see Davies, *Caroline Captivity of the Church*, pp. 210–18.

oath' among its new canons. This sixth canon was the only one which did not originate in the lower house of Convocation; and it proved by far the most divisive.[94] Whether or not we follow Julian Davies in speaking of 'Carolinism',[95] the King's personal involvement was as clear and as controversial in religion as in other aspects of policy. Its effect was to make the Caroline Church 'a very weird aberration from the first hundred years of the early reformed Church of England'.[96]

To locate Constitutional Royalism within its ideological and political context, it is necessary to examine the constitution and the successive monarchs of late sixteenth- and early seventeenth-century England. Throughout this chapter I have tried to argue four points. First, that the structures of the English Church and State rested on a number of delicate balances and blurred distinctions. Second, that because the monarchy was both 'personal' and 'mixed', it was acutely vulnerable if the monarch's personality did not 'mix' naturally with the attitudes of the leading subjects. Third, that this was largely achieved under Elizabeth I and James I, which strongly suggests that the constitution was not *inevitably* doomed to collapse. Fourth, that Charles I was much less suited to managing this system than his two immediate predecessors, and instead pursued policies which revealed the potential conflicts and tensions inherent in it. This was the broad backdrop against which Constitutional Royalism emerged during the 1640s. But before we turn to reconstruct its development in detail, we must first take stock of how the above discussion affects our view of England in the later 1630s.

To say that Charles I's personality and priorities generated instabilities and highlighted potential conflicts within Church and State is not to claim that the English constitution was about to collapse in 1637. I am not trying to resurrect the idea of a 'high road to civil war', charting its course from March 1625. Conrad Russell has recently argued convincingly that 'England in 1637 was a country in working order, and was not on the edge of revolution'.[97] While there 'were serious tensions', their 'resolution was not beyond all conjecture'.[98] There is no reason to doubt the sincerity of contemporary descriptions of England during the 1630s as peaceful and orderly, at any rate on the surface. Sir Henry Wotton wrote in 1633 that 'we know not what a rebel is; what a plotter against the common-weal: nor what that is, which grammarian[s] call treason: the names themselves are antiquated with the things'; while in October 1637, John Burghe told Viscount Scudamore of England's 'calmness' and 'quietness'.[99] Kevin Sharpe

---

[94] *Ibid.*, pp. 275–87; Sharpe, *Personal Rule*, pp. 877–84.
[95] Davies, *Caroline Captivity of the Church*, pp. 5–45.
[96] *Ibid.*, p. 3.   [97] Russell, *FBM*, p. 1.   [98] *Ibid.*, p. 13.
[99] Sir Henry Wotton, 'A Panegyrick to King Charles' (1633), in *Reliquiae Wottonianae*, ed. I. Walton (4th edition, 1685), p. 151 (Wing, W 3651); PRO, C 115/N4/861 (John Burghe to Viscount Scudamore, October 1637).

has demonstrated that these were not isolated comments, and has offered plentiful evidence that on the eve of the Scottish rebellion England was *quieter* than in 1625.[100]

But it was probably also less *stable*. John Reeve has suggested that the 1630s were almost too quiet, and that Charles was 'still traversing Indian country'.[101] Perhaps the best indicator of this lies in the level of political and religious debate which had emerged by the second half of the decade. We are not looking at a campaign of unrelieved criticism of Charles, let alone at the collapse of royal authority. It is clear that these debates were conducted 'within a context of loyalty to the King'.[102] But we can find evidence of divided opinions about the morality and legality of royal policy which went beyond the academic debates of the 'Jacobethan' period and confronted the day-to-day actions of the Caroline régime.

Three examples – one constitutional, the other two religious – will make the point. The first is taken from the commonplace book of Sir Roger Twysden, recently edited by Kenneth Fincham. This recounts the reaction of the Kentish gentry when Lord Keeper Weston informed them at Maidstone Assizes of the judges' decision upholding the legality of Ship Money in February 1637.[103] There was deep division:

> Some held my lord keeper's speech very moderate, that more could not bee hoped for from a prince then in causes of weight to proceed by the advise of hys judges and that the declaration the judges had made was fully to the poynt and by that the king had full right to impose it.

By contrast,

> others argued far differingly that it could not but bee expected that a just king would take councell of hys judges in a case of this weight, the greatest was ever herd at a common bar in England, that in a judgment that not may but doth touch every man in so hygh a poynt every man ought to be herd ... They confessed the last parliaments had beene much to blame in their caryages towards hys majestie, but the goodness of monarchs had formerly forgot as great errors ... that the whole discourse of Fortescue in the commendation of the lawes of England was to shew the king had not an absolute power, they considered in especiall the 9, 14, 18, 34, 35, 37, 53 chapters.

Both sides in this debate could claim a perfectly respectable pedigree in English constitutional thought, the first looking to those elements which made England a 'personal' monarchy, the second to those which made it a 'mixed' monarchy. What the dispute among these Kentish gentry surely

---

[100] Sharpe, *Personal Rule*, especially pp. 608–11.
[101] Reeve, *Road to Personal Rule*, p. 170.
[102] Sharpe, *Personal Rule*, especially pp. 690–702; quotation at p. 701.
[103] Kenneth Fincham, 'The judges' decision on Ship Money in February 1637: the reaction of Kent', *Bulletin of the Institute of Historical Research*, 57 (1984), 230–7, from which the following quotations are taken. The original MS is CKS, U 47/47 Z1, Z2.

reveals is that Charles's use of his emergency powers in a non-emergency situation had exposed a point of ambiguity within the 'ancient constitution' which would have been better left concealed. There simply was no way of resolving this debate over Ship Money, or of preventing people from extrapolating from it into a general discussion of the relationship between royal authority and the law. The really significant point is therefore not so much the correctness of either line of argument as the fact that the debate between them took place at all. Just as with Wentworth's comment in April 1628, the very formulation of the question presaged the disintegration of one of the 'ancient constitution's' cardinal assumptions.[104]

A comparable process was also at work within the Caroline Church. An exchange at the Sussex Quarter Sessions in 1639 affords a parallel with Twysden's account of the Maidstone Assizes. Anthony Stapley, a prominent member of the 'godly' gentry, used his opening speech as chairman of the Michaelmas sessions to deliver an outspoken attack on recent changes in the Church, protesting that 'the altering of the communion table alterwise was an innovation detracting from God's glory, and that some prelates in this kingdome did not approve of it'. He was immediately challenged by another JP, William White, who demanded 'what he meant to meddle with those businesses ther, which the Bench had nothing to doe withall'. Edward Burton, who reported the episode to Laud's chaplain, thought it symptomatic of the increased strength of 'the Puritane faction' on the Sussex Bench.[105] This in turn reflected the growing differences over religious issues which emerged during the reign of Charles I. Like the monarchy, the Church contained within it two potentially incompatible traditions. In the words of Conrad Russell, 'the division was not between the orthodox and the unorthodox: it was between rival claimants to the title of orthodox, and therefore between rival criteria of orthodoxy'.[106] As long as the Supreme Governor recognised each rival tradition as having a legitimate claim to orthodoxy, the Church would continue to run reasonably smoothly. But Charles I's policies in effect asserted that only the Laudian position was acceptable. This forced the 'godly' to reconsider their own position.

An excellent instance is found in our third example, Sir Benjamin Rudyerd's speech to the Commons in November 1640. During the 1620s, Rudyerd had advocated 'further reformation' of the Church, urging in particular the rooting out of 'scandalous livings' as an essential precondition

---

[104] For a contrasting interpretation of Twysden's account, see Sharpe, *Personal Rule*, pp. 720–1.
[105] PRO, SP 16/442/137 (Dr Edward Burton to Dr Bray, 27 January 1639/40). Cf. Anthony Fletcher, *Sussex, 1600–1660: A County Community in Peace and War* (1975), pp. 76, 93, 231.
[106] Russell, *Causes*, p. 84.

for a 'christian commonwealth'.[107] Yet this desire never precluded his feeling at home within the 'Jacobethan' Church. He conformed to the Church of England while seeking to reform it from within. Under Charles I, however, the boundaries of legitimate belief were moved, and many who hitherto saw themselves as loyal 'conformists'[108] suddenly found that they were branded as 'Puritans'. Rudyerd declared that the Laudians

have so brought it to pass that, under the name of Puritans, all our religion is branded ... Whosoever squares his actions by any rule, either divine or humane, he is a Puritan. Whoever would be governed by the King's laws, he is a Puritan. He that would not do whatsoever other men would have him do, he is a Puritan. Their great work, their masterpiece, now is, to make all those of the religion to be the suspected party of the kingdom.[109]

In other words, Charles and the Laudian clerics had challenged the validity of the 'godly' claim to orthodoxy in a way that would have been unthinkable under James or Elizabeth. This in turn forced Rudyerd to define his own feelings about official religious policy with unusual clarity:

We well know what disturbance hath been brought upon the Church for vain, petty trifles. How the whole Church, the whole kingdom, hath been troubled where to place "a metaphor" – an altar. We have seen ministers, their wives, children, and families undone, against all law – against conscience – against all bowels of compassion – about not dancing upon Sundays ... These inventions are but sieves made on purpose to winnow the best men, and that's the devil's occupation.[110]

This was precisely the sort of harmful division over official policy which James and Elizabeth had consistently sought to avoid. Rudyerd's speech shows that Charles I's religious policies – when applied to the delicate balance of the 'Jacobethan' Church – had polarised a previous spectrum of religious belief.

This probing of fault-lines within the Church and State, in turn triggering latent tensions and conflicts, was perhaps the most striking feature of the English political climate by the end of the 1630s. This did not mean that disaster was imminent. The commitment to harmony and balance

---

[107] *Sir Benjamin Ruddierd's speech in behalfe of the cleargy* (1628[/9]), pp. 3–4 (STC, 21435.7).
[108] For the value of the term 'conformist', see Peter Lake, *Anglicans and Puritans? Presbyterianism and English Conformist Thought from Whitgift to Hooker* (1988), p. 6; 'The Calvinist conformity of Robert Sanderson', *JBS*, 27 (1988), 114; S. Coolidge, *The Pauline Renaissance in England: Puritanism and the Bible* (Oxford, 1970), chapters 1–2; David L. Smith, 'Catholic, Anglican or Puritan? Edward Sackville, fourth Earl of Dorset and the ambiguities of religion in early Stuart England', *TRHS*, 6th series, 2 (1992), 120–4. I am most grateful to Conrad Russell and Richard Strier for discussions on this subject.
[109] *The Speeches of Sir Benjamin Rudyer in the High Court of Parliament* (1641), p. 3 (Wing, R 2200; BL, TT, E 196/2).
[110] *Ibid.*, p. 2.

which characterised the 'ancient constitution' was so innate that it could withstand a remarkable amount of buffeting before it collapsed. People retained an extraordinary degree of faith in the capacity of ancient institutions to remedy contemporary grievances, as the welcome accorded to the Short and Long Parliaments clearly shows. Sir Henry Slingsby wrote: 'great expectance their is of a happy Parliament where the subject may have a total redress of all his grievances';[111] while Francis Read reported 'a strong expectation of much ensuing good'.[112] But Charles I's personality and policies, and the responses which they engendered, did determine several things about the sort of difficulties which England would face if ever a major crisis blew up. They ensured that certain fundamental issues would dominate political and religious debate and would be discussed in unparalleled depth.

The first of these issues was the nature of royal authority and its relationship with the common law. Was Charles acting *pro bono publico* or *pro bono suo*? What was the extent of the royal prerogative, and in what situations could it be used? Had Charles I employed agreed powers in novel and unconstitutional ways? If so, should statutory guarantees be constructed to force him to respect the constitution; or would these by definition alter the fundamental nature of the constitution? Did the common law provide sufficient safeguards against unaccustomed uses of the royal prerogative? What were the limits, if any, of the subject's duty of obedience? Could the monarch be legitimately resisted, and if so in what circumstances? All of these became burning issues under Charles I; none of them found a clear-cut answer in early seventeenth-century English constitutional thought. Collectively they formed a cluster of doubts and anxieties which Glenn Burgess has labelled 'the crisis of the common law'.[113]

Second, the nature of Charles's policies meant that the future of certain key institutions became highly controversial. In particular, the relationship between the Crown on the one hand and Parliament and the common law on the other was probably more disputed by 1640 than for over a century. Above all, the future of the English Church was the subject of intense debate without parallel since the early sixteenth century. Should the current episcopate be purged while the existing structures remained basically unchanged; or did an institution which had fallen prey to the likes of Laud stand in need of 'root-and-branch' reform? By 1640, politicians could no longer evade such intractable problems.

At the heart of these debates lay a conundrum: did the externals of the English Church and State need to be redefined in order to preserve them; or

---

[111] *The Diary of Sir Henry Slingsby, of Scriven, Bart.*, ed. Daniel Parsons (1836), p. 64.
[112] PRO, SP 16/469/31 (Francis Read to [Robert Read], 4 October 1640).
[113] Burgess, *Politics of the Ancient Constitution*, pp. 210–30.

would this very process of redefinition change their fundamental nature? To this conundrum there were no obvious answers. Or rather, there were too many possible answers. The 'ancient constitution' and the Church of England embraced so many potentially incompatible traditions that it was quite easy to claim a distinguished lineage for several quite different solutions to these questions. This problem forms the natural context for a study of Constitutional Royalism: it should be seen as one of a number of competing solutions which emerged during the course of the 1640s. How it began to develop in the years immediately before the outbreak of the English Civil War, why its leading exponents came to converge, and what beliefs united them, will form the subject of the next two chapters.

─────────────────── ❈ *3* ❈ ───────────────────

Early careers of the main exponents

Having painted a broad-brush view of the early Stuart political and religious landscape, it is now time to add a series of cameos portraying individual reactions to it. This chapter will examine the early careers of those who later emerged as prominent Constitutional Royalists during the 1640s. It will analyse how these people perceived the developments described in chapter 2 and how they responded to them. What, if anything, did they have in common during the 1620s and 1630s? Did their backgrounds, beliefs or careers display shared characteristics which enable us to forecast their convergence on the eve of the Civil War? Can we establish any predictors of Constitutional Royalist attitudes, or was this a purely *ad hoc* political coalition? We will look at each of our ten leading Constitutional Royalists in turn, and analyse their political and religious attitudes, their public careers, their family backgrounds, their social and economic circumstances and their personalities. No infallible predetermining factors can be identified; but some intriguing patterns do emerge none the less.

Let us follow seventeenth-century precedence, and take the nobility first. James Stuart, Duke of Richmond and Lennox,[1] was born on 6 April 1612, a cousin of James I and Charles I. He had a claim to the Scottish but not the English throne, and from the start his royal blood was a crucial influence on his career. James I was sponsor at his christening, and later became his legal tutor and guardian.[2] Created an MA of the University of Cambridge by royal mandate in 1624,[3] and in receipt of a royal pension of £1,400 a year,[4] Richmond later became a Gentleman of the Bedchamber

---

[1] He became Duke of Lennox on his father's death in July 1624: *DNB*, X, 831. Charles I created him Duke of Richmond on 8 August 1641: see below, p. 93. To avoid confusion, I refer to him as Richmond throughout this book.
[2] G. E. C[okayne], *The Complete Peerage* (new edition, ed. Vicary Gibbs, H. A. Doubleday, Duncan Warrand, Lord Howard de Walden, Geoffrey H. White and R. S. Lea, 14 vols., 1910–59), X, 831; *DNB*, LV, 85.
[3] PRO, SP 14/176/66 (Dudley Carleton to Sir Francis Nethersole, 18 December 1624); J. Foster, ed., *Alumni Oxonienses, 1500–1714* (4 vols., Oxford, 1891–2), IV, 1423.
[4] PRO, SO 3/8 (Signet Office docquet book), unfol., March 1624/5; SP 16/389/137 (payments by Court of Wards, 7 May 1638). For a grant to Richmond of royal fee-farm

(April 1625),[5] a Privy Councillor (28 July 1633)[6] and a Knight of the Garter (November 1633).[7]

During the summer of 1633, he accompanied Charles to his Scottish coronation,[8] but was widely regarded as unsympathetic towards episcopacy. When, in September 1637, he attended his mother's funeral in Scotland, the ministers gave him

> supplications and remonstrances against the Service Booke into the King's hands ... both because the Ducke was a nobleman of a calme temper, and principled by such a tutor, Mr David Buchanan, as looked upon episcopacye and all the English ceremonyes with an evill eye.[9]

His strong support for Bishop Williams of Lincoln against Laud during the summer of 1637 would be entirely consistent with such a distaste for prelacy.[10] On the other hand, the supplicants also 'knew that besyde his neer relatione of blood to the Kinge, that the King held him in ane esteeme proportionable (if not greater) to his consanguinitye, besyde the advantage of his constant abode at courte'.[11] Peter Donald has suggested that the Covenanters' approaches to him in 1638 (like those to Hamilton and Morton) owed more to his courtly rank than to known religious sympathies.[12] Furthermore, in August 1641 his initial failure to swear the Covenant caused him to be refused entry to the Scottish Parliament.[13] Hyde's assessment of his character provides a possible explanation for this apparent inconsistency: 'he had so entire a resignation of himself to the King that he abhorred all artifices to shelter himself from the prejudice of those who ... failed in their duty to his Majesty'.[14] Or, in Keith Brown's words, 'the

rents worth nearly £1,500 per annum, see SO 3/11 (Signet Office docquet book), unfol., November 1637.
5 PRO, SP 16/1/80 (John Chamberlain to Sir Dudley Carleton, 23 April 1625).
6 PRO, SP 16/244/53 (Edward Nicholas to Sir John Pennington, 7 August 1633); PC 2/43 (Privy Council register), p. 178. I owe this last reference to John Scally.
7 Bodl. Lib., MS Ashmole 1111 (Order of the Garter papers), fo. 94v.
8 John Spalding, *Memorialls of the Trubles in Scotland and in England, A.D. 1624–A.D. 1645* (2 vols., Aberdeen, 1850–1), I, 35–6.
9 James Gordon, *History of Scots Affairs from MDCXXXVII to MDCXLI* (3 vols., Aberdeen, 1841), I, 18.
10 PRO, SP 16/363/119 (newsletter of C. Rossingham, 13 July 1637). I owe this reference to John Scally. Cf. Gardiner, *History*, VIII, 253.
11 Gordon, *History of Scots Affairs*, I, 18.
12 Peter Donald, *An Uncounselled King: Charles I and the Scottish Troubles, 1637–1641* (Cambridge, 1990), p. 69.
13 PRO, SP 16/483/99 (Diurnall Occurrences, August–September 1641); SP 16/483/91 (Thomas Wiseman to [Sir John Pennington], 26 August 1641); *The Nicholas Papers*, vol. I: *1641–1652*, ed. G. F. Warner (Camden Society, 2nd series, 40, 1886), 12–13 (Sir Henry Vane to Edward Nicholas, 17 August 1641). However, Richmond did eventually swear the Covenant: *The Historical Works of Sir James Balfour*, ed. J. Haig (4 vols., 1825), III, 46.
14 Clarendon, *History*, II, 528 (Book VI, §384).

Duke was a gut Royalist'.[15] This 'unspotted fidelity' to the Crown – reinforced by royal blood – may have dissuaded Richmond from co-operating with the Covenanters even if he had no great love for episcopacy or for Charles's policies towards the Scottish Kirk. He was not, it seems, prepared to let his private religious preferences compromise his public loyalty to the Crown. His reflex response to complaints about Caroline policy was the tactful assurance 'that the King was misinformed'.[16] It is worth noting, however, that this loyalty was not quite unconditional: Richmond 'seems to have questioned the wisdom of war with the Scots in November 1638 and again in May 1639'.[17] This eirenic attitude presumably owed much to Richmond's own Scottish roots; but it may also indicate a horror of a *bellum civile* which is helpful in understanding his later involvement in English peace negotiations.

Richmond's marriage to Buckingham's only daughter in August 1637 brought a £20,000 dowry which relieved him of financial worries until the mid-1640s.[18] He was also appointed to several local offices, notably those of Lord Lieutenant of Hampshire in May 1635, Keeper of Richmond Park in 1638 and Lord Warden of the Cinque Ports in June 1640.[19] He owned extensive estates in England,[20] yet lacked a consolidated territorial base. His country seat was at Cobham Hall in Kent, but his lands were scattered across nearly ten counties: Norfolk, Lincolnshire, Nottinghamshire, Bedfordshire, Huntingdonshire, Hampshire, Berkshire, Gloucestershire and Wiltshire.[21] This list includes both staunchly Parliamentarian areas and 'frontier' zones, and it would be difficult to posit any direct link between the location of Richmond's estates and his political behaviour.

He was, in short, a courtly figure whose actions were guided primarily

[15] Keith M. Brown, 'Courtiers and Cavaliers: service, anglicisation and loyalty amongst the Royalist nobility', in *The Scottish National Covenant in its British Context, 1638–51*, ed. John Morrill (Edinburgh, 1990), p. 159.
[16] *The Letters and Journals of Robert Baillie*, ed. D. Laing (3 vols., Edinburgh, 1841–2), I, 302.
[17] Donald, *An Uncounselled King*, p. 89, n. 47. The pacific speech often attributed to him in 1639 is, however, apocryphal: Bodl. Lib., MS Tanner 299 (Archbishop Sancroft's transcriptions), fos. 184r–185r. See also PRO, SP 16/537/147–9 (speech of 1639).
[18] Clarendon, *History*, II, 528 (Book VI, §384); Brown, 'Courtiers and Cavaliers', p. 159. Cf. PRO, SP 16/365/25 (newsletter of 5 August 1637). I owe this last reference to John Scally.
[19] J. C. Sainty, 'Lieutenants of counties, 1585–1642', *Bulletin of the Institute of Historical Research, Supplements*, 8 (1970), 23; G. E. C., *Complete Peerage*, X, 832; PRO, SP 16/456/44 (Edmund Rossingham to Viscount Conway, 8 June 1640); SP 16/457/104 (Rossingham to Conway, 23 June 1640); Bodl. Lib., MS Eng. hist. c. 230 (docquet book of warrants for letters patent), fo. 2r. 'Some others of the nobilitie' were 'ill satisfied' with this appointment: Henry E. Huntington Library, San Marino, California, Ellesmere MS 7837 (John Castle to the Earl of Bridgwater, 9 June 1640).
[20] His Scottish estates, by contrast, were 'small and unprofitable': Brown, 'Courtiers and Cavaliers', p. 159; David Mathew, *Scotland under Charles I* (1955), p. 240.
[21] PRO, SP 23/233 (Committee for Compounding papers), fo. 27r.

by loyalty to the Crown, and whose political influence was exercised mainly through personal access to the sovereign. Hyde wrote that he 'used to discourse with his Majesty in his bedchamber rather than at the Council-board'.[22] Richmond's significance during the 1620s and 1630s is well summed up by Keith Brown: 'he was bred at Court, and grew up to be an archetypal Caroline courtier whose portrait by Van Dyck epitomised the age'.[23]

In contrast to Richmond, William Seymour, third Earl and first Marquess of Hertford, could plausibly have been a pretender to the English but not the Scottish throne.[24] Born on 1 September 1587, he was the great-grandson of Edward VI's Protector Somerset.[25] A sense of this distinguished lineage undoubtedly coloured his political attitudes, and explains much of his bitterness at his own lack of preferment. His career throughout the early seventeenth century was a story of systematic exclusion from power and patronage at both central and local levels. He had, in Hyde's words, 'always undergone hard measure from the Court, where he received no countenance'.[26] An illicit marriage to James I's cousin Arabella Stuart in June 1610 led to Hertford's brief imprisonment in the Tower. He was then exiled in France from September 1611 until February 1616 when, following his wife's death, he was allowed to return to England.[27] His appointment to the Order of the Bath in November 1616 heralded his return to favour;[28] but the memory of this scandal seemed to dog him for his offices and honours remained meagre thereafter.

His career in the Parliaments of the 1620s tends to bear out Hyde's view that 'he had an aversion, even an unaptness, for business'.[29] He was elected MP for Marlborough in December 1620, but succeeded his grandfather as Earl of Hertford the following April.[30] In 1624, although the Prince of Wales helped restore him temporarily to favour,[31] Hertford attended the Lords only once, and there is no record that he spoke.[32] He was granted 'leave to be absent' from the 1625 Parliament, and attended none of its

---

[22] Clarendon, *History*, I, 207 (Book II, §113).
[23] Brown, 'Courtiers and Cavaliers', p. 159. Cf. the portrait in Mathew, *Scotland under Charles I*, pp. 236–42.
[24] Russell, *FBM*, p. 209.   [25] *DNB*, LI, 333; G. E. C., *Complete Peerage*, XII, part i, 70.
[26] Clarendon, *History*, II, 528 (Book VI, §385).
[27] There is a detailed account of this episode in Gardiner, *History*, II, 115–19. See also Ian McInnes, *Arabella: The Life and Times of Lady Arabella Seymour, 1575–1615* (1968), pp. 156–77.
[28] Foster, *Alumni Oxon.*, IV, 1336.   [29] Clarendon, *History*, II, 529 (Book VI, §385).
[30] Wallace Notestein, F. H. Relf and H. Simpson, ed., *Commons Debates, 1621* (7 vols., New Haven, 1935), V, 5; VI, 445–6.
[31] Russell, *Parliaments*, p. 152.
[32] *LJ*, III, 217; S. R. Gardiner, ed., *Notes of the Debates in the House of Lords in 1624 and 1626* (Camden Society, 2nd series, 24, 1879), 1–106.

sittings.[33] In 1626, however, his assistance to Arundel and Bristol as chairman of the Lords' committee for privileges marked him as an opponent of Buckingham.[34] Another symptom of this hostility was probably the fact that Hertford's contribution to the Forced Loan was paid very late, albeit in full.[35] Certainly in the 1628 Parliament – which he attended with unaccustomed assiduity[36] – Hertford consistently opposed the Duke. On 21 April, he joined Saye in arguing that the King could not 'commit without a cause expressed', which brought him into direct disagreement with Buckingham and Dorset.[37] Later, on 20 May, he spoke against a saving clause in the Petition of Right: 'I do not think the prerogative of the King is touched, and therefore there is no need of a saving.'[38] Hertford became widely perceived as one of Buckingham's enemies, but then lapsed back into inactivity during the session of 1629.[39] All in all, his career during the 1620s suggests a pronounced lack of political instinct and involvement; but where he did intervene, it was usually against the Court.

This stance probably owed much to his second marriage (April 1618) to Frances Devereux, sister of the third Earl of Essex.[40] His bond with another family excluded from Court – and his 'particular friendship' with his brother-in-law – ensured that Hertford's 'greatest acquaintance and conversation [was] with those who had the reputation of being best affected to the liberty of the kingdom, and least in love with the humour of the Court'.[41] In July 1629, he wrote warmly to Essex of 'two soe neerly linked in frendship and alliance as wee are'.[42] During the 1630s, Essex's visits to Hertford's Wiltshire houses,[43] his support for Hertford in a duel[44] and his ninety-nine year lease of part of Essex House to Hertford in return for

---

[33] Maija Jansson and William B. Bidwell, ed., *Proceedings in Parliament, 1625* (New Haven and London, 1987), pp. 45, 48, 596; *LJ*, III, 435–89.

[34] William B. Bidwell and Maija Jansson, ed., *Proceedings in Parliament, 1626* (3 vols., New Haven and London, 1991–2), I, 94, 227, 259, 303. See also Russell, *Parliaments*, pp. 285, 314, 434.

[35] Richard Cust, *The Forced Loan and English Politics, 1626–1628* (Oxford, 1987), pp. 102, 231.

[36] Mary Frear Keeler, M. J. Cole and W. B. Bidwell, ed., *Proceedings in Parliament, 1628* (6 vols., New Haven, 1977–83), V, 34–9.

[37] *Ibid.*, 313. Cf. David L. Smith, 'The fourth Earl of Dorset and the politics of the sixteentwenties', *Historical Research*, 65 (1992), 47.

[38] Keeler *et al.*, *Proceedings in Parliament, 1628*, V, 487.

[39] His attendances were quite frequent, but we have no evidence of any speeches: *LJ*, IV, 8–42; Wallace Notestein and F. H. Relf, ed., *Commons Debates for 1629* (Minneapolis, 1921).

[40] *DNB*, LI, 334.   [41] Clarendon, *History*, II, 529 (Book VI, §385).

[42] BL, Add. MS 46188 (Jessop Papers), fo. 114r (Hertford to Essex, 16 July 1629).

[43] PRO, SP 16/335/64 (John Nicholas to Edward Nicholas, 16 November 1636).

[44] HMC, *Manuscripts in Various Collections*, VII (1914), 414 (Ro[bert] Robotham to Sir Gervase Clifton, 26 May 1636); PRO, SP 16/536/41i (George Rawdon to Viscount Conway, 26 May 1636).

£1,100[45] all demonstrate the closeness of their relationship. This surely provides the crucial background to Hertford's decision to sign the Twelve Peers' petition in August 1640.[46]

Hertford's exclusion from the Court also extended to the Country. His estates were concentrated mainly in Wiltshire, but he was often in considerable debt.[47] Local politics in early Stuart Wiltshire were dominated by an ancient rivalry between the two great families of Herbert (the Earls of Pembroke) and Seymour. The third and fourth Earls of Pembroke served in turn as Lord Chamberlain of the King's Household,[48] and in Wiltshire their status as Lords Lieutenant reinforced their dominance of local patronage.[49] Only when Pembroke led a regiment of horse as the King's personal bodyguard during the first Bishops' War was Hertford appointed Lord Lieutenant of Somerset.[50] It is no coincidence that the people who were to benefit most directly from Pembroke's disgrace as Lord Chamberlain in July 1641 were Hertford and Essex.[51] This reversal of fortunes also spilled over into the provinces, as Pembroke, hitherto a courtier peer, gradually drifted away from the King, while it was Hertford who moved to implement the Commission of Array in Wiltshire.[52] The stock of these two families operated in inverse proportion to each other, and it is important to remember this when we come to explain Hertford's Royalism.

Hyde's portrait of Hertford is also very suggestive. He notes that Hertford 'was not to be shaken in his affection to the government of the Church, though it was enough known that he was in no degree biassed by any great inclination to the person of any churchman'.[53] This commitment to the *government* of the Church, but not to its leading *personnel*, was very

---

[45] C. L. Kingsford, 'Essex House, formerly Leicester House and Exeter Inn', *Archaeologia*, 73 (1923), 52–4.

[46] See below, pp. 66–7.

[47] Wiltshire RO, Ailesbury MS, WRO 1300/200A–B (two copies of Hertford's will); PRO, SP 23/3 (Committee for Compounding order book), p. 359; Russell, *Parliaments*, p. 195. Hertford was forced to sell lands in Shropshire in 1637: PRO, SP 16/352/29 (Matthew Nicholas to [Edward Nicholas], 4 April 1637).

[48] In 1615–26 and 1626–41 respectively: *DNB*, XXVI, 209, 229.

[49] For the third and fourth Earls of Pembroke as Lords Lieutenant of Wiltshire from 1621, see Sainty, 'Lieutenants of counties', 36–7; R. B. Pugh and Elizabeth Crittall, ed., *Victoria History of the County of Wiltshire*, V (1957), 80–1. For their immense clout as electoral patrons, see J. K. Gruenfelder, *Influence in Early Stuart Elections, 1604–1640* (Ohio, 1981), pp. 123–32; and Violet A. Rowe, 'The influence of the Earls of Pembroke on parliamentary elections, 1625–41', *EHR*, 50 (1935), 242–56.

[50] T. G. Barnes, *Somerset, 1625–1640: A County's Government during the 'Personal Rule'* (1961), pp. 99–101.

[51] For Pembroke's disgrace, see Clarendon, *History*, I, 345 (Book I, §213); for the preferment of Hertford and Essex, see below, p. 74.

[52] John Morrill, *The Revolt of the Provinces* (2nd edition, Harlow, 1980), pp. 42–3.

[53] Clarendon, *History*, I, 563–4 (Book IV, §295). Hyde refers elsewhere to 'the soundness of his religion': *ibid.*, III, 128 (Book VII, §155).

characteristic of the Constitutional Royalists. It certainly explains why Hertford later presented the Somerset petition on behalf of episcopacy to the House of Lords in December 1641.[54] Hyde also draws out Hertford's gentleness: 'he was a good scholar' who 'loved his book above all exercises', and 'cared not to discourse and argue in those points which he understood very well, only for the trouble of contending'. He concludes that 'pure zeal and affection for the Crown' was crucial in Hertford's acceptance of the Governorship of the Prince of Wales.[55] In sum, this loyalty to the Crown, an attachment to 'the Church by law established', a wish to regain some of the national and provincial eminence to which he thought his lineage entitled him, and a naturally mild and benign temperament seem to be the four most important elements behind Hertford's Constitutional Royalism.

The career of Hertford's younger brother, Sir Francis Seymour, was marked by an even deeper alienation from the Court. He sat in all the Parliaments of the 1620s except that of 1626, representing Wiltshire every time apart from 1624 when he was MP for Marlborough.[56] His basic political stance remained unchanged throughout this period. Conrad Russell has called him 'Buckingham's most consistent opponent' and a 'consistent wrecker' who had as great a claim as anybody to the title of 'opposition member'.[57] It seems that loyalty to his locality helps to explain both his prickliness in Parliament and his conscientiousness in provincial administration.[58] He opposed the Spanish war on the grounds of cost rather than ideology, and his own debts can only have strengthened this attitude.[59] Parliament he saw as a bulwark to guard the localities from excessive central demands. As he put it on 22 March 1628: 'this is the great council of the kingdom, and here, if not here alone, His Majesty may see, as in a true glass, the state of this kingdom'.[60] A concern for his locality underpinned his passionate hostility to Buckingham, which caused him to be pricked as a sheriff in February 1626 to exclude him from Parliament, and then to be removed from the Commission of the Peace the following

---

[54] *LJ*, IV, 469. This petition is discussed more fully below, pp. 84–5.
[55] Clarendon, *History*, I, 564 (Book IV, §296); III, 128 (Book VII, §156).
[56] G. E. C., *Complete Peerage*, XI, 640; Pugh and Crittall, *Victoria History of Wiltshire*, V, 80–1; *Return of Members of Parliaments of England, 1213–1702* (2 vols., 1878), I, 454, 461, 466, 478.
[57] Russell, *Parliaments*, pp. 151, n. 1, 242–3, 428.
[58] *Ibid.*, pp. 17, 34, 83, 223, 327, 425. Seymour acted as Sheriff for Wiltshire in 1624: PRO, SP 14/167/71 (commission of 16 June 1624); A. Hughes, ed., *List of Sheriffs for England and Wales from the earliest times to A.D. 1831* (PRO, Lists and Indexes, IX, repr. 1963), 154. For an instance of his assiduity as a Justice of the Peace in Wiltshire, see PRO, SP 16/4/125 (Sir Francis Seymour *et al.* to the Privy Council, 25 July 1625).
[59] Russell, *Parliaments*, pp. 152, 188, 195, 225, 247, 435.
[60] Keeler *et al.*, *Proceedings in Parliament, 1628*, II, 55.

July.[61] He also perceived Parliament as the guardian of legality, a stance which led him to refuse the Forced Loan, and which coloured his speeches in the 1628 Parliament.[62] He summed up his objections to recent royal policies on 22 March: 'when against a Parliament law the subject shall have taken from him his goods against his will, and his liberty against the laws of the land, shall it be accounted want of duty in us to stand upon our privileges hereditary to us, and confirmed by so many acts of Parliament?'[63] Parliament had a fundamental duty to defend 'the liberty of the subject'[64] and the rule of law, an outlook which is highly significant for Seymour's later political career.

Seymour's religious attitudes are also interesting. Although he regularly expressed anti-popish views, this was nearly always in the context of the Spanish war. Whereas Pym tended to conflate 'Arminianism' and 'popery', Seymour 'joined late into the protests against Arminianism'.[65] He was 'never very much in sympathy with godliness': 'he was a Calvinist, but not of a particularly heated sort'.[66] This was a man driven more by a wish to implement the laws against recusants than by zeal to create a godly commonwealth.[67]

Rather, it was concern for his locality and attachment to the rule of law which continued to guide Seymour's actions during the Personal Rule. In 1634 he led the opposition of Wiltshire justices against a royal commission sent in to reform the clothing industry. Seymour claimed that the commission was 'against the dignity of the office of a justice of peace', and was reported to be 'the most malitious man against the commission'.[68] He also became a prominent campaigner against Ship Money. In May 1639, following a complaint by the sheriff of Wiltshire that he 'refused to pay the shipping money, and that his example discouraged others', Seymour was summoned before the Privy Council. He informed the board that 'he had against his conscience, and upon the importunity of his friendes, paid that money twice, but now his conscience wold suffer him no more to doe a thing (as he thought) so contrary to law and to the liberty of the subject'.[69]

[61] Russell, *Parliaments*, p. 268; Cust, *Forced Loan*, p. 189. He was subsequently re-appointed as a Justice of the Peace: PRO, SP 16/405 (*Liber Pacis*, 1638), fo. 71v.
[62] Cust, *Forced Loan*, p. 189; Keeler *et al.*, *Proceedings in Parliament, 1628*, II, 246.
[63] Keeler *et al.*, *Proceedings in Parliament, 1628*, II, 56–7.
[64] *Ibid.*, 104, 311.
[65] Russell, *Parliaments*, pp. 173–4, 240, 406–7; *FBM*, pp. 100–1; Nicholas Tyacke, *Anti-Calvinists: The Rise of English Arminianism, c. 1590–1640* (Oxford, 1987), pp. 134, 136.
[66] Russell, *FBM*, p. 100.
[67] See, for example, Notestein and Relf, *Commons Debates for 1629*, p. 109.
[68] PRO, SP 16/267/15 (Anthony Wither's charge against Seymour, 2 May 1634); SP 16/267/17 (Seymour's information against Wither, 2 May 1634).
[69] Bodl. Lib., MS Clarendon 16, fos. 125v–126r (Windebank to Charles I, 24 May 1639). See also PRO, SP 16/407/41 (petition of Edmond Brunsdon, [? 1638]).

This statement goes to the very heart of Seymour's beliefs. As Hyde wrote, his 'parts and judgement were best in those things which concerned the good husbandry and the common administration of justice to the people'.[70] A deep attachment to legal propriety, allied to a concern for the 'liberty of the subject', continued to inform Seymour's speeches in the Short and Long Parliaments. Together with a certain lack of 'godly' zeal, they help to explain both his passionate denunciations of Ship Money, and his subsequent decision to join the King.

Our next figure, Thomas Wriothesley, fourth Earl of Southampton, was also notable for his defence of the law against royal policy during the 1630s. In his case, however, Charles demanded ship timber rather than Ship Money. Born on 10 March 1608, and educated at Eton and St John's College, Cambridge,[71] Southampton spent most of the late 1620s and early 1630s in France and the Low Countries before returning to England in 1634.[72] In debt following a rash bet at Newmarket, he began selling timber on his main estates at Titchfield in Hampshire.[73] The King took advantage of this to buy one thousand of Southampton's choicest oak trees for ship building at Portsmouth at a reduced price of £2,294 10s.[74] Had it stopped there, Southampton might have been grateful for the extra revenue. But he then fell victim to Charles's attempts to assert his forest claims. In October 1635, a forest court chaired by the Earl of Holland at Winchester challenged his title to the greater part of his estate at Beaulieu in the New Forest. Charles claimed that the lands were royal forest, which would reduce the rents paid to Southampton from £2,500 to £500 a year.[75] The King had exploited a legal technicality and forced Southampton to beg for the restitution of lands rightfully his. Although Charles relented in July 1636,[76] it is important to remember that Southampton had had personal experience of Charles's 'legal tyranny'. The Earl trod very carefully thereafter, and when he wished to fell more trees at Beaulieu in 1638, he approached Holland first to ask whether it would affect royal hunting

---

[70] Clarendon, *History*, II, 534 (Book VI, §392).
[71] J. Venn and J. A. Venn, ed., *Alumni Cantabrigienses. Part One: from the earliest times to 1751* (4 vols., Cambridge, 1922–7), IV, 479. For Southampton's career at St John's, see C. C. Stopes, *The Life of Henry, third Earl of Southampton, Shakespeare's Patron* (Cambridge, 1922), pp. 475–9.
[72] *DNB*, LXIII, 154.
[73] PRO, SP 16/263/20 (Charles Franckland to Richard Harvey, 20 March 1633/4); SP 16/267/24 (Kenrick Edisbury to Edward Nicholas, 3 May 1634); SP 16/275/29 (Navy officers to Lords of the Admiralty, 9 October 1634).
[74] PRO, SP 16/278/56 (John Chamberlain to Nicholas, 17 December 1634); SP 16/285/10 (Navy officers to Lords of the Admiralty, 17 March 1634/5); SP 16/290/82 (financial estimate, 12 June 1635).
[75] *The Earl of Strafforde's Letters and Despatches*, ed. W. Knowler (2 vols., 1739), I, 467 (Mr Garrard to Thomas Wentworth, 3 October 1635).
[76] PRO, C 66/2744 (Chancery Patent Roll), entry for 8 July 1636.

rights.[77] Southampton's own sense of bitterness may well help to explain why he was to insist in the Short Parliament that discussion of grievances precede supply.[78]

Hyde's portrait emphasises the importance of these experiences during the Personal Rule. By 1640, Southampton 'had never had any conversation in the Court, nor obligation to it; on the contrary he had undergone some hardness from it'. Like the Seymours, 'he had no relation to or dependence upon the Court'. Only belatedly (June 1641) did he become Lord Lieutenant of Hampshire.[79] He had 'a particular prejudice' against Strafford, but became alarmed 'as he saw the ways of reverence and duty towards the King declined'.[80] We shall see that one of the keys to the emergence of Constitutional Royalism lay in Charles's capacity to attract people hitherto excluded from the Court who came to fear a breakdown of law and order. In Southampton's case, this was closely linked to 'a perfect detestation of all the Presbyterian principles'.[81] He was 'a man of great and exemplary virtue and piety' who 'strictly observed the devotions prescribed by the Church of England' and was 'averse and irreconcileable to the sedition and rebellion of the Scots'.[82] This aversion ultimately overcame his initial alienation from the Court.

At the same time, Charles could also win support from long-established courtiers. Of our Constitutional Royalists, the peer who – along with Richmond – had the strongest position at Court during the 1620s and 1630s was Edward Sackville, fourth Earl of Dorset. I have examined his political career in detail elsewhere, and shall therefore concentrate here on drawing comparisons and contrasts with other Constitutional Royalists.[83] His precocious rise was temporarily halted by a duel (1613) in which he killed Lord Bruce of Kinloss. This necessitated a two-year exile – rather like Hertford's – and when he returned England was no longer dominated by his mother's family, the Howards. Strong support for aid to the Palatinate and a wish to clear James I of any blame for monopolies or corrupt legal practices brought him to the Crown's attention in the 1621 Parliament, and

---

[77] PRO, SP 16/384/40 (Earl of Holland to the verderors and foresters of the New Forest, 13 December 1638).
[78] See below, p. 65.   [79] Sainty, 'Lieutenants of counties', 23.
[80] Clarendon, *History*, II, 530 (Book VI, §386). Cf. *Life*, III, 232–3.
[81] Clarendon, *Life*, III, 238.   [82] *Ibid.*, 232, 238–9.
[83] See Smith, 'Dorset and the sixteen-twenties', 37–53; 'The fourth Earl of Dorset and the Personal Rule of Charles I', *JBS*, 30 (1991), 257–87; '"The more posed and wise advice": the fourth Earl of Dorset and the English Civil Wars', *HJ*, 34 (1991), 797–829; 'Catholic, Anglican or Puritan? Edward Sackville, fourth Earl of Dorset and the ambiguities of religion in early Stuart England', *TRHS*, 6th series, 2 (1992), 105–24. Some of the arguments of these papers are also fleshed out more fully in the same author's 'The political career of Edward Sackville, fourth Earl of Dorset (1590–1652)' (PhD thesis, University of Cambridge, 1990).

his career blossomed during the later 1620s. He became a Privy Councillor in 1626 and Lord Chamberlain of the Queen's Household in 1628; thereafter, his relative poverty and lack of involvement in local politics ensured that these offices remained the foundation of his political influence.[84]

That influence was deployed in remarkably subtle ways. Dorset was particularly close to Buckingham in 1626–8, and publicly supported the Forced Loan. Yet his private letters to Buckingham struck a more cautious note, stating tentatively that these policies '*in all probability* tend to happines'.[85] Dorset also assisted several people who refused the Loan – including Sir Thomas Wentworth and Sir John Strangways[86] – and came out against it in the 1628 Parliament.[87] He emerges from the debates on the Petition of Right as someone committed to the royal prerogative within the bounds of the common law. For example: 'the King cannot commit for any cause triable at common law, but for reason of state he may ... The King has as much right to *legem terrae* for matters of state as the subjects for their rights.' He advocated 'that a middle way be taken that his Majesty's right be preserved and the people's liberties'.[88] This was a man who disliked confrontations and definitions; someone perfectly acclimatised, in other words, to the 'Jacobethan' constitution.

Charles I's management of that constitution posed an intractable problem for Dorset. How could he reconcile his personal loyalty to the monarch with that particular monarch's tendency to subvert the constitution, while at the same time safeguarding his own position? Dorset's solution – a characteristic compromise – was to drop subtle hints to Charles. A paradigm of this strategy came in 1633, when Charles summarily dismissed Lord Keeper Coventry for refusing to issue pardons to various 'papists'. Dorset declared that 'he knew the King would not condemne any man without hearing him', and Coventry was promptly restored to office.[89] A belief that power and authority descended from the monarch is slightly more prominent in Dorset than in many other Constitutional Royalists, as his support for the Forced Loan, his acceptance of Ship Money, his suggestion that scutage be levied, and his horror of any insult to the King or Queen all show.[90] His official concern with public order also recurs throughout his Star Chamber sentences during the 1630s.[91] But along with these distinctive traits, he displayed much the same

---

[84] This paragraph is based on Smith, 'Dorset and the sixteen-twenties', *passim*.
[85] PRO, SP 16/74/62 (Dorset to Buckingham, 21 August 1627). My emphasis.
[86] See below, p. 58.   [87] Smith, 'Dorset and the sixteen-twenties', 45–9.
[88] Keeler *et al.*, *Proceedings in Parliament, 1628*, III, 237, 324.
[89] BL, Egerton MS 784 (diary of William Whiteway), fo. 94r.
[90] Smith, 'Dorset and the sixteen-twenties', 43–4; 'Dorset and the Personal Rule', 270–1, 276–7.
[91] Smith, 'Catholic, Anglican or Puritan?', 109–12.

concern for legality, for royal government within the law, and above all for constitutional balance as most of the others.

None of these attitudes endeared Dorset to the exponents of 'Thorough', and his influence was clearly waning by the later 1630s. He lamented that he was not of 'the Cabinett Counseyll', and was often baffled by Charles I's behaviour.[92] His relationship with Strafford gradually deteriorated; and he was apparently never close to Laud. His public praise of the Archbishop rings distinctly hollow, especially in the light of Dorset's help to a series of Laud's enemies, including Bishop Williams of Lincoln and four young gentlemen of Lincoln's Inn who drank to his 'confusion'. His leniency towards a godly minister (John Cotton of Boston) and a godly magistrate (Henry Sherfield of Salisbury), counterbalanced by firm links with several Catholics (especially Sir Kenelm Digby), suggest a commitment to the 'Jacobethan' Church which tolerated diverse strands of opinion within a broad national framework. This fits with Dorset's admiration of Sir Thomas Browne, who confessed in his *Religio Medici*: 'I could never divide my selfe from any man upon the difference of an opinion or be angry with his judgement for not agreeing with mee in that, from which perhaps within a few dayes I should dissent my selfe.'[93] This was as true of Dorset's approach to politics as of his religion. He was a 'conformist', wary of Laud, but with an apparent lack of godly zeal akin to that of many other Constitutional Royalists.[94] Above all, we are struck by his temperamental aversion to disputes and to confrontations, in which he resembles Hertford.

Dorset was sworn a Privy Councillor in 1626 during the wave of promotions of those thought sympathetic to Buckingham. Several new peers were created at the same time, including the father of our last peer, Montagu Bertie, second Earl of Lindsey. The first Earl became Lord Great Chamberlain in April 1627 and a Privy Councillor in July 1628.[95] He protested against the Militia Ordinance,[96] and became general of the King's forces on the outbreak of civil war.[97] However, he resented Charles's preference for Prince Rupert's advice on all military matters, and resigned shortly before the battle of Edgehill, at which he was killed.[98] Hyde called

---

[92] Smith, 'Dorset and the Personal Rule', 283–4.
[93] Sir Thomas Browne, *Religio Medici*, ed. J.-J. Denonain (2nd edition, Cambridge, 1955), p. 8; *Observations upon Religio Medici, occasionally written by Sir Kenelm Digby* (1643), pp. 2–3 (Wing, D 1422; BL, TT, E 1113/4).
[94] Smith, 'Dorset and the Personal Rule', 279–80; 'Catholic, Anglican or Puritan?', 117–24.
[95] BL, Egerton MS 2979 (Heath and Verney Papers), fo. 193; G. E. C., *Complete Peerage*, VIII, 16; APC, XLIV (1628–9), 42.
[96] *LJ*, IV, 627.
[97] BL, Add. MS 5752 (Musgrave Collection), fo. 211r; Clarendon, *History*, II, 214 (Book V, §375).
[98] Clarendon, *History*, II, 367 (Book VI, §90); HMC, *Ancaster Manuscripts* (1907), p. 410.

him 'a man of great honour' who 'spent his youth and vigour of his age in military actions and commands abroad'.[99] Sir Philip Warwick likewise remembered him as 'a man of undaunted courage, and of a good experience in soldiery'.[100] Only the fact that Dorset and Hyde were 'friends he loved well' suggests that he might have become more obviously a Constitutional Royalist had he lived. As it was, that role fell to his son.

Montagu Bertie, Lord Willoughby of Eresby,[101] was born in about 1608, and educated at Sidney Sussex College, Cambridge.[102] He was MP for Lincolnshire in 1624, and for Stamford in 1625–6,[103] but there is no evidence that he participated in any of these Parliaments. However, his father's clear enjoyment of royal favour and his own signing of a warrant for the arrest of those refusing rates for musters[104] both suggest that his basic political stance was favourable to the Court. This is borne out by numerous instances of royal goodwill during the 1630s: Charles hunted and dined with him on his way to Grantham in May 1633;[105] appointed him a Gentleman of the Privy Chamber and Warden of Waltham Forest in 1634;[106] and awarded him a royal pension.[107]

The family estates were in Lincolnshire, and the first Earl of Lindsey was appointed Lord Lieutenant in January 1629.[108] He and his son also became actively involved in fen drainage during the 1630s. This brought them into a furious dispute with the Berties' great rival in Lincolnshire, Theophilus Clinton, fourth Earl of Lincoln. As with the Herberts and Seymours in Wiltshire, the dynamics of local politics throw much light on choice of sides in 1642. From 1633, father and son had co-operated with the Earl of Lincoln in contracting with undertakers for the drainage of fenland.[109] However, by August 1638, there were clear signs that relations between the Berties and Lincoln had disintegrated.[110] This probably explains why a new division of shares in Lincolnshire fen drainage in November 1638

---

[99] Clarendon, *History*, II, 367 (Book VI, §90).
[100] Sir Philip Warwick, *Memoires of the Reigne of King Charles I* (1701), p. 228.
[101] This was his title from 1626 until his father's death in October 1642. To avoid confusion I shall refer to him throughout this book as Lindsey.
[102] G. E. C., *Complete Peerage*, VIII, 19; *DNB*, IV, 403; Venn and Venn, *Alumni Cant.*, I, 143.
[103] *Return of Members*, I, 458, 464, 470.
[104] Keeler *et al.*, *Proceedings in Parliament, 1628*, III, 363.
[105] PRO, SP 16/238/88 (Sir John Coke to Windebank, 17 May 1634).
[106] PRO, LC 5/134 (Lord Chamberlain's warrant book), p. 24; SP 16/275/21 (statement by Earl of Warwick, 5 October 1634). See also SP 16/289/32ii (Style of Forest Court, 23 May 1635).
[107] PRO, SP 16/389/137 (payments by Court of Wards, 7 May 1638).
[108] Sainty, 'Lieutenants of counties', 26.
[109] PRO, SP 16/232/39 (Charles I to commissioners of sewers in Lincolnshire, 12 February 1632/3).
[110] PRO, SP 16/397/12 (examinations of Margaret Cley and Anne Coleson, 4 August 1638).

excluded Lincoln.[111] Dorset's presence among the new share-holders
perhaps suggests that the enterprise was managed by those in favour at
Court. By January 1641, Lincoln was petitioning the House of Lords,
claiming that Lindsey's erection of dykes had protected his own fenland
but flooded Lincoln's 'sooner and longer and deeper ... than it hath been
heretofore'.[112] While a parliamentary committee began leisurely investigations, dispossessed commoners took the law into their own hands and
mounted sporadic attacks on Lindsey's drainage operations. These dis-
orders grew steadily worse as the nation slid into civil war.[113] But the
important point to emphasise here is that the first Earl of Lindsey and his
son were very much the agents of royal policy, quite unlike the Earl of
Lincoln, a man of deep godliness,[114] who had passionately opposed the
Forced Loan,[115] whose failure to sign the Twelve Peers' petition 'remains
mysterious',[116] and who was to gravitate towards Parliament in 1642 as
instinctively as the Berties rallied to the King.[117] The second Earl of
Lindsey, by contrast, displayed no apparent religious zeal, enjoyed royal
favour at both national and local levels, and provided the King with four
companies of lifeguards in the summer of 1639.[118] Of these traits, the military contribution was at once the most characteristic of his ancestry and
the least characteristic of the Constitutional Royalists in general.

We now turn to a Royalist who was only elevated to the peerage after
the Restoration: Edward Hyde.[119] He was born in February 1609, the son
of Henry Hyde of Wiltshire and nephew of Sir Nicholas Hyde, the Lord
Chief Justice of King's Bench. His uncle's influence helped to make the law
a central part of Hyde's life and thought. After Oxford – where royal
patronage failed to secure him a demyship at Magdalen College – he was
called to the bar (Middle Temple) in November 1633.[120] At about the same
time, he and Bulstrode Whitelocke organised a performance of James

---

[111] PRO, SP 16/401/54 (account of shares in fen drainage, 10 November 1638); SP 16/406/37
(calculation of shares, [? 1638]).
[112] PRO, SP 16/476/111 (Earl of Lincoln's petition, [January] 1641).
[113] Clive Holmes, *Seventeenth-Century Lincolnshire* (Lincoln, 1980), pp. 152–5; James S.
Hart, *Justice upon Petition* (1991), pp. 165, 173.
[114] Russell, *FBM*, p. 473.
[115] Cust, *Forced Loan*, especially pp. 170–5; Holmes, *Lincolnshire*, pp. 106–7.
[116] Russell, *FBM*, p. 155, n. 33.   [117] Holmes, *Lincolnshire*, p. 168.
[118] PRO, SP 16/426/81 (account of moneys due to troops, July 1639).
[119] For accounts of Hyde's life and career before 1640, cf. T. H. Lister, *Life and Administration of Edward, First Earl of Clarendon* (3 vols., 1837–8), I, 1–33; and Sir Henry Craik,
The Life of Edward, Earl of Clarendon, Lord High Chancellor of England (2 vols., 1911),
I, 1–62.
[120] PRO, SP 14/154/89 ([Secretary Conway] to Dr Langton, 27 November 1623); Foster,
Alumni Oxon., II, 780; H. A. C. Sturgess, ed., *Register of Admissions to the Honourable
Society of the Middle Temple* (3 vols., 1949), I, 117. See also BL, Add. MS 17017 (Hyde
Correspondence), fo. 1 (Edward Hyde to Henry Hyde, 15 May [1631]).

Shirley's *The Triumph of Peace* at the Inns of Court in protest against Prynne's attack on theatrical entertainments, and particularly on female actors.[121] Dorset, who detested Prynne,[122] would doubtless have approved. Hyde became keeper of the writs and rolls in the Court of Common Pleas in December 1635, and steadily built up a thriving practice.[123] In his native Wiltshire he also served as a Justice of the Peace.[124] Small wonder, then, that when he was returned to the Short Parliament as MP for Wootton Bassett, a newsletter identified him simply as 'Edw[ard] Hyde the lawyer'.[125]

Hyde's background as a lawyer helps to explain the view of the English constitution which he had formed by 1640. In his memoirs, he wrote that 'he had a most zealous esteem and reverence for the constitution of the government; and believed it so equally poised, that if the least branch of the prerogative was torn off, or parted with, the subject suffered by it, and that his right was impaired'. Furthermore, he was 'as much troubled when the crown exceeded its just limits, and thought its prerogative hurt by it: and therefore not only never consented to any diminution of the King's authority, but always wished that the King would not consent to it'.[126] It is in the development of this vision of the 'ancient constitution' – as well as in his belief in the rule of law – that we should locate the origins of Hyde's Royalism.

This constitutionalism strongly influenced Hyde's attitude towards the Church. Although he later insisted that he was 'always opposed' to 'all mutations in the Church' 'upon the impulsion of *conscience*',[127] the language of his opposition was secular and constitutional. He regarded the exclusion of bishops from the House of Lords as 'a violation of justice; the removing [of] a landmark; and the shaking [of] the very foundation of government'.[128] There is certainly no sign that Hyde ever felt drawn to godliness, again a trait which he shares with other Constitutional Royalists. Only his description of the Church as 'the most exactly formed and framed for the encouragement and advancement of learning and piety, and for the preservation of peace, of any Church in the world'[129] suggests that his religious attitudes can be distinguished – although not separated – from his sense of constitutional propriety. This religious position resembles that

---

[121] Bulstrode Whitelocke, *Memorials of the English Affairs from the beginning of the reign of Charles I* (4 vols., Oxford, 1853), I, 54–5.
[122] Smith, 'Catholic, Anglican or Puritan?', 111–12; 'Dorset and the Personal Rule', 270–1.
[123] Foster, *Alumni Oxon.*, II, 780; PRO, SP 16/447/84 ([Thomas] Triplet to Archbishop Laud, 10 March 1639/40).
[124] PRO, SP 16/405 (*Liber Pacis*, 1638), fo. 72v.
[125] PRO, SP 16/449/40 (John Nicholas to Edward Nicholas, 30 March 1640).
[126] Clarendon, *Life*, I, 109.   [127] *Ibid.*, 110. My emphasis.   [128] *Ibid.*
[129] *Ibid.*, 109.

associated with the Great Tew circle, and with the closest friend of Hyde's life, Lucius Cary, second Viscount Falkland.

Hugh Trevor-Roper has recently given us a sensitive and perceptive account of the coterie at Great Tew, emphasising the role of William Chillingworth as the circle's 'intellectual motor'.[130] In his most famous work, *The Religion of Protestants*, Chillingworth advanced a religious position based on tolerance and scepticism, arguing that 'we conceive a charitable judgement of our brethren and their errors, though untrue, much more pleasing to God then a true judgement, if it be uncharitable, and therefore shall alwaies choose (if we doe erre) to erre on the milder and more mercifull part'.[131] Falkland embraced the same outlook in his discourse on *The Infallibilitie of the Chvrch of Rome*. He could not see why someone 'should be saved, because, by reason of his parents' beleife, or the religion of the countrey, or some such accident, the truth was offered to his understanding, when had the contrary been offered he would have received that; and the other damned that beleeves falshood, upon as good ground as the other doth truth'.[132] Falkland followed this maxim in his own life, and 'never thought the worse, or in any degree declined the familiarity, of those who were of another mind'.[133] These words – very similar to those of Thomas Browne which Dorset liked so much – reflect an aversion to religious dogma characteristic of the Constitutional Royalists as a group. At the deepest level they rested on a distinction between essentials and inessentials which goes far to explain why these people both attacked Laudianism and later rallied to the defence of episcopacy.[134]

That said, Falkland's background was in many other respects unusual. He was born in about 1610 and admitted to St John's College, Cambridge in 1621. His father was appointed Lord-Deputy of Ireland in 1622, and Lucius was transferred to Trinity College, Dublin, graduating a BA three years later.[135] About the same time, his maternal grandfather, Sir Lawrence Tanfield, died, having entailed estates at Great Tew upon Lucius and his offspring. He took possession of this inheritance on the family's return from Ireland in November 1629.[136] However, his father left Ireland amid a violent quarrel with the Irish Privy Council and Lords Justices over the

---

[130] H. R. Trevor-Roper, *Catholics, Anglicans and Puritans* (1987), pp. 166–230; the quotation is at p. 169. Cf. Robert R. Orr, *Reason and Authority: The Thought of William Chillingworth* (Oxford, 1967), especially pp. 34–8.

[131] William Chillingworth, *The Religion of Protestants* (Oxford, 1638), p. 407 (*STC*, 5138).

[132] *Of the Infallibilitie of the Chvrch of Rome: A Discourse written by the Lord Viscount Falkland* (Oxford, 1645), p. 12 (Wing, F 322).

[133] Clarendon, *Life*, I, 49.   [134] Cf. Wormald, *Clarendon*, pp. 259–61.

[135] *DNB*, XI, 246; Venn and Venn, *Alumni Cant.*, I, 293.

[136] PRO, SP 16/151/81 (newsletter of 16 November 1629); Kurt Weber, *Lucius Cary, Second Viscount Falkland* (New York, 1940), pp. 3–4.

command of a company of five or six hundred men, and this led Lucius to challenge Sir Francis Willoughby – to whom the commission was granted – to a duel.[137] He was briefly imprisoned in 1630,[138] and this disillusionment with Irish politics may help to explain his subsequent hostility to Strafford, although it is difficult to establish a direct link.

When Falkland's father died in 1633, he left estates valued at nearly £57,000, with an annual income of £2,700, but encumbered with debts said to be over £3,000 a year.[139] Falkland claimed in December 1636 that what he had to pay to and for his mother 'was neere as much yearely as (my debts considerd) I had to maintaine my selfe, my wife, my children and my family'.[140] All in all, he was among the least affluent of the Constitutional Royalists.

He was also one of the least active in public life before 1640, and this makes it extremely hard to reconstruct his political opinions. He apparently played no part in local government and was not even a Justice of the Peace in Oxfordshire.[141] He refused to pay Ship Money for his lands at Aldenham, Hertfordshire, and 'the bayleiffe durst not distraine for feare of being sued'.[142] However, the fact that he paid in Oxfordshire,[143] and the heavy debts owed upon the Aldenham lands,[144] suggests that this was one of the numerous disputes over rating rather than a refusal to pay on principle.[145] Possibly more significant was his admission – on the recommendation of William Lenthall – to Lincoln's Inn on 18 January 1638.[146] This would have given him the acquaintance with the law which was to come through in his speeches of 1640–1, and which was fairly common among Constitutional Royalists. However, this was probably a less significant influence upon his later political relationships than the remarkable coterie of which he was so urbane a host.

We have already discussed the religious outlook of this circle, which articulated an ecumenical attitude seemingly widespread among those who became Constitutional Royalists. The circle also forged a number of ties which later became politically significant. Of these, by far the most important for the present analysis was the 'most entire friendship without

137 Weber, *Falkland*, pp. 57–9.   138 *APC*, XLIV (1629–30), 239, 247.
139 BL, Add. MS 29974 (Pitt Correspondence), fos. 144r-148r. See also Clarendon, *History*, III, 181 (Book VII, §222).
140 PRO, SP 16/337/40 (Viscount Falkland to the Privy Council, 16 December 1636). See also SP 16/537/3 (list of letters and certificates at Council chamber, January 1636/7).
141 PRO, SP 16/405, fos. 53r–54r.
142 PRO, SP 16/376/106 (Ship Money arrears in Hertfordshire, 1636).
143 PRO, SP 16/336/51 (Lewis Harris to Edward Nicholas, 26 November 1636).
144 PRO, SP 16/346/78i (order of Archbishop Laud, 31 May 1636).
145 For the widespread rating disputes, see Morrill, *Revolt*, pp. 24–8.
146 *The Records of the Honourable Society of Lincoln's Inn: Admissions, 1420–1893* (2 vols., 1896), I, 234.

reserve' between Hyde and Falkland.[147] This subsequently bore much fruit in the high politics of 1641–2.[148] We should also note the presence of William Chillingworth, who later helped Hyde on his journey to York in the summer of 1642.[149] On the other hand, the circle contained people like Edmund Waller who defended episcopacy in February 1641, but who ultimately remained with Parliament. This should make us wary of seeing Great Tew as a breeding ground for Constitutional Royalists. The friendships formed there do account for some of the religious stances and political alliances which became visible in the early 1640s; but the connection was an imperfect one and should not be overstated.

That there was no clear-cut link between the Great Tew circle and the Constitutional Royalists of 1641–2 is also borne out by the fact that neither Falkland nor Hyde had ever 'had the least acquaintance ... before the [Long] Parliament' with Sir John Culpepper, who was to become one of their closest allies on the eve of the Civil War.[150] Culpepper came from an old family prominent in Kent and Sussex. Born in 1600, he may have studied at Peterhouse, Cambridge (1611), and at Hart Hall, Oxford (1616).[151] He apparently then saw military service abroad.[152] After his first marriage in 1628, he settled at Hollingbourne in Kent; he was a Justice of the Peace in Kent by 1638.[153] He also served on the Sussex commission of sewers,[154] and made his services to the borough of Rye in that capacity the basis of his successful bid to represent the town in the Short Parliament.[155] Culpepper was even more deeply rooted in a particular locality than most MPs: he held little land outside Kent and Sussex,[156] and he made the grievances of Kent – the shire which he represented in the Long Parliament – the basis of his political interventions at the end of 1640.[157] There is, however, no evidence that he refused 'the heavy Tax of ship-mony' which he was later to condemn.[158]

---

[147] Clarendon, *Life*, I, 42.   [148] See below, pp. 86–91.
[149] Clarendon, *Life*, I, 138.
[150] *Ibid.*, 104. Culpepper's close links with Hyde and Falkland in 1641–2 are examined below, pp. 82–91.
[151] F. W. T. Attree and J. H. L. Booker, 'The Sussex Colepepers', *Sussex Archaeological Collections*, 47 (1904), 66–8; Venn and Venn, *Alumni Cant.*, I, 432; Foster, *Alumni Oxon.*, I, 303.
[152] Attree and Booker, 'Sussex Colepepers', 68.   [153] *Ibid.*; PRO, SP 16/405, fo. 36r.
[154] East Sussex RO, Rye Corporation MS, 47/118/35a/5 (Sir John Culpepper *et al.* to the Mayor and Jurats of Rye, 20 March 1634/5).
[155] *Ibid.*, 47/131/39/8 (Sir John Culpepper to the Mayor and Jurats of Rye, 8 January 1639/40).
[156] PRO, SP 23/78 (Committee for Compounding reports and petitions), p. 798; SP 23/206 (Committee for Compounding particulars of estates and fines), p. 502.
[157] See below, pp. 68–9. For Culpepper's election as MP for Kent, see BL, Stowe MS 184 (Dering papers), fos. 15r–17r; Stowe MS 743 (Dering correspondence), fos. 146r–159r.
[158] See below, pp. 64, 68, 70. His name does not appear in PRO, SP 16/319/90 (Ship Money arrears in Kent, 1636).

Hyde's portrait of Culpepper is one of his most penetrating. 'He was', we are told, 'of a rough nature, a hot head, and of great courage; which had engaged him in many quarrels and duels.' This irascible quality – 'a man of sharpness of parts, and volubility of language' – leaves the initial impression that the most 'moderate' thing about Culpepper was 'his estate'.[159] This certainly contrasts with the innate gentleness of personality which we have encountered several times in this chapter. But then we come to Culpepper's religious attitudes, which were almost exactly what we would expect:

In matters of religion he was, in his judgement, very indifferent; but more inclined to what was established, to avoid the accidents which commonly attend a change, without any motives from his conscience; which yet he kept to himself; and was well content to have it believed that the activity proceeded from thence.[160]

It is important to remember that Hyde wrote this passage in 1668, and therefore that the dig about Culpepper's lack of conscience almost certainly reflects the gulf which opened up between the two men during the course of the 1640s.[161] The really significant point, however, is that Culpepper clearly wished to preserve the existing government of the Church of England, a hallmark of the Constitutional Royalist perspective. This helps to compensate for the paucity of evidence for Culpepper's attitudes towards politics, the constitution and the law during the 1620s and 1630s.

We have much more to go on for the last of our Constitutional Royalists, Sir John Strangways. He was born in 1584, matriculated at Queen's College, Oxford in 1601, and was admitted to the Middle Temple in 1611.[162] His estates were at Chirk Castle and Melbury Sampford in Dorset,[163] and he rapidly established himself as a leading figure in local government. He became sheriff of Dorset in 1612–13, and served as a Justice of the Peace.[164] He represented Dorset in the Addled Parliament, and sat in all the Parliaments of the 1620s, for Dorset (1621, 1624, 1628–9), and for Weymouth and Melcombe Regis (1625, 1626).[165] He emerges throughout as one of 'the Duke's most vehement critics',[166] opposing the Spanish war and

---

[159] Clarendon, *Life*, I, 106. Compare Sir Philip Warwick's statement that Culpepper 'had an eagerness or ferocity, that made him less sociable than his other collegues': Warwick, *Memoires*, p. 195.
[160] Clarendon, *Life*, I, 107.
[161] Cf. Clarendon, *History*, IV, 206 (Book X, §57). The relationship between Hyde and Culpepper during the 1640s and 1650s is discussed below, pp. 86–91, 130–2, 280–3, 296.
[162] Foster, *Alumni Oxon.*, IV, 1433; Sturgess, *Admissions to the Middle Temple*, I, 96.
[163] Dorset RO, Fox-Strangways (Earls of Ilchester) MS, D 124, boxes 8–9.
[164] Hughes, *List of Sheriffs*, 39; Mary Frear Keeler, *The Long Parliament, 1640–1641: A Biographical Study of its Members* (Memoirs of the American Philosophical Society, 36, Philadelphia, 1954), p. 353.
[165] *Return of Members*, I, 451, 457, 463, 469, 475.   [166] Russell, *Parliaments*, p. 300.

actively working for Buckingham's impeachment.[167] He was a close friend of the Earl of Bristol, and this link with the Digbys probably explains why he later opposed the Commons' attempt to block Lord Digby's French embassy in July 1641.[168] Strangways's speech on 5 June 1626 tells us much about his constitutional beliefs. Replying to Sir Dudley Carleton's threat that the King might turn to 'new counsels', he recalled

a speech made by King James [in March 1610], viz.: All kings that are not tyrants or perjured, will keep themselves within the bounds of the laws of the[ir] own kingdoms, and those that counsel them to other ways are vipers fitting to be cast out, and pests of the commonwealth. I hope our King that now is, and I am confident that he will, [will] inherit his father's virtues as he did the crown, and that if any persuade him to new counsels that he will cast them out.[169]

I have already analysed the speech which Strangways had in mind, and argued that it perfectly captured the principles by which James I ruled England.[170] Strangways was calling for nothing less than a return to 'Jacobethan' government within the law. It seems likely that he had already recognised that Charles was a different man from his father, hence the Dorsetian hint in the final sentence of this passage.

Strangways's speeches of the later 1620s harp repeatedly on Charles's failure to rule within the law. He refused the Forced Loan, and was temporarily imprisoned and removed from the Commission of the Peace as a result.[171] This experience reinforced his growing sense of the threat to legality. He informed the Commons on 3 April 1628 that 'I myself was told because I refused the Loan, though I was imprisoned, yet that shortly we should not have the protection of the law'; and five days later read a letter from one of his constituents which expressed the fear that 'there is no judge in Israel'.[172] He believed that 'what has been acted to the prejudice of the liberties of the subject of late, had it been in former ages, had been sufficient to have shaken the frame and foundation of the kingdom'.[173] But he was equally convinced that 'our religion teaches us obedience, by lawful means and humble courses to redress our grievances'.[174] Such beliefs will help us to explain both Strangways's denunciation of recent royal policies in 1640-1, and his decision to join the King in 1641-2. His commitment to

---

[167] Ibid., pp. 172, 302, 307, 436.
[168] Ibid., p. 172; below, p. 79. See also PRO, SP 16/453/24 (Edmund Rossingham to Viscount Conway, 12 May 1640).
[169] Bidwell and Jansson, Proceedings in Parliament, 1626, III, 370.
[170] See above, pp. 22-3.
[171] Cust, Forced Loan, pp. 189, 335; Russell, Parliaments, p. 327. For Strangways's imprisonment, see APC, XLII (1627), 38, 40, 318-9, 395; APC XLIII (1627-8), 57, 217. It is interesting that Dorset conveyed the King's order for his release: APC, XLII, 424. Strangways was still off the Commission of the Peace in 1638: PRO, SP 16/405, fos. 16v-17v.
[172] Keeler et al., Proceedings in Parliament, 1628, II, 286, 365.   [173] Ibid., III, 197.
[174] Ibid.

royal government within the law made him yearn for 'Jacobethan' methods, but was to become a classic recipe for Constitutional Royalism in the Civil War.

His religious attitudes were consistent with this, for they rested on a commitment to non-Laudian episcopacy and a dislike of godly zeal. In his commonplace book, Strangways defended 'Church goverment' as 'an hedge or wall about the doctrine of religion: a curbe to licentious courses'.[175] During the 1640s he refused to countenance 'the extirpation of prelacie out of the Church of England' on the grounds that 'episcopacie is an apostolicall institution'; 'that the Church never soe flourished as within 500 yeares after Chryst, when it was governed by Bishoppes'; 'that our English episcopacie is justifyed by the pryme devynes of the Reformed Churches beyond the seas'; 'that our English Bishopps now and ever since the Reformation have disclaymed all papal dependencie'; and 'that the fowre Generall Councells (confirmed in England by Act of P[ar]liament [primo] Eliz[abeth]) assert episcopacie'.[176] Here is an eloquent defence of the institution of episcopacy in terms of legality, convenience and apostolic tradition. Strangways clearly felt no regard for the Laudians, and in the mid-1630s fought a prolonged battle with Bishop Coke of Bristol over the right of presentation to the rectory of Maiden Newton.[177] But equally, he could not accept that the Scottish kirk was 'according to the word of God';[178] during the Civil War Parliament sequestered two of the ministers whom he had presented to livings in Dorset.[179]

During the 1630s, Strangways had several brushes with the Caroline régime over a variety of issues. In 1634, 'desiring to keepe his Christmas in London', he 'desired leave of the King by the Earles of Dorset and Holland'.[180] This reveals another contact with Dorset. However, the King refused and ordered Strangways to 'keepe house in the countrey'.[181] It is uncertain whether Strangways paid Ship Money, although his stance in the Long Parliament and his son's purchase in 1638 of a copy of the arguments used by Hampden's counsel suggest not.[182] Certainly in 1637 he and three

---

175 Beinecke Library, Yale University, Osborn MS b. 304 (commonplace book of Sir John Strangways), p. 35.
176 *Ibid.*, p. 75.
177 For Strangways's side of this dispute, see BL, Add. MS 64911 (Coke MS), fo. 8r–v (Strangways to Sir John Coke, 6 October 1635). For the Bishop's position, see Add. MS 64910 (Coke MS), fos. 14r, 41r, 59r (Bishop Coke to Sir John Coke, 22 June; 3, 22 August 1635); Add. MS 64911, fo. 96r (Bishop Coke to Sir John Coke, 31 January 1635/6). Strangways apparently won the right of presentation: BL, Lansdowne MS 459 (Register of Church livings), fo. 23v.
178 Beinecke Library, Yale University, Osborn MS b. 304, p. 75.
179 BL, Lansdowne MS 459, fos. 23v, 26v.
180 BL, Egerton MS 784, fo. 110r. 181 *Ibid.*
182 See below, p. 70; Dorset RO, Fox-Strangways (Earls of Ilchester) MS, box 220, unfol. (accounts of Giles Strangways). It is not clear whether the 'Mr Strangways' listed

others were tried before Star Chamber for transporting a total of £200,000 in gold out of England.[183] Two years later, he ignored the King's request for a contribution to the war against the Covenanters.[184] In short, Strangways was a persistent critic of Caroline government, a man driven by a sense of legal propriety and a commitment to non-Laudian episcopacy. I will argue that this combination explains both his hostility to royal policy in 1640–1 and his support for the King in 1641–2.

Having reviewed the careers of these ten figures during the 1620s and 1630s, we must now assess whether there was anything which would allow us to predict their convergence as Constitutional Royalists in 1642. The first point which needs stressing is the obvious one that their backgrounds were in many ways highly contrasted. They did not share any common set of characteristics in terms of regional background, tenure of public office, or attitudes towards specific policies. The more we look at particular issues the more contradictory the picture becomes. Five had been MPs before 1640; five had not. Some supported the Forced Loan (Dorset) while others bitterly denounced it (Strangways, Seymour). Some were well-established figures at Court, such as Dorset and Richmond, whereas several others were either deeply estranged from it (Hertford, Seymour) or played little part in public affairs (Falkland). Their estates cut a broad swathe across eastern, southern and western England. It is worth noting that the north and the Welsh Marches are not represented at all; since those regions produced such inveterate Royalist warriors as the Earls of Worcester or Newcastle or Sir Marmaduke Langdale, this may indicate that Constitutional Royalism was a phenomenon of the areas either controlled or most immediately threatened by Parliament. But the economic circumstances and experiences of these ten figures – ranging from peers with far-flung estates to those with a consolidated territorial base, and from affluent to impoverished gentry – were so disparate that it is difficult to extrapolate this argument too far. Nor do the dates at which the peers' families were ennobled form a pattern: we have four pre-Stuart creations, three of whom were later elevated by James I or Charles I, and two Caroline creations. We are not dealing therefore with a political outlook typically associated with either the ancient or the new nobility.[185]

among the Ship Money defaulters in Dorset in 1636 was Sir John: PRO, SP 16/319/89 (Ship Money arrears in Dorset, 1636).
[183] PRO, SP 16/361/92 (newsletter of C. Rossingham, 15 June 1637); SP 16/362/31 (newsletter of C. Rossingham, 22 June 1637).
[184] Rushworth, III, 913.
[185] Pre-Stuart creations: the dukedom of Lennox (earldom created *c.* 1488; elevated to dukedom 1581, and to dukedom of Richmond 1641); the earldom of Hertford (1537; elevated to marquessate 1641); the earldom of Southampton (1547); the earldom of Dorset (1604; but the first Earl had been Baron Buckhurst since 1567). Stuart creations: the earldom of Lindsey (1626); Lord Seymour of Trowbridge (1641). This information is

We need to look beyond these externals and to explore the deeper assumptions which these people shared. These resolve themselves into two: a commitment to the rule of law, and an avoidance of the more extreme forms of godly zeal. The first was a very vague concept, and just about everybody in Tudor and early Stuart England claimed to believe in it. What distinguished these figures was their commitment to it above other loyalties, to Crown or Parliament, or to a particular faction. There was some difference over whether particular policies infringed the rule of law, as shown, for example, by contrasting attitudes towards the Forced Loan. But this was mainly the result of an ambiguous legal system which claimed to safeguard both personal monarchy and mixed monarchy, and left room for disagreement over the circumstances in which extra-parliamentary taxation was lawful. The important point is the priority accorded to the rule of law, rather than the specific political conclusions drawn from it. This outlook also coloured their religious attitudes, which were characterised by an attachment to the 'Church by law established' and by a general lack of zeal for 'further reformation'. The precise religious positions of these individuals varied: some accepted the existing structures of the Church of England primarily because they were part of the constitution; others because they approved of them on conscientious grounds; still others because they feared the upheaval of institutional change. These viewpoints were not, of course, incompatible, and often the distinction is one of emphasis. Once again, such inflections are less important than the underlying area of common ground: none was driven primarily by a desire to create a 'godly commonwealth'. An attachment to the rule of law and a lack of godly zeal form the common denominators of these ten figures, and they are the closest we can come to 'predictors' of Constitutional Royalism. Such attitudes shaped their perceptions of broader political and religious developments throughout the 1620s and 1630s. During the crisis of 1640–2, it was to be these same attitudes which would guide their reactions to events and underpin their emergence as Constitutional Royalists.

derived from the lists in E. B. Fryde, D. E. Greenway, S. Porter and I. Roy, ed., *Handbook of British Chronology* (3rd edition, 1986).

──────────────────── ❧ 4 ❧ ────────────────────

Formation and convergence, 1640–1642

I

Between the Short Parliament and the outbreak of the Civil War, a commitment to the rule of law and an absence of godly zeal continued to characterise those who became Constitutional Royalists. These attitudes informed both their attack on Charles I's recent policies and their subsequent opposition to the reforms sought by Pym's Junto. Certainly they all in varying degrees disliked Laudianism, and were thus able initially to co-operate with the likes of Pym in its destruction. But the reasons for their hostility towards Laud were quite different. Whereas Pym's perception of every issue was coloured by his religion,[1] these figures were driven by a vision of the constitution and the common law which was applied to various policies and institutions, including the Church. They did not feel overriding religious imperatives and wished to make the Caroline Church acceptable not to God but to 'Jacobethan' values.

This in turn reveals the inseparability of their spiritual and secular beliefs. Conrad Russell has written that in seventeenth-century England 'it was as ludicrous to talk of separating Protestantism from politics as it would be now to talk of separating Socialism from politics'.[2] In the case of the Constitutional Royalists this intertwining took the form of a defence both of the law and of the 'religion by law established'. The two attitudes reinforced each other: they were locked in a symbiotic relationship within which they were *distinguishable* but not *separable*. Together they came to form the bottom line of the Constitutional Royalist outlook, which was that the common law and God's law were compatible, and that loyalty to the monarch provided the best defence of both.

For Charles I's leading critics, that principle – a commonplace of sixteenth- and early seventeenth-century English thought – was to become untenable. By 1642, figures like Pym, Harley and Cromwell believed that it was only possible to defend God's law by adapting the common law; and

---

[1] Cf. Russell, *FBM*, pp. 100–1; *Causes*, pp. 58–9.   [2] Russell, *Causes*, p. 63.

in a political culture which abominated innovation, adaptation was tantamount to infringement. This was the conclusion to which Charles I's personality and policies had driven some people. But not everybody. During 1641–2, the respective actions of King Charles and 'King Pym' persuaded many previous opponents of Charles's 'legal tyranny' that the Junto's attempts to further God's law threatened to subvert the common law. If we wanted to frame a single question which determined political choices in 1642, it would perhaps be this: is it possible to obey both the common law and God's law; and if not, which takes priority? The Constitutional Royalists replied yes to the first half, and thus did not yet feel the need to answer the second. It was a response which made sense despite the apparent contrasts of their earlier careers, and it drove them decisively towards the King.

This is not to say that they thought Charles I beyond criticism. To read them another way, we might argue that throughout their careers they sought to restore the 'Jacobethan' synthesis which Charles had undermined. Some – like Strangways, Seymour and Hertford – drew the conclusion during the period before 1641 that this was best achieved by criticising official policy; others, of whom Dorset was the paradigm, that it was better to modify policy from a position of influence within Court and Council. It was a difference of means rather than of ends. By 1641–2, both types were persuaded that 'Jacobethan' methods were more likely to be restored by working with Charles I – 'warts and all' – rather than with his loudest critics. This led to the emergence of a Constitutional Royalist platform which asserted the legality and constitutional propriety of Charles I's kingship, and denied the legality of his leading critics. Such convictions were to find their classic expression in the King's *Answer to the XIX Propositions*. This chapter will investigate how these beliefs emerged; why a cluster of individuals committed to them converged in 1641–2; how these people became influential within the King's counsels; and the use which they made of this influence. It concludes with an assessment of why moderates on both sides were unable to prevent the outbreak of civil war by forming a united middle ground during the summer of 1642.

II

When the Short Parliament assembled, recent royal policies came under heavy criticism in the Commons. Future Constitutional Royalists were prominent among those who voiced a deep commitment to the rule of law and a desire to curb some of the uses to which Charles I had put his discretionary powers during the Personal Rule. In many cases, they made speeches wholly in keeping with their parliamentary performances of the

1620s. On 16 April, for example, Seymour advocated tough measures against evil advisers: 'though the King bee never so Just, his badd ministers may corrupt his Justice'.[3] Seymour's principal targets were those 'who tell [the King] his prerogative is above all Lawes and that his Subjects are but slaves to the distruccion of property'.[4] He wished to defend the rule of law against perceived encroachments from the royal prerogative. Ship Money was particularly resented on these grounds, and Seymour called the sheriffs 'as greivous a plague as the task masters of Egipt'.[5] Several other speakers then took up these themes, including Culpepper, Sir Henry Vane, John Pym and Sidney Godolphin.[6]   The Commons' unity of purpose was very striking, so much so that it is often difficult in this debate to distinguish between future Parliamentarians and future Royalists.

The same was true on 18 April, when two future Royalists provided important footnotes to Pym's major speech of the previous day.[7] Edward Hyde – making his parliamentary debut – added the further grievance of 'the Courte of Honour' (often called the Earl Marshal's court). According to Hyde, this had 'assumed power to fine and imprison what it listed ... Hee graunted the Courte was old, but the customes of it were newe.'[8] The arbitrary procedures of the court ensured that while it 'had such a power', 'for ought he knewe noe man but might be fined to his ruine and fewe dayes before to have spoken thus much would have undone him'.[9] Moments later, when the House went into Committee of the Whole to discuss grievances, Sir John Strangways supported Pym in raising the griev-ance of those MPs imprisoned after the incidents of 2 March 1629. Charles had tried to prevent the imprisoned members from pleading parliamentary privilege by having them charged with 'sedition'; when they sought bail on the grounds that sedition was a misdemeanour not a felony, Charles had them moved to another prison to give the judges time to answer this argu-ment.[10] Such behaviour is of a piece with the episodes recounted in chapter 2.[11] Strangways now offered a vigorous assertion of Parliament's role as guardian of the common law and bulwark against misuse of the royal prerogative: 'The Kinge may out of Parliament question Treason or felony in the Howse, but not misdemeanours, the howse was to be the sole judge hereof.'[12] This meant that royal discretionary powers of imprisonment were not unlimited. The King's right to levy revenue in national

---

[3] Cope, 140–1.   [4] Ibid., 142. Cf. Russell, FBM, p. 105.   [5] Cope, 143.
[6] Ibid., 143–5; Maltby, 5.
[7] For Pym's speech, see Cope, 148–57; Maltby, 8–10.
[8] Cope, 158. Cf. Maltby, 12; CJ, II, 6.
[9] Cope, 158.
[10] John Reeve, 'The arguments in King's Bench in 1629 concerning the imprisonment of John Selden and other Members of the House of Commons', JBS, 25 (1986), 264–87.
[11] See above, pp. 28–9.   [12] Cope, 159; cf. Maltby, 12–13.

emergencies had similar bounds: 'for if the Kinge be judge of the necessitye, wee have nothing and are but Tennants at will'.[13] In short, here we have two future Royalists working to uphold the rule of law against the 'legal tyranny' of Charles I.

Likewise, on 23 April a string of future Royalists took up the demand that redress of grievances precede supply.[14] Seymour believed 'the great trust of the Common wealth too great to be betrayed', and therefore 'thought fitt o[u]r Greivances to bee first and then his Majestyes supplye'.[15] Strangways asserted that 'to represent the greivances is the first parliamentary'. He hoped that the King would 'enable' them to give by guaranteeing their 'property'; in the meantime, however, 'greivances must precede'.[16] Most of the remaining speakers – including Edward Kirton and Sir Walter Erle – also became Royalists in the Civil War, although some, such as Sir John Wray, George Peard and John Glyn, remained at Westminster. Once again, there is no straightforward way of predicting Civil War allegiance from contributions to this debate.

A slightly different pattern emerges within the House of Lords. This was most clearly visible on Friday 24 April, when the King arrived unexpectedly, protesting that 'the necessitys ar[e] soe urgent that there can be no delay',[17] and calling on the Lords to give supply precedence over grievances. In the debate which followed, Privy Councillors such as Strafford, Dorset, Arundel and Bridgwater spoke for the King, apparently on his instructions, while Saye and Bristol spoke against.[18] When the House divided, sixty-one peers (including eighteen bishops) voted to give precedence to supply. The minority of twenty-five who wished to discuss grievances first included future Royalists – Hertford, Southampton, Bath, Dunsmore (later Earl of Chichester) – alongside such familiar critics of Charles I as Bedford, Essex, Saye, Brooke, Warwick, Bolingbroke, Mandeville and Howard of Escrick.[19] Thus, whereas in the Commons we find almost unrelieved criticism of recent royal policies, with future Royalists and future Parliamentarians working shoulder to shoulder, in the Lords we find a division of opinion over whether grievances or supply should take precedence, but it is one which does not allow us to predict later political behaviour.

Only when the Commons turned to religious issues, as on 29 April, can

---

13 Cope, 159.
14 For accounts of this debate, see Russell, *FBM*, pp. 109–11; and Kevin Sharpe, *The Personal Rule of Charles I* (New Haven and London, 1992), pp. 866–7.
15 Maltby, 38; Cope, 170.   16 Maltby, 38; Cope, 171.   17 Cope, 70.
18 *Ibid.*, 71–9; Russell, *FBM*, pp. 111–12; Sharpe, *Personal Rule*, p. 868.
19 PRO, SP 16/451/39 (Windebank's notes, 24 April 1640). See also *LJ*, IV, 67. Cf. Gardiner, *History*, IX, 109; Russell, *FBM*, p. 112.

we begin to forecast subsequent alignments.[20] This debate began with a discussion of the Laudian altar policy. Hyde argued that 'it is not Contrary to the Rubrick that the Communion Table stand alter wise'; and was supported by Falkland's advice 'to Read the Rubrick and then resolve'.[21] Then followed an impassioned speech from Sir Robert Harley that bowing at the altar amounted 'almost to idolatry', and Francis Rous, Sir John Wray, Sir William Masham and several others quickly followed in the same vein.[22] At that point the debate took a new turn as Strangways, Sir Richard Dyott and (probably) Hopton criticised current altar policy while defending everything that was warranted by law. This was an exact religious counterpart to the position which these men adopted on the relationship between royal discretionary powers and the common law. Strangways recalled the taking down of altars in 'Edward 6 time', pointed out '5 reazons not an altar in Foxes booke', and asked 'whether better reazons by those that have altered it, then those did it'.[23] Such a view was in marked contrast to that advanced by the likes of Harley, and was the first sign of a rift which would ultimately become unbridgeable: between those who objected to Laud's altar policy because they thought it idolatrous, and those who rejected it as contrary to law. Future Royalists were distinguished by a very literal attachment to the concept of 'religion by law established': unlike many future Parliamentarians, they did not attack the Church because they thought it failed to conform to the Scriptures or to the example of continental reformed Churches. The positions which people took during this debate corresponded very closely to their allegiance in 1642. But for some months this underlying divergence of attitudes was masked by a common hostility to Laudianism.

Another illustration of this phenomenon was the fact that one future Royalist, Hertford, was among the Twelve Peers who petitioned Charles in August 1640 to recall Parliament. Hertford joined Bedford, Essex, Warwick, Rutland, Exeter, Bolingbroke, Mulgrave, Saye, Mandeville, Howard of Escrick and Brooke in complaining of various 'evils and dangers', including the King's 'present expedition against the Scottish army'; 'the sundry innovations in matters of religion'; 'the urging of Ship Money'; and 'the great grief of your subjects by the long intermission of Parliaments'.[24] Hertford's signature probably owed much to his previous exclusion from the Court and his closeness to his brother-in-law, Essex.[25] Hertford even acted with Bedford as spokesman for the Twelve Peers

[20] Maltby, 87–97. Cf. the analysis in Russell, *FBM*, pp. 114–16. This debate was apparently unknown to Gardiner: *History*, IX, 111.
[21] Maltby, 88.   [22] *Ibid.*, 89.   [23] *Ibid.*, 90.
[24] This petition is printed in Gardiner, *Documents*, pp. 134–6. For the original, see PRO, SP 16/465/16. The petition is analysed in detail in Russell, *FBM*, pp. 149–50, 384–5.
[25] See above, pp. 42–4.

before the Privy Council on 7 September;[26] and his presence gainsays the view of the Twelve Peers as a 'company of Puritan rascalls'.[27] Yet he was an unusual case, for other future Royalists, such as Bristol, Bath and Hertford's own brother Sir Francis Seymour, refused to have anything to do with the petition.[28] Their reasons are difficult to reconstruct precisely. Those who later rallied to Charles were not necessarily hostile to the recall of Parliament, as Dorset's speech at the Privy Council meeting on 2 September shows.[29] There are, however, signs that some of them felt the Twelve Peers were proceeding in the wrong way.[30] It is also possible that the commitment to the English constitution, the English Church and the rule of English law consistently displayed by those who became Constitutional Royalists left them mistrustful of a petition which demanded 'the uniting of both [England and Scotland] against the common enemies of the reformed religion'.[31] Had they known about the secret contacts between some of the Twelve Peers and leading Covenanters their suspicions would have been all the greater.[32]

III

Charles responded to the petition by summoning a Great Council of peers to York, and on the very first day forestalled criticism by announcing the recall of Parliament.[33] When that Parliament assembled in early November, many of those who became Constitutional Royalists again emerged as highly critical of recent royal policies. On 7 November, Seymour lamented that 'the Counsell have not been good or else they would not suffer an army to come to this kingdome', and then warned: 'one may see what danger wee are in for religion Jesuites and Priests openly to walke abroad

---

[26] PRO, SP 16/466/65, 74, 75 (Windebank's notes, 6–7 September 1640); Bodl. Lib., MS Clarendon 19, fos. 23r–24v (Windebank to Charles I, 7 September 1640); CUL, Buxton MS (Corr.), Box 1, unfol. (William Le Neve to John Buxton, 8 September 1640).
[27] Russell, *FBM*, p. 150, n. 19.   [28] *Ibid.*, pp. 154–5.
[29] David L. Smith, '"The more posed and wise advice": the fourth Earl of Dorset and the English Civil Wars', *HJ*, 34 (1991), 803–4.
[30] Bodl. Lib., MS Clarendon 19, fos. 23r–24v (Windebank to Charles I, 7 September 1640), 27r–v (Windebank to Charles I, 9 September 1640), 29r–30v (Windebank to Charles I, 11 September 1640).
[31] Gardiner, *Documents*, p. 136.
[32] These contacts are discussed in Russell, *FBM*, pp. 60–4, 68–70, 151–3; and Peter Donald, *An Uncounselled King: Charles I and the Scottish Troubles, 1637–1641* (Cambridge, 1990), pp. 135–6, 184–5, 244–7.
[33] For the decision to summon a Great Council, see PRO, SP 16/466/28 (Privy Council minute, 3 September 1640). The King's speech on 24 September is found in Bodl. Lib., MS Ashmole 800 (miscellaneous collections), fo. 112r–v. For the Council's deliberations thereafter, see P. Yorke, ed., *Miscellaneous State Papers, 1501–1726* (2 vols., 1778), II, 208–98. See also Norfolk RO, Lee Warner MS 1/2 (diary of 1640), p. 6.

... What incouragement is this to our papists.'[34] He concluded by praising
Parliaments as the natural remedy for this problem of evil counsel: 'The
poore King and subjects poore by ill counsell. Parliament the great Phisi-
tian of the Commonwealth seldome Parliaments, and dissolucion of them
which is the cause of all mischief.'[35] Similarly, two days later Culpepper
accompanied his presentation of the Kentish petition with a lengthy statement of the 'grievances of the Church and Common-wealth'.[36] These he
defined as 'the greater increase of papists, caused by the remisse execution
of those lawes, which are made to represse them'; 'the obtruding and coun-
tenancing of many divers new ceremonies in matters of religion'; 'the new
canons'; 'military charges'; 'the heavy Tax of ship-mony' which, he
declared, 'strikes at ... our inheritance'; and lastly the monopolists, 'the
leeches that have suck'd the Common-wealth, that it's almost become
hereticall'.[37] Both these speeches attributed England's grievances to
breaches of the rule of law and thus differed subtly from the line taken by
Pym, who argued that all problems stemmed from 'a designe to alter the
kingdome both in religion and government'.[38]

As in the Short Parliament, it was on religious issues that the differences
between future Royalists and future Parliamentarians were most apparent.
The former tended to attack Laudian policies because they infringed existing laws. Unlike Pym, they did not object to the 1640 canons because they
thought they were ushering in popery or idolatry, but because they had
been promulgated by Convocation after the dissolution of the Short Parliament.[39] This divergence was to destabilise English politics during the
course of 1641; and it became pivotal in the emergence of Constitutional
Royalism. But in the short term it was concealed by two more immediate
concerns: the desire to enforce the existing laws against recusants, and the
wish to destroy the canons. When, on 1 December, Pym and Hopton
moved for 'some course ... to suppresse the growth of poperie', they were
supported by Culpepper, who advocated 'an humble remonstrance to the
King about the growing of poperie', and urged 'that an act may bee drawen
against the growth of poperie'.[40] Likewise, Strangways moved on 11 February 1641 for 'the papists to bee speedily disarmed', and was seconded by

[34] D'Ewes (N), p. 7.   [35] Ibid.
[36] See Russell, FBM, p. 219, n. 45, for a plausible case that this speech, though not mentioned in the diaries, was in fact delivered.
[37] Sir Iohn Cvlpeper His Speech in Parliament concerning the Grievances of the Church and
Common-wealth (1641), pp. 1–4 (Wing, C 5058; BL, TT, E 196/8). This speech is also
printed in Rushworth, IV, 33–4.
[38] D'Ewes (N), p. 8.
[39] Russell, FBM, pp. 220–1. For detailed accounts of the 1640 canons, see Julian Davies, The
Caroline Captivity of the Church (Oxford, 1992), pp. 251–87; and Sharpe, Personal Rule,
pp. 877–84.
[40] D'Ewes (N), p. 91.

Culpepper, who wished 'to disarme papists, hee desired also papists sent from Court and popish Lords putt from the Upper House'.[41] People whose political paths would shortly diverge dramatically could still at this stage unite against popery. Yet subtle differences of language already allow us to distinguish 'those whose first attachment was to the rule of law from those whose first attachment was to the creation of a godly commonwealth'.[42] Wherever we can recover the views of future Constitutional Royalists they were to be found among the former.

This was especially true of attitudes towards the canons. With the exception of Robert Holborne,[43] MPs unanimously condemned them. But the terms in which they did so are very revealing, as a comparison of the denunciations by the 'godly' MP for Truro, Francis Rous, and the future Royalist Seymour will illustrate. Rous objected mainly to the prescribed 'doctrine' and 'ceremonies', and wished to 'censure' the 'main contrivers of these wicked Canons'.[44] By contrast, Seymour's primary concern was with the illegal behaviour of a 'hollow-hearted synod' rather than the 'wickedness' of the canons, and he desired the 'reformation' of the clerics responsible rather than 'ther ruine'.[45] His reaction makes perfect sense in the light of his long-standing attachment to the rule of law and characteristic lack of godly zeal. This would ultimately make it impossible for Seymour to co-operate with people like Rous. In the short term they were agreed on what they did not want; but they would later disagree on what they did want.

This commitment to the rule of law also explains why future Royalists dominated the campaign against Ship Money during November–December 1640. The issue was referred to a committee which reported on 7 December.[46] This occasion witnessed a particularly 'notable speech' from Falkland.[47] He began by asserting that 'the constitution of this commonwealth hath established, or rather endeavoured to establish to us the security of our goods, and the security of those laws which would secure us and our goods'. However, by upholding Ship Money, the very judges 'who should have been as dogs to defend the sheep, have been as wolves to worry them'. Their judgement was contrary to statute, and also to 'apparent evidences', for they had supposed 'mighty and eminent dangers, in the most serene, quiet, and halcion days that could possibly be imagined'. Again, it was the uses to which Charles I had put his discretionary powers,

---

[41] *Ibid.*, p. 350.   [42] Russell, *FBM*, p. 228.   [43] *Ibid.*, pp. 232–3.
[44] D'Ewes (N), p. 125.
[45] *Ibid.*, p. 149.
[46] *CJ*, II, 38, 46; D'Ewes (N), p. 75; PRO, SP 16/539/31 (committee report, [7 December] 1640).
[47] D'Ewes (N), p. 117. I have followed the text in Rushworth, IV, 86–8. See also BL, Add. MS 64921 (Coke MS), fo. 136v (John Coke the younger to Sir John Coke, *c.* 15 December 1640).

rather than the existence or nature of those powers, which was at issue. Falkland summed up the situation in language which offers a fascinating contrast to Pym's perspective: 'the cause of all the miseries we have suffered, and the cause of all our jealousies we have had, that we should yet suffer, is, that a most excellent prince hath been infinitely abused by his judges, telling him that by policy he might do what he pleased'. There was a fundamental contrast between those who thought the root of England's problems lay in a 'design' to alter the nation's religion, and those who attributed them to infringements of the rule of law by a badly advised monarch. Both groups could unite against Ship Money; but because they did so for different reasons they could not remain united indefinitely.

Future Royalists dominated the rest of the debate on 7 December. Either Falkland or Culpepper (the sources disagree) called for the impeachment of Lord Keeper Finch as 'a Judas' among the twelve judges.[48] But perhaps the most significant contribution came from Hyde, who declared: 'all our sufferings from the original of ship-money. That property of subjects not in their Judgment, but Parliament's.'[49] Whereas for Pym Ship Money was one manifestation of a popish plot, Hyde thought it 'something evil in its own right'.[50]

The upshot of this debate was a resolution, nem. con., that 'the extrajudicial opinions of the Judges' on Ship Money were 'against the laws of the realm, the right of property, and the liberty of the subjects, and contrary to former resolutions in Parliament, and to the Petition of Right'. A committee was then appointed to 'know how' the judges were 'solicited or threatened, and in what manner, and by whom' to give their opinions.[51] This was chaired by Falkland, and included Hyde, Culpepper, Strangways and Seymour alongside such future Parliamentarians as Denzil Holles and Sir Arthur Hesilrige. The committee's findings, reported the next day, pointed to the central role played by Finch, and articles of impeachment were immediately drawn up against him. Hyde read these on 14 January 1641, and was followed by another remarkable speech from Falkland.[52] He described Finch's life as 'a perpetual warfare (by mines, and by battery, by battel, and by strategem) against our fundamental laws ... against the excellent constitution of this kingdom'. Finch had coerced the judges into signing 'opinions contrary to law', and had thus committed 'a treason as well against the king as against the kingdom; for whatsoever is against the

---

[48] Note Book of Sir John Northcote, ed. A. H. A. Hamilton (1877), p. 39; PRO, PRO 30/53/9/11 (diary of Lord Herbert), fo. 16v. Cf. Russell, FBM, p. 230.
[49] Note Book of Northcote, Hamilton, p. 38. Hyde's constituents acclaimed this speech: Bodl. Lib., MS Clarendon 19, fo. 140r (Sir John St John to Hyde, 15 December 1640).
[50] Russell, FBM, p. 230.   [51] CJ, II, 46.
[52] D'Ewes (N), p. 255. The most accessible, reliable version of Falkland's speech is in Rushworth, IV, 139–41. Hyde read the articles 'at the request of the Lord Falkland': CJ, II, 68.

whole, is undoubtedly against the head, which takes from His Majesty the ground of his rule, the laws'. Again, we find this view of the law as the foundation of the constitution, and the 'ground' of royal government. The primacy which Falkland accorded to this principle was not universally shared; but the hostility to Ship Money which it engendered apparently was. This is neatly symbolised by the four MPs whom the Commons singled out for special thanks 'for the great service they have performed, to the honour of this House, and good of the Commonwealth, in ... the Business of the Ship-Money': Falkland and Hyde were named alongside two future Parliamentarians, Bulstrode Whitelocke and Oliver St John.[53]

Yet the superficial unity reflected in the juxtaposition of these names concealed fundamental differences of perception and principle. Ever since the Short Parliament, religious issues had shown up the contrast between those whose main aim was to defeat a plot to alter the nation's religion, and those whose main objection was to lapses in the rule of law. Hostility to a range of common targets – Laud, recusants, papists, the altar policy, the canons of 1640 – initially masked this divergence. But on 8–9 February 1641 the Commons witnessed a full-scale confrontation on the *principle* of episcopacy which brought it dramatically into the open. The stance which people took during that two-day debate provides an almost perfect predictor of their allegiance in the Civil War.

IV

In December 1640, Alderman Pennington had tabled a petition from the City of London, reportedly bearing 15,000 signatures, which demanded the abolition of 'the government of archbishops and lord bishops, deans and archdeacons, etc ... with all its dependencies, roots and branches'.[54] After repeated delays, on 8 February 1641 the Commons finally debated whether the petition should be committed along with the 'godly' Ministers' Remonstrance presented on 23 January.[55] The most eloquent speech in favour of committing the root-and-branch petition came from Nathaniel Fiennes, who sought to 'represent unto you the evils and inconveniences that do proceed from the government and ceremonies of the Church'.[56] In marked

[53] *CJ*, II, 68.
[54] The root-and-branch petition is printed in Gardiner, *Documents*, pp. 137–44. For more detailed discussion of its contents, see David L. Smith, 'From Petition to Remonstrance', and Richard Strier, 'From diagnosis to operation', in *The Theatrical City: Culture, Theatre and Politics in London, 1576–1649*, ed. David L. Smith, Richard Strier and David Bevington (Cambridge, forthcoming).
[55] For the Ministers' Remonstrance, see Russell, *FBM*, pp. 188–90, 200; and W. A. Shaw, *A History of the English Church during the Civil Wars and under the Commonwealth, 1640–1660* (2 vols., 1900), I, 23–7. Its text is unfortunately now lost.
[56] Fiennes's speech is found in Rushworth, IV, 174–83.

contrast to those who wished to preserve the established laws, Fiennes insisted that 'the faults that I note in the ecclesiastical laws are that they hold too much of civil law and too much of the ceremonial law'. He concluded bluntly: 'To speak plain English, these Bishops, Deans and Chapters do little good themselves by preaching, or otherwise; and if they were felled, a great deal of good timber might be cut out of them for the use of the Church and kingdom at this time.'

By contrast, the names of those who opposed committing the petition read like a roll-call of future Royalists. Falkland declared himself 'content to take away all those things from them, which to any considerable degree of probability may again beget the like mischiefs, if they be not taken away'.[57] 'I am sure', he continued, 'neither their lordships, their judging of tythes, wills and marriages, no nor their voices in Parliaments are *jure divino*.' However, while they were not '*jure divino*', neither were they '*injuria humana*', and Falkland did not 'think it fair to abolish, upon a few days debate, an order which hath lasted . . . in most churches these sixteen hundred years'. He concluded that 'we should not root up this ancient tree, as dead as it appears, till we have tryed whether by this, or the like lopping of the branches, the sap which was unable to feed the whole, may not serve to make what is left both grow and flourish'. Hyde advised 'not to have it committed etc.',[58] while Culpepper – who had the previous week given 'offence to manye' by calling bishops 'maine columnes of the realme'[59] – spoke in the same vein.[60] Other future Royalists such as Edward Kirton also opposed committing the petition on 8 February.[61] The next day, Strangways, using an argument later made famous by Sir Thomas Aston's *Remonstrance against Presbytery*, argued that 'if wee made a paritie in the church wee must at last come to a paritie in the Commonwealth. And that the Bishops weere one of the three estates of the kingdome and had voice in Parliament.'[62] This provoked a furious rejoinder from the inexperienced Oliver Cromwell.[63] Finally, at Seymour's suggestion, the House resolved to commit the petition, while reserving 'to it selfe the consideration of the maine point of Episcopacie when this Howse shall thinke fitt'.[64]

It would be difficult to exaggerate the importance of this debate. For here those committed primarily to preserving the rule of law – hitherto on the offensive against Caroline innovations – were pushed on to the defensive by the spectre of radical religious reform. Such reform would involve

---

[57] For the text of his speech, see *ibid.*, 184–6.
[58] D'Ewes (N), p. 337. Cf. Clarendon, *History*, I, 270–1 (Book III, §66).
[59] D'Ewes (N), p. 315.   [60] *Ibid.*, p. 337.   [61] *Ibid.*
[62] *Ibid.*, pp. 339–40. For Aston's *Remonstrance against Presbytery*, see J. S. Morrill, *Cheshire, 1630–1660* (Oxford, 1974), pp. 49–51.
[63] D'Ewes (N), p. 340.   [64] *Ibid.*, p. 342.

fundamental institutional changes, rather than simply re-ordering the policies and advisers of a misguided monarch. A commitment to the rule of law involved turning the clock back to 1625, but no further; it involved a return to 'Jacobethan' values and methods. Root-and-branch reform, by contrast, implied that there was something fundamentally flawed about the English Reformation. This issue was peculiarly calculated to expose the difference between those who disliked Laudianism but wished to preserve the existing structures of the Church, and those who believed that a recurrence of Laudianism could only be prevented by uprooting those structures. Those whose primary attachment was to the rule of law were left fearing that the abolition of episcopacy would bring other long-established forms of government crashing down. From this moment, the cosmetic unity of the opening months of the Long Parliament was doomed.[65]

The debate was also significant because it was the first occasion on which we have some evidence of co-ordination between people who would shortly become close political allies. The Scottish minister Robert Baillie wrote that 'my Lord Digbie and Viscount Falkland, with a prepared companie about them, laboured, by premeditat speeches, and hott disputts, to have that petition cast out of the House without a hearing'.[66] I have not found any written evidence which proves collusion, but the number and similarity of the speeches in defence of episcopacy certainly make it plausible.

Conrad Russell has recently argued persuasively that there was a very close relationship between attitudes towards episcopacy and attitudes towards the Scottish Covenanters. This first became apparent a few weeks later on 27 February, when Hyde raised the question of a Scottish paper which demanded the execution of Strafford and root-and-branch reform in England. Culpepper, Arthur Capel, Hyde, Sir Hugh Cholmeley, Lord George Digby and Hopton all spoke against it, while Strangways attacked it particularly 'vehementlie' and 'invectively'.[67] This line-up is rather looser and broader than that of 8–9 February on episcopacy, for it includes several people who did not become Constitutional Royalists; but it does none the less demonstrate that 'the Royalist party was an anti-Scottish party before it was a Royalist party',[68] just as it was also a party committed to the preservation of non-Laudian episcopacy.

[65] Cf. Gardiner, *History*, IX, 281–2.
[66] *The Letters and Journals of Robert Baillie*, ed. D. Laing (3 vols., Edinburgh, 1841–2), I, 302. Cf. Anthony Fletcher, *The Outbreak of the English Civil War* (1981), pp. 98–9.
[67] D'Ewes (N), p. 417. Cf. the discussions of this debate in Russell, *FBM*, pp. 270–1; and of the general relationship between anti-Scots attitudes and Royalism in the Civil War in Russell, *Causes*, pp. 15–16.
[68] Russell, *Causes*, p. 15.

v

It is important, however, not to overplay the degree of political co-operation at this date, for the careers of those who collaborated in the defence of episcopacy against both the English 'godly' and the Scottish Covenanters were still moving on different trajectories. For example, the elevation of Seymour to the House of Lords in February 1641[69] is best understood as part of an attempt at bridge building which led Charles to appoint five of the Twelve Peers – Bedford, Essex, Saye, Mandeville and Seymour's own brother Hertford – as Privy Councillors.[70] During the summer of 1641, the King's rapprochement with Essex and the Seymours bore further fruit: Hertford, elevated to the rank of Marquess on 3 June,[71] was appointed Governor to the Prince of Wales on 10 August,[72] while Essex replaced Pembroke as Lord Chamberlain of the King's Household on 24 July.[73] Seymour was sworn a Privy Councillor on 8 August,[74] thus joining Hertford within the King's inner counsels rather earlier than figures such as Culpepper, Falkland, Hyde and Strangways.

Several of these changes were closely related to the stances which individuals adopted on Strafford's attainder. Hertford had absented himself from the crucial vote on 7 May 1641,[75] while Seymour had voted against the attainder. They were rewarded with office just as Pembroke – who had promised the crowds outside Parliament that he would 'move His Majesty that justice might be executed'[76] – was deprived of it. But attitudes towards Strafford are a very imperfect predictor of subsequent political allegiance. The positions of those who became Constitutional Royalists were extremely varied.

[69] *LJ*, IV, 169; Bodl. Lib., MS Eng. hist. c. 230 (docquet book of warrants for letters patent), fo. 17r. He took the title Baron Seymour of Trowbridge. I shall continue to refer to him throughout as Seymour.

[70] PRO, PC 2/53 (Privy Council register), p. 101. Cf. the discussion in Russell, *FBM*, p. 263.

[71] PRO, SO 3/12 (Signet Office docquet book), fo. 151r; BL, Add. MS 64922 (Coke MS), fo. 39r (John Coke the younger to Sir John Coke, 2 June 1641); Wiltshire RO, Ailesbury MS, WRO 1300/199 (creation of Marquessate of Hertford, 3 June 1641); *LJ*, IV, 266.

[72] PRO, SO 3/12, fo. 165r. For earlier rumours of this appointment, see PRO, SP 16/481/60 (Sidney Bere to Sir John Pennington, 24 June 1641); SP 16/482/5 (Edward Nicholas to Sir John Pennington, 1 July 1641).

[73] Bedfordshire RO, St John of Bletsoe MS, J 1383 (Thomas Jenyson to Sir Rowland St John, 10 June 1641); PRO, LC 5/135 (Lord Chamberlain's warrant book), p. 1.

[74] PRO, PC 2/53, p. 176; Christ Church Muniment Room, Oxford, Browne Letters, Box A–C, unfol. (Christopher Browne to Sir Richard Browne, 12 August 1641).

[75] *LJ*, IV, 236.

[76] *A Perfect Journall of the Daily Proceedings and Transactions in that Memorable Parliament, begun at Westminster, the third day of November 1640* (1659), CUL, Acton. d. 25. 109/1, p. 90. See also House of Lords RO, Braye MS 2 (John Browne papers), fo. 177r-v; PRO, SP 16/482/95 (Thomas Wiseman to Sir John Pennington, 29 July 1641); and Clarendon, *History*, I, 345 (Book III, §§213–14).

Southampton voted against the attainder and Richmond likewise 'stuck close and faithfully' to Strafford.[77] By contrast, Dorset and the first Earl of Lindsey apparently joined the many (including Essex, Warwick and Saye) who supported it.[78] The same diversity existed in the Lower House. On 23 February 1641, we find Culpepper urging the Commons to prepare answers to the Lords' objections to Strafford's impeachment.[79] By April, he supported a bill of attainder as 'the safest and the speediest way'.[80] Similarly, on 15 April Falkland had argued powerfully for the doctrine of cumulative treason: 'how many haires breadths makes a tall man, and how many makes a little man, noe man can well say, yet wee know a tall man when wee see him from a low man, soe 'tis in this, how many illegal acts makes a treason is not certainly well [known], but wee well know it when we see [it]'.[81] Four days later, Falkland stated bluntly: 'in equity lord Straford deserves to dye'.[82] When the bill came to its third reading on 21 April, it was carried by 204 votes to 59. The minority of 'Straffordians' included such future Royalists as Edward Kirton, Sir Edward Alford and Sir Frederick Cornwallis. But it also included the Parliamentarian John Selden. By contrast, Hyde, Culpepper, Falkland and Hopton all voted for the attainder. Sir John Strangways – who had earlier described Strafford's trial as a 'matter of bloud' – was anxious to refute charges that he was a 'Straffordian',[83] while on 29 April Hyde conveyed a message to the Lords regarding Strafford's 'alleged design to escape'.[84] In neither House can we predict future political behaviour from the positions adopted for or against Strafford's execution.[85]

It is rather easier to observe the characteristic concerns of future Constitutional Royalists on other issues during the summer of 1641. As before, wherever their attitudes can be reconstructed, they rested upon a deep attachment to the rule of law. When, on 3 May 1641, MPs learnt of Charles's complicity in the first Army Plot, Culpepper immediately moved 'for the remonstrance and peticon of rights to be forthwith read, and then to goe to the lordes and by that we may try the effeccon of the kinge, and

---

[77] Clarendon, *History*, I, 289 (Book III, §104); MP, April 1641 (notes of Strafford's trial), fo. 16; BL, Harl. MS 6424 (diary of a bishop), fo. 64v; Clarendon, *Life*, III, 232–3; Rushworth, IV, 257.

[78] MP, April 1641, fos. 15–19. I discuss Dorset's support for Strafford's attainder more fully in David L. Smith, 'The fourth Earl of Dorset and the Personal Rule of Charles I', *JBS*, 30 (1991), 281–2.

[79] D'Ewes (N), p. 390.

[80] See also *Notes of proceedings in the Long Parliament ... by Sir Ralph Verney*, ed. H. Verney (Camden Society, 1st series, 31, 1845), 50.

[81] *Ibid.*, 49.　　[82] *Ibid.*, 53.

[83] D'Ewes (N), p. 303; BL, Harl. MS 477 (diary of John Moore), fo. 49v.

[84] *CJ*, II, 130.

[85] Cf. the account in J.B. Crummett, 'The lay peers in Parliament, 1640–4' (PhD thesis, University of Manchester, 1972), pp. 314–21.

that if we should be dissolved, that we might be found doeinge the service we were hither sent for'.[86] Although it seems that he was not joined by other future Constitutional Royalists, Culpepper's response was entirely consistent with an overriding desire to preserve the rule of law against arbitrary royal actions.

Much the same was true of the attack on Star Chamber. The bill passed the Commons with virtually no resistance.[87] Hyde's attitude was probably typical: that the court 'whilst it was gravely and moderately governed was an excellent expedient to preserve the dignity of the king, the honour of his Council, and the peace and security of the kingdom', but that its recent 'exorbitances' and 'extraordinary courses' now made its abolition 'politic'.[88] The only strong support for preserving Star Chamber came from the Lord Privy Seal, the Earl of Manchester, who 'in defence thereof spake such high prorogative language that he was like to have bine called to the Barr'. Manchester 'affirmed the King's prorogative to be soe rivitted and inhaerent in him that it could not be limited by any lawe, that he might take any cause out of any C[ou]rt of Justice and judge it him selfe'.[89] But Manchester became a Parliamentarian in the Civil War. By contrast, Seymour lined up with Essex and Saye in condemning this 'high prorogative language', and attacked Manchester 'for the sorded bribery and corruption in his owne Co[u]rt'.[90] Manchester's belief that the King's prerogative 'could not be limited by any lawe' ultimately drove him to take up arms against Charles because it offered no means of restraint short of force. It was precisely that option which Hyde, Seymour and others left open by defending the concept of royal government within the rule of law.

This deep concern for legality was evident throughout the debates on the root-and-branch bill in May and June 1641. Future Constitutional Royalists consistently sought to remedy recent abuses without destroying long-established institutions. On 27 May, Hyde argued 'that the Church and State of England had flourished manye hundred yeares in much happines under the Church goverment wee now enioy'.[91] When the bill was referred to a committee, Hyde saw his appointment as chairman as a bid by the bill's supporters to silence his 'frequent speaking' against it.[92] Similarly, Culpepper moved on 11 June that the statement in the bill's preamble that 'the present goverment of the Church had been by *long* experience an hinderance to the full reformation of religion and to the civill state' be

---

[86] BL, Harl. MS 477, fo. 28r.   [87] *Two Diaries*, p. 120; *CJ*, II, 171.
[88] Clarendon, *History*, I, 374–5 (Book III, §§262–4).
[89] Bedfordshire RO, St John of Bletsoe MS, J 1386 (Thomas Jenyson to Sir Rowland St John, 24 June 1641).
[90] *Ibid.*   [91] BL, Harl. MS 163 (diary of Sir Simonds D'Ewes), fo. 238v.
[92] Clarendon, *History*, I, 362–3 (Book III, §240); *CJ*, II, 173.

rephrased 'by *late* experience'.[93] In other words, he did not want to overthrow the existing Church, but to return to 'Jacobethan' methods of running it. He believed that 'the grievances had growne from the abuse of the goverment and not from the goverment it selfe'.[94] On the whole, however, the supporters of episcopacy failed to apply the concerted pressure of 8–9 February. This prompted Falkland's savage comment that 'they who hated bishops hated them worse than the devil, and that they who loved them did not love them so well as their dinner'.[95]

How, then, did this commitment to non-Laudian episcopacy and to the Prayer Book develop into a fully fledged *political* programme based on a particular view of the constitution? This is an extremely difficult process to document, and different people made the crucial change of perspective at different times. But two factors above all appear to have provided the critical impetus: the growing plausibility of Charles I's claim to be the natural defender of the Church of England, together with his acceptance of the statutory changes of 1640–1; and a fear of religious violence in the English provinces, of a wave of popular iconoclasm which was seemingly accepted – if not encouraged – by many within Parliament.

By mid-1641, Charles had gone a long way towards removing those aspects of his rule to which people like Hyde, Falkland, Culpepper, Strangways and Seymour most objected. His assent to all the great constitutional measures of 1640–1 – the impeachment of leading advisers, the Triennial Act, the abolition of Ship Money, the Act against the dissolution of Parliament without its own consent, and the destruction of Star Chamber and High Commission – made him appear a monarch committed to ruling within the law. He had, in Conrad Russell's words, 'retreated to the point where members predominantly concerned with issues of legality ... were willing to work with him'.[96] They were all the more prepared to do so because Charles offered to protect the existing structures of the Church of England, especially non-Laudian episcopacy and the Prayer Book. His promise to 'reduce all things to the best and purest time, as they were in the time of Queen Elizabeth'[97] was all the more credible because he made no attempt to rescue Laud and instead promoted non-Laudians to the episcopate.[98] Charles's 'pious resolucon to mainteyne constantly ye doctrine & discypline of ye Church of England'[99] made him the natural rallying point

[93] BL, Harl. MS 164 (diary of Sir Simonds D'Ewes), fo. 217r (my emphasis).   [94] *Ibid.*
[95] Clarendon, *History*, I, 363 (Book III, §241).   [96] Russell, *FBM*, p. 401.
[97] This quotation is from the King's speech of 25 January 1641: Rushworth, IV, 155.
[98] For a list of the new bishops appointed during 1641, see *The Diary and Correspondence of John Evelyn*, ed. W. Bray (new edition, ed. H. B. Wheatley, 4 vols., 1906), IV, 99, n. 1. See also John Morrill, *The Nature of the English Revolution* (Harlow, 1993), pp. 158–9; and Fletcher, *Outbreak*, p. 121.
[99] *Diary of Evelyn*, Bray, IV, 111 (Nicholas to Charles I, 25 October 1641).

for those who had defended non-Laudian episcopacy on 8–9 February. His commitment to preserve the non-Laudian Church and to rule within the law was in effect a promise to re-establish 'Jacobethan' practices – which was exactly what the likes of Hyde had been trying to do in 1640–1.

This was all the more appealing because of the manifest dangers to the established Church which sprang up all over England during the spring and summer of 1641. John Morrill, Anthony Fletcher and David Underdown have described outbreaks of popular iconoclasm which brought England to the verge of anarchy.[100] The decisive political impact of this is most fully documented in the case of Sir Edward Dering, whose 'defection' from root-and-branch reform and subsequent allegiance to the King were caused primarily by warnings of 'disorder' from the Kentish minister Robert Abbot.[101] But Dering was very far from alone here. We can only understand the urgency of Culpepper's fear that people might 'speake and preach what they would against the . . . common prayer booke' and even come 'to open force and blowes' in the context of this terror that public order was about to collapse.[102] The indefatigable attachment to the rule of law voiced by many future Royalists loses much of its force and anxiety unless we appreciate how seriously provincial iconoclasm appeared to threaten it.

These two considerations – a sense of Charles I as a viable constitutional monarch committed to the Church, and a horror of popular violence against that Church – acted as push and pull factors driving people like Hyde towards the King. The translation of these motives into a full-blown political commitment happened earliest, perhaps, for Culpepper. His horror of popular hostility to the Church became clear on 18 June when he urged the Commons to send for a man who had told his minister that 'his function is Anti-Christian, his church noe church, and diverse other scandallous thinges'.[103] At almost exactly the same moment, we find him working frantically on a proposal to grant the King tonnage and poundage for three years, and to get this passed before the debate on root-and-branch could be concluded. This would have enabled the King to dissolve Parliament. Culpepper spoke in favour of the tonnage and poundage bill on 17 June,[104] and on 26 July reported confidently to Hamilton about the

---

[100] John Morrill, *The Revolt of the Provinces* (2nd edition, Harlow, 1980), pp. 31–51; Fletcher, *Outbreak*, pp. 91–124, 208–27; David Underdown, *Revel, Riot and Rebellion* (Oxford, 1985), pp. 136–41. See also Jacqueline Eales, 'Iconoclasm, iconography, and the altar in the English Civil War', in *The Church and the Arts*, ed. Diana Wood (Studies in Church History, 28, 1992), 313–27.
[101] Derek Hirst, 'The defection of Sir Edward Dering, 1640–1641', *HJ*, 15 (1972), 193–208.
[102] BL, Harl. MS 164, fo. 89r.
[103] BL, Harl. MS 478 (diary of John Moore), fo. 689r. Cf. Fletcher, *Outbreak*, p. 111.
[104] BL, Harl. MS 163, fo. 716v. Cf. Harl. MS 5047 (parliamentary diary), fo. 23v.

prospects for a new Book of Rates.[105] In the same letter, he warned that the 'bill of episcopacy' would 'bee ready for a report to the grand committee tomorrow or [the] nexte day'.[106] Shortly afterwards, however, Culpepper's proposals, embodied in the new Book of Rates, were shown to be financially unworkable and abandoned.[107] None the less, this episode apparently reveals the moment when his hatred of root-and-branch first translated into a bid to give political assistance to the Crown.[108] Not only do we find him keeping Hamilton informed of the progress of the Book of Rates and the root-and-branch bill,[109] but by September, Sir Edward Nicholas was passing his letters to Hamilton on to Charles, so that he 'may see all the passages of ye Com[m]ons House'.[110]

In Hyde's case also a wish to defend episcopacy was crucial in bringing him into the King's service. Charles summoned Hyde during the summer of 1641 and 'took notice of his affection to the Church', which 'he thanked him for more than for all the rest'. Hyde replied that 'he was very happy that His Majesty was pleased with what he did; but if he had commanded him to have withdrawn his affection, and reverence for the Church, he would not have obeyed him'. Charles replied that this only 'made him love him the better'.[111] Hyde's political allegiance to the King was thus inseparable from his loyalty to the Church.

For others, the Ten Propositions adopted by the Commons and presented to the Lords on 24 June were a crucial turning-point. Perhaps the most far-reaching was the third proposition, which requested Charles to dismiss 'such counsellors ... as have been active for the time past in furthering those courses contrary to religion, liberty [and] good government of the kingdom', and to appoint 'such officers and counsellors as his people and Parliament may have just cause to confide in'.[112] On 13 July, it was moved that the King should be asked specifically not to send Lord Digby as ambassador to France. Strangways acted as teller for the supporters of an amendment inserting the words 'for the present', but was defeated by 128 votes to 114.[113] He was clearly seeking to defend the King's discretionary power to choose such officials. However, this was not yet an issue which forced Charles's supporters to unite: Culpepper was far from

[105] Scottish RO, Hamilton MS, GD 406/1/1397 (Culpepper to Hamilton, 26 July 1641). I am most grateful to John Scally for showing me a xerox copy of this letter. See also Russell, *FBM*, pp. 348–9, 357.
[106] Scottish RO, Hamilton MS, GD 406/1/1397.   [107] Russell, *FBM*, pp. 357–9.
[108] Cf. Fletcher, *Outbreak*, pp. 115–17.
[109] Russell, *FBM*, pp. 348–9.
[110] *Diary of Evelyn*, Bray, IV, 86 (Nicholas to Charles I, 10 September 1641).
[111] Clarendon, *Life*, I, 93.
[112] The Ten Propositions are printed in Gardiner, *Documents*, pp. 163–6.
[113] BL, Harl. MS 163, fo. 397v. Strangways was a friend of the Digby family: see above, p. 58.

hostile to the Propositions,[114] while there is no sign that Hyde or Falkland even contributed to the debates on them.[115]

Pym's demands about counsel raised a disturbing new question: did the Junto now pose a greater threat to the rule of law and to constitutional balance than the King? One of the earliest answers in the affirmative is found in a poem composed during September 1641, although not published until the following year. Its author was Sir John Denham, who had been a witness for the defence in Strafford's trial. John Wallace has called Denham's *Coopers Hill* the 'manifesto of parliamentary royalism', and the language of its closing lines closely resembles the King's *Answer to the XIX Propositions*:

> Thus kings by grasping more then they could hould,
> First made their subjects by oppression bould,
> And popular sway by forcing Kings to give,
> More then was fitt for subiects to receave
> Ranne to the same extreame, & one excesse,
> Made both by striving to be greater, lesse:
> Nor any way but seeking to have more,
> Makes either loose, what they possest before.
> Therefore their boundles power lett princes draw
> Within the Chanell & the shoares of Lawe:
> And may that Law which teaches Kings to sway
> Their Septers, teach their subjects to obey.[116]

Here we have the commitment to a balanced constitution; the belief that monarchs and subjects should not exceed their respective powers; and the sense that the law was the natural guardian of these arrangements which later became the hallmarks of Constitutional Royalism. When the Long Parliament assembled, even the King's future supporters believed that his recent policies posed the greatest threat to the rule of law. But Denham's poem eloquently expressed a growing fear that the greater danger now came from Charles's leading critics within Parliament. As circumstances changed, a consistent commitment to the rule of law dictated different political alignments.

VI

We find abundant evidence of this change of attitude once Parliament re-assembled in October. Whereas news of the Scottish 'Incident' prompted

---

[114] Russell, *FBM*, pp. 352–3.   [115] Cf. Fletcher, *Outbreak*, p. 58.

[116] Brendan O Hehir, *Expans'd Hieroglyphicks: A Critical Edition of Sir John Denham's Coopers Hill* (Berkeley and Los Angeles, 1969), p. 90 (Draft I, lines 317–28). I am deeply grateful to the late John Wallace for drawing my attention to this poem, and for a most helpful discussion about its date and significance. See also John M. Wallace, 'Coopers Hill: the manifesto of parliamentary royalism, 1641', *ELH, A Journal of English Literary*

D'Ewes to advocate 'the setling of religion', Hyde and Falkland 'mooved that wee should leave the busines of Scotland to the Parliament there and not to take upp feares and suspicions without very certaine and undoubted grounds'.[117] As Gardiner observed, their language revealed 'that the Episcopalian party was in process of conversion into a Royalist party'.[118] This process was even more apparent in Hyde's speech of 28 October. In response to William Strode's demand that Parliament have 'a negative voice in the placing of the great officers of the King and of his Councellors', Hyde insisted that 'the choice of the great officers of the crowne ... by the King' was 'an hereditarie flowre of the crowne: and that the passing of the three bills against the Starre-chamber, the High-Commission Court and the shipp-monie wee had done verie much for the good of the subject: and hee thought all particulars weere in a good condition if wee could but preserve them as they weere'.[119] That same commitment to the rule of law which had earlier made Hyde attack policies such as Ship Money now inclined him to trust Charles I, and to regard the statutes of 1640–1 as sufficient to ensure royal government within the law. Those who could not accept this were those who sought 'further reformation' of the Church, and Conrad Russell has pointed to the extreme significance of D'Ewes's reply: 'For the Church I cannot agree with the gentleman over the way (viz. Mr Hide) who thinkes that all is well setled and constituted if wee cann but keepe them as they are; trulie I rather thinke the Church is yet full of wrinkles amongst us and needes a great deale of Reformation which I hope wee shall shortly see effected.'[120] There could be no clearer evidence of the gulf between those concerned primarily with the rule of law, and those whose overriding objective was to create a godly commonwealth.

This debate was also crucial in bringing Hyde and his allies to the King's attention as potential supporters. The very next day, Sir Edward Nicholas informed Charles

that the Lo[rd] ffalkland, S[i]r Jo[hn] Strangwishe, Mr Waller, Mr Ed[ward] Hide, & Mr Holborne, & diverse others stood as champions in maynten[a]nce of yo[u]r prerogative, and shewed for it unaunswerable reason and undenyable p[r]esedents, whereof yo[u]r Ma[jes]tie shall doe well to take some notice (as yo[u]r Ma[jes]tie shall thinke best) for their encouragm[en]t.[121]

The King then added in the margin: 'I co[m]mande you to doe it in my name, telling them that I will doe it myselfe at my returne.'[122]

Before Charles returned, however, the process of polarisation in the

History, 41 (1974), 494–540. For outlines of Denham's life, see O Hehir, pp. xix–xxi; and *DNB*, XIV, 346–9.
[117] D'Ewes (C), p. 15.   [118] Gardiner, *History*, X, 32. Cf. Fletcher, *Outbreak*, p. 133.
[119] D'Ewes (C), p. 45.   [120] *Ibid.*, p. 46; Russell, *FBM*, p. 413; *Causes*, p. 138.
[121] *Diary of Evelyn*, Bray, IV, 116 (Nicholas to Charles I, 29 October 1641).
[122] *Ibid.*

Commons was drastically accelerated by news of the Irish Rebellion, which arrived on 1 November. Five days later, Pym reported six proposed Instructions for the Committee of Both Houses attending the King in Scotland. The sixth made the unprecedented demand that 'ill Counsellors' be removed, or the Commons 'would not be obliged to ... releive Irelande'.[123] Culpepper immediately 'saied that hee thought Ireland to be a parte of England and that wee ought to defend it'.[124] This affirmation of Ireland as an English colony rather than a separate kingdom was clearly designed to answer any doubts about the Crown's obligation (and authority) to quell the rebellion. Pym responded on 8 November with a revised wording which threatened that 'wee should take such a course for the securing of Ireland as might likewise secure our selves'. This forced Culpepper to make his constitutional position more explicit: 'wee could nott desire this off Right. Power in the king alone in the Lords alone in the Commons alone; some in Lords and Commons, some in concurrency of all.' Culpepper then acted as teller against the motion, but was defeated by 151 votes to 110.[125] His views represented a notable stride towards a fully fledged doctrine of constitutional monarchy; they were shortly to crystallise further during the debates on the Grand Remonstrance.

The Remonstrance was the product of a lengthy gestation lasting over a year, and Pym's decision to bring it before the House on 8 November was precipitated by news of the Irish Rebellion.[126] The Remonstrance presented a comprehensive indictment of the misgovernment of one monarch: none of the grievances enumerated in it pre-dated 1625. All these 'evils' it blamed upon 'a malignant and pernicious design of subverting the fundamental laws and principles of government, upon which the religion and' justice of this kingdom are firmly rooted'. To foil this, the Remonstrance called for a 'reformation' of religion and requested that the King 'employ such counsellors, ambassadors and other ministers ... as the Parliament may have cause to confide in'.[127] During the fortnight after 8 November the opponents of the Remonstrance secured the deletion or dilution of several of its more extreme statements. For example, an article attacking the Prayer Book was removed;[128] and a denunciation of the Courts of Chancery, Exchequer and Wards as 'arbitrary' was changed to read 'grievous in exceeding their jurisdiction'.[129] On 16 November, Falkland and Culpepper

[123] D'Ewes (C), p. 99.   [124] Ibid.   [125] Ibid., pp. 104–5; CJ, II, 307.
[126] The context and contents of the Grand Remonstrance are discussed more fully in Smith, 'From Petition to Remonstrance' and Strier, 'From diagnosis to operation', in The Theatrical City, Smith et al.
[127] The Grand Remonstrance is printed in Gardiner, Documents, pp. 202–32. The quotations are taken from §§184–5, 197.
[128] D'Ewes (C), pp. 150–1; CJ, II, 317.
[129] D'Ewes (C), pp. 185–6, n. 18; CJ, II, 322. Cf. Morrill, Nature of the English Revolution, p. 294.

were added to the committee responsible for drafting the Remonstrance.[130] Their influence was discernible in a new article (§184) which, in Anthony Fletcher's words, 'was an extraordinary conjunction of different priorities'.[131] On the one hand it sought 'to unburden the consciences of men of needless and superstitious ceremonies, suppress innovations, and take away idolatry'. But it also, in language highly characteristic of those who became Constitutional Royalists, denied any 'desire to let loose the golden reins of discipline and government in the Church, to leave private persons or particular congregations to take up what form of Divine Service they please', and insisted 'that there should be throughout the whole realm a conformity to that order which the laws enjoin according to the Word of God'.[132] Despite this addition, Falkland and Culpepper both spoke against the final version of the Remonstrance when it was debated on 22 November. Falkland warned that it 'casts a concealing of delinquents uppon the king'.[133] Culpepper took a slightly different line, protesting 'against the forme off it'.[134] 'All remonstrances should bee addressed to the king', he argued, 'and not to the people, because hee only can redresse our greevances.'[135]

Culpepper concluded by denouncing the Remonstrance as 'daingerous for the publique peace'.[136] Hyde also 'spoke very vehemently against it', and advanced a view of constitutional balance which resembles that expressed a fortnight earlier by Culpepper: 'wee stand upon our liberties for the king's sake, least hee should bee king of meane subjects, or wee subjects of a meane king'.[137] The Remonstrance eventually passed by only 159 votes to 148, and caused a dramatic sharpening of political alignments. John Coke reported to his father: 'If yow sett Pimme Hollis and Hambden aside, the best of the house voted against it, as Sir Jo[hn] Culpeper, L[or]d Faulkland, Mr Crewe, Sir Robert Pye, Sir John Strangewaies, all the best lawiers.'[138] Hyde later recalled that 'the debate continued till after it was twelve of the clock, with much passion'.[139]

Then followed an even more heated debate over whether the Remonstrance should be printed. Hyde, Culpepper 'and divers others offered to enter their protestations against printing of it', but were told that there could be no such protestations without the consent of the House.[140]

---

[130] *CJ*, II, 317.   [131] Fletcher, *Outbreak*, p. 149.
[132] Gardiner, *Documents*, p. 229.
[133] *Verney's Notes*, Verney, 121.   [134] D'Ewes (C), p. 184.
[135] *Verney's Notes*, Verney, 122.
[136] *Ibid.*   [137] D'Ewes (C), p. 183; *Verney's Notes*, Verney, 121.
[138] BL, Add. MS 64922, fo. 65r (John Coke the younger to Sir John Coke, [? 22] November 1641).
[139] Clarendon, *History*, I, 419 (Book IV, §52).
[140] D'Ewes (C), p. 186; Clarendon, *History*, I, 419–20 (Book IV, §52); Wormald, *Clarendon*, pp. 28–9.

Geoffrey Palmer's dissent from this met with uproar, and he was briefly imprisoned in the Tower.[141] The principal objection to the printing was that voiced by Dering: that it was wrong to 'remonstrate downward' and 'tell stories to the people' without first sending the Remonstrance to the Lords.[142] Such fears reflected the increasing volatility of the London crowds in the last days of November. The demonstrators were concerned above all to exclude bishops from the Upper House, and on 29 November even overran the Court of Requests, yelling 'No Bishops'. Sir Philip Warwick 'saw old Sir John Strangewaies in the Court of Requests so crowded up into a corner by a multitude of people ... that I truly thought him in danger'.[143] In a passage which he later excised from his *Life*, Hyde recorded that the crowd then read a list of 'persons disaffected to the kingdom', of 'which Sir John Strangways was the first, and Mr Hyde was the second, and then the Lord Falkland and Sir John Culpepper'.[144] These names show that what the crowds meant by 'disaffected' was by now almost identical with what the King meant by 'well affected'.

An analogous pattern was evident in the Lords, where several peers who became leading Constitutional Royalists stood out against the abolition of bishops or their exclusion from the Upper House. On 2 November, Charles asked Nicholas 'to thanke Southampton in my name, for stopping the Bill against the Bishops: &, that at my coming, I will doe it myselfe'.[145] A peer who in April 1640 had insisted that redress of grievances precede supply[146] was now seeking to protect the legal and constitutional right of Bishops to sit in the Lords. By mid-November Henrietta Maria regarded Southampton's proxy as vitally important in the mobilisation of a Royalist party within the Upper House.[147] In December Hertford presented to the Lords a petition from Somerset reportedly bearing 14,350 signatures. This defended 'the present government of the Church' as 'the most pious, and the wisest, that any people or kingdom upon earth hath been blest withal since the Apostles' dayes'. While accepting the need for the Church to be 'restored to its former piety', the petitioners wished to preserve 'the Church government by Bishops' and hoped 'that the precious may be separated

---

[141] D'Ewes (C), pp. 186–7; Clarendon, *History*, I, 423 (Book IV, §58).
[142] Rushworth, IV, 425.
[143] Sir Philip Warwick, *Memoires of the Reigne of King Charles I* (1701), p. 186.
[144] Clarendon, *History*, I, 464 (section struck from MS of the *Life*).
[145] *Diary of Evelyn*, Bray, IV, 114 (Charles I, apostil of 2 November 1641 to Nicholas's letter of 27 October 1641). See also *ibid.*, 130 (Nicholas to Charles I, 8 November 1641).
[146] See above, p. 65.
[147] *Diary of Evelyn*, Bray, IV, 137 (Henrietta Maria to Nicholas, 12 November 1641). See also Guildford Muniment Room, Bray Deposit, 52/2/19/28 (Nicholas to Henrietta Maria, 22 October 1641). Cf. J.S.A. Adamson, 'Parliamentary management, men-of-business and the House of Lords, 1640–49', in *A Pillar of the Constitution: The House of Lords in British Politics, 1640–1784*, ed. Clyve Jones (1989), pp. 22–8.

from the vile, that the bad may be rejected, and the good retained'.[148] Dorset had defended the right of bishops to sit in the Lords the previous June;[149] and at the end of November he tried to disperse the crowds by ordering the guards outside Parliament to 'give fire', but it seems this instruction was disobeyed.[150] I have argued elsewhere that Dorset's order can be interpreted as another bid to protect the bishops' seats in the Lords, and that it was motivated by a commitment to constitutional balance and to the rule of law analogous to that of the four 'persons disaffected to the kingdom'.[151] But his action sharply divided members of both Houses. A mysterious entry in the House of Lords Manuscript Minutes for 2 December states that 'this Howse doth allowe and approve of what the E[arl] of Dorsett'. This unfinished sentence was then struck through, and no corresponding entry appears in the Journal, which perhaps indicates that a resolution to this effect was moved but then abandoned in the face of opposition.[152] Meanwhile in the Commons, D'Ewes condemned Dorset's 'late act of violence'.[153] However, Dorset found a supporter in Strangways, who insisted that 'the priviledge of Parliament was utterlie broaken if men might not come in safetie to give ther votes freelie'; and then 'informed the House that hee had received an information off some designe upon this House that did asperse some members off this House which on his Judgment did amount to high treason'.[154] The previous day, he had been 'encompassed with above 200 sworded and staved' who demanded that he 'give his vote against Bishopps'.[155] Just how tense the atmosphere had become is clear from an ugly exchange on 3 December between Strode and Culpepper over whether there had even been 'such tumults'.[156]

These developments can only have reinforced the crowds' view of Hyde, Falkland, Culpepper and Strangways as 'disaffected'. More and more, their commitment to the rule of law inclined them to resist Pym's Junto. Culpepper – while continuing to seek condign punishment for the army plotters – opposed the Militia Bill on the grounds that it would 'take the

---

[148] *LJ*, IV, 469; John Nalson, *An Impartial Collection of the Great Affairs of State* (2 vols., 1682–3), II, 726–7 (Wing, N 107). See also David Underdown, *Somerset in the Civil War and Interregnum* (Newton Abbot, 1973), pp. 26–7.

[149] BL, Sloane MS 1467 (speeches in Parliament), fo. 76v.

[150] D'Ewes (C), pp. 211–14, 225–6; Bodl. Lib., MS Rawlinson D 932 (diary of Sir John Holland), fo. 56r; Northamptonshire RO, Montagu MS 4, p. 6 (William Montagu to Lord Montagu, 2 December 1641). The King had entrusted Dorset, as Lord Lieutenant of Middlesex, with the command of these guards two days earlier.

[151] Smith, '"The more posed and wise advice"', 806–7, 828–9.

[152] House of Lords RO, MS Minutes, VIII, unfol. (2 December 1641); MS Lords Journal, XVIII, pp. 97–106; *LJ*, IV, 459–60. I am grateful to Conrad Russell for advice on this point.

[153] D'Ewes (C), pp. 225–6.   [154] *Ibid.*, p. 214.

[155] *Ibid.* See also Bodl. Lib., MS Dep. c. 165 (Nalson MS), fos. 81–2.

[156] D'Ewes (C), pp. 230–1.

King's lawfull power from him'.[157] He also joined Hyde and Falkland in defending the right of protestation in the Commons, a clear measure of how deeply the House was divided.[158] At the end of December, Strangways successfully blocked a bid to remove Bristol and Digby from the King's counsels.[159] A defence of the law was gradually becoming conflated with a defence of royal powers.

All this meant that if the King ever got sick of trying to conciliate Pym and his allies by means of 'bridge appointments' he now possessed a ready-made constituency in both Lords and Commons from which to choose advisers. This was precisely what happened at the turn of the year. Charles offered Pym the Chancellorship of the Exchequer one last time on 1 January 1642;[160] but when he refused appointed Culpepper instead.[161] The same day, Falkland was sworn a Privy Councillor, and became Secretary of State on 8 January.[162] Southampton was sworn a Gentleman of the Bedchamber on 30 December, and joined the Privy Council on 3 January.[163] It was rumoured that the King was also about 'to make him Groome of the Stoole, in the Earle of Hollandes place'.[164] Had he done so, it would probably have telescoped political developments by several months.[165]

The promotion of Falkland and Culpepper was the culmination of secret contacts between the King and those branded 'disaffected' by the London crowd. These contacts are very difficult to reconstruct, and the only reasonably reliable evidence is found in Hyde's memoirs. In a section later deleted from the *Life*, he wrote: 'Mr Hyde wished the Lord Digby to advise the King to call the Lord Falkland and Sir John Culpeper ... to his Council.'[166] Certainly we know that Hyde was 'well acquainted' with Digby,[167] and it seems likely that the idea of appointing Falkland and Culpepper – if not the precise timing – originated in Hyde's conversations

---

[157] *Ibid.*, pp. 245, 303.   [158] *Ibid.*, p. 322; *Verney's Notes*, Verney, 136.

[159] D'Ewes (C), pp. 361–3.

[160] Lambert B. Larking, ed., *Proceedings, principally in the county of Kent, in connection with the Parliaments called in 1640* (Camden Society, 1st series, 80, 1862), 68 (Sir Edward Dering to Lady Dering, 13 January 1641/2). The accuracy of Dering's account is not beyond doubt: see Russell, *FBM*, p. 447; Fletcher, *Outbreak*, p. 180.

[161] PRO, PC 2/53, p. 207; BL, Add. MS 64922, fo. 77v (Thomas Coke to Sir John Coke, 3 January 1641/2); Bodl. Lib., MS Clarendon 20, fo. 143r–v (Latin warrant of appointment). Culpepper was sworn a Privy Councillor at the same time.

[162] PRO, SO 3/12, fo. 183r; PC 2/53, pp. 207, 209; SP 16/488/27 (Thomas Wiseman to [Sir John Pennington], 6 January 1641/2); BL, Add. MS 64922, fo. 77v; Bodl. Lib., MS Clarendon 20, fo. 157r (Sir Henry De Vic to Falkland, 1 February 1641/2).

[163] PRO, LC 5/135, p. 5; PC 2/53, p. 207; Christ Church Muniment Room, Oxford, Browne Letters, Box A–C, unfol. (Christopher Browne to Sir Richard Browne, 6 January 1641/2).

[164] BL, Add. MS 64922, fo. 77v.

[165] See Russell, *Causes*, pp. 188–9; and *FBM*, pp. 502–3 for Holland's dismissal in April 1642.

[166] Clarendon, *History*, I, 457.   [167] Wormald, *Clarendon*, p. 30.

with Digby.[168] To advance people who were neither 'evil counsellors' nor associated with the Court promised to be a highly effective counter to Pym's complaints about 'ill advice'. These promotions greatly strengthened the influence of moderates within the King's counsels, and John Coke the younger reported that 'Hertford, Seymour, Southampton, Falkeland and Culpeper are the cheife councelors'.[169] To this list should certainly be added Hyde, who had turned down the office of Solicitor-General, and whose influence behind the new wave of appointments was considerable, though still largely invisible to outside observers.[170]

Unfortunately, as Anthony Fletcher has argued, Charles probably saw the appointments of Falkland and Culpepper as the flip-side of his attempted arrest of the Five Members.[171] This meant that the moderates were always trying to escape the circumstances of their own preferment, and only by breaking this link in the King's mind could they present him as a paragon of legality and constitutional rectitude. This was as necessary to satisfy their own belief in the rule of law as to achieve a settlement with the Junto. But the memory of 4 January died hard. Hyde later recalled the 'grief and anger' which Falkland, Culpepper and he felt that 'the violent party had by these late unskilful actions of the Court gotten great advantage and recovered new spirits'. Henceforth, they 'could not avoid being looked upon as the authors of those counsels to which they were so absolute strangers, and which they so perfectly detested'.[172] It is likely that the Queen and Digby lay behind the attempt on the Five Members,[173] but figures like Falkland and Culpepper were immediately suspect because of their status as royal officials.[174] It is no coincidence that on 11 January both men had to defend themselves against the charge of popery.[175] It was particularly difficult for Falkland to discharge his official duties as Secretary without incurring suspicion. For example, on 25 January he received 1,150 copies of the King's official messages relating to the Five Members.[176] But when the Commons discovered that these were being distributed it investigated whether Falkland had 'offended in breach of privilege of parliament'.[177] This shows that one of the issues dividing Falkland and

[168] Clarendon, *Life*, I, 98–100; *History*, I, 461–3 (Book IV, §§127–8); Wormald, *Clarendon*, p. 32.
[169] BL, Add. MS 64922, fo. 88r (John Coke the younger to Sir John Coke, 27 January 1641/2).
[170] Clarendon, *Life*, I, 100–4. Cf. Gardiner, *History*, X, 127–8.
[171] Fletcher, *Outbreak*, p. 180.
[172] Clarendon, *History*, I, 487 (Book IV, §158).
[173] *Ibid.*, I, 484–5 (Book IV, §§154–5); Gardiner, *History*, X, 133; Fletcher, *Outbreak*, p. 181.
[174] Clarendon, *History*, I, 487 (Book IV, §158); *Life*, I, 102–104.
[175] *PJ*, I, 33; Clarendon, *History*, I, 459 (Book IV, §125).
[176] BL, Add. MS 5756 (Musgrave Collection), fo. 132r.
[177] *PJ*, I, 323. The distribution of this material was probably part of the 'secrett service' for which Falkland received £700 a year: PRO, SO 3/12, fo. 183r.

Culpepper from the Junto was the extent to which loyalties to Crown and Parliament were still compatible.

This is closely linked to the question of when it is meaningful to speak of a Royalist party. Brian Wormald has argued brilliantly that Hyde always remained a Parliamentarian as well as a Royalist in the sense of upholding the place of that institution within the polity.[178] The King's withdrawal from London on 10 January none the less marked a watershed, for the physical separation of monarch and Parliament made it far more difficult to reconcile allegiance to both. For the first time, civil war between the two became *physically* possible. As Conrad Russell has observed, 'the identification of a "Royalist" party makes sense from the time of the King's departure from London'.[179] Henceforth, the King's moderate advisers needed constantly to allay fears that he would again resort to force. For example, Culpepper informed the House on 12 January 'that the king was indeed removing to Windsor and that there was no force with the King at the Court'.[180] This desire to prove the King's integrity probably explains why Culpepper advised Charles to assent to the Bishops' Exclusion Bill and the Impressment Bill.[181] To doubt whether the King could be trusted was to cut at the very root of this strategy, and when on 1 April Sir Peter Wentworth did precisely that, Culpepper 'wondered that any man should dare to speak such language within these walls'.[182]

This same insistence on Charles's respect for legal and constitutional propriety pervaded the public statements which Hyde, Falkland and Culpepper drafted on his behalf. Hyde wrote later that the three found 'themselves often of one opinion', and during 1642 they emerged as the King's leading apologists.[183] Hyde was initially the most active of the three, and drafted the majority of Charles's declarations from the end of 1641.[184] The reply he composed to Parliament's justification of the Militia Ordinance offers an ideal case-study of his beliefs and methods. Hyde's covering letter to the King sheds floods of light on the nature of Constitutional Royalism; on why its exponents rallied to the King; on what they wanted Charles to do; and on the underlying consistency of their views.

Your Ma[jes]ty well knowes that your greatest strength is in the heartes and affections of those persons who have bene the sevearest assertors of the publike libertyes, and so besides ther duty and loyalty to your person, are in love with your inclinacons to peace and iustice, and valew ther owne interests upon the preserva-

---

[178] Wormald, *Clarendon*, especially pp. 45–6, 93–100.
[179] Russell, *FBM*, p. 466, n. 55.
[180] *PJ*, I, 43.
[181] Clarendon, *Life*, I, 113–15. These two bills became 16 Car. I, cc. 27, 28 respectively. Cf. Wormald, *Clarendon*, pp. 58–61..
[182] *PJ*, II, 115.   [183] Clarendon, *Life*, I, 104.
[184] *Ibid.*, 97–100, 161–2. Cf. Warwick, *Memoires*, pp. 196–7.

con of your rights. These Your Ma[jes]ty will not loose by any acte which may begett iust feares in them; nether can ther be so cunninge a way founde out to assiste those who wish not well to Your Ma[jes]ty, (if any such ther be) as by givinge the least hinte to your people that you relye upon any thinge but the strength of your lawes, and ther obedyence.[185]

The declaration itself was designed to present exactly this image of kingship. Issued at Huntingdon on 15 March, it asserted that the King would 'leave no way unattempted, which may beget a good understanding betwixt him and his Parliament'. He in turn expected that his subjects would obey 'the laws established' and not let the Militia Ordinance lead them to 'do or execute what is not warranted by the laws'. Those laws cemented the mutual bond between monarch and people, 'His Majesty being resolved to observe the laws himself, and to require obedience to all of them from all his subjects'.[186]

For exponents of this ideal, the Militia Ordinance and Sir John Hotham's refusal to admit the King to Hull represented an intolerable encroachment on the King's lawful power of military command. When the Commons drafted a declaration defending Hotham's act, Falkland warned that 'we did not give his majesty reasons to satisfy him that what we did was according to law'.[187] Two weeks later, on 19 May, Culpepper and Strangways acted as tellers against a clause that the King's oath bound him to accept bills passed by both Houses for the good of the kingdom'.[188] Both these proposals were defeated; and the final exodus of most of this circle from the Commons began shortly afterwards. On 21 May, the King asked Hyde to 'make ... immediate repaire' to York.[189] That same day, a royal messenger visited Falkland in London, probably bearing a similar message.[190] It is likely that Hyde arrived in the last days of May, in time to draft the King's reply to the Houses' Remonstrance of 26 May. This answer culminated in the assertion that the Remonstrance's 'doctrine' rested upon seven axioms: 'that [the Houses] have an absolute power of declaring the law'; 'that no precedents can be limits to bound their proceedings'; 'that the Parliament may dispose of any thing wherein the King or subject hath a

---

[185] Bodl. Lib., MS Clarendon 20, fo. 191r (Hyde to Charles I, ? 9–15 March 1641/2).
[186] CJ, II, 481; LJ, IV, 647.
[187] PJ, II, 272 (4 May 1642).
[188] Ibid., 344; CJ, II, 580. The motion was defeated by 103 votes to 61.
[189] Bodl. Lib., MS Clarendon 21, fo. 62r (Charles I to Hyde, 21 May 1642). This letter, which Hyde received on 24 May, gainsays his later claim that Charles summoned him at 'about the end of April': Clarendon, Life, I, 135; Wormald, Clarendon, p. 111. Hyde had apparently ceased to attend the Commons in late March: CJ, II, 493, 504. See also Folger Shakespeare Library, Washington, DC, MS X.c.23 (Sir Giles Mompesson to Hyde, [?] April 1642).
[190] BL, Add. MS 64923 (Coke MS), fo. 14r (John Coke the younger to Sir John Coke, 24 May 1642).

right, for the public good'; 'that no member of either House ought to be troubled or meddled with or for treason, felony, or any other crime, without the cause first brought before them'; 'that the sovereign power resides in both Houses, and that His Majesty had no negative voice'; 'that the levying of forces against the personal commands of the King ... is not levying war against the King'; and 'that if they should make the highest precedents of other parliaments their patterns, there would be no cause to complain of want of modesty or duty in them'.[191] The thrust of this answer was that Parliament's demands were not merely unreasonable but actually illegal: it was the Junto which posed the greatest threat to the rule of law.

On 2 June, the Houses offered Charles fresh terms in the form of the *Nineteen Propositions*.[192] Shortly afterwards, Falkland and Culpepper joined the King at York and composed a reply to these terms which became a classic text in the history of Constitutional Royalism.[193] The King's *Answer to the XIX Propositions* is often located within the context of estates theory, and of ideas of mixed government.[194] It certainly contributed to both these ideologies. But it needs stressing that it was also the culminant statement of the principle of royal government within the law which had guided Falkland, Culpepper and others all along. The ideal of the monarch as guardian of the rule of law – and a corresponding belief in the Junto's illegality – form leitmotivs throughout the document.

The *Answer* began by condemning the Houses for trying to 'remove a troublesome rub in their way, the law'.[195] The Militia Ordinance 'in effect' constituted a claim 'to make laws without us'. But those laws were 'the birth-right of every subject in this kingdom', and ordinary people were thus endangered as much as the King. Falkland and Culpepper then condemned the *Nineteen Propositions* in terms of both the traditions analysed in chapter 2, arguing that they would overthrow *mixed* monarchy as well as *personal* monarchy. The terms formed 'a great chain ... by which our just, antient, regal power is endeavour'd to be fetch'd down to the ground'. But they were also inimical to the doctrine of King-in-Parliament, for the

---

[191] Clarendon, *History*, II, 163–4 (Book V, §315).
[192] For the text of the *Nineteen Propositions*, see Gardiner, *Documents*, pp. 249–54.
[193] Clarendon, *Life*, I, 145–52. It is difficult to date these movements precisely, but it seems that Culpepper attended the Commons for the last time on 2 June, and Falkland on 4 June: *PJ*, III, 2, 23, 111, n. 6. Hyde, Falkland and Culpepper were all recorded as absent from the Commons without leave on 16 June: *CJ*, II, 626; *PJ*, III, 454, 481.
[194] The classic work here is Michael Mendle, *Dangerous Positions: Mixed Government, the Estates of the Realm, and the Making of the Answer to the XIX Propositions* (Alabama, 1985); but see also Corinne Comstock Weston, 'The theory of mixed monarchy under Charles I and after', *EHR*, 75 (1960), 426–43; and Richard Tuck, *Philosophy and Government, 1572–1651* (Cambridge, 1993), pp. 232–3.
[195] In the following analysis, I have followed the most accessible reliable version of the *Answer*, which is found in Rushworth, IV, 725–35.

monarch was 'a part of the Parliament'. As a result, they directly threatened 'the antient, equal, happy, well-poised, and never enough commended constitution of the government of this kingdom'. By contrast, a 'regulated monarchy' was essential to 'preserve the laws in their force, and the subjects in their liberties and properties'. The *Answer* concluded with a firm commitment to 'the preservation of every Law'. Everything else stemmed from this axiom, including policy towards the Church. In words reminiscent of those which Falkland and Culpepper had added to the Grand Remonstrance, the *Answer* 'willingly' agreed to remove 'any illegal innovations which may have crept in'; but otherwise to preserve the existing features of the Church 'as they are here established by law'. In short, the *Answer* is the official expression of that commitment to the rule of law which had consistently guided the likes of Hyde, Falkland, Culpepper and Strangways, and which now caused them to rally to the King as a lesser danger to legality than the Junto.

This does not mean that these people saw eye to eye on everything. In particular, Hyde criticised that part of the *Answer* which discussed the estates of the realm. He argued that these were lords spiritual, lords temporal and commons; and that the definition in the *Answer* – monarch, lords and commons – was 'prejudicial to the King'.[196] Strangways would have shared this reservation.[197] Both models had a respectable ancestry within English political theory,[198] and we will see that this was a point on which Constitutional Royalists continued to differ during the years which followed.[199] However, this technical dispute in no way diminished the fundamental common ground which underpinned the emergence of Hyde, Falkland and Culpepper as the King's leading propagandists in 1642. They were, in Hyde's words, 'often of one opinion'.[200] The really important point is that they were united in seeing England as a limited monarchy where royal government operated within the rule of law, and in believing that Charles I was a more effective guardian of these arrangements than the Junto. This vision informed their various writings on the King's behalf and transcended their specific disagreement over the definition of the three estates.

VII

By the time the *Answer* was published on 18 June, Charles had also gained a substantial following among the peerage, and we must now examine how this came about. It would be impossible here to give a full account of how

---

[196] Clarendon, *Life*, I, 154–5.   [197] See above, p. 72.
[198] G. R. Elton, *The Parliament of England, 1559–1581* (Cambridge, 1986), pp. 17–23.
[199] See below, pp. 224, 229–31, 243 & n. 159.   [200] Clarendon, *Life*, I, 104.

and why two-thirds of the English nobility gravitated to the King in the summer of 1642. Rather, I will focus on the three peers who have already emerged in this chapter as influential royal advisers, Hertford, Seymour and Southampton; and on three other figures who would also play a key role in the peace negotiations of the Civil War years, but who were slightly less pre-eminent in 1642: the Duke of Richmond and Lennox, the Earl of Dorset and Lord Willoughby of Eresby, later second Earl of Lindsey. These six peers regularly operated as a coherent group after the outbreak of fighting, and it thus makes sense to concentrate on them. Here we need to examine how they came to join the King in the first place.

The fact that Hertford and Richmond could both have been pretenders to the thrones of England and Scotland respectively made the pattern of their careers unusual, and they are therefore best considered separately. The other four all displayed common traits. Parliament's attempts to wrest military command from the King and to assume control over the appointment of advisers were crucial in their decision to head north. They had hitherto resisted royal summonses: Southampton, for example, was given leave by both King and Lords to leave Westminster in February, but stayed put.[201] By contrast, Southampton joined Willoughby of Eresby, Seymour, Dunsmore (whose daughter he would shortly marry)[202] and several other future Royalist peers in protesting against putting the kingdom 'into a posture of defence' (2 March); and against the Militia Ordinance (5 March).[203] With the exception of Hertford, none of these peers was given the lieutenancy of his home county in the Militia Ordinance; the list of those who were appointed reads like a roll-call of peers whom the Junto felt able to trust.[204] The departure of the Royalist peers for York was neither simultaneous nor, it seems, co-ordinated; but it did in each case follow quite quickly upon these political reverses. Southampton obtained leave to go to York on 17 March and was there by the 27th.[205] Seymour had leave to visit his Wiltshire estates on 18 March, but was allegedly 'intercepted' by a royal messenger calling him to York. He returned briefly to the Lords on 4 April, only to be given further leave from which – despite promises to the contrary – he never returned.[206] Willoughby of Eresby, like

---

[201] PRO, SO 3/12, fo. 188r; LJ, IV, 562.

[202] BL, Add. MS 64923, fo. 7v (Edward Read to Sir John Coke, 24 April 1642).

[203] LJ, IV, 622, 627.

[204] The county of Sussex was entrusted to Northumberland rather than Dorset; Wiltshire to Pembroke rather than Hertford; Hampshire to Pembroke rather than Southampton; and Lincolnshire to Lincoln and Willoughby of Parham rather than Lindsey or Willoughby of Eresby: LJ, IV, 587–8. Hertford was offered the appointment of Lord Lieutenant of Somerset, but declined: see below, pp. 94–5.

[205] LJ, IV, 651; BL, Add. MS 64922, fo. 108v (John Coke the younger to Sir John Coke, 27 March 1642).

[206] LJ, IV, 653, 675, 679, 683, 697, 705; V, 19.

Hertford and Richmond, joined the King at Hull in April;[207] and on 2 May urged Dorset to 'make hast to York'.[208] Dorset had himself ceased to attend the Lords on 23 March, when he surrendered his commissions of lieutenancy.[209] He had earlier absented himself from the crucial vote on the Militia Ordinance,[210] and his departure from Westminster was rumoured from that moment.[211] In short, just as the 'Royalist exodus from the Lords' began when the House first voted for parliamentary control of the militia on 1 February,[212] so the Constitutional Royalist exodus was apparently triggered by the passage of the Militia Ordinance. There is little evidence that these departures were planned; but their timing strongly suggests the existence of shared perceptions and responses.

Now for the first of our two special cases: James Stuart, Duke of Richmond and Lennox. He was of the blood royal,[213] and his elevation to the dukedom of Richmond on 8 August 1641,[214] his receipt of much of the King's private correspondence during the Scottish visit,[215] and his appointment as Lord Steward of the King's Household in early December 1641[216] all reveal his closeness to the King. Richmond was among the first peers to follow the royal family from London to Windsor Castle in January 1642.[217] But shortly afterwards his position in the Lords was fatally compromised by a single rash intervention: on 26 January he moved to 'put the question whether we shall adjourn the Parliament for six months'.[218] Whether or not he acted on royal instructions is uncertain; either way,

---

[207] *PJ*, II, 255. The Lords had granted him leave on 2 April: *LJ*, IV, 693.
[208] CKS, Sackville MS, U 269/C7/1 (Lord Willoughby of Eresby to Dorset, 2 May 1640).
[209] *LJ*, IV, 664–5.   [210] House of Lords RO, MS Minutes VIII, unfol. (5 March 1641/2).
[211] PRO, SP 16/489/68 (Elizabeth, Queen of Bohemia to Sir Thomas Roe, 7 March 1641/2). Dorset's movements during the spring and summer of 1642 are discussed in more detail in Smith, '"The more posed and wise advice"', 807–11.
[212] Russell, *FBM*, pp. 470–1.
[213] This gave him a claim to the Scottish but not the English throne: see above, p. 39.
[214] CKS, Darnley MS, U 565/F52 (creation of Dukedom of Richmond, 8 August 1641); PRO, SP 16/483/34 (Thomas Smith to the Earl of Northumberland, 10 August 1641); BL, Harl. MS 6424, fo. 89r; Christ Church Muniment Room, Oxford, Browne Letters, Box A–C, unfol. (Christopher Browne to Sir Richard Browne, 12 August 1641).
[215] *Diary of Evelyn*, Bray, IV, 97 (Nicholas to Charles I, 3 October 1641; Charles I, apostil of 9 October 1641 to Nicholas's letter of 3 October 1641), 104–5 (Nicholas to Charles I, 15 October 1641). See also the sequences of letters from Richmond to Nicholas between August and November 1641 in Christ Church Muniment Room, Oxford, Nicholas Box, unfol.; and from Nicholas to Richmond in *The Nicholas Papers*, vol. I: *1641–1652*, ed. G. F. Warner (Camden Society, 2nd series, 40, 1886), 3–4, 8, 13–14, 32.
[216] PRO, LC 3/1 (Establishment of Charles I's Household, 1641), unfol.; SP 16/486/29 (Thomas Wiseman to Sir John Pennington, 9 December 1641); SP 16/486/93 (Sir Francis Windebank to Thomas Windebank, 24 December 1641); Christ Church Muniment Room, Oxford, Browne Letters, Box A–C, unfol. (Christopher Browne to Sir Richard Browne, 10 December 1641).
[217] Bodl. Lib., MS Tanner 66, fo. 242 (Josias Berners to John Hobart, 17 January 1641/2).
[218] *PJ*, I, 195.

there was an outcry in both Houses against this threat to Parliament's sitting, and some MPs demanded his impeachment.[219] In the event, he was required only to 'make an humble submission and acknowledgement' that he had spoken 'inconsiderately and inadvisedly', although twenty-two peers (including Warwick, Essex, Wharton, Pembroke and Brooke) protested that this was 'not a sufficient punishment'.[220] His parliamentary reputation in ruins, Richmond was given leave on 2 February and never attended the Lords again.[221] He apparently remained with the King thereafter, and was certainly at Hull by the last week of April.[222]

Hertford's career during the first half of 1642 was rather more complicated. His political significance hinged on his royal blood, which gave him a claim to the English but not the Scottish throne,[223] and on his position as Governor to the Prince of Wales. Parliament realised the extreme importance of this appointment – 'that trust that doth soe ymediatly concerne the present and future peace and safetie of the three kingdomes'[224] – and on 14 January ordered him to ensure that the Prince 'bee not carried out of the kingdome'.[225] Hertford tried desperately to reconcile his official duties with his family ties to Essex. When the King ordered him to bring the Prince and the Duke of York to Greenwich on 21 February, Hertford asked his wife to show Essex the letter 'and desire him to consider it'.[226] Parliament forbade the move to Greenwich, but a (diplomatic?) illness extricated Hertford from this clash of loyalties.[227] By the end of March, however, his position at Westminster was clearly disintegrating, at just the same time as his old rival Pembroke was becoming more and more influential on parliamentary committees.[228] As in many other cases, Parliament's bid to control the militia helped to drive Hertford towards the King. His appointment to the Lord Lieutenancy of Somerset in the Militia Ordinance probably reflected his political and dynastic importance, together with the influence of his brother-in-law, Essex.[229] But Hertford declined the office on the grounds that 'he was not at the debate of the militia, and therefore is

[219] *Ibid.*, 195–204. See also PRO, SP 16/489/2 (Sidney Bere to Sir John Pennington, 3 February 1641/2); *Verney's Notes*, Verney, 148–9; Clarendon, *History*, I, 544–8 (Book IV, §§255–61); and Fletcher, *Outbreak*, pp. 256–7.
[220] *LJ*, IV, 543. See also BL, Add. MS 64922, fo. 88r. It is interesting that Saye was not among those who protested: Russell, *FBM*, p. 470, n. 73.
[221] *LJ*, IV, 559, 568; House of Lords RO, MS Minutes, VIII, unfol.
[222] *PJ*, II, 255; *LJ*, V, 20.
[223] See above, p. 42.   [224] MP, 14 January 1641/2, fo. 21.
[225] *Ibid.*; *LJ*, IV, 513; *PJ*, I, 63–5, 69, 74; *Verney's Notes*, Verney, 145.
[226] HMC, *Bath (Longleat) Manuscripts*, Vol. IV: *Seymour Papers, 1532–1686* (1968), 217 (Charles I to Hertford, 21 February 1641/2; Hertford to the Marchioness of Hertford, 23 February 1641/2).
[227] *PJ*, I, 449–50, 455–7, 461–3, 465, 467, 470, 472; BL, Add. MS 64922, fo. 100r (John Coke the younger to Sir John Coke, 24 February 1641/2).
[228] Morrill, *Revolt*, pp. 43–4.   [229] *LJ*, IV, 587–8.

utterly ignorant of what hath passed in it'.[230] He surrendered his commission on 28 March,[231] and on 5 April protested against the Lords' vote that all Privy Councillors be 'displaced' by 'such persons' as both Houses 'recommended'.[232] Hertford left for York shortly afterwards and ignored parliamentary orders to return, claiming that he 'had ingaged [him] selfe to bringe' the Duke of York to the King.[233] Finally, on 3 May, he was forced to show his hand: he promised Essex that the Prince 'shall goe noe farther then his Majestie goeth, for soe it hath pleased his Majestie to assure me', but insisted that 'any other undertaking' was 'a thinge out of my powre'.[234] Ultimately his official duty to the monarch had overridden his loyalty to Essex and Parliament.

The distinctive circumstances and experiences of Richmond and Hertford apart, the Militia Ordinance emerges as the single most important catalyst of these peers' decision to join the King. They clearly believed in the monarch's prerogative to levy troops and all six – together with Falkland and Culpepper – engaged to provide horse on 22 June.[235] However, the influence of Constitutional Royalist ideas ensured that Charles did not claim this power on the grounds of prerogative alone.

Two days earlier, he had issued a proclamation justifying that most feudal of royal acts, the raising of troops by commissions to the nobility, in the language of constitutional government and legal propriety.[236] The masterly opening defended *both* a prerogative power *and* the rule of law: 'whereas, by the laws of this land, the ordering and governing of the militia of the kingdom, for the preventing and suppression of all invasions and rebellions, hath (as a most known and undoubted right and prerogative) belonged in all times solely to our self and our progenitors'. Moreover, although the Commission of Array had lapsed into disuse during the sixteenth century,[237] analogous commissions of lieutenancy had been issued under 'Queen Elizabeth and our dear father, both of happy memorie'. In other words, Charles promised to maintain the 'Jacobethan' synthesis in which the royal prerogative was compatible with the common law. Whereas Parliament's Militia Ordinance was 'void in law', the King had

[230] *Ibid.*, 666; MP, 24 March 1641/2, fo. 77r; *PJ*, II, 88. For Hertford's absence from the debate on the Militia Ordinance, see House of Lords RO, MS Minutes, VIII, unfol. (5 March 1641/2).
[231] *LJ*, IV, 677.　　[232] *Ibid.*, 700.
[233] *Ibid.*, 711, 714; MP, 11 April 1642, fo. 48r; BL, Add. MS 32093 (Malet Collection), fo. 194v (Hertford to the Marchioness of Hertford, 18 April 1642).
[234] *LJ*, V, 49; *PJ*, II, 285, 287; CUL, MS Mm. 1. 46 (Baker MS), p. 41.
[235] PRO, SP 16/491/29 (engagement to provide forces, 22 June 1642); BL, Egerton MS 2978 (Heath and Verney Papers, I), fo. 66r.
[236] For the text of this proclamation, see J. F. Larkin, ed., *Stuart Royal Proclamations*, vol. II: *Royal Proclamations of King Charles I, 1625–46* (Oxford, 1983), 777–81.
[237] See below, p. 157.

'resolved to rule and govern our subjects according to our known laws onely'. The proclamation concluded with a warning that 'justice' would 'be done' to those who disobeyed royal commands 'according to law', or obeyed the Militia Ordinance, 'contrary to law'.

This proclamation perfectly captures the complex nature of Royalism on the eve of the Civil War. At one level it represented a traditional call to arms by an anointed sovereign against those he declared rebels. But alongside this emerged another rationale for joining Charles I: a wish to defend the rule of law in both Church and State, and to preserve a delicate constitutional balance endangered more by the Junto's current demands than by Charles's earlier 'legal tyranny'. This did not involve seeing Charles as blameless, let alone exonerating the policies of 1625–40; but it did reflect a belief that the King was now a more convincing guardian of the law than Pym and his allies. That law in turn offered the only way to protect both the Crown's powers and the people's rights and liberties; it alone could restore the 'Jacobethan' polity which combined personal monarchy with mixed monarchy. Thus, while the powerful appeal of a monarch's call to arms attracted many like Sir Edmund Verney, whose conscience was 'only concerned in honour and in gratitude to follow [his] master',[238] there were others who rallied to the King in order to defend the constitution, the law and 'the Church by law established'. The second group thus felt a dual loyalty – to both Crown and constitution – and it is this which makes 'Constitutional Royalist' such an appropriate label for them.

VIII

We shall see that several of our Constitutional Royalists were prepared to take up arms in order to defend these beliefs. This was in no way incompatible with a deep commitment to negotiations between Crown and Parliament, and during the summer of 1642 Royalist moderates tried desperately to achieve an 'accommodation' with the Houses. Dorset, for example, wrote two important letters to the Earl of Salisbury, who had initially come to York but then returned to London in mid-June. Dorset begged him to 'study day and night, to keepe the more violent spiritts from passinge the Rubicon'. He stressed 'the tractable and councellable disposition of the King', while candidly admitting that Charles was 'apt to

---

[238] Clarendon, *Life*, I, 160. For other instances of such principles, see P. R. Newman, 'The King's servants: conscience, principle, and sacrifice in armed royalism', in *Public Duty and Private Conscience in Seventeenth-Century England: Essays Presented to G. E. Aylmer*, ed. John Morrill, Paul Slack and Daniel Woolf (Oxford, 1993), pp. 225–41.

take extempore resolutions, uppon the first impression'.[239] This difficulty of persuading the King to accept 'the more posed and wise advice' was to dog the Constitutional Royalists throughout the 1640s. Above all, Dorset wanted to find 'an easy and safe way' out of 'this darke and inextricable labyrinth'.[240] This in turn required moderation on both sides, and in a second letter Dorset lamented that 'there are to many hot headed people both heere and att London thatt advise and perswade desperate wayes'.[241] He feared 'soe universall a change both in government and familyes as a victory must make, on which side soever it happens', and the erection of 'an arbitrary government even on both sides'.[242] His horror of an absolute victory by either side thus led him to exploit contacts at Westminster in the search for 'an accommodation'.[243]

Exactly the same spirit lay behind Hertford's correspondence with Selden,[244] and led Hyde to hope that Pembroke might join the King.[245] But the most extensive recoverable contacts between York and London on the eve of the Civil War were apparently those effected by the Chief Justice of Common Pleas, Sir John Bankes. Bankes had not objected to the Militia Ordinance; but by May 1642 he was at York, convinced that 'there is no other way left but the way of accommodation', and anxious that 'the houses would set down their desires that they would fix upon'.[246] He did not believe 'that the differences between His M[ajes]ty and the Houses are so great in substance, but if there be a willingness on all parts, they may be reconciled'.[247] To this end, he wrote to several leading figures at Westminster, including Saye, Wharton, Northumberland and Denzil Holles. For example, on 20 June he assured Northumberland – one of the moderate (Constitutional?) Parliamentarians who was to participate repeatedly in peace talks – that 'as to the 19 propositions, some things therein will be granted, and the rest will bee left in the same condition as they have been in the time of his predecessors' kings of England'.[248] Northumberland's response (29 June) was equally conciliatory: 'all things desired in our 19 propositions are not absolutely necessarie for securing unto us our lawes,

---

[239] BL, Microfilm M 485 (Hatfield House, Cecil MS), vol. CXXXI, fo. 182v (Dorset to the Earl of Salisbury, 27 June 1642).
[240] *Ibid.*, fo. 183r–v.
[241] *Ibid.*, vol. CXCVII, fo. 129v (Dorset to the Earl of Salisbury, 4 August 1642).
[242] *Ibid.*, fos. 128r, 130r–v.   [243] *Ibid.*, fo. 129v.
[244] BL, Add. MS 4247 (miscellaneous papers), fo. 14 (Selden to Hertford, [?] June 1642). Cf. Clarendon, *History*, II, 205–6 (Book V, §365).
[245] BL, Stowe MS 142 (miscellaneous historical letters), fo. 47r (Hyde to Lady Carnarvon, 22 July [1642]). For the parallel activities of Falkland at the same time, see Society of Antiquaries of London, MS 140 (Lyttelton papers), fo. 22r (Falkland to Sir Thomas Lyttelton, 20 July 1642).
[246] G. Bankes, *The Story of Corfe Castle* (1853), p. 135.
[247] HMC, *Eighth Report* (1881), part I, 212.
[248] *Ibid.*, 211.

liberties, and priviledges, nor was it intended that those propositions should be insisted upon, they being petitions of grace, not of right'.[249] But Northumberland also condemned 'the greate numbers of horse that are providing in the North', and this fear of Charles's military mobilisation ultimately dissuaded such moderates from leaving London.[250] Bankes's own warning to Saye (11 July) that 'the King is now in a condition not to have anything inforced from him'[251] was hardly likely to inspire trust, and all his efforts to pursue 'the way of accommodation' came to nothing.

It is unlikely that these were isolated exchanges. As Conrad Russell has suggested, there was probably 'much more communication between London and York than now survives, and, one may suspect, much more than was ever on paper'.[252] Such informal contacts pose a question of fundamental importance: why did moderate Royalists and moderate Parliamentarians fail to unite in the summer of 1642? Why did the political middle ground not knit together to form a united front which could have either prevented the English Civil Wars or brought them to a much earlier conclusion?

The bonds of friendship and similarities of temperament between many Constitutional Royalists and their moderate counterparts at Westminster were very striking. Parliamentarian MPs such as Sir Simonds D'Ewes, Bulstrode Whitelocke, John Selden and Sir Benjamin Rudyerd all shared many fundamental assumptions about the English constitution with Royalist moderates. D'Ewes was 'a deeply conservative figure' in every respect except his religious zeal. Certainly he was intensely committed to the rule of law and during the years of civil war derived 'a sort of morbid pleasure from recording in his diary the successive outrages perpetrated ... on the body of his beloved mistress, the common law'.[253] Whitelocke and Hyde had been long-standing friends ever since they practised together as lawyers at the Middle Temple during the 1630s.[254] In 1642 Whitelocke 'stoutly opposed extremists on both sides'. He dissociated himself from the authors of the Militia Ordinance, and insisted that 'the power of the militia is neither in the King alone nor in the Parliament, but, if anywhere in the eye of our law, it is in the King and Parliament both consenting together'.[255] There was only a small but vital difference between this view and that of the Constitutional Royalists who saw control over the militia as an integral part of the royal prerogative, but to be exercised within

---

[249] Bankes, *Corfe Castle*, p. 138.   [250] *Ibid.*   [251] HMC, *Eighth Report*, part I, 212.
[252] Russell, *FBM*, p. 513.   [253] Morrill, *Revolt*, pp. 50, 53.
[254] Ruth Spalding, *The Improbable Puritan: A Life of Bulstrode Whitelocke, 1605–1675* (1975), pp. 31, 47–8, 50, 52, 54, 56, 64–5, 67, 70, 79–81. See also above, pp. 52–3.
[255] Spalding, *Improbable Puritan*, p. 80. See also *The Diary of Bulstrode Whitelocke, 1605–1675*, ed. Ruth Spalding (British Academy Records of Social and Economic History, new series, 13, Oxford, 1990), pp. 132–3.

limits defined by the law. Realising this, Hyde urged Whitelocke to leave Westminster in the spring of 1642. Such requests were in vain; yet Whitelocke none the less abhorred the 'spirit of division and contradiction' which reigned in England and became one of the Houses' most active commissioners in successive peace treaties.[256]

His outlook was very similar to that of another distinguished lawyer, John Selden. Here again there were close ties of friendship with leading Constitutional Royalists. Hyde later 'was wont to say that he valued himself upon nothing more than upon having had Mr Selden's acquaintance when he was very young'.[257] Selden was also in touch with Hertford on the eve of the Civil War,[258] and later referred to Dorset as 'comes mihi semper amicissimus'.[259] In the summer of 1642 he begged Parliament to 'think of some way of accommodating all matters of difference with His Majesty'.[260] On 9 July he acted with Strangways as teller against a proposal to raise an army of 10,000 volunteers. This proposal was carried by 125 votes to 45.[261] But whereas Strangways promptly withdrew to his home in Dorset and embarked on what the Commons later condemned as 'ill service',[262] Selden chose to remain at Westminster. This decision greatly troubled Hyde and he tried to exonerate it on the grounds that 'age obliged' Selden to take this course.[263] A real problem none the less remains: how could two lawyers, whose background and attitudes had so much in common, end up on different sides in the Civil War?

The career of another typical moderate Parliamentarian, Sir Benjamin Rudyerd, presents a similar puzzle. For here was 'a lerned lawyer' who perceived the 'reciprocation' between monarch and people as 'the strongest, the sweetest union';[264] who eulogised the constitutional reforms of 1641 as 'a dream of happinesse'; and who on 9 July 1642 begged the Houses 'to compose and settle these threatening ruining distractions' and 'make a fair way for the King's return hither'.[265] In the same speech,

---

[256] Spalding, Improbable Puritan, pp. 81–3. See also J.H. Hexter, The Reign of King Pym (Cambridge, MA, 1941), pp. 7–8, 40.

[257] Clarendon, Life, I, 35.

[258] BL, Add. MS 4247, fo. 14. Cf. Clarendon, History, II, 205–6 (Book V, §365).

[259] John Selden, Vindiciae Secundum Integritatem Existimationis Suae (1653), p. 31 (Wing, S 2444; BL, TT, E 719/1). I owe this reference to John Adamson.

[260] Richard Tuck, '"The Ancient Law of Freedom": John Selden and the Civil War', in Reactions to the English Civil War, 1642–1649, ed. John Morrill (1982), p. 149.

[261] CJ, II, 663; PJ, III, 191. See also Russell, FBM, p. 517.

[262] CJ, II, 685, 728–9; PJ, III, 252, 311. Strangways was disabled on 6 September 1642: CJ, II, 754; PJ, III, 446.

[263] Clarendon, Life, I, 35.

[264] Liber Famelicus of Sir James Whitelocke, ed. J. Bruce (Camden Society, 1st series, 70, 1858), 62; The Speeches of Sir Benjamin Rudyer in the High Court of Parliament (1641), p. 9 (Wing, R 2200; BL, TT, E 196/2).

[265] A Worthy Speech spoken in the Honourable House of Commons, by Sir Benjamin Rudyerd, this present July, 1642 (1642), pp. 2–3 (Wing, R 2206).

Rudyerd urged Parliament not to 'contend for such a hazardous, unsafe securitie as may endanger the losse of what we have already', and warned that they could never 'make a mathematicall securitie'.[266] This memorable phrase would surely have appealed to the Constitutional Royalists, whose whole conception of the polity – in which the monarch remained sovereign while governing within the law – was based on relationships which could not be mathematically defined. Rudyerd's speech was indeed welcomed at York, and reprinted there 'the week following for general distribution'.[267] During the Civil War, Rudyerd remained a passionate advocate of peace negotiations. On 17 February 1643, for example, he was to implore the Commons to consider 'who shall be answerable for all the innocent bloud which shall be spilt hereafter, if we doe not endeavour a peace, by a speedy treaty'.[268] He joined D'Ewes, Whitelocke and Selden in advising talks at every possible opportunity. These and many other moderate Parliamentarians shared the Constitutional Royalists' desperation to secure an 'accommodation' between Charles I and the two Houses. None of them would have dissented from Sir John Strangways's maxim that 'moderation is the inseparable attendant of trew wisdome and policie; and shee makes those counsells and those soveraigne courtes and p[ar]liaments happie wher she sitts in the chayre'.[269] Why, then, were people such as D'Ewes, Whitelocke, Selden and Rudyerd – prime examples of those who might be termed 'Constitutional Parliamentarians' – unable to form a united front with the Constitutional Royalists?

It needs stressing first of all that although both groups would have agreed that England was a limited monarchy governed according to fundamental laws, they meant subtly different things by that phrase. A shared vocabulary need not imply a shared set of meanings. The Constitutional Royalists' understanding of the English polity hinged on the idea that the monarch could still remain sovereign while being bound by the rule of law. Certain powers, such as control over the militia, were an inalienable part of the royal prerogative, but were also compatible with the processes of the common law. To erode those powers thus threatened the rule of law as well as the royal prerogative. Hence the claim repeatedly articulated by the Constitutional Royalists, that they wished to defend specific areas of royal authority not only as the rightful attributes of monarchy but also as an intrinsic part of England's fundamental laws. The position of the 'Constitutional Parliamentarians' was slightly different. They would have agreed

[266] *Ibid.*, p. 4. See also Fletcher, *Outbreak*, pp. 275–6.
[267] *Cobbett's Parliamentary History of England* (36 vols., 1806–20), II, 1416.
[268] *Sir Benjamin Rudyerd His Speech in the High Court of Parliament the 17 of February [1643], for a speedy Treaty of Peace with His Majestie* (1643), p. 5 (Wing, R 2195; BL, TT, E 90/15).
[269] Beinecke Library, Yale University, Osborn MS b. 304 (commonplace book of Sir John Strangways), p. 57.

with theorists such as Hunton and Herle that sovereignty was 'co-ordinate' between Crown, Lords and Commons.[270] Unlike the Constitutional Royalists, they believed that legislative authority was shared *equally* between Crown, Lords and Commons. Law-making was a collective process performed by the monarch and the two Houses as equal partners. By the summer of 1642, 'Constitutional Parliamentarians' thought it legitimate for the Lords and Commons to oversee senior civil and military appointments, the exercise of justice and the government of the Church – all areas which the Constitutional Royalists regarded as the unique preserve of the Crown. One side deemed such measures necessary to preserve the constitution; the other believed that they would destroy its very essence. As a result, the passionate commitment to peace negotiations displayed by moderates on both sides was only half the story. Their desire for peace was predicated on subtly contrasted ideas about the nature of a viable settlement; while they all sought an 'accommodation', they disagreed over the terms on which this could be achieved.

These divergent attitudes towards the constitution had dramatic implications for the political activities of moderates during the summer of 1642. According to each of these ideals, King Charles and 'King Pym' had both been found wanting. Charles's willingness to use force against his enemies, culminating in the attempt on the Five Members, and the Junto's bid to wrest military authority from the Crown were all violations of constitutional propriety. On the eve of the Civil War, moderates found that neither side had an unblemished record, and that they were therefore forced to choose between two evils. Had they been able to agree on which was the lesser evil, the moderate middle ground might have knitted together and thwarted the extremists at both Westminster and York. But such agreement proved elusive, as two quotations dramatically reveal. First, here is Brian Wormald's explanation of Hyde's decision to leave Westminster in the spring of 1642: 'While very far from absolving the King from responsibility, he could not but put most blame upon the reckless and relentless conduct of Parliament.'[271] Compare this with Richard Tuck's assessment of Selden:

To support Parliament was to choose the lesser of the two legal evils ... What led him to this commitment to war seems to have been his sense that while what the King was attempting was illegal, in the sense that it breached the legal rights of his subjects, Parliament's conduct was not illegal in the sense that it breached the King's rights.[272]

This inability to agree on who posed the greatest threat to England's constitution and fundamental laws prevented the moderates from forming a

---

[270] For Hunton and Herle, see below, pp. 228, 229, 230 n. 77, 323.
[271] Wormald, *Clarendon*, p. 99.
[272] Tuck, '"Ancient Law of Freedom"', pp. 153–4. Cf. *Philosophy and Government*, p. 219.

united middle ground. It was no accident that Hyde and Selden arrived at these contrasting positions. Their perspectives are entirely understandable in terms of their own characteristic views of the English polity. To anyone who believed that the relationship between Crown, Lords and Commons was that of co-ordinate powers, the King's readiness to contemplate the violent dissolution of an assembly whose existence was guaranteed by statute inevitably seemed more unconstitutional than any of the Junto's actions. By contrast, those like Hyde who regarded certain powers as the monarch's lawful prerogative, and who saw the Crown as sovereign over the two Houses, naturally perceived the Militia Ordinance as a more drastic threat to the constitution than Charles I's behaviour. We saw above that the Militia Ordinance was a vital catalyst in the decision of many moderate Royalists to leave Westminster. It offended their sense of constitutional propriety and the rule of law more deeply than the King's sabre rattling. Their Royalist allegiance thus reflected a different vision of the polity from that espoused by a Selden or a Whitelocke. But it was more complicated than that. For the differences between future Royalists and future Parliamentarians had first become visible on religious issues, and this brings us to another fundamental reason why moderates failed to unite in 1642.

I have argued that none of those who became Constitutional Royalists during the 1640s displayed the hallmarks of godly zeal. They were in varying degrees attached to the structures of the Church of England and did not seek root-and-branch reform. The fact that in 1640 they were able to join forces with Puritan zealots against Laudianism masked the fact that they did so for quite different reasons: whereas people like Hyde, Seymour and Culpepper denounced the religious policies of the Personal Rule as illegal, true religious radicals such as Pym attacked them as idolatrous. After the Laudian bogey-men had been removed, and the whole future of the established Church was called into question, the essential incompatibility of these two positions became obvious. The future Constitutional Royalists objected to Laudianism as one of a number of ways in which the Caroline régime had breached existing laws; but once this had been remedied they wished to preserve episcopacy as an essential part of the 'Church by law established'. By contrast, future Parliamentarians accorded a primacy to the religious issue and saw other unwelcome policies as manifestations of a 'popish' plot against Church and State. Moreover, the vast majority of them had consistently urged 'further reformation' of the Church to purge it of the traces of popery.[273]

This is true of all but one of the 'Constitutional Parliamentarians' examined above. D'Ewes displayed what Conrad Russell has called 'the

---

[273] Russell, *Causes*, pp. 222–4; Conrad Russell, 'Issues in the House of Commons, 1621–1629: predictors of Civil War allegiance', *Albion*, 23 (1991), 23–39.

diagnostic sign of a Parliamentarian' when he asserted that Elizabeth I had 'rather setled a beginning of a Reformation than a Reformation'. Or, as he put it in October 1641, the Church was 'yet full of wrinkles amongst us' and needed 'a great deale of Reformation'.[274] John Morrill cites D'Ewes as 'an extreme example of those men whose religious views in the end required them to stand out against the King'. He had been a Ship Money sheriff, he was deeply attached to the rule of law and yet 'he made austere adherence to a primitive reformed Church a prerequisite for settlement'.[275] Much the same was true of Whitelocke. The President of St John's College, Oxford, Dr Richard Bailie, remarked to him in 1634 that ever since his undergraduate days he had been 'always wont to have a puritanical jerk at the Church'. Whitelocke was passionately committed to freedom of conscience but was usually associated with the Erastians rather than the Independents in the Westminster Assembly.[276] His diary is shot through with an introspective Puritan piety which discerned the operation of God's providence in his own daily life as well as in national affairs.[277]

The case of Whitelocke's 'great and intimate friend' Selden[278] was rather more complex. He had enjoyed Laud's friendship and patronage during the 1630s,[279] and initially opposed root-and-branch reform.[280] However, during the summer of 1641 he began to move towards a more Erastian position, declaring:

It does not follow that we must have bishops still, because we have had them so long. They are equally mad who say that bishops are so *jure divino*, that they must be continued, and they who say, they are so antichristian, that they must be put away. All is as the state pleases.[281]

Selden rejected both divine right episcopacy and Presbyterian forms of government; and as a member of the Westminster Assembly he became a formidable advocate of an Erastian church settlement.[282] Richard Tuck has

---

[274] Russell, *Causes*, pp. 20, 138.
[275] Morrill, *Revolt*, pp. 25, 32, 50, 53, 70, 146. Cf. David Underdown, *Pride's Purge: Politics in the Puritan Revolution* (Oxford, 1971), pp. 8, 10, 16; and Sharpe, *Personal Rule*, pp. 691–4.
[276] Spalding, *Improbable Puritan*, pp. 96–7; Robert S. Paul, *The Assembly of the Lord* (Edinburgh, 1985), pp. 127–8, 271, 459–60, 495, 554.
[277] For a few examples, see *Diary of Whitelocke*, Spalding, pp. 107, 133, 153, 174, 176–7, 229, 287, 378, 389, 481.
[278] *Ibid.*, p. 403.
[279] Tuck, '"Ancient Law of Freedom"', p. 138; Richard Tuck, *Natural Rights Theories: Their Origin and Development* (Cambridge, 1979), p. 86; *Philosophy and Government*, p. 205.
[280] D'Ewes (N), p. 337.
[281] John Selden, *Opera Omnia*, ed. David Wilkins (6 vols., 1726), III, col. 2015. Cf. Tuck, '"Ancient Law of Freedom"', p. 155.
[282] Paul, *Assembly of the Lord*, especially pp. 269–71. On Selden's Erastianism, see also Sommerville, *Hobbes*, pp. 105, 123, 128; Tuck, *Philosophy and Government*, pp. 218–19; and *Natural Rights Theories*, pp. 86, 94. I owe this last reference to Nicholas Cranfield.

argued persuasively that his preference for this model over the episcopalian structures demanded by the Royalists 'must have acted as a powerful motive for remaining on the Parliamentary side'.[283] Yet this outlook rested on Erastianism and an obsessive concern for legalism rather than a desire for 'further reformation' *per se*. As Conrad Russell has suggested, Selden was 'highly untypical' of Parliamentarians in claiming that 'we charge the prelatical clergy with popery to make them odious, although we know they are guilty of no such thing'. Most appear to have believed that charge when they made it.[284]

With Sir Benjamin Rudyerd, on the other hand, we again return to a more representative figure. He had repeatedly sought further reformation and in particular urged measures against 'scandalous livings'. In January 1629, for example, he told a committee on religion that 'though christianity and religion bee established generally throughout this kingdome, yet untill it bee planted more particularly, I shall scarce thinke this a Christian Commonwealth'.[285] During the 1630s he became a member of the Providence Island Company;[286] and when the Long Parliament assembled he declared: 'let religion be our *primum quaerite*, for all things else are but *etcaeteras* to it'. This belief that all secular grievances sprang from a crisis in religion was highly characteristic of future Parliamentarians. As Rudyerd put it: 'if we secure our religion, we shall cut off and defeate many plots that are now on foot'.[287] His ideal was a primitive episcopacy 'according to the usage of ancient churches in the best times' rather than merely a return to 'Jacobethan' practice. Although he subsequently drew back from root-and-branch reform – 'I am as much for reformation, for purging and maintaining religion, as any man whatsoever: but I professe, I am not for innovation, demolition, nor abolition' – he remained committed to a programme of godly reformation and continued to pursue this as a member of the Westminster Assembly.[288]

The religious views of these four 'Constitutional Parliamentarians' thus differed perceptibly from those of the Constitutional Royalists. None gave the unequivocal endorsement of non-Laudian episcopacy associated with Hyde, Falkland and Culpepper; all sought either a parliamentary Erastianism or a programme of 'further reformation'. Contrasting religious attitudes are thus another crucial reason why moderates failed to coalesce in the summer of 1642. They disagreed first of all about the nature of the religious crisis: was this only one of several areas in which Charles I had infringed the rule of law, or was it the source of all the problems facing

---

[283] Tuck, '"Ancient Law of Freedom"', p. 155.
[284] Russell, *Causes*, pp. 20, 74–5, 226.
[285] *Sir Benjamin Ruddierd's speech in behalfe of the cleargy* (1628[/9]), p. 4 (*STC*, 21435.7).
[286] A. P. Newton, *The Colonising Activities of the English Puritans* (New Haven, 1914), pp. 67–8.
[287] *The Speeches of Sir Benjamin Rudyer in the High Court of Parliament*, pp. 2, 4.
[288] *Sir Benjamin Rudyerd's Speech; concerning Bishops, Deanes and Chapters* (1641), sigs. A3[r], [A4v] (Wing, R 2190; BL, TT, E 198/40); Paul, *Assembly of the Lord*, pp. 187, 508, 510, 529, 536, 554.

Church and State alike? Because they defined the question differently, they arrived at different answers, and were thus unable to agree on how the crisis should be resolved. More specifically, they were at odds over what should be the non-negotiable element within any religious settlement. Should it be the preservation of non-Laudian episcopacy even if this stymied further reformation; or should it be godly reform even at the cost of abolishing bishops? Without a common answer to this conundrum a united middle ground would remain elusive.

These religious attitudes were intimately bound up with the different constitutional paradigms examined above. There was a direct correlation between a religious position which stressed godly reform or a parliamentary Erastianism, and a view of the polity based on the 'co-ordinate' powers of Crown, Lords and Commons. If the Houses were equal as law-makers with the Crown, ran the Parliamentarian argument, they could justly demand that any religious reformation be acceptable to them. The Constitutional Royalists, on the other hand, thought that the clerical hierarchy was an intrinsic part of the 'Church by law established' and was guarded by the royal supremacy. Episcopacy was, as Hyde later put it, 'as much fenced and secured by the lawes as monarchy it selfe, and an entire part of the frame and constitucon of the kingdome';[289] its abolition would therefore violate the rule of law and strike a blow against the Crown. Conversely, the most effective way to defend bishops was to rally to Charles I — not just because he included this in his political platform but because the Constitutional Royalists held that the institutions of episcopacy and monarchy were symbiotically linked. These connections between ecclesiastical and constitutional beliefs were not the chance product of developments in the early 1640s; they possessed a logical coherence which events served to highlight and reinforce.

This integration of religious and secular attitudes was a characteristic which seems to have distinguished the moderates of 1642 from the extremists. The latter — those who forced the pace of events and ultimately took up arms — were apparently those whose religious beliefs were so powerful that they could override their secular preferences. The leaders of the two parties in Cheshire, Sir Thomas Aston and Sir William Brereton, dramatically illustrate the link between this trait and military activism.[290] Often this point is easier to demonstrate for Parliamentarian extremists like Oliver Cromwell or Sir Robert Harley;[291] among many Royalist activists it is more difficult to disentangle religious motives from secular concerns such as honour, loyalty to the sovereign, and fears for the social order.[292]

[289] Bodl. Lib., MS Clarendon 29, fo. 5r (Hyde to Nicholas, 12 December 1646).
[290] Morrill, *Nature of the English Revolution*, p. 68.
[291] *Ibid.*, pp. 118–47; and Jacqueline Eales, *Puritans and Roundheads: The Harleys of Brampton Bryan and the Outbreak of the English Civil War* (Cambridge, 1990), *passim*.
[292] J. G. Marston, 'Gentry honour and royalism in early Stuart England', *JBS*, 13 (1974), 21–43; G. E. Aylmer, 'Collective mentalities in mid-Seventeenth-Century England: II.

Nevertheless, many of those who implemented the Commission of Array were drawn to the King by his robust defence of episcopacy and the Prayer Book.[293] Thus, whether they fought for Crown or Parliament, such militants were often prepared to jettison the legal and constitutional assumptions of a lifetime in order to ensure a particular kind of Church settlement. The occupants of the middle ground, by contrast, never let their religious beliefs determine their agenda. Whereas the extremists (especially among the Parliamentarians) were those who allowed religious zeal to dictate their political behaviour, the moderates (especially among the Royalists) were those whose attitudes towards the Church dovetailed with their legal and constitutional assumptions to produce a single, harmonious outlook.

In the end, the failure of the middle ground to unite allowed the extremists to drive England into civil war. During July both sides became convinced that they could win an armed conflict; and on 22 August, with the encouragement of Henrietta Maria but to the dismay of his more moderate advisers, Charles raised his standard at Nottingham.[294] Hyde later lamented 'the melancholic state of the King's affairs';[295] while Dorset wrote to the Countess of Middlesex: 'Behold into whatt a sad condition blind zeale, pride, ambition, envy, malice and avarice ... hath plunged the honor, quiet, safety, peace, plenty, prosperity, piety of this late, very late, most happy kingdome.'[296] But the outbreak of civil war in no way blunted the Constitutional Royalists' resolve to achieve a settlement. It was logically impossible both to rally to the King in defence of the law and to jettison the concept of Parliament as a court of law. This did not, of course, imply an acceptance of the Junto's actions; but it did involve remaining a 'Parliamentarian' in the broadest sense of the word. Brian Wormald's point about Hyde holds good for other Constitutional Royalists.[297] The very assumptions which had impelled them to join the King in turn required that they continue negotiations with 'Constitutional Parliamentarians' at Westminster. The history of those talks, the ideas which informed them, and the issues over which they broke down, will form the subject of the second part of this book.

Royalist attitudes', *TRHS*, 5th series, 37 (1987), 1–30; Newman, 'The King's servants', pp. 225–41.
[293] Fletcher, *Outbreak*, pp. 369–406; Morrill, *Nature of the English Revolution*, p. 43; Newman, 'The King's servants', pp. 228–9.
[294] Russell, *FBM*, pp. 518–24; Conrad Russell, 'Why did Charles I fight the Civil War?', *History Today*, 34 (1984), 31–4; Fletcher, *Outbreak*, pp. 323–6; *Letters of Queen Henrietta Maria*, ed. Mary Anne Everett Green (1857), especially pp. 52–3, 55–7, 61, 95–7.
[295] Clarendon, *History*, II, 291 (Book V, §449).
[296] CKS, Uncatalogued Cranfield Papers: Dorset to the Countess of Middlesex, August 1642, fo. 1r–v. I am most grateful to Donald Gibson of the Centre for Kentish Studies for his assistance in using this collection.
[297] See above, p. 88.

Part II

CONSTITUTIONAL ROYALISM IN THEORY AND PRACTICE, 1642–1649

-- ⠀⠀⠀ 5 ⠀⠀⠀ --

Chronological outline: negotiations formal and informal

I

The aim of this chapter is to establish the basic narrative of peace talks between Royalists and Parliamentarians from the outbreak of the Civil War to the Regicide. It is written very much from the perspective of Constitutional Royalists, and seeks to recover their role in promoting and conducting such talks. It will analyse their involvement in informal peace initiatives as well as in the great set-piece treaties of Oxford, Uxbridge, Newcastle and Newport. Throughout, a familiar cast appears: Richmond, Southampton, Hertford, Lindsey and Dorset were the figures who most consistently urged Charles to keep talking with the two Houses. These peers emerge as the most important practitioners of Constitutional Royalist ideas during the period of the two Civil Wars, while Hyde, Falkland and Culpepper gradually became less influential and closely allied than they had been in 1642. By 1646 Falkland was three years dead, Hyde was increasingly isolated, and Culpepper was more closely aligned with Sir Henry Jermyn and John Ashburnham. All four were now in exile, and the main political exponents of Constitutional Royalism within England were a close-knit cluster of moderate peers.

II

Only three days after Charles raised his standard, Royalist moderates persuaded him to send peace commissioners to Westminster. Southampton advised the King that a message to Parliament 'might do good, and could do no harm';[1] while Culpepper 'was as earnest to persuade him to it as any man'.[2] Charles was 'offended' and 'exceedingly afflicted', but finally agreed to send Southampton and Culpepper – together with Dorset and Sir William Uvedale[3] – to inform the Houses of his 'constant and earnest care

[1] Clarendon, *History*, II, 300 (Book VI, §8).　　[2] *Ibid.*
[3] *Ibid.*, 301. Uvedale's presence is intriguing. He had been Treasurer for the Army in 1639–40, and many formal documents survive relating to this office (especially in PRO, SP

109

to preserve the publike peace'.[4] But on 27 August this message was received, in Hyde's words, 'with unheard of insolence and contempt'.[5] Southampton was ordered to leave the Lords, to pass the message to the gentleman-usher, and then 'forthwith to depart this town'.[6] In the Commons, Culpepper was permitted to deliver the message, but then told to withdraw.[7] The answer of the two Houses – which was drafted in the Lords and slightly amended by the Commons – insisted that they could not negotiate with the King until he retracted those proclamations declaring them 'traitors or otherwise delinquents' and took down his standard.[8] Charles 'believed that he should be no farther moved to make address to them',[9] but none the less sent Falkland with another declaration insisting that he had never intended to declare the Houses traitors or to raise his standard against them.[10] The Houses reiterated their refusal to negotiate until the offending proclamations were withdrawn and the standard taken down, and the negotiations reached deadlock.[11]

In these manoeuvres, the Constitutional Royalists stood wedged between a King who negotiated only with the greatest reluctance, and two Houses which refused to negotiate until the King rescinded his condemnation of them as traitors. In trying to reconcile these positions, they had to contend with the fact that Charles was receiving advice against further peace initiatives. Henrietta Maria feared that he would be 'ruined' by the message of 25 August, and that 'everybody [would] abandon' him.[12] The

16). His activities in the Long Parliament are difficult to uncover, although the fact that he had had an affair with Essex's wife during the 1630s may help to explain why he joined the King in 1642: J. Bruce, ed., *Letters and Papers of the Verney Family down to the end of the year 1639* (Camden Society, 1st series, 56, 1853), 168–70. However, he retained links with the Houses, and was eventually secluded at Pride's Purge: David Underdown, *Pride's Purge: Politics in the Puritan Revolution* (Oxford, 1971), pp. 71, 240, 388; Mary Frear Keeler, *The Long Parliament, 1640–1641: A Biographical Study of its Members* (Memoirs of the American Philosophical Society, 36, Philadelphia, 1954), 369–70. He certainly defies easy categorisation.

4 Clarendon, *History*, II, 305 (Book VI, §12); *His Majesties gracious message to both Houses of Parliament sent from Nottingham the 25 of August 1642, together with the answer of the Lords and Commons to the said message* (1642), pp. 2–3 (Wing, C 2332; BL, TT, E 116/2); *LJ*, V, 327–8; *CJ*, II, 745. For the original of the King's message, see MP, 25 August 1642, fo. 19. The message had been drafted by Hyde: Clarendon, *History*, II, 301.
5 Clarendon, *History*, II, 305 (Book VI, §12).
6 *LJ*, V, 326; Clarendon, *History*, II, 305 (Book VI, §12); Scottish RO, Hamilton MS, GD 406/1/1689 (Lanark to Hamilton, 31 August 1642). I owe this last reference to Conrad Russell.
7 *CJ*, II, 744; *PJ*, III, 320–3; Clarendon, *History*, II, 305 (Book VI, §12).
8 *LJ*, V, 328; *CJ*, II, 744–5; *PJ*, III, 323–4; Clarendon, *History*, II, 306–7 (Book VI, §14).
9 Clarendon, *History*, II, 307 (Book VI, §15).
10 *CJ*, II, 756; *PJ*, III, 333; Clarendon, *History*, II, 307–8 (Book VI, §§15–16).
11 *LJ*, V, 341; *PJ*, III, 333–4; Clarendon, *History*, II, 308 (Book VI, §18).
12 *Letters of Queen Henrietta Maria*, ed. Mary Anne Everett Green (1857), p. 110 (Henrietta Maria to Charles I, 3/13 September 1642).

Queen and other Royalist hard-liners exerted very considerable influence, as Lord Spencer reported on 21 September:

The King is of late very much averse to peace, by the persuasions of 102 and 111. It is likewise conceived that the King has taken a resolution not to do any thing in that way before the Queen comes, for people advising the King to agree with the Parliament was the occasion of the Queen's return. Till that time no advise will be received; nevertheless the honest men will take all occasions to procure an accommodation, which the King, when he sent those messages did heartily desire, and would still make offers in that way, but for 102, 111, and the expectation of the Queen.[13]

This reveals very clearly the difficulties which moderate Royalists faced in their search for a settlement. But even if the initiative of 25 August came to nothing, it had at least served to identify some of the Royalist peers most anxious to achieve an accommodation. Dorset's role almost certainly explains Essex's approaches to him in the autumn of 1642. This episode was typical of the informal contacts between the two sides which persisted throughout the 1640s; but it ultimately foundered on the same issue as the more public negotiations of late August.

At the request of both Houses, Essex wrote to Dorset on 26 September asking 'in what manner' the King would receive Parliament's terms and seeking 'safe convoy' for peace commissioners.[14] Dorset replied on Charles's behalf that the 'petitions of the houses shall never find his dower shutt against them', so long as they were not conveyed by 'those he hath by name accused of treason'.[15] The Houses then resolved that this qualification did 'not stand with the honour and privilege of Parliament'.[16] Essex relayed this resolution to Dorset, who reiterated Charles's refusal to 'receive any by the hands of such as he had, by name, proclaimed traitors', but insisted that 'his ear shall still be open to hear any fitting address from

---

[13] CKS, De L'Isle and Dudley MS, U 1475/Z53/92 (Lord Spencer to Lady Spencer, 21 September 1642). Tantalisingly, the numbers 102 and 111 were left undeciphered in the original manuscript. There is a very incomplete key to Lord Spencer's cipher in U 1475/O89/ 32, but unfortunately this does not include either of these numbers. Warburton believed that 102 and 111 were ciphers for Prince Rupert and Digby, identifications which become all the more plausible in the light of evidence discussed during the course of this chapter: *Memoirs of Prince Rupert and the Cavaliers*, ed. Eliot Warburton (3 vols., 1849), I, 338. Warburton's text was derived from *Letters and Memorials of State ... Written and Collected by Sir Henry Sydney*, ed. Arthur Collins (2 vols., 1746), II, 667. Warburton repeated several errors of transcription, including '202' instead of '102'. I am most grateful to Viscount De L'Isle for allowing me to consult and quote from his family muniments.

[14] *LJ*, V, 380.

[15] *Ibid.*; *CJ*, II, 791; Bodl. Lib., MS Tanner 64 (letters and papers), fo. 19r (Dorset to Essex, 28 September 1642).

[16] *LJ*, V, 384–5; *CJ*, II, 791; BL, Add. MS 18777 (diary of Walter Yonge), fo. 18v (I am most grateful to Christopher Thompson for providing me with a copy of his transcript of this diary); Staffordshire RO, Leveson-Gower Correspondence, D 868/4/5 (Stephen Charlton to Sir Richard Leveson, October 1642).

either or both Houses of Parliament'.[17] The Houses concluded on 20 October, that Charles 'doth refuse all addresses and petitions from the Parliament' and broke off negotiations.[18] Once again, the refusal of Charles and the Houses to compromise on the issue of proclaimed traitors had halted talks, and the battle of Edgehill followed three days later.

There was then a lull in peace talks through the winter of 1642–3. The King remained deeply suspicious of negotiations, and promised Henrietta Maria's confidant Newcastle that he would 'be wary of a Treatie'.[19] The Houses meanwhile drafted formal peace terms which were presented to Charles at Oxford on 1 February 1643. Their principal demands were that the King should 'disband' his armies (§I); 'settle' Church government and the militia on the advice of both Houses (§§IV, VII); make various named appointments in the judiciary (§VIII); grant a 'general pardon' for all offences committed before 10 January 1642 (§XIII); and 'restore such members of either House of Parliament to their several places of services and employment, out of which they have been put since the beginning of this Parliament' (§XIV).[20] The Houses had agonised over these terms for some weeks,[21] and they were finally presented by a broad-based committee comprising the Earls of Northumberland, Pembroke, Salisbury and Holland, Lords Wenman and Dungarvan, Sir William Lytton, Sir John Holland, Bulstrode Whitelocke, Richard Winwood, William Pierrepont and Edmund Waller.[22] But the King apparently decided almost immediately that the terms were unacceptable. After Northumberland read the propositions,[23] Charles replied that 'they that principally contrived and penned them had no thoughts of peace in their hearts, but to make things worse and worse. Yet I shall do my part, and take as much honey out of the gall as I can.'[24] In private he abandoned this tone of wounded right-eousness and forbearance, informing Ormond that 'no lesse power then his who made the worlde of nothing can draw peace out of thease Articles'.[25] His stance was shared by, among others, Secretary Nicholas, who the next day acclaimed Prince Rupert's capture of Cirencester on the grounds that

---

[17] *LJ*, V, 411–2.
[18] *Ibid.*, 412; *CJ*, II, 816. For an indication that Sir John Strangways was also involved in peace talks with Sir Walter Erle during October 1642, see BL, Add. MS 18777, fo. 27r.
[19] BL, Harl. MS 6988 (Royal letters and warrants), fo. 131v (Charles I to Newcastle, 29 December 1642). Newcastle's friendship with the Queen, and his consistent hostility to peace negotiations, are discussed more fully below, pp. 252–3.
[20] The Oxford Propositions are printed in Gardiner, *Documents*, pp. 262–7.
[21] The process of drafting may be reconstructed from *CJ*, II, 865–949, and *LJ*, V, 455–583.
[22] *CJ*, II, 949; *LJ*, V, 574–5; BL, Add. MS 18777, fo. 135r.
[23] Charles even interrupted this reading: *The Diary of Bulstrode Whitelocke, 1605–1675*, ed. Ruth Spalding (British Academy Records of Social and Economic History, new series, 13, Oxford, 1990), 142.
[24] *LJ*, V, 590.
[25] Bodl. Lib., MS Clarendon 98, fo. 12r (Charles I to Ormond, 2 February 1642/3).

this would 'worke better effects' upon the Parliamentarian commissioners than a more gracious reception.[26] In the event, the negotiations never got beyond Parliament's first proposition. On 6 February Charles replied with six demands, including the restoration to him of his 'own revenue, magazines, towns, forts and ships', and that 'a cessation of arms ... be first agreed upon'.[27] The Houses then drew up articles of cessation (28 February), making disbandment of Royalist armies a precondition for a cessation.[28] Charles confided to Henrietta Maria that he found these terms 'so unreasonable that I cannot grant them'.[29] The King therefore offered alternative articles of cessation (6 March) which included the demand that no subject be imprisoned 'otherwise than according to the known laws of the land'.[30] The Houses responded by drawing up new instructions to their commissioners (18 March) which stated explicitly that senior military offices should be held by 'such as both Houses shall confide in'.[31] Charles refused this, but the Houses nevertheless decided to begin a treaty on their first two propositions even though a cessation had not been agreed.[32] Charles made the restoration of his revenue, forts, ships and magazines a precondition for the disbandment of his armies, which the Houses refused unless they had guarantees of senior military officers in whom they could confide.[33] The removal of Richmond as Lord Warden of the Cinque Ports was explicitly requested.[34] Charles declared that he 'could not with justice remove [Richmond] from it until some sufficient cause were made appear to him'.[35] The Houses finally asked bluntly (29 March) whether Charles did 'intend that both Houses may express their confidence of the persons to whose trust those places are to be committed';[36] to which he replied equally bluntly that he did not, but was resolved only 'not to protect them against the

---

[26] BL, Add. MS 18980 (Prince Rupert Correspondence), fo. 18r (Nicholas to Prince Rupert, 3 February 1642/3).
[27] Rushworth, V, 168–70; *LJ*, V, 591; *CJ*, II, 958–9.
[28] Rushworth, V, 170–1; *LJ*, V, 625–6; *CJ*, II, 979–85. See also Henry E. Huntington Library, San Marino, California, Hastings MS, HA 9682 (Nicholas to Henry Hastings, 21 February 1642/3).
[29] *Letters of Henrietta Maria*, Green, p. 174 (Charles I to Henrietta Maria, 2/12 March 1642/3).
[30] Rushworth, V, 173; *LJ*, V, 644; *CJ*, II, 991.
[31] Rushworth, V, 175–7 (quotation at 177); *CJ*, III, 8. D'Ewes thought these terms 'so full of iustice and equalibrancie as that there was no probabilitie to the contrary but that His Ma[jes]tie would readily accept of them': BL, Harl. MS 164 (diary of Sir Simonds D'Ewes), fo. 334r.
[32] Rushworth, V, 177–9; *LJ*, V, 669; *CJ*, III, 17.
[33] Rushworth, V, 182–4; *LJ*, V, 673–4; *CJ*, III, 19.
[34] Rushworth, V, 205; *LJ*, V, 701–2.   [35] Rushworth, V, 200; *LJ*, V, 702.
[36] Rushworth, V, 200–1; *LJ*, V, 702.

publick justice'.[37] Unable to accept a cessation on these terms, the Houses sought (8 April) a positive answer to their demand for disbandment.[38] Charles refused (12 April) unless his revenue, magazines, ships and forts were returned to him; all members of either House expelled since 1 January 1642 were restored; and he and both Houses were 'secured' from 'tumultuous assemblies'.[39] The Houses rejected these terms and ordered their commissioners to return to Westminster (14 April),[40] so bringing the Treaty of Oxford to an end.

It is interesting to compare the first-hand accounts by Whitelocke and Hyde of why this treaty collapsed. Whitelocke thought that Charles 'shewed great abilities, in his apprehension, reason and judgement', but was led astray by his advisers. Often he appeared conciliatory, but 'some of his bedchamber, and some higher than they, doubting that the answear which he had promised to us might bring the Treaty to a good effect, which they sought to hinder, they left not to presse and perswade the King to alter ... his answear'.[41] Whitelocke offers no names, but notes that Charles 'had commonly waiting on him when he treated with the Com[missione]rs, Prince Rupert, the L[ord] Keeper Littleton, the E[arle] of Southampton, and the L[ord] Chiefe Justice Bankes, and severall other Lords of his Councell'.[42] The reference to highly placed figures and the controversy over the Lord Warden of the Cinque Ports make it probable that Richmond was among these others. But these advisers cannot be held wholly responsible for the failure of the treaty, for Charles's private thoughts revealed a deep-rooted unwillingness to compromise.

There were some issues on which Constitutional Royalists also resisted concessions. Hyde countered the 'opinion that the King was too severe in this treaty' by arguing that the Houses were simultaneously seeking fundamental reforms of the Church – including the 'total abolition and extirpation of archbishops, bishops, deans and chapters' – and many other measures 'contrary to common equity and the right of the subject'.[43] This, together with the limitations which the Houses imposed upon their commissioners' freedom to debate, persuaded Hyde that the Oxford Propositions did not constitute 'a means to have restored the kingdom to a

[37] Rushworth, V, 201; *LJ*, V, 702–3; *CJ*, III, 31.
[38] Rushworth, V, 191–2; *LJ*, V, 698; *CJ*, III, 36.
[39] Rushworth, V, 259–61 (mispagination; correct pages 209–11); *LJ*, V, 718; *CJ*, III, 44.
[40] *LJ*, V, 719; *CJ*, III, 44. See also *Mercurius Aulicus*, no. 15 (9–16 April 1643), pp. 189–91 (*STC (News)*, 275.115; BL, TT, E 99/22).
[41] *Diary of Whitelocke*, Spalding, pp. 145–6.   [42] *Ibid.*, p. 143.
[43] Clarendon, *History*, III, 9–13 (Book VII, §§21–3).

present peace, and the King to his just authority and rights'.[44] The Constitutional Royalists wanted peace;[45] but they did not want a sell out. At the same time, Hyde recognised that the search for settlement was a two-way business which required 'a receding mutually on both sides'.[46] He therefore advised Charles to make 'some condescensions in the point of the militia', and in particular to accept William Pierrepont's proposition that Northumberland be restored to the office of Lord High Admiral.[47] Hyde argued that such a gesture would bring Charles 'very notable advantages'. But the King refused, apparently because he had promised Henrietta Maria never to 'make any peace, but by her interposition and mediation'.[48] Hyde lamented that the rejection of this 'advantageous' proposal encouraged 'many ill humours and factions' in both camps.[49] Hard-line counsels at Oxford were further strengthened by the Queen's arrival there on 15 July 1643.[50] Her influence soon became apparent in the ennoblement of three of her closest allies, Jermyn, Henry Percy and Henry Wilmot, all of whom would emerge at various times as opponents of peace talks.[51]

A 'receding mutually on both sides' could only be achieved if the lines of communication between Oxford and Westminster remained open. For this reason, Hyde urged the King to respond graciously when three Parliamentarian peers, the Earls of Holland, Bedford and Clare, arrived at Oxford in August.[52] However, it seems that 'the Queen would not hear of it'.[53] The

---

[44] *Ibid.*, III, 12–13 (Book VII, §23). Hyde's own influence at this time should not be doubted. He became a Privy Councillor on 22 February 1643: Bodl. Lib., MS Clarendon 21, fo. 197r (minute of Privy Council meeting). Then, on 3 March, he replaced Culpepper as Chancellor of the Exchequer following the latter's appointment as Master of the Rolls: PRO, IND 4226 (Patent Office docquet book of warrants for the Great Seal), fo. 8r–v; Clarendon, *History*, II, 527 (Book VI, §382).

[45] Just how badly Falkland in particular wanted peace is apparent from the celebrated manner of his death at the first battle of Newbury on 20 September 1643. Hyde recounts that he would 'often, after a deep silence and frequent sighs, ingeminate the word Peace, Peace, and would passionately profess that the very agony of the war, and the view of the calamities and desolation the kingdom did and must endure, took his sleep from him, and would shortly break his heart': Clarendon, *History*, III, 189 (Book VII, §233). His death in battle was, in Gardiner's words, 'scarcely distinguishable from suicide': *DNB*, XI, 251.

[46] Clarendon, *Life*, I, 178.

[47] The King had dismissed Northumberland from this office at the end of June 1642: *LJ*, V, 169.

[48] Clarendon, *Life*, I, 181–7; *History*, III, 10–11 (Book VII, §§21–2).

[49] Clarendon, *Life*, I, 184.

[50] *Mercurius Aulicus*, no. 28 (9–15 July 1643), p. 373 (*STC (News)*, 275.128; BL, TT, E 62/3).

[51] Bodl. Lib., MS Ashmole 832 (creations of peers), fos. 181v–182v, 188v–190r; Clarendon, *History*, III, 194 (Book VII, §242). For their hostility to negotiations, see below, pp. 117, 118, 119.

[52] Clarendon, *History*, III, 146–56 (Book VII, §§178–90); 193–9 (Book VII, §§241–7).

[53] *Memoirs of Prince Rupert*, Warburton, II, 272.

peers were pardoned but not given offices or commands, and after a few months they returned disconsolately to Westminster. Their treatment was, in Hyde's words, 'a great error',[54] especially because Northumberland – notwithstanding the King's refusal to make him Lord High Admiral – was also seriously considering coming to Oxford. However, when he saw the cold reception accorded to these three peers he decided against it.[55] Charles's behaviour, in which he was supported by the Queen and the majority of the Privy Council,[56] offered no incentive for disillusioned Parliamentarians to defect to the King and thus destroyed an important opportunity for moderates on both sides to draw together.

Essex, for his part, clearly wished to keep talking with moderates at Oxford. In May 1643 he 'sent to his confident the Earl of Dorset concerning the exchange of some prisoners'.[57] This apparently bore fruit, for on 22 June Essex was able to write to Prince Rupert proposing detailed arrangements for the exchange.[58] When these were duly implemented a few weeks later, Lindsey was among the prisoners exchanged.[59] Yet there remained certain points on which Essex was not prepared to compromise, and when in August the Lords drew up peace proposals conceding everything Charles had demanded at Oxford, the Lord General joined the Commons in rejecting them.[60] Informal contacts between the two sides nevertheless continued to be made at the highest levels, culminating in a personal exchange between Charles and Essex during August 1644.

The first of these links was a secret negotiation between Thomas Ogle and the Earl of Bristol between November 1643 and January 1644.[61] Ogle, a prisoner in Winchester House whose background remains obscure, drew up propositions which differed little from those adopted by the Lords in August 1643. He wished

to settle ... a confidence in the people of his Ma[jes]t[ie]s reallitie in mayntenance of religion, the just priviledges of Parliament, the lawfull liberties and propertie of the subject, and his future government by the knowne lawes of the land, without

---

[54] Clarendon, *History*, III, 199 (Book VII, §248).
[55] *Ibid.*, III, 152–6 (Book VII, §§187–90); 200 (Book VII, §248); Gardiner, *Civil War*, I, 202.
[56] Clarendon, *History*, III, 146–52 (Book VII, §§178–86); 193–9 (Book VII, §§241–7); Sir Richard Bulstrode, *Memoirs and Reflections upon the Reign and Government of King Charles the Ist and K[ing] Charles the IId* (1721), pp. 96–8.
[57] BL, Add. MS 18980, fo. 60r (Nicholas to Prince Rupert, 11 May 1643).
[58] William Salt Library, Stafford, Salt MS 509 (Essex to Prince Rupert, 22 June 1643).
[59] Christ Church Muniment Room, Oxford, Evelyn Collection, Browne Letters, Box A–C, unfol. (Christopher Browne to Sir Richard Browne, 3 August 1643); *LJ*, VI, 151, 153.
[60] *LJ*, VI, 163, 171; *CJ*, III, 197; MP, 5 August 1643 (propositions drafted by Lords and reasons for Commons' rejection of them).
[61] The evidence relating to this negotiation, mainly derived from Bodl. Lib., MS Tanner 62, is printed in B. M. Gardiner, ed., 'A secret negotiation with Charles I, 1643–4', *Camden Miscellany*, VIII (Camden Society, 1st series, 31, 1883).

the alteracon of Episcopalle government, and the trust of the militia reposed in the Crowne.[62]

Possibly the most attractive aspect of these generous terms was their provision for a modified episcopacy, comprising 'the ablest and most conscientious divines' who would be shorn of coercive powers.[63] As we shall see, this bore some resemblance to the arrangements for Church government presented to Charles in the *Heads of the Proposals* of 1647.[64] Unfortunately, the negotiation became known to the Committee of Safety and rapidly collapsed in January 1644.[65]

However, the assembly of the Oxford Parliament on 22 January quickly led to further moves for peace among Charles's followers.[66] Culpepper soon found himself at odds with more hard-line Royalists over whether to embark on a treaty. He 'propounded' in the King's Council 'that they might presently fall upon propositions to be sent to the Parliament at Westminster'. As pledges of goodwill, he suggested that 'His Maiestie may pass an act against papists, and deliver up such delinquents as were proclaimed traitors by His Maiestie at the desire of both Houses, before this war begun, and are yet notwithstanding commanders in His Maiesties army.' However, 'the Lord Digby, Master Jermaine, Master Peircie, Secretarie Windebank etc. were not well pleased with the motion, and Her Maiestie much offended at it'.[67] There was thus considerable opposition within the King's counsels to the pursuit of a negotiated settlement, especially from Henrietta Maria and her circle.

Nevertheless, a few days later 44 peers (including Hertford, Lindsey, Dorset, Richmond, Southampton and Seymour) and 118 members of the House of Commons (including Hyde, Culpepper and Strangways) drafted a long letter to Essex asking him to join with them as 'happy instruments of our countries redemption from the miseries of warre, and restitution to the

---

[62] *Ibid.*, 9.   [63] *Ibid.*

[64] This parallel seems to me closer than that which Gardiner draws to 'the settlement of 1688': Gardiner, *Civil War*, I, 265.

[65] *CJ*, III, 378; BL, Add. MS 18779 (diary of Walter Yonge), fos. 52v–54r; Gardiner, *Civil War*, I, 264–75.

[66] It is a tragedy that the records of the Oxford Parliament were burnt prior to Oxford's surrender in June 1646: *The Life, Diary, and Correspondence of Sir William Dugdale*, ed. W. Hamper (1827), p. 87. One of the very few sources to survive is a diary covering 22–30 January 1644, possibly compiled by Lord Loughborough's medical attendant Philip Kinder: Huntington Library, Hastings MS, HA 8060. For the Oxford Parliament's opening, see Clarendon, *History*, III, 293–4 (Book VII, §370); for its membership, see *A Catalogue of the Names of the Knights, Citizens and Burgesses that have served in the last four Parliaments* (1656), pp. 20–5 (Wing, C 1394; BL, TT, E 1602/6).

[67] *The Kingdomes Weekly Intelligencer*, no. 41 (23–30 January 1644), pp. 314–15 (*STC (News)*, 214.041; BL, TT, E 30/19). This account was taken from an intercepted letter from Oxford to Lord Maynard.

blessings of peace'.[68] John Adamson has suggested that this letter's engrossment on parchment constituted an 'acknowledgement of Essex's protectoral status'.[69] Such a direct approach to Essex was certainly very shrewd, for Charles had shortly before told Richmond that he 'would take noe corespondence of the Lordes or house [of] Comons' and only deal 'with Lo[rd] Essex'.[70] However, Essex's reaction showed not that he aspired to 'protectoral status', but rather that he still saw himself very much as the servant of the Houses of Parliament. His immediate response was to desire 'the direction of' the House of Lords 'what to do herein'.[71] The 'packet' was referred to a committee, who opened it and – finding that it was 'without directions to the Parliament' – left it up to Essex to reply to the Earl of Forth.[72] Essex told Forth that he was unable to communicate the letter to the two Houses because it contained no 'acknowledgement of them'. He thus used his commitment to 'the maintenance of the Parliament of England, and of the privileges thereof' to avoid involvement in this peace initiative.[73] From a Royalist perspective, this episode clearly illustrates the influence of moderate counsels at Oxford, and it is probably no coincidence that January also saw the appointment of Dorset as Lord Chamberlain of the King's Household and of Hertford as Groom of the Stool.[74] The latter's elevation marked a defeat for the Queen's close ally, Jermyn.[75] The exchanges also demonstrate Essex's belief that he was directly accountable to the two Houses, and his deep reluctance to negotiate independently of them. This was to prove a recurrent problem during 1644.

Talks nevertheless continued among the nobility. That summer, amid

[68] A Copy of a Letter from the Members of both Houses to the Earle of Essex desiring a Treaty of Peace (Oxford, 1644), pp. 3–8 (Wing, E 1285; BL, TT, E 32/3); Clarendon, History, III, 294–7 (Book VII, §§371–4); Huntington Library, Hastings MS, HA 8060, unfol.

[69] J. S. A. Adamson, 'The baronial context of the English Civil War', TRHS, 5th series, 40 (1990), 109–10.

[70] Leeds Castle, Kent, MS C1/22 (Richmond to Prince Rupert, 12 November [1643]). I am most grateful to the Leeds Castle Foundation, and especially to Mr David A. H. Cleggett, for providing me with a xerox copy of this MS, and for permission to publish the above extract. Cf. Adamson, 'Baronial context', 111.

[71] LJ, VI, 399.

[72] LJ, VI, 400. See also The Kingdomes Weekly Intelligencer, no. 42 (30 January–7 February 1644), pp. 321–2 (STC (News), 214.042; BL, TT, E 31/21).

[73] LJ, VI, 404; Clarendon, History, III, 298 (Book VII, §377); Diary of Whitelocke, Spalding, p. 150.

[74] PRO, SP 16/500/30 (John Jones to Lord Hopton, 1 February 1643/4); BL, Add. MS 27962 K(i) (Salvetti Correspondence), fo. 222r–v; CKS, Sackville MS, U 269/C283/1 (John Jackman to the Countess of Bath, 24 January 1643/4); Huntington Library, Hastings MS, HAP, Box 18, folder 21; Letters of Henrietta Maria, Green, p. 230 (Henrietta Maria to the Marquis of Newcastle, 7 October [1643]).

[75] Clarendon, History, III, 194–5 (Book VII, §242).

Royalist campaigns which had been strongly supported by Digby and Wilmot but opposed by the likes of Culpepper,[76] there were signs of further communication between Essex and Dorset. The Lord General revealed in June that Lord Conway 'did give notice, in a letter to the Earl of Dorset at Oxford, of [Lord Chandos's] intention to come away [to Parliament]'.[77] I have argued elsewhere that the absence of evidence that this letter was intercepted suggests that Dorset permitted its contents to be leaked to Essex.[78] The Lords' examination of Chandos established that he had conversed with Lindsey and Dorset at Oxford, and that Dorset was also in touch with Conway.[79] The extent of these contacts is tantalisingly obscure, but they do at least suggest the existence of covert links between Essex and Dorset.

It was, however, with his brother-in-law Hertford that Essex had his closest contacts during the summer of 1644. It is well known that shortly before the surrender of Lostwithiel Charles invited Essex to 'join with me heartily and really in the settling of those things which we have both professed constantly to be our only aims', and promised 'such eminent marks of my confidence and value as shall not leave room for the least distrust amongst you'.[80] What needs stressing here is the part played by Constitutional Royalists in promoting and managing this initiative. The King may well have been acting on the advice of Hyde, Culpepper and Digby.[81] His message to the Lord General was conveyed by Hertford's son Lord Beauchamp, who was also Essex's nephew.[82] Furthermore, the nature of Essex's reaction to this offer – which was to decline 'any treaty with the King, having received no warrant for it from the Parliament' – was related by John Richard, who had apparently acted as Hertford's man-of-business

---

[76] BL, Add. MS 18981 (Prince Rupert Correspondence), fos. 99r–102r (Lord Digby to Prince Rupert, 25 March 1644); *Memoirs of Prince Rupert*, Warburton, II, 437–9 (Charles I to Prince Rupert, 14 June 1644); Sir Philip Warwick, *Memoires of the Reigne of King Charles I* (1701), pp. 274–5, 279; W. A. Day, ed., *The Pythouse Papers* (1879), pp. 62, 68; Clarendon, *History*, III, 345–6 (Book VIII, §30).
[77] *LJ*, VI, 577.
[78] See David L. Smith, '"The more posed and wise advice": the fourth Earl of Dorset and the English Civil Wars', *HJ*, 34 (1991), 821–2.
[79] *LJ*, VI, 592. See also Smith, '"The more posed and wise advice"', 821–2; and MP, 10 June 1644 (petition of Lord Chandos).
[80] The King's letter, dated 6 August 1644, is printed in Rushworth, V, 691–2; and in *LJ*, VI, 670. Cf. Adamson, 'Baronial context', 111–12.
[81] PRO, SP 16/502/46i (Charles I to Henrietta Maria, 25 June 1644).
[82] BL, Add. MS 27402 (miscellaneous historical papers), fo. 80r; Dr Williams's Library, London, MS 24.50 (diary of Thomas Juxon), fo. 23r; Bodl. Lib., MS Firth c. 7 (Prince Rupert Papers), fo. 139r (Ri[chard] Cave to Prince Rupert, 13 August 1644). I owe this last reference to Ian Gentles. Essex possessed portraits of both Hertford and Lord Beauchamp: Huntington Library, Hastings MS, Inventories, Box I, folder 20 (inventory of goods in possession of Essex's executors, 24 November 1646).

in London during the 1630s.[83] This approach was followed by further letters to Essex from Prince Maurice and others on 8 August,[84] and from the commanders of Charles's army the following day.[85] But always Essex's response was the same: that 'having no power from the Parliament (who have employed me) to treat, [I] cannot give way to it, without breach of trust'.[86]

Clearly there were limits to how far informal talks could hope to achieve a settlement, and moderates on both sides now recognised that their best chance lay in another set-piece treaty. By the autumn of 1644, many Royalists were increasingly hostile to Prince Rupert and attacked him as 'the only cause of war in this kingdom'.[87] In November the Houses took the initiative and despatched peace commissioners, including Holles and Whitelocke, to Oxford bearing propositions.[88] These were significantly tougher than those presented early in 1643, and reflected the Scottish influence on the Committee of Both Kingdoms.[89] The principal clauses required the King to 'swear and sign the late Solemn League and Covenant' (§2); to pass a bill 'for the utter abolishing and taking away of all Archbishops, Bishops' and other clerical offices stipulated by the Treaty of Edinburgh in November 1643 (§3); to accept the 'reformation of religion' as defined by the Westminster Assembly, and 'to endeavour the nearest conjunction and uniformity in matters of religion' between England and Scotland 'according to the Covenant' (§5); to prevent the saying of the Catholic Mass at Court and elsewhere (§10); and to assent to a series of named bills abolishing clerical pluralism and absenteeism, the Court of Wards and feudal tenures (§11). In addition, the Irish Cessation of September 1643 was to be declared void (§13); and fifty-eight named Royalists – including Hyde, Culpepper and Strangways – were to be exempted from any pardon (§14[i]). The clauses affecting the militia were equally rigorous. All military officers were to be 'persons of known integrity, and such as both kingdoms may confide in for their faithfulness to religion and peace of the kingdoms' (§17). This was to be ensured by a joint committee of representatives from both England and Scotland (§17[iv]). Finally, a series of civilian officers of state were to 'be nominated by both Houses of

---

[83] BL, Add. MS 27402, fo. 80r; Adamson, 'Baronial context', 112n. I am grateful to John Adamson for advice about the identity of John Richard.

[84] Devon RO, Seymour of Berry Pomeroy MS, 1392 M/L16/1644/54 (Prince Maurice *et al.* to Essex, 8 August 1644).

[85] This letter is printed in Rushworth, V, 692–3; and in *LJ*, VI, 671.   [86] *LJ*, VI, 671.

[87] *Memoirs of Prince Rupert*, Warburton, III, 28 (Prince Rupert to Will Legge, 16 October 1644). See also Bodl. Lib., MS Carte 12, fo. 462r (Arthur Trevor to Ormond, 13 October 1644).

[88] *Diary of Whitelocke*, Spalding, p. 155.

[89] These terms, subsequently discussed at the Treaty of Uxbridge and hence known as the Uxbridge Propositions, are printed in Gardiner, *Documents*, pp. 275–86.

Parliament' (§20). Such were the concessions which Lords and Commons now demanded of the King.

On their arrival at Oxford, the Parliamentarian commissioners received a warm welcome from the Constitutional Royalists. Hyde greeted them in person, while the wounded Lindsey sent a gentleman to see them.[90] Shortly afterwards, Whitelocke and Holles visited Lindsey, who treated them 'with extraordinary respect and courtesy'.[91] The King received the commissioners courteously, and requested a safe conduct for Richmond and Southampton to convey his formal answer to the Houses.[92] The Houses agreed, and on 14 December Richmond and Southampton arrived in London. Three days later, Richmond presented the King's answer to the propositions, which lamented that they 'import[ed] so great an alteration in Government, both in Church and State', but nevertheless asked Parliament to appoint commissioners for a fresh treaty.[93] The Houses agreed to this, but – anxious to prevent further informal contacts – ordered the two peers to return to Oxford immediately.[94]

That Richmond and Southampton had been sent at all was a significant victory for moderate counsels at Oxford. Henrietta Maria set her face firmly against any initiative which might involve acknowledging the Houses at Westminster as a legitimate Parliament;[95] while Sir Edward Walker later denounced the Royalists' 'untimely desire for peace'.[96] Charles nevertheless allowed the treaty to open at Uxbridge on 30 January 1645.[97] It was agreed to spend three days on religion, then three on the militia, followed by three on Ireland. Thereafter, the commissioners would

[90] *Diary of Whitelocke*, Spalding, p. 157.
[91] *Ibid.*, p. 158. Parliament's commissioners had been given no powers to negotiate, and this conversation subsequently led to charges of treachery against Whitelocke and Holles: *LJ*, VII, 416–31; MP, 12 June – 19 July 1645; *Diary of Whitelocke*, Spalding, pp. 168–77. See also BL, Add. MS 32093 (Malet Collection), fos. 218v, 227v–228r; Add. MS 37343 (Whitelocke's Annals), fo. 394r.
[92] *Diary of Whitelocke*, Spalding, pp. 158–60; Bodl. Lib., MS Clarendon 23, fo. 213 (Charles I to the Houses of Parliament, 27 November 1644). Dorset had earlier alerted the commissioners that Charles 'was resolved upon his answer': *CJ*, III, 710. The French ambassador thought that Dorset was also included in the King's request for safe conduct, but there is no evidence to support this: PRO, PRO 31/3/75, fo. 239v. For the King's instructions to Southampton and Richmond, drafted by Hyde, see Bodl. Lib., MS Clarendon 23, fos. 219r–222v.
[93] *LJ*, VII, 82, 92–3, 103; *CJ*, III, 712, 726; MP, 3, 10, 12 December 1644; BL, Add. MS 31116 (diary of Laurence Whitaker), fo. 180r; PRO, SP 21/8 (Committee of Both Kingdoms day book), pp. 27–8.
[94] *CJ*, III, 729–32; *Life of Dugdale*, Hamper, p. 76; Dr Williams's Library, London, MS 24.50, fo. 34r–v.
[95] *Letters of Henrietta Maria*, Green, p. 276 (Henrietta Maria to Charles I, 30 December 1644).
[96] Edward Walker, *Historical Discourses* (1705), p. 149.
[97] Huntington Library, Hastings MS, HA 9705 (Nicholas to Henry Hastings, [?] January 1644/5).

continue to discuss these subjects in rotation until they had talked for a total of twenty days.[98] Uxbridge was much the shortest of the formal treaties, lasting barely three weeks. The Royalist commissioners included many familiar names: Richmond, Southampton, Hertford, Seymour, Hyde and Culpepper.[99] They faced a well nigh impossible task. Charles's inner thoughts are clear from an apostil to Sir Edward Nicholas dated 6 February:

I should thinke, if in your privat discourses (I nowais meane in your publique meetings) with the London Comissioners, you would put them in mynde that they were arrant Rebelles and that their end must be damnation, ruine, and infamy, except they repented, and founde some way to free themselfes from the damnable way they ar in (this Treaty being the aptest) it might doe good; and cheefly, if Hertford or Southampton would doe it, though I belive it will have the owen operation by any of you.[100]

To expect this of two such moderate figures as Hertford and Southampton showed how completely Charles had misunderstood some of his closest advisers. The Constitutional Royalists did not want to cast Parliament's commissioners as 'arrant Rebelles', but to achieve an accommodation with them.

The difficulties attending this became immediately apparent. How were Charles's unshakeable commitment to episcopacy and Parliament's growing attachment to Presbyterianism to be reconciled? Discussion over the abolition of episcopacy quickly reached deadlock, and a desperate bid by Hertford to sidestep the point at issue by claiming that neither episcopacy nor presbytery existed *jure divino* failed to command agreement.[101] A similar impasse occurred over the militia.[102] The Royalist commissioners argued that Parliament's propositions 'import[ed] very great alterations in the main foundation of the frame of government of this kingdom, taking ... the whole military and civil power out of the Crown, without any limitation in time or reparation proposed'.[103] Parliament's commissioners replied that they intended only what was 'necessary at this time for the

[98] Rushworth, V, 807; *LJ*, VII, 163.
[99] PRO, C 231/3 (Crown Office docquet book), p. 142; Rushworth, V, 846; *LJ*, VII, 150–1; Clarendon, *History*, III, 469 (Book VIII, §211). See also Bodl. Lib., MS Dep. c. 160 (Nalson MS), fos. 12r–13r.
[100] *The Diary and Correspondence of John Evelyn*, ed. W. Bray (new edition, ed. H. B. Wheatley, 4 vols., 1906), IV, 149 (Charles I, apostil of 6 February 1644/5 to Nicholas's letter of 5 February 1644/5). Cf. Bodl. Lib., MS Clarendon 24, fo. 28r (Charles I to Nicholas, 5 February 1644/5).
[101] Religion was debated on 31 January and 1 and 3 February. For the papers exchanged, see Rushworth, V, 811–15; *LJ*, VII, 166–8, 170–3, 175–6. For Hertford's intervention, see *Diary of Whitelocke*, Spalding, p. 163.
[102] This was debated on 4, 5 and 6 February: Rushworth, V, 826–30; *LJ*, VII, 180–4; *CJ*, IV, 44.
[103] Rushworth, V, 826; *LJ*, VII, 181.

security of His Majesty's kingdoms',[104] and refused to place a limit on the period during which the militia was controlled by parliamentary nominees.[105] The furthest the King would go was to appoint twenty commissioners, half nominated by himself, half by the Houses, to control the militia for three years.[106] There was no way round the fundamental disagreement expressed in a head-on confrontation between Hyde and Whitelocke: 'Hyde affirmed the power of the Militia to be by Law unquestionably in the King only, Wh[itelocke] denyed this, as reflecting uppon the Parlements propositions, and not cleer by law where that power was.'[107] It was only thanks to Southampton, who moved 'that they might first see how neer they could come to a composure upon the buisnes of the Militia', that any progress at all was made on this issue.[108] Next, the commissioners turned to Ireland.[109] Here disagreement centred on whether the King had the power to make the Cessation with the Irish rebels, and on whether his motive was 'the good and safety of his Protestant subjects there' or 'the advantage of the Popish rebels'.[110] After three days, the two sides remained irreconcilable, and it was time to begin another cycle of debates.

The points at issue did not change during the next round of talks.[111] Charles defined his position in a memorandum to Nicholas on 17 February.[112] On 'Religion and Churche Governement', he would 'not goe one jott further, than what is offered … alreddy'. He likewise refused to compromise further on the militia, and reiterated his demand for 'free nomination of the full halfe' of the militia commissioners. Finally, he authorised Nicholas to promise some Parliamentarian commissioners 'rewards for performed services' – including official 'places' – provided these were not 'taken away from honnest men in possession'. Only Richmond, Southampton, Culpepper and Hyde were to be informed of 'this last'. In an eleventh hour attempt to keep the negotiations alive, the King's

---

[104] Rushworth, V, 826; *LJ*, VII, 182.   [105] Rushworth, V, 826–7; *LJ*, VII, 182.
[106] Rushworth, V, 827–8; *LJ*, VII, 182–3.
[107] *Diary of Whitelocke*, Spalding, p. 164. Cf. Clarendon, *History*, III, 486 (Book VIII, §233).
[108] *Diary of Whitelocke*, Spalding, p. 164. Charles wished that his commissioners had 'used more reservation concerning the militia': *Diary of Evelyn*, Bray, IV, 149–50 (Charles I to Nicholas, 8 February 1644/5).
[109] This was discussed on 7, 8 and 10 February: Rushworth, V, 843–6; *LJ*, VII, 188–9; *CJ*, IV, 47.
[110] Rushworth, V, 844–5; *LJ*, VII, 189.
[111] Following the agreed rota of issues, religion was discussed on 11, 12 and 13 February, the militia on 14, 15 and 17 February, and Ireland on 18, 19 and 20 February. The papers exchanged during these three sequences are found in: (1) Rushworth, V, 815–22; *LJ*, VII, 195–200; (2) Rushworth, V, 830–9; *LJ*, VII, 201–3, 211–15; (3) Rushworth, V, 846–64; *LJ*, VII, 231–8.
[112] *Diary of Evelyn*, Bray, IV, 152 (Charles I to Nicholas, 17 February 1644/5), from which the following quotations are taken.

commissioners suggested on 20 February that Charles would return to London provided that the armies on both sides were disbanded.[113] This was a desperate gamble, for the King was receiving trenchant advice from Henrietta Maria against disbandment or returning to London while the Long Parliament still sat. She warned Charles: 'If you consent to this, you shall be lost; they shall have the whole power of the militia; they have done, and will do whatsoever they will.'[114] On 19 February Charles assured his wife that: 'as for trusting the rebels, either by going to London or disbanding my army before a peace, do no ways fear my hazarding so cheaply or foolishly'.[115] In any case, the Houses rejected this Royalist proposal for disbandment, and the treaty came to an end on 22 February.[116]

The French ambassador Sabran blamed the failure of the Uxbridge talks on the hard-line advice which Charles received from Digby.[117] Certainly their collapse was a grievous blow to the Constitutional Royalists.[118] Richmond and Dorset reportedly thought the situation now seemed 'very dangerous', while Hyde later vowed that he would not 'buy a peace at a deerer pryze then was offred at Uxbridge'.[119] Two weeks after the treaty collapsed, on 5 March, the moderates began to fragment as Hyde and Culpepper accompanied the Prince of Wales on his journey 'towards the west'.[120] Such a move, which had been mooted for some months, was supported by Digby but strongly opposed by Richmond.[121] When the Prince was finally sent into the west with his own Council, Richmond and Southampton expressed a particular wish to remain with the King.[122] The departure of Hyde and Culpepper reduced their influence over the King, and even in the west effective power gradually passed to Goring.[123]

The erosion of moderate counsels at Oxford was soon evident. In April,

[113] Rushworth, V, 920-1; LJ, VII, 238; CJ, IV, 60.
[114] Letters of Henrietta Maria, Green, pp. 282-3 (Henrietta Maria to Charles I, [? February] 1644/5).
[115] Rushworth, V, 892.
[116] Rushworth, V, 922; LJ, VII, 239-40; CJ, IV, 60; Diary of Whitelocke, Spalding, p. 165.
[117] BL, Add. MS 5461 (Sabran despatches), fo. 110r (Sabran to Brienne, 2 March 1644/5).
[118] One newsbook reported that the King's commissioners were 'much discontented': A Perfect Diurnall of some Passages in Parliament, no. 83 (24 February – 3 March 1644[/5]), p. 557 (STC (News), 504.083; BL, TT, E 258/31).
[119] PRO, PRO 31/3/76, fo. 134v; Bodl. Lib., MS Clarendon 28, fo. 70r (Hyde to Nicholas, 1 June 1646). For the desire for peace at Oxford in February 1645, see PRO, SP 21/17 (Committee of Both Kingdoms letter book), pp. 215-16.
[120] Life of Dugdale, Hamper, p. 78; Warwick, Memoires, p. 284; Clarendon, Life, I, 230-1; The Memoirs of Edmund Ludlow, ed. C. H. Firth (2 vols., Oxford, 1894), I, 119.
[121] BL, Add. MS 18981, fo. 170r (Thomas Elyott to Prince Rupert, 7 May 1644).
[122] Clarendon, History, III, 525-6 (Book VIII, §280).
[123] Bodl. Lib., MS Clarendon 24, fos. 168r-169v (Council in the West to Charles I, [June] 1645); Clarendon, History, III, 501-3 (Book VIII, §§253-5); 524-6 (Book VIII, §§279-80); IV, 35-6 (Book IX, §30); Walker, Historical Discourses, p. 125; Bulstrode, Memoirs, pp. 135-7, 147-8.

Arthur Trevor reported that the King's advisers were 'at great faction', with 'Hertford and all the rest against Lords Digby and Cottington' over 'some interruption given to the renuing of the Treaty'.[124] By this time, Prince Rupert was increasingly committed to negotiations and as a result drew closer to Hertford, Richmond and Culpepper.[125] Contrary to Rupert's advice, but with the full support of Digby, Cottington and Ashburnham, Charles embarked on further military campaigns which culminated in the defeat at Naseby.[126] Yet even after this the King resisted the idea of further concessions. On 28 July, Rupert wrote to Richmond – who spent much of this summer journeying between Oxford and the King's camp[127] – urging him to persuade Charles that there was 'now no way left to preserve his posterity, kingdom, and nobility, but by treaty'.[128] Richmond showed the letter to Charles, who replied directly to Rupert.[129] He declared that he had no other quarrel 'but the defence of my religion, crown and friends'. While convinced 'as a mere soldier and statesman' that 'there is no probability but of my ruin', he believed 'as a Christian' that 'God will not suffer rebels to prosper, or this cause to be overthrown'. He was 'resolved' not to 'give over this quarrel … whatever it cost me', and insisted that he would 'not go less than what was offered in my name at Uxbridge'. It is clear that he had already embraced the role of martyr.

Charles's refusal to compromise with the Houses was supported by two figures in particular: the Queen and Lord Digby. Henrietta Maria continued to show 'little inclination … for peace'.[130] She preferred instead to seek aid from French Catholics and thus confirmed the worst fears of both Parliament and the Scots.[131] In the wake of Naseby, Digby likewise moved into what Ann Sumner has called his 'truly "Ultra-Royalist" phase'.[132] Even if he was not the extremist portrayed in Parliamentarian propaganda before 1645, he was nevertheless one of Charles's more hard-line

---

[124] Bodl. Lib., MS Carte 14, fo. 372v (Arthur Trevor to Ormond, 9 April 1645).

[125] *Ibid.*; *Memoirs of Prince Rupert*, Warburton, III, 132 (Charles I to Prince Rupert, 3 July 1645).

[126] Bodl. Lib., MS Carte 14, fos. 372v, 494v (Arthur Trevor to Ormond, 8 May 1645); Walker, *Historical Discourses*, p. 129.

[127] *Life of Dugdale*, Hamper, pp. 80–2; Walker, *Historical Discourses*, p. 136.

[128] *Memoirs of Prince Rupert*, Warburton, III, 149 (Prince Rupert to Richmond, 28 July 1645). See also *ibid.*, 151 (Prince Rupert to Will Legge, 25 July 1645); BL, Add. MS 18982 (Prince Rupert Correspondence), fo. 79r (Richmond to Prince Rupert, 3 August 1645); and Clarendon, *History*, IV, 74 (Book IX, §69).

[129] This letter is printed in Clarendon, *History*, IV, 74–5 (Book IX, §70), from which the following quotations are taken.

[130] 'The diplomatic correspondence of Jean de Montereul', ed. J. G. Fotheringham, *Publ. Scottish Record Society*, 29–30 (1898–9), I, 62, 66–9.

[131] *Letters of Henrietta Maria*, Green, p. 308; Gardiner, *Civil War*, III, 12–15.

[132] A. Sumner, 'The political career of Lord George Digby until the end of the first Civil War' (PhD thesis, University of Cambridge, 1985), p. 186. See also *ibid.*, pp. 278, 383, 393.

counsellors. We have already seen several occasions where he obstructed the search for a negotiated settlement; and his reaction after Naseby highlighted the contrast between his instincts and those of the Constitutional Royalists. In late August, he numbered himself among 'those few' who 'may be thought by our councells to fortifie the King in firmnesse to his principalls', and feared that other advisers including Rupert, Ormond and possibly Culpepper would help to impose 'such conditions as the rebells will give him'.[133] Such a view clearly distinguished Digby from the moderates, whose response to the King's continued intransigence during the autumn of 1645 was to seek peace by more drastic means.

Charles's tendency to perceive disloyalty among even his most faithful supporters placed them in a peculiarly difficult position. His treatment of Dorset – who confessed to feeling 'obliged' to Charles 'in honor, duty, piety and gratitude'[134] – perfectly illustrates this trait. When Charles returned to Oxford in November, Dorset 'expressed in a speech full of affection for the King the joy they ought all to feel on his arrival'; but the King 'replied to him coldly that he had the voice of Jacob, but that his hands were those of Esau'.[135] Shortly afterwards, Dorset bemoaned to Prince Rupert 'the disasterous condition' in which Charles's 'evill starrs have placed him'.[136] In early December the French Resident Montereul learned from the Countess of Devonshire that Dorset, Southampton, Hertford and Lindsey 'had pointed out to the King, in the first instance individually, and afterwards in council, the miserable state to which they were reduced by the continuance of the war, and the small prospect there was that they would be able to get out of it otherwise than by treating'.[137] Charles responded that he 'would place his crown on his head, and preserve it with his sword, if the swords of his friends failed him'. These peers therefore took the remarkable step of bypassing the King and negotiating directly with the Houses. They volunteered 'without the King's consent ... to offer to give him up to the Parliament, provided they may in so doing receive a general pardon, and be allowed to retain their possessions'. This expedient was presented 'under a pretext of honesty, by saying they are

---

[133] *The Lord George Digby's Cabinet and Dr Goff's Negotiations* (1646), p. 54 (Wing, B 4763; BL, TT, E 329/15). These three names are omitted in the printed version, but may be found in the original manuscript: PRO, SP 16/510/74 (Digby to Jermyn, 27 August 1645). Cf. Gardiner, *Civil War*, II, 303–4.

[134] CKS, Uncatalogued Cranfield Papers, Dorset to the Countess of Middlesex, [?] June–July 1645. This letter is quoted and discussed more fully in Smith, '"The more posed and wise advice"', 823; and below, pp. 210–11.

[135] 'Correspondence of Montereul', Fotheringham, I, 60.

[136] BL, Add. MS 18982, fo. 98r (Dorset to Prince Rupert, 25 November 1645).

[137] 'Correspondence of Montereul', ed. Fotheringham, I, 74.

taking care of the King's personal safety, and of his honour, while they are betraying him; because they pretend it is preferable for him to have been obliged by his friends to surrender to his enemies, than to have done so voluntarily'.[138] Charles learnt of the peers' initiative from his spy Sir William Vavasour, and tried to preempt it by writing to Parliament offering a fresh treaty.[139] But the Houses rejected this on the grounds that 'former treaties have been made use of by Your Majesty for other ends under the pretence of peace'.[140] A further exchange, in which the Houses insisted that the King must first give 'satisfaction and security' to both kingdoms before visiting London, likewise came to nothing.[141] His talks with Parliament at an end, Charles launched the negotiations with the Scots which led to his surrender at Newark in May 1646.[142] Meanwhile, a final attempt in late April by Southampton, Hertford, Richmond and Lindsey to reach agreement with the Parliamentarian army at Woodstock went seriously wrong,[143] and culminated in the last two 'cast[ing] themselves upon the mercy of the Parliament', only to be briefly imprisoned in Warwick Castle.[144] Back in Oxford, the King's remaining councillors nominated commissioners 'to treate for the delivery of Oxford' on 15 May.[145] The articles of capitulation were signed by, among others, Hertford, Dorset, Southampton and Seymour on 20 June, and the city formally surrendered four days later.[146] Thus ended the first Civil War.

---

138 *Ibid.*
139 *LJ*, VIII, 31; PRO, SP 16/511/87 (Charles I to the Speaker of the House of Lords, 5 December 1645); *Diary of Evelyn*, Bray, IV, 187–8.
140 *LJ*, VIII, 36. See also MP, 10 December 1645, fos. 46r–48v (drafts of Parliament's answer to Charles I); Bodl. Lib., MS Clarendon 26, fo. 80r (John Ashburnham to Culpepper, 13 December 1645).
141 *LJ*, VIII, 72, 99–100, 103–4, 108–9, 125–6, 132–3 (quotation at 99).
142 Gardiner, *Civil War*, III, 96–103.
143 Bodl. Lib., MS Clarendon 27, fo. 151r–v (instructions to Lindsey *et al.*, 25 April 1646); BL, Microfilm M 636/7 (Claydon House, Verney MS), unfol. (Sir Nicholas Crispe to Sir Ralph Verney, [? 7] May 1646); *A Narrative by John Ashburnham of his attendance on King Charles the first* (2 vols., 1830), II, 69–70; Bulstrode Whitelocke, *Memorials of the English Affairs from the beginning of the reign of Charles the first* (4 vols., Oxford, 1853), II, 12; *Life of Dugdale*, Hamper, pp. 85–6.
144 Whitelocke, *Memorials*, II, 13; MP, 7, 25 May 1646; *LJ*, VIII, 305, 335; HMC, *Ancaster Manuscripts* (1907), p. 413; *CSPV*, 27 (1643–7), 259; Dr Williams's Library, London, MS 24.50, fos. 74v–75v.
145 *Life of Dugdale*, Hamper, p. 87. See also Buckminster Park Estate Office, Lincolnshire, Tollemache MS 3750 (letters, orders and gifts of Charles I), fo. 10v (Charles I to the Governor of Oxford, 18 May 1646). I am most grateful to Sir Lyonel Tollemache for permission to consult his family muniments.
146 For the Oxford articles of surrender, see PRO, SP 16/514/27; Whitelocke, *Memorials*, II, 34–42; *A Full and True Relation of the Several Actions and Particulars of what was taken and done in Oxford* (1646), Wing, F 2330; BL, TT, E 342/9.

III

From this point, an analysis of Constitutional Royalism is greatly complicated by the diaspora of its principal exponents. Never again did they all
converge in the promotion and management of peace negotiations as they
did during the first Civil War. However similar their outlooks remained,
their physical and political paths were now diverging. Hyde and Culpepper
moved with the Prince of Wales to Jersey in mid-April 1646.[147] On 26 June,
the Prince set sail for France accompanied by Culpepper, Jermyn, Ashburnham and others.[148] Despite their contrasting attitudes hitherto, these
three increasingly acted as political allies, and their letters of advice to
Charles I in 1646–7 form one important strand of moderate Royalist
counsel. Hyde, by contrast, remained in Jersey, an increasingly isolated
figure,[149] absorbed in the writing of his *History*, in touch with like-minded
people in both England and France, but no longer politically active.[150] In
England, the circle of Constitutional Royalist peers comprising Richmond,
Southampton, Lindsey, Hertford, Seymour and Dorset remained close knit
and intervened at several key moments in 1647–9 to try to achieve a settlement. However, they kept in the shadows during much of 1646 and 1647,
and it fell to Culpepper, Jermyn and Ashburnham to advise Charles
regarding the Newcastle Propositions, which the Houses presented to him
on 13 July 1646, and which he only finally rejected in September 1647.[151]

The Newcastle Propositions were much the most stringent that Parliament had so far offered. The religious clauses required Charles to swear the
Solemn League and Covenant (§2); accept the 'reformation of religion,
according to the Covenant' (§5); and 'to endeavour the nearest conjunction
and uniformity in matters of religion' between England and Scotland (§6).
Parliament required that the militia be controlled for twenty years (equivalent to Charles's presumed lifespan) by 'such as shall act by the authority
or approbation of the said Lords and Commons' (§13). During the same
period, the Houses were to have absolute control over all armed forces,
and to suppress any forces raised against them either at home or abroad

---

[147] *Journal de Jean Chevalier*, ed. J. A. Messervy (9 fascicles, Jersey, 1906–14), p. 303;
Clarendon, *History*, IV, 169 (Book X, §5).
[148] *Journal de Chevalier*, Messervy, pp. 309–10; Clarendon, *History*, IV, 181–4 (Book X,
§§19–22).
[149] The King observed during the summer of 1647 that Hyde 'had but very few compaig-
nons': BL, Add. MS 35029 (letters of Charles I), fo. 2r (Charles I to Hyde, 19 August
1647).
[150] Clarendon, *Life*, I, 239–43. For his decision to begin writing the *History*, see Bodl. Lib.,
MS Clarendon 28, fos. 286r–289v (Hyde to Nicholas, 15 November 1646).
[151] The Newcastle Propositions are printed in Gardiner, *Documents*, pp. 290–306. For
Charles's three successive answers to them, see *ibid.*, pp. 306–8 (1 August 1646), 308–9
(20 December 1646), 311–16 (12 May 1647). For his final rejection, see *LJ*, IX, 434–5, 442.

(§13[i-iii]). Even after twenty years, the Houses were to organise new arrangements for military authority which would be implemented if necessary against the King's will (§13[iii]). There was to be a general pardon, but with a total of eleven qualifying clauses, the first of which exempted fifty-eight named Royalists, including Hyde, Culpepper and Ashburnham. Provision was also made for the sale of one-third of the lands of bishops and clergy (§16). The offices of state to be nominated by both Houses now included Culpepper's office of Master of the Rolls (§17). Finally, all grants and commissions passed under the King's Great Seal since 22 May 1642 were declared 'invalid' (§19).

Royalist reactions to these propositions varied. Culpepper, Jermyn and Ashburnham urged the King to use them as the basis for negotiations. They begged him 'not to consent to destroy your selfe and posterity',[152] and if necessary to compromise on Church government as the price of Scottish support:

The question in short is whether you will chuse to be a King of Presbitery or no King, ... We well know that if you part with the Militia and place [it] in the Parliament as is desryed you will thereby consent to change Monarchy into Aristocracy, nether, if you give satisfaction in the Church Governement, will you [be] much presed in the Militia, or your Party, as we are advysed from good hands at London.[153]

They were supported by Bishop Juxon of London and Dorset's former chaplain Brian Duppa, now Bishop of Salisbury, who assured the King that such concessions would impugn neither his coronation oath nor his conscience.[154] But Charles was intransigent, regarding the primary sticking-points as the militia and above all religion. In a series of exchanges with the Scottish divine Alexander Henderson between 29 May and 16 July 1646, Charles vigorously defended the English Reformation on the grounds that 'it was done ... legally and orderly', and 'retained nothing but according as it was deduced from the Apostles to be the constant and universall custome of the Primitive Church'. His conscience, by 'directing [him] to maintaine the lawes of the land', sustained his 'constant maintenance of episcopacy in England'. He regarded 'all popular Reformation' as 'little better than Rebellions', and this perceived link between Presbyterianism

---

[152] Bodl. Lib., MS Clarendon 91, fo. 26r (Culpepper, Jermyn and Ashburnham to Charles I, 27 July 1646).
[153] *Ibid.*, fo. 36r (Culpepper and Jermyn to Charles I, 18 September 1646). See also *ibid.*, fo. 45r (Culpepper and Jermyn to Charles I, 12 October 1646).
[154] *Ibid.*, fo. 43r (Juxon and Duppa to Charles I, 14 October 1646). For Duppa as Dorset's chaplain, see David L. Smith, 'Catholic, Anglican or Puritan? Edward Sackville, fourth Earl of Dorset and the ambiguities of religion in early Stuart England', *TRHS*, 6th series, 2 (1992), 114–15.

and sedition was to dog talks over the Newcastle Propositions.[155] As Charles put it to Culpepper, Jermyn and Ashburnham on 22 July:

It is not the change of Church Governement which is cheefly aymed at (though that were too much) but it is by that pretext to take away the dependancy of the Church from the Crowne, which, lett me tell you, I hould to be of equall consequence to that of the Militia, for people ar governed by Pulpits more then the sword, in tymes of peace ... I will lesse yeald to this then the Militia, my conscience being irreconciliably ingaged against it.[156]

He fastened on this point again and again through the summer and autumn of 1646: 'This alteration of Governement ... I belive to be as distructive to the Regall Power as the quitting of the Militia';[157] 'the giving such way to Presbiteriall Gover[nme]nt as will content the Scots is the absolut distruction of monarchy';[158] 'show me any president where ever Presbiteriall Governement and Regall was together without perpetuall rebellions ... the ground of theire doctrine is anty-monarchicall'.[159] Though willing to negotiate with the Houses, Charles declared that he would 'never condescend unto what is absolutely destructive to that just power which, by the laws of God and the land, he is born unto'.[160]

In making this stand, Charles was firmly supported by Henrietta Maria. Her advice all along was 'not to agree to the' Newcastle Propositions, on the grounds that if the King were 'resolved and constant' they could 'again be masters'.[161] She encouraged Charles to resist the more moderate counsels of Culpepper, Jermyn and Ashburnham.[162] Equally, it needs stressing that Hyde also found himself increasingly out of sympathy with the concessions advocated by these three. He told Nicholas on 1 June that he would never accept a peace 'at a deerer pryze then was offred at Uxbridge', as we have already noted, and thought it 'ill logic to infer, that because you

---

155 *The Papers which passed at Newcastle betwixt His Sacred Majestie and Mr Al[exander] Henderson: concerning the change of Church-Government* (1649), pp. 3–4, 38 (Wing, C 2535; BL, TT, E 1243/3). These exchanges were not published until 1649, and it is therefore not beyond doubt that they were touched up after the Regicide. However, I have found no evidence of this, and the balance of probability would seem to be that they are an authentic record of Charles's beliefs in the summer of 1646.
156 Bodl. Lib., MS Clarendon 91, fo. 23v (Charles I to Culpepper, Jermyn and Ashburnham, 22 July 1646).
157 Bodl. Lib., MS Clarendon 97, fo. 37v (Charles I to Culpepper, Jermyn and Ashburnham, 12 August 1646).
158 *Ibid.*, fo. 41r (Charles I to Culpepper, Jermyn and Ashburnham, 31 August 1646).
159 Bodl. Lib., MS Clarendon 91, fo. 33r (Charles I to Culpepper, Jermyn and Ashburnham, 7 September 1646). See also *Charles I in 1646: Letters of King Charles the first to Queen Henrietta Maria*, ed. J. Bruce (Camden Society, 1st series, 63, 1856), 70–1 (Charles I to Henrietta Maria, 17 October 1646).
160 Gardiner, *Documents*, p. 307.
161 *Letters of Henrietta Maria*, Green, p. 327 (Henrietta Maria to Charles I, 9/19 October 1646).
162 *Charles I in 1646*, Bruce, 94–5 (Henrietta Maria to Charles I, 20/30 November 1646).

cannot have it cheaper, therefore you must give whatsoever is asked'.[163] On 14 August he wrote bitterly that 'the imaginacon that it is possible for the kinge to submitt to those vyle proposicons is the next treason to the making [of] them'.[164] Again, on 12 December, he declared: 'episcopacy . . . is as much fenced and secured by the lawes as monarchy it selfe, and an entire part of the frame and constitucon of the kingdome: and when they have changed it (which I hope they will never be able to doe) I will not looke to see good dayes in England'.[165] Writing to Sir John Berkeley a fortnight later, Hyde opposed those 'who with great industry and activity shall perswade the King to consent to what will (under the spetious title of Peace) robb him of that peace which cannot otherwise bee taken from him', and argued that 'resolucon will sooner restore him to what hee hath lost then the signing the Proposicons will doe'.[166] Hyde expressed these feelings compellingly in a letter to Culpepper on 8 January 1647, which indicated just how far their political paths had diverged:

In Gods name let them have all circumstantiall temporary concessions, but let not the landmarkes bee removed, nor pillars upon which the fabrique relyes bee taken away; let him like a good pilot throwe over his goods and his merchandize, his officers and his honours, to save the ship, but if hee throwes over too his mariners and his passengers that the ship may bee the lighter, hee may bee in noe lesse danger after the tempest then hee was before.[167]

While there is no evidence that Culpepper and Hyde differed fundamentally in their ultimate goals, they clearly disagreed deeply about the most appropriate means to attain those goals, and above all over how far Charles should accept the Newcastle Propositions.

Religion – and more specifically ecclesiology – formed the core of this disagreement. Hyde refused to contemplate any structural alteration of the Church, and abhorred the idea that episcopal lands should be sold. Martin Dzelzainis has recently shown how this strong reaction against the Newcastle Propositions provides the ideological context for Hyde's *Of Sacrilege*, completed in 1648.[168] The point was not lost on Charles I, who had noted after the Treaty of Uxbridge Hyde's 'affection to the Church'.[169] By contrast, the King 'never . . . much esteemed' Culpepper 'in religion',[170] and even told Sir William Davenant that he thought 'Culpeper had no

---

[163] Bodl. Lib., MS Clarendon 28, fo. 70r (Hyde to Nicholas, 1 June 1646).
[164] Christ Church Muniment Room, Oxford, Evelyn Collection, Clarendon and Browne Letters, 1646–60, fo. 2r (Hyde to Sir Richard Browne, 14 August 1646).
[165] Bodl. Lib., MS Clarendon 29, fo. 5r (Hyde to Nicholas, 12 December 1646).
[166] *Ibid.*, fo. 30r (Hyde to Sir John Berkeley, 26 December 1646).
[167] *Ibid.*, fo. 55v (Hyde to Culpepper, 8 January 1646/7).
[168] Martin Dzelzainis, '"Undoubted Realities": Clarendon on sacrilege', *HJ*, 33 (1990), 515–40. *Of Sacrilege* is analysed more fully below, p. 151.
[169] Clarendon, *Life*, I, 213.
[170] *Charles I in 1646*, Bruce, 30 (Charles I to Henrietta Maria, 30 March 1646).

religion'.[171] The religious attitudes of these allies of 1642 had diverged significantly by the mid-1640s, indicating a gradual fragmentation within the Constitutional Royalist camp.

If Hyde was closer to the King's religious position than Culpepper, he was also more frequently in touch with the Constitutional Royalist peers back in England. As early as June 1646 we find him asking Nicholas to 'remember my service to my L[or]d Southampton'.[172] In mid-November he enquired again 'what my L[or]d South[amp]ton ... meanes to doe', and asked 'what doe my L[or]d Marquesse [of Hertford], Seymour, Dorsett, Chichester'.[173] The same day he wrote to Cottington wondering 'what intends my L[or]d Seymour', and 'will my L[or]d South[amp]ton trust himselfe betweene the feares and iealousyes of the Presbyterians and Independ[en]ts?'[174] Six weeks later he asked after 'my good Lord of Lindsey'.[175] These enquiries were far more than pleasantries, and reflected genuine ties with the Constitutional Royalist peers. Early in April 1647, when Hyde composed his 'will and last profession', he wrote letters to Richmond and Southampton to be opened in the event of his death, begging them to look after his 'poore wife and children'.[176] He also assured his wife that 'Lord Seymour will be ready to doe thee good offices.'[177] It was this circle to whom Hyde entrusted his family;[178] and it was these peers who, during the summer and autumn of 1647, attempted to bring Charles I to a settlement.

The identity of the authors and promoters of the Heads of the Proposals has long been the subject of vigorous debate. Historians have often argued that the terms were drafted within the Army Council and precisely reflected the ideals of men such as Cromwell and Ireton. Furious at the way the dominant Presbyterian faction within Parliament had treated the army,

[171] Clarendon, History, IV, 206 (Book X, §57).
[172] Bodl. Lib., MS Clarendon 28, fo. 70r (Hyde to Nicholas, 1 June 1646).
[173] Ibid., fo. 289r (Hyde to Nicholas, 15 November 1646). 'Chichester' was Francis Leigh, Lord Dunsmore (d. 1653), who was created a Privy Councillor in August 1641 and Earl of Chichester in June 1644. A Royalist commissioner at the Treaty of Uxbridge, he was also personally associated with some leading Constitutional Royalists: he was South-ampton's father-in-law and Hyde counted him among his 'good freinds'. See Bodl. Lib., MS Clarendon 29, fo. 80r–v (Hyde to Cottington, 28 January 1646/7); Clarendon, History, II, 533 (Book VI, §391); III, 469–70 (Book VIII, §§211, 213); and G.E. C[okayne], The Complete Peerage (new edition, ed. Vicary Gibbs, H. A. Doubleday, Duncan Warrand, Lord Howard de Walden, Geoffrey H. White and R. S. Lea, 14 vols., 1910–59), III, 193–4.
[174] Bodl. Lib., MS Clarendon 28, fo. 290v (Hyde to Cottington, 15 November 1646).
[175] Bodl. Lib., MS Clarendon 29, fo. 40r (Hyde to Nicholas, 1 January 1646/7).
[176] Ibid., fos. 172r (Hyde to Richmond, 4 April 1647), 174r (Hyde to Southampton, 3 April 1647). For Hyde's will, see ibid., fos. 180r–182r.
[177] Ibid., fo. 176r (Hyde to Lady Hyde, 3 April 1647).
[178] It is entirely consistent with these friendships that Hyde possessed portraits of Richmond, Lindsey and Dorset: Bodl. Lib., MS Clarendon 92, fo. 253r–v (list of pictures repaired for Clarendon).

senior officers attempted to reach their own settlement with the King. Some of these officers were themselves MPs, and they drew further support from among leading Independents at Westminster. Against this, it has been argued that the contents of the *Heads* were not merely supported but decisively shaped by this constituency in both Houses. The army acted in tandem with a bicameral faction in which peers such as Saye, Wharton and Northumberland exercised a crucial influence. Members of the nobility co-ordinated the formulation of the *Heads*, the negotiations with Charles, and the subsequent attempt to enact the main clauses in legislation.

The evidence relating to these issues is extremely complex and ambiguous. Some aspects of the origins and promotion of the *Heads* will probably always remain shrouded in mystery. But whereas a variety of contemporary evidence sustains the first reading, the second, more elaborate interpretation has yet to be satisfactorily demonstrated. In particular, the surviving sources do not prove beyond doubt that the Saye–Northumberland group oversaw the drafting of the first recension of the *Heads*; or that they co-ordinated meetings between officers and civilians immediately before the Army Council adopted a later recension; or that they masterminded the presentation of the terms to Charles.[179] Now this matters for our present discussion because the King is likely to have known where real responsibility for the proposals lay, and that in turn would have affected his reaction to them. Certainly he and his moderate advisers had no doubt that they were dealing directly with the army. Sir John Berkeley, who carried messages between the King and the army leaders, recorded that on about 25 July 1647 he 'procured His Majesty a sight of the Army's proposals' and hoped for a time when 'His Majesty and the Army were accorded'.[180] Similarly, John Ashburnham recalled that 'Cromwell and Ireton did expect His Majestie's consent to their proposalls'.[181] Hyde wrote to Sir John Berkeley: 'I have little hope of good by the conclusyons of the two Houses ... but from the Army my hopes are much greater.'[182] The King himself referred to

---

[179] Contrasting accounts of the genesis of the *Heads* may be found in Gardiner, *Civil War*, III, 330–41; C. H. Firth, *The House of Lords during the Civil War* (1910), pp. 172–9; Austin Woolrych, *Soldiers and Statesmen* (Oxford, 1987), pp. 152–3, 168–89; and Ian Gentles, *The New Model Army in England, Ireland and Scotland, 1645–1653* (Oxford, 1992), pp. 181–4. For the recent controversy, see: J. S. A. Adamson, 'The English nobility and the projected settlement of 1647', *HJ*, 30 (1987), 567–602; Mark A. Kishlansky, 'Saye what?', *HJ*, 33 (1990), 917–37; J. S. A. Adamson, 'Politics and the nobility in Civil-War England', *HJ*, 34 (1991), 231–55; Mark A. Kishlansky, 'Saye no more', *JBS*, 30 (1991), 399–448. See also Jonathan L. Dean, 'Henry Ireton, the Mosaic law, and morality in English civil politics from April 1646 to May 1649' (MLitt thesis, University of Cambridge, 1991), pp. 95–112.
[180] *Narrative by Ashburnham*, II, cl–clii.
[181] *Ibid.*, 91. Cf. Kishlansky, 'Saye no more', 432.
[182] Bodl. Lib., MS Clarendon 30/1, fo. 119r (Hyde to Sir John Berkeley, 6 October 1647).

the *Heads* as 'the proposals of the army';[183] and it was with the army's consent that a familiar cluster of Constitutional Royalist peers vainly urged Charles to use them as the basis for a settlement.

For over a year these peers had apparently had little direct contact with the King.[184] But in June 1647, following Charles's seizure from Holdenby House, the army permitted Richmond and Lindsey to attend him.[185] The King claimed that this was 'necessary for our service',[186] and the army's permission ran clean contrary to an order by the Commons.[187] Early the following October, the army again acquiesced when Charles summoned Richmond, Southampton, Dorset, Hertford, Ormond and Seymour to Hampton Court to 'advise, and consult withall as his privy councells'.[188] It was rumoured that 'they came to perswade or meditate with His Majesty to passe the Propositions [the *Heads of the Proposals*]' or to 'treat as commissioners on His Majesties behalfe with the commissioners of Parliament upon the Propositions and setling of peace if it should be accepted of'.[189] The peers were admitted on Thursday 7 October,[190] but departed on Saturday 9 October for reasons which are still not entirely clear. One Royalist agent picked up a report that 'the Agitators ... had an intent to sende for them back, to prevent which they came away of theire owne accord'; and another that 'the Propositions will be shortly with the King, and that His Ma[jes]tie being resolved to refuse them, hath sent them [the peers] away, least being with him, it might be thought to be done with theire Councell, and so might win them into the odium of the Parliament'.[191] The newsbooks, however, present contrasting stories. According to *Perfect Occurrences*, the peers never intended 'to stay above two or three

[183] *LJ*, X, 434–5.
[184] There was, however, some indirect communication, especially between Charles and Richmond: see Bodl. Lib., MS Clarendon 91, fo. 54r (Charles I to William Murray, 15 October 1646).
[185] Bodl. Lib., MS Clarendon 29, fos. 249, 256, 264r–265v (letters of intelligence, 28 June, 1, 8 July 1647); Whitelocke, *Memorials*, II, 175. See also W. C. Trevelyan and C. E. Trevelyan, ed., *Trevelyan Papers*, part III (Camden Society, 1st series, 105, 1872), 259. For Richmond's departure from the King in July, see Bodl. Lib., MS Clarendon 30/1, fo. 4r (letter of intelligence, 12 July 1647).
[186] Worcester College, Oxford, Clarke MS XLI (letters and papers, 1646–7), fo. 84v (Charles I to Fairfax, 17 June 1647).
[187] *CJ*, V, 226; Whitelocke, *Memorials*, II, 168.
[188] *A Perfect Diurnall of some Passages in Parliament*, no. 219 (4–11 October 1647), p. 1764 (*STC (News)*, 504.219; BL, TT, E 518/43). For the King's letter summoning Ormond, with whom he wished 'to speake ... concerning matters of speciall and great importance', see Bodl. Lib., MS Carte 21, fo. 478r (Charles I to Ormond, 2 October 1647).
[189] *A Perfect Diurnall*, no. 219, p. 1764.
[190] Bodl. Lib., MS Clarendon 30/1, fo. 124r–v (letter of intelligence, 7 October 1647).
[191] *Ibid.*, fo. 134v (letter of intelligence, 11 October 1647). That Charles wished them to depart is also corroborated by an Italian newsletter, cited in Gardiner, *Civil War*, III, 372–3, n. 5.

dayes';[192] while *A Perfect Diurnall* reported that because there was 'no satisfaction as yet given on His Majesty's behalfe to the Parliament or the army', the peers' presence 'was declared against by the army'.[193] A possible reconstruction, which reconciles these conflicting accounts, might perhaps run thus: the army officers permitted the peers to attend Charles believing they would encourage him to accept the *Heads*; but when he proved adamant the initiative fell apart, and eventually neither the army officers nor the King wished the peers to remain at Hampton Court. At any rate, the common denominators of the various versions are that these peers wished to secure Charles's consent to the *Heads*, and that Charles stubbornly refused to grant it.

Why should they have thought the *Heads* a viable basis for a settlement? The answer is almost certainly that these terms were much the most favourable ever presented to Charles I, by either the Houses or the army.[194] According to Sir Arthur Hopton, they contained 'better then ordinary good tearmes'.[195] The final recension of the *Heads* – approved by the Army Council on 1 August[196] – stood in marked contrast to all other propositions devised during the 1640s. Instead of transferring power from the Crown to the two Houses, they sought to clip Parliament's wings by repealing the Triennial Act (§I[1]), establishing biennial Parliaments sitting for between 120 and 240 days (§I[2]), and redistributing seats 'according to some rule of equality or proportion' so as to make 'the House of Commons ... an equal representative of the whole' (§I[5]). 'The power of the militia by sea and land' was to be transferred to the Houses 'during the space of ten years' (rather than twenty), and those lately in arms against Parliament were to be disabled from public office for five years (rather than for life) (§II). The Houses would control 'the great offices for ten years'; thereafter, they were 'to nominate three, and the King out of that number to appoint one for the succession upon any vacancy' (§IV). The abolition of the Court of Wards was confirmed 'provided His Majesty's revenue be not damnified therein' (§IX). It was, however, the religious clauses which differed most dramatically from those offered by Parliament. 'Bishops and all other Ecclesiastical Officers' were to be preserved, although shorn of 'all coercive power, authority, and jurisdiction' (§XI). Similarly, the use of the Prayer

---

[192] *Perfect Occurrences of Every Daie Iournall in Parliament*, no. 41 (8–15 October 1647), sig. R1 (*STC (News)*, 465.5041; BL, TT, E 518/44).
[193] *A Perfect Diurnall*, no. 219, p. 1764. This version is also found in Whitelocke, *Memorials*, II, 219.
[194] Cf. Gentles, *New Model Army*, p. 182.
[195] Christ Church Muniment Room, Oxford, Evelyn Collection, Browne Letters, Box D–L, unfol. (Sir Arthur Hopton to Sir Richard Browne, 11 November 1647).
[196] The text is printed in Gardiner, *Documents*, pp. 316–26. For an analysis of how this final recension differed from earlier ones, see J. S. A. Adamson, 'The peerage in politics, 1645–9' (PhD thesis, University of Cambridge, 1986), appendix C, pp. 298–9.

Book was permitted, but on an entirely voluntary basis (§XII). No Presbyterian structures were to be created, and 'the taking of the Covenant' was not to be 'enforced upon any' (§XIII). If all these demands were conceded, then the King and his family were to 'be restored to a condition of safety, honour and freedom ... without diminution to their personal rights, or further limitation to the exercise of the regal power' (§XIV). In other words, the royal veto would remain intact. The proposed treatment of Charles's followers was also incomparably more generous than that envisaged by the Houses. No more than five Royalists would be subject 'to the further judgement of the Parliament'; while 'the rates of all future compositions' were to 'be lessened and limited' (§XV[1–2]). The exceptions to 'a general Act of Oblivion' (§XVI) would thus be exceptionally few. Small wonder, then, that the Constitutional Royalist peers saw the *Heads* as a rare opportunity to achieve a negotiated settlement.

But the obstacle – as they discovered on their arrival at Hampton Court – lay in Charles I. Although he clearly preferred them to the Newcastle Propositions, throughout the summer and autumn of 1647 Charles withheld his consent to the *Heads*, stressing that the army could not achieve a settlement without him, and seeking a Church hierarchy guaranteed by law.[197] Instead, he opened negotiations with three Scottish commissioners, Loudoun, Lanark and Lauderdale.[198] However, on the evening of 11 November, fearing some 'bloody designes' against his person, he made the famous escape from Hampton Court, accompanied only by Berkeley, Ashburnham and Will Legge.[199] They reached Southampton's house at Titchfield in Hampshire on 12 November, and Charles sent Berkeley and Ashburnham to negotiate with Robert Hammond, Governor of the Isle of Wight.[200] In case these talks proved unsatisfactory, the King ordered a vessel to be prepared to take him to France.[201] However, when Hammond promised to give him 'whatever hee could expect from a person of honour and honestie', Charles agreed and arrived at Carisbrooke Castle on 14 November.[202]

---

[197] *LJ*, IX, 434–5; Bodl. Lib., MS Clarendon 30/1, fo. 124r (letter of intelligence, 7 October 1647); *Narrative by Ashburnham*, II, clx; Gardiner, *Civil War*, III, 333–4, 340–3, 372–3.

[198] Bodl. Lib., MS Clarendon 30/2, fos. 180r–181r (letter of intelligence, 11 November 1647); Gilbert Burnet, *The Memoirs of the Lives and Actions of James and William, Dukes of Hamilton and Castle-Herald* (Oxford, 1852), pp. 411–12 (Book V, §§122–3).

[199] Bodl. Lib., MS Clarendon 30/2, fo. 182v (letter of intelligence, 15 November 1647).

[200] *Memoirs of the Two Last Years of the Reign of King Charles I, by Sir Thomas Herbert*, ed. G. Nichol (1813), p. 54; *Narrative by Ashburnham*, II, 112–13, clxviii; *Memoirs of Ludlow*, Firth, I, 168. Southampton was not at Titchfield, but his mother was: Clarendon, *History*, IV, 264 (Book X, §127).

[201] *Memoirs by Herbert*, Nichol, p. 54; *Narrative by Ashburnham*, II, 118.

[202] *Memoirs by Herbert*, Nichol, p. 54; *Narrative by Ashburnham*, II, 114–19 (quotation at 115), clxxv–clxxvii; Clarendon, *History*, IV, 266–7 (Book X, §§129–30).

During the following month, Charles received the Houses' minimum terms contained in the *Four Bills*,[203] while simultaneously continuing to negotiate with the Scots. He was by this time truly 'an uncounselled king', for Hammond denied Charles's Constitutional Royalist advisers entry to Carisbrooke Castle. It was reported in mid-December that 'there is a very strict examinacon of all that goes and comes, and lately Coll[onel] Hammond refused to permitt the Ea[rl] of Southampton to come to attend His Ma[jes]tie there'.[204] Without such moderating counsels, Charles treated alone with Loudoun, Lauderdale and Lanark, who arrived at Carisbrooke on about 24 December. The King much preferred their terms to the *Four Bills*, for despite the Scots' religious demands they did at least offer to protect his military authority, his free choice of Privy Councillors, and his negative voice in Parliament.[205] On 26 December Charles therefore concluded an Engagement with the Scottish commissioners by which he agreed to establish 'Presbyterial government' for three years in return for guarantees of his 'honour, safety and freedom'. He also promised to 'endeavour a complete union of the kingdoms' and to allow one-third of his Privy Councillors and officers of state to be Scots.[206] Two days later, he rejected the *Four Bills* on the grounds that they would divest 'himself of all sovereignty'.[207] It seems that Charles did not consult any Constitutional Royalist advisers about these momentous steps. Hyde later condemned the Scottish commissioners – representatives of a 'watchful and crafty people' – for extracting 'so many monstrous concessions from the King'.[208] His reaction revealed a deep hostility both to 'Presbyterial government' and to any fundamental change in the existing constitutional relationship between England and Scotland.[209] Hyde also noted that the King's decisions encouraged 'a new spirit and temper in the House of Commons' which manifested itself in the Vote of No Addresses on 17 January 1648.[210]

---

203 The *Four Bills* passed the Lords on 14 December: *LJ*, IX, 574. They are printed in Gardiner, *Documents*, pp. 335–47. They demanded: (1) Parliamentary control of the militia for twenty years; (2) the voiding of 'all Oaths, Declarations, and Proclamations heretofore had or made against both or either of the Houses of Parliament'; (3) the voiding of all peerages granted since 20 May 1642 without the Houses' consent; (4) the right of the Houses to adjourn themselves 'to any other place of the kingdom of England' which they thought desirable. Charles rejected these terms on 28 December 1647 on the grounds that they entailed 'the divesting himself of all sovereignty' and the 'giving [of] an arbitrary and unlimited power to the two Houses for ever': *ibid.*, pp. 354–5.
204 Bodl. Lib., MS Clarendon 30/2, fo. 216r (letter of intelligence, 16 December 1647).
205 Burnet, *Memoirs of the Dukes of Hamilton*, pp. 400–23 (Book V, §§103–44); Gardiner, *Civil War*, IV, 1–2, 10, 37–41.
206 For the text of the Engagement, see Gardiner, *Documents*, pp. 347–53.
207 *Ibid.*, p. 354.
208 Clarendon, *History*, IV, 295, 302 (Book X, §§161, 167).   209 Cf. above, p. 67.
210 Clarendon, *History*, IV, 281 (Book X, §146). For the text of the Vote of No Addresses, see Gardiner, *Documents*, p. 356.

This vote – which forbade 'further addresses or applications to the King' and prescribed 'penalties of high treason' for those who breached it – drastically reduced the chances of a negotiated settlement. A peace initiative of March–April 1648 reveals just how much the political climate had changed by the eve of the second Civil War. Towards the end of March, Saye and several Commons allies – including Evelyn, Pierrepont and possibly Cromwell – attempted a personal approach to Charles I on the Isle of Wight in clear violation of the Vote of No Addresses.[211] They visited Southampton at Titchfield and 'earnestly solicited [him] to goe to the King to make way for a Treaty'.[212] Southampton declined to 'invite them to dinner', and finally replied: 'my lords doe you come to catch me, have you not made itt treason to make any addresse to the king; and would you bring me within the compasse of itt'.[213] Unmoved by promises of an 'exception' or a 'particular order', Southampton concluded by stating bluntly: 'my lords, I must tell you that I shall as a sworne privy councillor to his Ma[jes]tie give him such advise as is best and safest for him, but my lords you shall not heare nor be privy to what I say'.[214] The Vote of No Addresses thus ruled out another attempt at mediation, and there was now no way to avoid a second Civil War in which the Scots invaded England under the terms of the Engagement.[215]

There is no evidence that the Constitutional Royalist peers participated in that conflict,[216] and they only re-emerged as active politicians in the Treaty of Newport between 18 September and 5 December 1648.[217] Richmond, Hertford, Lindsey and Southampton headed the list of those permitted to attend the King on the Isle of Wight at the end of August.[218] They

[211] For Saye's involvement in this initiative, see Underdown, *Pride's Purge*, pp. 95–6. It is much less certain whether Cromwell actually travelled to the Isle of Wight: for contrasting views on this, see J. S. A. Adamson, 'Oliver Cromwell and the Long Parliament', in *Oliver Cromwell and the English Revolution*, ed. John Morrill (Harlow, 1990), pp. 76, 78; and Barry Coward, *Oliver Cromwell* (Harlow, 1991), pp. 59, 66–7.
[212] Bodl. Lib., MS Clarendon 31, fo. 51r (letter of intelligence, 13 April 1648).
[213] *Ibid.*, fo. 54v ([Sir Edward Forde] to [Lord Hopton], 16 April 1648).
[214] *Ibid.* The nature of Southampton's response is corroborated by S. R. Gardiner, ed., *The Hamilton Papers* (Camden Society, 2nd series, 27, 1880), 185–6 (anonymous letter to Lanark, 18 April 1648).
[215] Saye apparently made another unsuccessful approach to Southampton in July 1648: Clement Walker, *The Compleat History of Independency* (1661), part 1, 110–11 (Wing, W 324).
[216] For Richmond's refusal to 'entermeddle' in it, see below, p. 262.
[217] For an excellent modern study of this treaty, see Underdown, *Pride's Purge*, pp. 106–42. The papers exchanged during it are conveniently printed in Edward Walker, *Perfect Copies of all the Votes, Letters, Proposals and Answers ... that passed in the Treaty held at Newport* (1705). They are also found in *LJ*, X, 508–622. The selection printed in Rushworth, VII, 1299–1303, 1321–3, 1333–6 is very incomplete. As Gardiner pointed out, this volume of Rushworth is little more than a 'collection of newspaper cuttings': Gardiner, *Civil War*, IV, 260, n. 1.
[218] Rushworth, VII, 1241–2; *LJ*, X, 491.

were described simply as 'gentlemen of [the] bedchamber'.[219] Their aims throughout the ensuing treaty appear to have been twofold: to keep the talks going in order to promote a settlement; and to protect the King's person from increasingly restive elements within the army. They fostered close links with Parliament's commissioners. Richmond was 'very intimate' with Saye, and 'by him ... [Saye] conveyed his intelligence to the King', while Lindsey was similarly 'intimate' with Holles.[220] These personal contacts probably assisted the processes of negotiation, and led to the King's giving more ground than some of his other advisers thought prudent. Nicholas, for example, was 'very confident' that the treaty would fail, and could not 'comprehend' how Charles's 'concessions [could] be the way to good either for King or people'.[221] On 9 October, Charles agreed to parliamentary control of the militia for twenty years.[222] But little progress was made on the issue of Church government. Faced with a blunt demand that 'Reformation of Religion, according to the Covenant, be settled by Act of Parliament in England, Ireland and Wales, in such manner as both Houses have agreed',[223] Charles offered on 21 October to 'suspend the exercise of all episcopal government for the space of three years, and 'to confirm the form of Church government now presented to him for the said three years'.[224] He also conceded that 'in case no settlement shall be agreed on within the said three years, then after the said time, the power of ordination shall not be exercised by Bishops, without the counsel and assistance of presbyters'. Yet he still felt 'bound in conscience to uphold' the 'function of Bishops'.[225] While the Lords were amenable, the Commons rejected this answer on 27 October.[226] By that time, the treaty was nearing its allotted period of forty days, and on 2 November it was reported that 'Richmond is gon for London to procure (as is believed) an enlargement of time'.[227] The treaty was extended,[228] but both sides refused to compromise

---

[219] Rushworth, VII, 1241. For their closeness to the King during the negotiations see, for example, Francis Peck, ed., *Desiderata Curiosa* (2 vols., 1779), II, 392.

[220] Bodl. Lib., MS Dep. c. 169 (Nalson MS), fo. 181r–v (Thomas Coke's deposition, April 1651).

[221] Bodl. Lib., MS Carte 22, fos. 360v (Nicholas to Ormond, 12/22 October 1648), 632r (Nicholas to Ormond, 16/26 November 1648).

[222] Walker, *Perfect Copies*, p. 53; PRO, SP 16/516/97 (John Crewe to John Swynfen, 11 October 1648); SP 16/516/99 (Charles I's concessions, [13 October] 1648); Clarendon, *History*, IV, 440–3 (Book XI, §§173–5).

[223] Walker, *Perfect Copies*, p. 63; *LJ*, X, 560.

[224] Walker, *Perfect Copies*, p. 64; *LJ*, X, 561.

[225] Walker, *Perfect Copies*, p. 65; *LJ*, X, 561.   [226] *LJ*, X, 564–6; *CJ*, VI, 62–3.

[227] Bodl. Lib., MS Rawlinson Letters 47 (Warcup Correspondence), fo. 45r (anonymous letter of 2 November 1648). See also Bodl. Lib., MS Carte 22, fo. 572r (Nicholas to Ormond, 6/16 November 1648).

[228] *LJ*, X, 573.

on the future of the Church.[229] Charles told the Prince of Wales on 6 November that 'episcopacy was so interwoven in the lawes of this land, that wee apprehended the pulling out this thread was like to make the whole garment wravell'.[230] Furthermore, by mid-November the army officers and the Derby House Committee knew that Charles was plotting to escape from the Isle of Wight, and it was therefore resolved to secure his person.[231]

This imminent danger transformed the Constitutional Royalist peers from political advisers into personal protectors. On 30 November Charles heard of an army design to seize him 'that night', and immediately summoned Richmond and Lindsey.[232] Southampton was 'indisposed', while Hertford had 'left the Iland that morning'. The two other peers urged the King to escape, on the grounds that 'he would better bring about a personal treaty with the Parliament, which he so coveted, when out of the reach of the army, than when within their power; and this would certainly secure the safety of his person, which else might be very much in danger'. Finding Charles reluctant, Lindsey reminded him of 'Hampton Court, where your escape was your best security', while Richmond argued that 'an escape [was] feasible enough'. But the King remained adamant that 'he would not break his word', and retired for the night. At dawn on 1 December, troops entered his bedchamber and announced that they had instructions to remove him to Hurst Castle. Richmond, who 'was then in waiting', was permitted to accompany him for two miles, but 'was then told he must go no further'. The Duke returned to Lindsey's lodgings, and the two peers helped Colonel Cooke to draw up a narrative of these events.

A deep desire to protect the King's person characterised the peers' behaviour throughout the weeks that followed. As the army purged Parliament and then pressed for Charles's trial, they continued to perform their obligations of personal service to the monarch, and endeavoured up to the very last moment to save his life. As late as 12 January 1649, eight days before the King's trial began, it was reported that:

[229] For the final exchanges on the government of the Church, see Walker, *Perfect Copies*, pp. 83–7; *LJ*, X, 603–5.
[230] Bodl. Lib., MS Clarendon 32, fo. 10r (Charles I to the Prince of Wales, 6 November 1648).
[231] PRO, SP 21/25 (Derby House Committee letter book), p. 91 (Derby House Committee to Hammond, 15 November 1648); *Letters between Colonel Robert Hammond ... and the Committee ... at Derby-House* (1764), pp. 85–94.
[232] The following story is told in a detailed narrative by Colonel Edward Cooke, a Parliamentarian soldier who had come to sympathise with Charles I. His account – which was written within hours of the events it describes and endorsed as accurate by Richmond and Lindsey – was printed in *Memoirs of the Two Last Years of the Reign of ... King Charles I* (1702), pp. 165–83. Another version, with only minor variations, is found in Rushworth, VII, 1344–8. I have quoted from Rushworth throughout, as the more accessible edition.

the Duke of Richmond, Marquis Hertford, Dorset and divers others of the King's party, have sent to the Councell of the Army to engage both their persons and estates that the King shall performe whatsoever he yeilds unto. And the speech goes that they were to be at Whitehall as this day about the same business.[233]

The French agent, Grignon, reported that the peers were received politely, 'mais plustost suivant la coustume de Cromwell qui ne veut refuser d'entendre aucune proposition, que pour leur donner satisfaction'.[234] Indeed, it seems likely that the peers realised that their chances of success were virtually nil, but simply wished to demonstrate their personal loyalty to Charles. Grignon continued:

Quand les Principaux du Conseil de Guerre ne se seroient pas laissé entendre qu'ils sont résolus au refus, on n'auroit pas pour cela plus de subiet de s'en promettre quelque succes en l'estat que sont les affaires: et il est à croire que ces Seigneurs l'ont bien jugé ainsy, mais qu'ils ont mieux aimé tenter une chose qui ne devoit point réussir, que de manquer en ceste rencontre à quelque témoignage de leur affection envers leur Roy.[235]

Lord Craven realised that this initiative was Charles's very last chance,[236] and its failure opened the way to the King's trial. Nothing now could deflect the army's determination to bring 'Charles Stuart, that man of blood' to account.

Yet the peers remained in attendance right to the end. Richmond, Southampton, Lindsey and Hertford were with Charles during his trial, and presented their duty to him after the High Court of Justice had passed sentence.[237] Following the Regicide, Southampton stayed in the palace of Whitehall, where it is said he witnessed Cromwell approach the King's corpse, consider 'it attentively for some time', and then mutter the words 'cruel necessity'.[238] Finally, the four peers – together with Bishop Juxon – were permitted to attend the King's funeral at Windsor on 8 February. Hyde wrote that they 'had been of his bedchamber, and always very faithful to him', and were given 'leave to perform the last duty to their dead master, and to wait upon him to his grave'.[239] At the last, they were thus moved by a personal, almost feudal sense of loyalty to the sovereign, which

---

[233] Bodl. Lib., MS Clarendon 34, fo. 74r (John Lawrans to Nicholas, 12 January 1648/9). Another contemporary newsletter makes it clear that Lindsey and Southampton were among the 'divers others of the King's party': HMC, *Fifteenth Report* (1897), part II, 111.
[234] PRO, PRO 31/3/89, fo. 77v.   [235] *Ibid.*
[236] HMC, *Fifteenth Report*, part II, 111.
[237] *Memoirs of the Two Last Years of the Reign of ... King Charles I*, pp. 118–19; *Memoirs of Herbert*, Nichol, pp. 170–1; *A Perfect Diurnall of some Passages in Parliament*, no. 288 (29 January – 5 February 1648[/9]), p. 2315 (STC (News), 504.288; BL, TT, E 527/16).
[238] Joseph Spence, *Observations, Anecdotes, and Characters of Books and Men*, ed. James M. Osborn, I (Oxford, 1966), 244 (§586).
[239] Clarendon, *History*, IV, 492 (Book XI, §244). See also *Memoirs of Herbert*, Nichol, p. 202; PRO, PRO 31/3/89, fos. 128–30; CJ, VI, 134; Peck, *Desiderata Curiosa*, II, 412.

outlived any possibility of retrieving Charles's political position, or indeed the place of the monarchy within the constitution. For the day before the King's funeral, the Rump had voted to abolish the monarchy as 'unnecessary, burdensome, and dangerous to the liberty, safety, and publick interest of the people of this nation'.[240] The House of Lords had preceded the Crown into oblivion on 6 February.[241]

Where did the destruction of both the monarchy and the House of Lords, and the fundamental transformation of England's polity into a Commonwealth, leave this circle of peers committed to Constitutional Royalist ideals? We will take up their story again in Part Three of this book, which charts their experiences during the Interregnum and after the Restoration. But first, I want to examine more closely their motives and activities between 1642 and 1649. Chapter 6 will analyse the various sticking-points which impeded successive peace negotiations. What issues precluded settlement, and what stance(s) did the Constitutional Royalists adopt upon them? This chapter is organised thematically rather than chronologically. Then, in chapter 7, we will consider whether the attitudes expressed by Constitutional Royalists during the 1640s amounted to a coherent ideology – to an organised system of political thought – by examining the works of eight writers. My argument will be that in theory and practice alike, an identifiable Constitutional Royalist outlook existed throughout the years of civil war.

[240] *CJ*, VI, 132.   [241] *Ibid.*, 133.

⟫ 6 ⟫

Issues and sticking-points

I. RELIGION AND CHURCH GOVERNMENT

I argued in chapter 4 that loyalty to the Church 'by law established' and horror of root-and-branch reform were crucial in driving people towards the King during 1641–2. There was a direct correlation between commitment to the institution of episcopacy and commitment to Charles I. The Constitutional Royalists maintained this position throughout the peace negotiations of the 1640s. They abhorred Parliament's abolition of bishops, the alienation of episcopal lands, and the proscription of the Prayer Book. A willingness to treat with the Houses did not imply a readiness to surrender the ecclesiastical hierarchy. In the later 1640s, however, the Constitutional Royalists began to differ over whether the King should make a tactical retreat over episcopacy – whether he should surrender them now the better to preserve them later. After 1646 the Constitutional Royalists no longer presented a united front on the issue of Church government. But until then, this question had proved one of the primary – perhaps *the* primary – sticking-point in their negotiations with the Houses.

In the *Answer to the XIX Propositions*, Falkland and Culpepper had this to say on the King's behalf about the Church of England:

No Church could be found upon the earth, that professeth the true religion with more purity of doctrine than the Church of England doth, nor where the government and discipline are jointly more beautified, and free from superstition, than as they are here established by law; which (by the grace of God) we will with constancy maintain (while we live) in their purity and glory, not only against all invasions of popery, but also from the irreverence of those many schismaticks and separatists wherewith of late this kingdom and our City of London abounds.[1]

This was reiterated in many of Charles I's official statements. In his *Declaration to all his Loving Subjects* of 12 August 1642, he stated his intention to defend 'the true Reformed Protestant Religion, sealed by the bloud of so many Reverend Martyrs, and established by the wisdome and pietie of former blessed Parliaments', to stand by 'the book of common

[1] Rushworth, IV, 734.

143

prayer and the government of the Church', and to denounce the 'innovation in religion' planned by 'desperate persons' at Westminster.[2] His words were widely echoed, for example by Hertford, Seymour and the other Commissioners of Array for Somerset who, on 25 August 1642, declared that they had 'lived and [were] resolved to dy, as [their] fathers [had] done in the constant practise of the Protestant Religion, by which it is apparent that their quarrell [was] not to [them] but to the Church of England to which' they were 'knowne constantly to adhere'.[3]

It was therefore peculiarly unfortunate for the cause of peace that two weeks later the Houses issued a declaration to the Scottish General Assembly condemning bishops as 'evil and justly offensive and burthensome to the kingdom, a great impediment to reformation and growth of religion, [and] very prejudicial to the state and government of this kingdom'. The declaration concluded with a request that the Scots send 'some godly and learned divines' to the Westminster Assembly in order to promote 'an uniformity of Church Government' between the two kingdoms.[4] Then in January 1643 the Houses passed a bill for

the utter abolishing and taking away of all Archbishops, Bishops, their Chancellors and Commissaries, Deans, Sub-deans, Deans and Chapters, Archdeacons, Canons and Prebendaries, and all Chaunters, Chauncellors, Treasurers, Sub-treasurers ... and all other their under-officers, out of the Church of England.[5]

This was root-and-branch reform indeed; and the Houses resolved to demand the King's acceptance of this bill in the Oxford Propositions. They also required his consent to bills 'for taking away superstitious innovations', 'against scandalous ministers', 'against pluralities', and 'for consultation to be had with godly, religious and learned divines'. Charles was asked to pass such bills 'for the settling of Church Government' as were agreed by the Westminster Assembly and the Houses.[6] Hyde later portrayed these measures as a *quid pro quo* for Scottish military assistance to the Houses.[7] For him, the abolition of episcopacy demonstrated the aim of some at Westminster 'to make peace impossible': knowing 'the

[2] *His Majesties Declaration to all his Loving Subjects* [12 August 1642], pp. 67–8 (Wing, C 2241; BL, TT, E 115/11).
[3] MP, 25 August 1642 (declarations signed by Hertford, Seymour and the other Commissioners of Array for Somerset).
[4] LJ, V, 350; CJ, II, 754–5; PJ, III, 335.
[5] CJ, II, 947; LJ, V, 572, 582. For a detailed account of the origins and passage of this bill, see W.A. Abbott, 'The issue of episcopacy in the Long Parliament, 1640–1648' (DPhil thesis, University of Oxford, 1982), pp. 286–90.
[6] LJ, V, 582; Gardiner, *Documents*, pp. 263–4.
[7] Clarendon, *History*, II, 438–9 (Book VI, §229). Hyde was, however, writing after the Solemn League and Covenant, and in January 1643 there was no realistic prospect of Scottish military intervention. His account probably underestimates the strength of backbench pressure behind the bill: see Gardiner, *Civil War*, I, 84.

inclination and affection the King had to the Church', the bill showed a resolution 'that no peace could be safe for them but such a one as would be unsafe for the King'.[8]

In fact, as we saw in the previous chapter, the Treaty of Oxford was immediately deadlocked on the issue of what pledges should precede a cessation of arms. The talks never even got as far as the 'settling of Church Government'. However, Parliament's flexibility on the future of episcopacy was drastically curtailed by its Solemn League and Covenant with the Scots (September 1643), in which it agreed to endeavour 'the extirpation of Popery' and 'prelacy', defining the latter as 'Church government by Archbishops, Bishops, their Chancellors and Commissaries, Deans, Deans and Chapters, Archdeacons, and all other ecclesiastical officers depending on that hierarchy'.[9] This was a position from which the Houses would henceforth find it difficult to retreat.

While denouncing 'prelacy', the Solemn League and Covenant did not explicitly rule out the possibility of some form of 'primitive' episcopacy. This, together with a recognition of Royalist commitment to bishops, probably coloured the terms drafted by Thomas Ogle in the autumn of 1643. Presented to the Earl of Bristol, Ogle's terms proposed 'that all the ould Bishopps, what have brought in and practised the late innovations in the Church, whoe have tyranised and oppressed his Ma[jes]t[ie]s subjects in theire severall judicatures, bee forthwith displaced'. In their place, the King was asked to appoint 'the ablest and most conscientious divines, whoe through theire unblameable livs and doctrine have interest in the peoples affections'.[10] Those who had 'byn oppressed' under the Bishops' jurisdiction were to be 'repaied'. This vision of a moderated episcopacy bore some resemblance to that presented in the *Heads of the Proposals* in 1647.[11] It offered perhaps the only possibility of a compromise. As Bristol wrote to Ogle's accomplice Mosely, 'yow goe upon a good ground and such a one as must unite all honest Englishmen, although in other thinges of different mindes, which is not to be overrunn by an invasion of the Scotts, who if they should prevayle will tyranize both over our estates and consciences'.[12] Unfortunately, Ogle indicated that the Parliamentarian garrison of Aylesbury would be betrayed as proof of the serious intentions behind the proposals, and this intelligence quickly reached the Committee of Safety. The 'plot' collapsed and Ogle fled abroad early in January 1644.[13]

---

[8] Clarendon, *History*, II, 438–9 (Book VI, §229).   [9] Gardiner, *Documents*, pp. 268–9.
[10] B. M. Gardiner, ed., 'A secret negotiation with Charles I, 1643–4', *Camden Miscellany*, VIII (Camden Society, 1st series, 31, 1883), 9. See also BL, Add. MS 18779 (diary of Walter Yonge), fo. 53r (I am most grateful to Christopher Thompson for providing me with a copy of his transcript of this diary).
[11] See below, pp. 151–2.   [12] Gardiner, 'A secret negotiation', 25.
[13] *LJ*, VI, 367.

The failure of this negotiation stymied 'Independent' proposals for a moderated episcopacy until 1647. Instead, the Royalists were forced to treat with a Parliament increasingly influenced by Scottish demands. The Uxbridge Propositions clearly reflected the Covenanters' priorities: not only was the King again asked to accept the bill for the abolition of episcopacy, he was also required to 'endeavour the nearest conjunction and uniformity in matters of religion' between England and Scotland.[14] The Parliamentarian commissioners at Uxbridge included such prominent Covenanter peers as Argyll, Loudoun and Maitland, while Alexander Henderson was appointed to advise 'upon the propositions concerning religion'.[15] The unenviable task of the Constitutional Royalists was therefore to reconcile the King's (and their own) commitment to episcopacy with the Houses' commitment to Presbyterianism.

The magnitude of this problem was immediately apparent. On the very first day of negotiations (31 January) Henderson argued against episcopacy and for Presbyterianism, claiming that the latter existed *jure divino*. Hertford suggested that 'neither the one nor the other' was *jure divino*.[16] The commissioners then moved into detailed discussion. The Royalists maintained that the Houses' terms entailed 'the utter abolishing of that government, discipline and publick form of the worship of God, which hath been practised and established by law here ever since the Reformation'.[17] They stressed 'the injustice and inconveniency which would follow upon passing the bill for abolishing episcopacy';[18] and argued that they had so far seen no evidence 'that episcopacy is, or hath been, an impediment to a perfect reformation, to the growth of religion; or that it is prejudicial to the civil state'.[19] Instead, on 13 February they submitted fresh proposals for a 'regulated episcopacy'. It was, they suggested,

much better and more agreeable to Christian prudence and charity to remove those particulars from the present government, or to make such alterations therein, as may most probably give satisfaction to all persons seriously disturbed or afflicted in their consciences, than by destroying the whole, to give just offence and scandal to very many pious and religious persons.[20]

To this end, they proposed that 'freedom be left to all persons ... in matters of ceremony'; that bishops be obliged to reside in their dioceses; that no priest hold more than two livings; and that abuses in Church courts be reformed. These measures would, they believed, obviate the need for the

---

[14] Gardiner, *Documents*, pp. 275–6.   [15] *LJ*, VII, 143.

[16] *The Diary of Bulstrode Whitelocke, 1605–1675*, ed. Ruth Spalding (British Academy Records of Social and Economic History, new series, 13, Oxford, 1990), p. 163. See also Rushworth, V, 795.

[17] Rushworth, V, 814; *LJ*, VII, 172.   [18] Rushworth, V, 816; *LJ*, VII, 196.

[19] Rushworth, V, 817; *LJ*, VII, 196.

[20] Rushworth, V, 818; *LJ*, VII, 197.

King to take the Covenant, and for the introduction of a Directory of Public Worship. The proposals also show that the defence of episcopacy did not preclude a degree of religious toleration.[21] But the Parliamentarian commissioners regarded this response as a refusal of their terms, and pressed their case against bishops. Discussion ultimately focused on how far episcopacy was lawful, and whether it existed *jure divino*. The Royalists reiterated their view that 'no national Church' had been without bishops 'since the Apostles' time till within these few years'.[22] At that point, on 22 February, the time allotted for the treaty expired and talks came to an end.

The papers submitted by the King's commissioners at Uxbridge pose a major problem: how far did they reflect Charles's own convictions, and how far those of the commissioners themselves? Four pieces of evidence suggest that they do afford an accurate insight into Constitutional Royalist attitudes. First, the papers bear a striking resemblance to the pro-episcopal speeches of 1641–2 examined in chapter 4. Then, as at Uxbridge, episcopacy was defended on the grounds that it was lawfully established, that it had existed 'since the apostles' times', and that its abolition would involve a dangerous 'alteration' in Church government. Second, the previous year the members of the Oxford Parliament had declared their commitment 'to the maintenance of God's true religion, established by law within this kingdom'.[23] There is no evidence that this did not accurately express their own beliefs. Third, the King assured Henrietta Maria that his commissioners were 'so well chosen ... that they will neither be threatened nor disputed from the grounds I have given them ... And, in this, not only their obedience, but their judgments concur.'[24] He had no reason to believe that they were defending positions which they would not have adopted on their own. Finally, there is sometimes a direct correlation between the official papers presented at Uxbridge and the private words of the King's commissioners. For example, in the summer of 1645, Dorset wrote to the Countess of Middlesex: 'God and the King in my beleefe are both att stake, and if my life cann free them the one from beinge thrown out of his Church, and the other the State I will as hartely make itt a sacrifice as to wish my sinns in my last gaspe may bee forgiven mee.'[25] An even plainer link is found in Hyde's 'will and last profession' of April 1647, in which he professed

---

[21] Rushworth, V, 818–9; *LJ*, VII, 197–8. See also *Diary of Whitelocke*, Spalding, p. 164. These proposals were adapted and condensed from a scheme drawn up by the Oxford clergy: see S. R. Gardiner, 'A scheme of toleration propounded at Uxbridge in 1645', *EHR*, 2 (1887), 340–2.

[22] Rushworth, V, 823–4; *LJ*, VII, 244–5.   [23] Rushworth, V, 593.

[24] *The Harleian Miscellany* (12 vols., 1808–11), V, 521 (Charles I to Henrietta Maria, 25 February 1644/5).

[25] CKS, Uncatalogued Cranfield Papers: Dorset to the Countess of Middlesex, [?] June–July 1645. For the dating of this letter, see David L. Smith, '"The more posed and wise advice": the fourth Earl of Dorset and the English Civil Wars', *HJ*, 34 (1991), 823, n. 174.

to dye a true Protestant accordinge [to] the doctryne of the Church of Englande, established in the 39 Articles, and a sonn of that Church, which I doe in my soule believe to have bene (before it was invaded by this odious, unreasonable, and unchristian rebellion) both in doctryne and disciplyne, the most pure and perfecte in the Christian world.[26]

Such a correlation between public and private rhetoric cannot be documented in all cases, but it does suggest a personal commitment to the views expressed collectively by the Royalist commissioners.

Contemporaries were quick to recognise that religion had proved the most important single sticking-point at the Treaty of Uxbridge. A discussion paper drafted for the committee with the army in June 1645 argued that 'the greatest aversnes from agreement upon the kings p[ar]t' had been 'in the point of relig[ion]'; and that 'great industrie' had been 'used to sow sedition and raise jelousies betwixt the two kingdomes'. Hoping to exploit Parliament's recent victory at Naseby, the paper then advised that 'a new message might be sent to the King for setling of Relig[ion]'.[27] This was apparently not sent, but the King's response would have been predictable. He wrote to Nicholas on 25 August: 'Let my condition be never so low, my successes never so ill, I resolve (by the grace of God) never to yeald up this Church to the governement of Papists, Presbiterians, or Independants.'[28] This letter shows that he was already embracing the role of martyr by mid-1645.[29]

With the collapse of the Treaty of Uxbridge, talks on the future of Church government were effectively shelved until the following year. Then, as Charles embarked on negotiations with the Scots, he again had to confront the issue of episcopacy. As early as 10 January 1646, he told the French Resident Montereul – who acted as his go-between with the Scots – that 'the establishing of the Presbiteriall governm[en]t in England as it is in Scotland' was 'that which he cannot with the safety of his conscience condiscend unto'.[30] Eleven days later he repeated that 'you have all that my shopp can afforde, it is your part now to make the best bargaine you may'.[31] The most he would concede was a willingness 'to be instructed concerning the Presbyterian government' as soon as he joined the Scots' army.[32] Once at Newcastle, however, Charles exchanged a series of papers

---

[26] Bodl. Lib., MS Clarendon 29, fo. 180r (Hyde's will, April 1647).
[27] Henry E. Huntington Library, San Marino, California, Hastings MS, Military Papers, Box 1, folder 38 ('perticulars to be considered by the comittie with the armie', 29 June 1645).
[28] *The Diary and Correspondence of John Evelyn*, ed. W. Bray (new edition, ed. H. B. Wheatley, 4 vols., 1906), IV, 170 (Charles I to Nicholas, 25 August 1645).
[29] Cf. Russell, *Causes*, p. 199.
[30] Bodl. Lib., MS Clarendon 26, fo. 195r (Charles I to Montereul, 10 January 1645/6).
[31] Bodl. Lib., MS Clarendon 27, fo. 17r (Charles I to Montereul, 21 January 1645/6).
[32] *Clarendon SP*, II, 220 (Charles I's promise to Montereul, 1 April 1646).

with Alexander Henderson which showed him to be an unreceptive student of Presbyterianism. He insisted on 'the lawfulnesse, and succession of Episcopacy, and ... the necessity of it'; and argued that it was consistent with 'the universall practice of the Primitive Church'.[33] This uncompromising stance was to vitiate not only Charles's talks with the Scots, but also his negotiations over the Newcastle Propositions which the Houses sent him on 13 July 1646.

The religious demands contained in the Newcastle Propositions were identical with those of the Uxbridge Propositions. The King was asked to consent to the abolition of episcopacy; sign the Solemn League and Covenant and ensure that it was taken 'by all the subjects of the three kingdoms'; confirm 'the reformation of religion according to the Covenant'; and pass a series of bills against pluralism, absenteeism and 'innovations'.[34] We saw in chapter 5 that the King refused to compromise on Church government throughout the summer and autumn of 1646, despite repeated advice to the contrary. Culpepper and Jermyn told him bluntly: 'the question in short is whether you will chuse to be a King of Presbitery or no King'.[35] Charles's refusal hinged on the belief that Presbyterianism was incompatible with monarchy. It was an extension of his father's axiom 'No Bishop, no King'. As he put it on 7 September, 'the ground' of Presbyterian doctrine was 'anty-monarchicall'.[36] This was because the abolition of episcopacy entailed an assault upon the royal supremacy: 'I must make you acknowledge that the giving such way to Presbiteriall governm[en]t as will content the Scots, is the absolut distruction of monarchy, for with it Episcopasy must be totally abolished, the dependancy of [the] Church torne from the Crowne and the Covenant firmly established.'[37] There is no doubt that Charles viewed this as the single most important principle which had at all costs to be defended. As he wrote to the Prince of Wales on 26 August 1646,

the cheefest particular duty of a King is to maintaine the true religion (without which he can never expect to have God's blessing), so I asseur you, that this duty can never be right performed without the Church be rightly governed, not only in relation to consience but lykewais for the necessary subsistance of the Crowne. For take it as an infallible maxim from me that as the Church can never florishe

---

[33] *The Papers which passed at Newcastle betwixt His Sacred Majestie and Mr Al[exander] Henderson: concerning the change of Church-Government* (1649), pp. 18, 55–8 (Wing, C 2535; BL, TT, E 1243/3).
[34] Gardiner, *Documents*, pp. 291–3.
[35] Bodl. Lib., MS Clarendon 91, fo. 36r (Culpepper and Jermyn to Charles I, 18 September 1646).
[36] *Ibid.*, fo. 33r (Charles I to Culpepper, Jermyn and Ashburnham, 7 September 1646).
[37] Bodl. Lib., MS Clarendon 97, fo. 41r (Charles I to Culpepper, Jermyn and Ashburnham, 31 August 1646).

without the protection of the Crowne so the dependancy of the Church upon the Crowne is the cheefest support of regall authority.[38]

As so often with his letters to the Prince of Wales, this offers a very important indication of Charles's inner thoughts.[39] He put the same point more briefly in a letter to Juxon: 'God is my wittnes, my cheifest end in regaining my power is to doe the Church service.'[40] The only concession Charles was prepared to make, in 'privat instructions' to Will Murray, was the introduction of 'Presbiteriall governement' for five years provided that at the end of that time 'a regulated episcopacy ... be established'.[41] Henrietta Maria correctly perceived that this 'subtillty' would never 'satisfy the Presbiterians', and thought that any attempt to compromise on that issue was doomed.[42] In any case, despite this short-term concession, Charles told Will Murray that he would 'not abjure episcopacy, take, or establish the Covenant, nor consent to that undouted sacriledge of alienating the Church Lands'. Charles added: 'comunicat all things freely with the Duke of Richmond; with others as you shall see cause'.[43]

This instruction clearly illustrates the extent of Charles's personal trust in Richmond. However, by this time some other Constitutional Royalists were prepared to sacrifice episcopacy in order to reach a settlement, even if this meant modifying their earlier position. Culpepper was the most striking example of this change of emphasis. He had defended bishops in February 1641 as 'maine columnes of the realme';[44] yet by 1646 he denied that episcopacy was 'jure divino exclusive'.[45] But for others, most notably Hyde, compromise remained unthinkable. Perhaps deliberately recalling Culpepper's earlier metaphor, Hyde begged him not to let 'the landmarkes bee removed, nor pillars upon which the fabrique relyes bee taken away'.[46] Characteristically, the fact that bishops were lawfully established weighed very heavily with Hyde: he warned Nicholas that 'episcopacy ... is as much fenced and secured by the lawes as monarchy it selfe, and an entire part of the frame and constitucon of the kingdome'.[47]

Nor was it only the preservation of episcopacy which concerned Hyde.

---

[38] Bodl. Lib., MS Clarendon 91, fo. 30r–v (Charles I to the Prince of Wales, 26 August 1646).
[39] Cf. John Morrill, The Nature of the English Revolution (Harlow, 1993), p. 287.
[40] Bodl. Lib., MS Clarendon 91, fo. 40r (Charles I to William Juxon, 30 September 1646).
[41] Ibid., fo. 54r (Charles I to Will Murray, 15 October 1646).
[42] Charles I in 1646: Letters of King Charles the first to Queen Henrietta Maria, ed. J. Bruce (Camden Society, 1st series, 63, 1856), 98 (Henrietta Maria to Charles I, 4/14 December 1646).
[43] Bodl. Lib., MS Clarendon 91, fo. 54r. See also above, p. 134 n. 184.
[44] D'Ewes (N), p. 315.
[45] Bodl. Lib., MS Clarendon 91, fo. 35v (Jermyn and Culpepper to Charles I, 18 September 1646).
[46] Bodl. Lib., MS Clarendon 29, fo. 55v (Hyde to Culpepper, 8 January 1646/7).
[47] Ibid., fo. 5r (Hyde to Nicholas, 12 December 1646).

He also abhorred the vesting of bishops' 'lands and possessions upon trustees for the use of the commonwealth'.[48] Shortly afterwards, Hyde began work on his essay *Of Sacrilege*.[49] In defining sacrilege as 'the robbing and defrauding [of] the Church',[50] Hyde was able to draw on an extensive body of writings by figures as diverse as Richard Hooker, Lancelot Andrewes, Joseph Mede and Sir Henry Spelman.[51] Furthermore, the fear of committing sacrilege had exercised other individuals close to Charles I. Prominent among these was the first Viscount Scudamore who, racked with guilt at an estate comprised mainly of former monastic lands, threw himself into paying tithes and returning impropriations.[52] It seems that Hyde's views on sacrilege were also shared by other Royalists and former associates of the Great Tew circle such as Henry Hammond, Gilbert Sheldon, Richard Steward and Christopher Potter.[53] Hyde's tract explained not only his belief that Parliament's policies constituted sacrilege, but also the reasons why they had proved a sticking-point in peace negotiations with the King. 'It is observable', Hyde declared,

that in these violent and furious attempts against the Church, albeit His Majesty hath always publicly declared that his not complying with them in that particular (the doing whereof many have supposed would have procured him his desires in all other Parliaments) proceeds purely from matter of conscience, and principally from the conclusion that what they desire is sacrilege; there hath been no application to his person, nor any sober animadversions in writing, to inform his judgement that it is not sacrilege.[54]

We shall see below how this assertion that the Houses had not presented adequate justification for their actions also characterised Royalist arguments on several other issues.

In England, meanwhile, the King's political options changed dramatically during the summer of 1647. Charles and his advisers had long been aware that both Houses contained a significant body of opinion which was hostile to Presbyterianism and willing to contemplate a 'reduced episcopacy'. This anti-Presbyterian lobby embraced both Erastians and Independents, and included such figures as Northumberland, Saye, Wharton, Salisbury, Clare and Denbigh.[55] We have seen that several of these peers had

---

[48] *CJ*, IV, 677; *LJ*, VIII, 515.
[49] *A Compleat Collection of Tracts, by that Eminent Statesman the Right Honourable Edward, Earl of Clarendon* (1747), pp. 211–17.
[50] *Ibid.*, p. 213.
[51] Martin Dzelzainis, '"Undoubted Realities": Clarendon on sacrilege', *HJ*, 33 (1990), 520–7.
[52] Ian Atherton, 'Viscount Scudamore's "Laudianism": the religious practices of the first Viscount Scudamore', *HJ*, 34 (1991), 567–96.
[53] Dzelzainis, '"Undoubted Realities"', 528–31.
[54] *Compleat Collection of Tracts by Clarendon*, p. 217.
[55] The religious attitudes of these peers are discussed in J. S. A. Adamson, 'The peerage in politics, 1645–9' (PhD thesis, University of Cambridge, 1986), pp. 68–114, 290–2.

private contacts with Constitutional Royalists;[56] and Northumberland, Salisbury and Denbigh had also served as Parliamentarian commissioners in various formal treaties.[57] Their acceptance of a moderated episcopacy, provided that it safeguarded liberty of conscience, offered a more promising basis for negotiation than did Presbyterianism. Unfortunately, the King's rebuff of Clare and Northumberland in 1643, followed by the collapse of Ogle's initiative, precluded the exploration of this avenue for several years. In 1647, however, the *Heads of the Proposals* offered terms for a settlement of the Church along precisely these lines. Episcopacy was to be preserved, but an act passed 'to take away all coercive power, authority, and jurisdiction of Bishops and all other ecclesiastical officers whatsoever, extending to any civil penalties upon any'.[58] The Covenant would not be enforced; use of the Prayer Book would become voluntary; and all penalties 'for not coming to church, or for meetings elsewhere for prayer or other religious duties' were to be repealed. This vision embodied some measure of religious toleration, and was not very different from the scheme for a 'regulated episcopacy' which Hyde and his allies had advanced in February 1645. Certainly, as we have already seen, most of the Constitutional Royalists seem to have shared Sir Arthur Hopton's view that the *Heads* comprised 'better then ordinary good tearmes'.[59]

But still the King refused to compromise. When Sir John Berkeley gave him a preview of the *Heads* at Woburn in late July 1647, Charles retorted that 'though there was nothing done against the Church-government established, yet there was nothing done to assert it'. Berkeley fell back on the characteristic Constitutional Royalist argument that 'the law was security enough for the Church', adding that 'it was happy that men, who had fought against the Church, should be reduced (when they were superiors), not to speak against it'. The King's cryptic and singularly unhelpful response was that he should 'see them glad ere long to accept more equal terms'.[60] In his public dealings with the army officers on 2 August, however, Charles adopted the argument offered by Berkeley, 'that he would have the Church established according to law, by the Proposals'.[61] At this point the negotiations over the *Heads* ground to a halt.

The Houses meanwhile stuck uncompromisingly to their own terms. The Newcastle Propositions and then the *Four Bills* repeated the demand for Charles's assent to the bills for the abolition of episcopacy and for the alienation of the lands of bishops, deans and chapters.[62] The King's

[56] See above, pp. 96–8, 112, 115–16, 138–9.   [57] *LJ*, V, 574–5; VII, 136.
[58] This and subsequent quotations are taken from Gardiner, *Documents*, p. 321.
[59] See above, pp. 132–6.
[60] *A Narrative by John Ashburnham of his attendance on King Charles the first* (2 vols., 1830), II, cli–clii.
[61] *Ibid.*, cliv.   [62] Gardiner, *Documents*, pp. 291–2, 343.

answer, drafted by Hyde,[63] did not address the religious clauses explicitly but rejected these terms as 'against his honour and conscience'.[64] Instead, he signed the Engagement with the Scots, whereby he undertook to confirm the Solemn League and Covenant, to confirm 'Presbyterial government, the directory of worship, and Assembly of Divines at Westminster for three years', and to settle Church government thereafter in concert with the two Houses.[65] This agreement marked the culmination of the policy advocated by Jermyn and Culpepper: the temporary acceptance of Presbyterianism as the necessary price for Scottish assistance and longer-term military advantage. It was also to define the limits of the King's concessions on Church government at the Treaty of Newport.

The exchanges over religion were by far the most anguished part of this treaty. At one point, the King was in such 'a great perplexity about the point of abolishing episcopacy' that he burst into tears.[66] When the talks began, Charles signalled his willingness for the Directory of Worship to be used for three years, although without any compulsion, and for Church government in the meantime to be settled by the King and the two Houses.[67] But he emphatically did not want to sacrifice episcopacy. Instead, on 2 October, he requested to 'be satisfied in conscience that episcopacy might be lawfully taken away, and another government settled'.[68] 'If government presbyterial could be proved to be jure divino', he argued, 'he would yield the cause.'[69] Over the next few days, he insisted that the alienation of the bishops' lands was 'sacrilege', and thought 'it would be scandalous to take away episcopacy generally; never any such thing having been any where attempted'.[70] This view extended to the Prayer Book, 'which had been established in the glorious reformation of England and settled by five several acts of Parliament', and the abolition of which 'would be a great inlett and incouragement to popery'.[71] Charles restated his position on 9 October, advocating the moderate episcopacy he had been committed to since 1641. He argued that the substance of episcopacy 'consist[ed] in the power of ordination and jurisdiction as they were exercised by the apostles themselves', and his goal was 'the alteration and regulating of this present hierarchy and government, so as episcopacy reduced to the primitive usage may be settled and continued in this Church'.[72] The most he would

---

[63] For the draft, see Bodl. Lib., MS Clarendon 30/2, fos. 234–5. See also Clarendon, *History*, IV, 276–9 (Book X, §§141–3).
[64] Gardiner, *Documents*, p. 354.   [65] *Ibid.*, pp. 347–8.
[66] Francis Peck, ed., *Desiderata Curiosa* (2 vols., 1779), II, 392.
[67] Rushworth, VII, 1281.
[68] Peck, *Desiderata Curiosa*, II, 387; Rushworth, VII, 1281; PRO, SP 16/516/94 (John Crewe to John Swynfen, 7 October 1648).
[69] Peck, *Desiderata Curiosa*, II, 388.   [70] *Ibid.*, 389.   [71] *Ibid.*, 390.
[72] Edward Walker, *Perfect Copies of all the Votes, Letters, Proposals and Answers … that passed in the Treaty held at Newport* (1705), p. 49; LJ, X, 538–9.

concede, on 21 October, was 'to suspend the exercise of all episcopal government for the space of three years'.[73] He admitted to William Hopkins, at whose house he was lodging, that these concessions were 'merely in order to [his] escape' – a plot in which the Constitutional Royalist peers who attended Charles were implicated.[74] But there were limits to how far he would compromise on Church government: in his final answer on 18 November he insisted that he could not 'with a good conscience consent to the total abolition of the function and power of Bishops, nor to the entire and absolute alienation of their lands, as is desired, because he is yet persuaded in his judgment that the former is of apostolical institution, and that to take away the latter is sacrilege'.[75] This answer was communicated to the Houses on 27 November;[76] and their decision to press ahead with negotiations despite it precipitated Pride's Purge.

Yet the King's public position on the Church remained utterly consistent. From the scaffold, he urged his attendants to 'give God his due, by regulating rightly his Church (according to his Scriptures) which is now out of order'; and he claimed to 'die a Christian according to the profession of the Church of England, as I found it left to me by my father'.[77] This final pledge to maintain the 'Jacobethan' Church confirmed Charles's posthumous reputation as a martyr who had died defending the Church of England – 'that blessed martyr', as Hyde called him.[78] This in turn was to be a crucial dimension of the monarchy's popular appeal by the end of the 1650s.

Although significant divergences had opened up by the later 1640s, especially between Hyde and Culpepper, this section has surely demonstrated that there was an identifiable Constitutional Royalist position on the Church of England. It was not unique to the figures examined here, and was expressed in other works such as Sir Thomas Aston's *A Remonstrance against Presbytery*. This outlook was characterised first of all by a defence of the 'Church by law established'. The abolition of bishops and the alienation of their lands; the proscription of the Prayer Book; the establishment of Presbyterianism – all these infringed existing English laws. The preservation of these externals thus coincided with the powerful attachment to the rule of law which will form a recurrent theme throughout this chapter. This legal argument against radical reform of the Church was deployed again and again from the debates of 8/9 February 1641 onwards. As Aston put it, 'the removing of this order of Bishops would shake a great part of

[73] Walker, *Perfect Copies*, p. 64; *LJ*, X, 561.
[74] Gardiner, *Civil War*, IV, 220–3; Peck, *Desiderata Curiosa*, II, 392; see also above, p. 140.
[75] Walker, *Perfect Copies*, p. 83; *LJ*, X, 603.   [76] Walker, *Perfect Copies*, p. 98.
[77] Rushworth, VIII, 1429–30.
[78] Clarendon, *History*, IV, 488 (Book XI, §238).

the foundation of our common lawes'. Like the King's commissioners in successive treaties, he believed that the underlying aim of those who sought further reformation of the Church was to erect 'a meere arbitrarie government'.[79]

Such arguments were closely related to what may be termed the constitutional case in defence of episcopacy. This assumed that there was a fundamental link between episcopacy and monarchy via the royal supremacy. Because it was established by law, episcopacy was – in Hyde's phrase – 'an entire part of the ... constitucon of the kingdome'.[80] Any attack upon it violated the royal supremacy and was therefore an implicit attack on the monarchy. It was one of the fundamental tenets of Constitutional Royalism that the inverse equation was also true: that allegiance to the Crown represented the only viable defence of episcopacy. In other words, they believed in the symbiotic relationship which James I summed up in his celebrated maxim 'No Bishop, no King'. Aston argued that bishops 'appear to have an inseparable supportation by the King's most antient, most legall, prerogative'.[81] The rule of law was the mechanism by which the two were brought into harmony and preserved.

Two other contentions, although less often articulated, served to reinforce this legal–constitutional case. The first was the argument from antiquity: episcopacy was an ancient form of Church government which had been found satisfactory in many different nations for centuries. 'For fifteene hundred and odde yeares after Christ', declared Aston, 'the order of episcopacie was never questioned, nor paritie of ministers set a foote by any Church.'[82] To remove bishops would cut the Church of England adrift from its past and sever the umbilical chord which linked it to the pre-Reformation Church. This was, of course, precisely what many of those who remained at Westminster had come to want: they felt that the English Reformation had been totally inadequate and that 'further reformation' was imperative.[83] The Solemn League and Covenant with the Scots underlined the Houses' public commitment to this policy. But to the Constitutional Royalists reverence for the 'martyr-bishops' of the Reformation afforded a further argument against the abolition of episcopacy. Even if – as the Constitutional Royalists consistently argued – episcopacy was not established *jure divino*, how could an order which had produced the likes of Cranmer be abolished?

The second line of argument was to defend the government and

---

[79] Sir Thomas Aston, *A Remonstrance against Presbytery* (1641), p. 62, sig. L2[r] (Wing, A 4078; BL, TT, E 163/1, E 163/2).
[80] See above, p. 131.   [81] Aston, *Remonstrance*, p. 67.   [82] *Ibid.*, p. 12.
[83] For the link between this attitude and a decision to remain at Westminster after 1642, see Russell, *Causes*, pp. 222–4.

discipline of the Church as intrinsically beautiful and free from superstition. The argument was thus religious rather than ecclesiastical. It moved from externals to internals. It rested on a belief that the established Church of England was more acceptable to God than the alternatives on offer. This view is advanced particularly eloquently in the *Answer to the XIX Propositions* and in Hyde's correspondence. But in the public exchanges on Church government during the formal peace negotiations, we encounter it much less frequently than the legal–constitutional arguments against 'further reformation'.

This in turn raises the issue of how far religious motives can be separated from other, more secular considerations. Certainly the disagreement between Culpepper and Hyde from 1646 onwards rested in part on different readings of the political situation, and particularly of the strength of the King's bargaining position. There was a similar pragmatism underlying Charles's apparently generous concessions at Newport. But this was surely not the only level at which politics and religion were intertwined. The evidence presented here strongly suggests that it is quite inappropriate to try to segregate them, or to see one as determining the other. Rather, they emerge as different aspects of a single, unified and self-sustaining pattern of beliefs within which they were distinguishable but not separable. It is extraordinarily difficult to find a word which satisfactorily captures this ideological relationship. Perhaps the best summing up would be that an attachment to the law and the constitution *coloured* the Constitutional Royalists' attitude towards the Church. It certainly did not in itself dictate that attitude. But it did complement and reinforce the grounds on which they chose to justify the established order. Throughout the 1640s, it informed the contours of their defence of the Church and the idiom within which they expressed this.

II. THE MILITIA

Royal authority over the militia was a fiercely contested question long before the outbreak of civil war. Originally based on feudal tenure, the monarch's right to muster soldiers had been regulated by a series of medieval statutes, of which the most important was the Statute of Winchester (1285). A Marian Arms Act repealed these statutes in 1558 and established instead a county militia system organised on a territorial basis and administered by the lieutenancy. This Arms Act was itself repealed in 1604, as was the Statute of Winchester in 1624, thus creating an ambiguity over whether or not the other medieval statutes remained in force. This caused bitter controversy throughout the later 1620s over the King's right to raise soldiers. The fact that his authority over the militia was not clearly grounded in statute left Charles in a difficult position in 1642, and posed a tricky problem with which his apologists had to grapple.[84]

To surmount this obstacle, Charles – after consultation with 'some judges and lawyers of eminency'[85] – fell back on the Commission of Array. This expedient was originally devised by Edward I and later enshrined in a statute of 1405. It was frequently employed during the fifteenth century, but abandoned by the Tudors in favour of the lieutenancy. Its great advantage was that it conferred broad powers upon the Commissioners of Array, including the legal moving of militia all over the country in a way that was impossible under the lieutenancy.[86] But in 1642 it was widely perceived as a dangerous innovation, and Hyde later acknowledged that it had been a tactical error:

many did believe that if the King had resorted to the old known way of lord lieutenants and deputy lieutenants, his service would have been better carried on; the Commission of Array being a thing they had not before heard of, though founded upon an ancient Act of Parliament in the reign of Harry IV,[87] and so received with jealousy, and easily discredited by the glosses and suggestions of the Houses.[88]

This was a handicap which the Constitutional Royalists would have to try to overcome throughout the years of civil war.

By contrast, it was precisely the established system of Lords Lieutenant which formed the basis of Parliament's military organisation. The Militia Ordinance had been formulated in the wake of the King's attempt on the Five Members. This 'most dangerous and desperate design upon the House of Commons', it argued, necessitated drastic measures 'for the safety . . . of His Majesty's person, the Parliament and kingdom in this time of imminent danger'.[89] It then named new Lords Lieutenant for every county and empowered these to command the local militias. They could lead their troops into 'any other part of this realm of England or dominion of Wales, for the suppression of all rebellions, insurrections and invasions that may happen, according as they from time to time shall receive directions from the Lords and Commons'.

The King refused to pass this Ordinance on the grounds that it robbed

---

[84] This paragraph is based on Lindsay Boynton, *The Elizabethan Militia, 1558–1638* (1967), pp. 3–12, 209–97; A. Hassell Smith, 'Militia rates and militia statutes, 1558–1663', in *The English Commonwealth, 1547–1640*, ed. Peter Clark, A. G. R. Smith and Nicholas Tyacke (Leicester, 1979), pp. 93–110; and Richard Tuck, '"The Ancient Law of Freedom": John Selden and the Civil War', in *Reactions to the English Civil War, 1642–1649*, ed. John Morrill (1982), pp. 145–54.

[85] Clarendon, *History*, II, 196–7 (Book V, §364).

[86] J.S. Morrill, *The Revolt of the Provinces* (2nd edition, Harlow, 1980), pp. 40, 156–8.

[87] A reference to 4 Hen. IV, c. 13.   [88] Clarendon, *History*, II, 201–5 (Book V, §364).

[89] This and subsequent quotations from the Militia Ordinance are taken from the version printed in Gardiner, *Documents*, pp. 245–7.

him of powers with 'which God and the Law hath trusted us solely'; and insisted that 'we shall rely upon that royal right and jurisdiction which God and the law hath given us, for the suppressing of rebellion and resisting foreign invasion'.[90] Falkland and Culpepper took up this point in the *Answer to the XIX Propositions*, declaring that the King would 'no more part with' his powers 'in the point of the militia' than with his 'Crown, lest [he] enable others by them to take that from us'. They got round the fact that Charles's mobilisation of troops lacked clear statutory authority thus: 'If no forces must be levied till rebellions and invasions (which will not stay for the calling of Parliaments, and their consent for raising of forces) be actual, they must undoubtedly (at least most probably) be effectual and prevalent.'[91] This argument, that troops could be raised under the royal prerogative in a national emergency, had been used by Dorset to justify Charles's levies during the late 1620s. As Lord Lieutenant of Sussex he had first-hand experience of the difficulty of raising forces without clear statutory authority, and declared in May 1628: 'Yesterday in the King's Bench a man was returned for refusing to contribute to the musters upon a *habeas corpus*. Answered: because there is no law for it. So you see the King's prerogative is necessary.'[92] But despite the absence of such a statute, the framers of the *Answer to the XIX Propositions* nevertheless insisted that 'the laws of the realm' had vested the command of the militia in the Crown;[93] and this was to remain a central tenet of Constitutional Royalist attitudes throughout the 1640s.

It needs stressing first of all that those attitudes did not preclude active military service. It would be anachronistic to associate political moderation with pacifism or even neutralism. Hertford, Seymour, Lindsey and Falkland all combined a firm commitment to peace negotiations with active service in the Royalist armies.[94] This rested on an acceptance of the King's right to raise troops by means of the Commissions of Array. Lindsey, like his father the first Earl, had received and obeyed the Commission of Array in Lincolnshire in the summer of 1642.[95] But much the most

[90] *LJ*, V, 32.
[91] Rushworth, IV, 728, 730. See also Michael Mendle, 'The Great Council of Parliament and the first ordinances: the constitutional theory of the Civil War', *JBS*, 31 (1992), 133–62.
[92] David L. Smith, 'The fourth Earl of Dorset and the politics of the sixteen-twenties', *Historical Research*, 35 (1992), 48. For Dorset as Lord Lieutenant of Sussex, see the same author's 'The political career of Edward Sackville, fourth Earl of Dorset (1590–1652)' (PhD thesis, University of Cambridge, 1990), pp. 268–87.
[93] Rushworth, IV, 725.
[94] P.R. Newman, *Royalist Officers in England and Wales, 1642–1660: A Biographical Dictionary* (1981), pp. 26–7, 339–40.
[95] Lincolnshire Archives Office, Ancaster MS, 12/A/4–7 (Charles I's commissions to Lord Willoughby of Eresby, July–August 1642); CUL, Add. MS 89 (historical collections), fo. 32v; *LJ*, V, 120; *PJ*, III, 5–6, 13–14, 33, 175.

articulate defenders of the Commission among this group were Hertford and Seymour. Together with Lord Poulet, Sir Ralph Hopton, Edward Kirton and several other Royalist officers, they signed two declarations of 25 August 1642 which insisted that they were only obeying the King's 'iust authority' and 'iust commands'. They simply wished to quell a 'riotous and tumultuous . . . assembly' which was 'soe contrarie to lawe and His Ma[jes]ties commands'.[96] We cannot gain an authentic sense of Constitutional Royalism unless we appreciate that these sentiments – and the military activism which they spawned – were just as characteristic of it as the peace initiative which Dorset, Southampton and Culpepper led on the very same day. Equally, men like Lindsey, Hertford and Seymour were no less vigorous in the treaties of the 1640s than those whose activities were confined to the civilian sphere.

Following the outbreak of hostilities, the issue of disbandment inevitably loomed large in peace negotiations. The Oxford Propositions asked the King to disband his armies, return to London, and 'by Act of Parliament to settle the militia both by sea and land, and for the forts and ports of the kingdom, in such manner as shall be agreed on by both Houses'.[97] Charles immediately countered with six propositions, the first of which was that 'His Majesty's own revenue, magazines, towns, forts and ships which have been taken or kept from him by force be forthwith restored unto him.'[98] The Houses in turn proposed certain 'conditions and limitations' for a cessation of arms which confined Royalist forces to within twelve miles of Oxford.[99] Charles found these terms 'so unreasonable' that he could not grant them;[100] and instead offered alternative articles of cessation allegedly designed to further 'the good of his people'.[101] The Houses responded with new instructions to their commissioners which culminated in the demand that the King 'name persons of quality to receive the charge of the several offices and forts, castles, and towns, to be forthwith certified to the two Houses of Parliament, that thereupon they may express their confidence in those persons, or humbly beseech His Majesty to name others'. None of these persons could 'be removed during three years next ensuing without just cause to be approved by Parliament, and if any be so removed, or shall die within the said space, the person to be put into the same office shall be such as both Houses shall confide in'. Furthermore, all 'generals and commanders in any of the

---

[96] MP, 25 August 1642. See also David Underdown, *Somerset in the Civil War and Interregnum* (Newton Abbot, 1973), pp. 31–43.
[97] Gardiner, *Documents*, pp. 262, 264.   [98] Rushworth, V, 169; *LJ*, V, 591.
[99] Rushworth, V, 170–1; *LJ*, V, 625–6.
[100] *Letters of Queen Henrietta Maria*, ed. Mary Anne Everett Green (1857), p. 174 (Charles I to Henrietta Maria, 2/12 March 1642/3).
[101] Rushworth, V, 171–3; *LJ*, V, 644.

armies on either side', together with the Lord Admiral and the Lord Warden of the Cinque Ports, were to take an oath to preserve 'the true reformed Protestant religion' against all forces 'raised without His Majesty's authority and consent of the two Houses of Parliament'.[102] Charles refused all concessions which would infringe 'his honour, justice and duty to his Crown' and 'render him less able to protect his subjects', but offered a treaty even though a cessation of arms had not been agreed upon.[103] To this the Houses consented.[104] Thereafter, the talks reached an impasse over whether the King would appoint senior military officers in whom the Houses could confide. Charles refused to concede this authority to the Houses, and agreed 'only that they shall have liberty upon any just exceptions to proceed against any such persons according to law; His Majesty being resolved not to protect them against the publick justice'. He further insisted that 'the nomination and free election' to such offices constituted 'a right belonging to and inherent in His Majesty, and ... enjoyed by all his royal progenitors'.[105] In his final answer on 15 April, the day after the Houses withdrew their commissioners from Oxford, Charles refused to countenance arguments which 'might extend to the depriving him of, or at least, sharing with him in all his just regal power', and to contemplate divesting 'himself of those trusts which the law of the land hath settled in the Crown alone'.[106]

This last phrase was highly characteristic of Constitutional Royalist views on the militia. They emphasised that royal authority over the militia was guaranteed by English law, despite the uncertainty over whether or not the medieval statutes remained in force. Sir John Strangways characterised the difference between Royalists and Parliamentarians on this point thus: 'we have mayntayned the militia of the kingdome to belong to the King, they the contrary: our warrant is the statute of 7 Edw[ard] I and manie statutes since; and the practise of all tymes'.[107] This precluded parliamentary control over the militia, but it did not rule out the possibility of concessionary appointments. Hyde thought that 'some condescensions in the point of the militia' were 'the only substantial security' the Houses could have, and that 'nothing could be digested of that kind, which would not reflect both upon the King's authority and his honour'. But equally, he insisted that there were 'very notable advantages' in restoring Northumberland to the office of Lord High Admiral.[108] Such arguments contrasted

---

[102] Rushworth, V, 177; *CJ*, III, 8.   [103] Rushworth, V, 179; *LJ*, V, 660.
[104] Rushworth, V, 179–80; *LJ*, V, 669.
[105] Rushworth, V, 201; *LJ*, V, 702–3.   [106] Rushworth, V, 203.
[107] Beinecke Library, Yale University, Osborn MS b. 304 (commonplace book of Sir John Strangways), p. 45. This was an almost exact quotation from David Jenkins, *Lex Terrae* (1647), p. 17 (Wing, J 593; BL, TT, E 390/18). For this tract, see below, pp. 234–5.
[108] Clarendon, *Life*, I, 179–85.

dramatically with the advice of Henrietta Maria, whose main concern was that Charles should under no circumstances allow his 'army to be disbanded' until Parliament was dissolved.[109]

The close link which Royalist moderates forged between the King's military authority and the rule of law emerged even more clearly at the Treaty of Uxbridge. The Houses' Propositions required all forces at land and sea to be settled 'as both Houses shall think fit', and entrusted to commissioners who were to be 'persons of known integrity' nominated by both Houses. These commissioners would also form a joint committee with Scottish commissioners.[110] The tone of the Royalist response to these demands was set by an exchange between Hyde and Whitelocke on 4 February 1645. Hyde 'affirmed the power of the militia to be by law unquestionably in the King only'. Whitelocke 'denyed this, as reflecting uppon the Parlements propositions, and not cleer by law where that power was'.[111] As Hyde later summed it up: 'when the commissioners of the King ... made the demand appear to be without any pretence of law or justice, and asserted it to be vested in the king by the law', the Parliamentarian commissioners 'never offered to allege any other argument than the determination of the Parliament, which had declared the right of the militia to be in them, from which they could not recede'.[112] This assertion that the Houses had signally failed to present convincing arguments for their demands closely resembled Hyde's discussion of 'sacrilege', examined above.[113] Moreover, the papers exchanged at Uxbridge on the militia confirm the accuracy of his statement.

The King's commissioners' first reply stated that the propositions 'import[ed] very great alterations in the main foundation of the frame of government of this kingdom' by taking 'the whole military or civil power out of the crown without any limitation in time or reparation proposed'. They therefore asked for a time limit to be given for the settlement of the militia in this manner.[114] In a further paper two days later, they also requested that the commissioners number twenty – half of whom would be named by the King and half by the Houses – and that their powers be limited to three years.[115] The Parliamentarian commissioners found these terms 'very far differing from what we have proposed, and unsatisfactory to our just and necessary desires, for the securing the peace of the kingdoms', observing also that 'the kingdom of Scotland is wholly omitted'.[116] They demanded a straight answer to their original propositions, but the

[109] *Letters of Henrietta Maria*, Green, p. 182 (Henrietta Maria to Charles I, 8 April 1643).
[110] Gardiner, *Documents*, pp. 281–3.   [111] *Diary of Whitelocke*, Spalding, p. 164.
[112] Clarendon, *History*, III, 486 (Book VIII, §233).   [113] See above, p. 151.
[114] Rushworth, V, 826; *LJ*, VII, 181–2.
[115] Rushworth, V, 827–8; *LJ*, VII, 183.   [116] Rushworth, V, 829; *LJ*, VII, 183.

Royalist commissioners refused this until they received 'satisfaction by conference that it is reasonable for us to grant the nomination of the persons by the two Houses only, and that the time ought not to be limited'.[117] Alongside these exchanges, there was a parallel dispute over what powers should be entrusted to the commissioners for the militia. Here again, the thrust of the Parliamentarian response was simply to refer the King's commissioners to the Houses' original propositions.[118] This in turn elicited a final response from the King's commissioners which contains a particularly fine statement of the Constitutional Royalist position on the militia.[119]

Their paper began by declaring the original propositions relating to the militia 'unreasonable in many particulars'. They 'intrusted' the militia to persons 'nominated only by the two Houses'; the commissioners' powers were to be 'framed and altered as occasion serves by the two Houses only'; the King was 'absolutely excluded'; and no time limit was set for these arrangements. The upshot of this was that 'His Majesty for himself and his posterity should for ever part with their peculiar regal power of being able to resist their enemies, or protect their good subjects, and with that undoubted and never denied right of the Crown, to make war and peace.' However, in repudiating such a demand, they could only fall back on a request that the Houses trust Charles to make appropriate appointments. Parliament should rest assured 'that as he will name no man for this great trust against whom there can be just exception (if the persons are named equally between him and you) so if the whole nomination were left to him, he would pitch only upon such as both kingdoms might have great cause to confide in'. To restrict the King's choice any further, the paper concluded, would be 'destructive to the end for which' the Propositions had originally been devised, namely 'justice, peace [and] unity'.

The King's commissioners' paper stressed that royal authority over the militia was a 'right', a regal power which derived from both the law and God, and which was exercised for the good of his people. This authority had clearly been enjoyed by previous monarchs; and the Houses' claims to exercise it were unprecedented. Such beliefs were axiomatic within Constitutional Royalist thought. Although they entailed a rejection of the Houses' terms, they should be contrasted with the hard-line advice which Charles received from other quarters. Just before the Treaty of Uxbridge opened, Henrietta Maria begged Charles never to disband his army, for

---

[117] Rushworth, V, 830–2; *LJ*, VII, 184, 201, 203, 211–12, 214.
[118] Rushworth, V, 833–6; *LJ*, VII, 183, 201–3, 211–13.
[119] This answer, delivered on 17 February 1645, is printed in Rushworth, V, 838–9; and *LJ*, VII, 214–15. The same day, Charles informed Nicholas that he would not settle for less than 'the free nomination' of half the militia commissioners: *Diary of Evelyn*, Bray, IV, 152 (Charles I to Nicholas, 17 February 1644/5).

that would give Parliament 'the whole power of the militia', enabling them to 'do whatsoever they will'.[120] Similarly, Digby's hostility towards the Houses' terms rested exclusively on their subversion of 'monarchichall power' rather than an attachment to the rule of law.[121] This view was later reiterated by another consistent opponent of negotiations, the Marquess of Newcastle.[122] What distinguished these people from the Constitutional Royalists was their lack of emphasis on legal propriety and the statutory foundation of royal military authority.

Behind the Houses' demands lay a profound unwillingness to trust Charles with senior military appointments. This hardened in the wake of the first Civil War, as the Newcastle Propositions indicated. For the first time, the Houses' control over the armed forces was to be limited to twenty years, the remainder of the King's presumed lifetime. This appeared a generous concession, but there was a vital qualification: after twenty years, 'in all cases wherein the Lords and Commons shall declare the safety of the kingdom to be concerned', any bills passed relating to the armed forces were to 'have the force and strength of an Act or Acts of Parliament, and shall be as valid to all intents and purposes as if the royal assent had been given thereunto'. 'The like' provision was promised 'for the kingdom of Scotland, if the Estates of Parliament there shall think fit'.[123] Thus hedged about, the concession of a twenty-year time limit was more apparent than real.

Through the summer and autumn of 1646, Charles's correspondence returned again and again to the issue of the militia. He clearly regarded this as marginally more negotiable than the future of the Church: as he informed Jermyn, Culpepper and Ashburnham on 22 July, he would 'lesse yeald' to Presbyterian government 'then the militia'.[124] Or again, a month later, 'I am most confident that religion will much sooner regaine the militia then the militia will religion.'[125] Charles told the Prince of Wales: 'next to religion the power of the sword is the truest badge and greatest support of soveranity, which is unknowen to none (as it may bee that of religion is to some)'.[126] To Henrietta Maria he declared himself 'still of

---

[120] *Letters of Henrietta Maria*, Green, pp. 282–3 (Henrietta Maria to Charles I, [? February] 1644/5).
[121] Bodl. Lib., MS Carte 14, fos. 92r–93r (Digby to Ormond, 7 February 1644/5).
[122] Thomas P. Slaughter, ed., *Ideology and Politics on the Eve of the Restoration: Newcastle's Advice to Charles II* (Memoirs of the American Philosophical Society, 159, Philadelphia, 1984), 5–9.
[123] Gardiner, *Documents*, pp. 295–7.
[124] Bodl. Lib., MS Clarendon 91, fo. 23v (Charles I to Jermyn, Culpepper and Ashburnham, 22 July 1646).
[125] *Ibid.*, fo. 28r (Charles I to Jermyn, Culpepper and Ashburnham, 19 August 1646).
[126] *Ibid.*, fo. 30v (Charles I to the Prince of Wales, 26 August 1646).

opinion, that, except religion be preserved, the militia will not be much usefull to the Crowne; nay without that, this will be but a shaddow'.[127] The Queen disagreed. Only if Charles was 'as resolute in the affair of the militia' as 'for the bishops', she argued, could all 'yet be well'.[128] She remained convinced that superior military force would ultimately enable the King to defeat his enemies. Jermyn and Culpepper also opposed concessions, but for quite different reasons: 'if you part with the militia, and place [it] in the Parlament as is desyred you will thereby consent to change monarchy into aristocracy'.[129] This use of Aristotelian categories was strikingly reminiscent of the *Answer to the XIX Propositions* which Culpepper had drafted with Falkland, and it complemented the more usual Constitutional Royalist arguments based on law and antiquity. Hyde, for example, claimed that his advice regarding the militia proceeded from a desire that 'what was unquestionably [the King's] owne right, and that the lawes of the lande, and constitucons of the kingdome in Church and State might be intirely and inviolably preserved'.[130]

The King's only concession during this period came in a secret approach via Will Murray to the Scottish commissioners in London. Charles was 'content that the whole power, for ten yeares, be in the two Houses'. If this was not enough, he was prepared 'to change the terme of yeares unto all the tyme of my reing', in return for 'a cleare and perfect asseurance that it shall freely return to my sone and successors, as Queene Elizabeth and my father injoyed it'. This was, however, 'not to be mentioned except upon absolut necessety'.[131] Charles's offer 'greatly surprised' Henrietta Maria, who felt that he had 'cut [his] own throat'.[132] But nothing came of it, for the Scots refused to take up these terms.[133] Instead, Charles was forced back on to increasingly desultory negotiations with the two Houses which culminated in his third answer to the Newcastle Propositions on 12 May 1647. He rejected 'the proposition touching the militia' because

thereby he conceives he wholly parts with the power of the sword intrusted to him by God and the laws of the land for the protection and government of his people, thereby at once divesting himself and disinheriting his posterity of the right and prerogative of the Crown which is absolutely necessary to the kingly office, and so

[127] Bodl. Lib., MS Clarendon 97, fo. 54r (Charles I to Henrietta Maria, 21 November 1646).
[128] *Letters of Henrietta Maria*, Green, p. 336 (Henrietta Maria to Charles I, 1/11 December 1646).
[129] Bodl. Lib., MS Clarendon 91, fo. 36r (Jermyn and Culpepper to Charles I, 18/28 September 1646).
[130] Bodl. Lib., MS Clarendon 29, fo. 182r.
[131] Bodl. Lib., MS Clarendon 91, fo. 54r (Charles I to Will Murray, 15 October 1646).
[132] *Letters of Henrietta Maria*, Green, p. 335 (Henrietta Maria to Charles I, 1/11 December 1646).
[133] *Charles I in 1646*, Bruce, 73 (Charles I to Henrietta Maria, 1 November 1646).

weakening monarchy in this kingdom that little more than the name and shadow of it will remain.

Once again, he offered to concede 'the whole power of the militia' to 'such persons as the two Houses of Parliament' shall nominate, provided that it 'afterwards ... return to the proper channel again, as it was in the times of Queen Elizabeth and King James of blessed memory'.[134] This statement picked up several phrases which occur repeatedly in Charles's private correspondence. But it also employed two motifs which were highly characteristic of Constitutional Royalist thought. First, there was the emphasis on the 'laws of the land' as a foundation of 'the power of the sword'. We have seen how this was a recurrent concern for Hyde in particular. Second, the King's response took the reigns of his two immediate predecessors as an ideal, and this invocation of 'Jacobethan' practice again echoed the views of Constitutional Royalists since 1641. The fact that Charles wrote this letter at Holdenby House[135] – cut off even from such peers as Richmond – reveals the extent to which he was prepared to deploy the arguments of his more moderate advisers.

Once again, the terms which demanded least from the King were the *Heads of the Proposals*. These envisaged that 'the power of the militia by sea and land' would be 'disposed by the Lords and Commons' during 'the space of ten years next ensuing'. Furthermore, no specific provisions were sought beyond this ten-year period.[136] By any reckoning, this should have removed a major obstacle to all previous negotiations. Hyde recognised the opportunity, and wrote to Sir John Berkeley: 'I have little hope of good by the conclusyons of the two Houses, who can never thinke themselves secure but by such an absolute power as will leave nobody else secure: but from the Army my hopes are much greater.'[137] It is likely that Berkeley agreed. His memoirs suggest that the clauses relating to the militia were not Charles's principal objection to the *Heads*.[138] But even if it proved less of a sticking-point than the future of the Church, this could not prevent Charles's rejection of the terms. At almost exactly the same time as Hyde's letter to Berkeley, the moderate Royalist peers were actively seeking the King's acceptance of the *Heads*.[139] But, like Berkeley's, their attempts were in vain.

The Houses absolutely refused to compromise on parliamentary control over military appointments for twenty years, together with continued powers thereafter in all matters concerning 'the safety of the kingdom'.

---

[134] Gardiner, *Documents*, p. 314.   [135] For the letter's delivery, see *LJ*, IX, 193.
[136] Gardiner, *Documents*, pp. 318–19.
[137] Bodl. Lib., MS Clarendon 30/1, fo. 119r (Hyde to Sir John Berkeley, 6 October 1647).
[138] *Narrative by Ashburnham*, II, cli-clii.   [139] See above, pp. 132–6.

They reiterated these demands in the *Four Bills* of December 1647.[140] The King, in a response drafted by Hyde,[141] retorted that such measures would give 'an arbitrary and unlimited power to the two Houses for ever, to raise and levy forces for land and sea'.[142] Instead, Charles struck a much more attractive deal with the Scots: the Engagement explicitly defended 'the right which belongs to the Crown in the power of the militia'.[143] This provided the basis for Scottish military intervention in the second Civil War.

However, when Scottish arms had failed to bring victory, and when talks had resumed at Newport, Charles finally made a qualified concession on the militia. On 9 October he agreed that

> trusting in his two Houses of Parliament, that they will make no farther use of the powers ... mentioned after the present distemper's settled, then shall be agreeable to the legal exercise thereof in times past, and for the purposes particularly mentioned in your proposition; and to give satisfaction to his two Houses, that he intends a full security; and to express his real desire to settle the peace of the kingdom, His Majesty doth consent to this proposition touching the militia, as is desired.[144]

This was a remarkable casuistry. While it ostensibly granted the Houses' demand to control the militia for twenty years, it in fact conceded this only for the duration of 'the present distemper' and only insofar as it was consistent with legal precedents. This enabled Charles to square the circle by giving ground while preserving the rule of law. However, the Parliamentarian commissioners balked at an answer which they claimed would cause 'difference and dispute upon the interpretation of it'. According to Hyde, Charles was then persuaded – upon the 'importunity of friends as well as of enemies' – to issue his concession without this preamble.[145] This suggests that by the Treaty of Newport, some of the King's closest advisers were urging him to cut his losses and to make straight concessions over the militia without fudges or qualifications. Charles clearly saw his 'great concession' as 'merely in order to my escape, of which if I had not hope, I would not have done'.[146] As we saw in chapter 5, this was a plot in which Constitutional Royalist peers were implicated.

As on the future of the Church, the rule of law coloured the Constitutional Royalists' attitudes towards the King's military authority. Command of the militia was vested in the King by law; to try to wrest this

---

[140] Gardiner, *Documents*, pp. 336–8.
[141] For the draft, see Bodl. Lib., MS Clarendon 30/2, fos. 234–5. See also Clarendon, *History*, IV, 276–9 (Book X, §§141–3).
[142] Gardiner, *Documents*, p. 355.   [143] *Ibid.*, p. 349.
[144] Walker, *Perfect Copies*, p. 53.
[145] Clarendon, *History*, IV, 443 (Book XI, §175). Hyde's account is corroborated by the contemporary diary of the King's secretary, Nicholas Oudart: Peck, *Desiderata Curiosa*, II, 393.
[146] Quoted in Gardiner, *Civil War*, IV, 220–1.

from him was unprecedented and downright illegal. But it went deeper than that. God and the law were very often invoked in the same breath as the foundations of the King's military powers, making this one of the most striking areas in which divine law and the common law were thought to coincide. Furthermore, this aspect of the King's powers was essential for the protection of his subjects. It was part of the responsibilities bestowed upon him by God, and it was exercised *pro bono publico*. This proved a major sticking-point because the Houses distrusted Charles to such a degree that they were unable to accept that his control over the militia was in the public interest. For the Constitutional Royalists, on the other hand, these powers were divine in origin and statutory in force. They had been confirmed by a string of medieval statutes, and – despite the uncertainty over whether or not those statutes remained in operation – it was therefore possible to defend them on grounds of both the royal prerogative and the common law without any inconsistency.

In successive negotiations, this close link between divine and common law as legitimators of royal military powers enabled a form of words to be devised which would satisfy both Charles and his moderate advisers. The distinction between moderate and hard-line Royalists was not between those who wished to fight and those who wished to negotiate, but between differing levels of commitment to peace treaties and varying degrees of emphasis on the rule of law. We should not see Constitutional Royalism and what Peter Newman has recently termed 'Armed Royalism' as mutually exclusive.[147] It was perfectly possible – as the examples of Hertford, Seymour and Lindsey show – to combine active military service with energetic involvement in peace talks. For, whether on the battlefield or in the council chamber, what they wished to defend was a concept of the King's military powers legitimated by both God and the common law. With this forceful assertion of the symbiosis between royal powers and the rule of law, they cut through the doubts surrounding England's militia statutes and repudiated the Houses' demands for enhanced military authority.

III. PARLIAMENT: POWERS AND PRIVILEGES

The King's withdrawal from London and subsequent raising of his standard cast grave doubts on the status of the two Houses at Westminster. Did they remain a legitimate Parliament, or did that require the personal

---

[147] P. R. Newman, 'The King's servants: conscience, principle, and sacrifice in armed Royalism', in *Public Duty and Private Conscience in Seventeenth-Century England: Essays Presented to G. E. Aylmer*, ed. John Morrill, Paul Slack and Daniel Woolf (Oxford, 1993), pp. 225–41.

presence of the monarch? The question was further complicated from January 1644 by Charles's summoning of an alternative Parliament to Oxford. The Houses at Westminster consistently refused to recognise the legality of this assembly. Not only did these issues recur throughout the formal treaties; the problem of parliamentary privilege disrupted talks in all sorts of other ways, from Essex's persistent refusal to negotiate independently of the two Houses, to Southampton's reluctance to transgress Parliament's Vote of No Addresses in the spring of 1648. What looked a reasonably straightforward constitutional matter turned out to be a peculiarly complex and ramifying problem.

The *Answer to the XIX Propositions* defined the Houses of Parliament as the King's 'Great and Supreme Council'. It argued that the Commons were 'an excellent conserver of liberty, but never intended for any share in government, or the chusing of them that should govern'; while the Lords, 'being trusted with a judicatory power', formed 'an excellent skreen and bank between the prince and the people, to assist each against any incroachments of the other'.[148] The King did not wish to challenge what he saw as Parliament's existing place in the constitution, and was 'ever willing that . . . Parliament should debate, resolve and transact such matters as are proper for them, as far as they are proper for them'. But of late the Houses had thought 'that proper for [their] debates, which hath not used to be at all debated within those walls'. Furthermore, because laws were 'jointly made' by Crown, Lords and Commons, the King was very much 'a part of the Parliament'.[149] The doctrine of the three estates was thus invoked to safeguard the King's position. Hyde criticised Falkland and Culpepper for advancing a formulation which was 'prejudicial to the King': he asserted that the three estates were in fact lords temporal, lords spiritual, and commons, with the King 'as head and sovereign of the whole'.[150] Both these models were significantly different from that of Viscount Saye and Sele, who held to a view of the three estates as Crown, Lords Temporal and Commons. Saye's exclusion of bishops clearly distinguished him from the Constitutional Royalists, as did his belief that the second and third estates could act on their own initiative if royal authority failed.[151]

However, Hyde clearly did agree with Falkland and Culpepper in

---

[148] These and the following quotations are taken from the text of the *Answer to the XIX Propositions* as printed in Rushworth, IV, 725–35.

[149] Cf. Clarendon, *History*, II, 80 (Book V, §149); and Mendle, 'Great Council of Parliament', 150–62.

[150] Clarendon, *Life*, I, 154–5. For a discussion of these contrasting definitions of the three estates, see Michael Mendle, *Dangerous Positions: Mixed Government, the Estates of the Realm, and the Making of the Answer to the XIX Propositions* (Alabama, 1985), especially pp. 5–20.

[151] J. S. A. Adamson, 'The *Vindiciae Veritatis* and the political creed of Viscount Saye and Sele', *Historical Research*, 60 (1987), 54–5.

wishing to preserve what he termed 'the privilege, dignity and security of Parliament'.[152] Indeed, to people like Hyde the greatest threat to such privileges appeared to come from 'those few men who called themselves the two Houses of Parliament'.[153] Just as the Houses distinguished between the office and the person of the King, so the Constitutional Royalists distinguished between the Houses of Parliament and the Junto which controlled them. On 15 June 1642, for instance, Hertford, Southampton, Lindsey, Falkland, Richmond, Seymour, Dorset, Culpepper, Nicholas and Bankes all signed an engagement that the King intended to preserve 'the just privileges of Parliament' and 'the liberty of the subject'.[154] Two days later, Charles issued a declaration composed by Hyde which asserted that 'it is impossible for [the King] to subsist without the affections of his people, and that those affections cannot possibly be preserved or made use of but by Parliaments'.[155] The King's *Declaration* of 12 August – also drafted by Hyde – developed this point and listed occasions on which the Junto had infringed 'the dignity, privilege and freedom of Parliaments'. He lamented the 'injustice, injurie, and violence offered to Parliaments'; and insisted that Parliaments 'were so essentiall a part of the constitution of the kingdome that' he could 'attain to no happinesse without them, nor' would he 'ever make the least attempt (in [his] thought) against them'. The King and the two Houses, this *Declaration* concluded, 'were like Hippocrates twins, [they] must laugh and crie, live and die together'.[156] In short, if the Houses claimed to defend the office of King more effectively than Charles I, the Constitutional Royalists claimed to protect the privileges of Parliament more successfully than the Junto.

This became a recurrent theme of Royalist propaganda throughout the years of civil war. In his first answer to the Oxford Propositions, for example, Charles insisted that the 'laws, liberties, priviledges and safety of Parliament' had been already 'amply settled and established' before the taking up of arms.[157] The King's answers to the Newcastle Propositions reiterated his pledge to defend 'the just privileges of Parliament'.[158] There is no reason to doubt that the Constitutional Royalists were sincerely attached to such ends. The members who assembled at Oxford in 1644 described 'the Parliament of England' as 'indeed the foundation whereupon all our laws and liberties are supported'; and pledged themselves to

---

[152] Clarendon, *History*, II, 195 (Book V, §361).   [153] *Ibid.*

[154] *Ibid.*, 185–6 (Book V, §§345–6).

[155] *His Maiesties Answer to the Petition of the Lords and Commons in Parliament assembled* [17 June 1642], p. 9 (Wing, C 2137; BL, TT, E 152/3); Clarendon, *History*, II, 202 (Book V, §364). For Hyde's draft, see Bodl. Lib., MS Clarendon 21, fo. 69r–v.

[156] *His Majesties Declaration* [12 August 1642], p. 77.   [157] Rushworth, V, 168.

[158] Gardiner, *Documents*, pp. 306–9.

defend 'the just freedom, liberty and privilege of Parliament'.[159] Sir John Strangways recorded in his commonplace book: 'we love p[ar]laments'. But the Parliaments which they loved were not those of the Junto. They were Parliaments 'held in a grave ... manner, without tumults'. By contrast, the Junto 'allow[ed] multitudes of the meaner sort of people to come to Westminster to cry for justice if they cannot have their will'. Once again, the Junto's actions paradoxically served to undermine the liberties and privileges of Parliament.[160]

It was important, however, not to restrict the concept of parliamentary privileges to the two Houses at Westminster. The King was also part of Parliament, and Hyde warned Nicholas in February 1647 that 'the priviledge of Parliam[en]t is noe lesse violated by forcing [Charles's] opinion or conscience, then if the same force were used to either House'.[161] This may have signalled an implicit retreat from Hyde's position in the summer of 1642. Certainly he now saw the King's freedom of conscience as a vital aspect of parliamentary privilege. This notion of the Crown as an essential component of a legitimate Parliament in turn explains several issues which surfaced throughout the 1640s: whether the King should return to Westminster; whether the two Houses remained a legitimate Parliament in his absence; and whether the King could legally summon an alternative Parliament to Oxford.

Ostensibly, both sides wanted the King to rejoin his Parliament at Westminster. At the Treaty of Oxford, for example, Charles was requested to return to Parliament and assured that he could do so 'with honour and safety'.[162] Similarly, in his third answer to the Newcastle Propositions, Charles desired 'presently to be admitted to his Parliament at Westminster, with that honour which is due to their sovereign'.[163] In practice, however, each party always predicated this move on concessions which the other refused to grant. Thus at Uxbridge the King's commissioners made his return conditional upon 'the disbanding [of] all armies'.[164] Similarly, his offer to return of 26 December 1645 was conditional upon 'his free and safe repair' to Oxford, Worcester or Newark after forty days; that of 23 March 1646 upon 'an act of oblivion and free pardon'.[165] The Houses consistently rejected such conditions: only at Newport did they finally relent. On 15 November 1648, the Commons voted to grant the King his lands and legal revenues, to pass an Act of Indemnity and Oblivion, and to permit

[159] Rushworth, V, 583, 593.
[160] Beinecke Library, Yale University, Osborn MS b. 304, pp. 46–7. Again, this was an almost exact quotation from David Jenkins's *Lex Terrae*, p. 18. See below, pp. 234–5.
[161] Bodl. Lib., MS Clarendon 29, fo. 107r (Hyde to Nicholas, 24 February 1646/7).
[162] Rushworth, V, 194; LJ, V, 704.
[163] Gardiner, *Documents*, pp. 315–16.   [164] Rushworth, V, 867.
[165] LJ, VIII, 72, 235.

Charles's return to London 'in a condition of honour, freedom and safety'.[166] This concession was decisive in furthering a settlement, and was clearly perceived as such by moderates and radicals alike. As a result, the resolution of this particular sticking-point became a crucial step towards Pride's Purge.[167] The eventual reunion of monarch and Parliament thus precipitated the destruction of the former and the truncation of the latter.

The second problem lay in the legal status of the two Houses at Westminster during the monarch's absence. The King's declaration of 17 June 1642, drafted by Hyde, marvelled at the 'desperate and dangerous positions' adopted by the Houses. None the less, the King wished 'to be present at, and to receive advice from, both Houses of Parliament', and therefore proposed that they be 'adjourned to another place which may be thought convenient, where His Majestie will be present'. The volatility of the London crowds offered another reason why 'both for the liberty and dignity of Parliament that convention for a time should be in another place'.[168] This was typical of the Constitutional Royalists' position throughout the 1640s: in contrast to more hard-line Royalists, they did not deny that the Houses were a Parliament;[169] but they did insist that they were not a *free* Parliament.[170] The only way for this to be remedied was by adjournment to another location with the King. That was what Charles – acting upon Hyde's advice – attempted with the Oxford Parliament, but it in turn muddied the waters of parliamentary privilege still further.[171]

Charles's proclamation of 22 December 1643 summoned the members of both Houses to Oxford, and offered 'a free and general pardon' to all who arrived within one month.[172] About forty Lords and over a hundred Commons duly assembled in Christ Church on 22 January 1644.[173] Charles

---

[166] *CJ*, VI, 76–7.
[167] David Underdown, *Pride's Purge: Politics in the Puritan Revolution* (Oxford, 1971), p. 122.
[168] *His Maiesties Answer* [17 June 1642], pp. 11–12; Clarendon, *History*, II, 203–4 (Book V, §364). For Hyde's draft, see Bodl. Lib., MS Clarendon 21, fo. 69r–v.
[169] For examples of the more hard-line position, see *Letters of Henrietta Maria*, Green, p. 276 (Henrietta Maria to Charles I, 30 December 1644); and Gryffith Williams, *Jura Majestatis, the Rights of Kings both in Church and State* (Oxford, 1644), pp. 204–12 (Wing, W 2669; BL, TT, E 14/18*).
[170] Cf. B. H. G. Wormald, *Clarendon: Politics, History and Religion, 1640–1660* (Cambridge, 1951; repr. 1989), p. 157.
[171] Clarendon, *History*, III, 259–61 (Book VII, §§326–8).
[172] Rushworth, V, 559–60. See also PRO, SP 16/500/10 (M. R[ichard] to Mr Richard, 11 January 1643/4).
[173] A number of other members subsequently joined the Oxford Parliament: see Rushworth, V, 573–5; *A Catalogue of the Names of the Knights, Citizens and Burgesses that have served in the last four Parliaments* (1656), pp. 20–5 (Wing, C 1394; BL, TT, E 1602/6). For a slightly exaggerated estimate of its size, see PRO, SP 16/500/30 (John Jones to Lord [Hopton], 1 February 1643/4). See also Huntington Library, Hastings MS, HA 8060 (diary of [? Philip Kinder]), unfol.

welcomed them, seeking their frank advice, 'in presenting whereof they should use all that parliamentary freedom which would be due to them if they were with him at Westminster, and which with all their other privileges they should enjoy at Oxford, though they could not in the other place'.[174] A week later, the Oxford Parliament made an approach to Essex which foundered on the issue of parliamentary privilege.[175] Then, on 3 March, the King wrote to the Houses at Westminster requesting the appointment of peace commissioners. He was, he said, following 'the advice of the Lords and Commons of Parliament assembled at Oxford': he was anxious to discuss 'how all the members of both Houses might securely meet in a full and free convention of Parliament'; and he reiterated his commitment to 'the rights and privileges of Parliament'.[176] The letter was addressed to 'the Lords and Commons of Parliament assembled at Westminster' – a style, Hyde thought, which 'they could not reasonably except against'.[177] This was very much against Charles's better judgement: he and Nicholas argued that it was not 'fitting to call those sitting at Westminster a Parliament', but bowed to the wishes of the majority of Privy Councillors.[178]

The Houses' response indicated how extraordinarily tangled the whole question of parliamentary privilege had become.[179] It lamented that 'those persons now assembled at Oxford, who, contrary to their duty, have deserted your Parliament', were 'put into an equal condition with it'. Meanwhile, the Parliament at Westminster, 'convened according to the known and fundamental laws of the kingdom (the continuance whereof is established by a law consented unto by your Majesty)' was 'in effect denied to be a Parliament'. The King's wish to assemble 'a full and free convention of Parliament' implied that the Houses at Westminster did not fulfil this description, and could only do so through the return of the members who had 'deserted' to Oxford. Those at Westminster consistently refused to acknowledge the legitimacy of the Oxford Parliament.[180] According to Hyde, some referred to it as 'the mock Parliament at Oxford'.[181] The Newcastle Propositions included a demand that 'the late members, or any who pretended themselves members of either House of Parliament, who have sat in the unlawful assembly at Oxford, called or pretended by some to be a Parliament, and have not voluntarily rendered

[174] Clarendon, *History*, III, 294 (Book VII, §370).   [175] See below, pp. 173–4.
[176] *LJ*, VI, 451–2.
[177] Clarendon, *History*, III, 304 (Book VII, §391).
[178] *Memoirs of Prince Rupert and the Cavaliers*, ed. Eliot Warburton (3 vols., 1849), III, 42.
[179] *LJ*, VI, 459–60, from which the following quotations are taken.
[180] See, for example, BL, Add. MS 18779, fo. 48v.
[181] [Edward Hyde], *A Full Answer to an Infamous and Trayterous Pamphlet* (1648), p. 105 (Wing, C 4423; BL, TT, E 455/5).

themselves before the last of October 1644, be removed from His Majesty's counsels'.[182]

The members of the Oxford Parliament, by contrast, maintained that they should 'not be thought less Members of Parliament, tho[ugh] we are not at Westminster, than if that city were in the possession of a foreign enemy'. They claimed to have been driven away by 'those outrages and violences offered to our persons or our consciences, which take away all freedom and consequently all authority from those counsels'. The Junto had 'speciously pretended the defence of the rights and privileges of Parliament' while in reality 'cancelling all the liberties and privileges of Parliament'. Freedom from intimidation was a prerequisite for a true Parliament: the Oxford assembly therefore accounted itself 'the true and lawful members of Parliament', whereas the Houses at Westminster were 'not a full nor free convention'.[183] Unfortunately, a free Parliament offering frank advice was by no means good news for the King. The Oxford Parliament consistently urged Charles to continue peace talks with the Houses,[184] and he ultimately came to detest it. Henrietta Maria was 'always ... afraid of the assembly at Oxford';[185] following its second adjournment in March 1645, Charles expressed exasperation with its moderate advice and congratulated himself on being 'well freed from the place of base and mutinous motions'; he went so far as to call it a 'mungril Parliament',[186] implicitly challenging its status and very existence, which had in itself impeded negotiations with Westminster.

But this difficulty of determining which body constituted a legitimate Parliament was not the only way in which the issue of privilege stymied peace negotiations. At another level, it vitiated Royalist approaches to Essex on two key occasions during 1644. First, on 27 January the Oxford Parliament sent the Lord General a conciliatory letter seeking his help in a 'restitution to the blessings of peace' and asking him to convey their hopes for a treaty to 'those by whom you are trusted'.[187] This suggests that they addressed Essex not so much to acknowledge his 'vice-regal status', but rather to communicate with the Houses at Westminster in a way which avoided explicitly recognising (or denying) their legitimacy as a Parliament.[188] However, this initiative foundered on the Lord General's conviction that

---

[182] Gardiner, *Documents*, pp. 300–1.   [183] Rushworth, V, 589, 594–5.
[184] Gardiner, *Civil War*, II, 114, 181.
[185] *Letters of Henrietta Maria*, Green, p. 285 (Henrietta Maria to Charles I, 14 February 1644/5).
[186] Rushworth, V, 894.
[187] *A Copy of a Letter from the Members of both Houses to the Earle of Essex desiring a Treaty of Peace* (Oxford, 1644), pp. 4–5 (Wing, E 1285; BL, TT, E 32/3).
[188] Cf. J.S.A. Adamson, 'The baronial context of the English Civil War', *TRHS*, 5th series, 40 (1990), 108–10.

he was the servant of the two Houses. Essex replied to the Earl of Forth that since this letter bore no 'address to the two Houses of Parliament, nor therein there being no acknowledgement of them', he 'could not communicate it to them'. He continued: 'My Lord, the maintenance of the Parliament of England, and of the privileges thereof, is that for which we are all resolved to spend our blood; as being the foundation whereupon all our liberties and laws are built.'[189] Essex's unflinching sense of duty to Parliament led to an almost exact replay of this exchange the following summer. Faced with an initiative from the King, Prince Maurice, and many senior officers, Essex replied simply: 'I, having no power from the Parliament (who have employed me) to treat, cannot give way to it without breach of trust.'[190] The King may have addressed the Lord General 'in terms almost of equality'; but Essex continued to see himself as directly accountable to the two Houses.[191] In recognition, the Lords and Commons promptly wrote to the Earl 'taking notice of his great faithfulness to the Parliament, and to give him thanks and encouragement for the same'.[192]

This deference to parliamentary authority was no less of a sticking-point for the Constitutional Royalist peers. Perhaps the most striking instance of this came in the spring of 1648 when Southampton refused a peace initiative led by Saye, Evelyn, Pierrepont and possibly Cromwell on the grounds that this would breach the Vote of No Addresses: 'my lords doe you come to catch me', he asked, 'have you not made itt treason to make any addresse to the king; and would you bring me within the compasse of itt ... Recall the order you have made ag[ains]t the King, and then gett me a p[ar]ticular order to goe and I will goe.'[193] This literal adherence to a parliamentary vote went along with a pronounced reverence for statute. In April 1644, for example, the Oxford Parliament petitioned the King 'to hold and keep [our laws] inviolable and unalterable, but by Act of Parliament'. The following year, parliamentary statutes provided the organising principle for a tract in which Hyde argued that the Houses 'and their complices have spoken and acted nothing but rebellion and treason if examined and tryed by the lawes of the land'.[194] Hyde's respect for statutes extended to the reforming acts of 1640–1 which Henrietta Maria and other Royalist hard-liners were never able to countenance.[195] Similarly, Sir John

[189] *LJ*, VI, 404; Clarendon, *History*, III, 298 (Book VII, §377).   [190] *LJ*, VI, 671.
[191] Adamson, 'Baronial context', 111.
[192] *LJ*, VI, 669; *CJ*, III, 590.
[193] Bodl. Lib., MS Clarendon 31, fo. 54v ([Sir Edward Forde] to [Lord Hopton], 16 April 1648).
[194] [Edward Hyde], *Transcendent and Multiplied Rebellion and Treason, discovered by the Lawes of the Land* (1645), p. 22 (Wing, C 4428; BL, TT, E 308/29).
[195] *Letters of Henrietta Maria*, Green, pp. 144 (Henrietta Maria to Charles I, 3/13 November 1642), 182 (Henrietta Maria to Charles I, 8 April 1643); Slaughter, *Ideology and Politics*, pp. 49–55. See also below, pp. 180, 252–3.

Strangways based his point by point analysis of his own position on statutes.[196] Comparable views were expressed by Dorset in the wake of the riots in late July 1647 which forced many members of both Houses to withdraw from Westminster. 'Shall orders and ordinances prove feathers and weather-coks?', Dorset asked the Earl of Middlesex, 'shall the resolutions of soe venerable an assembly as the two houses of parlement florish in the morning, and bee revoked or contemned before the next evening? Shall apprentices turne privy councellors, and shall confusion become the mother of order?'[197] I have argued elsewhere that this letter must be understood in the context of Dorset's consistent hostility to any attack on Parliament's established composition and procedures.[198] Dorset returned to this theme in another letter to Middlesex two days later. He deplored the way in which members of both Houses had left the capital:

Itt seems a parlement may bee withoutt a broad seale, and itt seems this fixed parlement may move forth of London att the will and pleasure of a few private persons, for certaynly the speakers of both howses are nott qualifyed any where else butt in their severall howses, nor showld withdraw themselvs withoutt a plurality of votes, in ether howses, particularly to warrant there absences. I beleeve noe precedent cann bee found to iustify these proceedings, and God knowes what may bee the consequences, when foundations are shaken.[199]

Their hostility to Parliamentarian leaders notwithstanding, the customary structure of the Houses clearly formed part of the 'foundations' which the Constitutional Royalists sought to preserve. Indeed, they were hostile to those at Westminster precisely because they blamed them for damaging Parliament's legality and constitutional propriety.

This fundamental distinction between Parliament's structure and its existing leadership in turn helps to explain why Royalist moderates found the *Heads of the Proposals* so appealing. The thrust of the *Heads* was to preserve the place of Parliaments within the constitution while curtailing the life of the existing assembly. 'A certain period' was to 'be set for the ending of this Parliament'. Parliaments would henceforth meet biennially and sit for between 120 and 240 days. Elections were to be conducted 'according to some rule of equality or proportion' in order 'to render the House of Commons (as near as may be) an equal representative of the whole'.[200] The effect of these reforms was to exclude the current

---

[196] Beinecke Library, Yale University, Osborn MS b. 304, pp. 45–7. For further citations of statutes see, for example, *ibid.*, pp. 49, 52. Cf. Jenkins, *Lex Terrae*, pp. 17–19.
[197] CKS, Sackville MS, U 269/C248, unfol.: Dorset to the second Earl of Middlesex, 30 July 1647.
[198] Smith, '"The more posed and wise advice"', 825–6. Cf. above, p. 85.
[199] CKS, Sackville MS, U 269/C248, unfol.: Dorset to the second Earl of Middlesex, 1 August 1647.
[200] Gardiner, *Documents*, pp. 316–17.

Presbyterian leaders of the Commons, those who had sought Charles's acceptance of the Uxbridge and Newcastle Propositions. This should have made the issue of parliamentary privilege less of a sticking-point than in any earlier negotiations.

However, when he showed the Heads to Charles, Sir John Berkeley found that the King had received 'another advice' and objected to 'the excluding his party from being eligible in the next ensuing Parliament'. Berkeley answered that 'the next Parliament would be necessitated to lay great burdens upon the kingdom; and it would be a happiness to the King's party to have no voice in them'.[201] This was not a particularly strong argument, but it seems to have allayed the King's fears sufficiently for him to entertain the Heads as a possible basis for a 'personal treaty' with the Houses. He remained anxious, during the autumn of 1647, to affirm his desire to preserve 'the just privileges of Parliament'.[202] He further requested that the Houses consider 'the proposals of the army concerning the succession of Parliaments and their due elections'.[203] The army's allies within Parliament were anxious to enshrine these terms in legislation.[204] The Heads thus promised genuine headway towards a settlement regarding the duration and composition of Parliament. This prospect was, however, soon dashed by Charles's rejection of both the Heads and the Four Bills, and his Engagement with the Scots. Yet amid these complex tactical manoeuvres, Charles's basic position remained unchanged: the Engagement sought to establish 'a free and full Parliament in England' and to set 'a speedy period ... to this present Parliament'.[205] Indeed, he espoused this view to the very end: at his trial he rejected the charge that he had 'levied war against' Parliament, and argued instead that Pride's Purge and the establishment of a High Court of Justice violated 'the privileges of both Houses of Parliament'.[206] On the scaffold he declared that he 'never did begin the war with the two Houses of Parliament' and 'never did intend to incroach upon their privileges'.[207]

Throughout the years of civil war, the difficulty with this stance lay in how to offer a plausible defence of parliamentary privileges in theory while in practice rejecting the demands of the Junto on a whole range of issues. To resolve this apparent contradiction, the Constitutional Royalists fell back on a denial that the Houses at Westminster formed a full, free and legitimate Parliament. They recognised Parliament's importance within the constitution, but argued that this was a function of its ability to advise the

[201] *Narrative by Ashburnham*, II, cli–clii.   [202] Gardiner, *Documents*, p. 327.
[203] *Ibid.*, p. 332.
[204] *LJ*, IX, 481–3; *CJ*, V, 338. Cf. Adamson, 'Projected settlement', 586–8.
[205] Gardiner, *Documents*, p. 350.
[206] *Ibid.*, pp. 372, 375.   [207] Rushworth, VIII, 1429.

King freely. That could, they argued, only be achieved if the King were physically present with the Lords and Commons, and the deliberations of those Houses were carried on freely and without intimidation. The Houses at Westminster had ceased to fulfil these criteria following the mass demonstrations of late 1641 and the King's departure from London in January 1642. Insofar as the Junto had failed to ensure free debate and to facilitate the King's return to Westminster, it had *itself* subverted Parliament's powers and privileges. Insofar as the King had summoned a Parliament to his headquarters at Oxford away from the London crowds, he had given proof of his commitment to govern with the consent of a free Parliament. This argument was thus the exact mirror image of that which the Houses deployed to justify taking up arms against the King. Whereas the Junto argued that the only way to defend the King's office was to fight the person of Charles I, so the Constitutional Royalists argued that the privileges of Parliament could only be preserved by standing firm against the Junto. The King, in short, was a far more effective champion of Parliament's rights and liberties than those who held sway at Westminster.

This inevitably became a sticking-point in successive peace negotiations. The denial of the Houses' legitimacy informed the King's commissioners' rejection of any propositions which transferred authority from the Crown to Parliament. In particular, it justified their refusal to compromise on Church government, the militia, the legal system, and the right to appoint councillors. The dispute over Parliament's legitimacy thus helped to prevent a settlement on other issues as well. It also – as the talks involving Essex in 1644 and Southampton in 1648 show – caused confusion about how far private peace initiatives could contravene the Houses' orders.

Furthermore, the separation of the King from the two Houses highlighted an ambiguity in the application of estates theory to the English polity. Did the three estates consist of King, Lords and Commons, as Falkland and Culpepper argued in the *Answer to the XIX Propositions?* Or did they comprise lords temporal, lords spiritual, and commons, as Hyde asserted in 1642? Both models could trace respectable pedigrees within English political theory, although the second was 'the main accepted definition' during the sixteenth and early seventeenth centuries.[208] But we should not exaggerate the significance of this controversy: it is important not to lose sight of the large area of common ground which united both models. This rested on the assumption that the natural relationship between the monarch and the two Houses was one of harmonious collaboration. From the 1530s onwards, the King-in-Parliament formed the supreme legislative authority in England. The harmony within this 'mixed-

---

[208] G. R. Elton, *The Parliament of England, 1559–1581* (Cambridge, 1986), pp. 17–23 (quotation at p. 17).

sovereign'[209] was essential for the passage of statutes. The Constitutional Royalists – however they defined the three estates – wished to preserve existing statutes and the constitutional arrangements which had produced them. Unlike some Royalist hard-liners, they never sought the repeal of those statutory reforms to which Charles had assented in 1640–1. They recognised the interdependence of royal powers and parliamentary privileges. The insistence that Crown, Lords and Commons needed each other – and the corollary that the Houses could not legislate on their own – united the Constitutional Royalists and transcended the specific dispute over the definition of the three estates. The King could not rule effectively without Parliaments acting both as his Great Council and as a court of law. With the advice of Parliament he passed statutes which then constituted the highest form of law. This ideal was one aspect of the Constitutional Royalists' belief in the intimate relationship between royal powers and the English common law, which was itself another area of dispute.

IV. THE COMMON LAW

A commitment to the rule of law has already emerged at several points in this study as highly characteristic of the Constitutional Royalists. We saw in chapter 4 how it provided a major inducement for them to rally to the King in 1641–2; and it subsequently coloured their attitudes towards 'the Church by law established' and the military authority legally vested in the Crown. But the Constitutional Royalists' understanding of and attachment to the rule of law extended well beyond that. This section will concentrate on four areas and assess their impact upon peace negotiations: the interrelationship between the common law, the 'liberties of the subject' and the royal prerogative; the King's attempted adjournment of the common law courts to Oxford; the Houses' demands for certain named appointments to the judiciary; and Parliament's legal right (or not) to produce and use a new Great Seal.

It was one of the fundamental tenets of Constitutional Royalism that the rule of the Crown operated in symbiosis with the rule of law. The King's *Answer to the XIX Propositions* drove this point home again and again. Parliament's terms, it argued, would force the King 'to abandon that power which only can enable us to perform what we are sworn to in protecting our people and the laws'. The King was defending powers 'which are trusted wholly to us by the laws'. Those laws were 'jointly made' by King, Lords and Commons, and it was vital to maintain 'this kind of regulated monarchy . . . without which it would be disabled to preserve the laws

---

[209] *Ibid.*, p. 21.

in their force, and the subjects in their liberties and properties'. To transfer royal powers to the Houses 'would be a total subversion of the fundamental laws, and that excellent constitution of this kingdom'. Invoking the barons' maxim in the Statute of Merton (1236), the *Answer* summed up this commitment to law as follows:

Our Answer is, *Nolumus Leges Angliae mutari*: but this we promise, that we will be as careful of preserving the laws in what is supposed to concern wholly our subjects, as in what most concerns our self: for indeed we profess to believe that the preservation of every law concerns us, those of obedience being not secure when those of protection are violated.[210]

It was thus a powerful attraction of the rule of law that it protected *both* the royal prerogative *and* the subjects' liberties. The two were bolted together by 'fundamental laws'; and to harm one would therefore automatically harm the other.

The various declarations drafted by Hyde advanced almost identical arguments. That of 17 June 1642, for example, committed the King to 'the care of the laws and liberties of the kingdom'. It claimed that the King required nothing of his subjects but 'what their own dutie, guided by the infallible rule of the law, leads them to do'; whereas the Houses had voted 'all his legal power ... from him'.[211] Similarly, the Royalist engagement two days earlier had asserted that all the King's 'endeavours' tended towards 'the liberty of the subject, the law, peace, and prosperity of this kingdom'.[212] Hertford, Seymour and the other Commissioners of Array for Somerset insisted on 25 August 1642 that they would 'never bee brought to execute any thinge that shall anie way tend to the violation of the libertie or propriety of the subiect'.[213] The members of the Oxford Parliament likewise pledged themselves to 'the preservation of the liberty and property of the subject, settled and evident by the laws, statutes and customs of the realm'.[214] Private rhetoric precisely echoed these statements. In a codicil to his will of 6 April 1647, Hyde insisted that he had always desired 'that the frame and constitucons of the kingdome might be observed, and the knowne lawes the bounds betwene the Kings power and the subiects righte'.[215] Strangways wrote in his commonplace book: 'We of the Kings partie ... doe well know that our estates, lives and fames are preserved by the lawes; and that the King is bound by his lawes.'[216] This outlook stood in

[210] Rushworth, IV, 726, 731–2.
[211] *His Maiesties Answer* [17 June 1642], pp. 7–8, 11; Clarendon, *History*, II, 201–3 (Book V, §364). For Hyde's draft, see Bodl. Lib., MS Clarendon 21, fo. 69r–v.
[212] Clarendon, *History*, II, 185–6 (Book V, §345).   [213] MP, 25 August 1642.
[214] Rushworth, V, 593.
[215] Bodl. Lib., MS Clarendon 29, fo. 181v.
[216] Beinecke Library, Yale University, Osborn MS b. 304, p. 47. This was an almost exact quotation from David Jenkins's *Lex Terrae*: see below, p. 235.

marked contrast to that of Henrietta Maria, who condemned those 'persons about' Charles who did not 'wish [him] to be absolute'.[217] Similarly, her friend Newcastle felt that the King had 'the whole lawe to depend uppon' him, and stood 'above the law'.[218] It was, however, the more moderate idea of a legally limited monarchy which was consistently advanced on Charles's behalf during peace negotiations.

The concept of a symbiotic relationship between royal powers, popular liberties and the common law allowed Charles to maintain that he could safeguard his subjects' rights and freedom much more effectively than the two Houses. This coloured the King's responses at the Treaty of Oxford. Charles insisted that his desire had 'always been that all men should be tried by the known law', and proposed that everything 'done or published contrary to the known laws of the land, or derogatory to His Majesty's legal and known power and rights be renounced and recalled'. He demanded that 'whatsoever illegal power hath been claimed and exercised by, or over his subjects, [such] as imprisoning their persons without law ... be disclaimed, and all such persons so committed forthwith discharged'.[219] The Oxford talks then reached deadlock on the issue of a cessation of arms, which enabled the Houses to avoid answering these demands head on. However, the King continued to insist that during the cessation 'there should be no plundering or violence offered to any of his subjects ... contrary to the known laws of the land'.[220] At Uxbridge, the King repeated these propositions verbatim.[221] However, the programme for that treaty – with rotating negotiations on Church government, the militia and Ireland – precluded a detailed exploration of the legal issues which they raised. Even with a different agenda, however, it is very unlikely that agreement could have been reached for the Houses' respect for the rule of law was by this time rapidly disintegrating. As early as the summer of 1643, Lord Wharton had declared that 'they were not tied to a law for these were times of necessity and imminent danger'.[222] This principle was used to justify the many illegal measures – involving the infringement of virtually every clause in the Petition of Right – which the Houses adopted in order to win the first Civil War. These policies have been recounted in detail, especially by John Morrill and Robert Ashton, and here we should simply note the enormous

---

[217] *Letters of Henrietta Maria*, Green, p. 144 (Henrietta Maria to Charles I, 3/13 November 1642).

[218] Slaughter, *Ideology and Politics*, pp. 34, 54. Cf. *The Life of William Cavendish, Duke of Newcastle, ... by Margaret, Duchess of Newcastle*, ed. C. H. Firth (1907), p. 121. Other exponents of the belief that the monarch stood above human law are discussed below, pp. 244–54.

[219] Rushworth, V, 168–9; *LJ*, V, 591.   [220] Rushworth, V, 178.

[221] *Ibid.*, 804; *LJ*, VII, 151–2.

[222] Quoted in Morrill, *Revolt*, pp. 52, 82–3.

mileage which Royalist propaganda was able to derive from them.[223] The King repeatedly pledged his commitment to 'the freedom and propriety of the subject' and to 'the undoubted rights of every free-born man, how mean soever his birth be'.[224] For instance, Charles assured the High Sheriff of Worcestershire in December 1642 that he was 'resolved always to govern [his subjects in that county] by the known laws of the land, that thereby they may have a perfect enjoyment of their liberty and property'.[225] These arguments entirely accorded with the advice of moderates close to Charles. Thus the Oxford Parliament complained in the spring of 1644 that

> the Charter of our liberties, *Magna Charta*, so industriously and religiously preserved by our ancestors, and above thirty several times confirmed in Parliament, that rampire and bulwark of all the precious privileges and immunities which the subjects of this kingdom could boast of, and which distinguishes them from all the subjects of Christendom, is levelled and trampled under foot.[226]

Such words struck an immediate chord in the provinces. The earnest desire of the commissioners for the Marcher counties early in 1645 – 'that during this war your Majesty will order that as near as the necessity of the times can admit, our ancient laws shall be observed in force and reputation'[227] – was entirely typical of the sentiment which led many to see the King's rule as more law abiding than that of the Houses, and which was to culminate in pro-Royalist activism during the second Civil War.

This was not, of course, simply a matter of propaganda. There is no reason to doubt that Strangways meant every word when he wrote in his commonplace book:

> We mayntayne that noe man should be imprysoned, putt out of his lands, but by dew p[ro]cesse of law, and noe man ought to be adjudged to death, but by the lawes established in the land, the customs therof, or by act of parlament. They practise the contrary in London, Bristoll, Kent. Our warrant is Magna Charta cap. 29, the petition of right [ter]tio Car. and diverse lawes there mentioned.[228]

The same is surely true of Hyde's letter to Culpepper of 20 August 1648: 'If wee stand fast upon the old rock of established law, wee have advantage in the contencon, and shall still have a proporcon of hope, which will bee more comfortable then any security they can have who oppresse us.'[229] In the main, Royalist justice lived up to these high ideals in practice. Charles's

---

[223] *Ibid.*, especially pp. 52–88; Robert Ashton, 'From Cavalier to Roundhead tyranny, 1642–9', in *Reactions*, Morrill, pp. 185–207.

[224] For examples, see Gardiner, *Documents*, pp. 307–8.

[225] 'The Diary of Henry Townshend of Elmley Lovett, 1640–1663', ed. J. W. Willis Bund, *Publ. Worcs. Historical Society* (2 vols., 1916–20), II, 91.

[226] Rushworth, V, 590–1.   [227] Quoted in Morrill, *Revolt*, p. 83.

[228] Beinecke Library, Yale University, Osborn MS b. 304, pp. 46–7. Cf. Jenkins, *Lex Terrae*, pp. 18–19.

[229] Bodl. Lib., MS Clarendon 31, fo. 209r (Hyde to Culpepper, 20 August 1648).

sequestration policy rested on the principle that wherever possible his opponents should be formally indicted for treason by a jury at common law. If they had been sequestrated without such an indictment, they were allowed to appeal to the next assize. The King also sought local approval, usually by grand juries, for all financial contributions and forced loans.[230] This concern for legal propriety was in marked contrast to Parliament's wartime administration, which employed ordinances to cut loose from tradition and bypass the jury system.[231] In particular, ordinances enabled the Houses to redefine treason to cover all manner of offences against the Lords and Commons, and to use this charge to attack their own political enemies.[232]

Constitutional Royalists were not slow to grasp the public relations value of the King's record in this area. As Hyde told Lord Digby in November 1648, 'whilst wee keepe ourselves upon the old foundacon of the established governm[en]t, and the good knowne lawes, how weake soever wee are in *power*, wee shall bee strong in *reputacon*'.[233] This was a remarkably perceptive and prescient statement. It is no exaggeration to say that Hyde had identified one of the greatest appeals of Constitutional Royalism. On the scaffold, Charles I embraced exactly the same position when he claimed to desire the people's 'liberty and freedom as much as any body whomsoever'; but insisted that 'their liberty and freedom consists in having of government, those laws by which their life and their goods may be most their own'.[234] Monarchy was the best guardian of liberty and property because it was the best guardian of the rule of law. These words reveal the extent to which Charles had assimilated the views of his moderate advisers and – as we shall see below – they were to form a vital part of the long-term appeal of Royalism.

Hand in hand with this view of the King as the guardian of English laws and liberties went a belief that he was the fount of justice. Although laws were 'jointly made' by King, Lords and Commons,[235] justice was exercised in the King's name. The central law courts were the King's courts. Charles argued in turn that this entitled him to summon those courts to Oxford. On 27 December 1642 he issued a proclamation adjourning the Courts of Wards, Exchequer, Chancery, the Duchy of Lancaster and Requests to Oxford, 'where His Majesties residence now is'.[236] The Houses retorted

[230] Morrill, *Revolt*, pp. 80–4.
[231] *Ibid.*, pp. 54–80; Ashton, 'From Cavalier to Roundhead tyranny', pp. 187–202.
[232] Adele Hast, 'State treason trials during the Puritan Revolution, 1640–1660', *HJ*, 15 (1972), 37–53.
[233] Bodl. Lib., MS Clarendon 31, fo. 319v (Hyde to Lord Digby, 20 November 1648). My emphasis.
[234] Rushworth, VIII, 1429.   [235] *Ibid.*, IV, 731.
[236] J. F. Larkin, ed., *Stuart Royal Proclamations*, vol. II: *Royal Proclamations of King Charles I, 1625–46* (Oxford, 1983), 834–7. See also S. F. Black, 'The judges of Westminster Hall during the Great Rebellion, 1640–1660' (BLitt thesis, University of Oxford, 1970), pp. 54–5.

that the Lord Keeper, the Master of the Court of Wards, and the Supreme Judges of the Chancery and the Court of Wards were members of the Lords and therefore could not depart from Westminster 'without breach of privileges of Parliament ... unless they have leave of the said House of Peers'. Furthermore, the journey to Oxford through two armies would prove hazardous for both litigants and legal records; while in Oxford itself the Courts could not 'proceed ... with that freedom and liberty as Courts of Justice ought to do, there being an army in the said city'.[237] Charles's answer – drafted by Hyde – reiterated his personal need for all these officials in Oxford, and asserted 'his undoubted right to adjourn or remove the [law] terms to what place he please'. Again, the symbiosis between royal authority and the law was emphasised:

The reason of His Majesty's adjournment of the courts of law till *crastino purificationis* is for the great danger his good subjects must undergo by passing through the armies; and His Majesty much fears his good subjects will have little benefit by their legal proceedings whilst His Majesty and the law are no better able to defend one another.[238]

The King's right to remove the central law courts to a location of his choice thus rested on that same fundamental principle of reciprocity between prerogative and law.

The Houses retaliated on 21 January 1643 with an ordinance which argued that to adjourn the courts to Oxford tended 'much to the prejudice of the Commonwealth'. They repeated the claim that traversing two armies near Oxford would endanger both records and litigants, as well as remove those judges and other legal officials who were members of either House. They therefore declared those assisting the removal to be 'disturbers of the peace of the kingdom', and ordered that no judgements made by courts sitting 'out of the usual places' could 'bind any person' without their consent.[239]

This ordinance underpinned the Houses' subsequent peace terms relating to courts of law. The Uxbridge Propositions stipulated that all judges and legal officers who had 'deserted the Parliament and adhered to the enemies thereof' were to be 'made incapable of any place of judicature and office, towards the common law or civil'.[240] The Newcastle Propositions repeated this demand and imposed the additional penalty of a fine of one third of the value on the estates of all 'Judges and officers towards the law' who had 'deserted the Parliament'.[241] This in turn led to the issue of

[237] *LJ*, V, 548.
[238] *Ibid.*, 562. For Hyde's draft, see Bodl. Lib., MS Clarendon 21, fo. 69r–v. See also Black, 'Judges of Westminster Hall', p. 56.
[239] *LJ*, V, 567; Black, 'Judges of Westminster Hall', p. 56.
[240] Gardiner, *Documents*, pp. 280, 284.
[241] *Ibid.*, p. 303.

punishments for those who had adhered to the King, discussed in section VI below.

Throughout, the Constitutional Royalists still accepted and defended the King's right to determine the location of the common law courts. Several of them gained senior legal offices at Oxford. Falkland served as Lord Privy Seal from April to September 1643;[242] Culpepper was installed as Master of the Rolls on 28 January 1643;[243] and Seymour became Chancellor of the Duchy of Lancaster in April 1644.[244] The willingness to accept such appointments rested on two assumptions. The first was that the King was legally entitled to make them. In the *Answer to the XIX Propositions*, Falkland and Culpepper had asserted that 'power ... of making ... judges for law' was 'placed in the King'.[245] Second, they clearly thought that the Houses had obstructed the provision of justice. In the spring of 1644, the Oxford Parliament lamented that there was 'no face of justice over the land', for 'the Judges are prohibited to ride their circuits for the administration of that justice which the King owes his people, and they are bound to execute'.[246] It was therefore up to the King – insofar as he could – to supply the deficiency which Parliament had caused.[247]

In general, however, Charles's attempt to adjourn the common law courts to Oxford proved a failure. Such institutions could only be moved once a writ of adjournment had been read in open court, and this was difficult to perform at Westminster. Furthermore, the common law relied so heavily upon precedent that the impossibility of transporting bulky records through a hostile army severely hampered proceedings at Oxford. Similarly, the King's bid to maintain the assize circuits slowly disintegrated after 1643. The Houses refused to authorise any circuits during the first Civil War, and those despatched from Oxford were gradually curtailed by Parliamentarian victories. The Houses thus retained control of the central organs of legal administration throughout the 1640s, despite the fact that the majority of judges sided with the King.[248]

This brings us to the closely linked issue of the Crown's right to make appointments to the judiciary. For those at Westminster, this once again raised the question of whether they could trust the King. They remembered the numerous occasions on which Charles had interfered with due process of law.[249] It was not enough that the King had assented (on 15 January

---

[242] E. B. Fryde, D. E. Greenway, S. Porter and I. Roy, *Handbook of British Chronology* (3rd edition, 1986), p. 97.
[243] BL, Add. MS 18777 (diary of Walter Yonge), fo. 143v.
[244] PRO, SO 3/12 (Signet Office docquet book), fo. 264v.
[245] Rushworth, IV, 731.   [246] *Ibid.*, 591.
[247] Clarendon, *History*, II, 525–7 (Book VI, §§377–81).
[248] Black, 'Judges of Westminster Hall', pp. 44–8, 52–63, 76–7.
[249] For an analysis of Charles's 'legal tyranny', see Morrill, *Nature of the English Revolution*, pp. 287–91. See also above, pp. 28–9.

1641) that the judges of King's Bench, Common Pleas and Exchequer 'hold their places ... *quamdiu se bene gesserint*, and not *durante bene placito*'.[250] The whole power of royal nomination had to be changed, not just the terms of judicial tenure. The *Nineteen Propositions* requested that the Lord Keeper, the Chief Justices of King's Bench and Common Pleas, and the Chief Baron of the Exchequer be 'chosen with the approbation of both Houses'. All Judges were to 'hold their places *quamdiu se bene gesserint*'.[251] The King's *Answer* found this demand quite 'unreasonable', for it indicated 'that it is not with the persons now chosen, but with our chusing that you are despleased'. Indeed, the King would rather that he approve and the Houses nominate than vice versa, although he insisted that he would 'never grant either'.[252] However, Parliament's next set of terms, the Oxford Propositions, adopted this alternative strategy by presenting a slate of named appointments. They sought the appointment of Sir John Bramston as Chief Justice of King's Bench, of William Lenthall (Speaker of the Commons) as Chief Justice of Common Pleas, and of John Wilde (also a member of the Long Parliament) as Chief Baron of the Exchequer.[253] In addition, they requested that further named persons be either continued or appointed as Justices in each of these three Courts. The Justices were to hold their places *quamdiu se bene gesserint*, and those who currently held the offices at Oxford were to be removed.[254] The Uxbridge Propositions abandoned requests for specific appointments, but retained the principle of parliamentary nomination. They demanded that the 'Judges of both Benches and of the Exchequer ... be nominated by both Houses of Parliament, to continue *quamdiu se bene gesserint*.' The Newcastle Propositions repeated these demands almost word for word, but added the Chief Baron of the Exchequer and the Master of the Rolls to the list of nominated officers.[255] The latter position was at that time occupied by Culpepper, and the King was therefore being asked to sacrifice one of his closest advisers.[256] His reply to this demand remained what it had been in the *Answer to the XIX Propositions*, that he was 'resolved to be as careful of those we have chosen as you are of those you would chuse, and to remove

---

[250] *LJ*, IV, 132. Charles abided by this concession in his subsequent appointments: A. F. Havighurst, 'The judiciary and politics in the reign of Charles II', *Law Quarterly Review*, 66 (1950), 65. See also Black, 'Judges of Westminster Hall', pp. 26–8.

[251] Gardiner, *Documents*, pp. 251, 253.   [252] Rushworth, IV, 727–8.

[253] For Lenthall and Wilde, see Mary Frear Keeler, *The Long Parliament, 1640–1641: A Biographical Study of its Members* (Memoirs of the American Philosophical Society, 36, Philadelphia, 1954), 250, 394. The Houses had earlier nominated Lenthall to be Master of the Rolls in December 1642: *LJ*, V, 481; *CJ*, II, 880. This was reiterated in an ordinance of 8 November 1643: *LJ*, VI, 299–300. See also BL, Add. MS 18779, fo. 31r.

[254] Gardiner, *Documents*, p. 265.   [255] *Ibid.*, pp. 301, 304.

[256] The Chief Baron of the Exchequer, Sir Thomas Trevor, had remained in London: James S. Hart, *Justice upon Petition* (1991), pp. 178–9.

none till they appear to us to have otherwise behaved themselves, or shall be evicted by legal proceedings to have done so'.[257] A commitment to due process of law thus reinforced the defence of appointments which, it was in turn asserted, the King was legally entitled to make. This argument for a symbiosis between royal powers and the rule of law was beautifully coherent and self-sustaining.

A further aspect of the relationship between Crown and common law lay in the King's control over the Great Seal. In late May 1642, Lord Keeper Littleton had joined the King at York taking the Great Seal with him. The Lords immediately voted him a delinquent.[258] The Houses then faced the major problem that the Great Seal was essential for the authentication of many acts of the Crown, including all royal grants and all original writs.[259] The removal of this 'the ultimate symbol of sovereignty'[260] from London severely handicapped the Houses' executive activities. The Commons therefore urged that a new Great Seal be made, and – after prolonged hesitation in the Lords – this was enacted by ordinance on 10 November 1643.[261] The ordinance stated that the Great Seal 'ought to attend the Parliament, being the supreme court of justice and judicature within this realm, for the dispatch of the great and weighty affairs of the Commonwealth'. However, it was now being 'traiterously and perniciously abused, to the ruin and destruction of the Parliament and kingdom', especially by the issuing of Commissions of Array and of proclamations against the Houses. All acts issued under the Great Seal since 22 May 1642 were therefore declared void, and a new seal was to be made which would have the same 'force, power and validity' as the original. The office of Lord Keeper was entrusted to six commissioners, all of whom had impeccable Parliamentarian credentials.[262] This was a critical stage in the Houses' development into an executive body, and it greatly complicated peace negotiations with the King. For Parliament here 'laid claim to the highest symbol of sovereignty and to complete control of the judicial system'.[263] As Professor

[257] Rushworth, IV, 727.
[258] *LJ*, V, 80, 91, 93; BL, Add. MS 64923 (Coke MS), fo. 14r (John Coke the younger to Sir John Coke, 24 May 1642).
[259] G. R. Elton, *The Tudor Revolution in Government* (Cambridge, 1953), pp. 13–14; ed., *The Tudor Constitution* (2nd edition, Cambridge, 1982), pp. 117–18.
[260] Black, 'Judges of Westminster Hall', p. 34.
[261] For this ordinance, see *LJ*, VI, 301–2 (from which the following quotations are taken); BL, Add. MS 18778 (diary of Walter Yonge), fo. 87r–v; and Clarendon, *History*, III, 286–9 (Book VII, §369). For the Lords' hesitation, see Hart, *Justice upon Petition*, pp. 186–90. See also Black, 'Judges of Westminster Hall', pp. 62–6.
[262] *LJ*, VI, 301, 315; Clarendon, *History*, III, 251 (Book VII, §§315–16). The six commissioners were the Earls of Kent and Bolingbroke, Samuel Browne, Edmund Prideaux, Oliver St John and John Wilde. The political considerations behind their appointments are discussed in Black, 'Judges of Westminster Hall', pp. 63–6.
[263] Black, 'Judges of Westminster Hall', p. 67.

Hart has written, with this step the upper house 'committed itself to a decisive break with the Crown and the traditional vestiges of the law'.[264] To the Constitutional Royalists, the creation of a new Great Seal was not only totally illegal; it was also high treason. Hyde saw it as the Houses' bid to 'provide for their sovereign jurisdiction in civil matters as their security in martial'; and concluded that 'they would be absolute, and not joint-sharers in the sovereign power'.[265] He thus regarded the new seal as an assertion of parliamentary sovereignty and a direct assault upon the lawful powers of the Crown. The Oxford Parliament expressed a similar view in the spring of 1644. It complained that 'to make way' for the

> making void all civil rights and proprieties, and the better preparing the kingdom to be shared by strangers, a new Great Seal (the special ensign of monarchy, and the only way by which justice is derived and distributed to the people) is counterfeited and used, albeit it be by the express letter of the statute of the 25th year of King Edward the Third, declared to be high treason.[266]

Once again, a commitment to legal precedent and the rule of law was buttressed by the citation of a specific statute.[267]

The Houses, by contrast, demanded the recognition of the authority of their own seal and the nullification of all acts issued under the King's seal. The Uxbridge Propositions limited this to a requirement that all titles of honour conferred by the King since 20 May 1642 be declared null and void.[268] The Newcastle Propositions repeated this clause, but also demanded that all acts issued under the King's Great Seal since 22 May 1642 be declared void, and that the Great Seal used by the Houses be deemed 'of like force and effect' as 'any Great Seal of England in any time heretofore were or have been'.[269] The King never responded explicitly to this demand, but the Houses were able to force the issue because the Great Seal had been captured at the surrender of Oxford. On 11 August 1646 the Great Seal – together with the seals of the Courts of King's Bench, Exchequer, Wards and the Admiralty – was 'defaced and broken in the presence of both Houses'.[270] This was an extraordinary act of public vandalism against the symbols of royal justice.

To prevent the issue of any further acts did not, however, ensure the nullification of earlier acts or the King's recognition of the authority of the Houses' Great Seal. These concessions were specifically requested in the

---

[264] Hart, *Justice upon Petition*, p. 190.
[265] Clarendon, *History*, III, 250, 252 (Book VII, §§313, 317).
[266] Rushworth, V, 591. See also BL, Add. MS 18779, fo. 77r.
[267] The statute referred to was 25 Edw. III, c. 5. For identical use of this same statute, see Huntington Library, Hastings MS, HA 9691 (Nicholas to Falkland, 24 May 1643).
[268] Gardiner, *Documents*, p. 283.   [269] *Ibid.*, pp. 297, 305–6.
[270] *LJ*, VIII, 458; *CJ*, IV, 641.

Heads of the Proposals (§VII),[271] and also by the Houses in the *Four Bills*[272] and at Newport. Charles agreed on 12 May 1647 to confirm acts passed under Parliament's new Great Seal; but he refused to nullify the acts issued under his own Great Seal, arguing that he was 'obliged to maintain' them 'in honour and justice'. He also asked that the 'future government' of the Seal 'may be in His Majesty, according to the due course of law'.[273] Only at the Treaty of Newport did Charles finally agree to the nullification of acts passed under the Great Seal at Oxford. On 21 October 1648 he gave a blanket acceptance of all Parliament's demands relating to the Great Seal.[274] His motives may be inferred from those which he confessed regarding Church government and the militia. But these concessions came far too late. The army's convictions were such that every step Charles took towards a settlement with Parliament turned out to be a step to his own execution. But on the scaffold he drew a striking contrast between the 'arbitrary way' cut by 'the power of the sword', and his own unflinching desire to preserve 'the laws of the land' which now made him 'the martyr of the people'.[275]

Nothing could be more different from the advice which Charles had received from Strafford in 1640, that he was 'loose and absolved from all rules of government'.[276] It was axiomatic to Constitutional Royalism that royal powers were tempered by the rule of law and offered a far better guarantee of legal government than the Houses. Whereas many at Westminster adopted a position strangely analogous to that of Strafford – that infringements of law were permissible in national emergencies – men like Hyde consistently argued that royal powers and popular liberties existed within, and were guaranteed by, the common law. This idea of interdependence might be termed the law–liberty–prerogative nexus. It provided the principal grounds for the Royalists' objections to parliamentary violations of due process of law, and was the foundation of their claim that the King was the only effective defender of the 'fundamental laws'. While radicals from Strafford to Wharton were willing to subvert the rule of law, the Constitutional Royalists urged Charles to prove that the common law was safe in his hands.

The law–liberty–prerogative nexus found its institutional expression in the assertion that the King could determine the location of his law courts, could employ a new Great Seal, and could appoint judges and other legal officers without consulting Parliament. The Houses found such arguments

---

[271] Gardiner, *Documents*, pp. 320–1.   [272] *Ibid.*, pp. 337, 340–1.
[273] *Ibid.*, p. 315.
[274] Walker, *Perfect Copies*, p. 68; Peck, *Desiderata Curiosa*, II, 397.
[275] Rushworth, VIII, 1429.
[276] Gardiner, *History*, IX, 229.

abhorrent. How could you trust a monarch with such a record of manipulating due process of law? In documents like the Grand Remonstrance, they pointed to that string of incidents from the Five Knights' Case to the Army Plots which revealed Charles's willingness to violate the rule of law when it suited his political needs. But the Constitutional Royalists countered that Charles was a reformed character, a constitutional monarch wedded to royal government within the law. It was a role which, as we saw in chapter 4, Charles viewed with suspicion in 1640–1; but one which he came to embrace and defend eloquently from 1642 onwards. This marked a striking departure from Charles's 'legal tyranny' during the 1620s and 1630s,[277] and one which the Constitutional Royalists were at pains to underline in successive peace negotiations.

This in turn helps to explain a pronounced feature of the Constitutional Royalists' political behaviour: their legally based criticisms of Charles's Personal Rule in the opening weeks of the Long Parliament, followed by a readiness to rally to him thereafter. It was entirely consistent for people like Hyde to lead the attack on Ship Money as 'against the laws of the realm',[278] but then to draw closer to the King once they concluded that he posed a less serious threat to the rule of law than the Junto. A fervent commitment to legality underlay both positions. It rested upon a particular vision of the English common law as the partner of royal powers rather than their subordinate. This coloured the Constitutional Royalists' attitudes towards the Church, the militia and Parliament; and it will surface again in the remaining sections of this chapter. Any constitution, written or unwritten, rests upon its public laws; and this belief in a fundamental symbiosis between royal powers and the rule of law further suggests the appropriateness of the term 'Constitutional Royalist' as a label for its exponents.

V. COUNCIL AND COUNSEL

It was a commonplace of early seventeenth-century English political thought that the monarch could commit no wrong. Since the law courts were the King's courts, and since nobody could be tried or convicted in their own courts, it was technically impossible for him to do wrong. This meant that critics of royal policies had to direct their objections not against the sovereign but against the 'evil counsellors' who had allegedly led him astray. This doctrine was most eloquently expressed in the Grand Remonstrance, which blamed current 'dangers and distempers' on the 'mischievous devices' of 'a corrupt and ill-affected party'. The King's 'authority and trust' had 'been abused', and the only remedy was for him 'to employ such

---

[277] For this phrase, see above, n. 249.   [278] See above, p. 70.

persons ... in places of trust as ... Parliament may have cause to confide in'.[279] These ideas guided the Houses' decision to take up arms against a King who, 'seduced by wicked counsel, intend[ed] to make war against the Parliament'.[280] Exactly the same views were expressed in private correspondence. In June 1643, for example, Viscount Saye condemned 'those upstart evill counsellors' who were 'the cause of all our distractions and myseryes'.[281] Successive Parliamentarian peace propositions therefore demanded that evil advisers be replaced by those whom the Houses could trust.

The Constitutional Royalists' response to such claims was utterly consistent with their views on the appointment of military and legal officers: they asserted that it was the King's discretionary right to choose whoever he pleased to advise him. This authority was conferred by God, guaranteed by law, and essential for the well-being of the commonwealth. The seventeenth century, lacking modern professional demarcations, made no distinction between military, legal and civilian officials and bracketed them together as royal advisers offering counsel on different aspects of the King's responsibilities. Hence the Constitutional Royalists' statements on this issue often closely resembled those we have encountered in sections II and IV.

Their first line of defence was to deny the existence of any 'evil counsellors'. Hyde advanced this argument with particular force in his reply to the Houses' Remonstrance of 26 May 1642. He insisted that the Junto branded as 'the malignant party' all 'the members of both Houses who agreed not with them in their opinion'. This in practice meant those 'who had stood stoutly and immutably for the religion, the liberties, the laws [and] for all the public interests'. These were people, Hyde argued, 'to whose wisdom, courage, and counsel, the kingdom owed as much as it could to subjects. So much for the evil counsellors'.[282]

But the Houses' subsequent demands were not so easily deflected. The *Nineteen Propositions* requested the King's dismissal of all Privy Councillors except those 'approved of by both Houses of Parliament'; the limiting of the Privy Council to a maximum of twenty-five; and the removal of 'private men' and 'any unknown and unsworn councillors'. They also demanded that new Councillors take an oath 'agreed upon' by the Houses, and that sixteen named officers of state 'may always be chosen with the approbation of both Houses'.[283] This list included the Lord High

279 Gardiner, *Documents*, pp. 203–5.   280 *LJ*, V, 76.
281 Huntington Library, Stowe (Temple) MS, Box 12, item 781 (Viscount Saye and Sele to Sir Peter Temple, 21 June 1643).
282 Clarendon, *History*, II, 150 (Book V, §282).
283 These demands were contained in the first three of the *Nineteen Propositions*: Gardiner, *Documents*, pp. 250–1.

Constable, Lord High Steward and Earl Marshal,[284] the three officers empowered in the *Modus Tenendi Parliamentum* (*c*. 1322) to summon a commission of estates in the event of 'discord between the King and some magnates'.[285] Many antiquaries held that the Constable (an office vacant since at least 1521) also had the power to arrest the King if he violated his coronation oath and to bring him before his Parliament.[286] The inclusion of these three offices perhaps reflected a growing feeling within both Houses during the summer of 1642 that Charles might have to be compelled to return to Westminster. Furthermore, it is possible that competing groups in the Houses each had candidates in mind for at least some of these offices.[287]

The *Answer* which Falkland and Culpepper drafted on Charles's behalf set out very fully the Constitutional Royalist position on both the Council and counsel. It insisted that the King would 'be careful to make election of such persons in those places of trust as shall have given good testimony of their abilities and integrities'. If, by any chance, he were to be 'mistaken' in his 'election', he would happily leave the offending councillor to 'the justice of the law'. It would, however, be utterly wrong for the King to 'quit the power and right' which his predecessors had wielded 'of appointing persons in these places': such a concession would leave Charles 'but the out-side, but the picture, but the sign of a King'. Charles wished to 'retain [his] power ... of discoursing with whom' he pleased and 'of what' he pleased. He still intended to consult, at his discretion, those whose 'qualities, education, or other abilities may not make them so fit to be of' the Council; and he would certainly not confine himself to twenty-five councillors in a kingdom 'so replenished with judicious and experienced persons of several kinds'. Only with this counsel could he make mature and considered decisions on matters of state.

But the *Answer* did not confine itself to a point-by-point rejection of the Houses' demands relating to the composition of the Privy Council. It also argued that Parliament was trying to subvert existing notions of counsel. The role of councillors was to give advice, not to be 'tutors or guardians'; and the King was not their 'pupil or ward'. By removing the King's discretionary right to seek the counsel of whoever he chose, the *Nineteen Propositions* opened the way for a 'new-fangled kind of counsellors' who

[284] The other thirteen were the Lord Chancellor, Lord Treasurer, Lord Privy Seal, Lord Admiral, Warden of the Cinque Ports, Chief Governor of Ireland, Chancellor of the Exchequer, Master of the Wards, the two Secretaries of State, the two Chief Justices (of King's Bench and Common Pleas) and the Chief Baron (of the Exchequer): *ibid.*, p. 251.
[285] N. Pronay and J. Taylor, ed., *Parliamentary Texts of the Later Middle Ages* (Oxford, 1980), p. 87.
[286] Morrill, *Nature of the English Revolution*, pp. 11–12, 299–300.
[287] As suggested in Adamson, 'Baronial context', 98.

would be 'joint patentees with [Charles] in the regality'. Again, everything finally came down to the question of trust, and the King lamented that he was not 'trusted to chuse those who were to be trusted as much as we'.[288] But could Charles be trusted with the same discretionary powers as his predecessors?

The *Nineteen Propositions* not only demanded revolutionary changes to the existing nature of royal counsels; according to the Constitutional Royalists they also subverted the established relationship between the King's Great Council (Parliament) and his Privy Council. The *Answer* stressed that the Houses were seeking to arrogate to themselves affairs which were 'proper for [the] Privy Council'. Furthermore, parliamentary 'approbation' of councillors would return England 'to the worst kind of minority, and make [the King] despicable both at home and abroad'.[289] Hyde also took up this point in his declaration of 17 June: 'For the declining all other counsells, and the uniting his confidence to his Parliament, His Maiestie desires both his Houses of Parliament seriously and sadly to consider, that it is not the name of a great or little councell that makes the results of that councell just or unjust.'[290] The King was thus entitled to choose and consult his Privy Councillors without Parliamentary approval.

Hyde elaborated upon this argument in his *History*. No monarch, he suggested, could be 'too strict, too tender … in the constituting the body of their Privy Council'. A well-chosen Council was an essential foundation of constitutional monarchy. For a King could not be 'thought a great monarch when he follows the reins of his own reason and appetite, but when, for the informing his reason and guiding his actions, he uses the service, industry, and faculties of the wisest men'.[291] The counsel of those wise men had to be given independently of the King's Great Council of Parliament. Hyde argued that it was 'not only lawful for, but the duty of, the Privy Council, to give faithfully and freely their advice to the King upon all matters concluded in Parliament, to which his royal consent is necessary, as well as upon any other subject whatsoever'. This was not just 'the known practice'; it was also in the public interest thus to 'inform the understanding and conscience of the King'.[292] The King's discretionary right both to choose his advisers and to accept or reject their counsel was an integral part of this system. As Strangways wrote in his commonplace book, '*Conciliarij non sunt praeceptores: concilium non est praeceptum.*

---

[288] Rushworth, IV, 727–9. Cf. John Guy, 'The "Imperial Crown" and the liberty of the subject: the English constitution from Magna Carta to the Bill of Rights', in *Court, Country and Culture*, ed. B. Y. Kunze and D. D. Brautigam (Rochester, NY, 1992), pp. 80–1.
[289] Rushworth, IV, 730, 732. Cf. Mendle, 'Great Council of Parliament', 156–62.
[290] *His Maiesties Answer* [17 June 1642], p. 7.
[291] Clarendon, *History*, I, 260–1 (Book III, §§51, 53).   [292] *Ibid.*, 262–3 (Book III, §55).

The Councell may be good, the councell may be ill and therefore may be refused: and he who is consulted may approve of itt or reject itt: and soe hath it been done in all P[ar]laments from the beginning of P[ar]laments to this.'[293] Kings should be counselled, but not strait-jacketed.

The Houses' distrust of Charles made them loath to countenance such claims. Yet, on the nature of the Privy Council at least, the Oxford Propositions did mark a significant retreat from Parliament's demands of June 1642. All requests for parliamentary approbation of Privy Councillors and named officers of state were dropped; nor was the Privy Council obliged to take a new oath of office. This was a striking departure from the *Nineteen Propositions*, and reflected the political influence of the peace party at Westminster during the winter of 1642–3. The original proposals, drawn up in the House of Lords, stipulated that 'all acts of the Council table, that do concern government, may be attested under the hands of those who give advice'.[294] This bid to increase conciliar accountability was omitted from the final version, thus removing one major sticking-point.[295] However, the preamble to the Oxford Propositions still blamed the King's decision to leave London and take up arms on 'the persuasion of evil counsellors', and sought the removal of the Earl of Bristol from the King's 'counsels'.[296] This was one of the penalties imposed upon 'delinquents', another fiercely contested subject which will be discussed in section VI. Otherwise, the Oxford Propositions deliberately avoided the issue of counsel and, as we have seen, it was on the guarantees to precede a cessation of arms that this treaty foundered. Had the demands of the *Nineteen Propositions* regarding the Privy Council been revived, it is likely that the Constitutional Royalists' response would have been analogous to their position on parliamentary approval of senior military officers. As Falkland put it, 'well knowing that when any of those places shall be void, the nomination and free election is a right belonging to, and inherent in His Majesty, and having been enjoyed by all his royal progenitors, His Majesty will not believe that his well-affected subjects will desire to limit him in that right'.[297]

Subsequent peace propositions developed the Houses' strategy of seeking specific dismissals but not parliamentary control over the Privy Council. The Uxbridge Propositions required that all those still adhering to the King after 31 October 1644 'be removed from His Majesty's counsels' and cease to 'have any employment concerning the State or Commonwealth'.[298] These terms also contained a revised clause (§20) relating to officers of state. This time, the officers were to be *nominated* (rather than

[293] Beinecke Library, Yale University, Osborn MS b. 304, p. 42.   [294] *LJ*, V, 504.
[295] *Ibid.*, 582.
[296] Gardiner, *Documents*, pp. 262, 264.   [297] Rushworth, V, 201; *LJ*, V, 703.
[298] Gardiner, *Documents*, p. 280.

merely approved) by both Houses, and were to hold office *quamdiu se bene gesserint.*[299] Intriguingly, the Lord High Constable, Lord High Steward and Earl Marshal were omitted from the list of officers of state in the draft propositions prepared by the Committee of Both Kingdoms in April 1644, and never reinserted during the subsequent process of amendment in both Houses. The reason for this is elusive but if, as suggested above, these three officers had been named in the *Nineteen Propositions* for a rhetorical purpose specific to the circumstances of 1642, it is possible that they were now left out because in the changed context of 1644 they no longer seemed necessary.[300] The particular powers attributed to these three officers would explain why all three were dropped together,[301] and would probably have made that omission appear a conciliatory gesture to the King. However, the evidence does not permit a firm conclusion, and this interpretation must remain very tentative.

The structure of the Treaty of Uxbridge – cyclical talks on Church government, the militia and Ireland – meant that there was no discussion explicitly relating to officers of state. But because the Lord Deputyship of Ireland was one of the offices to which Parliament wished to nominate, Charles did address the issue in one of the sessions on Ireland during February 1645. He argued that 'when the power to reward those who are worthy of publick trust shall be transferred to others, and having neither force left us to punish nor power to reward, we shall be in effect a titular contemptible Prince'. Once again, he promised to 'leave all [his] ministers to the known laws of the land to be tryed and punished according to those laws if they shall offend'. But he absolutely refused to 'put so great a trust and power out of us' as his right to nominate the officers of state.[302] The rule of law guaranteed the King's rights; and it also afforded a sufficient – indeed the only – safeguard if they were to be abused.

The Houses were still not satisfied, and in the Newcastle Propositions

---

[299] *Ibid.*, p. 284.
[300] The propositions drafted by the Committee of Both Kingdoms were read in each House on 29 April 1644. At no stage during the preparation of these terms were these three offices listed among the offices of state: PRO, SP 16/501/88, 89 (draft propositions, 21, 29 April 1644); SP 21/7 (Committee of Both Kingdoms day book), pp. 49, 54, 58; *LJ*, VI, 533; *CJ*, III, 472. This demand was therefore not 'formulated contemporaneously with the military reforms over the winter of 1644–5', as suggested in Adamson, 'Baronial context', 118. Nor is it certain that the omission of these offices was intended to repudiate Essex's 'aspirations to constabular rank' (*ibid.*), especially as the Earl was present when the Committee of Both Kingdoms discussed the draft propositions on the afternoon of 22 April: PRO, SP 21/7, p. 54.
[301] It is important to note that the Earl Marshal was omitted as well as the 'two great military offices' of Constable and Steward: cf. Adamson, 'Baronial context', 118. This suggests that the reason was intimately bound up with the constitutional powers unique to those three offices rather than with Parliament's military reforms of 1644–5.
[302] Rushworth, V, 885.

they reiterated the demands that those supporting the King after 31 October 1644 be excluded from royal counsels, and that the officers of state be 'nominated by both Houses ... to continue *quamdiu se bene gesserint*'.[303] In addition, as part of honouring the Solemn League and Covenant, they requested the appointment of fifty-one 'commissioners for the kingdom of England, for conservation of the peace between the two kingdoms'. These included virtually all the leading Parliamentarian peers and MPs, notably Northumberland, Essex, Manchester, Wharton, St John and Holles. Charles's response was to concede such demands only insofar as they did not erode his discretionary powers: he accepted the commissioners for the two kingdoms 'upon confidence that all of them respectively with the same tenderness will look upon those things which concern His Majesty's honour'; and he promised to 'gratify' Parliament 'concerning the officers' of state – 'without destroying the relations which are necessary to the Crown'.[304] Still the King clung to his discretionary right to choose counsellors; and still the Houses balked at entrusting him with it.

As on so many other issues, the *Heads of the Proposals* marked an attempt to break this deadlock. They offered a radical new solution to the problem of counsel. The Privy Council was to be supplanted by a Council of State wielding direct control over the militia, and with sweeping powers over foreign policy except that it could not conclude war or peace without parliamentary consent. These powers were much more extensive than those of the old Privy Council, which could only transact business entrusted to it by the King.[305] The new Council was to 'be put into the hands of trusty and able persons now to be agreed on, and the same persons to continue in that power (*si bene se gesserint*) for the certain term not exceeding seven years'. The silence over parliamentary approval or nomination was deafening. The 'great offices' were still to be in the Houses' disposal, though only for ten years. Thereafter, the Houses were to nominate 'three and the King out of that number to appoint one for the succession upon any vacancy'.[306] The Royalist response to these clauses is difficult to recover explicitly. But we do know that they were not among Charles's principal objections to the *Heads*.[307]

At the same time, he continued to exercise his right to select Privy Councillors at his own discretion. In early October, he summoned Richmond, Hertford, Dorset, Southampton, Seymour and Lindsey to Hampton Court 'to advise and consult withall as his privy councells'. Observers believed

---

[303] Gardiner, *Documents*, pp. 301, 304.   [304] *Ibid.*, pp. 313, 315.
[305] Gardiner, *Civil War*, III, 331.
[306] Gardiner, *Documents*, p. 320.
[307] *Narrative by Ashburnham*, II, cli; Bodl. Lib., MS Clarendon 30/1, fo. 26r–v (Charles I to Sir Thomas Fairfax, 3 August 1647).

that these Constitutional Royalist peers 'had thoughts to settle there for a time in councell with His Majesty'.[308] As we saw in the previous chapter, the army allowed them access to Charles in the hope that they would persuade him to accept the *Heads of the Proposals*.[309] The important point to note here is that these peers were summoned as 'privy councells': regardless of successive peace terms, Charles was still treating this inner coterie of moderate peers as a *de facto* Privy Council. Furthermore, in seeking to promote a settlement on the basis of the *Heads*, these peers were perfectly happy to perform such a role.

There is some evidence, however, that the King did not regard the nature of his Council as quite so critical an issue as the future of Church government or control over the militia. On 17 November 1647, shortly after his flight from Hampton Court, Charles wrote to the Speaker of the House of Lords agreeing that 'for the securing all fears ... an Act of Parliament be passed for the disposing of the great offices of State, and naming of Privy Councillors for the whole term of his reign, by the two Houses of Parliament, their patents and commissions being taken from His Majesty, and after to return to the Crown'.[310] Yet it seems that this was only a tactical move, for the Engagement which Charles signed with the Scots barely a month later explicitly asserted the royal powers of 'bestowing of honours and offices of trust, [and] choice of Privy Councillors'.[311] The Houses, however, apparently regarded the issue as settled by the King's concessions of mid-November, for the *Four Bills* made no reference to either the Privy Council or the officers of state.

Even before the concessions at Newport concerning the Church and the militia, it seems that at least some Constitutional Royalists believed that the King was giving too much ground. Hyde complained to Sir John Berkeley in March 1648 that 'after [the King] hath quitted so much authority to other men and made them so much above him that it may bee questionable whether the exercise of any power over him bee an act of oppression'. He clearly blamed the King for this state of affairs: Charles's fate was in his own hands, and there was as 'yet noe example of any Kinge of Englande who hath bene destroyed without his owne consent'.[312] Nicholas likewise wished that Charles 'had kept firme to his princely and magnanimous resolucons' and not descended 'soe low'.[313] In a paper written shortly after the Vote of No Addresses, Nicholas included among the King's concessions

[308] *A Perfect Diurnall of some Passages in Parliament*, no. 219 (4–11 October 1647), p. 1764 (*STC (News)*, 504.219; BL, TT, E 518/43).
[309] See above, pp. 134–5.   [310] Gardiner, *Documents*, p. 331.   [311] *Ibid.*, p. 349.
[312] Bodl. Lib., MS Clarendon 30/2, fo. 311r ([Hyde] to Sir John Berkeley, 8 March 1647/8). Cf. [Hyde], *Full Answer*, p. 142.
[313] Christ Church Muniment Room, Oxford, Evelyn Collection, Letters from Nicholas to Browne, unfol. (Nicholas to Sir Richard Browne, 13 December 1647).

that 'for the civil governm[en]t he hath offred [the Houses] the nominacon of all those ministers by whom the kingdome is to be governed'.[314]

Notwithstanding such reservations, Charles confirmed and extended these concessions at Newport, although earlier sections of this chapter have revealed that his motives were less than idealistic. The Houses made no demands regarding the Privy Council, but they did ask that the officers of state 'be nominated by both Houses ... to continue *quamdiu se bene gesserint*, and in the intervals of Parliament, by such commissioners' as the Houses should nominate, subject to parliamentary approval in the next session. The King agreed to this provided that 'the time for nomination be limited to ten years'.[315] The Houses found this unsatisfactory, and so on 8 November Charles conceded parliamentary nomination of the officers of state for twenty years.[316] The debates on this issue at Newport were quickly settled, and there is no sign that they were anything like so contentious as those surrounding Church government, the militia, or the fate of delinquents. Furthermore, this was not a question which Charles chose to address in his final speech on the scaffold.[317]

This section has shown that the Constitutional Royalists' attitudes towards royal counsel closely resembled their position on the appointment of military officers and of senior legal officials: they held that the King had a discretionary right to choose whomever he pleased to advise him. This was not only 'the known practice' and an aspect of the royal prerogative. It was also clearly in the interests of the commonwealth that royal decisions should be taken after careful consultation. To establish parliamentary approval – let alone *nomination* – of Councillors would reverse the existing relationship between the Great Council and the Privy Council. The only safeguard against 'evil counsellors' (if any existed) was therefore the due process of law from which the King promised never to shelter proven offenders.

Yet this was a slightly different sticking-point from those examined in the first four sections of this chapter. After the *Nineteen Propositions*, the Houses dropped their demand to approve Privy Councillors. From the Uxbridge Propositions onwards, they revived a request to approve named officers of state. This, together with the radical solution of a Council of State offered in the *Heads of the Proposals*, meant that there was considerably more variation in the demands relating to counsel than on most other issues. The Constitutional Royalists therefore had less opportunity to

[314] Bodl. Lib., MS Clarendon 31, fo. 33r (draft paper by Nicholas, [January 1647/8]).
[315] Walker, *Perfect Copies*, pp. 66–7; *LJ*, X, 562; Peck, *Desiderata Curiosa*, II, 397; PRO, SP 16/516/104 (John Crewe to [John] Swynfen, 21 October 1648).
[316] Walker, *Perfect Copies*, pp. 77–8; *LJ*, X, 589; Peck, *Desiderata Curiosa*, II, 402.
[317] Rushworth, VIII, 1429–30.

develop a sustained response to them. The nature of counsel tended to be a less urgent issue than the Church or the militia, not least because the King appeared more willing to compromise on it. The disputes over royal counsel were ultimately not as prejudicial to the search for settlement as some other questions. Yet we should certainly not underestimate their broader significance. In the first place, we shall see in chapter 9 that many of the leading Constitutional Royalists gained key positions within royal counsels at the Restoration. Their role within the Privy Council during the years of civil war, and their views on the nature of counsel, provide an important context for their activities in office after 1660. Second, the issue of counsel cannot be seen in isolation. After abandoning the abortive demands of the *Nineteen Propositions*, the Houses concentrated their efforts on the removal of named individuals from the King's counsels. Several of the Constitutional Royalists were threatened not only with loss of office but also with severe penalties as 'delinquents'. The nature of those penalties, the debates about them in successive peace negotiations, and the extent to which they were implemented, will form the subject of the next section.

<h2 style="text-align:center">VI. THE FATE OF 'DELINQUENTS'</h2>

In his *History*, Hyde traced the Houses' use of the term 'delinquent' back to May 1641, the month of the Protestation Oath and the Act against the dissolution of the Long Parliament without its own consent. He argued that they applied it to 'whom they pleased', employing it interchangeably with 'evil counsellors', 'malignants' and 'cavaliers' as a generic term of abuse for 'all such who expressed any eminent zeal for [the King's] service'.[318] During the years of civil war, however, the Houses attached it more specifically to those of the King's adherents whom they wished to punish once peace was restored. Not surprisingly, these penalties became a major source of contention in peace talks, not least because many of the leading Constitutional Royalists were themselves among the prospective victims. They consistently sought to reduce the threatened punishments, and argued in particular against penalising those who were merely acting out of loyalty to Crown, Church and law. They wanted to see delinquents tried and sentenced by their peers according to due process of law. These attitudes must in turn be understood in the context of their own material sufferings at the hands of successive parliamentary committees.

The *Nineteen Propositions* demanded that 'the justice of Parliament may pass upon all delinquents, whether they be within the kingdom or fled out

---

[318] Clarendon, *History*, I, 356 (Book III, §231); I, 554 (Book IV, §279); II, 314 (Book VI, §31).

of it; and that all persons cited by either House of Parliament may appear and abide the censure of Parliament'.[319] In their *Answer*, Falkland and Culpepper did not rebut this clause head on, but responded with the general statement that 'there is no man so near to [the King] in place and affection, whom [he] will not leave to the justice of the law, if you shall bring a particular charge and sufficient proofs against him'.[320] This made an important distinction between justice under the common law and 'the justice of Parliament', implying that the King defended due process of law which stood higher even than Parliament. These competing notions of 'justice' were to characterise many of the subsequent exchanges over the fate of delinquents.

The outbreak of civil war brought a marked hardening in the Houses' attitude towards delinquents. On 6 September 1642 they declared that they would never lay down arms 'until His Majesty shall withdraw his protection from such persons as have been voted by both Houses to be delinquents, or that shall by both Houses be voted to be delinquents, and shall leave them to the justice of Parliament, to be proceeded with according to their demerits'.[321] Such demands were reiterated in the Oxford Propositions. These complained that the King had 'protected delinquents from the justice of' the Houses, and requested him to 'leave delinquents to a legal trial and judgment of Parliament'. They asked also that the Earl of Newcastle and George, Lord Digby be exempted from a 'general pardon'.[322] Again, the King's commissioners fired back with an alternative definition of justice, pledging that 'all such persons as, upon the treaty, shall be excepted out of the general pardon, shall be tried *per pares*, according to the usual course and known law of the land, and that it be left to that either to acquit or condemn them'.[323] On 23 March 1643, Charles likewise requested that none of his subjects be imprisoned during a cessation of arms 'otherwise then according to the known laws of the land'; and that 'no plundering or violence [be] offered to any of his subjects'. He included within this the 'impositions and taxes' which the Houses were already levying 'contrary to the known laws of the land'.[324] Declared delinquents were thus protected beneath an umbrella defence of property, freedom and due process of law.

Four days later, the Parliamentarian commissioners objected that since the King's understanding of 'the known laws of the land' precluded the Houses' raising arms, this apparent concession would in fact impose 'streight bonds upon the two Houses' while leaving Royalist officers 'as

[319] Gardiner, *Documents*, p. 253.   [320] Rushworth, IV, 727.
[321] *LJ*, V, 341. See also *CJ*, II, 752–3; *PJ*, III, 333–4.
[322] Gardiner, *Documents*, pp. 262–3, 266.   [323] Rushworth, V, 169; *LJ*, V, 591.
[324] Rushworth, V, 178; *LJ*, V, 660.

much liberty as before'.[325] The very same day, the Houses issued an ordinance for the sequestration of the estates of 'notorious delinquents'. These
they defined as all 'person or persons ecclesiasticall or temporall as have
raised or shall raise arms against the Parliament'; those voluntarily contri-
buting to the Royalist war effort; those who had joined in any oath or
association 'against the Parliament'; and those who enforced any taxes or
other levies to assist the King.[326] Some of the Constitutional Royalists,
most notably Hertford, Seymour, Lindsey and Falkland, had taken up
arms and therefore fell within the first category. Others, including Dorset,
Richmond, Southampton and Culpepper, had engaged in June 1642 to
provide the King with forces.[327] Hyde had contributed at least £2,000 'for
the King's service'.[328] All these people were thus liable to have their estates
'converted and applyed towards the supportation of the great charges of
the Common-wealth'.[329]

Over the next two-and-a-half years, most of the leading Constitutional
Royalists were subject to assessments by the Committee for the Advance of
Money, appointed in November 1642 to raise money from all who refused
to contribute voluntarily to Parliament's war effort.[330] On 10 July 1643,
Falkland was assessed at £300.[331] This was followed on 28 July 1644 by
assessments of £1,500 on Ashburnham, £2,000 on Culpepper, £800 on
Hyde, £4,000 on Strangways, £1,500 on Dorset's eldest son, Lord Buckhurst, and £1,000 on his secretary John White.[332] The peers generally suffered later but more severely. Dorset was assessed at £5,000 on 5 June
1644,[333] Richmond at £5,000 on 4 August 1645[334] and Hertford at £10,000
on 31 October.[335] On 17 November 1645, Seymour was assessed at £3,000,
and Lindsey and Southampton at £6,000 each.[336] However, there is no
evidence that any of these assessments was ever paid, or that the cases were
heard before the Committee for the Advance of Money.

Many of these people nevertheless suffered sequestration of their goods
and estates. The Committee for Sequestrations ordered Lindsey's goods to

---

[325] Rushworth, V, 183; LJ, V, 674.
[326] C. H. Firth and R. S. Rait, ed., Acts and Ordinances of the Interregnum, 1642–1660 (3 vols., 1911), I, 106–7.
[327] PRO, SP 16/491/29 (engagement to provide forces, 22 June 1642); BL, Egerton MS 2978 (Heath and Verney Papers), fo. 66r.
[328] Narrative by Ashburnham, II, iii.   [329] Firth and Rait, Acts and Ordinances, I, 106.
[330] For the development of the Committee for the Advance of Money, see Calendar of the Proceedings of the Committee for the Advance of Money, ed. M. A. E. Green (3 vols., 1888), I, vi–xvii.
[331] PRO, SP 19/61 (assessments by the Committee for the Advance of Money), fo. 23r.
[332] PRO, SP 19/65 (assessments by the Committee for the Advance of Money), fos. 123r, 124r, 126r, 128r, 129r.
[333] PRO, SP 19/65, fo. 64r.
[334] PRO, SP 19/69 (assessments by the Committee for the Advance of Money), fo. 66r.
[335] PRO, SP 19/69, fo. 100r.   [336] PRO, SP 19/69, fos. 108r, 109r, 110r.

be seized and inventoried on 29 May 1643.[337] The following September, the Commons confirmed the sequestration of Southampton's estate.[338] A month later, the Committee for Sequestrations refused to grant any relief on Falkland's estate on the grounds that 'he died in actuall warre against the parliam[en]t'.[339] A parliamentary order of 16 January 1644 provided for money to be raised out of Richmond's 'pictures and goods',[340] while another of 9 February stipulated that Culpepper's estate was to be sequestrated and his goods sold.[341] The Constitutional Royalists were thus incurring direct material losses as a result of their adherence to the King.

These experiences no doubt help to explain the tone of the declaration issued by the Oxford Parliament in March 1644. Members complained that their estates had been 'sequestred by persons of whom the law can take no notice'; and that 'committees, made by committees, rob, banish, and imprison the Lords and Commons of England'. These 'pernicious and publick enemies' had 'left themselves no other means to repay those vast sums they have extorted from the people, upon that they call publick faith, but out of the estates of those who have preserved their duty and loyalty entire'. The declaration concluded with a call to 'all good men who desire peace' to join 'in the suppressing these enemies of peace'.[342] A continuing commitment to peace talks did not make Royalist moderates any less hostile to the penalties imposed on delinquents.

Yet, for the Constitutional Royalists at least, material suffering only enhanced their determination to achieve a settlement. Nearly all the King's principal negotiators at Uxbridge were threatened with financial penalties of varying magnitude. The Uxbridge Propositions exempted fifty-eight individuals from any general pardon, ranging from such long-standing *bêtes noires* of Parliament as Bristol, Newcastle and Digby to quintessential moderates like Hyde, Strangways and Culpepper. Their estates, like those of papists in arms and plotters of rebellion in Ireland, were to be used 'to pay public debts and damages'. A further forty-eight named Royalists, including Nicholas, stood to lose a third of their estates. 'All other delinquents' would have 'a tenth part' of their estates sequestrated.[343] As at Oxford, the King's response was to fall back on due process of law. He once again asked that all those exempted from a general pardon 'be tried *per pares*, according to the usual course and known law of the land, and

---

[337] PRO, SP 20/1 (Committee for Sequestrations order book), p. 59. The Lords did, however, send the Gentleman Usher to ensure that this was done 'in a fair way, without any violence': *LJ*, VI, 66.
[338] *CJ*, III, 231, 238. See also PRO, SP 20/1, pp. 92–3. [339] PRO, SP 20/1, p. 104.
[340] *CJ*, III, 369.
[341] *Ibid.*, 394. [342] Rushworth, V, 591, 594–5.
[343] Gardiner, *Documents*, pp. 278–81.

that it be left to that either to acquit or condemn them'.[344] It was thus possible to shield delinquents behind the characteristic Constitutional Royalist defence of the rule of law.

As with several other key issues, the tight focus of the Uxbridge talks on the Church, the militia and Ireland precluded a specific discussion about the fate of delinquents. But the collapse of these talks, and the King's defeat at Naseby the following June, seem to have made Royalist moderates even more determined to achieve a settlement. The material penalties for allegiance to the King only strengthened their resolve. We saw in chapter 5 that early in December 1645, Dorset, Southampton, Hertford and Lindsey 'pointed out to the King, in the first instance individually, and afterwards in council, the miserable state to which they were reduced by the continuance of the war, and the small prospect there was that they would be able to get out of it otherwise than by treating'. When the King refused, they volunteered to surrender him to Parliament provided they were granted a full pardon and 'allowed to retain their possessions'.[345] The Houses' refusal to negotiate stymied this initiative, but it is none the less highly significant as evidence of the attitudes of leading Constitutional Royalist peers by the end of 1645. More specifically, it reveals that the financial penalties imposed upon them only sharpened their determination to restore peace.

This was not, however, the universal Royalist response. While the circle of Constitutional Royalist peers only became more desperate for peace in the aftermath of Naseby, others adopted a position which has been termed 'ultra-Royalist'. George, Lord Digby was perhaps the most striking exemplar of this shift.[346] His change of front has been plausibly linked to deteriorating relations with Prince Rupert, but it probably also owed much to the fact that Parliament consistently placed Digby high on its list of exemptions from pardon. Such a classification almost certainly proved self-fulfilling for Digby became more radical the more he had to lose from Charles's defeat. The King's declining military fortunes, and the proposed penalties for his adherents, thus served to widen the rift between those Royalists who were committed to a negotiated settlement and those who sought an outright military victory.

This process of polarisation became even more pronounced after the end of the first Civil War. The articles for the surrender of Oxford – signed by, among others, Hertford, Dorset, Southampton and Seymour – established

---

[344] *Ibid.*, p. 287.
[345] 'The diplomatic correspondence of Jean de Montereul', ed. J.G. Fotheringham, *Publ. Scottish Record Society*, 29–30 (1898–9), I, 74. See above, pp. 126–7.
[346] This paragraph is based on my interpretation of the evidence presented in A. Sumner, 'The political career of Lord George Digby until the end of the first Civil War' (PhD thesis, University of Cambridge, 1985), especially pp. 185–90, 390–3.

special terms for all those within the city when it capitulated. Apart from 'persons by name excepted by ordinance of Parliament from pardon', they were given six months during which they could 'compound for their estates' at the rate of two years' revenue (or one-tenth of their value). This applied only to estates of inheritance, and not to estates held for life or a term of years. They were to be free from 'oaths, engagements and molestations' for six months, and thereafter for as long as they swore 'not to bear arms against the Parliament' (the so-called 'Negative Oath').[347] Those exempted from pardon were to receive an indemnity for six months during which they could seek to compound for their estates, or obtain a pass 'to go beyond the seas'. A special clause included Richmond and Lindsey, then in prison, within these terms.[348] The Constitutional Royalist peers thus succeeded in significantly diluting the penalties for their own delinquency. Indeed, one-tenth was the lowest rate at which the Houses ever permitted any delinquent to compound.[349]

Not surprisingly, these peers were among the first to seek the benefit of the new terms. Between 22 September and 1 October 1646, Hertford, Seymour, Southampton, Lindsey, Dorset and Richmond all begged to compound under the Oxford Articles for their delinquency in adhering to the King.[350] They were all assessed at the rate of one-tenth, or the value of two years' income from their estates. Hertford's fine was set at £12,603 6s. 9d. on 21 November 1646, but subsequently reduced to £8,345 because part of his estate was held only for life.[351] Even allowing for his considerable wealth, this was one of the highest composition fines, but we have no firm evidence that it was ever paid.[352] Hertford's brother, Seymour, was fined £3,725 on 24 November;[353] two days later Southampton's fine was set at £6,466.[354] Dorset and Lindsey were both fined the same amount (£4,360) on the same day (7 December 1646).[355] These two cases proved particularly complex and protracted, dragging on into the early 1650s.[356] Richmond

---

347 The text of the Negative Oath is printed in Gardiner, *Documents*, pp. 289–90.
348 PRO, SP 16/514/27 (Oxford articles of surrender, 20 June 1646); Rushworth, VI, 282–4.
349 For a detailed account of the development of the composition system, see *Calendar of the Proceedings of the Committee for Compounding with Delinquents*, ed. M. A. E. Green (5 vols., 1889), I, v–xxiv.
350 PRO, SP 23/191 (Committee for Compounding particulars of estates and fines), pp. 600, 607–11, 782–3; SP 23/192 (Committee for Compounding particulars of estates and fines), p. 182; SP 23/193 (Committee for Compounding particulars of estates and fines), pp. 182, 236. Richmond's petition to compound is missing; but see SP 23/3 (Committee for Compounding order book), p. 248.
351 PRO, SP 23/3, p. 298; SP 23/191, pp. 595, 607–11. See also MP, 28 August 1648 (order and certificate regarding Hertford's delinquency).
352 Ian Ward, 'The English peerage, 1649–1660: government, authority and estates' (PhD thesis, University of Cambridge, 1989), pp. 330–1.
353 PRO, SP 23/3, p. 302.   354 PRO, SP 23/3, p. 307.   355 PRO, SP 23/3, p. 318.
356 See below, pp. 260–1, 267.

was the last to be fined and the first to pay up: assessed at £9,810 on
15 December 1646, he compounded and received letters of discharge in
May 1647.[357] Whatever their differing experiences, however, all these peers
clearly accepted the principle of composition and welcomed the opportunity to pay reduced fines at the rate of one-tenth.

This was not true of all the Constitutional Royalists, however. Writing
from Jersey in mid-November 1646, Hyde condemned those who 'foolishly, as well as impiously, make such hast to buy damnacon at two yeares
purchase'.[358] This suggests that Hyde thought that recent compounders
still had to take the Covenant as well as the Negative Oath, whereas the
Oxford Articles had in fact waived the requirement to take the former.[359]
The need to take the Covenant caused great anguish to many Royalists
who wished to compound but could not take advantage of the Oxford
Articles. The case of Sir John Strangways illustrates this predicament very
clearly. Taken prisoner in October 1645, he appealed to 'the Parlaments
mercie'.[360] He begged to compound without having to take the Covenant
and the Negative Oath.[361] Strangways could neither accept that 'the
worshippe, disciplyne and government of the Church of Scotland' was
'according to the Word of God', nor condone 'the extirpation of prelacie
out of the Church of England'.[362] Finally, in March 1648, he was allowed
to compound for a fine of £10,000, in return for which he and his son Giles
were pardoned for their delinquency and the sequestration was taken off
their estates.[363] There is no evidence that he was compelled to take the
Covenant, but such a dispensation was highly unusual.[364]

Another reason for Hyde's intemperate attitude was probably the fact
that composition at such a favourable rate was not open to him. The Newcastle Propositions again exempted fifty-eight named Royalists, including
Hyde, Culpepper, Nicholas and Ashburnham, from a general pardon and

[357] PRO, SP 23/3, p. 329; SP 23/233 (Committee for Compounding composition cases), fos.
27–8. See also *LJ*, IX, 35.
[358] Bodl. Lib., MS Clarendon 28, fo. 286v (Hyde to Nicholas, 15 November 1646).
[359] Hertford's case offers a good illustration of this: see Bodl. Lib., MS Clarendon 29, fo.
165r (letter of intelligence, 1 April 1647).
[360] Bodl. Lib., MS Dep. c. 156 (Nalson MS), fo. 89v (Sir John Strangways to Speaker
Lenthall, 28 November 1645); *CJ*, IV, 321, 357.
[361] Bodl. Lib., MS Tanner 58, fo. 758r (Strangways to Speaker Lenthall, [March] 1647/8);
CJ, V, 489; *LJ*, X, 113.
[362] Beinecke Library, Yale University, Osborn MS b. 304, p. 75. Strangways's views on
Church government are analysed more fully above, pp. 59–60.
[363] Bodl. Lib., MS Clarendon 31, fo. 41r (letter of intelligence, 29 March 1648); *CJ*, V, 489,
501, 534, 537; *LJ*, X, 236. See also Dorset RO, Fox-Strangways (Earls of Ilchester) MS,
Box 233/ii, Lady Strangways's correspondence, item 1 (Lady Strangways to Sir Thomas
Trenchard, [? 1647/8]).
[364] PRO, SP 23/120 (Committee for Compounding particulars of estates and fines), pp. 558,
575–6, 579.

deprived them of their entire estates. Another forty-eight individuals were to lose office together with one-third of their estates. In more elaborate clauses than those of the Uxbridge Propositions, further losses ranging from a half to a sixth of their estates were imposed on those who had assisted Parliament's enemies and 'not rendered themselves' before 1 December 1645.[365] By the time the Newcastle Propositions were presented to the King, Hyde and Culpepper were already in exile, leaving their goods and estates to the increasingly savage attentions of the parliamentary sequestrators.[366]

The King's response to these new demands struck a different note from all his earlier answers. Instead of arguing that delinquents should be tried by due process of law, he complained of 'the perpetual dishonour that must cleave to him if he should thus abandon so many persons of condition and fortune that have engaged themselves with and for him out of a sense of duty'. Instead, he suggested 'that a general act of oblivion and full pardon be forthwith passed by Act of Parliament'.[367] At this point, with the negotiations over the Newcastle Propositions in a state of deadlock, the army and its allies within the Houses offered radically different terms for delinquents in the *Heads of the Proposals*.

These were incomparably more generous than any parliamentary propositions. Those formerly exempted from composition would now be allowed to compound at a rate of 'not above a third part', while other categories of delinquent would be fined at rates of between a quarter and a tenth. Henceforth, those wishing to compound would not have to take the Covenant. 'All English' Royalists who were 'not worth £200 in land or goods' were to 'be at liberty and discharged'. A 'general Act of Oblivion' would 'absolve from all trespasses, misdemeanours etc. done in prosecution of the war', and only a handful of Royalists – seven in the first draft of the *Heads*, five in the final recension – would be exempted from this.[368] These individuals were never named. Small wonder, then, that moderate Royalists welcomed these terms and encouraged the King to accept them.

Yet when Berkeley showed a draft of the *Heads* to Charles, the King's first objection was 'the exception of seven, not named, from pardon'. Berkeley replied that 'after His Majesty and the army were accorded, it would be no impossible work to make them remit in the first point; and, if he could not, when His Majesty was reinstated in his throne, he might easily supply seven persons beyond the seas, in such sort as to make their

---

[365] Gardiner, *Documents*, pp. 298–303.
[366] For Hyde, see PRO, SP 23/162 (Committee for Compounding particulars of estates and fines), pp. 631, 633, 635. For Culpepper, see PRO, SP 23/88 (Committee for Compounding particulars of estates and fines), p. 170; *CJ*, III, 374, 394.
[367] Gardiner, *Documents*, p. 315.
[368] *Ibid.*, pp. 322–3; Adamson, 'Projected settlement', 586.

banishment supportable to them'.[369] This was an ingenious response, but not one calculated to satisfy the King. For, as Charles had told the Prince of Wales the previous year, he was resolved 'never to abandon the protection of [his] frends upon any pretention whatsoever'.[370] This pledge was indivisible: Charles rejected the exemption of *any* delinquents from pardon, whether they numbered five, seven or fifty-eight. A King who could tell army leaders that 'he would have no man to suffer for his sake, and that he repented of nothing so much as the bill against the Lord Strafford' was not likely to retreat from this position.[371]

Yet the Houses remained equally intransigent. In their minimum terms, the *Four Bills* of December 1647, they repeated the clauses of the Newcastle Propositions relating to delinquents.[372] The King did not answer these demands explicitly, but claimed that Parliament's proposals were 'utterly inconsistent with the liberty and prosperity of the subject, and His Majesty's trust in protecting them'.[373] Meanwhile, he signed the Engagement with the Scots which asserted that all those who joined 'in pursuance' of it would 'be protected by His Majesty in their persons and estates'. Charles also promised the introduction of an Act of Oblivion in both England and Scotland.[374] To Hyde, this offer only made Parliament's decision to turn its back on Charles in the Vote of No Addresses all the more reprehensible. He wrote in the spring of 1648 that 'the King hath often offered an Act of Oblivion, which will cut down all gallows, and wipe out all opprobrious tearms, and may make the very memory and mention of treason and traytors as penall as the crimes ought to have been; they who desire more aske impossibilities, and that which would prove their own destruction'.[375] Nevertheless, when the Houses did resume negotiations with the King, at Newport, their propositions regarding delinquents remained essentially unchanged.

By the time this treaty opened in the autumn of 1648, many of the Constitutional Royalist peers were in the process of compounding for their estates and securing individual pardons for their delinquency. The Commons accepted Seymour's fine of £3,725 and pardoned him in December 1647, but the case was respited in the Lords the following January until there was a full House.[376] The pace accelerated after the end of the second Civil War. During August and September 1648, the Commons accepted the composition fines imposed on Hertford, Richmond and Southampton. In each case, they ordered them to be pardoned for their

---

[369] *Narrative by Ashburnham*, II, cli–clii.
[370] Bodl. Lib., MS Clarendon 91, fo. 31r (Charles I to the Prince of Wales, 26 August 1646).
[371] *Narrative by Ashburnham*, II, cliv.   [372] Gardiner, *Documents*, p. 344.
[373] *Ibid.*, p. 355.
[374] *Ibid.*, p. 350.   [375] [Hyde], *Full Answer*, p. 138.   [376] *CJ*, V, 391; *LJ*, IX, 644.

delinquency and the sequestration to be taken off their estates.[377] However, the Lords again respited the cases of Richmond and Southampton until they returned from the Treaty of Newport.[378] This none the less shows that as the King's commissioners assembled at Newport, several were well on the way to securing the Houses' pardon for their delinquency. Parliament was less lenient towards some other categories of delinquent. At Newport, its commissioners proposed that fifty named Royalists be exempted from any pardon, including Strangways, Hyde, Culpepper, Ashburnham and Nicholas. A further forty-nine individuals were to be removed from the King's counsels. There was then a scale of punishments for other delinquents identical with those contained in the Newcastle Propositions and the *Four Bills*.[379] Charles accepted that those implicated in the Irish Rebellion should be exempted from pardon, but asked that all the other proposed exceptions 'may moderately compound for their estates'. He did, however, concede that 'such of them as the Houses of Parliament will insist upon' should be removed from his counsels and 'restricted from coming to the Court'.[380] The Houses found this answer unsatisfactory. They were willing to allow all Protestants on their original list of exceptions to compound at the rate of one-half of their estates; but they still wanted seven individuals exempted from pardon, including Newcastle and Digby.[381] Charles agreed to these terms, but asked that the seven might be admitted to compound for their estates. He added the by now familiar rider that

if any of them shall be proceeded against according to the ancient and established laws of this kingdom, His Majesty will not interpose to hinder any legal proceedings thereupon; but that His Majesty should join in any act for the taking away the life or estate of any that have adhered to them, or for the condemning of his own party, His Majesty cannot in justice and honour agree thereunto.[382]

Once again, a commitment to the rule of law and a desire to protect the King's adherents were inextricably linked.

This provides further evidence of the extent to which Constitutional Royalism embodied a nexus of interlocking assumptions rather than a series of discrete attitudes. Throughout the years of civil war, the King's answers drew a fundamental distinction between the justice of Parliament

---

[377] *CJ*, V, 683–4, 688; VI, 35–6. See also House of Lords RO, 8 September 1648, fos. 60, 62r (order and certificate regarding Richmond's delinquency). In Hertford's case, the Commons sent a similar draft ordinance to the Lords, but no action was apparently taken about it: MP, 28 August 1648 (order and certificate regarding Hertford's delinquency).
[378] *LJ*, X, 493, 532.   [379] Walker, *Perfect Copies*, pp. 57–60; *LJ*, X, 548–50.
[380] Walker, *Perfect Copies*, p. 61; *LJ*, X, 553.
[381] Walker, *Perfect Copies*, pp. 90–1; *LJ*, X, 573, 599–600.
[382] Walker, *Perfect Copies*, pp. 92–3; *LJ*, X, 620.

and justice by due process of law. His insistence that delinquents should be tried only by the latter was yet another aspect of the Constitutional Royalist commitment to the rule of law. The material hardship which so many of his moderate advisers suffered because of their allegiance only seems to have reinforced their dedication to the common law and their belief that the King was the most effective guardian of it.

But the issue went well beyond a desire to try delinquents by due process of law. It also raised the question of the King's attitude towards his friends and adherents. Haunted by what he termed the 'unjust sentence' on Strafford, Charles was determined never again to betray any of his followers. The exchanges over the fate of delinquents raised Strafford's ghost, and ultimately the King could only exorcise this by accepting an 'unjust sentence' on himself.[383] To the last, he never failed in his perceived duty to protect his own servants. As on several other issues, the common law offered the perfect justification for this stand. But the King's refusal to compromise also rested on his deep sense of honour as a private individual. Adherence to the monarch was a reciprocal relationship which brought obligations as well as benefits to both parties. At one level, Charles's attempts to mitigate the penalties on delinquents was an expression of his personal code of honour. Though complex and nebulous, this was intensely felt by King and Constitutional Royalists alike, and it forms the last of our seven sticking-points.

VII. THE KING'S 'HONOUR AND CONSCIENCE'

A wish to protect the King's honour and conscience has already emerged as an obstacle to settlement in earlier sections of this chapter. Powers as diverse as the choice of military officers and Privy Councillors, or the summoning of Parliament and the law courts to Oxford, were justified on the grounds of regal honour. It would be dishonourable, ran the argument, for Charles to surrender prerogative powers or to sacrifice his friends and adherents. Notions of honour were intimately related to the issue of the King's private conscience, which in turn was a crucial reason for Charles's refusal to compromise on the abolition of episcopacy. The defence of the King's honour and conscience derived much of its strength from his rights as a private individual; yet it was also inextricably bound up with public ideas about constitutional monarchy, the coronation oath and the rule of law. Hyde, for example, regarded the forcing of the King's conscience as a breach of parliamentary privilege. Furthermore, the issue had a direct bearing on political allegiance, for considerations of honour and

---

[383] Rushworth, VIII, 1429.

conscience inclined many to rally to Charles in the Civil Wars. This was, in short, the most intangible and elusive of all our sticking-points, but also among the most pervasive and multi-faceted.

In their *Answer*, Falkland and Culpepper summed up the *Nineteen Propositions* as terms which the King could not 'in honour, or regard to . . . regal authority . . . receive without just indignation'. They complained that the loss of his discretionary right to appoint 'great officers and ministers of state' overseas as well as at home would ensure that his 'dishonour' would not 'be bounded within this kingdom'. Nor was it just Charles's honour as a monarch which was at stake: for 'as neither care is taken for [his] rights, honour, nor safety as a prince, so [his] rights as a private person are endeavoured to be had from [him]'. This danger was yoked together with an attack on the English people, and Falkland and Culpepper condemned 'the subtile insinuations and secret practices of men who for private ends are disaffected to [the King's] honour and safety, and the peace and prosperity of [his] people'.[384] The *Answer* laid the foundations for a cluster of ideas which became fully developed during the 1640s: that Parliament's propositions infringed both Charles's public honour as a monarch and his private rights as an individual; and that by robbing him of powers exercised *pro bono publico* they also threatened the interests of his subjects.

The exchanges at the Treaty of Oxford extended and nuanced these arguments. The King was at pains to stress that he was 'less sollicitous for his own dignity and greatness than for his subjects' ease and liberty'. He promised to satisfy Parliament 'with such farther acts of grace as may agree with his honour, justice and duty to his Crown', and also 'not render him less able to protect his subjects according to his oath'.[385] Royal powers enhanced the monarch's honour and dignity, but they also safeguarded the subject's interests and the rule of law. As Falkland put it, the King could not 'devest himself of those trusts which the law of the land hath settled in the Crown alone, to preserve the power and dignity of the Prince, for the better protection of the subject and of the law'.[386] The rule of law formed a common denominator which ensured this symbiosis between royal honour and the public interest: it was – again in Falkland's words – 'always the most impartial judge between [the King] and his people'.[387] Charles wished to 'return to both Houses' whenever he could do so 'with honour and safety'. But he had been driven away by 'tumults . . . and what followed those tumults', and therefore could not return 'without more particular offers of security'.[388]

Among the most striking aspects of these statements is their fusion of

[384] *Ibid.*, IV, 725, 727, 730, 732.   [385] *Ibid.*, V, 179; *LJ*, V, 660.
[386] Rushworth, V, 203.
[387] *Ibid.*, 201; *LJ*, V, 703.   [388] Rushworth, V, 207, 209; *LJ*, V, 701.

arguments based on the King's dignity and honour with those derived from the rule of law. This blending of the regal and the legal was particularly apparent in a declaration issued by the Oxford Parliament in the spring of 1644. The members claimed that they sought 'the preservation of the religion, laws and safety of the kingdom', and were moved by 'zeal and tenderness of His Majesty's honour and safety' and 'affection and compassion of the bleeding condition of our miserable country'. They were 'absolutely obliged' and 'solemnly sworn' to protect 'the honour and safety of His Majesty's person'. Yet they spoke of 'the preservation of the liberty and property of the subject, settled and evident by the laws, statutes and customs of the realm' in the same breath as 'the defence of His Majesty's sacred person, his honour and just rights'.[389] These were not commitments running in parallel; they were interlocking components of a single ideological nexus.

The declaration of the Oxford Parliament also reveals that 'honour' and 'conscience' were not just royal attributes to be defended; they were also motives which inspired adherence to the King. The members had acted 'from that conscience, loyalty and duty' from which they could 'not swerve without the manifest breach of [their] allegiance'. Just like the King himself, they had found it impossible to remain at Westminster 'with honour, freedom and safety', and they were now prevented from returning there 'for [their] duty and loyalty to [their] sovereign'. Forced to leave London 'by reason of those outrages and violences offered to [their] persons or [their] consciences', they now urged 'all men of loyalty and conscience to be industrious and active on His Majesty's behalf against this horrid and odious rebellion'.[390] A wish to defend Charles's honour and conscience was precisely mirrored by a belief that these imperatives should also compel allegiance to the King.

There is considerable evidence that they did just that. We have already examined Sir Edmund Verney's remark of 1642 that 'my conscience is only concerned in honour and in gratitude to follow my master'.[391] Likewise, Lord Spencer wrote shortly after the outbreak of civil war that there was 'handsome occasion to retire' from the King's headquarters 'were it not for gaining honour', and that he would not 'continue [there] an hour' if 'there could be an expedient found to salve the punctillio of honour'.[392] Dorset expressed very similar sentiments when he told the Countess of Middlesex in the summer of 1645: 'I thank God my conscience wittnesseth unto mee,

[389] Rushworth, V, 582, 589, 593.   [390] *Ibid.*, 584, 589, 594.
[391] Clarendon, *Life*, I, 160. See above, p. 96.
[392] CKS, De L'Isle and Dudley MS, U 1475/Z53/92 (Lord Spencer to Lady Spencer, 21 September 1642). I am most grateful to Viscount De L'Isle for allowing me to consult and quote from his family muniments.

thatt in followinge my King, my master, my benefactor, I doe nothing butt whatt I am obliged to doe in honor, duty, piety and gratitude.'[393] Conscience, honour and duty were all intimately related for both the King and his adherents. Hyde later characterised the Royalists as those who had 'served [the King] faithfully, and out of the most abstract considerations of conscience and honour'. Ultimately, they 'for conscience sake ... lost all'.[394] Hyde's portraits of the leading Constitutional Royalists are steeped in a vocabulary of honour and fidelity. Dorset was a figure of 'much honour' and 'of most entire fidelity to the Crown'; Richmond was 'so punctual in point of honour that he never swerved a tittle' and lived 'with unspotted fidelity'; Hertford was 'a man of great honour and fortune'; Seymour 'remained firm in his fidelity'.[395] Such phrases were not empty rhetorical flourishes. These people genuinely believed that Charles was also a man of honour, a King who fully deserved the allegiance of honourable men. Hyde described him as 'an honest man' whose 'mind alwaies disdained even to prosper or be secure by any deviations from truth and honour'.[396] In seeking to defend the King's honour, the Constitutional Royalists were in part trying to preserve him as a worthy focus for their own honourable loyalty.

In the early years of the Civil War, Charles's honour – both as a monarch and as a private individual – thus became a major subject of debate. But from the Treaty of Uxbridge onwards, the closely related issue of his conscience also came to the fore. This was primarily because these and subsequent talks, unlike those at Oxford, addressed Parliament's proposed changes to the government of the Church of England. The King reduced the issue of Church government to two principles: 'conscience and policy'.[397] His commissioners insisted that they would only consent to such reforms 'as may stand with the glory of God, and in truth be for the honour of the King and the peace and happiness of his kingdoms'. Their argument against the abolition of episcopacy rested on 'conscience, law [and] reason': such a fundamental change would not, they asserted, be 'agreeable to conscience and justice'.[398] But it was not just the King's conscience which had to be safeguarded. As with Charles's honour, the royal and public interests were inseparable. The Royalist commissioners at Uxbridge repeatedly urged that 'another bill may be framed for the ease of tender

---

[393] CKS, Uncatalogued Cranfield Papers, Dorset to the Countess of Middlesex, [?] June–July 1645. The date of this letter is discussed in Smith, '"The more posed and wise advice"', 823.
[394] [Hyde], *Full Answer*, pp. 137, 186 (correct pagination 166).
[395] Clarendon, *History*, I, 76 (Book I, §131); II, 528 (Book VI, §§384–5); II, 534 (Book VI, §392).
[396] *Ibid.*, IV, 489 (Book XI, §239); [Hyde], *Full Answer*, p. 80.   [397] Rushworth, V, 891.
[398] *Ibid.*, 816–18; *LJ*, VII, 196–7.

consciences'.[399] They were anxious to 'give satisfaction to all persons seriously disturbed or afflicted in their consciences', but believed that the abolition of episcopacy would only offend 'very many pious and religious persons'.[400] The protection of conscience underpinned the Constitutional Royalists' acceptance of a measure of religious toleration,[401] and they saw it as a right enjoyed by the King and his subjects alike.

At the Treaty of Uxbridge, the question of honour figured most prominently in the exchanges over the Irish Cessation. Once again Charles reduced the issue to two principles, this time 'honour and policy'.[402] The Houses asked Charles to 'make void the Cessation' which he had signed with the Irish rebels on 15 September 1643.[403] The Royalist commissioners retorted by asking 'how that Cessation can be declared void without a breach of faith and honour in His Majesty?'[404] They could not 'apprehend how His Majesty can, with justice and honour, declare the same to be void'.[405] The Parliamentarian commissioners' response was highly revealing: they condemned the Cessation as 'only for the advantage of the popish rebels, to the high dishonour of God, the disservice of His Majesty, and evident prejudice of his three kingdoms'.[406] This answer boded ill for an early settlement. Not only did it duck the question of the King's honour; by alluding to 'the high dishonour of God' it raised the problem of what to do if royal and divine honour became incompatible. Throughout their statements, the Royalist commissioners never addressed this danger. Indeed, their constant talk of duty to God and to the King in the same breath suggests that they thought it a logical impossibility. But as long as what the Royalist commissioners believed necessary for the King's honour required what the Parliamentarian commissioners saw as a dishonour to God, a settlement would elude them.

None the less, towards the end of 1645, the Constitutional Royalist peers persuaded Charles to launch another peace initiative.[407] In a message to the Speaker of the House of Lords, Charles attributed his raising arms to 'the necessary defence of God's true religion, His Majesty's honour, safety and prosperity', and 'the peace, comfort and security of his people'.[408] Again, his own interests and those of his subjects were bracketed together. Charles subsequently requested a 'personal treaty' based on the three 'heads' used

[399] Rushworth, V, 804; LJ, VII, 152.   [400] Rushworth, V, 818; LJ, VII, 197.
[401] See above, pp. 146–7, 151–2.
[402] Rushworth, V, 891.
[403] Gardiner, Documents, p. 278. For the Cessation, see Gardiner, Civil War, I, 225; and David Stevenson, Scottish Covenanters and Irish Confederates (Belfast, 1981), pp. 137–9, 145–50.
[404] Rushworth, V, 844; LJ, VII, 189.   [405] Rushworth, V, 845; LJ, VII, 189.
[406] Rushworth, V, 845; LJ, VII, 189.
[407] The background to this initiative is discussed above, pp. 126–7, 202.
[408] LJ, VIII, 46.

at the Treaty of Uxbridge.[409] But he insisted that his terms were now 'as low as he [could] goe with preservation of his conscience and honor'.[410] He had reached an irreducible core on which he refused to compromise further. Yet, as we saw in chapter 5, the Houses felt unable to accept the King's invitation until he gave 'satisfaction and security' to both England and Scotland.[411]

The issues of honour and conscience recurred throughout the summer and autumn of 1646 as the King stood firm in rejecting the Newcastle Propositions. On 10 October, for example, Charles assured Jermyn, Culpepper and Ashburnham that he would never sacrifice his 'conscience, crowne and frends' for 'the forsaking of any one of them looses the other two'.[412] Despite assurances from Bishops Juxon and Duppa that concessions regarding Church government would not vitiate either the King's conscience or his coronation oath,[413] Charles stubbornly refused to countenance the introduction of Presbyterianism or the abolition of episcopacy. He clung to the doctrine of mental reservation,[414] and warned against those who mistook 'courage and morall honesty for conscience', a distinction which reveals something of his own idea of conscience and helps to explain why it was so difficult for others to discuss such matters on Charles's behalf.[415] There was a point beyond which negotiations became impossible with a monarch who could write: 'I have long agoe resolved rather to shipwracke my person, than either my conscience or honnor.'[416] Charles's letters displayed extraordinary conviction and confidence throughout these months. He seemed to sense the long-term – even posthumous – rewards of his stand on points of principle. As he told Henrietta Maria, 'I am confident that within a very small time I shall be recalled with much honour, and all my friends will see that I have neither a foolish nor peevish conscience.'[417] The word 'recalled' is another indication of how far Charles had already embraced the role of martyr by the end of 1646.

The fullest public elaboration of these themes came in Charles's third answer to the Newcastle Propositions in May 1646. The King found

[409] *Ibid.*, 72.
[410] Bodl. Lib., MS Clarendon 26, fo. 97r (reasons why Charles I sent propositions of 20 December [1645]).
[411] *LJ*, VIII, 99; above, p. 127.
[412] Bodl. Lib., MS Clarendon 91, fo. 51r (Charles I to Jermyn, Culpepper and Ashburnham, 10 October 1646).
[413] *Ibid.*, fo. 43r (Bishops Juxon and Duppa to Charles I, 14 October 1646).
[414] Keith Thomas, 'Cases of conscience in seventeenth-century England', in *Public Duty and Private Conscience*, Morrill *et al.*, p. 33.
[415] Bodl. Lib., MS Clarendon 91, fo. 47r (Charles I to Jermyn, Culpepper and Ashburnham, 3 October 1646).
[416] *Ibid.*, fo. 70v (Charles I to William Murray, 22 October 1646).
[417] *Charles I in 1646*, Bruce, 81–2 (Charles I to Henrietta Maria, [21 November] 1646).

himself unable to accept the Houses' terms 'without disclaiming that reason which God hath given him to judge by for the good of him and his people, and without putting the greatest violence upon his own conscience'. Once again, the King's interests and those of his subjects were identified as one and the same, while the link between 'conscience' and 'reason' recalls the Royalist commissioners' defence of episcopacy at Uxbridge. The King was prepared to return to London, but only 'upon confidence' that 'those things which concern His Majesty's honour' be looked upon 'with tenderness'. He could not yet give an answer regarding the Covenant, 'because, it being a matter of conscience', he would first need to consult with his chaplains. The protection of delinquents was another point of honour, and Charles warned of 'the perpetual dishonour that must cleave to him, if he should ... abandon so many persons of condition and fortune that have engaged themselves with and for him out of a sense of duty'.[418] Henrietta Maria reinforced Charles's resolve by reminding him 'how much [his] honour and justice' were at stake.[419] Honour obliged the King to protect his followers just as it obliged them to defend him.

At this point, with talks between Charles and the Houses at a standstill, the *Heads of the Proposals* adopted a different approach. They explicitly guaranteed that 'His Majesty's person, his Queen, and royal issue, may be restored to a condition of safety, honour and freedom in this nation, without diminution to their personal rights'.[420] This removed the threat to the King's honour, just as the preservation of a modified episcopacy and the non-enforcement of the Covenant lifted that to his conscience.[421] This was yet another way in which the *Heads* were the most generous terms ever presented to Charles. Small wonder, then, that shortly before the King's flight from Hampton Court in November 1647, John Ashburnham was confident that a settlement could be achieved if Charles informed the Lords that 'hee would come in person to the House, and with reservation of his conscience and honour, would give them all other imaginable settlement'.[422]

Characteristically, when Charles did act on this advice, it was too late.[423] On 17 November, he wrote to the Speaker of the Lords insisting that he could not accept the abolition of episcopacy 'both in relation as he is a Christian and a King'. Once again, his private rights and public duties pointed to exactly the same response. So, too, did his obligations to his

[418] Gardiner, *Documents*, pp. 312–13, 315.
[419] *Letters of Henrietta Maria*, Green, p. 333 (Henrietta Maria to Charles I, [?] 1646).
[420] Gardiner, *Documents*, pp. 321–2.   [421] See above, p. 152.
[422] *Narrative by Ashburnham*, II, 104.
[423] For a discussion of this trait, cf. Russell, *Causes*, pp. 208–9.

subjects: while he was prepared for episcopal powers to 'be so limited that they be not grievous to the tender consciences of others', he none the less saw 'no reason why he alone, and those of his judgement, should be pressed to a violation of theirs'.[424] Regarding the militia, Charles was 'willing to concur in any thing that can be done without the violation of his conscience and honour'. Similarly, he could not 'consent in honour and justice' to nullify all grants under his Great Seal since 22 May 1642. But, as before, he desired 'a personal treaty at London with his two Houses in honour, freedom and safety'.[425]

The same qualifications recur throughout the King's Engagement with the Scots and his answer to Parliament's *Four Bills*. In the Engagement, Charles promised to confirm the Solemn League and Covenant 'so soon as he can with freedom, honour and safety be present in a free Parliament'. In return, the Scots would demand 'that His Majesty might come to London in safety, honour and freedom for a personal treaty', and that his Queen and children might remain in either kingdom 'with safety, honour and freedom'.[426] As before, these considerations moved the King's adherents as much as Charles himself: the Scottish signatories engaged themselves upon their 'honour, faith and conscience, and all that is dearest to honest men'.[427]

What made the Engagement attractive to Charles was precisely what made the *Four Bills* unacceptable. Although he credited the Houses with not wishing 'to force other things from him, which are either against his conscience or honour', the King complained of the 'strange condition' into which these terms would cast him 'and all his subjects'. Charles was convinced that a refusal was the only possible response; and one, moreover, which entirely accorded with the duties incumbent on each of the monarch's two bodies. 'His Majesty is very much at ease within himself', Charles's reply concluded, 'for having fulfilled the offices both of a Christian and of a King'.[428] His conscientious scruples as a monarch and as a private person were indivisible.

These issues were as important to the Constitutional Royalists as they were to Charles. For Hyde they lay at the heart of the conflict between Crown and Parliament. As he wrote to Culpepper in August 1648: 'For God's sake, remember that the quarrell hath always been, and still is, that the King bee not by force compelled to any thing contrary to his conscience, honour, and judgm[en]t.' This was not a matter of prerogative rights; it was pivotal to the idea of constitutional monarchy governing within the law. For with this Hyde associated a second issue: 'that the people may not bee compelled to submitt to any determinacons, contrary

---

[424] Gardiner, *Documents*, p. 329.   [425] *Ibid.*, pp. 330, 332.   [426] *Ibid.*, pp. 347–9.
[427] *Ibid.*, p. 352.   [428] *Ibid.*, pp. 354–6.

to the lawes established, which have not his royall assent'.[429] The granting or withholding of the royal assent thus safeguarded the rule of law, which in turn guaranteed the rights and liberties of the subject.

The issue of royal honour again loomed large in the exchanges which led to the Treaty of Newport. In mid-August 1648, Charles asked how he could 'treat with honour, so long as people [were] terrified by votes and orders to come, speak or write to [him]'. He also questioned whether he was 'honourably treated, so long as there [were] none about [him] ... that ever [he] named, to wait upon [him]'.[430] A fortnight later, the Houses acknowledged the force of these arguments by granting safe conduct to all persons summoned by Charles, except for Ashburnham and William Legge.[431]

During the talks which followed, the King's 'conscience' emerged as the main stumbling block in the debates over Church government. The arguments against episcopacy did not satisfy Charles's conscience, and his concessions always included a reservation that neither his own nor his subjects' consciences were to be violated.[432] A similar correlation between royal and popular rights was evident on 21 November when Charles declared himself 'well pleased that he be settled in a condition of honour, freedom and safety, agreeable to the laws of the land'.[433] The same assumption that royal dignity and the rule of law were in harmony lay behind the King's protection of delinquents on the grounds of 'honour and justice'.[434] These represented the final sticking-points at Newport, for it was only on issues which involved his honour or conscience that Charles found himself unable to compromise.

These themes formed a leitmotiv through the King's last public utterances. At his trial, he insisted that 'the duty' which he owed 'to God in the preservation of the true liberty of [his] people' would not suffer him 'to be silent'. Charles claimed to speak not for his 'own right alone', but 'also for the true liberty of all [his] subjects'; and he promised to 'defend the ancient laws and liberties of this kingdom together with [his] own just right'.[435] On the scaffold, Charles stated his desire to clear himself 'both as an honest man, a good King, and a good Christian', and concluded by saying that he had 'delivered [his] conscience'.[436] Such words no doubt contributed to Marvell's later tribute that Charles 'nothing common did or mean / Upon that memorable Scene'.[437]

[429] Bodl. Lib., MS Clarendon 31, fos. 208v–209r (Hyde to Culpepper, 20 August 1648).
[430] Walker, Perfect Copies, p. 4; LJ, X, 437.   [431] CJ, V, 694; LJ, X, 484.
[432] Walker, Perfect Copies, pp. 65, 83, 85–6, 98; LJ, X, 561, 603, 605, 622.
[433] Walker, Perfect Copies, p. 88; LJ, X, 606.
[434] Walker, Perfect Copies, p. 93; LJ, X, 620.
[435] Gardiner, Documents, pp. 374–6.   [436] Rushworth, VIII, 1429–30.
[437] The Poems and Letters of Andrew Marvell, ed. H. M. Margoliouth (2 vols., Oxford, 1927), I, 88 ('An Horatian Ode upon Cromwel's Return from Ireland', lines 57–8). For

Honour and conscience in a sense made strange bedfellows. They derived their force from contrasting value systems and ideological traditions. The notion of honour drew ultimately on a medieval, chivalric ethos.[438] Conscience, on the other hand, was a spiritual and religious imperative which was thought to rest on the law of nature and on God's law.[439] Yet within Constitutional Royalism they became welded together into an organic whole. A man of honour had to listen to his conscience. Furthermore, these attributes were expected of both the monarch's two bodies, of Charles I as a sovereign and as a man. His integrity as a ruler and as an individual Christian were thus indivisible. These were tied neatly together by his coronation oath, a public declaration which yet depended on the monarch's private conscience to honour it. The oath bound the monarch to uphold the 'fundamental laws' of England, and in this way honour and conscience in turn became inseparable from the rule of law.[440]

That law ensured that the interests of monarch and subjects operated symbiotically. It followed from this that honour and conscience applied with equal rigour to the King and to his people. They imposed obligations of mutual defence on both parties: the King was bound to protect his people and rule them according to established law; but conscience and honour also required the subjects to rally to the sovereign against rebels. The invocations of honour and conscience by Charles and his close advisers were thus designed not only to give him the moral high ground and to portray him as intrinsically worthy of allegiance. They also formed one half of a reciprocal relationship in which these same qualities impelled adherence to the Crown. Again and again, the Constitutional Royalists reminded listeners that Charles had honoured his side of the bargain.

Such patterns and connections once again illustrate the extraordinary degree to which Constitutional Royalist attitudes operated in series rather than in parallel. As so often in this study, we are looking at a nexus of interlocking ideas rather than a set of separable beliefs. The issues of honour and conscience also posed two specific problems in successive peace negotiations. First, they were quite intangible, and led into the murkiest reaches of Charles's complex and enigmatic personality. Conrad

contrasting analyses of these lines, see John M. Wallace, *Destiny his Choice: the Loyalism of Andrew Marvell* (Cambridge, 1968), p. 78; and Blair Worden, 'Andrew Marvell, Oliver Cromwell, and the Horatian ode', in *The Politics of Discourse: The Literature and History of Seventeenth-Century England*, ed. Kevin Sharpe and Steven N. Zwicker (Berkeley, 1987), pp. 179–80.

[438] Cf. Mervyn James, *Society, Politics and Culture* (Cambridge, 1986), pp. 308–415.
[439] Thomas, 'Cases of Conscience', pp. 30–1; Patricia Crawford, 'Public Duty, Conscience, and Women in Early Modern England', in *Public Duty and Private Conscience*, Morrill *et al.*, p. 68.
[440] Cf. Kevin Sharpe, 'Private conscience and public duty in the writings of James VI and I', in *Public Duty and Private Conscience*, Morrill *et al.*, pp. 80–7.

Russell has recently drawn attention to the difficulty 'of how we identify the point where conscience, fear and self-will meet'.[441] In the end, only Charles could say whether or not a demand was compatible with his conscience and honour, and this made it extremely difficult to discuss these matters on his behalf. Furthermore, so many other subjects ultimately held implications for the King's honour and conscience. One way or another, this seventh sticking-point had a bearing on all the previous six. Perhaps it was therefore appropriate that it should prove the final obstacle to settlement in the last formal treaty of the 1640s.

On the scaffold, Charles dismissed the distinction between his person and his office, and offered a defiant assertion of his integrity in *both* his bodies. The Constitutional Royalists believed passionately in Charles I as both a King and a man of honour, just as they believed in their own duty to protect and advise him. That bond was a reciprocal one, and ultimately it proved indestructible. For just as Charles always honoured his pledge that 'he would have no man to suffer for his sake', so at the last four Constitutional Royalist peers carried his coffin to the grave. For Richmond, Hertford, Southampton and Lindsey, this was a fitting expression of their own honour and conscience.

[441] Russell, *Causes*, p. 200.

⟪⟫ *7* ⟪⟫

The theory of Constitutional Royalism

The four peers who acted as the King's pallbearers, together with Dorset and Seymour, remained a close-knit political grouping throughout the 1640s. But that decade saw a gradual disintegration of the broad Constitutional Royalist front which had existed in the summer of 1642. From 1645–6 onwards, Hyde was exiled and isolated; Culpepper remained influential but henceforth in association with Jermyn and Ashburnham; and Strangways was in prison. The Constitutional Royalists increasingly formed discrete clusters of individuals, small political constellations which had similar values, but scarcely collaborated with each other. They were ideologically aligned, but not politically co-ordinated.

This brings us to the question of how far there was a coherent theory of Constitutional Royalism during these years. This chapter will suggest that a number of writers advanced ideas very similar to those of the King's moderate advisers. Eight authors stand out as the leading exponents of Constitutional Royalist theory: John Bramhall, Sir Charles Dallison, Dudley Digges the younger, Henry Ferne, James Howell, David Jenkins, Jasper Mayne and Sir John Spelman. None of these was a member of the Long Parliament, nor were they ever involved in peace negotiations. The majority of them had works published at Oxford during the first Civil War. These were nearly all produced by the printer to Oxford University, Leonard Lichfield, who also printed the King's declarations and proclamations during these years. It would be unwise to attribute much significance to this beyond the fact that Lichfield clearly did not print things which the Court found objectionable: writers at Oxford would naturally have used Lichfield and this fact does not in itself reveal much about their attitudes or connections.[1] I have found no evidence which proves that these writers worked at the behest of particular patrons or an identifiable political group. Nevertheless their writings do provide a theoretical justification for the political activities examined above, just as those activities offer a context within which the texts may be understood. Without losing

[1] For details of Lichfield, see *DNB*, XXXIII, 220–1. I am most grateful to Sheila Lambert for advice on this point.

sight of the differences between these eight writers, they did share important areas of common ground with the practical exponents of Constitutional Royalism on whom we have so far concentrated.

These shared attitudes may be briefly characterised as a belief that royal powers should be guided and limited by the rule of law, and that Charles I's actions posed less of a threat to legality than those of the Houses; the combination of a respect for Parliament's place in the constitution with an abhorrence of the Junto; a defence of the existing Church of England and the Protestant religion 'by law established'; a wish to preserve the royal discretionary powers to appoint Privy Councillors and senior military and legal officers; and a conviction that armed resistance to the sovereign ran contrary to both the common law and God's law. In essentials, these principles represent a development of the position outlined in the *Answer to the XIX Propositions*; and they provide the central themes of the extensive body of writings analysed in this chapter. They stood in marked contrast to other strands within Royalist thought, and the final section of the chapter will analyse the views of several writers who defended absolute monarchy against the exponents of limited monarchy. Prominent among these were John Maxwell, Griffith Williams, Michael Hudson, and above all Sir Robert Filmer and Thomas Hobbes.

Probably the best known of our eight theorists of Constitutional Royalism was John Bramhall. Alone among this group, he has had his works collected posthumously and has been the subject of a full-length biography.[2] The latter portrayed Bramhall as a divine right theorist; but two more recent studies have persuasively identified him as a moderate or Constitutional Royalist writer of major significance.[3] A graduate of Sidney Sussex College, Cambridge, Bramhall became chaplain to Wentworth in Ireland in 1634, and Bishop of Derry the following year. He was impeached and imprisoned by the Irish Commons in 1641 for alleged unconstitutional acts in the recovery of Church property, but Archbishop Ussher later secured his release. He then joined the English Royalists until July 1644 when he went abroad. In 1661 he became Archbishop of Armagh, a position which he held until his death two years later.[4]

Bramhall was a very considerable preacher and theologian. But by far

[2] *The Works of the Most Reverend Father in God, John Bramhall, D.D.*, ed. A. W. H. (5 vols., Oxford, 1842–5); W. J. Sparrow Simpson, *Archbishop Bramhall* (1927).
[3] J. W. Daly, 'John Bramhall and the theoretical problems of Royalist moderation', *JBS*, 11 (1971), 26–44; John Sanderson, '*Serpent-Salve*, 1643: the Royalism of John Bramhall', *Journal of Ecclesiastical History*, 25 (1974), 1–14.
[4] This biographical outline is derived from Sparrow Simpson, *Bramhall, passim*; DNB, VI, 203–6; and J. Venn and J. A. Venn, ed., *Alumni Cantabrigienses. Part One: from the earliest times to 1751* (4 vols., Cambridge, 1922–7), I, 204. For Bramhall's activities during the 1630s, see also Hugh F. Kearney, *Strafford in Ireland, 1633–41* (Manchester, 1959), pp. 113–26, 183, 187, 211.

his most important work for our present purpose is *The Serpent-Salve*,[5] a point-by-point refutation of Henry Parker's *Observations upon some of His Majesties late answers and expresses*.[6] His central theme was the threat which Parker's arguments posed to England's 'ancient, glorious, well-tempered and settled monarchy'.[7] He asserted the need for obedience to 'his Sacred Majesty', for 'what can the poor kingdom expect, when the person of the prince is not held sacred, but combustion and confusion?'[8] All claims 'that subjects who have not the power of the sword committed to them, after a long time of obedience and lawful succession, after oaths of allegiance, may use force to recover their former liberty, or raise arms to change the laws established' were 'both false and rebellious'.[9] Bramhall insisted that there were no circumstances in which armed resistance was permissible: even 'if a sovereign shall persecute his subjects for not doing his unjust commands, yet it is not lawful to resist by raising arms against him'.[10]

Equally, the law served to protect England from royal tyranny. The monarchy was legally limited, for 'His Majesty is bound in conscience both by his oath and office, not only to protect his people committed to his charge in wealth, peace and godliness, but also to promote their good; but this protection must be according to law, this promotion according to law.'[11] Bramhall nevertheless argued that the King retained some discretionary powers. Although 'his office and authority may be limited by law ... a King without personal authority is a contradiction rather than a King'.[12] The corollary of this was that 'the law hath no coercive power over him'. However, 'the law hath a directive power over kings; and all good kings will follow it, for example'[s] sake to their subjects, for conscience'[s] sake to themselves'.[13] Good monarchs would respect the rule of law; but the law could not sanction armed resistance against bad monarchs. Bramhall thus evolved what James Daly has called 'a concept of self-limited sovereignty'.[14]

Of central importance within this process of self-limitation were the Houses of Parliament. Bramhall was at pains to deny that his treatise was 'intended to the prejudice of the lawful rights and just privileges of Parliament'. Indeed, 'the very name of a Parliament was music in our ears; at the summons thereof our hearts danced for joy'. On the other hand, he warned against those who 'idolized Parliaments, and trusted more in them than in

[5] [John Bramhall], *The Serpent-Salve, or, A Remedie for the Biting of an Aspe* (1642), Wing, B 4236; printed in *Works of Bramhall*, III, 289–496.
[6] [Henry Parker], *Observations upon some of His Majesties late answers and expresses* (1642), Wing, P 412; BL, TT, E 153/26.
[7] *Works of Bramhall*, III, 299.   [8] *Ibid.*, 350, 455.   [9] *Ibid.*, 341–2.
[10] *Ibid.*, 352.
[11] *Ibid.*, 337.   [12] *Ibid.*, 356.   [13] *Ibid.*, 363.   [14] Daly, 'Bramhall', 35.

God for our temporal well being'.[15] Bramhall quoted approvingly Charles's (Hyde's) statement that 'Parliaments are so essential a part of the constitution of this kingdom that we can attain no happiness without them.' But this was not to grant them 'superiority above kings, or equality with kings'.[16] The monarch remained 'undoubtedly the *primum mobile*'; while the Houses of Parliament were 'the lower spheres' which 'by their transverse yet vincible motions, ought to allay the violence of the highest orb for the good and preservation of the universe'.[17] It was therefore vital that Charles retain a 'negative voice', the removal of which would leave England 'open and stark naked to all those popular evils, or epidemical diseases, which flow from ochlocracy'.[18] Bramhall disliked 'arbitrary government much in one, but twenty times worse in more', for there was 'no tyranny like many-headed tyranny'.[19] The King's 'negative voice' would prevent anarchy, whereas the 'cure' for royal tyranny lay in 'the mixture of governments'.[20]

The laws which guaranteed this 'mixture' also underpinned Church government. Episcopacy was 'woven and riveted into the body of our law', or – to vary the metaphor – 'cemented into our laws'.[21] Furthermore, just as 'conscience' obliged the King to govern lawfully, so it also bound him to defend the Church by reason of his coronation oath.[22] Similarly, bishops were 'bound to proceed according to law', and even if they were 'not necessary, yet at the least they [were] lawful'.[23] Exactly like the Constitutional Royalists in the root-and-branch debates of 1641, Bramhall distinguished carefully between the 'function' and the 'abuses' of bishops. He declared that 'no form of government' kept out 'all abuses', and that 'errors of religion' could therefore not be 'imputed to the government of the Church'. Far from abolishing episcopacy, as Parliament demanded, Bramhall concluded that 'the present condition of England doth plead more powerfully for Bishops than all that have writ for episcopacy since the Reformation of our Church'.[24]

A condemnation of armed resistance against the Crown; the concept of a legally limited monarchy; respect for the role of Parliament within a 'mixture of governments'; and a rejection of calls to abolish episcopacy: all these attitudes clearly align Bramhall's position in The Serpent-Salve with that of the Constitutional Royalists. Like them, Bramhall assumed that God's law and the English common law were synchronised, and that Charles was the most effective defender of both. By contrast, he regarded

[15] Works of Bramhall, III, 299.
[16] Ibid., 386. The quotation came from His Majesties Declaration of 12 August 1642: see above, p. 169.
[17] Works of Bramhall, III, 404.   [18] Ibid., 416.   [19] Ibid., 381–2.
[20] Ibid., 380.
[21] Ibid., 468–9.   [22] Ibid., 419.   [23] Ibid., 477, 485.   [24] Ibid., 490, 492–3.

Parker's views as 'not warranted by the laws of God' and 'most repugnant to the known laws and customs of this realm'.[25]

Another writer who replied to Parker's *Observations* was Dudley Digges the younger, son of the distinguished judge, diplomat and MP Sir Dudley Digges.[26] A brilliant mathematician, the younger Digges was elected a Fellow of All Souls' College, Oxford in 1633, at the age of twenty.[27] He was admitted to Gray's Inn in March 1641. Richard Tuck has uncovered his association with the Great Tew circle, which has already emerged as a possible though by no means necessary qualification for Constitutional Royalism during the 1640s. Digges's fame rests on three eloquent treatises; and his early death from camp fever in October 1643 robbed the Royalist cause of one of its most articulate apologists.

The first tract, which Digges wrote in collaboration with Falkland and Chillingworth, was another systematic rebuttal of Henry Parker entitled *An Answer to a printed book, intituled Observations upon some of His Majesties late answers and expresses*.[28] While accepting that sovereignty originated in the people, the *Answer* argued against armed resistance on the grounds that 'a people ... cannot resume that authority which they have placed in another'. Digges admitted that 'the subject [had] groaned under some grievances', but neatly turned this to advantage by asserting that 'we owe to the goodnesse of His Majesty that we are free even from the feare of them for the future'. This was a legally limited monarchy in which the King was 'bound to maintaine the rights and liberty of the subject'; but it was emphatically not a contractual monarchy, for the King's authority was not 'capable of forfeiture upon a not exact perform-ance of covenant'.[29] Furthermore, the King would defend his people from 'arbitrary power', and was 'resolved never to make use of it' himself. The King was 'a part of the State', and therefore 'the other part hath not any

---

[25] *Ibid.*, 289.
[26] For the elder Digges, see *DNB*, XV, 68–9. For discussions of his son's political thought, see John Sanderson, *'But the People's Creatures': The Philosophical Basis of the English Civil War* (Manchester, 1989), pp. 73–85; Margaret Atwood Judson, *The Crisis of the Constitution: An Essay in Constitutional and Political Thought in England, 1603–1645* (New Brunswick, NJ, 1949), pp. 384–96; Richard Tuck, *Natural Rights Theories: Their Origin and Development* (Cambridge, 1979), pp. 101–111, 115–16; *Philosophy and Government, 1572–1651* (Cambridge, 1993), pp. 273–4; and I. D. Brice, 'Political Ideas in Royalist pamphlets of the period 1642–1649' (BLitt thesis, University of Oxford, 1970), pp. 13–20.
[27] *DNB*, XV, 70; Venn and Venn, *Alumni Cantab.*, II, 42; J. Foster, ed., *Alumni Oxonienses, 1500–1714* (4 vols., Oxford, 1891–2), I, 403; Joseph Foster, ed., *The Register of Admissions to Gray's Inn, 1521–1889* (1889), p. 230.
[28] [Dudley Digges], *An Answer to a printed book, intituled Observations upon some of His Majesties late answers and expresses* (Oxford, 1642), Wing, D 1454; BL, TT, E 105/5. For the collaboration between Digges, Falkland and Culpepper, see *The Complete Prose Works of John Milton*, vol. II: *1643–1648*, ed. Ernest Sirluck (New Haven, 1959), 34–5.
[29] [Digges], *An Answer*, pp. 1, 7, 11.

power warranted by law to doe what they thinke fit to his prejudice, upon pretence of publique extremity'. Similarly, the two Houses alone were 'not the Parliament'. Rather, 'the subject of such power is the entire body, which consists of three estates'.[30] Like Falkland and Culpepper, Digges thus defined the three estates as King, Lords and Commons. This was integral to his concept of a legally limited monarchy.

Digges explored these issues further in his second refutation of Parker, *A Review of the Observations upon some of His Majesties late answers and expresses, written by a gentleman of quality*.[31] This again argued that 'in every state there are three parties capable of just, or unjust soveraignty; that is to say, some Princes, the nobles, and the people'. These 'three parties' were 'admitted to a participation' of sovereignty; yet they were 'so admitted as that still the soveraignty should cleerely remain to him that ought to be the soveraign'. However, the law had established 'the frame of State and government' in such a way that 'the Prince should have his hands bound up from using the legislative power without the concurrence of the peers and commons'. This was designed to 'prevent the evil' of 'absolute power'. To ensure that the Houses might 'not themselves become that evil which they were called to prevent, the law gave to them no more interest in the legislative power than it had stil left in the hands of the Prince'. In other words, King, Lords and Commons possessed 'an equall power of assent or dissent in making of new law', thus ensuring 'a ballancing of their powers one against another'.[32] The law safeguarded this system, and thus formed 'the best boundary of regall power against any irregularity whatsoever'. It could 'no way be in the power of the King to take away the least right, much lesse the being of Parliaments'. Equally, the King was 'our soveraign lord' and 'the only supream vice-gerent of the great and supream judge', and Digges concluded with an impassioned plea that he might be 'in righteousness, in judgement, in true religion, and in peace for ever established over us'.[33]

It followed from these principles that armed resistance against the sovereign could never be justified, and this formed the central argument of Digges's longest and most famous work, *The Unlawfulnesse of Subjects taking up armes against their Soveraigne*.[34] Here Digges contended that it was 'unlawfull to resist him or them in whom the supreame authority (that

---

[30] *Ibid.*, pp. 39, 43, 51.

[31] [Dudley Digges], *A Review of the Observations upon some of His Majesties late answers and expresses, written by a gentleman of quality* (Oxford, 1643), Wing, D 1459; BL, TT, E 97/11.

[32] *Ibid.*, p. 9.   [33] *Ibid.*, pp. 19, 24.

[34] [Dudley Digges], *The Unlawfulnesse of Subjects taking up armes against their Soveraigne, in what case soever* (Oxford, 1643[/4]), Wing, D 1462; BL, TT, E 128/42.

is, all the *legall* power of the kingdome in order to raise armes) is placed'.[35] He made much play of the Pauline doctrine that 'the powers that be are ordained of God',[36] culminating in the injunction: 'We render to Caesar the things which are Caesar's, and to God the things which are God's. Be subject to every ordinance of man for the Lord's sake.'[37] But Digges also advanced the more utilitarian claim that 'non-resistance to the supream power [is] essentiall to the preservation of order'.[38] Armed resistance against the sovereign was thus contrary both to God's law and to public order.

Digges then embarked on a detailed exploration of the nature of monarchy. He argued that there could not 'be such a thing as *mixtum imperium*'. Rather, by 'mixt monarchy' he meant 'a government not arbitrary, but restrained by positive constitutions, wherein a prince hath limited himselfe by promise or oath not to exercise full power'.[39] The King was 'under God and the law because the law makes him King'. In a passage explicitly derived from Bracton, Digges wrote: 'That the King is *sub lege*, under the law, hath this sense, that he ought to governe according to those standing rules.' However, this was only a moral obligation, for 'if he should swerve from these rules, he is not liable to any punishment, nor compellible by strong hand'. The subject thus possessed 'no legall remedy'.[40] However, to argue that the King wielded 'supreame power' did not vitiate the idea of a legally limited monarchy: 'a mixt monarchy' was 'a contradiction', and denoted simply 'a restrained and limited monarchy' in which the King had 'supreme' but 'not absolute power'.[41]

The Unlawfulnesse of Subjects taking up armes was completed shortly after the Treaty of Oxford, and Digges's argument concluded with a systematic account of how Parliament's propositions violated these constitutional principles. The abolition of episcopacy threatened 'the foundation' of 'the ecclesiasticall and civill State' because 'a presbyteriall government' would 'prove extremely prejudiciall to monarchy'. Furthermore, the King had 'sworne to preserve the rights and immunities of the Church intire', and therefore could not consent 'to lessen or abrogate them'. The nomination of officers of state was 'his undoubted right, happily enjoyed by all his royall progenitors', while the Houses' demands regarding the militia were 'destructive of that fundamentall law, which intrusts this power in the Crowne alone to enable the King to protect his subjects and the lawes'.[42] In this final section, Digges applied his general theory of the constitution to the particular terms presented to Charles in

[35] *Ibid.*, p. 10. My emphasis.   [36] *Ibid.*, pp. 11–12, 44–8.   [37] *Ibid.*, p. 13.
[38] *Ibid.*, p. 32.
[39] *Ibid.*, p. 68.   [40] *Ibid.*, pp. 76–7.   [41] *Ibid.*, pp. 59, 138–9.
[42] *Ibid.*, pp. 163–7.

February 1643. He thus offered an ideological framework which justified the responses of the Royalist commissioners during the Treaty of Oxford. Once again, political theory and practice informed and reinforced each other.

Another writer who closely resembled Digges in his constitutional ideas and in his response to Parker, and who also died prematurely of camp fever, was Sir John Spelman.[43] The son of the historian and antiquary Sir Henry Spelman, he was educated at Trinity College, Cambridge and then Gray's Inn. He served as MP for Worcester in 1625. He was knighted in December 1641, and following the outbreak of civil war, Charles ordered him to remain in Norfolk. However, Spelman was later summoned to Oxford and was about to be appointed Secretary of State when he died on 25 July 1643. He has received much less attention than Bramhall and Digges; yet his four tracts of 1642–3 certainly merit inclusion in this discussion.[44]

The earliest of these was entitled *A Protestants Account of his Orthodox Holding in Matters of Religion*, and presented a sustained defence of existing forms of Church government. Spelman asserted that 'though the whole form and frame of [episcopacy] is not so expressely prescribed, but that the Church may, in many things, have power of making therein accommodations to the times and exigence of State', yet 'may not those acts of accommodation amount to such a height as to subvert or abolish the government which by the judgement of her members, then infallible, was set on foot'.[45] He attacked the exponents of root-and-branch reform as 'fighters against the Spirit of God'. Furthermore, like many other Constitutional Royalists, he assumed that the common law coincided with divine law. He insisted that 'the liturgie of our Church' had been established 'by the laws of this kingdome'.[46] England's laws thus underpinned both episcopacy and the Prayer Book.

This concern for the rule of law loomed equally large in Spelman's three political treatises. The first, *Certain considerations upon the duties both of*

---

43 The details of this paragraph are derived from *DNB*, LIII, 333–4; Venn and Venn, *Alumni Cantab.*, IV, 130; Foster, *Alumni Oxon.*, IV, 1397; and Foster, *Admissions to Gray's Inn*, p. 119. See also BL, Add. MS 34599 (Sir Henry Spelman Correspondence), fo. 92r (Spelman to Sir Henry Spelman, 11 May 1625); Bodl. Lib., MS Tanner 64, fo. 145r (Spelman to Sir John Potts, 2 February 1642/3); and *CJ*, II, 813.

44 The fullest account of his political thought is Brice, 'Political ideas', pp. 21–9. There is no reference to him in Judson, *Crisis of the Constitution*; and only a glancing one in Corinne Comstock Weston, *English Constitutional Theory and the House of Lords, 1556–1832* (1965), p. 34.

45 [Sir John Spelman], *A Protestants Account of his Orthodox Holding in Matters of Religion, at this present in difference in the Church* (Cambridge, 1642), p. 22 (Wing, S 4939; BL, TT, E 129/23).

46 *Ibid.*, pp. 23–4.

Prince and people, was offered by a self-styled 'wel-wisher both to the King and Parliament'.[47] The same symmetry was evident in Spelman's assertion that 'the rights and manners of kingdoms' were 'to be observed as well of the Prince as of the people', and that 'the establishment of a kingdom depends upon the observance of the rights thereof as well by the one as by the other'. He then argued, in terms reminiscent of the *Answer to the XIX Propositions*, that 'the composite forme' was 'the only firme and durable forme', and that 'of the three powers, regall, aristocraticall or popular, any of them prevailing so far as to be wholly free from being qualified or tempered by some operation of the other two, corrupted the legitimate forme into a tyrannicall'.[48] 'Absolute power' tended 'not to prosperity but to the destruction of it selfe'. The monarch's authority was therefore not 'without law' but subject to limitations: the laws were 'most sacred and binding even to Kings themselves'. However, this was 'to be understood in safety, in honour, in conscience betweene God and them', and there was no way that 'in their default, the people can become authorised'.[49] While Spelman was a 'wel-wisher' to Parliament, he rejected the Junto's claim to exercise sovereignty on the monarch's behalf.

This conviction in turn led Spelman – like Bramhall and Digges – to compose a refutation of Parker's *Observations*.[50] Spelman's express purpose was 'to vindicate the King's just rights and priviledges', and he began by insisting that although the King and the Houses of Parliament formed one body, 'yet is the King the head of that body'.[51] This was not to claim 'a power to make lawes and lay taxes without the consent of Parliament', but only 'a negative voice, that they without him may not make any lawes, or charge his subjects, but that all be done by the joynt consent of him and his people'.[52] 'Active resistance by taking up armes against a lawful soveraign Prince though tyranizing over his subjects' could never be sanctioned.[53] Moreover, there was 'a bridle to restraine the licencious will of ambitious Princes, and that's the law, but the reynes must not be layd in the hands of subjects'. Once again, however, this concept of legally limited monarchy went along with a firm belief that God was 'the author and efficient cause of kingly power', and that Kings were 'properly accountable to him alone'.[54] Certain powers, such as control over the militia, were 'by the fundamentall law immovably setled in the Crowne'.[55] But this was

---

[47] [Sir John Spelman], *Certain considerations upon the duties both of Prince and people, written by a gentleman of quality, a wel-wisher both to the King and Parliament* (Oxford, 1642), Wing, S 4938; BL, TT, E 85/4.
[48] *Ibid.*, p. 18.   [49] *Ibid.*, pp. 18–20.
[50] [Sir John Spelman], *A View of a printed book intituled Observations upon His Majesties late Answers and Expresses* (Oxford, 1642), Wing, S 4941; BL, TT, E 245/22.
[51] *Ibid.*, pp. 2, 8.   [52] *Ibid.*, p. 23.   [53] *Ibid.*, sig. D3[r].   [54] *Ibid.*, sig. E2[r].
[55] *Ibid.*, sig. F3[r].

perfectly compatible with a defence of mixed monarchy. Echoing Falkland and Culpepper, Spelman wrote that 'monarchy ... tempered and mixt ... is the constitution of government in England, so well poysed and molded by the wisdome of our ancestors as that it gives to this kingdome the conveniences of all [forms] without the inconveniences of any one'.[56] Once again, the *Answer to the XIX Propositions* provided the framework for his analysis of English government.

Spelman developed these points more fully in his final political work, *The Case of our Affaires*.[57] He reiterated that 'even by the declaration of our lawes', the King was 'a supreme head, a soveraigne' whose crown was 'an imperiall crown, the kingdom *his* kingdom, *his* realme, *his* dominion, the people *his* people, the subject *his* subject'.[58] Hence 'the soveraignity of this State' was 'clearly vested in the King, by law established in him, and inseparably annexed to his person'.[59] The existence of a 'great restraint of regall absolutenesse ... in the two points of declaring and making of law' did not detract 'any whit' from this 'soveraignity'.[60] By the same token, the Houses of Parliament were 'meerly instruments of regulation and qualification of the King's legislative absolutenesse' and 'no sharers with him in the soveraignity'. Royal powers were thus 'not as properly said to be restrained as regulated'.[61] Not only were they guaranteed by the 'positive lawes of the kingdome'; religion also 'fortifie[d] and enforce[d] all those bonds of duty and obedience'.[62] God's law and the common law merged in condemning any form of armed resistance to the sovereign. Here, as in his other writings, Spelman laid out two aspects of Constitutional Royalist thought with particular clarity: first, that mixed monarchy did not imply shared sovereignty; and second, that the concept of legally limited monarchy involved a regulation rather than a restriction of the monarch's powers. These principles sharply distinguished him and our other seven writers from those Parliamentarian pamphleteers who either asserted the sovereignty of the two Houses (Parker), or argued that King, Lords and Commons were 'co-ordinate' (Herle, Hunton).[63]

A fourth writer who responded vigorously to Parliamentarian polemic was Henry Ferne. Educated at Uppingham and St Mary Hall, Oxford, he later became a Fellow of Trinity College, Cambridge and in 1641

[56] *Ibid.*, sig. E2[v].
[57] [Sir John Spelman], *The Case of our Affaires, in law, religion, and other circumstances briefly examined, and presented to the conscience* (Oxford, 1643), Wing, S 4936; BL, TT, E 30/14.
[58] *Ibid.*, p. 1. Original emphasis.   [59] *Ibid.*, p. 2.   [60] *Ibid.*, p. 3.
[61] *Ibid.*, p. 5.
[62] *Ibid.*, p. 17.
[63] See especially Judson, *Crisis of the Constitution*, pp. 396–436; and Weston, *English Constitutional Theory*, pp. 36–9.

archdeacon of Leicester. He joined the Royalist forces at Nottingham and served as chaplain-extraordinary and then chaplain-in-ordinary to Charles I, as a result of which he lost his living at Medbourne (Leicestershire) in March 1646. He spent the later 1640s and the 1650s in retirement in Yorkshire. Like Bramhall, the Restoration brought him rapid preferment: Master of Trinity College, Cambridge in 1660, Dean of Ely in 1661, and finally Bishop of Chester in 1662, the year of his death.[64]

Ferne's first pamphlet, *The Resolving of Conscience*,[65] began from the premise that armed resistance to the sovereign was 'against the Apostles' expresse prohibition' and also 'limited and circumscribed by the established laws of the land'.[66] As a result, 'conscience cannot find clear ground to rest upon for making resistance: for it heares the Apostle expressely say, whosoever shall resist shall receive to themselves damnation [Romans, XIII, 2]: and it cannot find any limitation in Scripture that will excuse the resistance of these dayes'.[67] Ferne then turned to the nature of royal authority, and argued that 'the power of the Prince' received 'qualification by joynt consent of himself and the people' and was 'limited by the laws made with such consent'. However, 'the power itself is of God originally and chiefly'.[68] There could be no 'absolute means of safety and securitie in a State', but the 'fundamentals of ... government' ensured this 'by that excellent temper of the three estates in Parliament, there being a power of denying in each of them, and no power of enacting in one or two of them without the third'.[69] This suggests that Ferne at that date defined the three estates as Crown, Lords and Commons, and believed that the mixture between them tempered and moderated royal powers.

But to say that the three estates were *mixed* did not imply that they were *equal*, as Ferne showed the following year in *Conscience Satisfied*.[70] He was replying to Charles Herle who, like many Parliamentarian writers, argued that King, Lords and Commons were 'co-ordinate'.[71] Ferne immediately stated his desire, which he took to be that 'of the King

---

[64] This paragraph is derived from *DNB*, XVIII, 372–3; Venn and Venn, *Alumni Cantab.*, II, 133; Foster, *Alumni Oxon.*, II, 493; and A. G. Matthews, *Walker Revised* (Oxford, 1948; repr. 1988), p. 235. For an analysis of Ferne's political thought, see Brice, 'Political ideas', pp. 3–11.

[65] H[enry] F[erne], *The Resolving of Conscience* (Cambridge, 1642), Wing, F 800. This tract led the House of Commons to summon Ferne as a delinquent: *CJ*, II, 900.

[66] F[erne], *Resolving of Conscience*, sig. ¶2[r].   [67] *Ibid.*, p. 5.   [68] *Ibid.*, p. 15.

[69] *Ibid.*, pp. 25–6.

[70] Henry Ferne, *Conscience Satisfied, that there is no warrant for the armes now taken up by subjects* (Oxford, 1643), Wing, F 791; BL, TT, E 97/7.

[71] [Charles Herle], *A Fuller Answer to a Treatise written by Doctor Ferne* (1642), pp. 3–5 (Wing, H 1558; BL, TT, E 244/27). For discussions of Herle's political thought, see Judson, *Crisis of the Constitution*, pp. 419–33; and Weston, *English Constitutional Theory*, pp. 35–6.

himselfe, that Parliaments should flourish in their due power and free-dom'.[72] He granted 'that the two Houses of Parliament' were 'in some sort co-ordinate with His Majesty', in that their role in the 'making of lawes by yeelding their consent' was guaranteed 'by a fundamentall constitution'. They did not, however, enjoy 'a fellowship with His Majesty in the supre-macy it selfe', nor 'a power of resistance reserved at first to supply His Majesty's refusals'.[73] Thus it did 'not follow if there be a mixture in [the monarchy]' that it was therefore 'one of equall ingredients'. The King remained 'supream, or the higher power' because although not 'sole and absolute in making or imposing laws', he was 'still, notwithstanding the consent of the two Houses, required to that act or exercise of supream power'.[74] The King was 'bound by oath to protect' his subjects, and 'accordingly [had] the power of the sword and the defending of armes'.[75] At the same time, 'the law or constitution of government' cast 'a restraint' upon 'the governing power', and Ferne concluded with a prayer that peace would shortly be restored 'not through an absolute prevailing of either side by armes', but by the 'loyall submission' of those who had 'done the wrong to His Majesty and his people, by the lawlesse resistance'.[76] This fear of an outright victory by either side was highly characteristic of Constitutional Royalism, a point to which we shall return.

Ferne's fullest examination of the issue of mixed government came in his *Reply unto several treatises*.[77] 'Limitation in government', he argued, bounded 'the will of the monarch for those particulars that law concernes'. Similarly, 'mixtures' were achieved by 'persons joyned to the monarch for certaine acts and purposes'. But such persons did not 'have a share with the monarch in the soveraigne power': this could not 'consist with that supre-macy which is supp[os]ed to be in the monarch, for it would make severall independent powers in the same State or kingdome'. Rather, 'the concur-rence and consent of such persons' would be 'sufficient to make a mixture in the government'.[78] Ferne then turned to discuss the King's *Answer to the XIX Propositions*. He praised the 'limitations and mixtures of this govern-ment', but stressed that the King never used the term 'three estates' 'with any intent of diminution to his supremacy and headship'. Ferne echoed Hyde in reminding readers that 'properly the prelates, Lords and

---

[72] Ferne, *Conscience Satisfied*, sig. §3[r].   [73] *Ibid.*, p. 6.   [74] *Ibid.*, pp. 15, 20.
[75] *Ibid.*, p. 84.   [76] *Ibid.*, pp. 46, 83.
[77] H[enry] F[erne], *A Reply unto severall treatises pleading for the armes now taken up by subjects in the pretended defence of religion and liberty* (Oxford, 1643), Wing, F 799; BL, TT, E 74/9. Ferne's principal target here was Philip Hunton, especially his *A Treatise of Monarchie* (1643), Wing, H 3781; BL, TT, E 103/15. There is an excellent analysis of this tract in J. W. Allen, *English Political Thought, 1603–1660*, vol. I: *1603–1644* (1938), 449–55.
[78] F[erne], *A Reply*, p. 17.

Commons are the three estates of this kingdome, under His Majesty as their head'. This may have marked a shift from his own earlier position; and there was clearly some disagreement among the Constitutional Royalists on the composition of the three estates. But this does not negate their broad consensus on the nature of legally limited monarchy. As Ferne put it, 'limitations and mixtures in monarchy' did not imply 'a forceable constraining power in subjects' but only 'a legall or morall restraint upon the power of the monarch'.[79] Armed resistance could therefore never be justified: it was expressly forbidden in Romans, XIII; and it would be 'worse then the disease, and more subversive of a State, then if [the subjects] were left without it'.[80]

Towards the end of his *Reply*, Ferne described the King's supporters as those who defended 'the established religion and governement of this Church and State'.[81] He amplified this point the following year in *Episcopacy and Presbytery considered*.[82] Here, Ferne's central theme was that 'the practice and continuance of episcopall government [was] most evident in all the Ancient Fathers, all the Councells, all the histories of the Church'. Furthermore, it 'most willingly acknowledge[d] a dependance on, and subordination to the Soveraigne power of Majesty'; and 'long experience' had shown how well it had 'agreed with the monarchicall government of the kingdome'.[83] Episcopacy was thus so bound up with the State that there were constitutional as well as religious objections to its abolition.

Ferne's final publication of 1644 – a sermon preached at Oxford on 12 April[84] – is interesting because it reveals the nature of his personal commitment to peace negotiations. He warned that 'if no peace' could 'be had with the refusers of peace but upon unjust tearmes', then he would therefore have to recommend 'resolutions for a necessarie warre'. However, he insisted that this was not 'to cast out ... thoughts of peace, but in order to them', just as 'the sword must sometimes make the way to peace'.[85] These arguments did not vitiate the clear preference for peace negotiations so characteristic of the Constitutional Royalists; rather, they show how those moderates who did accept military commissions were able to reconcile this with their involvement in successive treaties.

Another, more minor, cleric of Constitutional Royalist views who preached at Oxford during these years was Jasper Mayne. A graduate of

---

[79] *Ibid.*, pp. 32, 39, 42.   [80] *Ibid.*, pp. 67–83, 90.   [81] *Ibid.*, p. 97.
[82] [Henry Ferne], *Episcopacy and Presbytery considered* (Oxford, 1644), Wing, F 793; BL, TT, E 400/11.
[83] *Ibid.*, pp. 5, 22.
[84] Henry Ferne, *A Sermon preached at the publique fast the twelfth day of April [1644] at St Maries Oxford, before the members of the honourable House of Commons there assembled* (Oxford, 1644), Wing, F 805; BL, TT, E 46/5.
[85] *Ibid.*, p. 25.

Christ Church, Oxford, Mayne was the author of two plays, the comedy *The Citye Match*, and the tragicomedy *The Amorous Warre*.[86] In 1639 he became Rector of Cassington (Oxfordshire) and turned to political writing. He was ejected from Cassington in 1648, but became Rector of another Oxfordshire living, Pyrton, from which he was in turn ejected in 1656. At the Restoration, he was reinstated in both benefices and appointed canon of Christ Church, Oxford, archdeacon of Chichester, and chaplain-in-ordinary to Charles II.[87]

By far his most important political tract was Οχλο-μαχια, or *The Peoples War*.[88] This advanced the familiar arguments that armed resistance against the sovereign could never be justified, and that the English monarchy was legally limited. Mayne began by pointing out that liberty did not mean 'an exemption from all Governement'. Indeed, 'a subjection with security hath alwayes, by wise men, been preferr'd before liberty with danger'.[89] Tyranny was thus always preferable to anarchy. Tyranny was however prevented by the rule of law: 'the fundamentall lawes, or custfomes, of this kingdome ... stand the land-marks and markes of partition between the King's prerogative and the liberty of the subject'.[90] But once again, this concept of a legally limited monarchy did not deny that the Crown was the senior partner within a mixed government. Mayne agreed that the King's was 'but a regulated power' which could 'rise no higher' 'than a trust committed by the lawes of this kingdome, for the governement of it, to the King'. Nevertheless, just 'as in the making of these lawes he holds the first place, so none of these rights which he derives from them can without his consent be taken from him'. The logical consequence of this was that the two Houses did not have 'a legall power, in defence of their liberty, to take up armes against the King'.[91]

In his other writings and sermons of 1646–7, Mayne turned to the issue of Church government. Preaching at Oxford on 9 August 1646, he wondered 'what hath crumbled us asunder, and turn'd one of the purest and most flourishing Churches of the world into a heap of heresies'. He concluded with an eloquent plea to rally to the established Church of England: 'to divide and separate yourselves from the communion of our Church, if it had been guilty of a mole or two, is as unreasonable as if you should quarrell the moon out of her orb, or think her unworthy of the skies

---

[86] [Jasper Mayne], *The Citye Match* (Oxford, 1639), STC, 17750; *The Amorous Warre* (1648), Wing, M 1463.

[87] *DNB*, XXXVII, 162–4; Venn and Venn, *Alumni Cantab.*, III, 169; Foster, *Alumni Oxon.*, III, 995; Matthews, *Walker Revised*, p. 298. For Mayne's political thought, see Brice, 'Political ideas', pp. 43–6.

[88] Jasper Mayne, Οχλο-μαχια, or *The Peoples War* (1647), Wing, M 1472; BL, TT, E 398/19.

[89] *Ibid.*, pp. 4, 9–10.   [90] *Ibid.*, p. 11.   [91] *Ibid.*, pp. 14, 24.

because she wears a spot or two writ on a glorious ball of light'.[92] Mayne developed this point powerfully in another sermon preached 'shortly after the surrender of' Oxford. 'I cannot think the sunne', he declared, 'in all his heavenly course, for so many years, beheld a Church more blest with purity of religion for the doctrines of it, or better establisht for the government and discipline of it, then ours was.' He condemned those who sought 'to alter the whole frame and government of a State', and argued that 'to change the universally received government of a Church meerly for change sake, and that things may be new not that they may be better, is a vanity'. Just as the law regulated the monarch's powers, so it also buttressed an established Church which promoted true religion and 'sound doctrine'.[93]

This second sermon elicited a hostile correspondence from the Parliamentarian chaplain and member of the Westminster Assembly Francis Cheynell.[94] Mayne subsequently published Cheynell's letters together with his own response in which he claimed only to 'contend for the restitution of the true Protestant religion, and contend for the civill right which we have to exercise the true Protestant religion'. He vigorously defended episcopacy as 'an order of the Church ancient as the Christian Church itselfe', and likened root-and-branch reform to the view that 'there was no way left to reforme drunkenness in their State but utterly to root up and extirpate and banish vines'. The introduction of Presbyterianism would, he argued, 'be but a wild vine ingrafted into a true. Upon which unequall, disproportioned incorporation, we may as well expect to gather figs or thistles, or grapes of thornes, as that the one should grow so southerne, the other so northerne.' He concluded by telling Cheynell: 'what errors in government or discipline were committed by the prelates I know not; neither have you proved them hitherto chargeable with any'.[95]

This attachment to episcopacy was closely linked to a defence of the royal supremacy. In *The Difference about Church Government ended*, Mayne argued that 'the government in all things in a Christian kingdom is and ought to be in the civill magistrate'. He then advanced from this premise to a full-blown Erastianism:

[92] Jasper Mayne, *A Sermon concerning Unity and Agreement, preached at Carfax Church in Oxford, August 9 1646* (Oxford, 1646), pp. 35, 43 (Wing, M 1476; BL, TT, E 355/30).
[93] Jasper Mayne, *A Sermon against False Prophets, preached in St Marjes Church in Oxford, shortly after the surrender of that garrison* (Oxford, 1646[/7]), pp. 17, 20, 37 (Wing, M 1473; BL, TT, E 371/8).
[94] For Cheynell, see *DNB*, X, 222–4; and Robert S. Paul, *The Assembly of the Lord* (Edinburgh, 1985), pp. 83, 180, 547, 556.
[95] Jasper Mayne, *A Late Printed Sermon against False Prophets, vindicated by letter from the causeless aspersions of Mr Francis Cheynell* (1647), pp. 9, 21, 48 (Wing, M 1471; BL, TT, E 392/15).

As it is lawfull for the civill magistrate to take all the government into his hands, even in things ecclesiasticall ... so it is most expedient for us in the ministry that they should so doe, because being exempt from this trouble, we shall be the more free to prayer, reading, meditation, preaching, and other holy offices properly belonging to our function.[96]

In this way, episcopacy and the royal supremacy protected and reinforced each other within a structure underpinned equally by God's law and the common law. The foundations of royal authority were thus the same in both religious and secular affairs.

While three of our eight writers were clergy, it was not surprising that the heavy emphasis upon the rule of law within Constitutional Royalism should also appeal to those who either had a legal training (such as Spelman) or had actually practised as lawyers. Of the latter, much the most distinguished was David Jenkins. He was educated at St Edmund Hall, Oxford, and called to the bar at Gray's Inn in 1609.[97] Like several other Constitutional Royalists, he opposed the Forced Loan and the 'excesses' of some Laudians. In March 1643 he became judge of the Great Sessions for Carmarthen, Pembroke and Cardiganshire, in which capacity he indicted several Welsh Parliamentarians of high treason. He was captured at Hereford in December 1645 and imprisoned until the Restoration. He was tried in King's Bench and then in the Commons, but consistently maintained that the House had no right to try him.[98] During the later 1640s he wrote a number of political tracts vindicating his position, many of which were published in a collected edition of 1648.[99]

Jenkins's longest and most important work was *Lex Terrae*. He began by asserting that 'this law of royall government is a law fundamentall', and condemned the Newcastle Propositions as 'contrary to the lawes and [the King's] prerogative'. 'Supreme power' was vested in the monarch alone, and 'the regality of the Crowne of England' was 'immediatly subject to God and to none other.' This meant that there could no more be a 'Parliament without a King' than 'a body without a head'. Similarly, 'all commissions to levy men for the warre are awarded by the King', and 'the power of warre only belongs to the King'.[100] But these principles went hand in

---

[96] J[asper] M[ayne], *The Difference about Church Government ended* (1646), pp. 10–11 (Wing, M 1470; BL, TT, E 339/8).

[97] This paragraph is derived from *DNB*, XXIX, 298–300; and Foster, *Alumni Oxon.*, II, 807.

[98] For Jenkins's imprisonment and trials, see *CJ*, IV, 396, 398; V, 153, 220, 432, 437, 465, 466–70; *LJ*, X, 72, 79; and S. F. Black, 'The judges of Westminster Hall during the Great Rebellion, 1640–1660' (BLitt thesis, University of Oxford, 1970), pp. 88–9.

[99] *The Works of that Grave and Learned Judge Jenkins, prisoner in Newgate, upon divers statutes, concerning the liberty and freedome of the subject* (1648), Wing, J 574; BL, TT, E 1154/2.

[100] David Jenkins, *Lex Terrae* (1647), pp. 1, 4, 5, 9, 10 (Wing, J 593; BL, TT, E 390/18). This tract is reprinted in *Works of Jenkins*, pp. 5–46.

hand with a firm commitment to the rule of law. Jenkins argued that for 'the King's party' the 'law of the land' formed 'their byrth-right' and 'their guide'. The King's own position rested upon the same bases: he was 'King by an inhaerent birth-right, by nature, by God's law, and by the law of the land'. In a phrase later quoted by Strangways, he insisted that 'we of the King's party did and do detest monopolies, and ship money, and all the grievances of the people as much as any men living, we do well know that our estates, lives and fortunes are preserved by the lawes, and that the King is bound by his lawes'.[101] It was axiomatic that 'the law is above the King' and that 'the King is subject to law and sworne to maintaine it'. The Houses threatened to destroy this constitutional arrangement by robbing Charles of 'his kingly power by sea and land', by levying 'what taxes they thinke meete', and by seeking 'to abolish the Common-prayer booke, to abolish episcopacy, and to introduce a Church-government . . . such as they shall agree on'.[102]

Jenkins reiterated these ideas in several other tracts of 1647–8. He argued consistently that 'the supreame and only power by the lawes of this land is in the King', and that the monarch was 'the only supreame governour, the fountaine of justice, and the life of the law'.[103] It followed from this that the King was an integral part of Parliament, and that 'no act of Parliament bindes the subjects of this land without the assent of the King, either for person, lands, goods or fame'.[104] Hence 'the two Houses are no more a Parliament than a man without a head a man', and 'without the King' there could be 'no colour of a Parliament'.[105] Similarly, 'the King and his progenitors' possessed authority over the militia, for 'the lawes [had] fixed it upon them'.[106] Nevertheless, Jenkins maintained that this was a legally regulated monarchy: 'the King is not above the law, nor above the safety of his people; the law and the safety of his people are his safety, his honour and his strength'.[107] The fact that the law ensured this symbiosis between royal and popular interests in turn impelled allegiance

---

[101] Jenkins, *Lex Terrae*, pp. 17, 19, 21. For Strangways's use of this last phrase, see above, p. 179 & n. 216. See also above, pp. 160 & n. 107, 170 & n. 160, 174–5 & n. 196, 179 & n. 216, 181 & n. 228.

[102] Jenkins, *Lex Terrae*, pp. 25, 33.

[103] David Jenkins, *The Vindication of Judge Jenkins Prisoner in the Tower, the 29 of April 1647* (1647), pp. 1–2 (Wing, J 613; BL, TT, E 386/6). This tract is reprinted in *Works of Jenkins*, pp. 64–74.

[104] Jenkins, *Vindication*, p. 6.

[105] David Jenkins, *An Apology for the Army, touching the Eight Quaeres, etc.* (1648), p. 3 (Wing, J 582; BL, TT, E 396/18). This tract is reprinted in *Works of Jenkins*, pp. 152–69.

[106] David Jenkins, *Judge Jenkin's Plea delivered in to the Earle of Manchester, and the Speaker of the House of Commons* (1647[/8]), p. 7 (Wing, J 598; BL, TT, E 427/12). This tract is reprinted in *Works of Jenkins*, pp. 170–6.

[107] [David Jenkins], *The Cordiall of Judge Jenkins for the good people of London* (1647), p. 22 (Wing, J 586; BL, TT, E 391/11). This tract is reprinted in *Works of Jenkins*, pp. 99–136.

to the King. Jenkins urged his readers to 'be wise in time: without the King and the lawes, you will never have one houre of safety for your persons, wives, children or estates'.[108] This concern for the rights and property of the subject made Jenkins very sympathetic to the Army's plight in 1647–8. Twice he publicly defended the Army's actions.[109] He rejected charges that the Army resembled Jack Cade; he promised that the King would 'pay the arreares of the Army'; and he praised those who 'to their eternall honour have freed the King from imprisonment at Holmby'.[110] His writings also show with remarkable clarity why Constitutional Royalists thought the *Heads of the Proposals* a viable basis for settlement. Nearly all his tracts of 1647–8 conclude with a stock peroration along the following lines: 'without an Act of Oblivion, a gratious generall pardon from His Majesty, the arreares of the souldiers paid, a favourable regard had to tender consciences, there will be neither truth nor peace in this land, nor any man secure of any thing he hath'.[111] All these terms were enshrined in the *Heads.*[112] The passage indicates how far the immediate political goals of Constitutional Royalists and Army officers converged during the summer and autumn of 1647; and it thus throws further light on the moderate attempts to secure Charles's acceptance of the *Heads* examined above.[113]

Jenkins remained an ardent supporter of peace negotiations even after the King's rejection of the *Heads.* On the eve of the Treaty of Newport he published a short treatise which highlighted the close similarities between the declarations issued by the King and the two Houses since the summer of 1642, and argued that 'the King and the two Houses of Parliament declaring mutually that they took up armes for the same reasons, intents and purposes, 'tis a wonder how at first they fell out, and a greater wonder that hitherto they are not reconciled'.[114] He concluded with a plea that if the two Houses promised to 'maintaine and defend the King, the Crown, His Majesties Honour and Estate, his authority, power and greatnesse', then 'an agreement and peace' would 'follow thereupon'.[115] Equally,

[108] Jenkins, *Apology for the Army*, p. 5.
[109] [David Jenkins], *The Armies Indempnity* (1647), Wing, J 584; BL, TT, E 390/10 (this tract is reprinted in *Works of Jenkins*, pp. 75–86); and *Apology for the Army.*
[110] Jenkins, *Apology for the Army*, pp. 2, 5–7, 8; *The Armies Indempnity*, p. 4.
[111] This is taken from David Jenkins, *A Discourse touching the Inconveniences of a long continued Parliament* (1647), p. 10 (Wing, J 590; BL, TT, E 392/30). This tract is reprinted in *Works of Jenkins*, pp. 137–51. For almost identical examples, see *The Armies Indempnity*, p. 5; *Apology for the Army*, p. 10; *Cordiall of Judge Jenkins*, p. 24; *Judge Jenkin's Plea*, p. 7; and *Vindication of Judge Jenkins*, p. 8.
[112] Gardiner, *Documents*, pp. 321, 323, 325–6.   [113] See above, pp. 132–6.
[114] Da[vid] J[enkins], *A Preparative to the Treaty: or, A short, sure, and conscientious expedient for Agreement and Peace; tendred to the two Houses of Parliament* (1648), p. 1 (Wing, J 600; BL, TT, E 463/17).
[115] *Ibid.*, p. 4.

Jenkins believed that such concessions had to be reciprocal, and on 12 October he wrote 'humbly beseeching His Majesty to salve up the sores of this kingdom, in this present personall treaty, and to embrace the opportunity now on foot'.[116] Like other Constitutional Royalists, Jenkins thus combined a desire to protect the King's place within the constitution with a fervent commitment to peace negotiations. He saw both the *Heads* and the Treaty of Newport as opportunities to realise his vision of a legally limited monarchy. But his high hopes were soon dashed. He remained one of the seven delinquents whom the King eventually agreed to exempt from pardon.[117] He spent most of the Interregnum in prison; and after the Restoration retired to Glamorganshire, where he died in 1663.[118]

The second and less eminent of the two lawyers was the Recorder of Lincoln, Sir Charles Dallison. Alone among our eight writers, he does not receive an entry in the *Dictionary of National Biography*.[119] Born into a Lincolnshire family, he was admitted to Gray's Inn in February 1620. He subsequently became one of the City of Lincoln's counsel in 1631, and City Recorder in 1637.[120] By June 1642, local Parliamentarians regarded him as 'popishly inclined',[121] and the following month Dallison welcomed Charles to Lincoln in a speech pledging military assistance. Yet his words afford further evidence that a willingness to bear arms was perfectly compatible with Constitutional Royalist attitudes.

Dallison compared England to 'a man in perfect health, yet who doth fancie himselfe sicke of a consumption; who (if his fortune be to light on a skilfull and honest physitian) is in no danger; but if upon an empricke, it is like his body shall be brought into that condition, which before he did but fancy himselfe to be in'. Fortunately, the King's recent declarations had promised 'to maintaine and governe by the knowne lawes of this realme; to defend the true Protestant religion established by law: by which meanes your loyall subjects shall be preserved and protected from arbitrary government'. On behalf of the City of Lincoln, Dallison then offered 'all we have to be disposed of by your Majesty for the maintenance and

---

[116] *The Declaration of David Jenkins, late prisoner in the Tower of London* (1648), p. 6 (Wing, J 589; BL, TT, E 467/31). This letter, which was intercepted, was written at Wallingford Castle, where Jenkins had been taken the previous day: Bodl. Lib., MS Tanner 57, fo. 356r (Ar[thur] Evelyn to Speaker Lenthall, 11 October 1648).

[117] *LJ*, X, 600; above, p. 207.

[118] For the sequestration and dismemberment of Jenkins's estates in 1651–3, see the *Calendar of the Proceedings of the Committee for Compounding with Delinquents*, ed. M. A. E. Green (5 vols., 1889), III, 2176–80. His final years are described in *DNB*, XXIX, 299.

[119] But see the helpful entry in P. R. Newman, *Royalist Officers in England and Wales, 1642–1660: A Biographical Dictionary* (1981), p. 99.

[120] Foster, *Admissions to Gray's Inn*, p. 158; Sir Francis Hill, *Tudor and Stuart Lincoln* (Cambridge, 1956; repr. Stamford, 1991), p. 122, n. 1.

[121] *LJ*, V, 131.

preservation of your just rights and prerogative, which cannot be maintained but thereby the priviledges of your subjects be likewise defended; the same law defending both'.[122] Dallison was subsequently knighted, and served with the Royalist horse during the first Civil War.[123] But, like his neighbour the Earl of Lindsey, Dallison's readiness to fight did not weaken his conviction that royal prerogatives and popular liberties were reconciled and protected by the law, and that this constitution, like the Church of England, was best safeguarded by Charles I.

For the House of Commons, however, the taking up of arms was sufficient proof of delinquency, and on 14 September 1642 Dallison was impeached 'for levying war against the King and Parliament'. Three months later he was deprived of his Recordership.[124] When he was captured at the siege of Lincoln in the summer of 1644, the Commons ordered that he should not be discharged without its consent.[125] It was while he was in prison, with his estates under sequestration,[126] that Dallison composed his most significant political work, entitled *The Royalist's Defence*.[127]

This tract began by striking a familiar balance between royal sovereignty and the rule of law: 'by the constitutions of this realm, our King hath inherently in his person the soveraigne powers of government, but he hath not authority to judge the law'. Rather – and here we catch the voice of the Recorder – 'the judges of the realme declare by what law the King governs, and so both King and people [are] regulated by a known law'.[128] Hence royal sovereignty and legally limited monarchy were not incompatible. The King was 'the only supreame governour' and 'the supreamacy' was in his person. But 'he neither hath nor claimes an unlimited power. The people are governed under him, but that government is directed by a known law, of which law the King is not judge, nor can he by himselfe alone alter that law'.[129] The King's 'authority and interest' was 'regulated by a known law' which thus protected 'the subject from tyranny and arbitrary power'.[130] By contrast, 'the people of England, under the government claimed by the members of the two Houses, [were] absolute slaves' for the Houses had 'usurped an arbitrary power'.[131] By thus 'setting aside the King', the Houses had perpetrated 'an absolute subversion both of law and

---

[122] *Mr Charles Dallison Record[e]r of Lincoln, His Speech to the King's Majesty* (1642), Wing, D 139. Cf. Clive Holmes, *Seventeenth-Century Lincolnshire* (Lincoln, 1980), p. 149.
[123] *LJ*, V, 375; Hill, *Tudor and Stuart Lincoln*, pp. 150–1.   [124] *CJ*, II, 766, 890.
[125] *Ibid.*, III, 550.
[126] See the *Calendar of the Committee for Compounding*, Green, II, 1339–40.
[127] [Charles Dallison], *The Royalist's Defence* (1648), Wing, D 138. For a discussion of this tract, see Brice, 'Political ideas', pp. 34–8.
[128] [Dallison], *Royalist's Defence*, sig. A2[r].   [129] *Ibid.*, pp. 69, 80.
[130] *Ibid.*, pp. 128, 140.
[131] *Ibid.*, pp. 128, 139.

government' which could only be cured 'by restoring the King again'.[132]
Dallison, writing in the year of the second Civil War, concluded with this
injunction to overthrow Parliament's tyranny: 'so long as the people continue in this slavery, they are not onely their owne wilfull tormentors, but
disobeyers of the lawes of God and man. And by quitting themselves from
bondage (which is at every instant in their power to do) they performe their
duty to both.'[133] Once again, God's law and the common law coincided in
demanding allegiance to the King.

Dallison suffered extensive material losses for his Royalist allegiance.
His composition fine was set at £465 15s. in May 1649, reduced the following year to £351 16s. 8d.[134] At the Restoration he complained that he had
'ingaged with others in bondes for the King and his service to the value of
sixteene thousand poundes'; had lost his professional livelihood for
eighteen years; and had been 'plundred of a personall estate worth 100-
0li'.[135] Like so many other former Royalists, he received no reparation
beyond the restitution of his office as Recorder of Lincoln.[136] Thereafter,
he remained active in local government and the law until his death in
January 1669.[137]

The last and possibly the most colourful of our eight writers was James
Howell. Born around 1594, he graduated from Jesus College, Oxford in
1613 and became a Fellow there ten years later.[138] He travelled widely on
the continent, undertaking a diplomatic mission to Spain in 1622–4 and
acting as secretary on Leicester's embassy to Denmark in 1632. Back in
London, he moved in literary circles which included Ben Jonson and Sir
Kenelm Digby. On 1 January 1642, his own literary activities assumed a
political dimension when he presented the King with a poem entitled *The
Vote*. This sought

---

[132] *Ibid.*, p. 136.   [133] *Ibid.*, p. 142.
[134] *Calendar of the Committee for Compounding*, Green, II, 1339–40.
[135] PRO, SP 29/45/78 (Sir Charles Dallison's case presented to Sir Edward Nicholas,
20 December 1661).
[136] Hill, *Tudor and Stuart Lincoln*, p. 171.
[137] PRO, SP 29/115/56 (Sir Charles Dallison *et al.* to Attorney-General Palmer, 20 March
1664/5); Hill, *Tudor and Stuart Lincoln*, pp. 173, 175; A. R. Maddison, ed., *Lincolnshire
Pedigrees*, vol. I (Harleian Society, L, 1902), 287. I owe this last reference to Dr G. A.
Knight of the Lincolnshire Archives Office.
[138] For two excellent appraisals of different aspects of Howell's life and writings see Daniel
Woolf, 'Conscience, constancy, and ambition in the career and writings of James
Howell', in *Public Duty and Private Conscience in Seventeenth-Century England: Essays
Presented to G. E. Aylmer*, ed. John Morrill, Paul Slack and Daniel Woolf (Oxford,
1993), pp. 243–78; and Michael Nutkiewicz, 'A rapporteur of the English Civil War: the
courtly politics of James Howell (1594?–1666)', *Canadian Journal of History/Annales
canadiennes d'histoire*, 25 (1990), 21–40. I am most grateful to Daniel Woolf for this last
reference, and for much helpful advice about Howell. See also *DNB*, XXVIII, 109–114;
Foster, *Alumni Oxon.*, II, 755; and Brice, 'Political ideas', pp. 39–42. For Howell's link

> to vindicat the truth of Charles his raigne,
> From scribling pamphletors,

and concluded by hoping that King and Parliament might henceforth

> propp each other,
> And like the Grecian's twins live, love together.
> For the chief glory of a people is
> The power of their King, as theirs is his.[139]

Charles was evidently pleased, for on 30 August 1642 Howell was promised the position of clerk to the Privy Council. However, early the following year he was arrested while visiting London and committed to the Fleet. He remained in prison until 1651, and devoted this enforced leisure to writing political tracts.

The first work which Howell completed during his imprisonment was a collection of *Parables*.[140] Perhaps the most pointed of these was entitled 'Ορνιλογια, or The Great Councell of Birds'. This contrasted those 'most eager to attempt ... high insolences against Jove's Bird who had been stark naked, and as bare as cootes, unlesse he had feathered them' with 'the high-borne birds ... and all the ancient birds of the mountains' who 'remained faithfull and firme to the Eagle'. A marginal note included Hertford and Southampton among the latter. The 'morall' of this parable was that 'moderation is that Golden Rule whereby all great counsells should square their deliberations'; and that 'in a successive hereditary monarchy, when subjects assume regall power, and barre the Holy Church of her rights ... it is the most compendious way to bring all things to confusion, and consequently to an inevitable ruine'.[141] Another parable – 'Ανθολογια, the gathering together, or Parlement of Flowers' – applied these general principles to the specific issue of the militia: it warned that this was 'an inherent inalienable strength' in the monarch, and that 'for him to transmit this strength to any other is the only way to render him inglorious and despicable'.[142] All these themes were to recur throughout Howell's subsequent writings.

He created another appealing literary device in *Englands Teares, for the Present Wars*, in which the narrator adopted the voice of England. In the climacteric passage, England desired 'my high councell to consider that the royall prerogative is like the sea, which, as navigators observe, what it

with Ben Jonson, see BL, Add. MS 5947* (historical collections), fos. 106v–108r (Howell to Sir Thomas Hawk, 5 April 1636).

[139] [James Howell], *The Vote, or A Poeme Royall, presented to His Maiestie for a New-yeares-Gift* (1642), pp. 5, 9 (Wing, H 3128; BL, TT, E 238/7).

[140] [James Howell], *Parables, reflecting upon the Times* (Paris, 1643), Wing, H 3099; BL, TT, E 67/16.

[141] *Ibid.*, pp. 10–11.   [142] *Ibid.*, p. 13.

loseth at one time or in one place gets alwaies in some other'. By the same token, England then urged 'my deare King to consider that the priviledge of Parlement, the laws and liberties of the subject, is the firmest support of his Crown, that his great councell is the truest glasse wherin he may discerne his peoples love, and his own happinesse'. The moral was that Crown and Parliament should together 'strike saile in so dangerous a storme' in order to 'avoyd shipwrack'.[143] Reciprocal concessions, arbitrated by the laws, were now essential, for 'where there is no obedience, subordination, and restrictive lawes to curb the changeable humours and extravagancies of men, there can be no peace or piety'.[144]

Howell was again at pains to show that he was no enemy to Parliament in another tract of 1644, *The Preheminence and Pedigree of Parlement*. Rebutting William Prynne's accusation of 'malignancy',[145] he argued that 'the power, priviledges and jurisdiction' of Parliament stood 'in equall balance with the lawes, in regard it is the fountaine whence they spring'. Parliament formed 'the bulwarke of our liberties, the maine boundary and banke which keeps us from slavery, from the inundations of tyrannicall rule, and unbounded will-government'. But the King also derived great benefits from it, for Parliament 'rendreth him a King of free and able men, which is far more glorious than to be a King of slaves, beggars and bankrupts'. It was, moreover, a vital 'point of contact' which 'encreaseth love and good intelligence twixt him and his people'.[146] Parliament was nothing less than 'the principall fountaine whence the King derives his happinesse and safety'. Echoing the words of Henry VIII in 1542, Howell concluded that in Parliament the King 'appeares as the sun in the meridian, in the altitude of his glory, in the highest state royall, as the law tels us'.[147] This was the lost ideal which the Constitutional Royalists believed to be enshrined in English law, and which they desperately wished to restore.

But such effusive praise for Parliament did not detract one iota from the Crown's rights and authority. During the autumn of 1648, Howell published *The Instruments of a King*, in which he argued that sword, sceptre and crown were 'inalienable from the person of the King'.[148] In practice, this meant that the King possessed 'sole authority of making lawes' which therefore had 'no life at all in them till the King puts breath

---

[143] J[ames] H[owell], *Englands Teares, for the Present Wars* (1644), p. 14 (Wing, H 3070; BL, TT, E 253/10).
[144] *Ibid.*, pp. 16–17. Cf. Woolf, 'Conscience, constancy, and ambition', pp. 258–9.
[145] Nutkiewicz, 'Rapporteur', 26; Woolf, 'Conscience, constancy, and ambition', pp. 257–60.
[146] James Howell, *The Preheminence and Pedigree of Parlement* (1644), pp. 1, 2, 8 (Wing, H 3106; BL, TT, E 253/2).
[147] *Ibid.*, p. 10. Henry VIII's words are discussed above, p. 19.
[148] [James Howell], *The Instruments of a King: or, A Short Discourse of the Sword, the Scepter, the Crowne* ([16 September] 1648), p. 1 (Wing, H 3083; BL, TT, E 464/7).

and vigour into them'. The law thus presumed 'the King to be alwaies the sole Judge Paramount, and Lord Chief Justice of England'. Howell then defended the monarch's military authority on the grounds that crown and sceptre were 'but unweildy and impotent naked indefensible things without the sword'.[149] It was very much in his subjects' interests that the King should possess such authority, for 'with this sword he shields and preserves all his people that ev'ry one may sit quietly under his own vine, sleep securely in his own House, and enjoy sweetly the fruits of his labours'.[150] Royal powers were thus to be exercised *pro bono publico*. Writing on the eve of the Treaty of Newport, Howell urged: 'let the King be restor'd, and ev'ry one will com to his own, all interests will be satisfied, all things quickly rectified'. But until this was done, it would be 'as absurd to attempt the setling of peace as if one shold go about to set a watch by the gnomon of an horizontall diall when the sun is in a cloud'.[151]

In 1647, Howell reiterated the need for reciprocal concessions by the King and Parliament in *Down-right Dealing, or The Despised Protestant Speaking Plain English*. This culminated in the plea: 'Let soveraigns seek the good of their subjects, and subjects the honour and peace of their soveraigns. Let Parliaments be faithful, and people peaceable.'[152] Nevertheless, it is clear that he still blamed the Houses more than Charles for causing England's calamity. In a public letter to Pembroke published the same year, he attacked the Earl for flouting his oaths of office as Privy Councillor and Lord Chamberlain; worshipping 'the beast with many heads'; and hating 'that reverend order in God's Church which is contemporary with Christianity it self'.[153] It is likely that his hostility towards Pembroke was sharpened by the latter's prominence in the campaign against Howell's old friend Strafford in 1641.[154] Howell went on to denounce the 'monstrousness' of the Newcastle Propositions 'wherein no lesse then Crown, Scepter, and Sword, which are things inalienable from Majesty, are in effect demanded'. This was entirely characteristic of two Houses which had 'broken all the fundamentall rules, and priviledges of Parliament, and dishonoured that high Court more then anything else'. By 1647, the Parliamentarians had 'ravish'd Magna Charta which they are sworn to maintaine, taken away our birth-right, and transgressed all the

---

[149] *Ibid.*, pp. 3, 5.   [150] *Ibid.*, p. 7.   [151] *Ibid.*, p. 11.

[152] J[ames] H[owell], *Down-right Dealing, or The Despised Protestant Speaking Plain English* (1647), p. 16 (Wing, H 3069; BL, TT, E 408/17). I owe this reference to Daniel Woolf. Cf. Woolf, 'Conscience, constancy, and ambition', pp. 266–7.

[153] [James Howell], *A Letter to the Earle of Pembrooke Concerning the Times, and the sad condition both of Prince and People* (1647), sig. A3[r–v], p. 5 (Wing, H 3085; BL, TT, E 522/5).

[154] I owe this suggestion to Daniel Woolf. Cf. Woolf, 'Conscience, constancy, and ambition', pp. 246, 256, 261–6. Pembroke's support for Strafford's attainder is discussed above, p. 74.

lawes of heaven and earth'.[155] Only the King could remedy these disasters and re-establish the rule of law.

If Pembroke was an example of the treacherous counsellor whom Howell had denounced in his parable 'Ορνιλογια', a Constitutional Royalist peer, the Earl of Dorset, represented his ideal of a moderate and responsible adviser. Dorset had also criticised Pembroke's political pragmatism in 1647;[156] and after his death in 1652 Howell wrote an elegy praising this 'most accomplish'd and heroick Lord'. Dorset was a figure of 'princely, hospitable and brave mind', and

> his person with it such a state did bring
> That made a Court as if he had bin King.

With these words, a theorist of Constitutional Royalism extolled the 'admired perfections' of one of its leading practitioners.[157] But unlike his subject, Howell lived to see the Restoration of the Stuarts: he was appointed Historiographer Royal in 1661, and died in London five years later.[158]

It should by now be clear that notwithstanding certain differences of emphasis the writings analysed in this chapter expressed a number of shared themes, attitudes and assumptions. Briefly stated, these 'common denominators' comprised the beliefs that the monarch's powers were sovereign yet legally limited; that episcopacy should be retained as an integral part of the existing Church 'by law established'; and that constitutional monarchy protected the property and freedom of the subjects and the privileges of Parliament much more effectively than the Junto. The rule of law guaranteed each of these elements and held them together in constitutional equilibrium. The common law was perceived as an expression of natural and divine law, and armed resistance to the monarch was deemed contrary to both. Monarchy, Church and the law were thus taken to be interdependent structures. This web of interlocking beliefs coloured the idiom in which each was expressed, and it is therefore impossible to separate them, or to assign a prior importance to any one, without doing violence to their intrinsic nature. There were perceptible variations between the different writers, most strikingly on the composition of the three estates and on the need to ensure 'liberty for tender consciences'.[159] But these

---

[155] [Howell], *Letter to the Earle of Pembrooke*, pp. 10–11.
[156] Dorset wrote of Pembroke: 'Paraselsus himselfe cowld never have fixed the mercuriall spirit thatt predominates in his breast: if hee weere alive to practise on him'. CKS, Sackville MS, U 269/C248, unfol.: Dorset to the second Earl of Middlesex, 1 August 1647.
[157] [James Howell], *Ah, Ha; Tumulus, Thalamus: Two Counter-Poems* (1654), sigs. [A2r–A3r] (Wing, H 3054; BL, TT, E 228/1).
[158] Woolf, 'Conscience, constancy, and ambition', pp. 275–8; *DNB*, XXVIII, 112.
[159] On the first, the attitude of Ferne was particularly fluid, and he seems to have moved away from the position associated with Digges and Spelman. Jenkins stressed the second

partly reflected the polemical contexts of individual tracts, and they were easily accommodated within a broad framework of agreed ideas.

That framework may be contrasted with other strands within Royalist thought during the 1640s. In particular, a number of writers advanced a significantly different view of the nature of royal authority and the constraints upon it. Ian Brice has classified them as apologists for 'absolute monarchy', in contradistinction to 'legally limited monarchy'.[160] The majority were clergy, and they closely resembled the apologists for the divine right of kings who wrote before 1640.[161] A detailed examination of their ideas would be inappropriate in a study devoted to Constitutional Royalism, and here there is only space to consider a handful of representative works.

The first was written by John Maxwell, formerly Bishop of Ross and a supporter of Charles I's Scottish Prayer Book. In 1640 he had gone to Ireland as Bishop of Killala and Achonry, and was wounded in the Ulster rebellion. Eventually he arrived at Oxford where he served as a royal chaplain.[162] Here he used his formidable theological erudition to advance a theory of divine right monarchy in a series of tracts of which the most important was *Sacro-sancta Regum Majestas*. This argued vigorously that 'the King is onely and immediately dependent from Almighty God, the King of Kings, and Lord of Lords, and independent in his soveraigntie and power from the communitie'.[163] Royal sovereignty derived directly from God and the monarch was thus 'no creature of the people's making'. Sovereignty was indivisible, and the only limitations upon it were imposed by God: 'Almighty God as he investeth the soveraigne with entire soveraignty, so hath he set the bounds of it, defined it.'[164] This then enabled Maxwell to invoke St Thomas Aquinas's axiom that the monarch was *legibus solutus*: 'the power of all monarchs and of every monarch is *legibus soluta*, subject to no over-ruling power of man. Conceive it not so, that Kings are free from the direction of and obligation to the law of God, nature and common equitie; but from coercion humane, or any humane

issue more than the other writers, although most of those alive from the mid-1640s onwards were probably willing to accept a measure of religious toleration on condition that episcopacy were preserved. The Royalist commissioners likewise advocated a 'liberty for tender consciences' during peace negotiations: see above, pp. 146–7, 151–2.

160 Brice, 'Political ideas', chapter 2.
161 J. P. Sommerville, *Politics and Ideology in England, 1603–1640* (Harlow, 1986), chapter 1.
162 These biographical details are derived from *DNB*, XXXVII, 128–30. For Maxwell's political thought, see Brice, 'Political ideas', pp. 55–8; and Allen, *English Political Thought*, 509–11.
163 [John Maxwell], *Sacro-sancta Regum Majestas: or; The Sacred and Royall Prerogative of Christian Kings* (Oxford, 1644), p. 6 (Wing, M 1384; BL, TT, E 30/22).
164 *Ibid.*, pp. 19, 125.

coactive power to punish, censure or dethrone them.'[165] Thus although Maxwell accepted that royal powers were subject to limitations, he believed that those limitations were exclusively divine and not human in nature. This distanced him decisively from the advocates of a legally limited monarch who argued that royal powers were regulated by the laws of the land as well as by the laws of God.

Another divine who expressed almost identical views was Griffith Williams. A cleric of high church views, who had been suspended as early as 1616 for antagonising the godly, Williams became a royal chaplain in 1636 and Bishop of Ossory in 1641. However, the outbreak of rebellion in Ireland later that year forced him to flee to England, where he joined the King during the autumn of 1642.[166] His views alarmed Royalist moderates, and Falkland urged Charles to suppress Williams's *Discovery of Mysteries* in 1643.[167] This tract bitterly condemned 'the plots and practices of a prevalent faction in this present Parliament'.[168] Williams alleged that this faction harboured a 'grand designe' for 'the subversion of our monarchicall government' in order to create 'a paritie among all men both in Church and Commonwealth', and he warned that 'we must not idolize the Parliament as if it were a kinde of omnipotent creature'.[169] These sentiments were hardly likely to appeal to those, such as Falkland, who were desperately trying to keep open the lines of communication between Oxford and Westminster. But Charles apparently liked this work and ignored Falkland's advice. Williams's most important tract, published in 1644 under the title *Jura Majestatis*, was even more forceful. Like Maxwell, Williams began by asserting that 'the institution of Kings is immediately from God'. He insisted that 'of all sorts of government the monarchie is absolutely the best' because it was 'the first in nature' and also 'the prime and principall ordinance of God'.[170] Sovereignty was 'fixed in the King', and because 'divers supreme powers are not compatible in one State, nor allowable in our State; the conceit of a mixed monarchie is but a sopperie'.[171] Williams's concept of the legal limitations upon the monarch's authority was quite different from that of the Constitutional Royalists. He acknowledged that 'though the supreme majestie be free from lawes, *sponte*

---

[165] *Ibid.*, p. 140. For the use of Thomist doctrine to advance a theory of absolutism, especially in the writings of Suárez, see Quentin Skinner, *The Foundations of Modern Political Thought* (2 vols., Cambridge, 1978), II, 178–84.

[166] For biographical details, see DNB, LXI, 401–3; Venn and Venn, *Alumni Cantab.*, IV, 415. For Williams's political thought, see Brice, 'Political ideas', pp. 47–55.

[167] Gr[iffith] Williams, *The Discovery of Mysteries* (1643), Wing, W 2665; BL, TT, E 60/1, E 104/27; DNB, LXI, 402.

[168] Williams, *Discovery of Mysteries*, title page.   [169] *Ibid.*, pp. 55, 59, 107.

[170] Gryffith Williams, *Jura Majestatis, the Rights of Kings both in Church and State* (Oxford, 1644), pp. 14, 20 (Wing, W 2669; BL, TT, E 14/18*).

[171] *Ibid.*, p. 133.

tameniis accommodare potest, the King may of his owne accord yeild to observe the same'. But while 'that rule which formerly was arbitrary is now become limited', it was 'limited by their owne lawes and with their owne wills, and none other wise'. The King 'gives the law' to his subjects but 'takes none from them', and thus 'the power of making lawes was never yeilded out of the King's hands'. It followed from this that in the making of legislation 'the King worketh and acteth . . . absolutely by the power of his owne inherent soveraignty'.[172] Once again, the only limitations upon the monarch's powers were those imposed by God's law; as regards human law, the King was *legibus solutus*.

It was however a third divine, Michael Hudson, who wrote what has been described as 'the most complete exposition of divine right absolute monarchy to be put forward during the Civil War period'.[173] A graduate and later a Fellow of Queen's College, Oxford, Hudson served as tutor to Charles I's eldest son for a time during the early 1630s.[174] He joined the King at the start of the Civil War and was shortly afterwards appointed scout-master to the Royalist army in the North. Together with John Ashburnham, Hudson accompanied Charles to Newark in April 1646 prior to his surrender to the Scots.[175] Hudson was twice captured and imprisoned in 1646–8, and after twice escaping he raised forces for the King in Lincolnshire during the second Civil War. He was killed at the siege of Woodcroft House (Northamptonshire) in June 1648.[176] The previous year Hudson had published *The Divine Right of Government*, the express purpose of which was to assert 'the divini[t]y or divine right of government (and particularlie of monarchie)'.[177] This tract contained a lengthy discussion of the different forms of government and various types of divine right which culminated in the definition of monarchy as 'a politick government instituted and approved by God, consisting in the prudentiall administration and exercise of the supream power and authority of one person over all others within the same society, for the preservation of peace and unity in order to God's glory, the King's honour, and the people's welfare'.[178]

---

[172] *Ibid.*, pp. 146, 149.   [173] Brice, 'Political ideas', p. 73.
[174] For the following biographical details, see *DNB*, XXVIII, 152–3; Foster, *Alumni Oxon.*, II, 759; Matthews, *Walker Revised*, p. 252.
[175] Edward Walker, *Historical Discourses* (1705), p. 153; Sir Richard Bulstrode, *Memoirs and Reflections upon the Reign and Government of King Charles the 1st and K[ing] Charles the IId* (1721), p. 158.
[176] *LJ*, X, 313–14; Holmes, *Seventeenth-Century Lincolnshire*, p. 200; E.W. Hensman, 'The East Midlands and the Second Civil War, May to July, 1648', *TRHS*, 4th series, 6 (1923), 133–7.
[177] Mich[ael] Hudson, *The Divine Right of Government* (1647), sig. B2[r] (Wing, H 3261; BL, TT, E 406/24). For a discussion of this tract, see Tuck, *Philosophy and Government*, pp. 269–70.
[178] Hudson, *Divine Right of Government*, p. 67.

Hudson argued that it was 'the very essence of monarchie that one man should enjoy the supremacy'. Sovereignty could thus be neither shared nor divided. Laws should be 'revoked by the King if they [were] prejudiciall to his owne honour; for all such lawes are supposed to be fraudulently procured'. Furthermore, it was 'a sacriledge of an high nature to violate and invade the sacred power and prerogative of Kings'.[179] Hudson's tract advanced a full-blown theory of divine right monarchy in which the King was answerable to God alone and limited by divine law but not by the laws of the land.

Finally, we turn to a tract which has been justly labelled the 'apotheosis' of the absolutist strain within Royalist thought during the 1640s.[180] Its author was Sir Robert Filmer, a prosperous Kentish gentleman best known for his classic work *Patriarcha*. This treatise, possibly written in about 1628–31, advanced a theory of patriarchalism which drew a parallel between royal and fatherly authority and argued that both were derived from God.[181] However, *Patriarcha* was not published until 1680, twenty-seven years after Filmer's death, and of the works which appeared in his own lifetime the one which concerns us here was entitled *The Anarchy of a Limited or Mixed Monarchy*. Written while Filmer was imprisoned in 1643–4, and published in April 1648, this was another explicit attack on Hunton's *Treatise of Monarchie*.[182] But in denouncing Hunton, the *Anarchy* also repudiated many of the assumptions which underpinned Constitutional Royalism. Filmer began by asserting that the 'doctrine of limited and mixed monarchy is an opinion but of yesterday, and of no antiquity, a mere innovation of policy, not so old as New England, though calculated properly for that meridien'. Rather, he defined 'monarchy' as 'the government of one alone', and insisted that 'the monarch must not only have the supreme power unlimited, but he must have it alone – without any companions'. The idea of a legally limited sovereign was a contradiction in terms, 'for to govern, is to give a law to others, and not to

---

179 *Ibid.*, pp. 111, 190, 191.
180 John M. Wallace, *Destiny his Choice: The Loyalism of Andrew Marvell* (Cambridge, 1968), p. 14.
181 The best scholarly edition of *Patriarcha* is now Sir Robert Filmer, *Patriarcha and other Writings*, ed. Johann P. Sommerville (Cambridge, 1991), pp. 1–68. I here follow Sommerville's tentative dating, justified in *ibid.*, pp. xxxii–xxxiv. For the most recent works in the on-going controversy over the date of *Patriarcha*, see John M. Wallace, 'The date of Sir Robert Filmer's *Patriarcha*', *HJ*, 23 (1980), 155–65; James Daly, 'Some problems in the authorship of Sir Robert Filmer's Works', *EHR*, 98 (1983), 737–62; and Richard Tuck, 'A new date for Filmer's *Patriarcha*', *HJ*, 29 (1986), 183–6.
182 [Sir Robert Filmer], *The Anarchy of a Limited or Mixed Monarchy* (1648), Wing, F 910; BL, TT, E 436/4. The following discussion is based on the text in Filmer, *Patriarcha and other Writings*, pp. 131–71. Its context and composition are analysed in *ibid.*, pp. xi–xii, xv–xx; in James Daly, *Sir Robert Filmer and English Political Thought* (Toronto, 1979), pp. 12–14, 29–30, 52; and in Tuck, *Philosophy and Government*, pp. 262–6.

have a law given to govern and limit him that governs. And to govern alone is not to have sharers or companions mixed with the governor.' This position in turn rested on a view of the common law which differed fundamentally from that of the Constitutional Royalists. According to Filmer, 'the common law is generally acknowledged to be nothing else but common usage or custom, which by length of time only obtains authority. So that it follows in time after government, but cannot go before it and be the rule to government by any original or radical constitution.' This was in stark contrast to the belief in the rule of law and in a harmony between the common law and divine law which characterised the Constitutional Royalists. Instead, Filmer's sense of divine law inclined him to 'embrace' Hunton's definition of 'absolute monarchy' as 'when the sovereignty is so fully in one, that it hath no limits or bounds under God but his own will'.[183] The views advanced in *The Anarchy* had affinities both with English absolutist writings prior to 1640 (which probably included *Patriarcha*) and with the theories of Bodin. Indeed, only four months later, in August 1648, Filmer published a collection of extracts from Richard Knolles's English translation of Bodin's *Six Livres de la République* (1576).[184] Like Maxwell, Williams, Hudson and a number of other writers, Filmer thus demonstrated that theorists of absolute monarchy were alive and well in seventeenth-century England,[185] and that the experiences of the 1640s drove them to present their beliefs with a new sophistication and urgency.

The most famous apologist for absolute sovereignty to emerge in this period was, of course, Thomas Hobbes. A great deal has already been written on his political thought, and it would be impossible to attempt a detailed analysis here. But it is worth briefly examining Hobbes's attitude towards the Constitutional Royalists and also – insofar as we can reconstruct it – their view of him. In his *Behemoth*, completed towards the end of the 1660s, Hobbes offered this assessment of 'the King's counsellors, lords and other persons of quality and experience' during the Civil Wars:

They thought the government of England was not an absolute, but a mixed monarchy ... This opinion, though it did not lessen their endeavour to gain the victory for the King in a battle, when a battle could not be avoided, yet it weakened their endeavour to procure him an absolute victory in the war. And for this cause, notwithstanding that they saw that the Parliament was firmly resolved to take all

---

[183] Filmer, *Patriarcha and other Writings*, pp. 134, 135, 137, 146, 153.

[184] This collection was entitled *The Necessity of the Absolute Power of all Kings: and in particular of the King of England* (1648), Wing, F 917; BL, TT, E 460/7. For a modern edition, see Filmer, *Patriarcha and other Writings*, pp. 172–83. The text is discussed in *ibid.*, pp. xii, xvi.

[185] Cf. Sommerville, *Politics and Ideology*, pp. 46–50; 'Absolutism and royalism', in *The Cambridge History of Political Thought, 1450–1700*, ed. J. H. Burns and Mark Goldie (Cambridge, 1991), pp. 347–73; James Daly, 'The idea of absolute monarchy in seventeenth-century England', *HJ*, 21 (1978), 227–50.

kingly power whatsoever out of his hands, yet their counsel to the King was upon all occasions to offer propositions to them of treaty and accommodation, and to make and publish declarations; which any man might easily have foreseen would be fruitless ... Those which were then likeliest to have their counsel asked in this business were averse to absolute monarchy, as also to absolute democracy or aristocracy, all which governments they esteemed tyranny; and were in love with mixarchy, which they used to praise by the name of mixed monarchy, though it were indeed nothing else but pure anarchy. And those men, whose pens the King most used in these controversies of law and politics, were such (if I have not been misinformed) as having been members of this Parliament, had declaimed against shipmoney and other extra-parliamentary taxes as much as any; but when they saw the Parliament grow higher in their demands than they thought they would have done, went over to the King's party.[186]

It would be difficult to better this summary in terms of facts if not of opinions. The motives and behaviour of the Constitutional Royalists are described accurately enough, albeit from an obviously hostile perspective. Yet Hobbes's account needs to be located within its polemical context; for during his life he locked horns with one of the leading theorists of Constitutional Royalism (Bramhall) and was later denounced by one of its most distinguished practitioners (Hyde).

Bramhall and Hobbes had first clashed in the mid-1640s over the issues of free will and determinism.[187] This controversy culminated in the publication of Bramhall's massive *Castigations of Mr Hobbes* in 1657.[188] The following year saw Bramhall launch an incisive attack on Hobbes's most famous work in a piece entitled *The Catching of Leviathan*.[189] This began with a denunciation of Hobbes's religious views. Bramhall regarded 'Hobbian principles' as 'destructive to Christianity and all Religion', and argued that 'without religion, societies are but like soapy bubbles, quickly dissolved'. He then turned to Hobbes's theory of sovereignty. Bramhall insisted that its effect was to make 'the power of kings to be so exorbitant that no subject, who hath either conscience or discretion, ever did or can

---

[186] Thomas Hobbes, *Behemoth, or The Long Parliament*, ed. Ferdinand Tönnies (Chicago, 1990), pp. 114–17.

[187] Samuel I. Mintz, *The Hunting of Leviathan: Seventeenth-Century Reactions to the Materialism and Moral Philosophy of Thomas Hobbes* (Cambridge, 1962), pp. 11–12, 110–23.

[188] John Bramhall, *Castigations of Mr Hobbes his last Animadversions, in the Case concerning Liberty, and Universal Necessity* (1657), Wing, B 4214. This tract is reprinted in *Works of Bramhall*, IV, 197–506. For the earlier contributions to this debate, see *ibid.*, 3–196; and *The English Works of Thomas Hobbes*, ed. W. Molesworth (11 vols., 1839–45), IV, 229–384; V, *passim*.

[189] John Bramhall, *The Catching of Leviathan, or the Great Whale*, printed as a sequel to the 1658 edition of *Castigations of Mr Hobbes*, pp. 449–573 (Wing, B 4215; BL, TT, E 1757/1). This tract is reprinted in *Works of Bramhall*, IV, 507–97. For discussions, see John Bowle, *Hobbes and his Critics: A Study in Seventeenth-Century Constitutionalism* (1951), pp. 114–33; and Mark Goldie, 'The reception of Hobbes', in *The Cambridge History of Political Thought*, Burns and Goldie, pp. 589–615.

endure; so to render monarchy odious to mankind'. Against this, Bramhall re-asserted the Constitutional Royalist vision of a monarchy which was 'more aptly called a temperated or moderated sovereignty rather than "divided" or "mixed"'. The 'three estates of the kingdom' which assembled in Parliament 'were but suppliants to the King, to have such or such laws enacted'. Yet the monarch 'hath restrained himself in the exercise of his legislative power, that he will govern by no new laws other than such as they should assent unto'. Such principles were clearly incompatible with Hobbes's 'state of nature', a concept which Bramhall dismissed as 'a bundle of absurdities'. The 'law of nature' was as central to Hobbes's position as the rule of law was to Constitutional Royalism, and Bramhall concluded by condemning Hobbes's 'gross mistake of the laws of nature' which would make 'a moral heathen . . . blush for shame'.[190] The notion of an absolute sovereignty justified by natural law alone was utterly inimical to the Constitutional Royalists' ideal of a monarchy limited by both divine law and the common law.

Not surprisingly, this was a theme which 'Hyde the lawyer'[191] also took up in his *Brief View and Survey of the Dangerous and Pernicious Errors* in Hobbes's *Leviathan*, completed during Hyde's second exile and published in 1676.[192] Hobbes's doctrines were, he argued, 'so contrary to all the laws established in his country' that they would 'make all laws cobwebs, to be blown away by the least breath of the governor'. His vision of 'an absolute dictatorship' would 'overthrow and undermine all those principles of government which preserv'd the peace of this kingdom through so many ages' and 'destroy the very essence of the religion of Christ'. Hyde insisted that Hobbes's paradigm would prove much less attractive to both monarch and people than England's existing constitutional arrangements. The laws already provided 'so many limitations and restraints of the sovereign power' and ensured 'that happy and beneficial agreement between the soveraign power and the naked subject'. This was the great advantage of a legally limited monarchy, in which 'the strength of the laws and the good

---

[190] *Works of Bramhall*, IV, 519–20, 560, 564, 573, 594.
[191] For this phrase, see PRO, SP 16/449/40 (John Nicholas to Edward Nicholas, 30 March 1640).
[192] Edward, Earl of Clarendon, *A Brief View and Survey of the Dangerous and Pernicious Errors to Church and State, in Mr Hobbes's Book, entitled Leviathan* (Oxford, 1676), Wing, C 4420. For discussions of this work, see Bowle, *Hobbes and his Critics*, pp. 157–73; Mintz, *Hunting of Leviathan*, pp. 37–8; and above all Perez Zagorin, 'Clarendon and Hobbes', *Journal of Modern History*, 57 (1985), 593–616. Although this was Hyde's only published attack on Hobbes, he also compiled his own private dossier of anti-Hobbesian materials: see Martin Dzelzainis, 'Edward Hyde and Thomas Hobbes's *Elements of Law, Natural and Politic*', *HJ*, 32 (1989), 303–17. The intellectual context of Hyde's critique of Hobbes is discussed in J. C. Hayward, 'New directions in studies of the Falkland circle', *The Seventeenth Century*, 2 (1987), 19–48; and in Johann P. Sommerville, 'Further light on Hobbes', *HJ*, 36 (1993), 736.

constitutions of the government ... resisted the operation and malignity' of the monarch's sovereignty. Hyde's final point was that *Leviathan* was as detrimental to the Church as to the State. He thought the work 'very pernicious and destructive to the very essence of religion', and felt that 'it was below the education of Mr Hobbes, and a very ungenerous and vile thing, to publish his *Leviathan* with so much malice and acrimony against the Church of England, when it was scarce strugling in its own ruines'. This was both an expression of beliefs which 'destroy[ed] the very essence of the religion of Christ' and another aspect of Hobbes's onslaught upon the laws of England. Caught between 'that mischievous doctrine' of 'a co-ordinate power' between Crown, Lords and Commons on the one hand, and Hobbes's vision of an 'absolute soveraign' on the other, Hyde vigorously reiterated the Constitutional Royalist belief that a sovereign yet limited monarchy ruling within the law conferred unrivalled benefits upon monarchs and their subjects alike.[193]

Constitutional Royalism and Hobbes's critique of it both grew out of the disintegration of England's 'ancient constitution' during the 1640s and 1650s. Hobbes's doctrine of the 'laws of nature' and the Constitutional Royalists' attempts to restore limited monarchy under the rule of law were different products of what Glenn Burgess has called 'the crisis of the common law'.[194] Once doubts emerged about whether the common law could provide a viable solution to the nation's political problems, people were forced either to re-assert its validity as the foundation of England's polity and the guarantor of constitutional balance, or alternatively to adopt what Mark Goldie has termed 'Hobbes's bullish irreverence for common law'.[195] Both these lines of argument could draw on existing traditions within English political thought. The former looked to the long-standing claims that England was a limited monarchy, a *dominium politicum et regale*, while the latter equated the law with the sovereign's command and thus built on the ideas of earlier absolutist thinkers such as Bodin and Filmer.[196] But of these two responses, the first – that of the Constitutional Royalists – had much the longer future before it. The *de facto* theories of political obligation, to which Hobbes's ideas have been so

---

[193] Clarendon, *Brief View and Survey*, pp. 6, 16, 39, 96, 98, 111, 130–1, 133, 292, 305.
[194] Glenn Burgess, *The Politics of the Ancient Constitution: An Introduction to English Political Thought, 1603–1642* (1992), pp. 212–31.
[195] Goldie, 'Reception of Hobbes', p. 596. For Hobbes's views on the common law, see Thomas Hobbes, *A Dialogue between a Philosopher and a Student of the Common Laws of England*, ed. Joseph Cropsey (Chicago, 1971). I am most grateful to Mark Goldie for this reference and for advice on Hobbes's thought.
[196] For Filmer, see above, pp. 247–8. The affinities between Hobbes and earlier theorists of absolutism are discussed in Johann P. Sommerville, *Thomas Hobbes: Political Ideas in Historical Context* (1992), pp. 96–100.

convincingly related,[197] had much less direct influence upon the long-term development of English government than the Constitutional Royalists who returned to prominence in 1660. Accused of heresy and atheism, Hobbes was 'forbidden to publish works on sensitive political issues in England'.[198] His ideas, like those of Maxwell, Williams, Hudson and Filmer, differed markedly from those of the Constitutional Royalists – with their emphasis on legally limited monarchy, on the rightful powers of Parliament and on the rule of law – and indicate the richness and diversity of Royalist thought during the period of the English Civil Wars.

Hobbes's career also illustrates the close link which often existed between political theory and practice. He served as tutor, adviser and financial agent to the Cavendish family from around 1608, and later became closely associated with William Cavendish, first Marquess of Newcastle.[199] Throughout his life, the Marquess gave robust counsel to both Charles I and his eldest son. Hyde wrote that Newcastle was 'without any reverence or regard for the Privy Council', thought 'all business ought to be done by councils of war', and 'was always angry when there were any overtures of a treaty'.[200] On the eve of the Restoration, he was to present Charles II with a book of *Advice* which urged him to avoid his father's 'errors off state' and to remember that he, like all governments, was 'above the law'.[201] Such attitudes helped to make Newcastle a close friend and ally of Henrietta Maria during the 1640s.[202] He had been implicated in the first Army Plot; and in 1645 married one of the Queen's Maids of Honour, Margaret Lucas.[203] It was almost certainly through Newcastle that Hobbes gained an entrée to Court circles and became tutor in mathematics to the

[197] See especially Quentin Skinner, 'Conquest and consent: Thomas Hobbes and the Engagement controversy', in *The Interregnum: The Quest for Settlement, 1646–1660*, ed. G. E. Aylmer (1972), pp. 79–98; and 'The ideological context of Hobbes's political thought', *HJ*, 9 (1966), 286–317.

[198] Sommerville, *Hobbes*, pp. 26–7. See also Richard Tuck, *Hobbes* (Oxford, 1989), pp. 32–9; and *Philosophy and Government*, pp. 335–45.

[199] Tuck, *Philosophy and Government*, pp. 280–4, 294–8, 314–15; *Hobbes*, pp. 4, 11–13, 24–5; Sommerville, *Hobbes*, pp. 6–23.

[200] Clarendon, *History*, III, 383 (Book VIII, §86). See also Sir Philip Warwick, *Memoires of the Reigne of King Charles I* (1701), pp. 235–8.

[201] Thomas P. Slaughter, ed., *Ideology and Politics on the Eve of the Restoration: Newcastle's Advice to Charles II* (Memoirs of the American Philosophical Society, 159, Philadelphia, 1984), pp. 49, 54. For a brilliant discussion of this work, see Conal Condren, 'Casuistry to Newcastle: "The Prince" in the world of the book', in *Political Discourse in Early Modern Britain*, ed. Nicholas Phillipson and Quentin Skinner (Cambridge, 1993), pp. 164–86.

[202] Clarendon, *History*, II, 466–7 (Book VI, §§264–5). For examples of the Queen's letters to Newcastle, see *Letters of Henrietta Maria*, Green, pp. 121, 127–8, 134–5, 181, 195–7, 206–8, 218–21, 223–39, 261.

[203] Russell, *FBM*, p. 356; *Unrevolutionary England, 1603–1642* (1990), pp. 289–90; Tuck, *Philosophy and Government*, p. 321.

Prince of Wales in 1646.[204] These links were reflected in Hobbes's writings. By implication, his attack on Constitutional Royalism in *Behemoth* offered a retrospective justification for Newcastle and Henrietta Maria's hostility towards peace treaties.[205]

The same intertwining of theory and practice was evident among more moderate Royalists. The ideas of the Constitutional Royalist writers bore a striking resemblance to those advanced by the King's commissioners during successive negotiations. Nor was this restricted to constitutional issues such as the nature of royal powers, the future of Church government, and the rule of law. It extended to a profound fear of total victory by *either* King *or* Parliament. Ferne was far from alone in his reluctance to see 'an outright prevailing of either side by armes'.[206] His concern was shared by some of the moderate peers close to Charles. Dorset, for example, had warned Salisbury in August 1642 that 'none butt the desperate every way can hope for amelioration by the ruines of soe many, and soe universall a change both in government, and familyes as a victory must make, *on which side soever itt happens*'. This was the worst possible outcome, 'for to breath under such an arbitrary government, *even on both sides*, as wee miserable subiects doe, is to languish not live'.[207] Another figure who voiced almost identical sentiments was Sir John Strangways. On 23 November 1646, while incarcerated in the Tower, he wrote a poem 'concerning the ending of our unhappie differences by peace'. ''Tis not safe for the state', he declared,

> to make the sword the judge of this debate.
> If in this warre the parlement prevayle,
> To us and ours they doe the warre intayle.

But the opposite extreme was no better, for

> if the King regayne his Crowne by armes
> Then we may thanke our selves for all our harmes
> For having soe gott all into his hands
> He is made lord of all our lives and lands
> And we our lawes and lybertyes . . . have lost.

The corollary of this abhorrence of military victory by either side was an intense desire to see a negotiated settlement. Strangways believed that if the war were ended 'by treatie' then

---

[204] Tuck, *Philosophy and Government*, pp. 320–2; *Hobbes*, p. 25; Sommerville, *Hobbes*, pp. 22–3.
[205] See above, pp. 110–11, 112, 115–17, 121, 125, 130, 163, 180.
[206] Ferne, *Conscience Satisfied*, p. 83.
[207] BL, Microfilm M 485 (Hatfield House, Cecil MS), vol. CXCVIII, fos. 128r, 130r–v (Dorset to the Earl of Salisbury, 4 August 1642). My emphasis.

> we may with safetie our affaires attend:
> And we agayne a glorious state shall see,
> If King and people by this meanes agree.[208]

A Constitutional Royalist theory of the polity thus found its practical application in the promotion and management of peace negotiations. Strangways's poem concluded with the hope that

> none wilbe found soe mad,
> To hazard all, for what cannot be had.[209]

The enemies to a negotiated settlement were not only the Junto; they were the hardliners on *both* sides. This symmetry within Constitutional Royalist thought was especially clear in Dorset's words to Salisbury of August 1642:

Bee nott an actor or adviser in extreeme courses thatt will sett all on fire and burne the authors in there owne flames first or last bee they whome they will, *ether on one side or other*, for noe doupt there are to many hot headed people *both heere and att London*, thatt advise and perswade desperate wayes.[210]

These 'hot headed people' included hard-line Royalists as well as Parliamentarian extremists. The former were those Royalist advisers who at various times sought an outright military victory and opposed peace talks with the Houses. They were the practical counterparts to theorists such as Maxwell, Hudson, Williams, Filmer and Hobbes. James Daly has reminded us of the difficulty of categorising these as 'Ultra-Royalists' and argued persuasively that they remained a highly amorphous, shifting group.[211] The present study has amply confirmed that figures such as John Ashburnham and Henry Jermyn cannot be consistently associated with any single political position. Similarly, we have seen that by the summer of 1645 Prince Rupert, often seen as the quintessential 'ultra', was collaborating with Richmond in urging Charles to make peace.[212] Furthermore, self-interest mingled with issues of principle to a degree which makes it impossible to prove that a person was motivated by ideology alone. Equally, the pragmatism of individuals does not gainsay the existence of consistent strands of opinion among English Royalists. A coherent body of ideas stood opposed to further treaties with Parliament, even if the exponents of those ideas varied through time and acted from a plurality of motives.

Similarly, between 1642 and 1649 an outlook identifiable as Constitutional Royalism led a number of advisers to urge Charles repeatedly to treat with the Houses. It is important to distinguish between those

---

[208] Beinecke Library, Yale University, Osborn MS b. 304 (commonplace book of Sir John Strangways), p. 92.
[209] *Ibid.*   [210] BL, M 485, vol. CXCVIII, fo. 129r–v. My emphasis.
[211] James Daly, 'The implications of Royalist politics, 1642–6', *HJ*, 27 (1984), 745–55.
[212] See above, p. 125.

counsellors who at one time or another advocated peace negotiations, but who on other occasions were either lukewarm or downright hostile, and those whose consistent preference was for talks. Royalists were perfectly capable of adapting their strategies in response to changing circumstances; but the Constitutional Royalists were distinguished by their unswerving commitment to talks with the Houses and later with the Army. For these advisers the promotion of peace talks amounted to a knee-jerk reflex. They became less and less co-ordinated politically as the decade progressed; but they always retained a common perception of the English Civil Wars and a shared sense of how that conflict should be brought to an end. They sought a negotiated peace which would enshrine their view of the constitution by guaranteeing a sovereign yet legally limited monarchy, the rightful powers of Parliament, an episcopalian Church, and the rule of law. In theory and practice alike, these were the fundamental hallmarks of the Constitutional Royalist outlook. They formed an attitude or frame of mind as much as a series of ideological tenets, and their exponents attempted to realise them by avoiding an outright military victory for either side and searching instead for a negotiated settlement. Pride's Purge, followed by the trial and public execution of Charles I, marked the ultimate failure of this search. An army coup which breached parliamentary privilege, stopped peace negotiations in their tracks, and paved the way for an act of regicide which violated both human and divine law represented the negation of all that the Constitutional Royalists stood for. It signalled the triumph of fanaticism over moderation and of martial law over the rule of law.

Yet these cataclysmic events belied the fundamental resilience of the Constitutional Royalist outlook. In the longer term, such attitudes proved far more influential upon England's political and constitutional development than their temporary eclipse in 1649 suggested. Their exponents retreated, regrouped and awaited more propitious times. Precisely how Constitutional Royalism survived the 1650s, re-emerged at the Restoration, and came into its own after 1660 will be explored in the last part of this book.

Part III

CONSTITUTIONAL ROYALISM IN PERSPECTIVE

―――――――――――――― ⚜ 8 ⚜ ――――――――――――――

Epilogue: Constitutional Royalism from Regicide to Restoration

I

This chapter extends the biographical sketches presented in chapter 3 down to the Restoration of Charles II. It will look in turn at the experiences of those Constitutional Royalists who lived through the 1650s, and analyse how they came to terms with the Commonwealth and Protectorate. My argument will be that the Constitutional Royalists typically survived these years by retreating into seclusion, by withdrawing into a private world of friendships and political quiescence. Many of them were utterly convinced that times would change and the monarchy would ultimately be restored. But in the meantime they preferred to live quietly and have as little as possible to do with the Interregnum régimes, in the belief that co-operation would compromise their principles while an insurrection could only jeopardise Charles II's eventual return. This characteristic response was celebrated in Royalist poetry of the period; and it is remarkable how infrequently it was punctuated by attempts to foment disorder and to subvert the republic.

II

This retirement from public life forms a leitmotiv in Sir Edward Walker's account of the Knights of the Garter in these years. It is described particularly vividly in the cases of two peers who died during the Interregnum, Dorset and Richmond. According to Walker, 'after the barbarous murder of the King his master' Dorset 'never stirred out of his house' in London.[1] There is plentiful evidence in the records of Chancery to support this statement. For example, in May 1649, the court subpoenad Dorset for failing to pay forty shillings' costs to three defendants whom he had prosecuted in

---

[1] BL, Stowe MS 580 (Sir Edward Walker papers), fo. 30v. The following account of Dorset's final years is a heavily condensed version of that found in David L. Smith, 'The political career of Edward Sackville, fourth Earl of Dorset (1590–1652)' (PhD thesis, University of Cambridge, 1990), pp. 441–51.

his capacity as the Earl of Arundel's executor.[2] Five months later a 'commission of rebellion' was issued to 'attach' Dorset.[3] However, the commissioners were unable to find him, and so in January 1650 the Serjeant-at-Arms was ordered to arrest Dorset for contempt of court unless good reason to the contrary were shown within eight days.[4] Yet there is no sign that he was actually arrested, and instead Chancery found that the costs had been paid, and the case was dismissed.[5]

Dorset's withdrawal from litigation continued thereafter. Between February 1651 and his death in July 1652, Chancery dismissed no fewer than three suits begun by Dorset 'for want of further prosecution'.[6] The fact that one of these bills was filed as late as November 1650 raises an intriguing problem about Dorset's attitude towards the republic. From 2 January 1650, all adult males aged eighteen and over were required to sign an Engagement to 'be true and faithful to the Commonwealth of England as it is now established without a King or House of Lords' in order to hold public office or to launch proceedings in a court of law.[7] It is possible that Dorset refused to engage and that Chancery turned a blind eye. Equally, it was far from uncommon for Royalist peers to engage in order to begin litigation.[8] For Dorset we have no evidence either way. Whatever the truth, there was clearly no legal obstacle to his continuing suits already commenced, and other evidence suggests rather that he was simply too weary and too impoverished to proceed further.

By the early 1650s, the Sackville estates in both Kent and Sussex showed the combined effects of neglect and of Parliamentarian depredations.[9] After the settlement of impropriated rectories, Dorset's composition fine had been reduced to £775 in November 1647.[10] Yet it took him until May 1650 to pay this sum and secure his discharge.[11] It is likely that growing poverty

---

2 PRO, C 33/191 (Chancery entry book of decrees and orders), fo. 672v. For Dorset's original bill of complaint, see C 8/99/6 (Chancery proceedings, Mitford's Division).
3 PRO, C 33/193 (Chancery entry book of decrees and orders), fo. 20v.
4 *Ibid.*, fo. 294v. 5 *Ibid.*, fo. 416r.
6 PRO, C 33/195 (Chancery entry book of decrees and orders), fo. 356v; C 33/197 (Chancery entry book of decrees and orders), fos. 149v, 1159r. Dorset had begun these suits in February 1642, July 1647 and November 1650 respectively: PRO, C 2, Chas. I, D 9/6; C 2, Chas. I, D 24/63 (Chancery proceedings, series I); and C 7/330/105 (Chancery proceedings, Hamilton's Division).
7 C. H. Firth and R. S. Rait, ed., *Acts and Ordinances of the Interregnum, 1642–1660* (3 vols., 1911), I, 325–8.
8 Ian Ward, 'The English peerage, 1649–1660: government, authority and estates' (PhD thesis, University of Cambridge, 1989), pp. 64–8.
9 For examples, see PRO, E 317/SUSSEX/26 (Parliamentary survey of Sussex); SP 18/17/38–41 (Navy Commissioners' papers, 1651); CKS, Sackville MS, U 269/C61/2 (William Bloome to the fifth Earl of Dorset, [?] November 1652).
10 PRO, SP 23/4 (Committee for Compounding order book), fos. 140v–141r.
11 PRO, SP 23/43 (accounts of fines received by Treasurers at Goldsmiths' Hall), unfol., 31 May 1650; SP 23/8 (Committee for Compounding order book), p. 106.

was the reason for this long delay.[12] Driven further and further into debt, Dorset was forced to borrow heavily,[13] and in February 1652 he bemoaned his fate as 'a poore unsuccessefull Cavalier'.[14] Five months later, he died peacefully at Dorset House.[15] A will of March 1625 was apparently not located and he was declared intestate.[16] His son inherited estates saddled with debts, and towards the end of the Protectorate lamented that he was 'one of the poorest Earls in England'.[17] Impoverished and dispirited, the fifth Earl followed his father's example of retirement from public life, and apart from a brief visit to France lived quietly at his homes in London and Kent until the Restoration.[18]

Another peer who withdrew from public life was the Duke of Richmond. Walker wrote that 'after the murther of the King he retyred unto his house at Cobham Hall in Kent, seldome ever appearing abroad'.[19] However, the régime was markedly more suspicious of Richmond than of Dorset and monitored his activities much more closely. Although Richmond was determined to lead a quiet life, he was regularly approached by Royalist activists. Thus in November 1649, Sir Gilbert Talbot, a Gentleman of the Bedchamber, hoped that the exiled King would 'fix a councell of some few sober and discreet men' in England 'as the meanes to unite the heartes of all the sober Royalysts'. He suggested that the exiled Charles write 'in privat' to Richmond, together with Hertford and Southampton, but warned that 'all the difficulty will be to make these noblemen engage'.[20] These fears turned out to be fully justified. In July 1650, as

---

[12] Smith, 'Political career of Dorset', pp. 432–41.
[13] CKS, Sackville MS, U 269/F3/3 (notebook of the fifth Earl of Dorset), unfol., 4 September 1651.
[14] CKS, Sackville MS, U 269/C8 (Dorset to William Bloome, 16 February 1651/2).
[15] Bodl. Lib., MS Clarendon 43, fo. 215r (letter of intelligence, 16 July 1652); CKS, De L'Isle and Dudley MS, U 1475/F24 (journal of the Earl of Leicester), p. 85. I am most grateful to Viscount De L'Isle for allowing me to consult his family muniments.
[16] CKS, Sackville MS, U 269/T83/5 (holograph will of the fourth Earl of Dorset); PRO, PROB 6 (Prerogative Court of Canterbury, act books of administrations), 1653–4, vol. III, fo. 115r.
[17] Castle Ashby, Northampton, Compton MS 1084, fo. 21r (Richard Sackville, fifth Earl of Dorset, to the Countess of Northampton, 5 November 1657). I am grateful to Ian Ward for showing me his transcript of this letter. For the fifth Earl of Dorset's strained finances during the 1650s, see Ward, 'English peerage', pp. 368, 380–2, 397–403, 440–8, 535; 'Rental policy on the estates of the English peerage, 1649–60', *The Agricultural History Review*, 40 (1992), 23–4, 28–30.
[18] C. J. Phillips, *History of the Sackville Family* (2 vols., 1930), I, 393–7.
[19] Bodl. Lib., MS Ashmole 1110 (Order of the Garter papers), fo. 167r.
[20] *The Nicholas Papers*, vol. I: *1641–1652*, ed. G. F. Warner (Camden Society, 2nd series, XL, 1886), 154–5 (Gilbert Talbot to Sir William Coventry, 12 November 1649). Nicholas and a group of Presbyterian exiles in Holland shared these hopes: PRO, SP 18/9, fo. 20v (Nicholas's statement regarding Presbyterians in Holland, 5 March 1649/50); *The Diary and Correspondence of John Evelyn*, ed. W. Bray (new edition, ed. H. B. Wheatley, 4 vols., 1906), IV, 195 (Nicholas to Charles II, 31 January 1649/50).

Charles was assembling an army in Scotland, the double agent Thomas Coke allegedly asked Richmond to 'undertake the commaund of such forces' as could be raised in Kent, Surrey and Sussex to join up with the King's Scottish troops. But the Duke replied that 'hee meddled not in any countrey affaires and did desire but to live quietly amongst them or to that purpose'.[21] Coke reported that Richmond had also declined to take the Engagement.[22] The Duke added that he had 'refused to entermeddle' in the Kentish rising of 1648, and warned Coke of the 'danger himselfe would bee in, if hee should negotiate or act any thing of that nature ag[ains]t the present governem[en]t, and what a severe eye there was upon all endeavours of that nature'. The conversation then turned to news and reminiscences, and after he left Cobham Hall Coke heard nothing further from the Duke.[23]

This is an utterly characteristic instance of the unwillingness of Royalist peers within England to participate in conspiracies against the republic. But it was enough to make the Council of State highly suspicious of Richmond's political loyalties when Coke revealed this conversation to it in May 1651. That same month, Richmond was summoned before the Committee of Examinations to respond to Coke's deposition.[24] The Duke insisted that Coke had never visited him and that no conversation had taken place between them. He also stated that he knew nothing about the 1648 rising 'before the same was, nor was moved to bee a Generall for the Kinge in those parts'. Asked whether he had taken the Engagement, he desired 'to bee excused at the present from giveinge answere to it'.[25] The Council was clearly unhappy with these evasive answers, for they bailed Richmond on a bond for £10,000, with two sureties for £5,000 each, and even considered whether he should 'continue to have his residence' in Kent for the next six months.[26] The following October, Richmond was again summoned before the Council, but replied that he was too ill to attend.[27] Upon the production of a doctor's certificate, the Council 'thought fit to dispence with [the Duke's] appearance'.[28] Another summons in December 1651 was again declined owing to 'want of health'.[29] The Council

[21] Bodl. Lib., MS Dep. c. 169 (Nalson MS), fo. 197v (Thomas Coke's depositions before the Council of State, 28 May 1651).
[22] Bodl. Lib., MS Clarendon 40, fo. 137r (Thomas Coke to Charles II, 2 August 1650).
[23] Bodl. Lib., MS Dep. c. 169, fo. 198r.
[24] PRO, SP 25/19 (Council of State draft order book), p. 155.
[25] Bodl. Lib., MS Dep. c. 169, fo. 200v (examination of Richmond before the Council of State, 24 May 1651). There is apparently no evidence that Richmond ever took the Engagement: see Ward, 'English peerage', p. 512.
[26] PRO, SP 25/19, p. 158.
[27] PRO, SP 25/96 (Council of State letter book), pp. 587, 591; SP 18/16/79 (Richmond to the Council of State, 24 October 1651).
[28] PRO, SP 25/96, p. 593.
[29] PRO, SP 25/66 (Council of State fair order book), p. 133; SP 25/97 (Council of State letter book), pp. 49, 53.

apparently made no further attempt to secure Richmond's attendance, but there are signs that it remained deeply mistrustful of him. In August 1652 it ordered an inventory to be taken of his goods at Dunbarton Castle;[30] and late in 1653 General Marceline was given leave to visit Richmond 'before his departure out of England'.[31] Richmond was evidently being kept under close surveillance.

These exchanges between the Duke and the Council of State took place alongside extremely complicated proceedings in the Committee for Compounding with Delinquents.[32] Richmond's original fine of £9,810 was confirmed in April 1650, and his estate was discharged two months later on payment of this sum.[33] Thereafter he faced numerous creditors entering claims on his property, especially for the lands at Sutton Marsh in Lincolnshire. The dispute originated in Richmond's attempts to drain these lands and dated back to the early 1640s.[34] It seems that Richmond's tenants took advantage of his sequestration to seek redress of a long-standing grievance.[35] The case dragged on, drawing in the Lincolnshire County Committee, and was still unsettled at the time of the Duke's death.[36]

There are some signs that Richmond assisted Church of England clergy during the 1650s. The future Bishop of Worcester, James Fleetwood, acted as tutor to the Duke's children.[37] Richmond's chaplain, Herbert Thorndike, dedicated two discourses to him in 1650. Thorndike's purpose, as expressed in his epistle dedicatory, was 'of a civil and moderate nature'; and his work also carried an open letter 'to the lovers of peace and truth'. He went on to defend episcopacy as 'delivered in Scripture by the agreement of historicall truth and primitive practice'.[38] Yet Richmond does not seem to have been as active an ecclesiastical patron as some other Constitutional Royalist peers, most notably Hertford.

Richmond's final years were dogged by ill health. Walker wrote that he suffered for a long time 'with a quartern ague'.[39] According to Robert

---

[30] PRO, SP 25/31 (Council of State draft order book), p. 86.

[31] PRO, SP 25/72 (Council of State fair order book), p. 173.

[32] Richmond's case is summarised in *Calendar of the Proceedings of the Committee for Compounding with Delinquents*, ed. M. A. E. Green (5 vols., 1889), II, 1526–34.

[33] PRO, SP 23/7 (Committee for Compounding order book), p. 98; SP 23/8, p. 163.

[34] See *LJ*, IV, 176, 177, 181, 204, 221, 223, 231, 257, 262, 270, 277, 280, 284, 296, 300, 304, 307; V, 39, 45, 83, 592; VI, 174, 492; VIII, 493.

[35] *Calendar of the Committee for Compounding*, Green, II, 1529–34.

[36] *Ibid.* See also PRO, SP 18/100/120 (John Bellerby's complaint regarding Sutton Marsh, 13 September 1655); and *CJ*, VII, 208.

[37] A. G. Matthews, *Walker Revised* (Oxford, 1948; repr. 1988), p. 304; Ward, 'English peerage', p. 214.

[38] Herbert Thorndike, *Two Discourses, the one of the Primitive Government of Churches, the other of the service of God at the Assemblies of the Church* (Cambridge, 1650), sigs. ˟2[r], ˟3[r], p. 128 (Wing, T 1057).

[39] Bodl. Lib., MS Ashmole 1110, fo. 167r.

Baillie, by the summer of 1654, the Duke was living in Kent as quietly 'as a man buried'.[40] He died at Cobham Hall on 30 March 1655,[41] and was buried on 18 April in Henry VII's chapel at Westminster Abbey.[42] It was at first rumoured that he had appointed Southampton and Lindsey as his executors,[43] but in fact 'hee made the Dutchess his absolute executrise and left the children to her disposall and government'.[44] The Duchess suffered growing hardship in the later 1650s: the timber at Cobham Hall was plundered for Cromwell's navy, and by 1658 the family had sold off most of its Scottish lands.[45] She seems to have lived very quietly, and in the summer of 1658 moved to Paris where she spent the rest of the Interregnum.[46]

The initial reports about Richmond's will indicated how closely he was still associated with allies such as Southampton and Lindsey. Like the Duke, Southampton had been suggested in 1649–50 as a possible royal counsellor within England.[47] Nicholas wished to create 'a more full councell' comprising 'able, grave and experienced persons of unblemished integrity'.[48] Although, like Richmond, Southampton apparently shied away from involvement in such schemes, the Council of State still kept an eye on his activities.[49] In March 1651, for example, he was granted a licence to 'repaire to Tichfield in the county of Hants. to see his mother now lying sicke, and to remayne there for the space of one moneth'.[50] In fact, like other Constitutional Royalist peers, Southampton's political activities were extremely limited throughout the Interregnum. There is certainly no reason to doubt his deep personal loyalty to Charles II. In October 1651, during the King's flight after the battle of Worcester, Southampton sent word from Titchfield that 'he had a ship ready, and if the King

[40] The Letters and Journals of Robert Baillie, ed. D. Laing (3 vols., Edinburgh, 1841–2), III, 249.

[41] Clarendon, History, IV, 494 (Book XI, §245); A Collection of the State Papers of John Thurloe, Esq., ed. T. Birch (7 vols., 1742), III, 312.

[42] G.E. C[okayne], The Complete Peerage (new edition, ed. Vicary Gibbs, H. A. Doubleday, Duncan Warrand, Lord Howard de Walden, Geoffrey H. White and R. S. Lea, 14 vols., 1910–59), X, 833.

[43] The Nicholas Papers, vol. II: January 1653–June 1655, ed. G. F. Warner (Camden Society, 2nd series, 50, 1892), 250 (Andrew Johnson to Nicholas, 2 April 1655).

[44] Ibid., 255 (Percy Church to Nicholas, 16 April 1655).

[45] PRO, SP 18/141/155 (John Taylor to the Commissioners for the Admiralty, 21 June 1656); Letters and Journals of Baillie, Laing, III, 387.

[46] Thurloe State Papers, Birch, I, 734; Bodl. Lib., MS Clarendon 53, fo. 243v (John Jennings to Hyde, 24 January 1656/7); MS Clarendon 58, fos. 232v ([Nicholas] to Hyde, 28 August 1658), 271r ([John Cosin] to Hyde, 3 September 1658); MS Clarendon 71, fo. 326r (Thomas Kingstonn to [Hyde], 20 April 1660).

[47] Nicholas Papers, I, Warner, 155; PRO, SP 18/9, fo. 20v.

[48] Diary of Evelyn, Bray, IV, 195.

[49] David Underdown, Royalist Conspiracy in England, 1649–1660 (New Haven, 1960), p. 20; PRO, SP 25/8 (Council of State draft order book), p. 8.

[50] PRO, SP 25/65 (Council of State fair order book), pp. 71, 74.

came to him he should be safe'. However, Charles had already secured a boat to take him to France; but he 'ever acknowledged the obligation with great kindness, he being the only person of that condition who had the courage to solicit such a danger'.[51] After the King's 'miraculous escape', Southampton 'used to say' that 'how dismal soever the prospect was, he had still a confidence of His Majesty's restoration'.[52] Yet the Earl was, in Hyde's words, 'of a nature very much inclined to melancholic',[53] and as a result felt highly pessimistic about any possibility of overthrowing the republic in the immediate future. Typically, he wanted the King to wait patiently for his fortunes to improve, not to work actively for the new régime's collapse. His advice to Charles was always 'to sit still, and expect a reasonable revolution, without making any unadvised attempt', and he 'industriously declined any conversation or commerce with any who were known to correspond with the King'.[54] After a while, Royalist activists ceased even to mention him in their correspondence.[55]

In general, this passivity also characterised Southampton's relationship with the new régime. According to Hyde, 'after the murder of the King' Southampton 'remained in his own house, without the least application to those powers which had made themselves so terrible'.[56] Although there is no evidence that his composition fine was ever paid, the Committee for Compounding apparently ceased to harry him.[57] Southampton was not among those Royalists known to have taken the Engagement.[58] Hyde tells us that Cromwell 'courted' the Earl, but that Southampton 'could never be persuaded so much as to see him; and when Cromwell was in the New Forest, and resolved one day to visit him, he being informed of it or suspecting it, removed to another house he had at such a distance as exempted him from that visitation'.[59] Yet there were exceptions to this political quietism. Just as Southampton had earlier fallen foul of Charles I's claims to royal forests,[60] so in November 1655 he refused to give Major-General Kelsey a 'perticular of his estate' to permit assessment for the Decimation Tax. As a result, he was briefly imprisoned in the Tower. Southampton claimed that the Decimation Tax violated the Oxford Articles, under which he had surrendered and compounded for his estates, and also the Rump Parliament's Act of General Pardon and Oblivion.[61] Southampton's

[51] Clarendon, *History*, V, 211 (Book XIII, §106). See also Allan Fea, *After Worcester Fight* (1904), pp. 38, 139–40.
[52] Clarendon, *Life*, III, 237.   [53] Clarendon, *History*, II, 529 (Book VI, §386).
[54] Clarendon, *Life*, I, 338–9.
[55] Underdown, *Royalist Conspiracy*, p. 156.   [56] Clarendon, *Life*, III, 236.
[57] *Calendar of the Committee for Compounding*, Green, II, 1507–8.
[58] Ward, 'English peerage', p. 512.   [59] Clarendon, *Life*, I, 338.
[60] See above, pp. 47–8.
[61] *Thurloe State Papers*, Birch, IV, 234; 'The Diary of Henry Townshend of Elmley Lovett, 1640–1663', ed. J. W. Willis Bund, *Publ. Worcs. Historical Society* (2 vols., 1916–20), I,

attitude grew out of a lifelong attachment to the rule of law, and we shall see that it was shared by other Constitutional Royalists such as Hyde. A consistent defence of legal propriety led such people to challenge the levies imposed by the Caroline and Cromwellian régimes alike.

Southampton was at liberty again by the end of 1655,[62] and from then until the Restoration he lived very quietly. We catch a brief glimpse of him towards the end of June 1656 visiting John Evelyn in London to see his garden.[63] Southampton's wife died late in 1658, and the following year he married Hertford's daughter Frances.[64] By this stage of his life, Southampton was clearly concerned primarily with his family and friends. Yet his determination to keep out of public affairs in no way diminished other Royalists' regard for him. Thus in June 1659, shortly before Booth's Rebellion, Hyde assured one of the leading conspirators John, Viscount Mordaunt, that he would find Southampton 'one of the most excellent persons living. Of great affection to the King; of great honor; and of an understanding superior to most men.'[65] Not surprisingly, there is no evidence to implicate the Earl in this rising.[66] But Hyde greatly valued Southampton's advice and regularly asked for his opinions.[67] He often enquired about the Earl and hoped that he was enjoying good health.[68] The fact that Southampton was held in such esteem within the exiled Court is crucial in explaining his appointment as Lord Treasurer at the Restoration.[69]

Richmond's other supposed executor, the Earl of Lindsey, had similarly chequered experiences during the Interregnum. Walker wrote that 'after the horrid murther of the King, this nobleman retired and lived privately, expecting and endeavouring the happy change of governm[en]t by His Ma[jes]t[ie]s restitucon'.[70] This perhaps hints that Lindsey made more active efforts to subvert the republic than Dorset, Richmond and Southampton, and although there is no direct evidence to sustain this, the

---

30–1. For the Act of General Pardon and Oblivion (24 February 1652), see Firth and Rait, *Acts and Ordinances*, II, 565–77.

[62] Underdown, *Royalist Conspiracy*, p. 165.   [63] *Diary of Evelyn*, Bray, II, 84.

[64] Christ Church Muniment Room, Oxford, Evelyn Collection, Nicholas to Browne Letters, unfol. (Nicholas to Sir Richard Browne, 18 December 1657); G. E. C., *Complete Peerage*, XII, part i, 133.

[65] HMC, *Tenth Report* (1887), part VI, 204 (Hyde to Mordaunt, 6 June 1659). For Mordaunt and Booth's Rebellion, see Underdown, *Royalist Conspiracy*, pp. 254–85; and J. S. Morrill, *Cheshire, 1630–1660* (Oxford, 1974), pp. 301, 303, 307, 311.

[66] Despite some unsuccessful attempts to involve him: see HMC, *Tenth Report*, part VI, 204; and *The Letter-Book of John Viscount Mordaunt, 1658–1660*, ed. Mary Coate (Camden Society, 3rd series, 69, 1945), 19 (Mordaunt to Charles II, 6 June 1659).

[67] Bodl. Lib., MS Clarendon 70, fo. 83r (Hyde to Lady Willoughby, 3 March 1659/60); MS Clarendon 71, fo. 61v ([Edward Villiers to Hyde], 28 March 1660).

[68] See, for example, Bodl. Lib., MS Clarendon 58, fo. 30v (Hyde to [Edward Villiers], 29 April 1658); and MS Clarendon 60, fo. 171r (Hyde to Villiers, 28 February 1658/9).

[69] See below, pp. 295–6.   [70] Bodl. Lib., MS Ashmole 1110, fo. 174v.

Council of State certainly monitored his movements very closely throughout the decade. On 3 February 1651, for example, Lindsey was granted 'libertie to remain in [London] to the end of this terme, which is granted unto him upon the motion of Sir Henri Vane, to the end hee may passe a recoverie upon some land sold by the said Earle'. A week later this licence was extended for another ten days; and on 24 February for five more days.[71] The other peers had never had their presence in the capital limited to such short periods of time. It seems that Lindsey needed to be in London to settle two rectories as well as to sell Bellew Abbey and other lands to Vane.[72] Once he had done that, and paid his composition fine, his estate was discharged from sequestration on 27 May. In August, following an approach to Bulstrode Whitelocke on Lindsey's behalf, this decision was confirmed provided that he really had settled the rectories on Vane and others as ordered.[73]

Lindsey's activities as a plaintiff in Chancery and Exchequer from 1652 onwards make it probable that he took the Engagement.[74] But his relationship with the government steadily deteriorated thereafter. In September 1653 Jeremiah Gosse, the minister at Heckfield in Hampshire, complained to the Committee for Compounding that Lindsey had refused to pay him his augmentation due on the Rectory at Edenham (Lincolnshire).[75] The Committee immediately ordered that if Lindsey did not pay Gosse within fourteen days they would instruct the County Commissioners to levy the amount with damages from the Earl's estates.[76] There is no evidence of such an instruction, which suggests that Lindsey paid up. But the government's continued mistrust of him was dramatically illustrated during June 1655. In the wake of Penruddock's Rising, and amid rumours of a plot to assassinate Cromwell, a number of prominent Royalists were arrested.[77] Accounts differ about what exactly happened to Lindsey. Lord Hatton informed Nicholas that he had been 'mildly bid keepe home', a story which Nicholas subsequently repeated to John Jane.[78] Other versions claimed

---

[71] PRO, SP 25/17 (Council of State draft order book), pp. 25, 57; SP 25/65, p. 24.

[72] *Calendar of the Committee for Compounding*, Green, II, 1503.

[73] *The Diary of Bulstrode Whitelocke, 1605–1675*, ed. Ruth Spalding (British Academy Records of Social and Economic History, new series, 13, Oxford, 1990), p. 276; PRO, SP 23/12 (Committee for Compounding order book), pp. 220–1, 287; *CJ*, VII, 170.

[74] Ward, 'English peerage', pp. 512, 515. See also BL, Add. MS 21427 (Baynes Correspondence), fos. 139v–145r.

[75] PRO, SP 23/87 (Committee for Compounding reports and petitions), p. 533. The Committee had ordered Lindsey to pay £40 a year to the minister at Heckfield out of Edenham Rectory on 14 January 1651: SP 23/12, p. 94.

[76] PRO, SP 23/25 (Committee for Compounding order book), fo. 189r.

[77] Underdown, *Royalist Conspiracy*, pp. 159–66.

[78] *The Nicholas Papers*, vol. III: *July 1655–December 1656*, ed. G. F. Warner (Camden Society, 2nd series, 57, 1897), 5 (Lord Hatton to Nicholas, 22 June 1655); PRO, SP 84/160, fo. 196r (Nicholas to John Jane, 29 June 1655).

that Lindsey was among those arrested and 'committed prisoners' in Oxfordshire.[79] How long this confinement lasted is not certain, but early in 1656 Robert Whitley reported that Lindsey, along with several other peers, had obtained letters from Cromwell 'to the Major Generalls and commissioners of the respective counties where they are concerned that they proceed not against them as to the matter of security, nor (as I take it) about theire tenths'.[80] As with Southampton, Cromwell's respect for Lindsey's status as a peer helped to soften the government's treatment of him. But Lindsey was not exempted from the Decimation Tax altogether. The Council of State subsequently allowed him to compound for the tax by paying a lump sum of £1,200.[81] It remained highly suspicious of the Earl and his family, especially whenever it faced the threat of Royalist conspiracies. Thus in August 1659, during Booth's Rebellion, the Council intercepted Lindsey's correspondence.[82] It also suspected that there had 'been attempts made to perswade' his eldest son Lord Willoughby 'to ioyne with the enemyes of the Commonwealth', and therefore required him to take an 'engagem[en]t upon his honor not to act ag[ains]t the Parlam[en]t and Commonwealth'. If Lord Willoughby refused this, his person was to be secured.[83] But it seems that Lindsey himself had nothing to do with the rising. Similarly, at the end of that year, he rejected the approaches of a group of Presbyterian peers – led by Northumberland and Manchester – who wished to negotiate with Charles on the basis of the Treaty of Newport.[84] Like Southampton, Lindsey wished to retire from politics and live quietly. Certainly this passivity was sometimes interrupted by moments of non-co-operation with the régime, as over the Decimation Tax. But in neither case did this extend to active resistance. The fact that Lindsey and Southampton were both briefly imprisoned during 1655 reflects less insurrectionary zeal on their part than the government's anxieties in the wake of Penruddock's Rising.

Another Constitutional Royalist peer who distanced himself from Northumberland and Manchester late in 1659 was the Marquess of Hertford.[85] This was entirely characteristic of Hertford's behaviour throughout the Interregnum. Like Richmond and Southampton, he had been perceived

[79] *Thurloe State Papers*, Birch, III, 537; *The Perfect Diurnall of some Passages and Proceedings*, no. 288 (11–18 June 1655), p. 4425 (*STC (News)*, 503.288; BL, TT, E 843/4). Cf. Underdown, *Royalist Conspiracy*, p. 163.
[80] *Nicholas Papers*, vol. III, Warner, 254 (Robert Whitley to Nicholas, 14 January 1655/6).
[81] PRO, SP 25/77 (Council of State fair order book), pp. 217, 355, 575.
[82] Bodl. Lib., MS Clarendon 63, fo. 163r (Major Gladman to the President of the Council of State, 9 August 1659).
[83] PRO, SP 25/98 (Council of State letter book), p. 95.
[84] *Letter-Book of Viscount Mordaunt*, Coate, 96 (Mordaunt to Charles II, 5 November 1659).
[85] *Ibid.*

in 1649–50 as a potential royal counsellor within England.[86] But, unlike them, Hertford was also a powerful landowner, with extensive lands concentrated in Somerset and Wiltshire, and this made him a much greater potential threat to the government. In March 1650, Presbyterian exiles suggested the Marquess as 'a very acceptable person' to become General of the King's forces.[87] For the next twelve months the Council of State kept him under close surveillance. In July 1650 he was ordered to 'make choyce of anie of the houses belonging unto [him] in Wiltshire' and to retire there.[88] Hertford chose his seat at Netley, and the following November the Council issued a recognizance for £20,000, together with two sureties for £10,000 each, for him to remain there until April 1651 on condition that he 'act nothing to the prejudice of the Commonwealth and present government thereof'.[89] Shortly before this licence expired, the Council informed Hertford that it would not be 'for the quiet and peace of the Commonwealth and the security of those parts' for him to 'continue there any longer', and ordered him to move to another house in Wiltshire. He was also told to prevent the resort of 'many dangerous and disaffected persons' to his house, and to 'give security for his acting nothing prejudiciall to the Commonwealth'.[90] Hertford's potential strength as a local magnate clearly remained formidable. In April 1651, Thomas Coke informed the Council of State that 'the Marquess of Hartford and his sonn are look't upon as persons of greatest interest for the Kinge in the County of Somersett'. In Wiltshire the Seymours likewise 'generally sway', especially Hertford and his brother Lord Seymour.[91]

It was, however, Hertford's eldest son Lord Beauchamp rather than the Marquess himself who involved the Seymour interest in conspiracy during 1650–1. Beauchamp took command of the Western Association, formed in May 1650, and built up an extensive network throughout the west of England.[92] However, his hopes were dashed by the King's inability to provide military assistance from the Continent.[93] Furthermore, Beauchamp's web of contacts was soon infiltrated by government agents.[94]

[86] *Nicholas Papers*, vol. I, Warner, 155; PRO, SP 18/9, fo. 20v.
[87] PRO, SP 18/9, fo. 20v.
[88] PRO, SP 25/8, p. 8.
[89] PRO, SP 25/13 (Council of State draft order book), p. 24; SP 25/120 (Council of State recognizances), p. 52.
[90] PRO, SP 25/65, p. 108; SP 25/96, pp. 48–9.   [91] Bodl. Lib., MS Dep. c. 169, fo. 184v.
[92] For the formation of the Western Association, see PRO, SP 18/9, fos. 88r–89r (account by Colonel Keyne, 10 May 1650).
[93] *Nicholas Papers*, vol. I, Warner, 178 (Lord Beauchamp to Charles II, 31 May 1650), 180–1 (Charles II to Lord Beauchamp, [? June] 1650), 231–2 (Nicholas to [Lord Beauchamp], 24 March 1650/1); Bodl. Lib., MS Clarendon 40, fo. 127r–v (Charles II to the Prince of Orange, [? July] 1650).
[94] There is a detailed account of the Western Association and of Beauchamp's role within it in Underdown, *Royalist Conspiracy*, pp. 31–5.

Despite the Council's suspicions, there is no evidence that Hertford was directly involved with Beauchamp's activities. In March 1650 he had encouraged his son to come to Netley, a place 'neither unpleasant nor unsafe' which had 'the advantage [of] being out of all roads'.[95] When, in April 1651, Beauchamp was denounced by Thomas Coke and imprisoned in the Tower,[96] Hertford wrote wryly to his son:

I am very gladd toe heare that you have your health soe well in the Towre. It seems it is a place entailed upon our famylie, for wee have now helde it five generations, yeat toe speake the truth I like not the place soe well but that I coulde be very well contented the entayle should be cutt off and settled upon some other familie that better deserves it.[97]

This letter illustrates both Hertford's sense of his own distinguished lineage and his conviction that political prominence had proved a mixed blessing for the Seymours. Beauchamp was granted the liberty of the Tower in June 1651.[98] He was finally released in September 1651 after swearing the Engagement and a bond of £10,000 together with two sureties of £5,000 each.[99] But within two years Beauchamp's health was failing, and he died in March 1654.[100] Brian Duppa, formerly chaplain to Dorset and a friend of Hertford, mourned Beauchamp as 'the only blossom left that looked like any thing of tru nobility'.[101] Insofar as 'tru nobility' could be equated with a willingness to take up arms against the republic, Beauchamp clearly was, as Dorothy Osborne observed, 'an extreordinary person' within the English peerage.[102]

The exiled Court was devastated by the news of Beauchamp's death. Charles II expressed his condolences to Hertford and promised always to

---

[95] HMC, *Fifteenth Report* (1897), part VII, 156 (Hertford to Lord Beauchamp, 25 March 1650).

[96] PRO, SP 25/65, pp. 250, 273, 278–9, 319, 334.

[97] HMC, *Twelfth Report* (1891), part IV, 47 (Hertford to Lord Beauchamp, 15 June 1651).

[98] PRO, SP 25/20 (Council of State draft order book), p. 8; HMC, *Twelfth Report*, part IV, 48 (Hertford to Lord Beauchamp, 27 July 1651).

[99] PRO, SP 25/22 (Council of State draft order book), pp. 39, 59.

[100] For an indication of Beauchamp's deteriorating health, see HMC, *Fifteenth Report*, part VII, 158 (Hertford to Lord Beauchamp, 31 July 1650). For his final illness, see HMC, *Bath (Longleat) Manuscripts*, vol. IV: *Seymour Papers, 1532–1686* (1968), 222–3 (Marchioness of Hertford to Thomas Gape, 16 February, 9 March 1653/4).

[101] 'The Correspondence of Bishop Brian Duppa and Sir Justinian Isham', ed. G. Isham, *Publ. Northamptonshire Record Society*, 17 (1955), 85 (Duppa to Isham, 11 April 1654). Duppa was successively Bishop of Chichester (1638), Salisbury (1641) and Winchester (1660). For his association with Hertford, see BL, Add. MS 32093 (Malet Collection), fo. 418. His link with Dorset and his theological views are analysed in David L. Smith, 'Catholic, Anglican or Puritan? Edward Sackville, fourth Earl of Dorset, and the ambiguities of religion in early Stuart England', *TRHS*, 6th series, 2 (1992), 114–15.

[102] *The Letters of Dorothy Osborne to William Temple*, ed. G. C. Moore Smith (Oxford, 1928), p. 158 (2 April 1654).

protect a family which had served him so loyally.[103] Hyde deplored the passing of 'a most excellent young man', and feared that it would leave 'all the businesse of the West without any order'.[104] Another who mourned the 'very great loss' of Lord Beauchamp was Sir Edward Nicholas. He lamented that henceforth 'the West will be much unprovided', but added that 'some others may be thought on; and, if once things were ripe for it, I am confident the Marquis of Hertford, though he be old, would not be idle'.[105] In the event, however, Hertford proved a disappointment. Although he was 'engaged' in Penruddock's Rising, and had some contact with its leader,[106] he appears to have kept his distance and communicated with the conspirators mainly through go-betweens.[107] Hopeful reports of Hertford appearing in Wiltshire 'at the head of five thousand men' proved unfounded, and Royalist exiles complained that 'men of condition' failed to provide leadership for the rising.[108] Major-General Desborough tried in vain to implicate the Marquess and Lord Seymour, but found that they had 'little stomach to meddle' in Royalist conspiracy.[109] All the signs are that Hertford wished to avoid an open confrontation with the régime. This is further suggested by his readiness to pay £515 towards the Decimation Tax in May 1656. His compliance was in marked contrast to Southampton's principled stand against the tax. Equally, the Somerset commissioners treated Hertford 'very mildly' by assessing him according to a 'particular but of a third part of his estates' rather than 'the lands' value'.[110] Similarly, when Seymour requested exemption from the tax, Cromwell personally instructed the Wiltshire commissioners 'to forbear the assessing' of him despite their open hostility.[111] This is another instance of Cromwell's willingness to bend rules in order to protect Royalist peers.[112]

The Lord Protector's wish to befriend Hertford, and the Marquess's equally strong desire to have as little as possible to do with the régime, were most clearly illustrated by an episode of about 1655. When Cromwell heard of Lord Beauchamp's death, he sent Sir Edward Sidenham to offer his condolences to Hertford. The Marquess 'would have been glad, Cromwel had spared that ceremony: but however received it in the best

---

[103] Bodl. Lib., MS Clarendon 48, fo. 232r (Charles II to Hertford, 21 May 1654).
[104] *Ibid.*, fo. 185r (Hyde to Nicholas, 28 April 1654).
[105] *Nicholas Papers*, vol. II, Warner, 66 (Nicholas to Hyde, 4 May 1654).
[106] *Nicholas Papers*, vol. III, Warner, 161–5 (examinations of Henry Manning, 8–9 December 1655).
[107] Underdown, *Royalist Conspiracy*, pp. 156–7.
[108] *Ibid.*; Bodl. Lib., MS Clarendon 50, fo. 17r ([Sir John Henderson to Thurloe], 30 March 1655).
[109] A. A. Locke, *The Seymour Family* (1911), p. 138.
[110] HMC, *Bath (Longleat) Manuscripts*, vol. IV, 281–2.
[111] PRO, SP 25/77, p. 102; *Thurloe State Papers*, Birch, IV, 609–10.
[112] For a discussion of this, see Ward, 'English peerage', especially pp. 85–124.

manner hee could, and returned a suitable acknowledgem[en]t for the same'. 'Some time after this', Cromwell invited Hertford to dinner. Hertford, 'considering it was in Cromwels power to ruine him and al his family', reluctantly accepted, and was greeted 'with open armes'. The Lord Protector then sought 'his advice what to do'. Hertford replied that 'he had served King Charles all along, and been of his private Council, and that it was no way consistent with his principles, that either the Protector should aske, or hee, the Marquis, adventure to give him any advice'. But Cromwell 'would receive no excuses nor denyals', and so Hertford eventually responded thus: 'Our young Master, that is abroad, that is, my Master, and the Master of us all, restore him to his crownes, and by doing this, you may have what you please.' Cromwell seemed in 'no way disturbed' by this answer, but replied calmly that 'hee had gone so farre, that the young gentleman could not forgive'. 'Thus they parted', Hertford's secretary recorded, 'and the Marquis had never any prejudice hereby so long as Cromwel lived.'[113] If reconciliation and co-operation were out of the question, the Protectorate did at least allow passive Royalists to live quietly and free from persecution.

From 1656 onwards, Hertford increasingly lapsed into what David Underdown has called 'senescent inactivity'.[114] His correspondence became gradually less concerned with national affairs and more preoccupied with his family and friends.[115] He was still interested in the fate of old allies, and in May 1656 was delighted to hear that Southampton was 'abroad again' after 'a violent fit of the stone'.[116] But in general it was very much a tale of retirement and quiescence. Hertford showed relatively little interest even in the problems of his estates. His composition fine had been reduced from £12,603 6s. 9d. to £8,345 in January 1648, but there is no evidence that this was ever paid.[117] His total debts probably stood at about £19,000 by 1652.[118] Ian Ward has argued that Hertford's estates revealed the limitations of a fine-based rental income. In particular, they illustrated the obstacles facing any attempt to rack-rent existing copyhold tenancies.

---

[113] BL, Add. MS 32093, fo. 348r–v. This is a post-Restoration account by Hertford's secretary, Dr Thomas Smyth, of a conversation which the British Library catalogue suggests may have occurred in 1656 or 1657. This is based on Smyth's statement that the dinner took place 'some time after' Lord Beauchamp's death, which he mistakenly dates to 1656 (rather than March 1654). Once this error is taken into account, 1655 emerges as a possible date for the encounter, a hypothesis which is reinforced by Hertford's declining activity from 1656 onwards. This must, however, remain highly speculative.

[114] Underdown, *Royalist Conspiracy*, p. 31.

[115] See especially HMC, *Bath (Longleat) Manuscripts*, vol. IV, 221–6.

[116] *Ibid.*, 225 (Hertford to the Marchioness of Hertford, 11 May 1656).

[117] PRO, SP 23/191 (Committee for Compounding particulars of estates and fines), p. 595.

[118] The following discussion of Hertford's estates is based on Ward, 'Rental policy', 30–2; 'English peerage', pp. 330–5, 364–7, 382–4, 404–11, 448–53; and 'Settlements, mortgages and aristocratic estates, 1649–1660', *The Journal of Legal History*, 12 (1991), 25–8.

To overcome these difficulties, Hertford fell back on a device which Ward has called 'the fulcrum of aristocratic settlements', the trust for debt.[119] Hertford established such trusts in 1652 and 1654 to mitigate debts, but severe financial problems still remained, obliging him to secure loans with bonds. Yet the Marquess became increasingly detached from such problems. He was twice reported to have gone abroad in 1656–7 in order to escape his creditors; his wife gradually took over the management of the Seymour estates, taking policy decisions and corresponding with stewards. By the Restoration, Hertford was at least as indebted as during the early 1650s.[120]

Notwithstanding this financial hardship, he nevertheless ranked as 'one of the most dependable patrons of distressed clergy' during the Interregnum.[121] It is probable that Hertford was involved in the charitable network for dispossessed clerics established by the high churchman Henry Hammond. Certainly a number of ministers, such as George Mason of St Clement Dane's in London, received regular payments from the Marquess and his wife. In 1657 another cleric, Thomas Pestell, applied to Hertford for 'relief and consolation in this world of hard bowells and encreasing misery'. Hertford seems to have been very ecumenical in his patronage: he befriended leading high churchmen such as Hammond and Duppa, but he was also associated with more moderate Church of England divines like John Gauden. Such an impressive list of clients and associates suggests that Hertford was rather more active in assisting impoverished clergy than the other Constitutional Royalist peers.

Where he was even less active than the others was in any bid to subvert the Commonwealth and Protectorate. Like Southampton, he advised the King 'to sit still, and expect a reasonable revolution, without making any unadvised attempt', and 'industriously declined any conversation or commerce with any who were known to correspond with the King'.[122] The report in March 1658 that he would 'bee stirring ass soone ass anie' proved to be groundless,[123] although the government's edginess may help to explain why a licence for his brother Seymour to visit London shortly afterwards was limited to 'the space of one moneth'.[124] Mordaunt hoped to rouse Hertford in May 1659, but he was old and unwilling to correspond.[125] Reluctant to contemplate active resistance, the Seymours instead

---

[119] Ward, 'Settlements', 28.
[120] Ward, 'English peerage', pp. 384, 406, n. 1, 408–10, 450–1.
[121] *Ibid.*, p. 214. This paragraph offers my interpretation of the evidence presented in *ibid.*, pp. 210–11, 214–18.
[122] Clarendon, *Life*, I, 338–9.
[123] Bodl. Lib., MS Clarendon 57, fo. 260r (Daniel O'Neale to Hyde, [? 3] March 1657/8).
[124] PRO, SP 25/78 (Council of State fair order book), p. 578.
[125] *Letter-Book of Viscount Mordaunt*, Coate, 14 (Hyde to Mordaunt, 13 May 1659).

placed their faith in an eventual change in the political climate which would restore the monarchy. Lord Seymour, in a book of meditations and prayers dictated to his daughter Frances beginning on 3 May 1655 insisted: 'Let our troubls heare be what they will, this must bee our comfort, that noe power whatsoever can keepe us from goeinge unto God, and from powringe forth our supplyecations unto him; whoe in his owne good time will answer us.' Afflictions were positively to be welcomed, for they were sent by God as 'fatherly corrections proceedinge from love; not from anger'. Seymour therefore hoped that his fellow Royalists would rejoice that they were 'counted worthy to suffer in a good cause'.[126] Similarly, barely two months before the Restoration, Hertford told Duppa 'with a great deal of chearfullness what comforts he found when he repeated the 57th Psalme, particularly in those words, "Under the shadow of thy wings shall be my refuge, till this tyranny be overpast"'.[127] The story of Constitutional Royalists in England during the 1650s could be written around that remark. Their refusal to subvert or confront the republic was founded on an underlying conviction that the Stuarts would ultimately return, and that a premature insurrection could only endanger this outcome.

III

By contrast, this was an issue which proved more divisive within the exiled Court. One group, known as the 'Louvre' party, believed that the King should seek a military alliance with the Scots and later with the French in order to regain his throne by force. The 'Louvre' was led by Henrietta Maria and Henry Jermyn, but also included Lords Percy and Culpepper. It was opposed by an 'Old Royalist' group which believed that such alliances involved compromising fundamental political and religious principles. These Royalists – of whom Hyde was the most articulate and influential – felt instead that the King should wait patiently until a change in the political climate brought his peaceful restoration. Between these two groups stood a third, the so-called 'Swordsmen' led by Prince Rupert, which tended to adopt a less principled line and to attack whichever of the other factions currently held sway. Although, as Ronald Hutton has recently reminded us, these groupings were never watertight and individuals sometimes moved between them, they do represent the basic alignments. The dynamics of these three parties during the Interregnum have been analysed

---

[126] BL, Egerton MS 71 (meditations and prayers of Lord Seymour), fos. 4r–5r.
[127] 'Correspondence of Duppa and Isham', Isham, 85 (Duppa to Isham, 27 February 1659/60).

in detail elsewhere.[128] Here I just want to delineate the attitudes of the two exiles who had been most closely associated with Constitutional Royalism in the 1640s, Hyde and Culpepper, and to explore how they perceived developments during the next decade.

In general, Hyde's position was very comparable to that of the Constitutional Royalists who remained in England.[129] He later characterised it as the belief

that the King had nothing at this time to do but to be quiet, and that all his activity was to consist in carefully avoiding to do any thing that might do him hurt, and to expect some blessed conjuncture from the amity of Christian princes, or some such revolution of affairs in England by their own discontents and divisions amongst themselves, as might make it seasonable for His Majesty again to show himself.[130]

As Brian Wormald has argued,[131] this was not a retrospective self-justification: there is plentiful evidence that Hyde expressed such views in both public and private throughout the 1650s. But they were not calculated to find favour at Court in 1649–51. Instead, these years saw a disastrous Scottish alliance which culminated in the battle of Worcester. Hyde's political eclipse was signalled by his embassy to Madrid in May 1649.[132]

During his stay in Madrid, he resumed work on his *Contemplations and Reflections upon the Psalms of David*, and completed the commentaries on Psalms IX–LXVII.[133] These meditations throw floods of light on Hyde's frame of mind at the start of the 1650s. Above all, they emphasise the need for courage in adversity and the importance of waiting patiently on God. He placed his hopes in 'some sudden revolution of providence', trusting that 'when God pleases he can appear and manifest himself in all this terrible equipage for the preservation of those who entirely rely and depend on him'.[134] God thus acted as 'a second, who never fails if we call upon

[128] See Underdown, *Royalist Conspiracy*, especially pp. 10–12, 60–3, 243–4, 303–6; Richard Ollard, *Clarendon and his Friends* (1987), pp. 123–219; and Ronald Hutton, *Charles II: King of England, Scotland, and Ireland* (Oxford, 1989), pp. 34–132.
[129] For detailed accounts of Hyde's career during the Interregnum, see especially T. H. Lister, *Life and Administration of Edward, First Earl of Clarendon* (3 vols., 1837–8), I, 326–517; Sir Henry Craik, *The Life of Edward, Earl of Clarendon, Lord High Chancellor of England* (2 vols., 1911), I, 319–94; and Ollard, *Clarendon and his Friends*, pp. 123–219.
[130] Clarendon, *History*, V, 240 (Book XIII, §140).
[131] B. H. G. Wormald, *Clarendon: Politics, History and Religion, 1640–1660* (Cambridge, 1951; repr. 1989), p. 204.
[132] Bodl. Lib., MS Clarendon 37, fo. 94r (letters patent appointing Hyde and Cottington ambassadors to Spain, 10 May 1649). See also *Nicholas Papers*, vol. I, ed. Warner, 124–5 (Hyde to Nicholas, 27 March 1649).
[133] The *Contemplations* are printed in *A Compleat Collection of Tracts, by that Eminent Statesman the Right Honourable Edward, Earl of Clarendon* (1747), pp. 349–768. For discussions of them, see Ollard, *Clarendon and his Friends*, pp. 134–40; and Wormald, *Clarendon*, pp. 165–70, 175–7.
[134] *Compleat Collection of Tracts by Clarendon*, pp. 419, 421 (Psalm 18).

him as we ought; and knows well how to grapple with our fair-speaking adversaries, and to proportion punishments to their transgressions'.[135] In due course, the Royalists would 'find that our constancy and patience for suffering in a good cause hath made God propitious to us, and provided a Crown of Glory for our reward', whereas their enemies would be 'confounded with shame and sorrow'.[136] However, in order to deserve 'this wonderful vindication of providence', the exiles had to be 'honest as well as miserable'.[137] The best remedy for their 'low and even hopeless condition' lay in prayer; for when God saw their 'single and entire confidence in him', he would sow 'jealousies and divisions amongst our enemies'.[138] In the meantime, Hyde urged his fellow exiles to 'make the right use of our affliction, and improve our selves, and grow the better by them'.[139] They could turn their suffering to advantage, for 'adversity is the natural parent of reformation in understanding and affections, it refines and purifies men's natures, and begets a warmth and light of piety and religion'. It was possible to 'hallow and consecrate any wilderness into a Temple'.[140] Robbed of property and political power, exiled from England and her Church, the Royalists were thrown back on to their own personal piety: they turned inward, to prayer and contemplation, in preparation for 'some sudden revolution of providence'. This was the spiritual counterpart to the political retreat so characteristic of those Royalists who remained in England. Like them, Hyde felt an inner confidence that the tide of events would ultimately turn in their favour, and thought that in the meantime they should wait patiently and make themselves worthy of such a happy outcome.

The same themes pervaded Hyde's private correspondence during the Interregnum. Writing to his wife in May 1650, he confided: 'seriously I do not in the least degree despayre that God Almighty will bringe those rogues to confusion, and restore the Kinge, albeit, he hath a very harde journy, and a melancholique prospecte towards it'.[141] Three months later he told Nicholas:

Wee must only rely upon God Almighty, who will in the end bringe light out of this darkenesse, and I am confident, they who shall in spight of all evill examples continue honest and steady to ther good principles, what distresses soever they may for a tyme suffer, will in the end finde happinesse even in this world, and that all your dextrous complyers will be exposed to the infamy they deserve.[142]

---

[135] *Ibid.*, p. 517 (Psalm 58).   [136] *Ibid.*, p. 521 (Psalm 59).
[137] *Ibid.*, p. 421 (Psalm 18).
[138] *Ibid.*, p. 509 (Psalm 54).   [139] *Ibid.*, p. 468 (Psalm 37).
[140] *Ibid.*, pp. 530–1 (Psalm 63).
[141] HMC, *Manuscripts of the Marquis of Bath*, vol. II (1907), 91 (Hyde to Lady Hyde, 13 May 1650).
[142] Bodl. Lib., MS Clarendon 40, fo. 141r (Hyde to Nicholas, 6 August 1650).

Royalists would do well to remember that there was 'another Court to appeare in when we are out of this'. But if they held tight to 'foundacons of virtue and innocense' they would 'live to see exemplary judgem[en]ts upon this proiecting, restlesse, vayne people'.[143] Meanwhile, he knew 'not how to give a man better counsell then to sitt still',[144] and advocated a life of retirement and contemplation. In the early 1650s, he looked forward to 'livinge a yeare together with' Nicholas, 'studyinge harde, and mendinge one another, upon recollection of all that is past'. But above all he hoped that they would 'yet ... live to inioy each other in our owne country'.[145] Hyde felt the experience of exile – with all its Biblical resonances – very keenly, and lamented that he 'could be as well contented to lyve in poore Wiltshyre as in any place' he had seen.[146] But a return to England was contingent upon the patience and piety of the Royalist party in general and of Charles II in particular. As Hyde warned the King in November 1651: 'Your Ma[jes]ties owne fate, and that of your three kingdomes depends now purely upon your owne virtue.'[147] As always, Hyde believed that monarchs could not do as they pleased, but had to follow certain codes in both their personal and political conduct. He lamented the King's pursuit of pleasure and unwillingness 'to write himself three or fowre howres together'.[148] But the importance of royal 'virtue' went well beyond this, for it was also intimately related to the whole notion of a legally limited monarchy.

Hyde's constitutional beliefs remained absolutely consistent throughout the Interregnum. An unpublished declaration which he drafted at the beginning of March 1649 clearly expressed his position shortly after the 'odious and execrable murther' of Charles I.[149] Characteristically, he began by condemning the 'inconvenience and mischieve of departinge from the knowne rule of the law'. The Church of England, which had been 'as full of learninge and true piety and as voyde of errour and corrupcion as God had voutsafed to any people since the tyme of his Apostles' had been overthrown, and 'all the errors, heresyes and schismes which had bene ever heard of in the world' revived. Similarly, Parliament's privileges could never be maintained 'by those who denyed and snatched away all

[143] Bodl. Lib., MS Clarendon 39, fo. 112r (Hyde to the Countess of Morton, 8 March 1649/50).
[144] Bodl. Lib., MS Clarendon 42, fo. 168v (Hyde to Nicholas, 14 October 1651).
[145] Bodl. Lib., MS Clarendon 41, fo. 177v (Hyde to Nicholas, 30 January 1650/1).
[146] HMC, *Manuscripts of the Marquis of Bath*, vol. II, 85 (Hyde to Lady Hyde, 1 October 1649).
[147] Bodl. Lib., MS Clarendon 42, fo. 191r (Hyde to Charles II, 31 October 1651).
[148] Bodl. Lib., MS Clarendon 45, fo. 199r (Hyde to Nicholas, 18 March 1652/3).
[149] S. R. Gardiner, 'Draft by Sir Edward Hyde of a Declaration to be issued by Charles II in 1649', *EHR*, 8 (1893), 300–7 (printing Bodl. Lib., MS Clarendon 37, fos. 24r–27r), from which the following quotations are taken.

priviledge from the heade of the Parliament'. 'Religion, Law, Liberty, Lords and Parliament' had all lost 'ther true vigour and lustre . . . from the tyme that the King's power was eclipsed', and an army which dissolved 'all knowne lawes' had replaced 'the King that governed by law'. Only Charles II could 'vindicate the knowne and confessed lawes of the kingdome'. In terms which prefigured the Declaration of Breda, Hyde promised on the King's behalf 'a full and free convention of Parliament'; a 'Nationall Synod' to resolve 'the differences and disputes in religion'; and a 'full and gratious pardon to all . . . persons' other than those 'enimyes to mankinde' the regicides. However, the King's councillors registered so many objections – not least that Hyde's praise of the Church of England might endanger the Scottish alliance – that the 'declaration slept'.[150] Yet although never issued, the draft remains significant as a summary of Hyde's political and ecclesiastical attitudes in the immediate aftermath of the Regicide.

The remarkable consistency of Hyde's constitutional views – and above all his intense commitment to the rule of law – is most strikingly evident in *A Letter from a True and Lawfull Member of Parliament*, published anonymously in 1656.[151] Here he assumed the voice of a moderate Parliamentarian who had remained at Westminster during the 1640s and been expelled at Pride's Purge. This fictitious Parliamentarian had sided with those 'who were believed most intent and solicitous to free the subject from the vexations and pressures he had been made liable to'. But he now found that the Decimation Tax infringed the rule of law more violently than any Caroline levies. It was 'inconsistent with the elements of law, equity and religion', and uprooted 'all the laws and foundations of right, which are the onely security of every honest and free-born Englishman'.[152] This desire to protect the rule of law represented the hard core of Hyde's constitutional thought. It had motivated his attack on Charles I's policies in 1640–1, and his subsequent defence of the Crown's legal powers during successive peace negotiations. Now it prompted him to denounce the Lord Protector's introduction of a tax which 'pulls up all property and liberty by the roots, reduces all our law, common and statute, to the dictates of your own will, and all reason to that which you, and you alone, will call reason of State, and which we are obliged in the next place to examine, as our *Parva Charta*, and the funeral oration upon Parliaments, law, conscience and equity'.[153] As a result, 'the large bulk of our laws and records, which establish our liberty and our property, may be reduced into a very small

---

[150] Clarendon, *History*, V, 39–43 (Book XII, §§41–6).
[151] [Edward Hyde], *A Letter from a True and Lawfull Member of Parliament* (1656), Wing, C 4424; BL, TT, E 884/2. Hyde's authorship of this tract is established by the survival of his original manuscript in Bodl. Lib., MS Clarendon 50, fos. 256r–269v.
[152] [Hyde], *Letter*, pp. 5, 7, 10.   [153] *Ibid.*, p. 38.

volume'. The levy 'which came nearest' to the Decimation Tax, 'yet strayed at a great distance from it', was Ship Money, and Hyde condemned both for exactly the same reasons.[154] As we have seen, other Constitutional Royalists such as Southampton shared this objection to the Decimation Tax as a violation of the rule of law.

The *Letter* also revealed Hyde's continuing devotion to the role of Parliament within the polity. He complained that Cromwell had 'pulled up Parliaments by the roots, which are the onely natural security the nation can have against oppression and tyrannie, and which we thought we had exactly provided for by the Triennial Bill'.[155] Once again, his support for the constitutional reforms of 1640–1 was clear. Hyde expressed a similar view to Ormond in March 1656 as he considered the possibility of a rapprochement with the Levellers: 'You cannot extoll the priviledges of *Magna Charta* to much, nor make to ample promises for the confirmacon of them; magnify the power of free Parliam[en]ts as much as they and attribute as much to them.'[156] He felt able to contemplate such an arrangement because these were ideals which he consistently espoused himself.

On the other hand, Hyde believed that the King should avoid strategic alliances which involved in any way compromising these fundamental principles. In September 1649 he urged Charles 'to treat with noe party which shall refuse frankly and entirely to joyne with his Majesties party'.[157] The following year he hoped that the King would not make 'such concessions' to the Scots 'as may by degrees produce a resurrection of that accursed Parliam[en]t in England'.[158] With the disastrous defeat of the Scottish alliance at Worcester, Hyde's policy stood vindicated, and from the end of 1651 he dominated the King's counsels. He had several prominent enemies at Court, most notably Jermyn.[159] But nobody seriously doubted that he was 'Charles Stuart's great confident'; or, as Thurloe's spy Henry Manning put it, one of 'that faccion' who 'rule the roaste'.[160]

Manning also observed that Hyde 'designe[d] for the King in England';[161] and it seems that by the mid-1650s he was actively encouraging Royalists to conspire. He was involved with the Sealed Knot from

---

[154] *Ibid.*, pp. 44, 46.   [155] *Ibid.*, pp. 68–9.
[156] Bodl. Lib., MS Clarendon 51, fo. 100v (Hyde to the Earl of Ormond, 7 March 1655/6).
[157] *Nicholas Papers*, vol. I, Warner, 146 (memorandum by Hyde, 30 September 1649).
[158] Bodl. Lib., MS Clarendon 39, fo. 110r (Hyde to Henrietta Maria, 8 March 1649/50).
[159] See, for example, *Nicholas Papers*, vol. I, Warner, 128 (Lord Hatton to Nicholas, 26 May 1648), 294 (Nicholas to Lord Hatton, 15 April 1652).
[160] *Thurloe State Papers*, Birch, II, 327; *Nicholas Papers*, vol. III, Warner, 177–8 (examinations of Henry Manning, 8–9 December 1655). Cf. PRO, SP 18/77/52 (Nicholas to John Jane, 8 December 1654); SP 77/32, fo. 56r (Gilbert Talbot to Nicholas, 5 March 1657/8); and *Letters and Journals of Baillie*, Laing, III, 387.
[161] *Nicholas Papers*, vol. III, Warner, 178.

1654 onwards,[162] and was widely perceived as 'if not the sole, yet the cheife manager of' Penruddock's Rising.[163] By the end of 1655, Hyde and Ormond were thought to be 'the engines' who wished to promote further risings.[164] But although they did not rule out foreign alliances, they relied primarily upon the King's friends within England. Hyde's correspondence during the later 1650s is littered with regrets about the passivity of English Royalists, and approaches to individuals who might be persuaded to conspire. In September 1656, for example, we find him asking one of his closest contacts, Sir Marmaduke Langdale, for the names of individuals in Northern England 'upon whose interest and discrecon wee may well depende'.[165] Hyde realised that without 'some good accidents in England on our behalfe' a Royalist expedition from the Spanish Netherlands was quite impossible.[166] But such 'extraordinary accidents'[167] were difficult to foresee, and Hyde lamented in January 1659 that the Royalists had 'not yett founde that advantage by Cromwell's death as [they] reasonably hoped for'. If anything, they were 'the worse for it, and the lesse esteemed, people imagininge by the greate calme that hath followed, that the nacon is united, and that in truth the Kinge hath very few frends'.[168] Ironically, it was precisely because English Royalists embraced the quietism which Hyde himself had advocated that they felt unable to subvert the republic. The disastrous failure of Booth's Rebellion in August 1659 only seemed to confirm that a restoration of the monarchy was as far away as ever.[169] Hyde recorded that at the beginning of 1660 the Royalists were 'totally suppressed and dispirited' for they 'looked upon the government as more securely settled against domestic disturbances ... than it had been under Cromwell himself'.[170] At that stage, upheavals which might benefit the King were 'but faint hopes, and grounded upon such probabilities as despairing men are willing to entertain'.[171]

Only one prescient Royalist had foreseen what would happen next. A few days after Cromwell's death, Culpepper advised Hyde 'not [to] be over hasty in doing any thing in England, neither by proclayming the King, nor by any other publick act, untill you shall trewly and particularly know the

---

[162] Clarendon, *Life*, I, 339–40; Underdown, *Royalist Conspiracy*, pp. 87–90.
[163] *Nicholas Papers*, vol. II, Warner, 267 (Peter Mews to Nicholas, 23 April 1655).
[164] *Thurloe State Papers*, Birch, IV, 169.
[165] Folger Shakespeare Library, Washington, DC, MS X.d.18 (Clarendon correspondence), items 2, 3 (Hyde to Sir Marmaduke Langdale, 11, 18 September 1656).
[166] Bodl. Lib., MS Clarendon 61, fo. 84r (Hyde to [Alan Brodrick], 3 June 1659).
[167] Bodl. Lib., MS Clarendon 57, fo. 362v (Hyde to Mordaunt, 12 April 1658).
[168] Bodl. Lib., MS Clarendon 59, fo. 417r (Hyde to [William Howard], 12 January 1658/9).
[169] For Booth's Rebellion, see Underdown, *Royalist Conspiracy*, pp. 254–85; and Morrill, *Cheshire*, pp. 300–25.
[170] Clarendon, *History*, VI, 163 (Book XVI, §§111, 113).
[171] *Ibid.*, 164 (Book XVI, §115).

state of affaires there'. He warned against a premature strike which would 'only serve to unite our ennemyes and confirme their new governement by a victory over us, whereby wee shall be utterly disabled to doe our duty when the trew season shall come, which I doute not will quickly be, if wee have but the patience to waite for it'. Then followed this remarkable passage:

The person that my eye is cheefly on, as able alone to restore the King, and not absolutely avers to it, neither in his principles nor in his affections . . . is Monke, who commandeth absolutely at his devotion a better army . . . then that in England is, and in the King's quarrell can bringe with him the strength of Scotland, and soe protect the northerne countyes that he cannot faile of them in his march, the reputation whereof (if he declare) will as much give the will to the appearing of the King's party in the rest of England, as the drawing the army from the southerne, westerne and easterne countyes will give them the meanes to appeare in armes. Thus the worke will be certainly donne in spight of all opposition that can be apprehended, and the gaining of one man will alone make sure worke of the whole.[172]

This predicted with astonishing accuracy the chain of events which would lead to Charles II's restoration nearly two years later. It was possibly Culpepper's shrewdest political insight, and one of his finest moments in a decade which had seen his influence wax and wane dramatically.

Culpepper was closely associated with the 'Louvre' group, led by Jermyn and Henrietta Maria, which dominated the King's counsels in the immediate aftermath of the Regicide.[173] In November 1649 they were, one observer noted, 'fixed and rivetted into the King's court'.[174] Culpepper's principal goal in these years was to promote a rapprochement with the Scots, a policy which marked a continuation of his stance during the later 1640s.[175] But Culpepper was anxious to secure alliances with other powers as well: he was 'angry and offended' not to be sent as ambassador to Spain in the spring of 1649; and the following year he was despatched to Moscow 'to borrow money of that Duke'.[176] This mission proved highly successful. Culpepper was feted in Moscow – one meal consisted of a hundred dishes of meat – and he returned triumphantly in July 1650 with a loan of twenty thousand roubles.[177] But with the King's defeat at Worcester the advice of the 'Louvre' group was discredited and its influence began to decline. In

---

[172] Bodl. Lib., MS Clarendon 58, fos. 345v–346v (Culpepper to Hyde, 10 September 1658).
[173] Underdown, *Royalist Conspiracy*, pp. 10–11.
[174] *Nicholas Papers*, vol. I, Warner, 152 ([? Lord Hatton] to Nicholas, 1 November 1649).
[175] *A Collection of Original Letters and Papers*, ed. Tho[mas] Carte (2 vols., 1739), I, 213; *Nicholas Papers*, vol. I, Warner, 117 (Lord Hatton to Nicholas, 27 February 1648/9). Cf. above, pp. 129–32, 149–50.
[176] Clarendon, *History*, V, 36 (Book XII, §38), 233 (Book XIII, §130).
[177] A detailed account of Culpepper's embassy to Moscow may be found in *Nicholas Papers*, vol. I, Warner, 182–5. See also Bodl. Lib., MS Dep. c. 169, fo. 176r (Thomas Coke's depositions before the Council of State, April 1651).

April 1652 Nicholas wrote bluntly to Hyde: 'I believe all those lords [Culpepper, Percy and Jermyn] go upon as ill principles as may be; for I doubt there is few of them that would not do anything almost, and advise the K[ing] to do anything, that may probably recover his or their estates.'[178] Nicholas found Culpepper 'not only unfortunate in his counsels but incompatible in business', and remained opposed to his preferment.[179] Hyde took a more relaxed view and argued that Culpepper and Jermyn had already lost much of their former influence, 'the Kinge very sufficiently knowing [them], and trusting them accordingly'.[180] An attempt to resurrect 'the whole businesse of Sco[t]l[an]d' in May 1654 proved abortive;[181] and a further symptom of Culpepper's dwindling power came the following October when he urged Lord Percy 'to come to the King's Court for he needs helpe'.[182] Although in December 1655 Henry Manning listed Culpepper among 'that faccion' who 'rule the roaste',[183] it is clear that he was a much more marginal figure from the mid-1650s. He professed himself 'a great stranger to all busines, especially designes in England, and was very seldom' at Court.[184] Thereafter, as Richard Ollard writes, he 'remained in touch with the Court rather than a member of it'.[185]

Throughout the decade his relationship with Hyde was ambivalent. After the Restoration, Hyde claimed that although they were 'not thought to have the greatest kindness for each other, yet he knew he could agree with no other man so well in business, and was very unwilling [Culpepper] should be from the person of the King'.[186] Hyde described him as 'a man of great parts, a very sharp and present wit, and an universal understanding'.[187] It is difficult to assess how far Hyde's memory deceived him. Certainly contemporaries frequently remarked on his poor relations with Culpepper. Lord Hatton even thought Culpepper 'a sworne enemy to Sir E[dward] H[yde] even to death'.[188] Yet by the late 1650s they were more closely aligned politically than at any stage during the Interregnum. Culpepper warmly congratulated Hyde on his appointment as Lord Chancellor in January 1658.[189] Far from chivvying for immediate expeditions,

---

178 *Nicholas Papers*, vol. I, Warner, 293–4 (Nicholas to Hyde, 8 April 1652).
179 *Ibid.*, 315 (Nicholas to Hyde, 14 October 1652); *Nicholas Papers*, vol. II, Warner, 18 (Nicholas to Hyde, 4 August 1653).
180 Bodl. Lib., MS Clarendon 45, fo. 6r (Hyde to Nicholas, 24 December 1652).
181 Bodl. Lib., MS Clarendon 48, fo. 185r (Hyde to Nicholas, 28 April 1654).
182 *Nicholas Papers*, vol. II, Warner, 113 (Lord Hatton to Nicholas, 20 October 1654).
183 *Nicholas Papers*, vol. III, Warner, 177–8.
184 *Nicholas Papers*, vol. II, Warner, 252 (Joseph Jane to Nicholas, 13 April 1655).
185 Ollard, *Clarendon and his Friends*, p. 179.
186 Clarendon, *History*, V, 37 (Book XII, §38).
187 Clarendon, *Life*, I, 319.
188 *Nicholas Papers*, vol. II, Warner, 101 (Lord Hatton to Nicholas, 16 October 1654). See also PRO, SP 18/99/34 ([Andrew Manning to Thurloe], 10 July 1655).
189 PRO, SP 77/32, fo. 14v (Culpepper to [Nicholas], 8 January 1657/8).

the following March Culpepper warned that no further design should be attempted 'except some happy accidents in England should soone open [the King] a doore there'.[190] His attitude thus coincided perfectly with Hyde's. For neither of them, however, did this preclude negotiations with the French and Spanish monarchs, and in the autumn of 1659 Culpepper made a trip to Spain explicitly 'to serve the Chancelor'.[191] He kept Hyde closely briefed throughout that trip.[192] Then, as events at home began to unfold exactly as he had predicted, Culpepper contemplated the future with confidence: 'God keep you', he wrote to Sir Richard Browne in April 1660, 'and bringe us together quietly at Whitehall.'[193]

IV

Meanwhile, back in England, the last of our Constitutional Royalists, Sir John Strangways, lived in retirement throughout the Interregnum. Following his release from the Tower and permission to compound for £10,000 in March 1648,[194] he immediately returned to his seat at Melbury Sampford in Dorset.[195] The following May, having paid £5,000 and secured the rest, Strangways's sequestration was discharged.[196] In October 1649 he told Sir Simonds D'Ewes, a distant relative with whom he shared a love for antiquarianism, that 'the greatest part' of his collection of 'old evidences' had been 'either burnt or plundered', and the rest 'throwne into one heape' and 'tumbled into a great chest'. Furthermore, he had suffered 'a long desperate sickness' from which he was 'not yett fully recovered'.[197] Thereafter, like the other Constitutional Royalists, he seems to have become a recluse. When the King visited Melbury Sampford during his flight after Worcester it fell to Strangways's eldest surviving son Giles to give him £100 in gold and to apologise for being unable to provide the fleeing monarch with a boat.[198] Certainly the family's political loyalties were firm, although

[190] *Ibid.*, fo. 76r (Culpepper to Nicholas, 18 March 1657/8).
[191] Christ Church Muniment Room, Oxford, Evelyn Collection, Browne Letters, R–W, unfol. (Edmund Windham to Sir Richard Browne, 13 October 1659).
[192] *The Nicholas Papers*, vol. IV: *1657–1660*, ed. G.F. Warner (Camden Society, 3rd series, 31, 1920), 186 (Culpepper to Nicholas, 22 October 1659).
[193] Christ Church Muniment Room, Oxford, Evelyn Collection, Nobility Letters, A–H, fo. 67r (Culpepper to Sir Richard Browne, 3 April 1660).
[194] See above, p. 204.
[195] PRO, SP 23/120 (Committee for Compounding particulars of estates and fines), pp. 558, 575–6.
[196] *Ibid.*, pp. 573, 579; PRO, SP 23/4, fo. 202r–v.
[197] *The Autobiography and Correspondence of Sir Simonds D'Ewes, Bart.*, ed. J. O. Halliwell (2 vols., 1845), II, 317 (Strangways to Sir Simonds D'Ewes, 23 October 1649). Cf. Dorset RO, Fox-Strangways (Earls of Ilchester) MS, D 124, box 263, unfol. (account of Strangways's estate in verse, 1 May 1650).
[198] Fea, *After Worcester Fight*, pp. 188–9; *The Flight of the King* (1897), pp. 121–3, 271, 280.

covert. Colonel Keyne listed Giles Strangways among those who acted 'very zealously to advance the King's business' in the west.[199] Small wonder, then, that even though Sir John Strangways apparently played no part in Penruddock's Rising, he was one of the Dorset gentry rounded up and incarcerated in Dorchester gaol in the wake of that rising.[200]

While once more in prison, Strangways wrote a poem which captured the mood of Constitutional Royalists during the mid-1650s as vividly as *Coopers Hill* had that of 1641. Entitled 'Upon a private and retyred life', this declared that to 'seeke lost creditt to regayne' was to 'spend tyme in vayne'. Rather, Strangways vowed that:

> for ease and quyett I will trade
> From hence-forth in the darke and silent shade.

It was

> a safe way in this distemper'd tyme,
> To keepe me from suspicion of a cryme
> He that from all men hydes, none seekes to find,
> For he that's out of sight, is out of mind.

He hoped that such a retreat would enable him to

> Avoyd the stroakes of publique enmitie,
> Whereas if I lye buskinge in the sunne,
> Tis ten to one, but I shalbe undone.

This did not imply that he was indifferent to 'whither good men speake well or ill of me', for he wished to merit 'all good men's good thoughts'. But he was convinced that any fresh charges against him could only arise

> From base-false feares, and feigned jealosyes:
> And tis my comfort they will find noe cause
> To warrant their proceedings by the lawes.

Characteristically, Strangways perceived the rule of law as his best protection against the Interregnum régimes. Like Hyde, he put his faith in the long-term rewards which patience and virtue would surely receive:

> Pure innocence is long breath'd and itt will
> Runne long, and strong against a Craggie Hyll.

With that assurance, and trusting in 'God's grace', he rejoiced that 'on my sufferings I may sitt and smile'.[201]

Strangways was one of about twenty Dorset gentry summoned before

---

[199] PRO, SP 18/9, fo. 88r.
[200] David Underdown, *Fire from Heaven: The Life of an English Town in the Seventeenth Century* (1992), p. 215.
[201] Beinecke Library, Yale University, Osborn MS b. 304 (commonplace book of Sir John Strangways), pp. 138–9.

Desborough in December 1655. He pleaded 'his integrity', but after the Major-General 'dealt very plainly and indeed roundly' with him he finally agreed to pay the Decimation Tax and was released.[202] Thereafter, he apparently lived in retirement at Melbury Sampford until the Restoration. But the attitudes expressed in his poem had a broader significance that transcended the particular circumstances of its composition. His feelings were broadly shared by each of the Constitutional Royalists examined in this chapter. Furthermore, his philosophy of present retreat and trust in future rewards was a central theme of Royalist literature during the Interregnum. It was bound up with delight in a private world of inner peace and piety, often in the country, where strength was drawn from God, family and friends. It would be impossible here to do full justice to this aspect of the 'Cavalier mode'; but a discussion of Strangways and his poem leads us naturally to a handful of examples which illustrate how closely the outlook of leading Constitutional Royalists was mirrored in contemporary poetry and prose.[203]

Henry Vaughan, the metaphysical poet who wrote two poems entitled 'Retirement' and one called 'The Retreat', makes a good starting-point.[204] He practised as a lawyer and as a doctor before turning to poetry in the mid-1640s.[205] Shortly after the Regicide, probably in March 1649,[206] he wrote the poem which is most directly relevant to this discussion, entitled 'To his Retired Friend, an Invitation to Brecknock'. Vaughan urged the friend (whose identity remains unknown) to leave 'thy close retirements' and to cease lurking 'like a badger' in a 'dark hole . . . rooting up of books'. Instead, the friend should 'leave this sullen state' and come to Brecknock. But the town is described in such unattractive terms that the irony of Vaughan's invitation is immediately apparent. For this was a town full of noise

> Of banged mortars, blue aprons, and boys,
> Pigs, dogs, and drums.

---

[202] *Thurloe State Papers*, Birch, IV, 336–7.

[203] In the following discussion, I am indebted to Earl Miner, *The Cavalier Mode from Jonson to Cotton* (Princeton, 1971). I am most grateful to Richard Strier for this reference, and for much helpful advice on this subject.

[204] *Henry Vaughan: The Complete Poems*, ed. Alan Rudrum (Harmondsworth, 1976), pp. 172–3, 222–3, 369–70.

[205] For accounts of Vaughan's life, see *DNB*, LVIII, 164–6; F. E. Hutchinson, *Henry Vaughan: A Life and Interpretation* (Oxford, 1947); and Kenneth Friedenreich, *Henry Vaughan* (Boston, 1978).

[206] This date is not, however, beyond doubt. The case for it is made – to my mind very persuasively – in Hutchinson, *Vaughan*, pp. 82–3, 89; and in Friedenreich, *Vaughan*, p. 94. But for an alternative dating, see *The Secular Poems of Henry Vaughan*, ed. E. L. Marilla (Essays and Studies of English Language and Literature, 21, Uppsala, 1958), pp. 189–90.

The moral was clear: the country was really the best place in which to endure 'winter's frosty pangs', a metaphor perhaps for the Royalists' political and military defeat.[207] As Vaughan put it in another poem appropriately called 'Retirement (II)',

> If Eden be on earth at all,
> 'Tis that, which we the country call.

Amid 'fresh fields and woods' it was possible to survive political misfortunes and to draw on inner resources; for

> rural shades are the sweet fence
> Of piety and innocence.[208]

This praise of a pastoral idyll encouraged a number of Royalist poets to look to classical models depicting a rural Arcadia. One of the most popular of these was the lyric about a grasshopper by the Greek poet Anacreon (*c*.582 – *c*.485 BC), which inspired no fewer than three translations or adaptations during the 1650s. The most literal rendering of Anacreon's original text was by Thomas Stanley and appeared in 1651.[209] A rather freer version was published in 1656 by Abraham Cowley, a former Fellow of Trinity College, Cambridge, who had lived in France since 1646 and who served as a Royalist spy in the mid-1650s.[210] He was imprisoned in the wake of Penruddock's Rising and, as Thomas Corns has recently argued, the publication of his *Poems* the following year should be seen in the context of first-hand experience of defeat.[211] Cowley's 'The Grashopper' lauded a 'happy insect' which, 'fed with nourishment divine', could

> drink, and dance, and sing;
> Happier then the happiest King!

The 'happy insect' was fortunate indeed, for after its 'summer feast' it 'retir'est to endless rest' and thus would 'neither age, nor winter know'.[212]

---

[207] *Vaughan: Complete Poems*, Rudrum, pp. 77–9 ('To his Retired Friend, an Invitation to Brecknock', lines 15–17, 28, 39–40, 55, 74). For discussions of this poem, see Miner, *Cavalier Mode*, pp. 299–300; Friedenreich, *Vaughan*, pp. 20–1, 94–9; and D. C. Allen, 'Richard Lovelace: "The Grasse-hopper"', in *Seventeenth-Century English Poetry: Modern Essays in Criticism*, ed. William R. Keast (New York, 1962), pp. 280–9.

[208] *Vaughan: Complete Poems*, Rudrum, p. 369 ('Retirement [II]', lines 1, 21–2, 27–8).

[209] *The Poems and Translations of Thomas Stanley*, ed. Galbraith Miller Crump (Oxford, 1962), p. 94 ('The Grassehopper XLIII'). See also Miner, *Cavalier Mode*, pp. 109–11. Biographical details of Stanley may be found in *DNB*, LIV, 78–81.

[210] For Cowley's life, see *DNB*, XII, 379–82; and Arthur H. Nethercot, *Abraham Cowley: The Muses's Hannibal* (Oxford, 1931). For his activities as a Royalist spy, see Underdown, *Royalist Conspiracy*, pp. 207, n. 10, 318; and Nethercot, *Cowley*, pp. 142–57.

[211] Thomas N. Corns, *Uncloistered Virtue: English Political Literature, 1640–1660* (Oxford, 1992), pp. 253–5.

[212] *The English Writings of Abraham Cowley*, ed. A. R. Waller (2 vols., Cambridge, 1905–6), I, 57 ('The Grashopper', lines 1, 3, 9–10, 27–8, 33–4). For discussions of this poem, see Miner, *Cavalier Mode*, pp. 148–9; and James G. Taaffe, *Abraham Cowley* (New York, 1972), pp. 44–5.

Like Vaughan, Cowley here developed the metaphor of a 'Cavalier winter', a season in which the bitter frosts of political defeat could best be endured at a country retreat.[213]

It was, however, the third version of 'The Grasshopper' which departed furthest from Anacreon's text, and in the process achieved possibly the finest evocation of Royalist quietism and retirement written during the 1650s. Its author was Richard Lovelace, originally a courtier and playwright who had borne arms for the King on various occasions since 1639 and been several times imprisoned.[214] The poem, in Manfred Weidhorn's words, 'sounds the mid-seventeenth-century Royalist retreat from affairs of state, society, and war'.[215] Scholars have seen the grasshopper as a symbol of the Royalist party or even of Charles I himself.[216] Either way, its transient happiness – 'merry dayes' in which it 'mak'st merry men' – is cut short by 'the sickle' and then by 'green ice'. Yet this fate could be transcended by withdrawing into an inner world of friendship and conviviality. Lovelace addressed 'The Grasse-hopper' 'to my noble friend, Mr Charles Cotton', and declared:

> Thou best of Men and Friends! we will create
> A Genuine Summer in each others breast;
> And spite of this cold Time and frosen Fate
> Thaw us a warme seate to our rest.

This inner summer recaptured the grasshopper's lost idyll, and would prove more lasting than the transient 'Cavalier winter'. For in the long term Royalists could look forward to a reversal of their fortunes. Christmas would be celebrated once again:

> Dropping December shall come weeping in,
> Bewayle th'usurping of his Raigne;
> But when in show'rs of old Greeke we beginne,
> Shall crie, he hath his Crowne againe!

In the meantime, their private world contained modest pleasures that were far more genuinely valuable than the temporary rewards of political ascendancy:

> Thus richer than untempted Kings are we,
> That asking nothing, nothing need.[217]

[213] For this concept, see Miner, *Cavalier Mode*, pp. 282–97.
[214] For biographical details of Lovelace, see *DNB*, XXXIV, 168–72; *The Poems of Richard Lovelace*, ed. C. H. Wilkinson (Oxford, 1930), pp. xiii–lxxi; and Manfred Weidhorn, *Richard Lovelace* (New York, 1970), pp. 15–30.
[215] Weidhorn, *Lovelace*, p. 55.
[216] For these contrasting interpretations see, respectively, *ibid.*, pp. 54–5; and Miner, *Cavalier Mode*, pp. 285–93.
[217] *Poems of Lovelace*, Wilkinson, pp. 38–40 ('The Grasse-hopper', lines 11, 13, 17, 21–4, 29–32, 37–8).

Retirement would foster virtue, piety and simplicity. But, like so many other Royalists, Lovelace's short-term strategy of retreat rested upon an unshakeable faith in the long-term restoration of monarchy.[218]

Friendships, congenial company and the peace of the countryside afforded wonderful solace during the 'Cavalier winter'. Lovelace's 'The Grasse-hopper' was one of several treatments of the theme of retreat dedicated to fellow Royalists. Its addressee, Charles Cotton, was a considerable poet in his own right and later composed a verse 'To the Memory of my worthy Friend, Colonel Richard Lovelace'.[219] Cotton is however best known for his friendship with Izaak Walton, to whom he dedicated no fewer than three poems.[220] Possibly the finest of these was entitled 'The Retirement'. Cotton began by bidding 'farewell' to the 'busie world' and exchanging it for 'solitude, the Soul's best friend'. 'Here in this despis'd recess' it was possible to survive 'winter's cold, and the summer's worst excess', to 'contented live, and then contented die'. Such seclusion also permitted him to sit 'upon [the] flow'ry banks' of the river Dove in the Derbyshire Peaks and indulge in his favourite pursuit of angling.[221] The two friends delighted in this pastime, and in the 1670s Cotton wrote a sequel to Walton's The Compleat Angler. The original had first appeared in 1653, and has been described by Derek Hirst as 'the classic Royalist-Anglican literary product of these years'.[222]

Born in 1593, Walton worked as a draper and then an ironmonger in London until the early 1640s. He was a devoted Royalist who became 'not only unreconciled but unreconcilable' to the republic.[223] This prompted him to leave London and to compose the famous treatise on 'the art of angling', which he subtitled 'the contemplative man's recreation'. During the Interregnum he was secluded but not alone: his work takes the form of a dialogue between Piscator and Viator, and on the very first page Walton cites the maxim that 'good company makes the way seem the shorter'. This provided the perfect motto for Royalists as they negotiated the long and difficult road towards the Restoration. Meanwhile, angling would enable them to emulate 'Primitive Christians', those 'quiet men' who 'followed peace' and 'were too wise to sell their consciences to buy riches for vexation, and a fear to die'. It was thus 'a recreation that became a

---

[218] Cf. the discussion in Corns, Uncloistered Virtue, pp. 68–79, 244–56.
[219] Poems of Charles Cotton, ed. John Buxton (1958), pp. 112–13.
[220] Ibid., pp. 27–9, 48–51, 123–8.
[221] Ibid., pp. 48–51 ('The Retirement: Stanzes Irreguliers to Mr Izaak Walton', lines 1, 22, 36, 80–2, 87).
[222] Derek Hirst, Authority and Conflict: England, 1603–1658 (1986), p. 353.
[223] Owen Chadwick, The Fisherman and his God: Izaak Walton (1984), p. 2. For biographical details of Walton, see DNB, LIX, 273–7; and John R. Cooper, The Art of The Compleat Angler (Durham, NC, 1968), pp. 13–28.

Church-man',[224] and angling was commonly associated with the seques- tered clergy during these years.[225] Walton recounted how it had enabled Dean Nowell of St Paul's and the former diplomat and Provost of Eton Sir Henry Wotton to attain peace of mind.[226] Walton developed this theme more fully in his *Lives* of Wotton, Donne, Hooker, George Herbert and Robert Sanderson, biographical studies written between 1640 and 1678 which emphasised 'the vanity of ambition and the wisdom of retiring from the rat-race'.[227] Walton even used the word 'retiredness' to describe Donne's withdrawal from the busy world.[228] Such a retreat had strong religious overtones, as was evident in the closing lines of *The Compleat Angler*, where Walton bestowed Christ's blessing 'upon all that hate contentions, and love quietnesse, and vertue, and angling'.[229]

V

Throughout this chapter we have been looking at variations on the theme of 'retiredness'. Whether expressed by the Constitutional Royalist peers tucked away in their country seats, or by influential voices within the exiled Court, or by the Royalist poets of retreat, there was a broadly shared response to the experience of military and political defeat. Many diverse people came to terms with the new republic in similar ways and devised common strategies for surviving the 'Cavalier winter'. Certain differences of emphasis notwithstanding, these strategies all rested upon the same decision to retire from public activity in the short term, and the same unshakeable optimism that the monarchy would ultimately be restored in the long term. The Constitutional Royalists believed that a premature insurrection could only endanger this outcome. In the meantime, they could turn misfortune to advantage by cultivating their own virtue and piety, and by enjoying the modest pleasures of friends, family and rural life. This often went together with a commitment to the old Church of England, and a wish to protect some of its dispossessed clergy. The Constitutional Royalists' deep faith in the return of the Stuarts was triumphantly vindicated in 1660. How far the ideology of Constitutional Royalism was also vindicated in the aftermath of the Restoration is a much more complex question and will form the subject of the next chapter.

---

[224] Izaak Walton, *The Compleat Angler*, ed. Bryan Loughrey (Harmondsworth, 1985), pp. 23, 25–6.
[225] Cooper, *Art of* The Compleat Angler, pp. 27–8.
[226] Walton, *Compleat Angler*, Loughrey, pp. 35–6.
[227] Izaak Walton, *The Lives of John Donne, Sir Henry Wotton, Richard Hooker, George Herbert and Robert Sanderson*, ed. George Saintsbury (Oxford, 1927); Chadwick, *Fisherman*, p. 4.
[228] Chadwick, *Fisherman*, p. 4.   [229] Walton, *Compleat Angler*, Loughrey, p. 123.

—————————— ⤜⤜ *9* ⤛⤛ ——————————

Legacy: an ideology vindicated?

The Constitutional Royalism of the 1640s was in part a response to a specific set of political circumstances. It involved an attempt to guide Charles I towards a distinctive vision of constitutional monarchy characterised by royal sovereignty within the rule of law, a symbiotic relationship between the Crown and Parliament, and the preservation of an episcopalian Church of England. Though these ideas drew upon earlier traditions within English political and religious thought, the form in which they were expressed and the urgency with which they were advanced owed much to the particular climate of England before and during the Civil Wars. Constitutional Royalist attitudes can only be fully understood against this background. Equally, it is important to recognise that the view of the constitution which they embraced remained widespread after 1660. This chapter will examine the extent to which Constitutional Royalism influenced the Restoration settlement, the appointment of some of its leading protagonists to senior offices of state, and the continuing influence of their ideas through the later seventeenth century and beyond.

The platform on which Charles II was restored received its classic expression in the Declaration of Breda on 4 April 1660. This was, so to speak, the manifesto of the Restoration régime. It was drafted by the King with the advice of Hyde, Ormond and Nicholas,[1] and to be understood fully it needs to be seen less as a strategic masterstroke than as another expression of the Constitutional Royalist vision of Church and State. Read within such a context, it takes on some remarkable resonances which mark it as the culmination of two decades of constitutional and religious thought. It has striking affinities both with the King's commissioners' utterances during the peace negotiations of the 1640s and with Hyde's private counsel throughout the Interregnum.

[1] For Hyde's drafts, see Bodl. Lib., MS Clarendon 71, fos. 127r–132r. The genesis of the Declaration is described in John Price, *The Mystery and Method of His Majesty's Happy Restauration, Laid Open to Publick View* (1680), pp. 143–4 (Wing, P 3335); Ronald Hutton, *Charles II: King of England, Scotland, and Ireland* (Oxford, 1989), pp. 128–9; and *The Restoration: A Political and Religious History of England and Wales, 1658–1667* (Oxford, 1985), pp. 107–8.

The Declaration rested first of all on the assumption that the King's rights and those of his subjects were naturally harmonised under the rule of law. This was the interlocking cluster of ideas which I have called the law–liberty–prerogative nexus; and we have seen that it was asserted time and again in successive peace treaties to counter the Houses' claims that enhanced parliamentary authority was essential to preserve popular liberties. Hyde adopted a similar position in his private advice to the exiled Charles II. In his draft declaration of March 1649, for instance, Hyde had argued that 'it could not be possible that the people could have any security or assurance of ther property or liberty, whilst the King's just rights and power was taken from or denied to him'. By the same token, the King would 'not be more sollicitous' to 'recover [his] owne rights and just power to protecte [his] people' than 'to vindicate the knowne and confessed lawes of the kingdome, and to establish [his] subjects in a full possessyon of ther property and liberty'.[2] This promise surfaced clearly in the Declaration of Breda where, in a passage suggested by Hyde, the King renounced any desire 'to enjoy [more] what is ours, than that all our subjects may enjoy what by law is theirs, by a full and entire administration of justice throughout the land, and by extending our mercy where it is wanted and deserved'.[3]

This promise of clemency led directly to the King's offer of 'a free and general pardon' for any 'crime whatsoever committed against us or our royal father', extending to all but certain named exceptions.[4] Again, this clause had a long pedigree within Constitutional Royalist thought. During the Civil Wars, the promise of an act of general pardon and oblivion had appeared regularly both in peace treaties and in theoretical tracts. Similarly, in his 'advices' to Charles in September 1649, Hyde had urged that 'a full Act of Pardon and Indempnity' be granted to all except 'those who sate as Judges or Assistants or Ministers in that execrable Court which directed the murther of his Majestie, and of those who in the House of Commons consented to the erecting [of] that odious judicatory'.[5] The restriction of penalties to the regicides and the avoidance of a vindictive settlement had long been central to the thinking of Royalist moderates.

So, too, had the commitment to a free Parliament. This was a direct continuation of the Constitutional Royalists' attempts during the 1640s to show their support for the role of Parliaments within the polity. This in no

---

[2] S. R. Gardiner, 'Draft by Sir Edward Hyde of a Declaration to be issued by Charles II in 1649', *EHR*, 8 (1893), 302, 304 (printing Bodl. Lib., MS Clarendon 37, fos. 24r–27r).
[3] Gardiner, *Documents*, p. 465. For Hyde's responsibility for this passage, see BL, Egerton MS 2542 (Nicholas Papers), fo. 328r.
[4] Gardiner, *Documents*, pp. 465–6.
[5] *The Nicholas Papers*, vol. 1: *1641–1652*, ed. G. F. Warner (Camden Society, 2nd series, 40, 1886), 139, 142.

way diminished their hostility to the Junto: indeed, they claimed to defend the cause of free Parliaments far more effectively than those who held sway at Westminster. Hyde's draft declaration of March 1649 had likewise envisaged 'a full and free convention of Parliament, wher wee shall most willingly apply all proper and naturall remedyes to the diseases which have growne out of the late distempers'.[6] The following September, Hyde had urged the King to promise 'a free and full Parliament', and to guarantee 'the frequent and constant calling of Parliaments, and the continuance of them for such a competent tyme as shalbe necessary for the publique'.[7] This again became a key pledge within the Declaration of Breda, which sought 'the resettlement of our just rights' and those of the subject 'in a free Parliament, by which, upon the word of a King, we will be advised'.[8] The protection of the rule of law and of the subjects' interests was thus accompanied by the defence of Parliament, an institution which was both the highest court of law and the 'representative of the whole realm'.

Finally, we come to perhaps the most famous promise in the Declaration of Breda, that of 'a liberty for tender consciences'. We have seen that a number of Constitutional Royalists were prepared to countenance a measure of religious toleration as one aspect of a moderated episcopacy. They also saw the protection of conscience as a right enjoyed by the King and his subjects alike. If, during the 1640s, many Constitutional Royalists apparently gave less weight to toleration than to the survival of episcopacy, this was surely because at that time the latter was under greater threat and therefore needed defending more strongly. There seems no reason to doubt their sincere commitment to liberty of conscience; and this was another pledge which Hyde contributed to the Declaration of Breda.[9] The crucial clause stated that 'because the passion and uncharitableness of the times have produced several opinions in religion', the King would 'declare a liberty for tender consciences' which would ensure that 'no man shall be disquieted or called in question for differences of opinion in matter of religion, which do not disturb the peace of the kingdom'.[10] Once again, this was a measure which Hyde had long advocated. In September 1649 he had suggested that the King assent to an Act 'for the ease of tender consciences in the circumstances of divine worshipp'.[11] The inwardness of this commitment is soon clear when we remember Hyde's links with the Great Tew circle and in particular with William Chillingworth.[12] Their values, and those of his beloved friend Falkland, continued to influence

---

[6] Gardiner, 'Draft by Hyde', 304.   [7] *Nicholas Papers*, vol. I, Warner, 142–3.
[8] Gardiner, *Documents*, p. 466.
[9] BL, Egerton MS 2542, fo. 328v.   [10] Gardiner, *Documents*, p. 466.
[11] *Nicholas Papers*, vol. I, Warner, 142.
[12] See above, pp. 53–6.

Hyde.[13] In his *Commentaries and Reflections upon the Psalms of David*, Hyde had written in terms highly reminiscent of Great Tew:

That any man should be punished meerly for error in opinion, seems to be not only against the uncontroulable liberty of the soul of man, which cannot be restrained or constrained to other thoughts than what result from the natural faculties of the understanding, but against the elements of justice, and the nature and definition of punishment it self.[14]

Once these arguments are remembered, Hyde's commitment to a 'liberty for tender consciences' in 1660 looks less like a strategic political device to facilitate the King's restoration than an attempt to realise a dream long cherished on religious and philosophical grounds.

The values embodied in the Declaration of Breda had thus been axiomatic to Constitutional Royalist thought since the 1640s. As a programme it closely resembled that advocated, for example, in the stock conclusion to David Jenkins's works.[15] The concept of the law as the reconciler and guardian of the interests of Crown and subject; the promise of a general pardon extended as broadly as possible; the commitment to the role of a *free* Parliament within government; and the wish to preserve an episcopalian Church while also guaranteeing 'liberty for tender consciences': all these principles were defended by the King's commissioners in various peace negotiations as well as by theorists of Constitutional Royalism.

With the Restoration of Charles II in May 1660, these ideas resurfaced in print. Most notably, a tract possibly written in the 1640s as a rebuttal of Hunton's *Treatise of Monarchie* was published for the first time in England.[16] This was entitled *The Kings Supremacy Asserted*, and its author was Robert Sheringham, a graduate and Fellow of Caius College, Cambridge, who had spent most of the Interregnum in Holland after being ejected from his Fellowship in 1644.[17] His treatise presented arguments almost identical to those advanced by writers such as Ferne, Digges and Spelman. Like them, his central contention was that royal sovereignty was entirely compatible with the rule of law. He started from the premise that

---

[13] For Chillingworth's influence on Hyde, see B. H. G. Wormald, *Clarendon: Politics, History and Religion, 1640–1660* (Cambridge, 1951; repr. 1989), especially pp. 313–23.
[14] *A Compleat Collection of Tracts, by that Eminent Statesman the Right Honourable Edward, Earl of Clarendon* (1747), p. 539 (Psalm 67).
[15] See above, p. 236.   [16] For Hunton, see above, p. 230, n. 77.
[17] Robert Sheringham, *The Kings Supremacy Asserted. Or, A Remonstrance of the King's Right against the pretended Parliament* (1660), Wing, S 3237; BL, TT, E 1043/5. For analyses of this tract, see Corinne Comstock Weston, *English Constitutional Theory and the House of Lords, 1556–1832* (1965), pp. 82–3; and J. W. Daly, 'The origins and shaping of English Royalist thought', *Historical Papers/Communications Historiques* (1974), 29. Biographical details of Sheringham may be found in *DNB*, LII, 89–90; and J. Venn and J. A. Venn, ed., *Alumni Cantabrigienses. Part One: from the earliest times to 1751* (4 vols., Cambridge, 1922–7), IV, 61.

'the King alone is by the lawes of the land the only supreme lord and governour of England, and ... there is no mixture at all in the rights of soveraignty; for in respect of the power itself, the monarchy is absolute, simple, pure, independent'. The 'rights of soveraignty' were 'so inseparably annexed to his royal person by the lawes of the land, that they cannot be separated from him by any Act of Parliament'.[18] The King was thus 'legally invested with all the particular rights of soveraignty'. One of these was authority over the militia, which was 'inherent in the crown, setled upon it by the fundamental laws of the land, and confirmed by so many several acts of Parliament'. Nevertheless, the King was 'limited in the exercise of his power so as he cannot make laws without the assent of the Lords and Commons assembled in Parliament'.[19] This led to the familiar paradox that the monarch's powers were sovereign yet limited: 'the monarchie is absolute in respect of the power ... but yet the English monarchie is limited in respect of the use and exercise of power, the King being obliged to govern according to the laws of the land, which although they doe not diminish majesty *in essentialibus*, yet they do diversly qualifie, and modificate it'.[20] The appearance of this tract in 1660 was highly significant because it indicated the currency of Constitutional Royalist attitudes at the time of Charles II's return.

Likewise, the new régime swept aside the ideas which Sheringham had sought to refute. In particular, the concept of co-ordination between Crown, Lords and Commons was systematically undermined. The enacting clause of statutes assumed a standard form which studiously avoided any implication that the monarch was one of the three estates, and asserted instead his role as the sovereign law-maker. The formula now used universally had existed before as just one possible option. It read: 'Be it enacted by the King's most excellent majesty by and with the advice and consent of the lords spiritual and temporal and the commons in this present Parliament assembled and by the authority of the same'. As Corinne Comstock Weston has observed, the return of bishops to the Lords in 1660 only made this definition more plausible.[21] Furthermore, the guilt of a regicide like Henry Vane was compounded by his advocacy of co-ordination at his trial. An anonymous diarist recorded that Vane's 'asserting ... the co-ordinate, and, in some cases, superior authority of Parliament, with the uncourtly position, that all power is derived from the people, were treasons of too

---

[18] Sheringham, *Kings Supremacy Asserted*, pp. 12–13.   [19] *Ibid.*, pp. 23–5.
[20] *Ibid.*, p. 84.
[21] This form was adopted from 13 Car. II, s. 2, c. 2 onwards: Corinne Comstock Weston and Janelle Renfrow Greenberg, *Sovereigns and Subjects* (Cambridge, 1981), p. 159. For earlier practice, see G. R. Elton, *Studies in Tudor and Stuart Politics and Government* (4 vols., Cambridge, 1974–92), III, 142–55.

high a nature to be uttered with impunity'.[22] Vane was executed in June 1662. The revised Prayer Book of that year was similarly amended to establish that the monarch was not one of the three estates. For example, the thanksgiving for the foiling of the Gunpowder Plot now referred to 'the happy deliverance of the King, and the three estates of the realm'.[23] In short, the Restoration régime explicitly espoused Hyde's definition of the three estates, and emphatically endorsed the Constitutional Royalists' attack on the doctrine of co-ordination.

The resurgence of Constitutional Royalism at the Restoration was also clearly apparent in the personnel who dominated the new régime. Even before the King landed at Dover, John Rivett hoped that Hertford, Southampton 'and the rest of that classis' would soon sit in the House of Lords once again.[24] He was not disappointed. The Upper House was re-opened on 25 April;[25] and in the weeks that followed the survivors from the familiar circle of Constitutional Royalist peers – Southampton, Hertford, Lindsey and Seymour – all received honours and senior offices of state. All of them were sworn Privy Councillors shortly after the King's arrival.[26] Hertford was appointed a Knight of the Garter in late May and the following September was restored to the Dukedom of Somerset by a private Act of Parliament.[27] In giving his assent, Charles declared that this was an honour 'of an extraordinary nature ... for an extraordinary person, who hath merited as much of the King my father and myself as a subject can do'.[28] But Hertford was too old and ill to enjoy his new status: Hyde wrote that he 'was seldom out of his lodging after His Majesty came to Whitehall', and he died at Essex House on 24 October 1660.[29] It was ironic that he should end his days back in London, at the house of his late brother-in-law, whose career had diverged so dramatically from his own. Hertford's younger brother Seymour was appointed Chancellor of the Duchy of Lancaster on 9 July.[30] Lindsey received the Order of the Garter,[31]

---

[22] Weston and Greenberg, *Subjects and Sovereigns*, p. 157.   [23] *Ibid.*, p. 160.

[24] Bodl. Lib., MS Clarendon 72, fo. 82r (John Rivett to [Hyde], 27 April 1660).

[25] *LJ*, XI, 1; James S. Hart, *Justice upon Petition* (1991), p. 218.

[26] 'The Diary of Henry Townshend of Elmley Lovett, 1640–1663', ed. J. W. Willis Bund, *Publ. Worcs. Historical Society* (2 vols., 1916–20), I, 46.

[27] House of Lords RO, 12 Car. II, Original Act 10; Bodl. Lib., MS Ashmole 1110 (Order of the Garter papers), fo. 168v; *LJ*, XI, 156–9, 171; 'Diary of Townshend', Willis Bund, I, 50, 61–2; Clarendon, *History*, VI, 233 (Book XVI, §245).

[28] *LJ*, X, 173.

[29] PRO, SP 77/33, fo. 126r ([Nicholas] to Sir Henry De Vic, 26 October 1660); Clarendon, *History*, IV, 494 (Book XI, §245). For Hertford's burial at Bedwyn Magna in Wiltshire, see *Wiltshire: The Topographical Collections of John Aubrey, F.R.S.*, ed. J. E. Jackson (Devizes, 1862), p. 378.

[30] *LJ*, XI, 158–9; R. Somerville, *Office-holders in the Duchy and County Palatine of Lancaster from 1603* (1972), p. 3.

[31] Bodl. Lib., MS Ashmole 1110, fo. 174v.

and (following a dispute with the Earl of Oxford) was admitted to his father's old office of Lord Great Chamberlain, in which capacity he officiated at Charles II's coronation on 23 April 1661.[32] The highest promotion of all among this circle went to Southampton, who in addition to becoming a Knight of the Garter[33] was also appointed Lord Treasurer in September 1660.[34] The bonds between these peers, and their enduring loyalty to the Crown, were further demonstrated late in 1660 when Lindsey and Southampton visited Windsor Castle to try to find Charles I's burial place. But

the confusion that they had at that time observed to be in that church, all things pulled down which distinguished between the body of the church and the quire, and the small alterations which were begun to be made towards decency, so totally perplexed their memories, that they could not satisfy themselves in what place or part of the church the royal body was interred.[35]

The King's final resting-place was never discovered. Yet this story shows that Charles I's surviving pallbearers remained faithful to his memory when they found themselves honoured and rehabilitated by his son.

The same rapid preferment was the lot of other Constitutional Royalists. Most importantly, Hyde was confirmed as Lord Chancellor, the office which he had held since January 1658, and was elevated to the peerage as Earl of Clarendon in April 1661.[36] His growing closeness to Culpepper, evident towards the end of the 1650s, was reflected in the latter's appointment as Chancellor of the Exchequer in June 1660.[37] We will never know how this political relationship, so significant for Constitutional Royalism during the early 1640s but so variable thereafter, would have developed following the Restoration, for Culpepper died on 11 July 1660.[38] Lastly, Sir John Strangways also emerged from retirement. On 14 May 1660 he read the proclamation of Charles II at Sherborne and in the celebrations which followed he 'rode along the streets, encourag[ing] and commend[ing] the

---

[32] PRO, SP 29/35/38 (claims at Charles II's coronation), fo. 4v; BL, Add. MS 29775 (order of Charles II's coronation procession); *LJ*, XI, 220, 226–30, 280, 283, 288–9.

[33] BL, Add. MS 37998 (Sir Edward Walker papers), fos. 116r–117r; Clarendon, *History*, VI, 233 (Book XVI, §245).

[34] 'Diary of Townshend', Willis Bund, I, 59; J. C. Sainty, *Treasury Officials, 1660–1870* (1972), p. 18.

[35] Clarendon, *History*, IV, 494–5 (Book XI, §245).

[36] G. E. C[okayne], *The Complete Peerage* (new edition, ed. Vicary Gibbs, H. A. Doubleday, Duncan Warrand, Lord Howard de Walden, Geoffrey H. White and R. S. Lea, 14 vols., 1910–59), III, 264. Clarendon was introduced in the Lords on 11 May 1661: *LJ*, XI, 264.

[37] BL, Egerton MS 2551 (Nicholas Papers), fo. 25r (warrant to Sir Jeffrey Palmer, 11 June 1660).

[38] 'Diary of Townshend', Willis Bund, I, 55; F. W. T. Attree and J. H. L. Booker, 'The Sussex Colepepers', *Sussex Archaeological Collections*, 47 (1904), 68.

people of Sherborne for their hearty and constant loyalty to the King'.³⁹ Subsequently he served as MP for Weymouth and Melcombe Regis in the Cavalier Parliament until his death on 30 December 1666.⁴⁰ These appointments in turn exerted a powerful influence upon the making of government policy. In essence, the official position of the Restoration régime was based on Constitutional Royalist principles. It was therefore no accident that the Restoration settlement consciously sought to restore the *status quo* of 1641, not that of either 1640 or 1642. It thus incorporated the constitutional measures of the first six or seven months of the Long Parliament – those demanded by the Constitutional Royalists and accepted by Charles I – but not the later reforms which had divided the Houses and driven the Constitutional Royalists into the arms of Charles I. Star Chamber, High Commission, prerogative taxation: all the things which Clarendon and others had denounced in 1640–1 were permanently destroyed. On the other hand, innovations such as the Triennial Act remained (albeit in modified form). Thus, as Paul Seaward has recently argued, 'in both religion and politics, if the government could have been said to have had a policy in the early 1660s, it was Clarendon's'.⁴¹

The Lord Chancellor's public utterances during the early 1660s bore all the characteristic hallmarks of Constitutional Royalism, and developed the principles adumbrated in the Declaration of Breda. Clarendon was at pains, first of all, to stress 'the government's firm commitment to the laws of the country and to the settled ways of the constitution'.⁴² He urged new judges and officers of the law to be 'strict and precise in their administration of justice according to the law, with all equality and without respect of persons'. Lawyers should dispose the people to 'such reverence of the laws, and such an estimation of the persons who justly execute those laws, that they may look upon those who could pervert the laws at home, as enemies of the same magnitude, as those who would invade the country from abroad'.⁴³ Likewise, Clarendon's speeches to the Convention and the Cavalier Parliament eulogised the harmonious relationship between Crown and Parliament under the law. This was, he argued, the greatest 'manifestation of an excellent temper and harmony of affections throughout the

³⁹ *Mercurius Publicus*, no. 21 (17–24 May 1660), pp. 329, 331 (*STC (News)*, 378.121; BL, TT, E 183/17).
⁴⁰ *Return of Members of Parliaments of England, 1213–1702* (2 vols., 1878), I, 522; *The History and Antiquities of the County of Dorset ... by John Hutchins, M.A.*, ed. W. Shipp and J. W. Hodson (3rd edition, 4 vols., 1861–70), II, 662; PRO, SP 29/289/73 (John Pocock to James Hickes, 26 January 1666/7). Strangways had previously represented Weymouth and Melcombe Regis in 1625 and 1626: see above, p. 57.
⁴¹ Paul Seaward, *The Cavalier Parliament and the Reconstruction of the Old Régime, 1661–1667* (Cambridge, 1989), p. 34.
⁴² *Ibid.*, p. 18.   ⁴³ Quoted in *ibid.*, p. 19.

nation'.[44] The King was his subjects' 'greatest security and protection from injury and injustice, and for the enjoying whatsoever is due to them by the law'.[45] Clarendon hoped that the Convention would 'join with him in restoring the whole nation to its primitive temper and integrity, to its old good manners, its old good humour, and its old good nature'.[46] Of central importance in this process of reuniting the nation was the Act of Indemnity and Oblivion, a measure which Clarendon carefully steered through the Convention.[47] Only fifty-one named individuals were excepted from its terms. With the Act's passage in August 1660, the secular programme laid out at Breda was well on the way to making the transition from paper to practice.[48]

The other most influential Constitutional Royalist after 1660 was Southampton. Although he made far fewer public statements than Clarendon, he was clearly working in the same spirit as the Lord Chancellor. Ludlow praised Southampton's 'courage' and magnanimity for insisting in August 1661 that those exempted from the general pardon be given fourteen days 'for saving themselves'.[49] Six months later, the Lord Treasurer opposed the excessive use of force to suppress Venner's Rising in terms which were utterly consistent with his earlier principles. 'They had', he said, 'felt the effects of a military government, though sober and religious, in Cromwell's army: he believed vicious and dissolute troops would be much worse: the King would grow fond of them, and they would quickly become insolent and ungovernable: and then such men as he was must be only instruments to serve their ends.'[50] Southampton begged Clarendon to avoid any hint of arbitrary rule and instead to preserve lawful, constitutional government. Not surprisingly, the Lord Chancellor 'was persuaded he was in the right'.[51] Burnet, who tells this story, later claimed that Southampton had blamed 'all the errors' of Charles II's reign on his 'coming in without conditions', and criticised Clarendon for giving so favourable an impression of the King in 1660 that these were not deemed necessary.[52] Even allowing for the fact that Burnet had a Whiggish axe to grind, it is clear that Southampton never compromised his constitutional principles during the 1660s.

[44] *Cobbett's Parliamentary History of England* (36 vols., 1806–20), IV, 170.
[45] *Ibid.*, 174.
[46] *Ibid.*, 126.
[47] PRO, SP 29/4/83 (Clarendon's draft message to the House of Commons, [18 June 1660]); *Cobbett's Parliamentary History*, IV, 103–6.
[48] 12 Car. II, c. 11. For a discussion of this statute, see Hutton, *The Restoration*, pp. 132–8.
[49] *The Memoirs of Edmund Ludlow*, ed. C. H. Firth (2 vols., Oxford, 1894), II, 290; Edmund Ludlow, *A Voyce from the Watch Tower. Part Five: 1660–1662*, ed. A. B. Worden (Camden Society, 4th series, 21, 1978), 180.
[50] Gilbert Burnet, *Burnet's History of my own Time*, ed. Osmund Airy (2 vols., Oxford, 1897–1900), I, 280.
[51] *Ibid.*   [52] *Ibid.*, 162.

Burnet wrote that 'he was an incorrupt man, and during seven years management of the treasury he made but an ordinary fortune out of it'.[53] Furthermore, he was committed to 'moderating matters both with relation to the government of the Church and the worship and ceremonies'.[54] This brings us to what is easily the most controversial question surrounding the Restoration settlement: why was the King unable to fulfil his promise to grant a 'liberty for tender consciences'?

As Paul Seaward has recently argued, if the thrust of government policy in the early 1660s was Clarendonian, the great obstacle to that policy lay in the Cavalier Parliament.[55] There is no sign that the Lord Chancellor anticipated trouble when the Parliament assembled in May 1661. His opening speech took up a number of his favourite constitutional themes: he welcomed members as 'the great physicians of the kingdom', and 'the only means to restore the nation to its happiness, to itself, to its honour, and even to its innocence'.[56] He hoped that the Parliament would introduce a moderate Church settlement that ensured that 'every little difference in opinion, or practice in conscience or religion' did not 'presently destroy conscience and religion'.[57] Yet, over the next twelve months, a narrow and intolerant Church was established, accompanied by progressively harsher penalties for those unable to conform to it. These measures became known collectively as the 'Clarendon Code', yet the extent of the Lord Chancellor's responsibility for them has divided historians ever since.

More than thirty years ago, Robert S. Bosher argued that both Charles II and Clarendon had been strongly influenced by 'Laudian' divines during the Interregnum, and that insofar as they were prepared to tolerate dissent from a rigid Church this was for pragmatic rather than principled reasons. Their aim all along was to impose a 'Laudian' settlement, and they bided their time until they were in a position to revoke earlier concessions to the Presbyterians.[58] Against this, G. R. Abernathy and D. T. Witcombe have both suggested that the King and the Lord Chancellor sought a comprehensive Church, with toleration for nonconformists, but were thwarted by the uncompromising stance of the Cavalier Parliament.[59] In essence, this is also

---

[53] *Ibid.*, 171. [54] *Ibid.*, 316.
[55] Seaward, *Cavalier Parliament*, especially pp. 35–70.
[56] *Cobbett's Parliamentary History*, IV, 181, 183. [57] *Ibid.*, 183.
[58] Robert S. Bosher, *The Making of the Restoration Settlement* (1951). Cf. Anne Whiteman, 'The Restoration of the Church of England'; E. C. Ratcliff, 'The Savoy Conference and the revision of the Book of Common Prayer'; Geoffrey F. Nuttall, 'The first nonconformists'; and R. Thomas, 'Comprehension and indulgence', all in *From Uniformity to Unity, 1662–1962*, ed. Geoffrey F. Nuttall and Owen Chadwick (1962).
[59] G. R. Abernathy, *The English Presbyterians and the Stuart Restoration, 1648–1663* (Transactions of the American Philosophical Society, new series, 55, Part ii, Philadelphia, 1965), especially pp. 79–93; 'Clarendon and the Declaration of Indulgence', *Journal of*

the explanation favoured by Ronald Hutton.[60] By contrast, Ian Green presents a more complex reading of Clarendon's behaviour: he suggests that the Lord Chancellor acted as the King's mouthpiece by publicly advocating toleration, while secretly preferring the harsher policy of the Cavalier Parliament. As that policy gradually won the day, so Clarendon allowed his sympathy for it to become more overt.[61] Most recently, Paul Seaward has offered yet another interpretation: that Clarendon's loyalty to the law and the constitution overrode his eirenic religious attitudes and ultimately led him to oppose Charles's Declaration of Indulgence.[62]

This last scenario probably comes closest to the truth. We have already seen a duality within Hyde's religious thought. He combined intense loyalty to the Church of England with a desire to make that Church as comprehensive as possible. Equally, this commitment was coloured by a reverence for constitutional propriety and the rule of law, hence his defence of episcopacy on the grounds that 'it was a parte of the government of England'.[63] During the 1640s and 1650s, when the first priority was to protect this vision of the Church from the alternatives advanced by Presbyterians and Independents alike, the potential contradiction between these two aspects of Clarendon's thought remained concealed. But after the Restoration they became progressively harder to reconcile. It is likely that the magnitude of this problem only gradually dawned on the Lord Chancellor. There is a remarkable passage in his opening speech to the Cavalier Parliament which indicates the inner tension between his religious and constitutional instincts. The result sounds rather as though two people were battling for access to the same microphone:

> If the present oaths have any terms or expressions in them that a tender conscience honestly makes scruple of submitting to, in God's name let other oaths be formed in their places, as comprehensive of all those obligations which the policy of government must exact: but still let there be a yoke: let there be an oath, let there be some law, that may be the rule to that indulgence, that, under pretence of liberty of conscience, men may not be absolved from all the obligations of law and conscience.[64]

Liberty should not run to licence, and the rule of law had to be preserved at all costs. It was thus respect for the law which marked the boundaries of religious toleration. Hyde went on to condemn 'the seditious preachers,

Ecclesiastical History, 11 (1960), 55–73; D. T. Witcombe, *Charles II and the Cavalier House of Commons, 1663–74* (Manchester, 1966), pp. 4–10.

[60] Hutton, *Charles II,* pp. 176–84; *The Restoration*, pp. 166–80.

[61] I. M. Green, *The Re-establishment of the Church of England, 1660–1663* (Oxford, 1978), especially pp. 203–36.

[62] Seaward, *Cavalier Parliament*, pp. 27–34, 180–3.

[63] Bodl. Lib., MS Clarendon 30/2, fo. 284v (Hyde to Lord H[atton], 4 February 1647/8).

[64] *Cobbett's Parliamentary History*, IV, 184.

who cannot be contented to be dispensed with for their full obedience to some laws established, without reproaching and inveighing against those laws, how established soever'. He warned that if the Cavalier Parliament did 'not provide for the thorough quenching [of] these firebrands, King, Lords and Commons shall be their meanest subjects, and the whole kingdom kindled into one general flame'.[65] 'Liberty for tender consciences' was one thing; lawlessness quite another.

There is no reason to doubt Clarendon's sincere commitment to the ideal of a comprehensive Church which offered generous concessions to coax as many Presbyterians into the fold as possible. To this end he tried hard to moderate the Act of Uniformity. In March 1662 he moved an amendment to the Act which would allow the King to grant individual ministers exemption from wearing the surplice and using the cross in baptism, as the Prayer Book required. This passed the Lords but was defeated in the Commons. The following month he sought a similar exemption from the renunciation of the Covenant, but again in vain.[66] Nonconformists saw Clarendon as a patron, with some justification.[67] During the summer of 1661 he had 'much discourse' with his old friend Bulstrode Whitelocke about 'the phanatickes and liberty of conscience', while the following year he used Whitelocke as an intermediary in talks with London nonconformists. Throughout, he 'professed himselfe a great friend to' liberty of conscience.[68] He thus attempted to fulfil his pledge in the Declaration of Breda, and to implement the eirenic strand within his religious thought which may be traced back to his links with Falkland and the Great Tew circle.

But the Lord Chancellor's reverence for the rule of law and for the supremacy of statute was, if anything, even deeper than his religious principles. Once the Act of Uniformity passed both Houses and received the royal assent,[69] he 'thought it absolutely necessary to see obedience paid to it without connivance'.[70] The most he could do was to hope that the King would interpret it in a liberal spirit. As he told the Cavalier Parliament at the close of its first session in May 1662:

You have done your parts like good physicians, made wholesome prescription for the constitution of your patients; well knowing, that the application of these remedies, the execution of these sharp laws, depends upon the wisdom of the most discerning, generous, and merciful prince, who, having had more experience of the nature and humour of mankind than any prince living, can best distinguish

---

[65] *Ibid.*, 184–5.   [66] Seaward, *Cavalier Parliament*, pp. 175–8.   [67] *Ibid.*, p. 179.
[68] *The Diary of Bulstrode Whitelocke, 1605–1675*, ed. Ruth Spalding (British Academy Records of Social and Economic History, new series, 13, Oxford, 1990), pp. 631, 635, 644–8. Cf. Seaward, *Cavalier Parliament*, p. 29.
[69] 14 Car. II, c. 4.   [70] Clarendon, *Life*, II, 147.

between the tenderness of conscience and the pride of conscience, between the real effects of conscience and the wicked pretences of conscience.[71]

However, the scope of these royal discretionary powers was circumscribed by the operation of the laws. Clarendon believed that 'it was not in the King's power to give any dispensation to any man, that could preserve him against the penalty in the Act of Uniformity'.[72] Hence, when the King issued a Declaration of Indulgence in December 1662, and then proposed a bill to enforce it the following February, Clarendon and Southampton 'were very warm against it, and used many arguments to dissuade the King from prosecuting it'.[73] When the Lords debated this bill on 12 March, the Lord Chancellor 'thought it a very unreasonable and unjust thing to commit such a trust to the King'. Then, in a passage which illustrates the remarkable consistency of his legal and constitutional attitudes, Clarendon denounced 'the wildness and unlimitedness of the bill', and declared that 'it was Ship Money in religion, that nobody could know the end of, or where it would rest'.[74] He was attacking royal policies on exactly the same grounds as in 1640–1. As Paul Seaward has written, Clarendon thought 'it was possible to accept occasional and temporary irregular alterations to the law, but not something which would make irregularity regular'.[75] This remained true throughout his career.

Yet, in the summer of 1663, Clarendon was still discussing the possibility of extending 'such liberty as may be safe to men of peaceable spirits, though they differ in judgment'.[76] What appears to have changed his outlook decisively was the Yorkshire rising of the following October. Investigations revealed that the conspirators included Presbyterians as well as more extreme zealots.[77] Sedition was the unacceptable face of religious radicalism, and thereafter Clarendon lost his optimistic belief that it was possible for nonconformists to be 'peaceable'. Instead, the government embarked on progressively harsher measures against dissenters, culminating in the Conventicle Act (1664) and the Five Mile Act (1665).[78] By May 1665, Clarendon was writing that 'without doubt without a severe execution at present, the law and the government will fall into great contempt'.[79] Two months later, he ordered that ministers of conventicles were to be 'proceeded against with the utmost rigour accordinge to the letter of the

---

[71] *Cobbett's Parliamentary History*, IV, 252.   [72] Clarendon, *Life*, II, 140.
[73] *Ibid.*, 344.
[74] *Ibid.*, 348.   [75] Seaward, *Cavalier Parliament*, p. 184.
[76] HMC, *Manuscripts of the Marquess of Ormonde*, vol. III (1904), 71 (Earl of Anglesey to Ormond, 11 August 1663).
[77] Seaward, *Cavalier Parliament*, p. 190.
[78] *Ibid.*, pp. 189–93; Hutton, *The Restoration*, pp. 204–14.
[79] Quoted in Seaward, *Cavalier Parliament*, p. 192.

Acte of Parliam[en]t'.[80] He had abandoned the attempt to establish a comprehensive Church and henceforth viewed the Presbyterians reproachfully as 'a packe of knaves'.[81]

The years from 1662 onwards marked the defeat not just of the government's bid to achieve ecclesiastical as well as political unity, but also of Clarendon's wish to reconcile his religious ecumenicism with his reverence for the constitution and the rule of law. Two imperatives which he had hitherto regarded as inseparable were now tugging in opposite directions. In the end, he had to compromise one or the other. If, as has been argued throughout this study, the rule of law represented the bottom line of his thought, it is not surprising that this consideration came first and guided his actions during the creation of the Restoration Church settlement. The outcome was not the one that he would have preferred. But insofar as it was one that he sanctioned, and in part reflected the resolution of a conflict within himself, it may fairly be termed the 'Clarendon Code'.

Yet, if the Lord Chancellor was forced to abandon his religious ecumenicism, these same years saw the vindication of his constitutionalism and respect for the rule of law. It is remarkable how much of the programme espoused by the Constitutional Royalists during the 1640s was cast in stone after 1660. Howard Nenner has revealed how the values and attitudes of the common law pervaded the political culture of Restoration England. The law provided 'analogues and metaphors' which were applied directly to political processes.[82] Although a comprehensive Church eluded him, Clarendon did at least see the ecclesiastical hierarchy re-established by law, and the principle recognised that the monarch could only dispense from the Act of Uniformity in exceptional circumstances. As Alan Cromartie has argued, Charles II's reign marked an emphatic re-assertion of the rule of law and demonstrated the resilience and adaptability of the common law tradition.[83] The common law courts regained much of their old vitality while the prerogative courts lay buried forever. In particular, the House of Lords resumed its role as the highest court of appeal with extraordinary speed and success.[84] The cardinal principle of Constitutional Royalism – the maintenance of royal powers within the law – was enshrined in legislation such as the Triennial Act of 1664, and bolstered by Charles's respect

---

[80] PRO, SP 29/126/109 (note on letter from Deputy Lieutenants of Somerset to Lord Arlington, 15 July 1665).

[81] T. H. Lister, *Life and Administration of Edward, First Earl of Clarendon* (3 vols., 1837–8), III, 483 (Clarendon to Lord Cornbury, 10 June 1671).

[82] Howard Nenner, *By Colour of Law: Legal Culture and Constitutional Politics in England, 1660–1689* (Chicago, 1977), especially chapter 2.

[83] See A. D. T. Cromartie, 'Sir Matthew Hale (1609–76)' (PhD thesis, University of Cambridge, 1991), especially pp. 88–151.

[84] Hart, *Justice upon Petition*, pp. 218–58.

for Parliament and the constitution.[85] The creation of a standing army reflected the political élite's acceptance of the military authority vested in the monarchy.[86] But, as in religious affairs, that authority was always tempered by the law. Similarly, the King surrendered all claims to prerogative taxation and feudal dues in return for a permanent annual revenue.[87] Once again, the object was to create a strong and effective Crown operating within legally defined limits. As Roger North put it, 'all that was done for church and crown [was] true English policy for the preservation of law and property and not ... the result of chimeric loyalty'.[88] This marked the practical realisation of an ideal memorably expressed by Falkland in April 1643, that 'the laws and statutes of the kingdom ... will be always the most impartial judge between [the King] and his people'.[89] In short, the Restoration settlement signalled the victory of Clarendonian principles. As Paul Seaward has written, the Lord Chancellor 'constantly defended the sanctity of the law'. Like other Constitutional Royalists, he sought 'the Crown's military, constitutional, and financial security within a respect for the law, liberty, and property', and 'the restoration of stability and unity to the country by the reconstruction of a strong monarchy beside a powerful law'.[90]

It is important, however, to recognise the limits of this period of reconstruction. Paul Seaward has argued that the year 1667 marked a watershed in which war and agricultural crisis brought Clarendonian policies to an end. The Lord Chancellor's impeachment followed a series of deaths which had already removed the leading Constitutional Royalists of the 1640s from the political scene. Seymour died on 12 July 1664, and was buried like his elder brother at Bedwyn Magna in Wiltshire.[91] Lindsey died on 25 July 1666,[92] and Southampton on 16 May 1667.[93] Clarendon mourned the Lord Treasurer as 'a person of extraordinary parts, of faculties very discerning and a judgment very profound', and 'a man of great and exemplary virtue and piety'.[94] The Lord Chancellor's own resignation and impeachment on charges of corruption and incompetence followed a

[85] John Miller, 'Charles II and his Parliaments', *TRHS*, 5th series, 32 (1982), 1–23; 'The potential for "Absolutism" in later Stuart England', *History*, 69 (1984), especially 205; Wormald, *Clarendon*, p. xxxiii.
[86] John Childs, *The Army of Charles II* (1976), pp. 7–20.
[87] Seaward, *Cavalier Parliament*, chapter 5.
[88] Quoted in John Miller, 'The later Stuart monarchy', in *The Restored Monarchy, 1660–1688*, ed. J. R. Jones (1979), p. 31.
[89] Rushworth, V, 201.   [90] Seaward, *Cavalier Parliament*, p. 323.
[91] Somerville, *Office-holders in the Duchy of Lancaster*, p. 3; *Wiltshire Collections of Aubrey*, Jackson, p. 378.
[92] PRO, SP 29/165/12 (newsletter of 27 July 1666).
[93] BL, Sloane MS 1116 (Glisson medical papers), fo. 46r. For details of Southampton's funeral, see BL, Add. MS 12514 (heraldic and historical collections), fo. 316r–v.
[94] Clarendon, *Life*, III, 229, 238.

few months later.[95] He was made a scapegoat for the failures of the second Dutch War and in particular for the Dutch attack on Chatham in May 1667. Thus, by the close of 1667, that generation of Constitutional Royalists who had converged in 1641–2, conducted peace negotiations on Charles I's behalf during the Civil Wars, and re-emerged triumphantly on the Restoration of his son, was no longer represented among the major officers of state.

The year 1667 undoubtedly saw 'the end of an administration and of a policy'.[96] But there is much evidence that the ideology which had inspired that administration and policy lived on. J. R. Jones has shown that Clarendon's fall prompted the coalescence of a political grouping which came to be labelled the 'Friends of the Constitution in Church and State'. These 'Friends' were numerically significant in the Commons, but lacked both talent and leadership. Jones's analysis of their attitudes reveals that they were, in effect, Constitutional Royalists *après la lettre*. For 'the main principles of the Friends were based on the concept of the essential interdependence of Church, monarchy and the law'. They agreed with the Bishops 'on all fundamental principles', and shared 'a determination to safeguard the laws and the Church against all encroachments from any quarter, not least the Court'. On ecclesiastical matters, they experienced the same conflict of loyalties as Clarendon in 1661–2. They strongly defended the Act of Uniformity and believed that 'the status of the Church depended absolutely on statute'. The enactment of the Conventicle Act in 1670 can be seen as 'the peak of [their] achievement'. Equally, many of the Friends 'who supported the Act admitted the need for some measures of ecclesiastical reform ... and favoured concessions to the Presbyterians'. But because they saw the Church as a 'legal entity', they opposed 'any form of statutory indulgence' as 'an alteration of the government'. Exactly like the Constitutional Royalists, therefore, the core of their position lay in a deep attachment to 'a strict legalism'.[97]

Such 'Clarendonian' attitudes ceased to exert such a direct influence on government policy during the years of the Cabal and Danby ministries.[98] Yet they resurfaced at times of crisis and made a significant contribution to the course and outcome of both the Exclusion Crisis and the Glorious

---

[95] For accounts of Clarendon's fall, see Seaward, *Cavalier Parliament*, pp. 320–2; Lister, *Life of Clarendon*, II, 383–469; and Sir Henry Craik, *The Life of Edward, Earl of Clarendon, Lord High Chancellor of England* (2 vols., 1911), II, 287–308.

[96] Seaward, *Cavalier Parliament*, p. 323.

[97] J. R. Jones, 'The Friends of the Constitution in Church and State', in *Public and Private Doctrine: Essays in British History presented to Maurice Cowling*, ed. Michael Bentley (Cambridge, 1993), pp. 17–33, quotations at pp. 22–5. I am greatly indebted to Professor Jones for showing me a copy of this paper prior to publication.

[98] For an account of these years, see J. R. Jones, *Country and Court: England, 1658–1714* (1978), pp. 164–96.

Revolution. Charles I's *Answer to the XIX Propositions* proved a highly controversial text in this process. In May 1679 the Shaftesbury Whigs used a lengthy extract from the *Answer* to support their demand for Danby's impeachment.[99] This was typical of the way in which Falkland and Culpepper's definition of the three estates as King, Lords and Commons could be employed as a handle against the Crown. These years saw a remarkable efflorescence of the doctrine of co-ordination in Whig writings such as William Petyt's *Antient Right* (1680).[100] By contrast, the Clarendonians were anxious to repudiate this definition of the three estates,[101] and as the movement for Exclusion gathered momentum, it was to these former 'Friends of the Constitution in Church and State' that Charles II turned for support against the Whigs.[102] The Tory cry of '1641 is come again' is here highly revealing, for that year had witnessed the parting of the ways for Constitutional Royalist members of the Long Parliament. Like 1641, 1680–1 marked a watershed at which the demands made upon the Crown ceased to be either constitutional or reasonable. The argument against Exclusion rested above all on the analogy between the rules of royal inheritance and the subject's right of real property.[103] As we have seen, this equation between royal and popular rights was frequently reiterated by Constitutional Royalists. There were also direct parallels, as Mark Goldie has argued, between the attempts in both 1641–2 and 1678–81 to exclude bishops from the Lords.[104] The Tory ecclesiology expressed, for example, in William Falkner's *Christian Loyalty* had close affinities with that espoused by Clarendon and his allies. Like Falkland and several other speakers on 8–9 February 1641, Lawrence Womack defended bishops in 1680 as 'a fundamental and essential part of our English Parliament'. Such continuities bear out Jonathan Scott's thesis that the Exclusion Crisis 'followed the pattern of its Caroline predecessor'.[105] What was so different was that in the latter crisis the equivalent of the Constitutional Royalists – those branded 'episcopal tantivies' by their Whiggish enemies – carried the day.[106]

---

[99] Weston, *English Constitutional Theory*, pp. 93–103.
[100] Weston and Greenberg, *Subjects and Sovereigns*, pp. 182–221. See also B. Behrens, 'The Whig theory of the constitution in the reign of Charles II', *Cambridge Historical Journal*, 7 (1941–3), 42–71.
[101] Cf. Mark Goldie, 'John Locke and Anglican Royalism', *Political Studies*, 31 (1983), 69–71.
[102] Jones, 'Friends of the Constitution', pp. 29–33.
[103] Nenner, *By Colour of Law*, pp. 141–54.
[104] Mark Goldie, 'Danby, the bishops and the Whigs', in *The Politics of Religion in Restoration England*, ed. Tim Harris, Paul Seaward and Mark Goldie (Oxford, 1990), pp. 75–105.
[105] Jonathan Scott, *Algernon Sidney and the Restoration Crisis, 1677–1683* (Cambridge, 1991), p. 11.
[106] Goldie, 'Danby, the bishops and the Whigs', pp. 87, 96–7.

That victory ushered in the so-called 'Tory Reaction', a surge of loyalty to the twin lodestars of Church and Crown. This was linked to an attack on those theories of mixed monarchy which saw the powers of King, Lords and Commons as 'co-ordinate'. The discovery in 1683 of the Rye House Plot to murder Charles II and the Duke of York brought matters to a head. On 21 July 1683, the University of Oxford condemned certain books for preaching 'damnable' doctrines. These included that familiar target of Constitutional Royalist polemic, Hunton's *Treatise of Monarchie*.[107] So great was the concern to repel this danger, that Charles II's violation of the Triennial Act in 1684–5 passed almost entirely unremarked. Only the Lord Privy Seal, Halifax, was privately 'very earnest with the King for a Parlament, but to noe purpas'.[108] Otherwise, the spirit of Charles's rule generally inspired confidence that Church and State would be protected. He was 'ostentatiously devoted' to the laws enforcing religious uniformity.[109] The trials of Algernon Sidney and Lord William Russell in 1683 proved that the rule of law remained intact. These were not judicial murders: no more than any of his predecessors since Henry VIII could Charles II flout due process of law and arbitrarily pronounce 'off with his head'.[110] Yet there were times during the last few years of his reign when Royalism loomed larger than constitutionalism. From 1676 judges were appointed *durante bene placito* rather than *quamdiu se bene gesserint*, thereby re-asserting a power which Charles I had consistently claimed in theory but relinquished in practice after January 1641.[111] Moreover, between 1676 and 1683 the Crown unilaterally removed no fewer than eleven senior members of the judiciary.[112] Such actions dovetailed with the national mood expressed in the many loyalist addresses to Charles published during 1681. One 'well-wisher to the King and kingdom' declared that 'if it be the undoubted prerogative of the King to call, adjourn, prorogue, and dissolve Parliaments at his will and pleasure; it is a high impudence in any subject, or assembly of men, to take upon them to advise him (unasked) how and when to execute his power'.[113] Another Royalist pamphleteer wrote:

107 Weston, *English Constitutional Theory*, pp. 111–12. For Hunton, cf. above, pp. 101, 228, 230 n. 77, 247–8, 293.
108 *Memoirs of Sir John Reresby*, ed. Andrew Browning (Glasgow, 1936), p. 327.
109 Hutton, *Charles II*, p. 424.
110 Lois G. Schwoerer, 'The trial of Lord William Russell (1683): judicial murder?', in *Restoration, Ideology, and Revolution*, ed. Gordon J. Schochet (Folger Shakespeare Library, Washington, DC, 1990), pp. 169–98; Scott, *Sidney and the Restoration Crisis*, pp. 317–47. Cf. Russell, *FBM*, p. 506.
111 See above, pp. 184–5.
112 A. F. Havighurst, 'The judiciary and politics in the reign of Charles II', *Law Quarterly Review*, 66 (1950), 230–1, 247.
113 Quoted in Scott, *Sidney and the Restoration Crisis*, p. 75.

> Under five hundred Kings three Kingdoms groan,
> Go, Finch, dissolve them, Charles is on the throne,
> And by the grace of God will reign alone.[114]

The 'Tory Reaction' thus teetered on the brink of replaying Charles I's Personal Rule.[115] Furthermore, it unleashed a widespread campaign in the localities for the issuing of new borough charters on terms which benefited the Tories.[116] At the same time, in his relaxed personal style and willingness to avoid confrontations Charles II resembled his grandfather more than his father. The architects of the Restoration settlement had sought a return to the situation of 1641, which was itself an attempt to restore the *status quo ante* 1625.[117] However, the 'Tory Reaction' indicated that they had been only partially successful. There remained the real danger that a hard-line loyalism to Church and Crown would submerge Constitutional Royalism.

Ironically, what saved the day were the policies of James II which quickly made those two loyalties incompatible. Instead, his reign – and the revolution which it precipitated – ultimately demonstrated the resilience of Constitutional Royalist attitudes. Whigs and Tories alike derived inspiration from different elements within that tradition. Weston has shown that over a dozen pamphlets published in 1688–9 drew explicitly on the King's *Answer to the XIX Propositions*. She makes a persuasive case for believing that the *Answer* was known to the authors of the Bill of Rights. The idea of co-ordination between King, Lords and Commons was especially attractive to the Whigs as they advanced towards a notion of contractual monarchy.[118] This in turn gave rise to a distinctive resistance theory which legitimated the use of force against James II.[119]

However, this does not necessarily justify Weston's claim that the doctrine of the three estates as King, Lords and Commons 'triumphed after the Revolution of 1689'.[120] We should not underestimate the degree to which the Tories of 1688–9 were heirs of Constitutional Royalists, or the extent of their contribution to the Revolution settlement. For them, the principal objection to James's policies lay in his flouting of the rule of law. As under Charles II, the notion that the monarch could regularly dispense from statute law in order to extend religious toleration was abhorrent.

[114] Quoted in Keith Feiling, *A History of the Tory Party, 1640–1714* (Oxford, 1924), p. 198. 'Finch' is a reference to Heneage Finch, first Lord Finch, who held the offices of Attorney-General (1670), Lord Keeper (1673) and Lord Chancellor (1675) until his death in 1682. He was created Earl of Nottingham in 1681.
[115] Cf. Scott, *Sidney and the Restoration Crisis*, pp. 75–7.
[116] John Miller, 'The Crown and the Borough Charters in the reign of Charles II', *EHR*, 100 (1985), 53–84.
[117] Scott, *Sidney and the Restoration Crisis*, p. 6.
[118] Weston, *English Constitutional Theory*, pp. 116–23.
[119] Weston and Greenberg, *Subjects and Sovereigns*, pp. 261–6.
[120] Weston, *English Constitutional Theory*, p. 113.

Archbishop Sancroft and six bishops justified their refusal to read James's Declaration of Indulgence on the grounds that it was 'founded upon such a dispensing power as hath been often declared illegal in Parliament and particularly in the years 1662 and 1672'.[121] In other words, they were the direct heirs of the Clarendonians. Similarly, if the Whigs argued that James had violated his 'original contract' with his people, the Tories preferred the formula that he had 'violated the fundamental laws of the kingdom'.[122] James's remarkable achievement lay in uniting these essentially irreconcilable positions. Whigs and Tories could agree that the King had 'endeavoured to subvert the constitution of the kingdom', and this allowed them to take concerted action against him.

During the construction of the Revolution settlement, the Tory horror of a violation of the rule of law emerged alongside the Whig ideal of a contractual monarchy. A draft survives of a speech probably delivered on 24 December 1688 by one leading Tory, the second Earl of Nottingham, which reveals how much his agenda for a political settlement owed to Constitutional Royalism.[123] Henry Horwitz has even labelled him the 'counsel for the constitution'. Nottingham began by insisting that 'all laws civil or ecclesiastical be ratified and established', and that 'all the late violations of the laws and the pretences of prerogative and power by which they have been effected shall be declared void'. His preferred solution to the question of evil advisers closely resembled the Constitutional Royalists' proposals regarding the regicides and others guilty of treason: 'that notorious offenders be brought to condign punishment by due course of law or as shall be adjudged by Parliament'. The Prince of Orange was to possess those legitimate royal powers of 'the sole disposal and ordering of all forces by sea and land', and 'the disposal and nomination of all officers civil and military, and all the preferments in the Church to which the King had a right'. At this date, Nottingham still believed that James might return. He rejected the Whigs' claim that the throne was now 'vacant', but laid conditions for the King's return. In particular, he stipulated that 'the King will hearken to the advice of his Parliament in such other matters as shall be reasonable for the security of the Protestant religion and the rights, laws, and liberties of the subject'. He added the demands that 'the King will return to his people and forthwith call a free Parliament', and that Parliaments henceforth meet under the terms of the Triennial Act. All these points echoed the programme advanced by Constitutional Royalists

---

[121] W. A. Speck, *Reluctant Revolutionaries: Englishmen and the Revolution of 1688* (Oxford, 1988), p. 67.

[122] *Ibid.*, p. 98.

[123] This draft is printed in full in Henry Horwitz, *Revolution Politicks: The Career of Daniel Finch, Second Earl of Nottingham, 1647–1730* (Cambridge, 1968), p. 69, from which the following quotations are taken. I am most grateful to Craig Rose for this reference.

throughout the 1640s. They were founded upon an ideology of constitutional monarchy, in which the royal prerogative operated within the law, and Church, Parliament and the law protected and reinforced each other.

In a sense, the great achievement of the Bill of Rights, and of the Revolution settlement in general, was the reconciliation of this cluster of ideas with the Whig ideology of contractual monarchy. As Hugh Trevor-Roper has recently reminded us, the Revolution could not have happened without the Tories.[124] To put it another way, the Revolution enshrined the constitutional arrangements sought by Clarendon and his allies. Constitutional Royalists had always had to grapple with the fact that there were no safeguards to ensure that the monarch ruled within the law and used his legitimate powers in the public interest. As we saw in chapter 2, this was one of the most striking features of the 'ancient constitution'. Unfortunately, the Restoration settlement was too successful a restoration of the 'ancient constitution' in the sense that this problem was reintroduced in 1660–2. This is a point recently made with great force by Jonathan Scott who writes: 'the Restoration ... succeeded too well, for it restored not only the structures of early Stuart government, but subsequently its fears, divisions and crises'.[125] Only after 1688 was this remedied. Only then were constitutional guarantees established – what Brian Wormald called 'necessary conventions'[126] – to ensure that the monarch respected the rule of law and governed in a constitutional manner. The Declaration of Rights of 1689 stated that James 'did endeavour to subvert and extirpate ... the laws and liberties of this kingdom'. In words which echoed Clarendon in 1662–3, the Declaration then pronounced categorically that 'the pretended power of dispensing with laws or the execution of laws by regal authority as it has been assumed and exercised of late is illegal'. It likewise proscribed as 'illegal and pernicious' the King's 'Court of Commissioners for Ecclesiastical Causes'.[127] This was of a piece with the Constitutional Royalists' implacable opposition to the prerogative courts of Star Chamber and High Commission. For the first time, the monarch was actually obliged to rule within the law. As Professor Speck has written, 'what triumphed in the Revolution settlement was a version of the rule of law which saw the King as beneath and not above it'.[128] The really ingenious part of the settlement was that it was presented as simply an affirmation of established practice. This overcame the fears of people like Nottingham that England's 'old and legall foundations' would be destroyed,[129] and formed a programme on

---

[124] Hugh Trevor-Roper, 'Epilogue: the Glorious Revolution', in *The Anglo-Dutch Moment: Essays on the Glorious Revolution and its World Impact*, ed. Jonathan I. Israel (Cambridge, 1991), pp. 490–1.
[125] Scott, *Sidney and the Restoration Crisis*, p. 8.   [126] Wormald, *Clarendon*, p. xxxvi.
[127] Quoted in Speck, *Reluctant Revolutionaries*, pp. 141, 143–4.   [128] *Ibid.*, p. 165.
[129] Nenner, *By Colour of Law*, p. 173.

which all parties could agree.[130] Yet there were small but vital changes, such as those contained in the coronation oath. Whereas James II and his predecessors had undertaken to 'grant and keep' the 'laws and customs ... granted by the Kings of England', William and Mary swore that they would 'govern the people of this kingdom of England ... according to the statutes in Parliament agreed on, and the laws and customs of the same'.[131] The Constitutional Royalists had never asked for anything more.

Or at least not as far as legal and constitutional issues were concerned. But there are also the religious aspects of the Revolution to be considered. Here the situation was more ambivalent. Mark Goldie has recently reconstructed the political and religious thought which prompted 'Anglican' resistance to James's policies. At one level this involved a defence of episcopacy and the assertion – for example in Samuel Hill's *The Catholic Balance* (1687) – that an apostolic succession was essential for the preservation of orthodox doctrine. Yet James's policies also prompted a critique of the whole notion of a royal supremacy. There emerged as a result what Goldie has called 'Anglo-Catholicism'. This rested on the belief that the Church of England was, in Samuel Freeman's phrase, 'not a civil or secular, but a distinct, spiritual society'.[132] Such views diverged significantly from the Constitutional Royalist position, which defended hierarchy of the Church on the grounds that it formed an essential part of English government. What derived much more directly from Constitutional Royalism was the parallel defence of the Church as 'by law established', and the insistence that James was subverting it 'by assuming, and exercising a power of dispensing with, and suspending of laws, and the execution of laws, without consent of Parliament'.[133] We have already seen that the Declaration of Rights declared these powers illegal. In that sense the Revolution settlement resoundingly upheld the Act of Uniformity and the narrowly defined Church of England established in 1662.

Yet the same ambivalence which had dogged Clarendon in the wake of the Restoration now returned to haunt his successors. For the affirmation of the Act of Uniformity was accompanied by the passage in 1689 of a Toleration Act; and Nottingham's stance on these measures reflected precisely the same dilemma as had earlier confronted Clarendon.[134] Like the

---

[130] Speck, *Reluctant Revolutionaries*, p. 113.
[131] Lois G. Schwoerer, 'The coronation of William and Mary, April 11, 1689', in *The Revolution of 1688–9: Changing Perspectives*, ed. Schwoerer (Cambridge, 1992), p. 128. Cf. Speck, *Reluctant Revolutionaries*, p. 165.
[132] Mark Goldie, 'The political thought of the Anglican revolution', in *The Revolutions of 1688*, ed. Robert Beddard (Oxford, 1991), pp. 102–36.
[133] Quoted in Weston and Greenberg, *Subjects and Sovereigns*, p. 253.
[134] The following discussion of Nottingham is based on Horwitz, *Revolution Politicks*, pp. 86–95.

former Lord Chancellor, Nottingham coveted the ideal of a comprehensive Church with liberty for peaceful nonconformists. To these ends, he laid before the Lords a bill for toleration on 28 February 1689, followed by another for comprehension on 11 March. Yet when William then proposed the abolition of the sacramental test for public office, Nottingham objected that 'since our religion is the established religion ... [it is] impracticable and dangerous to admitt any kind of dissenters in to any share of the government'. This was the Clarendonian paradox all over again: peaceful dissenters could be tolerated, but not at the cost of weakening the rule of law or the government of the Church of England. The outcome of this controversy was similarly complex. A diluted version of the Toleration Bill was duly passed; but the proposal for comprehension was referred to Convocation where it was defeated.[135] Nottingham was justifiably disappointed. Yet if the Toleration Act was very limited in its concessions, it none the less dealt a major blow to the Church of England. As John Morrill has written, 'it caused the corrosion of Anglican triumphalism; it recognised, and in the decades that followed it inculcated the recognition, that it was no longer possible for English governors to seek to recreate a confessional state'.[136] It is precisely this ambivalence which is so reminiscent of Constitutional Royalist attitudes. The measures of 1689 marked a reworking of the balance between enforcing conformity to the Church and guaranteeing limited toleration for nonconformity; and it produced a settlement possibly closer to Clarendon's own preferences than that over which he had himself presided.

There is surely some truth, therefore, in G.M. Trevelyan's conclusion that 'the ecclesiastical settlement of 1689 was a compromise inclining to the Church and Tory side of things, whereas the dynastic settlement had inclined to the Whig side'.[137] Certainly Weston endorses the latter point and argues that the Glorious Revolution marked the victory of the doctrine of co-ordination between the three estates of Crown, Lords and Commons. She suggests that this cleared the way for the classic theory of constitutional checks and balances which pervaded eighteenth-century thought. She thus emphasises the Whig achievement in the wake of the Revolution, and concludes that 'it was the theory of mixed monarchy expounded by the Parliamentarians in the civil-war period, not the Royalist theory of mixed government, that triumphed either in the Revolution of 1689 or very shortly afterwards'.[138] But this statement may require some qualification.

[135] For the Church of England's consistent hostility to comprehension, and the relationship between this issue and the 1689 Toleration Act, see John Spurr, 'The Church of England, comprehension and the Toleration Act of 1689', *EHR*, 104 (1989), 927–46.
[136] John Morrill, *The Nature of the English Revolution* (Harlow, 1993), p. 445.
[137] Quoted in *ibid.*, p. 443.
[138] Weston, *English Constitutional Theory*, pp. 87–137.

Jonathan Clark has recently alerted us to the durability of Royalist values and categories throughout England's *ancien régime*. He points to the persistence of entrenched loyalties to Church and Crown.[139] Without wishing to replace one ideological monolith with another, it is important to acknowledge the survival of this tradition alongside that delineated by Weston. In particular, the legacy of Constitutional Royalism into the eighteenth century needs to be recognised. One specific case-study will illustrate what is meant.

The centrepiece of Weston's discussion is an analysis of Sir William Blackstone's *Commentaries on the Laws of England*.[140] 'It was', she writes, 'Sir William Blackstone, sometimes called the high priest of the cult of constitutionalism, who gave Montesquieu's separation of powers its classical English form.'[141] Yet these *Commentaries* – which began life as lectures at Oxford in 1753 and were subsequently published in 1765–9 – in fact presented an account of the polity which closely resembled that associated with Constitutional Royalism. It needs stressing, first of all, that Blackstone's definition of the three estates was not that of Falkland and Culpepper (King, Lords and Commons), but that of Clarendon (lords spiritual, lords temporal and commons).[142] Blackstone then embarked on a brief history of the 1640s which might almost form an apologia for the activities of the Constitutional Royalists:

The Long Parliament of Charles I, while it acted in a constitutional manner, with the royal concurrence, redressed many heavy grievances and established many salutary laws. But when the two Houses assumed the power of legislation, in exclusion of the royal authority, they soon after assumed likewise the reins of administration; and, in consequence of these united powers, overturned both Church and State, and established a worse oppression than any they pretended to remedy.[143]

In other words, 1641 marked the point at which the desirable reforms sought by the Long Parliament – those vigorously demanded by the Constitutional Royalists and accepted by Charles I – gave way to unjustified and illegal encroachments upon the powers of the Crown. That year saw a shift away from measures designed to restore the 'Jacobethan' ideal towards fundamental innovations in government, and these in turn impelled the Constitutional Royalists to withdraw from the Long Parliament.

Blackstone's description of the royal prerogative showed exactly why he believed this. For 'the powers which are invested in the Crown by the laws

---

[139] J. C. D. Clark, *English Society, 1688–1832* (Cambridge, 1985), especially chapters 3–4.
[140] Weston, *English Constitutional Theory*, pp. 126–8.
[141] *Ibid.*, p. 126. For a contrasting account of Blackstone, see Clark, *English Society*, pp. 204–9.
[142] William Blackstone, *Commentaries on the Laws of England* (4 vols., Oxford, 1765–9), I, 153.
[143] *Ibid.*, 154.

of England are necessary for the support of society; and do not intrench any farther on our natural liberties than is expedient for the maintenance of our civil'.[144] The royal prerogative amounted to 'that special pre-eminence which the King hath, over and above all other persons, and out of the ordinary course of the common law, in right of his regal dignity'. Blackstone trusted that he would not 'be considered as an advocate for arbitrary power' when he laid 'it down as a principle, that in the exertion of lawful prerogative, the King is and ought to be absolute; that is, so far absolute, that there is no legal authority that can either delay or resist him'. This was precisely the paradox of a sovereign yet limited monarch which had been addressed by Sheringham and other theorists of Constitutional Royalism. Blackstone summed it up thus:

> In the execution ... of those prerogatives which the law has given him, the King is irresistible and absolute, according to the forms of the constitution. And yet, if the consequence of that exertion be manifestly to the grievance or dishonour of the kingdom, the Parliament will call his advisers to a just and severe account.[145]

This shows the remarkable durability of the doctrines that the King could do no wrong and that wrongful policies should therefore be blamed on 'evil advisers'. More generally, these quotations reveal that the funda-mental tenets of Constitutional Royalism – that the monarch wielded sovereign but not unlimited powers commensurate with the rule of law – were advocated by the leading legal authority of mid-eighteenth-century England.

Blackstone's *Commentaries* are also interesting for his discussion of when constitutional reality most closely approximated to these ideals. He identified this moment as the reign of Charles II in general, and the year 1679 in particular:

> the constitution of England had arrived to its full vigour, and the true balance between liberty and prerogative was happily established by law, in the reign of King Charles the Second ... The point of time, at which I would chuse to fix this theoretical perfection of our public law, is the year 1679; after the *habeas corpus* act was passed, and that for the licensing of the press had expired: though the years which immediately followed it were times of great *practical* oppression.[146]

The Habeas Corpus Act – or, to give its full title, the 'Act for the better secureing the Liberty of the Subject and for Prevention of Imprisonments beyond the Seas' – had been passed in 1679,[147] while the Licensing Act of 1662 had expired in May 1679.[148] As we noted above, there was some justice in Blackstone's fears that the 'Tory Reaction' threatened the ideals of Constitutional Royalism. He correctly perceived the influence of those

---

[144] *Ibid.*, 237.   [145] *Ibid.*, 239, 250–1.   [146] *Ibid.*, IV, 432.   [147] 31 Car. II, c. 2.
[148] 14 Car. II, c. 33. For this act's expiry, see Havighurst, 'Judiciary and Politics', 235.

ideals upon the Restoration settlement, while also recognising the ambivalent developments of Charles II's final years.[149] None the less, Blackstone's *Commentaries* demonstrate that Constitutional Royalist attitudes and categories not only survived the 'Tory Reaction' and the Glorious Revolution, but continued to shape English constitutional thought at the start of George III's reign.

The doctrines of Clarendon and his allies can thus be seen as a link between the 'ancient constitution' of the early seventeenth century and the ideology of 'checks and balances' which characterised the eighteenth. This is, perhaps, the true vindication of the Constitutional Royalists of the 1640s. Their vision of the English polity proved influential over an exceptionally long timespan. As Brian Wormald has written, 'it was precisely Hyde's conception of the constitution rather than that of anybody else which came to be permanently adopted ... The true bridge between the non-resistance of the epoch of the Tudor rulers and the eighteenth-century was the non-violent, the bridge-building parliamentarism of Hyde.'[150] We can trace a direct thread of continuity leading from Clarendon to Nottingham and on to Blackstone.

Yet, if eighteenth-century constitutional thought was more pluralistic than Weston concedes, it was also less monolithic than Clark suggests. Blackstone presented only one among several competing interpretations of the English constitution. The views of such writers as Louis De Lolme, William Paley and Edmund Burke owed more to the 'co-ordination' theorists of the 1640s than to the Constitutional Royalists.[151] Furthermore, Blackstone's *Commentaries* should be seen less as an authoritative definition of the English polity than as one contribution to an on-going debate. For they triggered a vigorous riposte from Jeremy Bentham, who denied a fundamental tenet of Constitutional Royalism by arguing that 'freedom in government depends not upon any limitation to the Supreme Power'. He thus jettisoned that cluster of ideas which I have termed the law–liberty–prerogative nexus.[152] Instead, he asserted that 'the principle of utility, accurately apprehended and steadily applied, ... affords the only clue to guide a man' on the issue of legislative authority.[153] In taking utility as an end in itself, Bentham had broken decisively with notions of an 'ancient constitution' and advanced an entirely novel theory of political legitimacy.

By the opening decades of the nineteenth century, Blackstone's views

---

[149] Cf. Robert Willman, 'Blackstone and the "Theoretical Perfection" of English law in the reign of Charles II', *HJ*, 26 (1983), 39–70.
[150] Wormald, *Clarendon*, p. 153.
[151] Weston, *English Constitutional Theory*, pp. 128–37.
[152] See above, pp. 188, 291.
[153] Jeremy Bentham, *A Fragment on Government*, ed. J. H. Burns and H. L. A. Hart (Cambridge, 1988), pp. 96–7.

were clearly losing ground to those of the Whigs. Thus in 1823 John Cartwright wrote contemptuously that 'Blackstone was an eloquent writer, but
a mere practical lawyer who, when he ventured beyond forms, practice,
and technicalities, got out of his depth'. Cartwright found Blackstone's
account of the royal prerogative 'a very lame attempt at a definition'; and
offered instead a lengthy comparison between the English monarchy and
the Presidency of America.[154] A few years later, on the eve of the Great
Reform Act, John Allen likewise distanced himself from the paradox of a
sovereign monarch limited by the law which Blackstone had derived from
Constitutional Royalism. In practice, Allen argued, this formula simply did
not work: 'the ideal King of the lawyers is a King above law; the real King
of the constitution is a King subject to law'. Instead, Allen asserted the
principle of co-ordination between the three estates of Crown, Lords and
Commons: 'The King is our sovereign lord; but he does not possess the
sovereign authority of the commonwealth, which is vested, not in the King
singly, but in the King, Lords and Commons jointly.'[155] By the final days of
England's *ancien régime*, the attitudes associated with Constitutional Royalism were clearly losing much of their currency.

The watershed of 1832 completed this process of decline. It changed the
political landscape beyond recognition and created an entirely new context
to which the Crown had henceforth to adapt. As David Cannadine has
shown, the monarchy now confronted a quite different matrix of issues in
defining its relationship to Parliament, the Church and the legal system.[156]
Constitutional Royalism had presented one highly durable answer for
England's constitutional arrangements; but the question had now been
fundamentally rephrased. In an age of mass enfranchisement, economic
transformation, and the many other profound changes caused by imperial
growth, the monarchy seemed at times almost an irrelevance. Only by
altering its primary function from political influence to public display was
it able to survive into the twentieth century. Constitutional Royalism in the
seventeenth-century sense had effectively disappeared when Walter
Bagehot could analyse the monarchy thus: 'the functions of English royalty
are for the most part latent ... It is commonly hidden like a mystery, and
sometimes paraded like a pageant, but in neither case is it contentious ...
Its mystery is its life. We must not let in daylight upon the magic.'[157] With

---

[154] John Cartwright, *The English Constitution produced and illustrated* (1823), pp. 247–9,
264, 325.
[155] John Allen, *Inquiry into the Rise and Growth of the Royal Prerogative in England*
(1830), pp. 36, 167.
[156] David Cannadine, 'The context, performance and meaning of ritual: the British
monarchy and the "Invention of Tradition", *c.* 1820–1977', in *The Invention of Tradition*, ed. E. J. Hobsbawm and T. Ranger (Cambridge, 1983), pp. 101–64.
[157] Walter Bagehot, *The English Constitution* (4th edition, 1885), pp. 45, 59.

these words, written during the 1860s, we have clearly entered a different world from that inhabited by the likes of Clarendon.

Yet to admit that the legacy of Constitutional Royalism had its limits is not to lose sight of its very real impact on English political and constitutional development. Forged during the Civil Wars of the 1640s and then eclipsed during the Interregnum, it returned in 1660 to shape the Restoration settlement and later helped to resolve what Jonathan Scott has called the second and third 'crises of popery and arbitrary government'.[158] It provided a recipe for peaceful constitutional change which retained its currency well into the reign of George III. To that extent, it contributed to the 'exceptionally complex process' whereby 'the political chaos of the late seventeenth century was transformed into the adamantine stability of eighteenth-century oligarchy'.[159] That legacy, surely, is sufficient vindication of its place in history.

[158] Scott, *Sidney and the Restoration Crisis*, p. 3.
[159] J. H. Plumb, *The Growth of Political Stability in England, 1675–1725* (1967), p. 2.

─────────────── ❧ *10* ❧ ───────────────

Conclusion: assessment and evaluation

I have argued throughout this book that Constitutional Royalism was a cluster of interdependent ideas whose secular and religious aspects can be distinguished but not separated. It is impossible to isolate any one element within Constitutional Royalism without doing violence to its intrinsic nature. The beliefs that the royal prerogative and the subjects' liberties operated in symbiosis; that the monarch's powers were sovereign yet consistent with the rule of law; that to abrogate those powers therefore violated both the constitution and the laws; that monarchy and episcopacy were bound together by the royal supremacy enshrined in statute – all these components meshed to form one coherent whole. If there was a single principle underpinning these ideas, colouring them and holding them in equilibrium, it was the rule of law, understood to be an amalgam of God's law and the English common law. Constitutional Royalism had affinities with both the so-called 'common law mind'[1] and the values of the Great Tew circle, yet remained distinct from both. It drew on earlier traditions within English political and religious thought, but also represented a response to the specific developments of the 1640s. It was guided by a temperate spirit which saw unity and reciprocity as the normative relationship between monarch and people, Crown and Parliament, Church and State.[2] In that sense, it was an outlook rather than an ideology, a frame of mind rather than a creed.

This last point in turn suggests other parallels, other contexts within which Constitutional Royalism may be understood. In particular, its spirit of moderate constitutionalism has marked affinities with the 'loyalism' which John Wallace has discerned in the career of Andrew Marvell. Wallace begins his study by comparing Marvell with Hyde, and argues that 'loyalism, whether of Clarendon's or Marvell's variety, is intimately

---

[1] For this concept, see Glenn Burgess, *The Politics of the Ancient Constitution: An Introduction to English Political Thought, 1603–1642* (1992), p. 58.
[2] The theme of harmony in early seventeenth-century English thought is surveyed in James Daly, *Cosmic Harmony and Political Thinking in Early Stuart England* (Transactions of the American Philosophical Society, new series, 69, Part vii, Philadelphia, 1979).

connected with [the] centre and may be said to arise from it'. It was 'an expression of the centre of moderation in seventeenth-century politics'.[3] Wallace's conclusion that 'decorum, modesty, and moderation were the qualities that excited [Marvell's] life-long regard, and which he consistently sought to apply to the inflammations of the time'[4] would be equally applicable to the Constitutional Royalists examined in this book. Yet it must be remembered that there was a subtle difference between 'loyalism' and Royalism. As the poet and pamphleteer John Hall put it in 1656, 'the way to be a constant Royalist is to be a constant Loyalist; not to respect the power or place for the persons sake, but the person for the place and power[s] sake'. 'Loyalism' and Royalism both 'presupposed subjection to a single person as the head of state'; but whereas 'the obedience of the royalist was to the King's person, the loyalist's was to his office and authority'.[5] 'Loyalism' therefore cannot explain fully the almost feudal allegiance to the King's person which characterised a number of Constitutional Royalists, especially among the peerage. The term was sufficiently broad to cover those, including Marvell, who did not join Charles I in the Civil War; indeed, it could be employed to support the distinction between the King's office and person with which the Houses justified their resort to arms. Thus, if Royalist moderates were among those whose attitudes might be labelled 'loyalist', they also cherished beliefs which distinguished them from the likes of Marvell. Constitutional Royalism and 'loyalism' overlapped, but the two categories cannot be simply equated or used interchangeably.

Another parallel, which again is illuminating if not entirely straightforward, is that with the 'Trimmers' of the 1680s. This word was used in two distinct ways: as a pejorative term by Tory writers such as Sir Roger L'Estrange and John Dryden; or much more positively by the Marquess of Halifax to describe a principled political response. Yet, whether loved or loathed, the nature of 'Trimmer' attitudes was generally agreed. John Wallace has suggested that 'Marvell was among the few, only later to be known as trimmers, who believed that moderation was the very essence of government', and their values also bear a striking resemblance to those of the Constitutional Royalists. Two texts will serve to illustrate this point. Here, first of all, is L'Estrange's satirical speech by 'Trimmer', which appeared in the *Observator* for 13 November 1682:

Nay I am for moderate councells I declare it; and for gaining upon people by the ways of lenity and indulgence. I am against violent courses on one side as well as on t'other. I would have the people enjoy their rights; and God forbid but the King

---

[3] John M. Wallace, *Destiny his Choice: The Loyalism of Andrew Marvell* (Cambridge, 1968), pp. 1–2, 8.
[4] *Ibid.*, p. 255.   [5] *Ibid.*, p. 5.

should enjoy his. I wish, with all my heart, that they would leave writing on both sides. It does but enflame differences, and beget heats, and animosities ... 'Tis true, we have a gracious prince; but yet he may have ill advisers about him ... But these are matters out of my reach. I pray for peace, and quietness; and that we may be govern'd by the law; and protestants live comfortably one with another.⁶

Now some brief excerpts from Halifax's much more sympathetic *Character of a Trimmer*, composed two years later but not published until 1688:

Our Trimmer hath a great veneration for laws in general, as he hath more particularly for our own ... They are a sanctuary to which the Crowne hath occasion to resort, as often as the people, so that it hath an intrest as well as a duty to preserve them ... Our Trimmer admireth our blessed constitution, in which dominion and liberty are so happyly reconciled ... The Crown hath power sufficient to protect our liberties, the people have so much liberty as is necessary to make them usefull to the Crown ... Our Trimmer is a freind to Parliaments ... [and] cannot helpe thinking, it had been better, if the Trienniall Act had been observed⁷ ... Our Trimmer would have those mistaken men [Dissenters] ready to throw themselves into the armes of the Church, and he would have those armes as ready to receave them ... [But he] is not so unreasonably indulgent to the Dissenters as to excuse the irregularities of their complaints, or to approve their threatning stile.⁸

Although written from contrasting perspectives, the two passages are largely in agreement on the actual content of 'Trimmer' beliefs; and these beliefs are in turn analogous to those of the Constitutional Royalists. The concern for moderate counsels; the belief that the interests of Crown and people were naturally compatible; the wish to avoid extremes and to prevent an outright victory by either side; the need to preserve the rule of law; and the search for an ecumenical religious settlement have all emerged as themes throughout this study. But a problem remains. For Trimmers are often identified not with the moderate Tories – who I suggested were the successors of the Constitutional Royalists – but with their enemies the Whigs. This equation may be traced back to L'Estrange's assertion that 'there goes no more then a little change of weather, to the turning of a Whig into a Trimmer, or of a Trimmer back again, into a Whig'. Trimming was, he believed, 'a more insidious form of Whiggery'.⁹ L'Estrange's assumption that Whigs and Trimmers were synonymous has proved highly influential and informs, for example, John Wallace's statement that the Whigs' 'ultimate position ... is to be identified with that of the trimmers, to whom the future of Whig constitutionalism belonged'.¹⁰

⁶ Quoted in Donald R. Benson, 'Halifax and the Trimmers', *Huntington Library Quarterly*, 27 (1963–4), 119.
⁷ For Halifax's attempt to uphold the Triennial Act in 1684, see above, p. 307.
⁸ *The Works of George Savile, Marquis of Halifax*, ed. Mark N. Brown (3 vols., Oxford, 1989), I, 180, 182, 194, 196, 198, 203, 209.
⁹ Quoted in Benson, 'Halifax and the Trimmers', 121.
¹⁰ Wallace, *Destiny his Choice*, p. 226.

However, Mark N. Brown has brilliantly challenged the perceived correlation between Trimmers and Whigs. He points out that many of those accused of Trimming were in fact Tories, and that 'Tory principles were not inconsistent with ... deploring the acrimony of partisan conflict'. Far from attacking the Whigs as such, L'Estrange's aim was 'to discredit moderation and compromise among members of the loyal party and established church'. He and other Tory propagandists sought to issue 'an implicit warning to Tories and Anglicans who did not whole-heartedly go along with *quo warrantos*, purges of Whigs from corporations, suppression of conventicles, or persecution of Protestant Dissenters'.[11] In other words, the charge of Trimming was used by the leaders of the Tory Reaction to discredit more moderate Tories. It was a weapon deployed against the heirs of the Constitutional Royalists, and is therefore another manifestation of the conflicts between the Crown's supporters in the wake of the Exclusion Crisis. While some Tories desired a more authoritarian style of government, others remained loyal to the constitutional inheritance of the Clarendonians. We saw in chapter 9 that the outcome of this tussle was far from clear; and the attempt to blacken moderate Tories as self-interested hypocrites was one reflection of how bitter it became during Charles II's final years.

The continuities between Constitutional Royalism and moderate Toryism can be drawn out even more explicitly. In ecclesiastical affairs the heirs of Constitutional Royalism remained committed to the ideals of tolerance and comprehension which proved elusive in 1660–2 and again in 1688–9. The correlation between this outlook and the 'conformist' attitudes of the period before 1640 – and indeed with the whole 'Jacobethan' ideal of the Church – was not lost on contemporaries. An anonymous pamphlet of May 1682, sometimes attributed to L'Estrange, denounced such people as 'Grindallizers', after Elizabeth I's Archbishop of Canterbury. These 'Grindallizers' were defined as 'conforming non-conformists, or rather such as are conformists in their profession, half-conformists in their practice, non-conformists in their judgment'.[12] As I argued above, the term 'conformist' accurately captures the religious attitudes of Constitutional Royalists such as Dorset.[13] They were willing to tolerate a diversity of opinion within a broad national framework, and at the Restoration sought to create a comprehensive Church comparable to that which had existed under Elizabeth I and James I. Although they were defeated,

---

[11] Mark N. Brown, 'Trimmers and moderates in the Reign of Charles II', *Huntington Library Quarterly*, 37 (1973–4), 312–13, 316.
[12] *Ibid.*, 322.
[13] See above, p. 50; and David L. Smith, 'Catholic, Anglican or Puritan? Edward Sackville, fourth Earl of Dorset and the ambiguities of religion in early Stuart England', *TRHS*, 6th series, 2 (1992), 120–4.

Clarendonians and moderate Tories continued to hanker after such a settlement, as Nottingham's bills for toleration and comprehension in 1689 clearly show.

Similar continuities are apparent when we turn to legal and constitutional issues. Those branded 'Trimmers' included 'men of some moderation' within the Tory party such as Lord Keeper Guilford. Again, his beliefs closely resembled those of the Constitutional Royalists. According to his brother Roger North, the Lord Keeper wished 'to give the Crown all its lawful prerogatives' but was 'equally just to the people in all their rights'. His 'chief blame' was 'only that he would not sacrifice the law to the iniquity of the times'. This attachment to the rule of law ultimately alienated him from more authoritarian Tories. He remained a Tory as long as he believed that the party 'pursued the true interest of England, that is to support the Church and Crown'. But when 'some pretended leaders' sought to exalt 'the power of the Crown above the law' he 'turn'd Trimmer'.[14] These attitudes – and especially the belief that the rule of law ensured equilibrium between the monarch and his subjects – again illustrate the link between Constitutional Royalism and the moderate Toryism which in the 1680s was branded 'Trimming'.

The case of Lord Keeper Guilford also helps to refute the charge that Trimmers were self-interested hypocrites. Trimming emerges instead as a highly principled and dynamic response to political and religious upheaval. Halifax, another moderate Tory, proudly presented it as a strategy which would protect the nation's interests:

This innocent word Trimmer signifieth no more than this, that if men are together in a boat, and one part of the company would weigh it down on one side, another would make it lean as much to the contrary, it happneth there is a third opinion, of those who conceave it would do well, if the boat went even, without endangering the passengers.

He could not imagine how this could be seen as 'a fault' or 'thought a heresie'.[15] Such a defence of 'Trimming' in turn illuminates the Constitutional Royalism of the 1640s. In particular, it helps to explain that wish to avoid 'an absolute victory' by either side which Hobbes observed in the King's moderate advisers. The analogy with 'Trimming' throws light, for example, on Dorset's words to Salisbury in August 1642: 'None butt the desperate every way can hope for ammelioration by the ruines of soe many, and soe universall a change both in government, and familyes as a victory must make, on which side soever itt happens.'[16] The following year, Henry Ferne likewise urged that 'peace may be restored', but 'not through an

---

[14] Brown, 'Trimmers and moderates', 329.   [15] _Works of Halifax_, Brown, I, 179.
[16] BL, Microfilm M 485 (Hatfield House, Cecil MS), vol. CXCVII, fo. 130r–v (Dorset to the Earl of Salisbury, 4 August 1642).

absolute prevailing of either side by armes'.[17] The notion of 'Trimming', of adjusting one's position in order to preserve balance, provides a useful context within which this horror of an outright victory by either side may be understood.

Yet it would not tell the whole story about Constitutional Royalism. For while he eschewed an 'absolute prevailing' by either Crown or Parliament, Ferne nevertheless desired the 'loyall submission of that side which has done the wrong to His Majesty and his people by this lawlesse resistance'.[18] The Houses posed the greater threat to England's fundamental laws by taking up arms, and the onus was therefore on them to submit. This perception in turn highlights an important contrast between 'Trimming' and Constitutional Royalism. The idea of adjusting one's weight to preserve balance necessarily implied a view of the constitution in which Crown, Lords and Commons were equal partners. Although Halifax thought 'coordination . . . an unmannerly word' he accepted the idea which lay behind it. As he wrote in some private reflections on the royal prerogative during James II's reign, 'though the quality of trustees may bee unequall, yet the power of the trust may be equall'.[19] In terms of the debates in the 1640s, he would stand nearer to Hunton or Herle than to Ferne or Hyde on this issue. For, despite some disagreement over the composition of the three estates, the majority of Constitutional Royalists thought that the monarch remained sovereign above the lords spiritual, lords temporal and commons. Collaboration in the process of law-making did not imply equipollence. Although limited by the rule of law, the monarch nevertheless retained 'supream, or the higher power';[20] he still held 'the first place'.[21] Hence, while they were dedicated to harmony and horrified at the prospect of an outright victory by either side, Charles I's moderate advisers still believed that the monarch occupied a unique place within the polity, set apart from and above the Houses of Parliament. This demonstrates that Constitutional Royalism and the 'Trimming' of a figure like Halifax were not identical. It also shows the lasting influence of Parliamentarian theorists such as Hunton.[22] John Wallace has argued that 'among earlier writers' he 'most clearly foreshadows Marvell's position'.[23] 'Trimming', whether practised by Marvell or Halifax, ultimately rested on the idea of

---

[17] H[enry] Ferne, *Conscience Satisfied, that there is no warrant for the armes now taken up by subjects* (Oxford, 1643), p. 83 (Wing, F 791; BL, TT, E 97/7).
[18] *Ibid.* [19] *Works of Halifax*, Brown, II, 63. See also *ibid.*, I, 192.
[20] Ferne, *Conscience Satisfied*, p. 20.
[21] Jasper Mayne, *Οχλο-μαχια, or The Peoples War* (1647), p. 14 (Wing, M 1472; BL, TT, E 398/19).
[22] The influence of the concept of co-ordination is surveyed in Corinne Comstock Weston and Janelle Renfrow Greenberg, *Sovereigns and Subjects* (Cambridge, 1981).
[23] Wallace, *Destiny his Choice*, p. 205.

co-ordinate powers vested in Crown, Lords and Commons. It diminished the uniqueness of the Crown's position to a degree which Constitutional Royalism could not countenance. Thus, while sharing much common ground with 'Trimming' as well as with 'loyalism', Constitutional Royalism was still distinguishable from both.

This in turn explains why the problem which faced Constitutional Royalists in the peace negotiations of the 1640s was likewise a highly distinctive one. Their concern was not simply to preserve constitutional equilibrium, but to do so in ways which reconciled two potentially contradictory needs: to safeguard the King's lawful powers and to guarantee that he genuinely did pose a lesser threat to the rule of law than the Houses. They wished to achieve this without surrendering to the doctrine of 'co-ordination'. Instead, they denied the possibility of ever attaining what Rudyerd called 'a mathematicall securitie'. As Ferne observed in 1642, 'we cannot expect absolute means of safety and securitie in a State, but such as are reasonable'.[24] They had to find a means to defend the rule of law which did not encroach upon the King's powers. Their constitutional beliefs rested upon the assumption that this was not only perfectly realisable but actually the best arrangement. Yet how could it be sustained when many thought that Charles I's understanding and employment of his own powers were incompatible with the rule of law? What defeated the peace treaties one after the other was the fact that Parliament's commissioners demanded a level of control over royal action which the Constitutional Royalists deemed inimical to the established polity. They insisted that Charles I could be trusted to rule within the customs and laws of England, and hence that there was no inconsistency in the concept of a legally limited sovereign who yet possessed discretionary powers. Their Parliamentarian counterparts, by contrast, argued that unless this King was shorn of his discretionary powers the notion of legal limitation would be empty rhetoric and the rule of law would remain vulnerable to royal authoritarianism. They pointed to earlier instances of Charles's 'legal tyranny' to justify this fear. The gulf between these two positions, which stemmed from conflicting perceptions of Charles I, obstructed treaties from Oxford to Newport. Later it led Hobbes to conclude that attempts at accommodation were doomed from the outset.

Yet to assert that their failure could have been 'easily ... foreseen' is perhaps to adopt the wisdom of hindsight. The attitudes which underpinned Constitutional Royalism were not impossibly idealistic. They corresponded closely to political and religious realities prior to 1625; and they were again to inform government policy after 1660. Constitutional

---

[24] H[enry] Fern[e], *The Resolving of Conscience* (Cambridge, 1642), p. 25 (Wing, F 800).

Royalism represented a justification for a reality which existed at several times during the seventeenth century, rather than pipe-dreams which were never actually put into practice. Nor was it unreasonable to hope that the large middle ground of moderate opinion, which embraced both Constitutional Royalists and Constitutional Parliamentarians, would knit together during the 1640s. We have seen that they shared many common values and assumptions, and above all that there were striking affinities of temperament between them. Their coming together would have permitted a settlement similar to that achieved in the Glorious Revolution. The years 1688–9 saw just such an 'alliance of moderates' accomplish 'a centrist compromise'.[25] Moderate Tories like Nottingham – the successors of the Constitutional Royalists – contributed to the Revolution settlement alongside moderate Whigs. Yet what proved possible under James II had remained elusive under his father, which brings us back once again to the particular difficulties generated by Charles I's personality and policies.

As Conrad Russell and Kevin Sharpe have recently reminded us, the problem was certainly not that Charles I refused to listen to critical counsel.[26] He never shut his ears to the advice of Constitutional Royalists. We have seen how he assembled a number of moderate advisers at the turn of 1641–2 who subsequently became his principal propagandists throughout the first Civil War. A King who could authorise the *Answer to the XIX Propositions* to be issued in his name was clearly not wedded in any simplistic sense to a concept of absolute monarchy. The responses of the King's commissioners during peace talks were sanctioned by him but generally did not involve compromising their own private beliefs. It was not that the King was saying and doing one thing and his moderate advisers another. Rather, the dilemma which the Constitutional Royalists faced was one familiar to earlier advisers such as Hamilton and Traquair, namely Charles's reluctance to accept one line of counsel to the exclusion of all others.[27] Time and again, he adopted a mixture of moderate and hard-line advice which proved less successful than either would have done if pursued in isolation.[28] It was impossible for the Houses to forget that Charles had been implicated in the Incident and the Army Plots, and had attempted to arrest the Five Members, when his own commitment to peace treaties was often so suspect. The King's concessions came belatedly and

[25] Morrill, *Nature of the English Revolution*, p. 441.
[26] Russell, *Causes*, especially pp. 193–4; *FBM*, pp. 4–6; and Sharpe, *Personal Rule*, pp. 706–8.
[27] Peter Donald, *An Uncounselled King: Charles I and the Scottish Troubles, 1637–1641* (Cambridge, 1990), especially pp. 43–118, 320–7; Russell, *FBM*, pp. 89–93. I have also profited from reading John Scally, 'The early career of James, third Marquis and first Duke of Hamilton' (PhD thesis, University of Cambridge, 1993).
[28] Cf. Wormald, *Clarendon*, pp. 104–5, 231.

with obvious reluctance: they would have carried far more credibility had they not been accompanied by grudging utterances and underhand negotiations with other interest groups.[29]

But the root of the difficulties extended even deeper into Charles's personality, for it gradually became clear that the most intractable sticking-points were those most closely related to his own 'conscience' and 'honour'. These included the fate of 'delinquents', the protection of lawful royal powers within secular government and over the militia, and above all the preservation of the existing Church of England. Unfortunately, these were precisely the issues on which moderate Parliamentarians and moderate Royalists found it hardest to agree. One of the few areas where they had differed throughout their earlier careers was the nature of the Church. Many of those who became Constitutional Royalists had first emerged as an identifiable grouping within the House of Commons over the issue of root-and-branch reform on 8–9 February 1641. The passage of the Militia Ordinance in March 1642 marked another critical turning-point and precipitated the final departure of many Royalists from both Houses to York. It revealed profound disagreements over whether the Junto was now behaving more illegally than Charles. The King took his firmest stand on precisely those issues about which the moderate middle ground proved unable to agree; the very considerations which divided people like Hyde and Selden over whether the monarch or the Houses posed the greater danger to England's fundamental laws and constitution. Once Charles had embraced the role of a martyr who would rather die than sacrifice his conscience, his Church or his friends – which he certainly had by mid-1645 at the latest[30] – compromise became virtually impossible. Yet, as the progress made over the *Heads of the Proposals* and later at the Treaty of Newport clearly reveals, settlement was not actually ruled out until fanatical elements within the Army decided that they had no option but to destroy 'Charles Stuart, that Man of Blood'.

All this amounts to saying that Charles I was an exceptionally difficult monarch for any Constitutional Royalist to serve. His propensity for trying to combine incompatible counsels and for taking what Dorset termed 'extempore resolutions'[31] impeded and ultimately thwarted their search for settlement. Yet under subsequent monarchs the basic strength and resilience of Constitutional Royalist attitudes became evident. They provided the guiding values of the Restoration régime, especially in its early years, under a monarch who had espoused them to a greater degree than many within the political nation. After Clarendon's fall, his ideas were

---

[29] Cf. Russell, *Causes*, pp. 208–9.   [30] See above, pp. 125, 148.
[31] BL, Microfilm M 485, vol. CXXXI, fo. 182v (Dorset to the Earl of Salisbury, 27 June 1642).

carried on by the 'Friends of the Constitution in Church and State', and by the moderate Tories who attempted to apply a brake during Charles II's final years. Under James II, the potential for moderate opinion to form a united middle ground was resoundingly demonstrated. Unlike his father, James did not take his stand on issues which divided moderates but on far-reaching concessions to Catholics against which they could readily unite. It was as if Charles I had adopted a more extreme position in 1642, and the commissioners at the Treaty of Oxford had then been able to formulate an agreed response. In the wake of the Glorious Revolution, Constitutional Royalist attitudes continued to be influential well into the eighteenth century, as Blackstone's *Commentaries* show. This should not, of course, be exaggerated: the remarkable durability of 'co-ordination' theory indicates how complex and pluralistic English constitutional thought remained. None the less, the ideas expressed by Hyde and his allies were to find exponents throughout the years of England's *ancien régime*.

That said, Constitutional Royalism was very much a product of the seventeenth century. Couched in the idiom and coloured by the experiences of the Stuart age, it can only be fully understood against this specific background. It in turn throws light on the political contours of the seventeenth century and on the contrasting characteristics of the Stuart monarchs. A study of Constitutional Royalism gives an unusually vivid sense of the *shape* of the seventeenth century. It lends support, first of all, to the recent rehabilitation of James I's reputation as monarch, politician and Supreme Governor of the Church. His assertion of royal powers as far as they were compatible with the rule of law, his willingness to work with Parliaments, and his tolerance of diverse religious opinions within the framework of the established Church all marked a continuation of Elizabethan practice and identified James as a close approximation to the Constitutional Royalists' ideal monarch. I have argued elsewhere that Dorset may be labelled a 'Jacobethan', and the same would be true of other Constitutional Royalists.[32] They were consistently spurred into action whenever the policies of any ruler violated 'Jacobethan' norms. This was evident in the aspects of Charles I's rule which they chose to criticise. They did not fear a 'popish plot' or the introduction of idolatry so much as the systematic infringement of the rule of law in both Church and State. During the 1620s and 1630s they held different views about what policies actually violated the law, and never formed a common front on issues such as the Forced Loan. But in the first six months of the Long Parliament their criticism of recent royal policies, especially Ship Money and the 1640 canons, was primarily on the grounds of legality. These were two key

[32] David L. Smith, 'The fourth Earl of Dorset and the politics of the sixteen-twenties', *Historical Research*, 65 (1992), 53; 'Catholic, Anglican or Puritan?', 121–2.

areas – the pursuit of national extra-parliamentary taxation and the dramatic narrowing of legitimate religious belief – in which Charles I departed most signally from his father's practices. But after Charles had renounced the policies of the Personal Rule, abandoned the prerogative courts and assented to statutory guarantees of Parliament's existence, and when simultaneously the Junto launched an assault on the 'Church by law established', precisely the same considerations drove the Constitutional Royalists to rally to the King. Having tried to protect the rule of law and 'the pure religion of Elizabeth and James'[33] from King Charles, they now sought to defend them against King Pym. This is a shift which Hobbes's account identifies very clearly. What he misses is the fact that identical motives lay behind the Constitutional Royalists' search for settlement during the ensuing years of civil war. Their promotion of peace treaties, like their criticism of royal policies during 1640–1 and their hostility to the Junto from 1641 onwards, were all part of a consistent attempt to re-establish the 'Jacobethan ideal'; to recover a lost paradigm founded on royal government with Parliaments and within the law, and on religious ecumenicism within an established episcopalian Church.

But an accommodation between King and Parliament proved impossible when the elements in that equation were Charles I and the Junto. Each side distinguished between the institution of the other (which could be trusted) and its current occupant(s) (which could not). With mistrust so inextricably linked to particular personalities, there could be no agreement over whether a 'mathematicall securitie', ensuring parliamentary approval of royal action, was desirable or even possible. This conundrum defeated the search for settlement in the short term. Yet the Constitutional Royalists' principles remained consistent and shaped their response to successive régimes after 1649. It is very striking that their general passivity under the Commonwealth and Protectorate was interrupted – most vehemently in the cases of Hyde and Southampton – by bitter condemnation of the Decimation Tax. They denounced it for exactly the same reasons that they had previously criticised Charles I and then the Junto. Hyde explicitly drew the parallel with Ship Money and objected that the Decimation Tax represented 'the funeral oration upon Parliaments, law, conscience and equity'.[34] Once again, it was the violation of 'Jacobethan' practice which forced Constitutional Royalists to break their silence.

In 1660 these 'good principles' returned to favour and provided the guiding philosophy of the Restoration régime. Charles II emerges from this study as a monarch who had internalised Constitutional Royalism – and with it 'Jacobethan' values – far more effectively than his father. If 1625

---

[33] Cf. Morrill, *Nature of the English Revolution*, p. 148.   [34] See above, p. 278.

marked a significant departure from earlier practice, the years after 1660 saw a conscious attempt to restore the political and religious stability of 'Jacobethan' England. Official policy emphasised the Clarendonian tenets of strong royal government under the rule of law, an assured role for Parliaments, and toleration of a spectrum of religious opinion within a broad national Church. The last objective was not achieved, but this does not negate the fact that the agendas of both King and Lord Chancellor were profoundly influenced by the model of 'Jacobethan' rule. Even as a personality, Charles II – with his easy-going, accessible manner, promiscuous private life and capacity to live with compromises and blurred distinctions – resembled his grandfather much more closely than his father. The parallels are not, of course, exact: Charles II was forced to accept a narrow, intolerant Church which never received the wide support possible before 1625. Furthermore, Constitutional Royalism enjoyed its greatest influence during the years of Clarendon's Lord Chancellorship; its impact on the rest of Charles's reign, and especially after 1681, was rather more mixed. None the less, the similarities between James I and Charles II repay careful examination, and the fact that both died peacefully in their beds surely owed much to their pursuit of policies compatible with Constitutional Royalist ideals.

When these ideals were again jettisoned by James II, another revolution resulted. Once more, an exploration of Constitutional Royalism serves to highlight the broader patterns within seventeenth-century political history. Just as it reveals the analogies between James I and Charles II, so it also prompts comparisons between Charles I and James II. For here were two monarchs who stumbled into unprecedented difficulties after unprecedentedly smooth accessions. They did so by subverting the rule of law and by drastically reforming the Church of England in ways which weakened its defences against popery. Both were conviction politicians, ideologues with a high-flown sense of their own powers and ill at ease with the rough and tumble which religious ecumenicism, collaboration with Parliaments and the exercise of royal powers within the law all required. No less than 1625, 1685 saw the accession of a monarch ill-suited to practise 'Jacobethan' methods. In terms of personality, a bluff, genial, outgoing monarch was again succeeded by one who was cold, brittle and aloof. This ultimately forced moderate Tories, the heirs of the Constitutional Royalists, to take drastic action. They were able to agree with moderate Whigs more easily than their predecessors had with moderate Parliamentarians; but their contributions to the Revolution settlement again bore the distinctive fingerprints which we have noted throughout this book. While many Whigs in 1688–9 could trace their ideological ancestry back to the 'co-ordination' theorists of the 1640s, the calls by Nottingham, the 'counsel for the constitution', that 'all laws civil or ecclesiastical be ratified and established' and that 'violations of the laws' be redressed all echoed the central tenets of Constitutional Royalism. That it was Nottingham who also introduced measures for toleration and comprehension early in 1689 affords further evidence that we should not underestimate the Tory contribution to the Revolution settlement. The problems of 1688–9 were posed by the particular personality and policies of James II; but among the solutions offered was one which harked back to the ideas which had proved so successful under James I and Charles II. At one level, moderate Tories thus saw the Glorious Revolution as another attempt to achieve the 'Jacobethan' ideal.

The outcome, however, was complex and ambiguous. Although the Revolution settlement did not of itself establish a fully constitutional monarchy, the following decade saw a series of measures which imposed new limitations upon royal actions. Angus McInnes has argued that 'in the 1690s England finally swung away from royal government and turned instead to mixed government'.[35] Under the pressure of war against Louis XIV, Parliament became 'an essential and omnipresent part of the constitution':[36] the Triennial Act (1694) obliged the Crown to call a new Parliament at least every three years; and the Civil List Act (1698) established the principle of annual votes of income to the crown and marked the abandonment of the ancient distinction between ordinary and extraordinary revenue. Although the extent to which William III willingly became 'the betrayer of English absolutism' remains controversial,[37] the significance of the constitutional measures during his reign is clear. They culminated in the 'Act for the further limitation of the Crown and better securing the Rights and Liberties of the Subject' in 1701.[38] This statute compelled the monarch to 'join in communion with the Church of England as by law established' and abrogated the royal powers to dismiss judges, to pardon those impeached by the Commons, or to declare war for the defence of foreign territories without parliamentary consent. At a stroke, this removed many of the principal sources of political instability which had dogged seventeenth-century England. We have only to examine the tensions generated by a monarch's dubious Protestant credentials, or by the burdens of war, or by the relationship between the Crown and the judiciary to appreciate why this was a critical turning-point. It rounded off a

---

[35] Angus McInnes, 'When was the English Revolution?', *History*, 66 (1982), 377–92; quotation at 390. Cf. Jennifer Carter, 'The Revolution and the Constitution', in *Britain after the Glorious Revolution, 1689–1714*, ed. Geoffrey Holmes (1969), pp. 39–58.
[36] McInnes, 'When was the English Revolution?', 388.
[37] This epithet was coined in *ibid.*, 392. For a review of alternative interpretations, see Morrill, *Nature of the English Revolution*, p. 429.
[38] 12 & 13 Gul. III, c. 2.

decade of rapid change in which the echoes of a personal monarchy gradually gave way to the more dominant strain of mixed monarchy.

From the perspective of Constitutional Royalism, however, these developments were distinctly ambivalent. The need for the monarch and the Church to operate in symbiosis; the commitment to Parliament's place within the constitution; the reciprocity between the monarch's powers and the subjects' rights and liberties; the defence of the rule of law – all these key axioms of Constitutional Royalism were enshrined in statute during the 1690s. The reign of William and Mary saw the establishment of what Brian Wormald has called the 'necessary conventions' which ensured royal government within the law.[39] By imposing statutory guarantees that the monarch would rule according to constitutional norms, the political nation had at last achieved the 'mathematicall securitie' against royal whim which Rudyerd had thought unattainable and the Constitutional Royalists undesirable. This was the final paradox. Men like Hyde and Culpepper, Dorset and Southampton believed in a monarchy limited by the rule of law and in harmony with Church and Parliament; but they did not believe in legislation to ensure this. They stoutly opposed Parliamentarian demands for such steps during the 1640s on the grounds that these would fundamentally alter the nature of the polity, and that any well advised monarch would naturally protect the law, the Church and the constitution. When these conditions were ultimately guaranteed by statute at the end of the century, it was therefore in a way which they could not have countenanced.

Nevertheless, we have seen that ideas similar to those of the Constitutional Royalists retained their currency well into the eighteenth century, especially in the writings of lawyers such as Blackstone. In that sense, Brian Wormald was undoubtedly correct to stress the long-term influence of Clarendonian ideas, and to conclude that 'the true bridge between the nonresistance of the epoch of the Tudor rulers and the eighteenth century constitution was the non-violent, the bridge-building parliamentarism of Hyde'.[40] In the end, Constitutional Royalism thus possesses a twofold significance. It opens up an important strand of political theory and practice which contributed to the search for settlement during the 1640s. The fact that it failed in the short term does not justify its long neglect. And second, it can trace a lengthy descent through English political and constitutional development into the eighteenth century. This is not to claim that its central ideas were eventually adopted in their entirety, but simply that Constitutional Royalism possessed an influence beyond the particular circumstances within which it originated, and that it was one of the threads which bound the English polity of the seventeenth century to that of

---

[39] Wormald, *Clarendon*, p. xxxvi.   [40] *Ibid.*, p. 153.

today.[41] Which is why, three-and-a-half centuries after the outbreak of the English Civil War, it is still worth reconstructing 'the more posed and wise advise of those thatt stud[ied] how to preserve things from extremity'.[42]

[41] Cf. J. W. Daly, 'The origins and shaping of English Royalist thought', *Historical Papers/ Communications Historiques* (1974), pp. 30–1.
[42] BL, Microfilm M 485, vol. CXXXI, fo. 183r (Dorset to the Earl of Salisbury, 27 June 1642).

BIBLIOGRAPHY

This bibliography makes no claim to comprehensive coverage of the vast body of material bearing on Constitutional Royalism, let alone that relating to English political and constitutional history during the 1640s. Rather, it contains full details of all the sources cited in the footnotes of this book. It is divided into three sections: manuscript sources, printed primary sources and secondary sources.

MANUSCRIPT SOURCES

BRITISH NATIONAL COLLECTIONS

Public Record Office (Chancery Lane)

C 2 (Chancery proceedings, series I)
C 7 (Chancery proceedings, Hamilton's Division)
C 8 (Chancery proceedings, Mitford's Division)
C 33 (Chancery entry books of decrees and orders)
C 66 (Chancery Patent Rolls)
C 115 (Chancery Masters' Exhibits, Duchess of Norfolk deeds: Scudamore newsletters)
C 231/3 (Crown Office docquet book)
E 317 (Parliamentary surveys)
IND 4226 (Patent Office docquet book of warrants for the Great Seal)
LC 3/1 (Establishment of Charles I's Household, 1641)
LC 5/134–135 (Lord Chamberlain's warrant books)
PC 2/53 (Privy Council register)
PRO 30/53/9 (diary of Lord Herbert)
PRO 31/3 (Baschet's French transcripts)
PROB 6 (Prerogative Court of Canterbury, act books of administrations)
SO 3/8–12 (Signet Office docquet books)
SP 14 (State Papers Domestic, James I)
SP 16 (State Papers Domestic, Charles I)
SP 18 (State Papers Domestic, Interregnum)
SP 19 (Committee for the Advance of Money papers)
SP 20 (Committee for Sequestrations papers)
SP 21 (Committee of Both Kingdoms and Derby House Committee papers)
SP 23 (Committee for Compounding papers)
SP 25 (Council of State papers)
SP 29 (State Papers Domestic, Charles II)

SP 77 (State Papers Foreign, Flanders)
SP 84 (State Papers Foreign, Holland)

British Library

Additional MS 4247 (miscellaneous papers)
Additional MS 5461 (Sabran despatches)
Additional MS 5752 (Musgrave Collection)
Additional MS 5756 (Musgrave Collection)
Additional MS 5947* (historical collections)
Additional MS 12514 (heraldic and historical collections)
Additional MS 17017 (Hyde correspondence)
Additional MSS 18777–18779 (diary of Walter Yonge)
Additional MSS 18980–18982 (Prince Rupert correspondence)
Additional MS 21427 (Baynes correspondence)
Additional MS 27402 (miscellaneous historical papers)
Additional MS 27962 (Salvetti correspondence)
Additional MS 29775 (order of Charles II's coronation procession)
Additional MS 29974 (Pitt correspondence)
Additional MS 31116 (diary of Laurence Whitaker)
Additional MS 32093 (Malet Collection)
Additional MS 34599 (Sir Henry Spelman correspondence)
Additional MS 35029 (letters of Charles I)
Additional MS 37343 (Whitelocke's Annals)
Additional MS 37998 (Sir Edward Walker papers)
Additional MS 46188 (Jessop papers)
Additional MSS 64870–64924 (Coke MS, series I)
Additional MSS 69868–69935 (Coke MS, series II)
Additional MSS 69936–69998 (Coke MS, series III)
Egerton MS 71 (meditations and prayers of Lord Seymour)
Egerton MS 784 (diary of William Whiteway)
Egerton MSS 2533–2562 (Nicholas papers)
Egerton MSS 2978–2979 (Heath and Verney papers)
Harleian MSS 162–164 (diary of Sir Simonds D'Ewes)
Harleian MSS 476–479 (diary of John Moore)
Harleian MS 5047 (parliamentary journal)
Harleian MS 6424 (diary of a bishop)
Harleian MSS 6802–6804 (Royalist Council of War papers)
Harleian MSS 6851–6852 (Royalist Council of War papers)
Harleian MS 6988 (Royal letters and warrants)
Lansdowne MS 459 (register of Church livings)
Sloane MS 1116 (Glisson medical papers)
Sloane MS 1467 (speeches in Parliament)
Stowe MS 142 (miscellaneous historical letters)
Stowe MS 184 (Dering papers)
Stowe MS 580 (Sir Edward Walker papers)
Stowe MS 743 (Dering correspondence)
Microfilm M 485 (Hatfield House, Cecil MS)
Microfilm M 636 (Claydon House, Verney MS)

Bodleian Library, Oxford

MS Ashmole 800 (miscellaneous collections)
MS Ashmole 830 (miscellaneous collections)
MS Ashmole 832 (creations of peers)
MSS Ashmole 1110–1112 (Order of the Garter papers)
MS Ashmole 1132 (Order of the Garter papers)
MSS Carte 10–22 (Ormond papers)
MSS Clarendon 1–93 (Clarendon State Papers)
MSS Clarendon 97–98 (select Clarendon papers)
MSS Dep. c. 152–176 (Nalson MS)
MS Eng. hist. c. 230 (docquet book of warrants for letters patent)
MSS Firth c. 6–8 (Prince Rupert papers)
MS Rawlinson C 956 (diary of Sir John Holland)
MS Rawlinson D 932 (diary of Sir John Holland)
MS Rawlinson D 1099 (diary of Sir John Holland)
MS Rawlinson Letters 47 (Warcup correspondence)
MSS Tanner 51–66 (letters and papers)
MS Tanner 299 (Archbishop Sancroft's transcriptions)

Cambridge University Library

Add. MS 89 (historical collections)
Buxton MS (Corr.), Box 1 (miscellaneous correspondence)
MS Mm. 1. 46 (Baker MS)

House of Lords Record Office

Braye MS 2 (John Browne papers)
Historical Collection MS 65 (Sir Edward Walker papers)
House of Lords Main Papers
House of Lords Manuscript Journals
House of Lords Manuscript Minutes, VII–XI (1641–5)
Original Acts of Parliament

Lambeth Palace Library

MS 943 (Laud papers)

Scottish Record Office, Edinburgh

GD 406 (Hamilton MS)

BRITISH LOCAL AND PRIVATE COLLECTIONS

Bedfordshire Record Office, Bedford

J 1382–1386 (St John of Bletsoe MS)

Devon Record Office, Exeter
1392 M/L16 (Seymour of Berry Pomeroy MS)

Dorset Record Office, Dorchester
D 124 (Fox-Strangways [Earls of Ilchester] MS)

Centre for Kentish Studies, Maidstone
U 269 (Sackville MS)
U 565 (Darnley MS)
U 1475 (De L'Isle and Dudley MS)
Uncatalogued Cranfield papers

Leeds Castle, Kent
MS C1 (letters to Prince Rupert)

Lincolnshire Archives Office, Lincoln
Ancaster MS

Buckminster Park Estate Office, near Grantham, Lincolnshire
Tollemache MS

Dr Williams's Library, 14 Gordon Square, London
MS 24.50 (diary of Thomas Juxon)

Society of Antiquaries of London, Burlington House, Piccadilly, London
MS 140 (Lyttelton papers)

Norfolk Record Office, Norwich
Lee Warner MS 1/2 (diary of 1640)

Castle Ashby, Northampton
Compton MS 1084 (Compton correspondence)

Northamptonshire Record Office, Northampton
Montagu MS 4 (Montagu correspondence)

Christ Church Muniment Room, Oxford
Evelyn Collection, Browne correspondence
    Clarendon and Browne letters
    Nicholas Box
    Nicholas to Browne letters
    Nobility letters

Worcester College, Oxford
Clarke MS XLI (letters and papers, 1646–7)

Staffordshire Record Office, Stafford
D 868 (Leveson-Gower correspondence)

William Salt Library, Stafford
Salt MS 509 (Essex to Prince Rupert, 22 June 1643)

Surrey Record Office: Guildford Muniment Room
Bray Deposits 52/2/19; 85/5/2 (Nicholas MS)

East Sussex Record Office, Lewes
Rye Corporation MS 47 (Rye Corporation correspondence)

Wiltshire Record Office, Trowbridge
WRO 1300 (Ailesbury MS)

Longleat House, Warminster, Wiltshire
Seymour MS

UNITED STATES OF AMERICA

Beinecke Library, Yale University
Osborn MS b. 304 (commonplace book of Sir John Strangways)

Folger Shakespeare Library, Washington, DC
MS X.c.23 (Sir Giles Mompesson to Edward Hyde, [?] April 1642)
MS X.d.18 (Clarendon correspondence)

Henry E. Huntington Library, San Marino, California
Ellesmere MS
Hastings MS
Stowe (Temple) MS

PRINTED PRIMARY SOURCES

SIXTEENTH AND SEVENTEENTH-CENTURY SOURCES PUBLISHED BEFORE 1700

Aston, Sir Thomas, *A Remonstrance against Presbytery* (1641), Wing, A 4078; BL, TT, E 163/1, E 163/2

Aylmer, John, *An Harborowe for Faithfvll and Trewe Subiectes* (Strasburg, 1559), STC, 1005

Bramhall, John, *Castigations of Mr Hobbes his last Animadversions, in the Case concerning Liberty, and Universal Necessity* (1657), Wing, B 4214

The Catching of Leviathan, or the Great Whale (1658), printed with *Castigations of Mr Hobbes his last Animadversions, in the Case concerning Liberty, and Universal Necessity* (1658), Wing, B 4215; BL, TT, E 1757/1

[Bramhall, John], *The Serpent-Salve, or, A Remedie for the Biting of an Aspe* (1642), Wing, B 4236

A Catalogue of the Names of the Knights, Citizens and Burgesses that have served in the last four Parliaments (1656), Wing, C 1394; BL, TT, E 1602/6

[Charles I, King], *His Maiesties Answer to the Petition of the Lords and Commons in Parliament assembled* [17 June 1642], Wing, C 2137; BL, TT, E 152/3

His Majesties Declaration to all his loving subjects on the causes which moved him to dissolve the last Parliament (1640), CUL, Syn. 7. 64. 73/43

His Majesties Declaration to all his Loving Subjects [12 August 1642], Wing, C 2241; BL, TT, E 115/11

His Maiesties gracious message to both Houses of Parliament sent from Nottingham the 25 of August 1642, together with the answer of the Lords and Commons to the said message (1642), Wing, C 2332; BL, TT, E 116/2

Chillingworth, William, *The Religion of Protestants* (Oxford, 1638), STC, 5138

A Copy of a Letter from the Members of both Houses to the Earle of Essex desiring a Treaty of Peace (Oxford, 1644), Wing, E 1285; BL, TT, E 32/3

Culpepper, Sir John, *Sir Iohn Cvlpeper His Speech in Parliament concerning the Grievances of the Church and Common-wealth* (1641), Wing, C 5058; BL, TT, E 196/8

Dallison, Charles, *Mr Charles Dallison Record[e]r of Lincoln, His Speech to the King's Majesty* (1642), Wing, D 139

[Dallison, Charles], *The Royalist's Defence* (1648), Wing, D 138

The Lord George Digby's Cabinet and Dr Goff's Negotiations (1646), Wing B 4763; BL, TT, E 329/15

Digby, Sir Kenelm, *Observations upon Religio Medici, occasionally written by Sir Kenelm Digby* (1643), Wing, D 1422; BL, TT, E 1113/4

[Digges, Dudley], *An Answer to a printed book, intituled Observations upon some of His Majesties late answers and expresses* (Oxford, 1642), Wing, D 1454; BL, TT, E 105/5

A Review of the Observations upon some of His Majesties late answers and expresses, written by a gentleman of quality (Oxford, 1643), Wing, D 1459; BL, TT, E 97/11

The Unlawfulnesse of Subjects taking up armes against their Soveraigne, in what case soever (Oxford, 1643[/4]), Wing, D 1462; BL, TT, E 128/42

Falkland, Lucius Cary, second Viscount, *Of the Infallibilitie of the Chvrch of*

Rome: A Discourse written by the Lord Viscount Falkland (Oxford, 1645), Wing, F 322

Ferne, Henry, *Conscience Satisfied, that there is no warrant for the armes now taken up by subjects* (Oxford, 1643), Wing, F 791; BL, TT, E 97/7

A Reply unto severall treatises pleading for the armes now taken up by subjects in the pretended defence of religion and liberty (Oxford, 1643), Wing, F 799; BL, TT, E 74/9

The Resolving of Conscience (Cambridge, 1642), Wing, F 800

A Sermon preached at the publique fast the twelfth day of April [1644] at St Maries Oxford, before the members of the honourable House of Commons there assembled (Oxford, 1644), Wing, F 805; BL, TT, E 46/5

[Ferne, Henry], *Episcopacy and Presbytery considered* (Oxford, 1644), Wing, F 793; BL, TT, E 400/11

[Filmer, Sir Robert], *The Anarchy of a Limited or Mixed Monarchy* (1648), Wing, F 910; BL, TT, E 436/4

The Necessity of the Absolute Power of all Kings: and in particular of the King of England (1648), Wing, F 917; BL, TT, E 460/7

A Full and True Relation of the Several Actions and Particulars of what was taken and done in Oxford (1646), Wing, F 2330; BL, TT, E 342/9

Grimston, Harbottle, *Master Grimston his worthy and learned Speech ... concerning troubles abroad and grievances at home* (1641), Wing, G 2051

Hacket, John, *Scrinia Reserata: A Memorial Offer'd to the Great Deservings of John Williams, D.D.* (1693), Wing, H 171

[Herle, Charles], *A Fuller Answer to a Treatise written by Doctor Ferne* (1642), Wing, H 1558; BL, TT, E 244/27

Howell, James, *Down-right Dealing, or the Despised Protestant Speaking Plain English* (1647), Wing, H 3069; BL, TT, E 408/17

Englands Teares, for the Present Wars (1644), Wing, H 3070; BL, TT, E 253/10

The Preheminence and Pedigree of Parlement (1644), Wing, H 3106; BL, TT, E 253/2

[Howell, James], *Ah, Ha; Tumulus, Thalamus: Two Counter-Poems* (1654), Wing, H 3054; BL, TT, E 228/1

The Instruments of a King: or, A Short Discourse of the Sword, the Scepter, the Crowne ([16 September] 1648), Wing, H 3083; BL, TT, E 464/7

A Letter to the Earle of Pembrooke Concerning the Times, and the sad condition both of Prince and People (1647), Wing, H 3085; BL, TT, E 522/5

Parables, reflecting upon the Times (Paris, 1643), Wing, H 3099; BL, TT, E 67/16

The Vote, or A Poeme Royall, presented to His Maiestie for a New-yeares-Gift (1642), Wing, H 3128; BL, TT, E 238/7

Hudson, Michael, *The Divine Right of Government* (1647), Wing, H 3261; BL, TT, E 406/24

[Hunton, Philip], *A Treatise of Monarchie* (1643), Wing, H 3781; BL, TT, E 103/15

[Hyde, Edward, Earl of Clarendon], *A Brief View and Survey of the Dangerous and Pernicious Errors to Church and State, in Mr Hobbes's Book, entitled Leviathan* (Oxford, 1676), Wing, C 4420

A Full Answer to an Infamous and Trayterous Pamphlet (1648), Wing, C 4423; BL, TT, E 455/5

A Letter from a True and Lawfull Member of Parliament (1656), Wing, C 4424; BL, TT, E 884/2

Transcendent and Multiplied Rebellion and Treason, discovered by the Lawes of the Land (1645), Wing, C 4428; BL, TT, E 308/29

Jenkins, David, *An Apology for the Army, touching the Eight Quaeres, etc.* (1648), Wing, J 582; BL, TT, E 396/18

   The Armies Indempnity (1647), Wing, J 584; BL, TT, E 390/10

   The Cordiall of Judge Jenkins for the good people of London (1647), Wing, J 586; BL, TT, E 391/11

   The Declaration of David Jenkins, late prisoner in the Tower of London (1648), Wing, J 589; BL, TT, E 467/31

   A Discourse touching the Inconveniences of a long continued Parliament (1647), Wing, J 590; BL, TT, E 392/30

   Judge Jenkin's Plea delivered in to the Earle of Manchester, and the Speaker of the House of Commons (1647[/8]), Wing, J 598; BL, TT, E 427/12

   Lex Terrae (1647), Wing, J 593; BL, TT, E 390/18

   A Preparative to the Treaty: or, A short, sure, and conscientious expedient for Agreement and Peace; tendred to the two Houses of Parliament (1648), Wing, J 600; BL, TT, E 463/17

   The Vindication of Judge Jenkins Prisoner in the Tower, the 29 of April 1647 (1647), Wing, J 613; BL, TT, E 386/6

   The Works of that Grave and Learned Judge Jenkins, prisoner in Newgate, upon divers statutes, concerning the liberty and freedome of the subject (1648), Wing, J 574; BL, TT, E 1154/2

The Kingdomes Weekly Intelligencer, no. 41 (23–30 January 1644), STC (News), 214.041; BL, TT, E 30/19

The Kingdomes Weekly Intelligencer, no. 42 (30 January–7 February 1644), STC (News), 214.042; BL, TT, E 31/21

[Maxwell, John], *Sacro-sancta Regum Majestas: or; The Sacred and Royall Prerogative of Christian Kings* (Oxford, 1644), Wing, M 1384; BL, TT, E 30/22

Mayne, Jasper, *The Difference about Church Government ended* (1646), Wing, M 1470; BL, TT, E 339/8

   A Late Printed Sermon against False Prophets, vindicated by letter from the causeless aspersions of Mr Francis Cheynell (1647), Wing, M 1471; BL, TT, E 392/15

   Οχλο-μαχια, *or The Peoples War* (1647), Wing, M 1472; BL, TT, E 398/19

   A Sermon against False Prophets, preached in St Marjes Church in Oxford, shortly after the surrender of that garrison (Oxford, 1646[/7]), Wing, M 1473; BL, TT, E 371/8

   A Sermon concerning Unity and Agreement, preached at Carfax Church in Oxford, August 9 1646 (Oxford, 1646), Wing, M 1476; BL, TT, E 355/30

[Mayne, Jasper], *The Amorous Warre* (1648), Wing, M 1463

   The Citye Match (Oxford, 1639), STC, 17750

Mercurius Aulicus, no. 15 (9–16 April 1643), STC (News), 275.115; BL, TT, E 99/22

Mercurius Aulicus, no. 28 (9–15 July 1643), STC (News), 275.128; BL, TT, E 62/3

Mercurius Publicus, no. 21 (17–24 May 1660), STC (News), 378.121; BL, TT, E 183/17

Nalson, John, *An Impartial Collection of the Great Affairs of State* (2 vols., 1682–3), Wing, N 106–107

The Papers which passed at Newcastle betwixt His Sacred Majestie and Mr Al[exander] Henderson: concerning the change of Church-Government (1649), Wing, C 2535; BL, TT, E 1243/3

[Parker, Henry], *Observations upon some of His Majesties late answers and expresses* (1642), Wing, P 412; BL, TT, E 153/26

The Perfect Diurnall of some Passages and Proceedings, no. 288 (11–18 June 1655), STC *(News)*, 503.288; BL, TT, E 843/4

A Perfect Diurnall of some Passages in Parliament, no. 83 (24 February–3 March 1644[/5]), STC *(News)*, 504.083; BL, TT, E 258/31

A Perfect Diurnall of some Passages in Parliament, no. 219 (4–11 October 1647), STC *(News)*, 504.219; BL, TT, E 518/43

A Perfect Diurnall of some Passages in Parliament, no. 288 (29 January–5 February 1648[/9]), STC *(News)*, 504.288; BL, TT, E 527/16

A Perfect Journall of the Daily Proceedings and Transactions in that Memorable Parliament, begun at Westminster, the third day of November 1640 (1659), CUL, Acton. d. 25. 109/1

Perfect Occurrences of Every Daie Iournall in Parliament, no. 41 (8–15 October 1647), STC *(News)*, 465.5041; BL, TT, E 518/44

Price, John, *The Mystery and Method of His Majesty's Happy Restauration, Laid Open to Publick View* (1680), Wing, P 3335

Rudyerd, Sir Benjamin, *Sir Benjamin Ruddierd's speech in behalfe of the cleargy* (1628[/9]), STC, 21435.7

Sir Benjamin Rudyerd's Speech; concerning Bishops, Deanes and Chapters (1641), Wing, R 2190; BL, TT, E 198/40

Sir Benjamin Rudyerd His Speech in the High Court of Parliament the 17 of February [1643], for a speedy Treaty of Peace with His Majestie (1643), Wing, R 2195; BL, TT, E 90/15

The Speeches of Sir Benjamin Rudyer in the High Court of Parliament (1641), Wing, R 2200; BL, TT, E 196/2

A Worthy Speech spoken in the Honourable House of Commons, by Sir Benjamin Rudyerd, this present July, 1642 (1642), Wing, R 2206

Rushworth, John, *Historical Collections of private passages of State* (8 vols., 1680–1701), Wing, R 2317–2319

Selden, John, *Vindiciae Secundum Integritatem Existimationis Suae* (1653), Wing, S 2444; BL, TT, E 719/1

Sheringham, Robert, *The Kings Supremacy Asserted. Or, A Remonstrance of the King's Right against the pretended Parliament* (1660), Wing, S 3237; BL, TT, E 1043/5

[Spelman, Sir John], *The Case of our Affaires, in law, religion, and other circumstances briefly examined, and presented to the conscience* (Oxford, 1643), Wing, S 4936; BL, TT, E 30/14

Certain considerations upon the duties both of Prince and people, written by a gentleman of quality, a wel-wisher both to the King and Parliament (Oxford, 1642), Wing, S 4938; BL, TT, E 85/4

A Protestants Account of his Orthodox Holding in Matters of Religion, at this present in difference in the Church (Cambridge, 1642), Wing, S 4939; BL, TT, E 129/23

A View of a printed book intituled Observations upon His Majesties late Answers and Expresses (Oxford, 1642), Wing, S 4941; BL, TT, E 245/22

Thorndike, Herbert, *Two Discourses, the one of the Primitive Government of Churches, the other of the service of God at the Assemblies of the Church* (Cambridge, 1650), Wing, T 1057

Walker, Clement, *The Compleat History of Independency* (1661), Wing, W 324

Williams, Griffith, *The Discovery of Mysteries* (1643), Wing, W 2665; BL, TT, E 60/1, E 104/27

Jura Majestatis, the Rights of Kings both in Church and State (Oxford, 1644), Wing, W 2669; BL, TT, E 14/18*

Wotton, Sir Henry, 'A Panegyrick to King Charles' (1633), in *Reliquiae Wottonianae*, ed. I. Walton (4th edition, 1685), Wing, W 3651

SOURCES PUBLISHED SINCE 1700

The Acts of the Privy Council of England, 1542–1631, ed. J. R. Dasent, E. G. Atkinson, J. V. Lyle, R. F. Monger and P. A. Penfold (46 vols., 1890–1964)

Allen, John, *Inquiry into the Rise and Growth of the Royal Prerogative in England* (1830)

A Narrative by John Ashburnham of his attendance on King Charles the first (2 vols., 1830)

The Short Parliament (1640) Diary of Sir Thomas Aston, ed. Judith D. Maltby (Camden Society, 4th series, 35, 1988)

Wiltshire: the Topographical Collections of John Aubrey, F.R.S., ed. J. E. Jackson (Devizes, 1862)

Bagehot, Walter, *The English Constitution* (4th edition, 1885)

The Letters and Journals of Robert Baillie, ed. D. Laing (3 vols., Edinburgh, 1841–2)

The Historical Works of Sir James Balfour, ed. J. Haig (4 vols., 1825)

Bentham, Jeremy, *A Fragment on Government*, ed. J. H. Burns and H. L. A. Hart (Cambridge, 1988)

Bidwell, William B. and Jansson, Maija, ed., *Proceedings in Parliament, 1626* (3 vols., New Haven and London, 1991–2)

Blackstone, William, *Commentaries on the Laws of England* (4 vols., Oxford, 1765–9)

The Works of the Most Reverend Father in God, John Bramhall, D.D., ed. A. W. H. (5 vols., Oxford, 1842–5)

Browne, Sir Thomas, *Religio Medici*, ed. J.-J. Denonain (2nd edition, Cambridge, 1955)

Bruce, J., ed., *Letters and Papers of the Verney Family down to the end of the year 1639* (Camden Society, 1st series, 56, 1853)

ed., *Notes of the Treaty carried on at Ripon ... taken by Sir John Borough* (Camden Society, 1st series, 100, 1869)

Bulstrode, Sir Richard, *Memoirs and Reflections upon the Reign and Government of King Charles the Ist and K[ing] Charles the IId* (1721)

Burnet, Gilbert, *Burnet's History of my own Time*, ed. Osmund Airy (2 vols., Oxford, 1897–1900)

The Memoirs of the Lives and Actions of James and William, Dukes of Hamilton and Castle-Herald (Oxford, 1852)

Calendar of the Proceedings of the Committee for the Advance of Money, ed. Mary Anne Everett Green (3 vols., 1888)

Calendar of the Proceedings of the Committee for Compounding with Delinquents, ed. Mary Anne Everett Green (5 vols., 1889)

Calendar of State Papers Venetian, ed. Rawdon Brown, Horatio F. Brown and Allen B. Hinds (40 vols., 1864–1940)

Carte, Thomas, ed., *A Collection of Original Letters and Papers* (2 vols., 1739)

Cartwright, John, *The English Constitution produced and illustrated* (1823)

The Life of William Cavendish, Duke of Newcastle ... by Margaret, Duchess of Newcastle, ed. C. H. Firth (1907)

Charles I in 1646: Letters of King Charles the first to Queen Henrietta Maria, ed. J. Bruce (Camden Society, 1st series, 63, 1856)

Journal de Jean Chevalier, ed. J. A. Messervy (9 fascicles, Jersey, 1906–14)

Clarendon, Edward, Earl of, *A Compleat Collection of Tracts, by that Eminent Statesman the Right Honourable Edward, Earl of Clarendon* (1747)

The History of the Rebellion and Civil Wars in England, ed. W. Dunn Macray (6 vols., Oxford, 1888)

The Life of Edward, Earl of Clarendon ... Written by himself (3 vols., Oxford, 1827)

State Papers collected by Edward, Earl of Clarendon (3 vols., Oxford, 1757)

Coates, Willson H., Young, Anne Steele and Snow, Vernon F., ed., *The Private Journals of the Long Parliament* (3 vols., New Haven and London, 1982–92)

Cobbett's Parliamentary History of England (36 vols., 1806–20)

C[okayne], G. E., *The Complete Peerage* (new edition, ed. Vicary Gibbs, H. A. Doubleday, Duncan Warrand, Lord Howard de Walden, Geoffrey H. White , and R. S. Lea, 14 vols., 1910–59)

Journals of the House of Commons (1803–)

Cope, Esther S., ed., *Proceedings of the Short Parliament of 1640* (Camden Society, 4th series, 19, 1977)

Poems of Charles Cotton, ed. John Buxton (1958)

The English Writings of Abraham Cowley, ed. A. R. Waller (2 vols., Cambridge, 1905–6)

Day, W. A., ed., *The Pythouse Papers* (1879)

The Autobiography and Correspondence of Sir Simonds D'Ewes, Bart., ed. J. O. Halliwell (2 vols., 1845)

The Journal of Sir Simonds D'Ewes from the beginning of the Long Parliament to the opening of the trial of the Earl of Strafford, ed. Wallace Notestein (New Haven, 1923)

The Journal of Sir Simonds D'Ewes from the first recess of the Long Parliament to the withdrawal of King Charles from London, ed. Willson H. Coates (New Haven, 1942; repr. Hamden, 1970)

The Life, Diary and Correspondence of Sir William Dugdale, ed. W. Hamper (1827)

'The correspondence of Bishop Brian Duppa and Sir Justinian Isham', ed. G. Isham, *Publ. Northamptonshire Record Society*, 17 (1955)

The Diary and Correspondence of John Evelyn, ed. W. Bray (new edition, ed. H. B. Wheatley, 4 vols., 1906)

Filmer, Sir Robert, *Patriarcha and other Writings*, ed. Johann P. Sommerville (Cambridge, 1991)

Firth, C. H. and Rait, R. S., ed., *Acts and Ordinances of the Interregnum, 1642–1660* (3 vols., 1911)

Foster, J., ed., *Alumni Oxonienses, 1500–1714* (4 vols., Oxford, 1891–2)

ed., *The Register of Admissions to Gray's Inn, 1521–1889* (1889)

Fryde, E. B., Greenway, D. E., Porter, S. and Roy, I., ed., *Handbook of British Chronology* (3rd edition, 1986)

Gardiner, B. M., ed., 'A secret negotiation with Charles I, 1643–4', *Camden Miscellany*, VIII (Camden Society, 1st series, 31, 1883)

Gardiner, S. R., 'Draft by Sir Edward Hyde of a Declaration to be issued by Charles II in 1649', *EHR*, 8 (1893), 300–7

Gardiner, S. R., ed., *Constitutional Documents of the Puritan Revolution, 1625–1660* (3rd edition, Oxford, 1906)

ed., *The Hamilton Papers* (Camden Society, 2nd series, 27, 1880)

ed., *Notes of the Debates in the House of Lords in 1624 and 1626* (Camden Society, 2nd series, 24, 1879)

Gordon, James, *History of Scots Affairs from MDCXXXVII to MDCXLI* (3 vols., Aberdeen, 1841)

Letters between Colonel Robert Hammond . . . and the Committee . . . at Derby-House (1764)

The Harleian Miscellany (12 vols., 1808–11)

Letters of Queen Henrietta Maria, ed. Mary Anne Everett Green (1857)

Memoirs of the Two Last Years of the Reign of King Charles I, by Sir Thomas Herbert, ed. G. Nichol (1813)

Historical Manuscripts Commission, *Eighth Report* (1881)

Tenth Report (1887)

Twelfth Report (1891)

Fifteenth Report (1897)

Ancaster Manuscripts (1907)

Manuscripts of the Marquess of Bath, vol. II (1907)

Bath (Longleat) Manuscripts, vol. IV: *Seymour Papers, 1532–1686* (1968)

Manuscripts of the Marquess of Ormonde, vol. III (1904)

Manuscripts in Various Collections, vol. VII (1914)

Hobbes, Thomas, *Behemoth, or The Long Parliament*, ed. Ferdinand Tönnies (Chicago, 1990)

A Dialogue between a Philosopher and a Student of the Common Laws of England, ed. Joseph Cropsey (Chicago, 1971)

The English Works of Thomas Hobbes, ed. W. Molesworth (11 vols., 1839–45)

Hooker, Richard, *Of the Laws of Ecclesiastical Polity*, ed. Arthur Stephen McGrade (Cambridge, 1989)

Hughes, A., ed., *List of Sheriffs for England and Wales from the earliest times to A.D. 1831* (PRO, Lists and Indexes, IX, repr. 1963)

The History and Antiquities of the County of Dorset . . . by John Hutchins, M.A., ed. W. Shipp and J. W. Hodson (3rd edition, 4 vols., 1861–70)

Jansson, Maija, ed., *Two Diaries of the Long Parliament* (Gloucester and New York, 1984)

Jansson, Maija and Bidwell, William B., ed., *Proceedings in Parliament, 1625* (New Haven and London, 1987)

Keeler, Mary Frear, Cole, M. J. and Bidwell, W. B., ed., *Proceedings in Parliament, 1628* (6 vols., New Haven, 1977–83)

Larkin, J. F., ed., *Stuart Royal Proclamations*, vol. II: *Royal Proclamations of King Charles I, 1625–46* (Oxford, 1983)

Larking, Lambert B., ed., *Proceedings, principally in the county of Kent, in connection with the Parliaments called in 1640* (Camden Society, 1st series, 80, 1862)

The Works of William Laud, ed. W. Scott (7 vols., Oxford, 1847–60)

The Records of the Honourable Society of Lincoln's Inn: Admissions, 1420–1893 (2 vols., 1896)

Journals of the House of Lords (1846)

The Poems of Richard Lovelace, ed. C. H. Wilkinson (Oxford, 1930)
The Memoirs of Edmund Ludlow, ed. C. H. Firth (2 vols., Oxford, 1894)
Ludlow, Edmund, *A Voyce from the Watch Tower. Part Five: 1660–1662*, ed. A. B. Worden (Camden Society, 4th series, 21, 1978)
Maddison, A. R., ed., *Lincolnshire Pedigrees*, vol. I (Harleian Society, L, 1902)
Manning, J. A., ed., *Memoirs of Sir Benjamin Rudyerd* (1841)
The Poems and Letters of Andrew Marvell, ed. H. M. Margoliouth (2 vols., Oxford, 1927)
Matthews, A. G., *Walker Revised* (Oxford, 1948; repr. 1988)
Memoirs of the Two Last Years of the Reign of ... King Charles I (1702)
The Complete Prose Works of John Milton, vol. II: *1643–1648*, ed. Ernest Sirluck (New Haven, 1959)
'The diplomatic correspondence of Jean de Montereul', ed. J. G. Fotheringham, *Publ. Scottish Record Society*, 29–30 (1898–9)
The Letter-Book of John Viscount Mordaunt, 1658–1660, ed. Mary Coate (Camden Society, 3rd series, 69, 1945)
Nelson, C. and Seccombe, M., ed., *British Newspapers and Periodicals, 1641–1700: A Short-Title Catalogue of Serials Printed in England, Scotland, Ireland and British America* (New York, 1987)
The Nicholas Papers, ed. G. F. Warner: vol. I: *1641–1652* (Camden Society, 2nd series, 40, 1886); vol. II: *January 1653–June 1655* (Camden Society, 2nd series, 50, 1892); vol. III: *July 1655–December 1656* (Camden Society, 2nd series, 57, 1897); vol. IV: *1657–1660* (Camden Society, 3rd series, 31, 1920)
Note Book of Sir John Northcote, ed. A. H. A. Hamilton (1877)
Notestein, Wallace and Relf, F. H., ed., *Commons Debates for 1629* (Minneapolis, 1921)
Notestein, Wallace, Relf, F. H. and Simpson, H., ed., *Commons Debates, 1621* (7 vols., New Haven, 1935)
O Hehir, Brendan, *Expans'd Hieroglyphicks: A Critical Edition of Sir John Denham's Coopers Hill* (Berkeley and Los Angeles, 1969)
The Letters of Dorothy Osborne to William Temple, ed. G. C. Moore Smith (Oxford, 1928)
Peck, Francis, ed., *Desiderata Curiosa* (2 vols., 1779)
Pollard, A. W. and Redgrave, G. R., ed., *A Short-Title Catalogue of Books Printed in England, Scotland and Ireland and of English Books Printed Abroad, 1475–1640* (2nd edition, ed. W. A. Jackson, F. S. Ferguson and K. F. Pantzer, 2 vols., 1976–86)
Pronay, N. and Taylor, J., ed., *Parliamentary Texts of the Later Middle Ages* (Oxford, 1980)
Relf, F. H., ed., *Notes of the Debates in the House of Lords, 1621–9* (Camden Society, 3rd series, 42, 1929)
Memoirs of Sir John Reresby, ed. Andrew Browning (Glasgow, 1936)
Return of Members of Parliaments of England, 1213–1702 (2 vols., 1878)
Memoirs of Prince Rupert and the Cavaliers, ed. Eliot Warburton (3 vols., 1849)
Sainty, J. C., 'Lieutenants of counties, 1585–1642', *Bulletin of the Institute of Historical Research, Supplements*, 8 (1970)
Treasury Officials, 1660–1870 (1972)
The Works of George Savile, Marquis of Halifax, ed. Mark N. Brown (3 vols., Oxford, 1989)
Selden, John, *Opera Omnia*, ed. David Wilkins (6 vols., 1726)
Slaughter, Thomas P., ed., *Ideology and Politics on the Eve of the Restoration:*

Newcastle's Advice to Charles II (Memoirs of the American Philosophical Society, 96, Philadelphia, PA, 1984)

The Diary of Sir Henry Slingsby, Bart., ed. Daniel Parsons (1836)

Spalding, John, *Memorialls of the Trubles in Scotland and in England, A.D. 1624–A.D. 1645* (2 vols., Aberdeen, 1850–1)

Spence, Joseph, *Observations, Anecdotes, and Characters of Books and Men*, ed. James M. Osborn, I (Oxford, 1966)

The Poems and Translations of Thomas Stanley, ed. Galbraith Miller Crump (Oxford, 1962)

The Earl of Strafforde's Letters and Dispatches, ed. W. Knowler (2 vols., 1739)

Sturgess, H. A. C., ed., *Register of Admissions to the Honourable Society of the Middle Temple* (3 vols., 1949)

Letters and Memorials of State ... Written and Collected by Sir Henry Sydney, ed. Arthur Collins (2 vols., 1746)

A Collection of the State Papers of John Thurloe, Esq., ed. T. Birch (7 vols., 1742)

'The Diary of Henry Townshend of Elmley Lovett, 1640–1663', ed. J. W. Willis Bund, *Publ. Worcs. Historical Society* (2 vols., 1916–20)

Trevelyan, W. C. and Trevelyan, C. E., ed., *Trevelyan Papers*, part III (Camden Society, 1st series, 105, 1872)

The Secular Poems of Henry Vaughan, ed. E. L. Marilla (Essays and Studies of English Language and Literature, 21, Uppsala, 1958)

Henry Vaughan: The Complete Poems, ed. Alan Rudrum (Harmondsworth, 1976)

Venn, J. and J. A., ed., *Alumni Cantabrigienses. Part One: from the earliest times to 1751* (4 vols., Cambridge, 1922–7)

Notes of proceedings in the Long Parliament ... by Sir Ralph Verney, ed. H. Verney (Camden Society, 1st series, 31, 1845)

Walker, Edward, *Historical Discourses* (1705)

Perfect Copies of all the Votes, Letters, Proposals and Answers ... that passed in the Treaty held at Newport (1705)

Walton, Izaak, *The Compleat Angler*, ed. Bryan Loughrey (Harmondsworth, 1985)

The Lives of John Donne, Sir Henry Wotton, Richard Hooker, George Herbert and Robert Sanderson, ed. George Saintsbury (Oxford, 1927)

Warwick, Sir Philip, *Memoires of the Reigne of King Charles I* (1701)

The Diary of Bulstrode Whitelocke, 1605–1675, ed. Ruth Spalding (British Academy Records of Social and Economic History, new series, 13, Oxford, 1990)

Whitelocke, Bulstrode, *Memorials of the English Affairs from the beginning of the reign of Charles I* (4 vols., Oxford, 1853)

Liber Famelicus of Sir James Whitelocke, ed. J. Bruce (Camden Society, 1st series, 70, 1858)

Wing, Donald, ed., *A Short-Title Catalogue of Books Printed in England, Scotland, Wales and British America and of English Books Printed Abroad, 1641–1700* (2nd edition, 3 vols., New York, 1972–88)

Yorke, P., ed., *Miscellaneous State Papers, 1501–1726* (2 vols., 1778)

SECONDARY SOURCES

BOOKS AND ARTICLES

Abernathy, G. R., 'Clarendon and the declaration of indulgence', *Journal of Ecclesiastical History*, 11 (1960), 55–73

The English Presbyterians and the Stuart Restoration, 1648–1663 (Transactions of the American Philosophical Society, new series, 55, Part ii, Philadelphia, PA, 1965)

Adamson, J. S. A., 'The baronial context of the English Civil War', *TRHS*, 5th series, 40 (1990), 93–120

'The English nobility and the projected settlement of 1647', *HJ*, 30 (1987), 567–602

'Oliver Cromwell and the Long Parliament', in *Oliver Cromwell and the English Revolution*, ed. John Morrill (Harlow, 1990), pp. 49–92

'Parliamentary management, men-of-business and the House of Lords, 1640–49', in *A Pillar of the Constitution: the House of Lords in British Politics, 1640–1784*, ed. Clyve Jones (1989), pp. 21–50

'Politics and the nobility in Civil-War England', *HJ*, 34 (1991), 231–55

'The *Vindiciae Veritatis* and the political creed of Viscount Saye and Sele', *Historical Research*, 60 (1987), 45–63

Allen, D. C. 'Richard Lovelace: "The Grasse-hopper"', in *Seventeenth-Century English Poetry: Modern Essays in Criticism*, ed. William R. Keast (New York, 1962), pp. 280–9

Allen, J. W., *English Political Thought, 1603–1660*, vol. I: *1603–1644* (1938)

Ashley, M., *Rupert of the Rhine* (1976)

Ashton, Robert, 'From Cavalier to Roundhead Tyranny, 1642–9', in *Reactions to the English Civil War, 1642–1649*, ed. John Morrill (1982), pp. 185–207

Atherton, Ian, 'Viscount Scudamore's "Laudianism": the religious practices of the first Viscount Scudamore', *HJ*, 34 (1991), 567–96

Attree, F. W. T. and Booker, J. H. L., 'The Sussex Colepepers', *Sussex Archaeological Collections*, 47 (1904), 47–81

Aylmer, G.E., 'Collective mentalities in mid-seventeenth-century England: II. Royalist attitudes', *TRHS*, 5th series, 37 (1987), 1–30

Bankes, G., *The Story of Corfe Castle* (1853)

Barnes, T. G., *Somerset, 1625–1640: A County's Government during the 'Personal Rule'* (1961)

Bartlett, Robert, 'Lordship and law in medieval England', *JBS*, 30 (1991), 449–54

Behrens, B., 'The Whig theory of the constitution in the reign of Charles II', *Cambridge Historical Journal*, 7 (1941–3), 42–71

Benson, Donald R., 'Halifax and the Trimmers', *Huntington Library Quarterly*, 27 (1963–4), 115–34

Bloch, Marc, *Les rois thaumaturges* (Strasburg, 1924)

Bosher, Robert S., *The Making of the Restoration Settlement* (1951)

Bowle, John, *Hobbes and his Critics: A Study in Seventeenth-Century Constitutionalism* (1951)

Boynton, Lindsay, *The Elizabethan Militia, 1558–1638* (1967)

Brown, Keith M., 'Courtiers and Cavaliers: service, anglicisation and loyalty amongst the Royalist nobility', in *The Scottish National Covenant in its British Context, 1638–51*, ed. John Morrill (Edinburgh, 1990), pp. 155–92

Brown, Mark N., 'Trimmers and moderates in the Reign of Charles II', *Huntington Library Quarterly*, 37 (1973–4), 311–36

Brownley, M. W., *Clarendon and the Rhetoric of Historical Form* (Philadelphia, PA, 1985)

Burgess, Glenn, *The Politics of the Ancient Constitution: An Introduction to English Political Thought, 1603–1642* (1992)

348   Bibliography

Cameron, Euan, *The European Reformation* (Oxford, 1991)
Cannadine, David, 'The context, performance and meaning of ritual: the British monarchy and the "Invention of Tradition", c. 1820–1977', in *The Invention of Tradition*, ed. E. J. Hobsbawm and T. Ranger (Cambridge, 1983), pp. 101–64
Carlton, Charles, *Going to the Wars: The Experience of the British Civil Wars, 1638–1651* (1992)
Carter, Jennifer, 'The Revolution and the Constitution', in *Britain after the Glorious Revolution, 1689–1714*, ed. Geoffrey Holmes (1969), pp. 39–58
Chadwick, Owen, *The Fisherman and his God: Izaak Walton* (1984)
Childs, John, *The Army of Charles II* (1976)
Christianson, Paul, 'Royal and parliamentary voices on the ancient constitution, c. 1604–1621', in *The Mental World of the Jacobean Court*, ed. Linda Levy Peck (Cambridge, 1991), pp. 71–95
Clark, J. C. D., *English Society, 1688–1832* (Cambridge, 1985)
Collinson, Patrick, *Archbishop Grindal, 1519–1583* (1979)
   The Religion of Protestants (Oxford, 1982)
Condren, Conal, 'Casuistry to Newcastle: "The Prince" in the world of the book', in *Political Discourse in Early Modern Britain*, ed. Nicholas Phillipson and Quentin Skinner (Cambridge, 1993), pp. 164–86
Coolidge, S., *The Pauline Renaissance in England: Puritanism and the Bible* (Oxford, 1970)
Cooper, J. P., *Land, Men and Beliefs*, ed. G. E. Aylmer and J. S. Morrill (1983)
Cooper, John R., *The Art of The Compleat Angler* (Durham, NC, 1968)
Corns, Thomas N., *Uncloistered Virtue: English Political Literature, 1640–1660* (Oxford, 1992)
Coward, Barry, *Oliver Cromwell* (Harlow, 1991)
Craik, Sir Henry, *The Life of Edward, Earl of Clarendon, Lord High Chancellor of England* (2 vols., 1911)
Crawford, Patricia, 'Public duty, conscience, and women in early modern England', in *Public Duty and Private Conscience in Seventeenth-Century England: Essays Presented to G. E. Aylmer*, ed. John Morrill, Paul Slack and Daniel Woolf (Oxford, 1993), pp. 57–76
Cust, Richard, 'Charles I and a draft Declaration for the 1628 Parliament', *Historical Research*, 63 (1990), 143–61
   'Charles I, the Privy Council and the Parliament of 1628', *TRHS*, 6th series, 2 (1992), 25–50
   The Forced Loan and English Politics, 1626–1628 (Oxford, 1987)
Daly, James W., *Cosmic Harmony and Political Thinking in Early Stuart England* (Transactions of the American Philosophical Society, new series, 69, Part vii, Philadelphia, PA, 1979)
   'The idea of absolute monarchy in seventeenth-century England', *HJ*, 21 (1978), 227–50
   'The implications of Royalist politics, 1642–6', *HJ*, 27 (1984), 745–55
   'John Bramhall and the theoretical problems of Royalist moderation', *JBS*, 21 (1971), 26–44
   'The origins and shaping of English Royalist thought', *Historical Papers/ Communications Historiques* (1974), pp. 15–35
   Sir Robert Filmer and English Political Thought (Toronto, 1979)

'Some problems in the authorship of Sir Robert Filmer's Works', *EHR*, 98 (1983), 737–62

Davies, Julian, *The Caroline Captivity of the Church* (Oxford, 1992)

Dean, D. M., and Jones, N. L., ed., *The Parliaments of Elizabethan England* (Oxford and Cambridge, MA, 1990)

Dictionary of National Biography, ed. L. Stephen and Sidney Lee (63 vols., 1885–1900)

Donald, Peter, 'The Scottish National Covenant and British politics', in *The Scottish National Covenant in its British Context, 1638–51*, ed. John Morrill (Edinburgh, 1990), pp. 90–105

An Uncounselled King: Charles I and the Scottish Troubles, 1637–1641 (Cambridge, 1990)

Dzelzainis, Martin, 'Edward Hyde and Thomas Hobbes's *Elements of Law, Natural and Politic*', *HJ*, 32 (1989), 303–17

'"Undoubted Realities": Clarendon on Sacrilege', *HJ*, 33 (1990), 515–40

Eales, Jacqueline, 'Iconoclasm, iconography, and the altar in the English Civil War', in *The Church and the Arts*, ed. Diana Wood (Studies in Church History, 28, 1992), 313–27

Puritans and Roundheads: The Harleys of Brampton Bryan and the Outbreak of the English Civil War (Cambridge, 1990)

Edgar, F. T. R., *Sir Ralph Hopton: The King's Man in the West, 1642–52* (Oxford, 1968)

Elton, G. R., *England under the Tudors* (3rd edition, 1991)

The English (Oxford, 1992)

The Parliament of England, 1559–1581 (Cambridge, 1986)

Studies in Tudor and Stuart Politics and Government (4 vols., Cambridge, 1974–92)

'Tudor Government', *HJ*, 31 (1988), 425–34

The Tudor Revolution in Government (Cambridge, 1953)

Elton, G. R., ed., *The Tudor Constitution* (2nd edition, Cambridge, 1982)

Fea, Allan, *After Worcester Fight* (1904)

The Flight of the King (1897)

Feiling, Keith, *A History of the Tory Party, 1640–1714* (Oxford, 1924)

Fergusson, B.E., *Rupert of the Rhine* (1952)

Fielding, John, 'Arminianism in the localities: Peterborough Diocese, 1603–1642', in *The Early Stuart Church, 1603–1642*, ed. Kenneth Fincham (1993), pp. 93–113

'Opposition to the Personal Rule of Charles I: the diary of Robert Woodford, 1637–1641', *HJ*, 31 (1988), 769–88

Fincham, Kenneth, 'Episcopal government, 1603–1640', in *The Early Stuart Church, 1603–1642*, ed. Kenneth Fincham (1993), pp. 71–91

'The judges' decision on Ship Money in February 1637: the reaction of Kent', *Bulletin of the Institute of Historical Research*, 57 (1984), 230–7

Prelate as Pastor: The Episcopate of James I (Oxford, 1990)

Fincham, Kenneth and Lake, Peter, 'The ecclesiastical policies of James I and Charles I', in *The Early Stuart Church, 1603–1642*, ed. Kenneth Fincham (1993), pp. 23–49

'The ecclesiastical policy of King James I', *JBS*, 24 (1985), 169–207

Firth, C. H., *The House of Lords during the Civil War* (1910)

Fletcher, Anthony, *The Outbreak of the English Civil War* (1981)

Sussex, 1600–1660: A County Community in Peace and War (1975)

Foster, Andrew, 'Church policies of the 1630s', in *Conflict in Early Stuart England*, ed. Richard Cust and Ann Hughes (Harlow, 1989), pp. 193–223

Friedenreich, Kenneth, *Henry Vaughan* (Boston, 1978)

Gardiner, S. R., *History of England from the accession of James I to the outbreak of the Civil War, 1603–1642* (10 vols., 1883–4)

History of the Great Civil War, 1642–1649 (4 vols., 1893)

'A scheme of toleration propounded at Uxbridge in 1645', *EHR*, 2 (1887), 340–2

Gentles, Ian, *The New Model Army in England, Ireland and Scotland, 1645–1653* (Oxford, 1992)

Goldie, Mark, 'Danby, the bishops and the Whigs', in *The Politics of Religion in Restoration England*, ed. Tim Harris, Paul Seaward and Mark Goldie (Oxford, 1990), pp. 75–105

'John Locke and Anglican Royalism', *Political Studies*, 31 (1983), 61–85

'The political thought of the Anglican Revolution', in *The Revolutions of 1688*, ed. Robert Beddard (Oxford, 1991), pp. 102–36

'The reception of Hobbes', in *The Cambridge History of Political Thought, 1450–1700*, ed. J. H. Burns and Mark Goldie (Cambridge, 1991), pp. 589–615

Graves, Michael A. R., *Elizabethan Parliaments, 1559–1601* (Harlow, 1987)

Green, I. M., *The Re-establishment of the Church of England, 1660–1663* (Oxford, 1978)

Gruenfelder, J. K., *Influence in Early Stuart Elections, 1604–1640* (Ohio, 1981)

Guy, John, 'The "Imperial Crown" and the liberty of the subject: the English constitution from Magna Carta to the Bill of Rights', in *Court, Country and Culture*, ed. B. Y. Kunze and D. D. Brautigam (Rochester, NY, 1992), pp. 65–87

'The origins of the Petition of Right reconsidered', *HJ*, 25 (1982), 289–312

Haigh, Christopher, *Elizabeth I* (Harlow, 1988)

Harris, R. W., *Clarendon and the English Revolution* (1983)

Harriss, Gerald, 'Political society and the growth of government in late medieval England', *P&P*, 138 (1993), 28–57

Hart, James S., *Justice upon Petition* (1991)

Hassell Smith, A., 'Militia rates and militia statutes, 1558–1663', in *The English Commonwealth, 1547–1640*, ed. Peter Clark, A. G. R. Smith and Nicholas Tyacke (Leicester, 1979), pp. 93–110

Hast, Adele, 'State treason trials during the Puritan Revolution, 1640–1660', *HJ*, 15 (1972), 37–53

Havighurst, A. F., 'The judiciary and politics in the reign of Charles II', *Law Quarterly Review*, 66 (1950), 62–78, 229–52

Hayward, J. C., 'New directions in studies of the Falkland circle', *The Seventeenth Century*, 2 (1987), 19–48

Hensman, E. W., 'The East Midlands and the Second Civil War, May to July, 1648', *TRHS*, 4th series, 6 (1923), 126–59

Hexter, J. H., *The Reign of King Pym* (Cambridge, MA, 1941)

Hill, Sir Francis, *Tudor and Stuart Lincoln* (Cambridge, 1956; repr. Stamford, 1991)

Hirst, Derek, *Authority and Conflict: England, 1603–1658* (1986)

'The defection of Sir Edward Dering, 1640–1641', *HJ*, 15 (1972), 193–208

Holmes, Clive, *Seventeenth-Century Lincolnshire* (Lincoln, 1980)

Holt, J. C., *Magna Carta and Medieval Government* (1985)

Horwitz, Henry, *Revolution Politicks: The Career of Daniel Finch, second Earl of Nottingham, 1647–1730* (Cambridge, 1968)

Hughes, Ann, 'Thomas Dugard and his circle in the 1630s – a "parliamentary-puritan" connexion?', *HJ*, 29 (1986), 771–93

Hutchinson, F. E., *Henry Vaughan: A Life and Interpretation* (Oxford, 1947)

Hutton, Ronald, *Charles II: King of England, Scotland, and Ireland* (Oxford, 1989)

'Clarendon's *History of the Rebellion*', *EHR*, 97 (1982), 70–88

The Restoration: A Political and Religious History of England and Wales, 1658–1667 (Oxford, 1985)

The Royalist War Effort, 1642–1646 (Harlow, 1982)

'The structure of the Royalist Party, 1642–6', *HJ*, 24 (1981), 553–69

James, Mervyn, *Society, Politics and Culture* (Cambridge, 1986)

Jones, J. R., *Country and Court: England, 1658–1714* (1978)

'The Friends of the Constitution in Church and State', in *Public and Private Doctrine: Essays in British History presented to Maurice Cowling*, ed. Michael Bentley (Cambridge, 1993), pp. 17–33

Jones, N. and Dean, D., ed., *Parliamentary History*, special issue on 'Interest groups and legislation in Elizabethan Parliaments: essays presented to Sir Geoffrey Elton', 8, part ii (1989)

Judson, Margaret Atwood, *The Crisis of the Constitution: An Essay in Constitutional and Political Thought in England, 1603–1645* (New Brunswick, NJ, 1949)

Kearney, Hugh F., *Strafford in Ireland, 1633–41* (Manchester, 1959)

Keeler, Mary Frear, *The Long Parliament, 1640–1641: A Biographical Study of its Members* (Memoirs of the American Philosophical Society, 36, Philadelphia, PA, 1954)

Kenyon, J. P., ed., *The Stuart Constitution* (2nd edition, Cambridge, 1986)

Kingsford, C. L., 'Essex House, formerly Leicester House and Exeter Inn', *Archaeologia*, 73 (1923), 1–54

Kishlansky, M. A., *The Rise of the New Model Army* (Cambridge, 1979)

'Saye no more', *JBS*, 30 (1991), 399–448

'Saye what?', *HJ*, 33 (1990), 917–37

Klein, William, 'The ancient constitution revisited', in *Political Discourse in Early Modern Britain*, ed. Nicholas Phillipson and Quentin Skinner (Cambridge, 1993), pp. 23–44

Koenigsberger, H.G., *Politicians and Virtuosi* (1986)

Lake, Peter, *Anglicans and Puritans? Presbyterianism and English Conformist Thought from Whitgift to Hooker* (1988)

'Calvinism and the English Church, 1570–1635', *P&P*, 114 (1987), 32–76

'The Calvinist conformity of Robert Sanderson', *JBS*, 27 (1988), 81–116

'The Laudians and the argument from authority', in *Court, Country and Culture*, ed. B. Y. Kunze and D. D. Brautigam (Rochester, NY, 1992), pp. 149–75

'The Laudian style: order, uniformity and the pursuit of the beauty of holiness in the 1630s', in *The Early Stuart Church, 1603–1642*, ed. Kenneth Fincham (1993), pp. 161–85

Moderate Puritans and the Elizabethan Church (Cambridge, 1982)

Lambert, Sheila, 'Richard Montagu, Arminianism and censorship', *P&P*, 124 (1989), 36–68

Lister, T. H., *Life and Administration of Edward, First Earl of Clarendon* (3 vols., 1837–8)

Locke, A. A., *The Seymour Family* (1911)

Malcolm, J., *Caesar's Due: Loyalty and King Charles, 1642–6* (1983)

Manning, Brian, 'The nobles, the people, and the constitution', *P&P*, 9 (1956), 42–64

Marston, J. G., 'Gentry honour and royalism in early Stuart England', *JBS*, 13 (1974), 21–43

Mathew, David, *Scotland under Charles I* (1955)

McInnes, Angus, 'When was the English Revolution?', *History*, 66 (1982), 377–92

McInnes, Ian, *Arabella: The Life and Times of Lady Arabella Seymour, 1575–1615* (1968)

Mendle, Michael, *Dangerous Positions: Mixed Government, the Estates of the Realm, and the Making of the Answer to the XIX Propositions* (Alabama, 1985)

'The Great Council of Parliament and the first ordinances: the constitutional theory of the Civil War', *JBS*, 31 (1992), 133–62

'Parliamentary sovereignty: a very English absolutism', in *Political Discourse in Early Modern Britain*, ed. Nicholas Phillipson and Quentin Skinner (Cambridge, 1993), pp. 97–119

Miller, John, 'Charles II and his Parliaments', *TRHS*, 5th series, 32 (1982), 1–23

'The Crown and the Borough Charters in the reign of Charles II', *EHR*, 100 (1985), 53–84

'The later Stuart monarchy', in *The Restored Monarchy, 1660–1688*, ed. J. R. Jones (1979), pp. 30–47

'The potential for "Absolutism" in later Stuart England', *History*, 69 (1984), 187–207

Miner, Earl, *The Cavalier Mode from Jonson to Cotton* (Princeton, 1971)

Mintz, Samuel I., *The Hunting of Leviathan: Seventeenth-Century Reactions to the Materialism and Moral Philosophy of Thomas Hobbes* (Cambridge, 1962)

Morrah, P., *Prince Rupert of the Rhine* (1976)

Morrill, John, *Cheshire, 1630–1660* (Oxford, 1974)

The Nature of the English Revolution (Harlow, 1993)

The Revolt of the Provinces (2nd edition, Harlow, 1980)

Morrill, John, ed., *Reactions to the English Civil War, 1642–1649* (1982)

Nenner, Howard, *By Colour of Law: Legal Culture and Constitutional Politics in England, 1660–1689* (Chicago, 1977)

Nethercot, Arthur H., *Abraham Cowley: The Muse's Hannibal* (Oxford, 1931)

Newman, P. R., 'The King's servants: conscience, principle, and sacrifice in armed royalism', in *Public Duty and Private Conscience in Seventeenth-Century England: Essays Presented to G. E. Aylmer*, ed. John Morrill, Paul Slack and Daniel Woolf (Oxford, 1993), pp. 225–41

Royalist Officers in England and Wales, 1642–1660: A Biographical Dictionary (1981)

Newton, A. P., *The Colonising Activities of the English Puritans* (New Haven, 1914)

Nutkiewicz, Michael, 'A rapporteur of the English Civil War: the courtly politics of James Howell (1594?–1666)', *Canadian Journal of History/Annales canadiennes d'histoire*, 25 (1990), 21–40

Nuttall, Geoffrey F., 'The first nonconformists', in *From Uniformity to Unity, 1662–1962*, ed. Geoffrey F. Nuttall and Owen Chadwick (1962), pp. 149–87

Ollard, Richard, *Clarendon and his Friends* (1987)

Orr, Robert R., *Reason and Authority: The Thought of William Chillingworth* (Oxford, 1967)

Paul, Robert S., *The Assembly of the Lord* (Edinburgh, 1985)

Phillips, C. J., *History of the Sackville Family* (2 vols., 1930)

Plumb, J. H., *The Growth of Political Stability in England, 1675–1725* (1967)

Pocock, J. G. A., *The Ancient Constitution and the Feudal Law* (2nd edition, Cambridge, 1987)

Porter, H. C., *Reformation and Reaction in Tudor Cambridge* (Cambridge, 1958)

Pugh, R. B. and Crittall, Elizabeth, *Victoria History of the County of Wiltshire*, V (1957)

Ratcliff, E. C., 'The Savoy Conference and the revision of the Book of Common Prayer', in *From Uniformity to Unity, 1662–1962*, ed. Geoffrey F. Nuttall and Owen Chadwick (1962), pp. 89–148

Reeve, L. John, 'The arguments in King's Bench in 1629 concerning the imprisonment of John Selden and other Members of the House of Commons', *JBS*, 25 (1986), 264–87

Charles I and the Road to Personal Rule (Cambridge, 1989)

Richards, Judith, '"His Nowe Majestie" and the English monarchy: the kingship of Charles I before 1640', *P&P*, 113 (1986), 70–96

Rowe, Violet A., 'The influence of the Earls of Pembroke on parliamentary elections, 1625–41', *EHR*, 50 (1935), 242–56

Roy, I., 'The Royalist Council of War, 1642–6', *Bulletin of the Institute of Historical Research*, 35 (1962), 150–68

Russell, Conrad, *The Causes of the English Civil War* (Oxford, 1990)

'Divine Rights in the early seventeenth century', in *Public Duty and Private Conscience in Seventeenth-Century England: Essays Presented to G. E. Aylmer*, ed. John Morrill, Paul Slack and Daniel Woolf (Oxford, 1993), pp. 101–20

The Fall of the British Monarchies, 1637–1642 (Oxford, 1991)

'Issues in the House of Commons, 1621–1629: predictors of Civil War allegiance', *Albion*, 23 (1991), 23–39

Parliaments and English Politics, 1621–1629 (Oxford, 1979)

Unrevolutionary England, 1603–1642 (1990)

'Why did Charles I fight the Civil War?', *History Today*, 34 (1984), 31–4

Salt, S. P., 'The origins of Sir Edward Dering's attack on the Ecclesiastical Hierarchy, c. 1625–1640', *HJ*, 30 (1987), 21–52

Sampson, Anthony, *The Changing Anatomy of Britain* (Coronet edition, 1983)

Sanderson, John, *'But the People's Creatures': The Philosophical Basis of the English Civil War* (Manchester, 1989)

'*Serpent-Salve*, 1643: the Royalism of John Bramhall', *Journal of Ecclesiastical History*, 25 (1974), 1–14

Schwoerer, Lois G., 'The coronation of William and Mary, April 11, 1689', in *The Revolution of 1688–9: Changing Perspectives*, ed. Lois G. Schwoerer (Cambridge, 1992), pp. 107–30

'The trial of Lord William Russell (1683): judicial murder?', in *Restoration, Ideology and Revolution*, ed. Gordon J. Schochet (Folger Shakespeare Library, Washington, DC, 1990), pp. 169–98

Scott, Jonathan, *Algernon Sidney and the Restoration Crisis, 1677–1683* (Cambridge, 1991)

Seaward, Paul, *The Cavalier Parliament and the Reconstruction of the Old Régime, 1661–1667* (Cambridge, 1989)

Sembower, Charles Jacob, *The Life and the Poetry of Charles Cotton* (New York, 1911)

Sharpe, Kevin, 'Archbishop Laud', *History Today*, 33 (1983), 26–30

'The image of virtue: the court and household of Charles I, 1625–1642', in *The English Court from the Wars of the Roses to the Civil War*, ed. David Starkey (Harlow, 1987), pp. 226–60

The Personal Rule of Charles I (New Haven and London, 1992)

'Private conscience and public duty in the writings of James VI and I', in *Public Duty and Private Conscience in Seventeenth-Century England: Essays Presented to G. E. Aylmer*, ed. John Morrill, Paul Slack and Daniel Woolf (Oxford, 1993), pp. 77–100

Shaw, W. A., *A History of the English Church during the Civil Wars and under the Commonwealth, 1640–1660* (2 vols., 1900)

Skinner, Quentin, 'Conquest and Consent: Thomas Hobbes and the Engagement controversy', in *The Interregnum: The Quest for Settlement, 1646–1660*, ed. G. E. Aylmer (1972), pp. 79–98

The Foundations of Modern Political Thought (2 vols., Cambridge, 1978)

'The ideological context of Hobbes's political thought', *HJ*, 9 (1966), 286–317

Smith, David L., 'Catholic, Anglican or Puritan? Edward Sackville, fourth Earl of Dorset, and the ambiguities of religion in early Stuart England', *TRHS*, 6th series, 2 (1992), 105–24

'The fourth Earl of Dorset and the Personal Rule of Charles I', *JBS*, 30 (1991), 257–87

'The fourth Earl of Dorset and the politics of the sixteen-twenties', *Historical Research*, 65 (1992), 37–53

'From Petition to Remonstrance', in *The Theatrical City: Culture, Theatre and Politics in London, 1576–1649*, ed. David L. Smith, Richard Strier and David Bevington (Cambridge, forthcoming)

'"The more posed and wise advice": the fourth Earl of Dorset and the English Civil Wars', *HJ*, 34 (1991), 797–829

Somerville, R., *Office-holders in the Duchy and County Palatine of Lancaster from 1603* (1972)

Sommerville, Johann P., 'Absolutism and royalism', in *The Cambridge History of Political Thought, 1450–1700*, ed. J. H. Burns and Mark Goldie (Cambridge, 1991), pp. 347–73

'Further light on Hobbes', *HJ*, 36 (1993), 733–6

Politics and Ideology in England, 1603–1640 (Harlow, 1986)

Thomas Hobbes: Political Ideas in Historical Context (1992)

Spalding, Ruth, *The Improbable Puritan: A Life of Bulstrode Whitelocke, 1605–1675* (1975)

Sparrow Simpson, W. J., *Archbishop Bramhall* (1927)

Speck, W. A., *Reluctant Revolutionaries: Englishmen and the Revolution of 1688* (Oxford, 1988)

Spurr, John, 'The Church of England, comprehension and the Toleration Act of 1689', *EHR*, 104 (1989), 927–46

Starkey, David, 'A reply: Tudor government: the facts', *HJ*, 31 (1988), 921–31

Starkey, David, ed., *The English Court from the Wars of the Roses to the Civil War* (Harlow, 1987)

Stevenson, David, *Scottish Covenanters and Irish Confederates* (Belfast, 1981)

Stopes, C. C., *The Life of Henry, Third Earl of Southampton, Shakespeare's Patron* (Cambridge, 1922)

Strier, Richard, 'From diagnosis to operation', in *The Theatrical City: Culture, Theatre and Politics in London, 1576–1649*, ed. David L. Smith, Richard Strier and David Bevington (Cambridge, forthcoming)

Taaffe, James G., *Abraham Cowley* (New York, 1972)

Thomas, Keith, 'Cases of conscience in seventeenth-century England', in *Public Duty and Private Conscience in Seventeenth-Century England: Essays Presented to G. E. Aylmer*, ed. John Morrill, Paul Slack and Daniel Woolf (Oxford, 1993), pp. 29–56

Thomas, R., 'Comprehension and indulgence', in *From Uniformity to Unity, 1662–1962*, ed. Geoffrey F. Nuttall and Owen Chadwick (1962), pp. 189–253

Thomson, G. M., *Warrior Prince: Prince Rupert of the Rhine* (1976)

Trevor-Roper, Hugh, *Catholics, Anglicans and Puritans* (1987)

'Epilogue: the Glorious Revolution', in *The Anglo-Dutch Moment: Essays on the Glorious Revolution and its World Impact*, ed. Jonathan I. Israel (Cambridge, 1991), pp. 481–94

Tuck, Richard, '"The Ancient Law of Freedom": John Selden and the Civil War', in *Reactions to the English Civil War, 1642–1649*, ed. John Morrill (1982), pp. 137–61

Hobbes (Oxford, 1989)

Natural Rights Theories: Their Origin and Development (Cambridge, 1979)

'A new date for Filmer's *Patriarcha*', *HJ*, 29 (1986), 183–6

Philosophy and Government, 1572–1651 (Cambridge, 1993)

Tyacke, Nicholas, *Anti-Calvinists: The Rise of English Arminianism, c. 1590–1640* (Oxford, 1987)

'Archbishop Laud', in *The Early Stuart Church, 1603–1642*, ed. Kenneth Fincham (1993), pp. 51–70

'Puritanism, Arminianism and counter-revolution', in *The Origins of the English Civil War*, ed. Conrad Russell (1973), pp. 119–43

Ullmann, Walter, *Principles of Government and Politics in the Middle Ages* (2nd edition, 1986)

'"This Realm of England is an Empire"', *Journal of Ecclesiastical History*, 30 (1979), 175–203

Underdown, David, *Fire from Heaven: The Life of an English Town in the Seventeenth Century* (1992)

Pride's Purge: Politics in the Puritan Revolution (Oxford, 1971)

Revel, Riot and Rebellion (Oxford, 1985)

Royalist Conspiracy in England, 1649–1660 (New Haven, 1960)

Somerset in the Civil War and Interregnum (Newton Abbot, 1973)

Wallace, John M., 'Coopers Hill: the manifesto of parliamentary royalism, 1641', *ELH, A Journal of English Literary History*, 41 (1974), 494–540

'The date of Sir Robert Filmer's *Patriarcha*', *HJ*, 23 (1980), 155–65

Destiny his Choice: The Loyalism of Andrew Marvell (Cambridge, 1968)

Ward, Ian, 'Rental policy on the estates of the English peerage, 1649–60', *The Agricultural History Review*, 40 (1992), 23–37

'Settlements, mortgages and aristocratic estates, 1649–1660', *The Journal of Legal History*, 12 (1991), 20–35

Weber, Kurt, *Lucius Cary, Second Viscount Falkland* (New York, 1940)

Weidhorn, Manfred, *Richard Lovelace* (New York, 1970)
Weston, Corinne Comstock, 'England: ancient constitution and common law', in *The Cambridge History of Political Thought, 1450–1700*, ed. J. H. Burns and Mark Goldie (Cambridge, 1991), pp. 374–411
English Constitutional Theory and the House of Lords, 1556–1832 (1965)
'The theory of mixed monarchy under Charles I and after', *EHR*, 75 (1960), 426–43
Weston, Corinne Comstock and Greenberg, Janelle Renfrow, *Subjects and Sovereigns* (Cambridge, 1981)
White, Peter, *Predestination, Policy and Polemic: Conflict and Consensus in the English Church from the Reformation to the Civil War* (Cambridge, 1992)
'The rise of Arminianism reconsidered', *P&P*, 101 (1983), 34–54
'The *via media* in the early Stuart Church', in *The Early Stuart Church, 1603–1642*, ed. Kenneth Fincham (1993), pp. 211–30
Whiteman, Anne, 'The restoration of the Church of England', in *From Uniformity to Unity, 1662–1962*, ed. Geoffrey F. Nuttall and Owen Chadwick (1962), pp. 21–88
Willman, Robert, 'Blackstone and the "Theoretical Perfection" of English law in the reign of Charles II', *HJ*, 26 (1983), 39–70
Witcombe, D. T., *Charles II and the Cavalier House of Commons, 1663–74* (Manchester, 1966)
Woolf, Daniel, 'Conscience, constancy, and ambition in the career and writings of James Howell', in *Public Duty and Private Conscience in Seventeenth-Century England: Essays Presented to G. E. Aylmer*, ed. John Morrill, Paul Slack and Daniel Woolf (Oxford, 1993), pp. 243–78
Woolrych, Austin, *Soldiers and Statesmen* (Oxford, 1987)
Worden, Blair, 'Andrew Marvell, Oliver Cromwell, and the Horatian ode', in *The Politics of Discourse: The Literature and History of Seventeenth-Century England*, ed. Kevin Sharpe and Steven N. Zwicker (Berkeley, 1987), pp. 147–80
The Rump Parliament, 1648–53 (Cambridge, 1974)
Wormald, B. H. G., *Clarendon: Politics, History and Religion, 1640–1660* (Cambridge, 1951; repr. 1989)
Zagorin, Perez, 'Clarendon and Hobbes', *Journal of Modern History*, 57 (1985), 593–616

UNPUBLISHED WORKS

Abbott, W. A., 'The issue of episcopacy in the Long Parliament, 1640–1648', DPhil thesis, University of Oxford, 1982
Adamson, J. S. A., 'The peerage in politics, 1645–9', PhD thesis, University of Cambridge, 1986
Black, S. F., 'The judges of Westminster Hall during the Great Rebellion, 1640–1660', BLitt thesis, University of Oxford, 1970
Brice, I. D., 'Political ideas in Royalist pamphlets of the period 1642–1649', BLitt thesis, University of Oxford, 1970
Cromartie, A. D. T., 'Sir Matthew Hale (1609–76)', PhD thesis, University of Cambridge, 1991
Crummett, J. B., 'The lay peers in Parliament, 1640–4', PhD thesis, University of Manchester, 1972

Dean, Jonathan L., 'Henry Ireton, the Mosaic law, and morality in English civil politics from April 1646 to May 1649', MLitt thesis, University of Cambridge, 1991

Roy, I., 'The Royalist army in the First Civil War', DPhil thesis, University of Oxford, 1963

Scally, John, 'The early career of James, third Marquis and first Duke of Hamilton', PhD thesis, University of Cambridge, 1993

Smith, David L., 'The political career of Edward Sackville, fourth Earl of Dorset (1590–1652)', PhD thesis, University of Cambridge, 1990

Sumner, A., 'The political career of Lord George Digby until the end of the first Civil War', PhD thesis, University of Cambridge, 1985

Ward, Ian, 'The English peerage, 1649–1660: government, authority and estates', PhD thesis, University of Cambridge, 1989

INDEX

358

Cambridge Studies in Early Modern British History

Titles in the series

Printed in the United Kingdom
by Lightning Source UK Ltd.
109960UKS00001BA/209

9 780521 893398